CORE
Visual C++® 6

ISBN 0-13-085859-5

PRENTICE HALL PTR
CORE SERIES

Core PHP Programming, Atkinson

Core Java Media Framework, deCarmo

Core Jini, Edwards*

Core Web Programming, Hall

Core Java 2 Volume 1: Fundamentals, Horstmann & Cornell*

Core Java 2 Volume 2: Advanced Features, Horstmann & Cornell*

Core Visual C++ 6, Klander

Core Java Web Server, Taylor & Kimmet

Core CSS, Schengili-Roberts

Core Java Foundation Classes, Topley

Core Swing: Advanced Programming, Topley

Core Web 3D, Walsh

---

* Sun Microsystems Press/Prentice Hall title.

CORE
Visual C++ 6

LARS KLANDER
MCSD, MCT

Prentice Hall PTR
Upper Saddle River, NJ 07458
www.phptr.com

Library of Congress Cataloging-in-Publication Data

Klander, Lars.
  Core Visual C++ 6 / Lars Klander.
     p. cm. -- (Prentice Hall PTR core series)
  ISBN 0-13-085859-5
  1. C++ (Computer program language) 2. Microsoft Visual C++. I. Title. II. Series.
QA76.73.C153 K58 2000
658'.0552768--dc21

                                         99-052125

Production Editor and Compositor: *Vanessa Moore*
Acquisitions Editor: *Jill Pisoni*
Editorial Assistant: *Linda Ramagnano*
Marketing Manager: *Lisa Konzelmann*
Buyer: *Maura Goldstaub*
Cover Design: *Talar Agasyan*
Cover Design Direction: *Jerry Votta*
Art Director: *Gail Cocker-Bogusz*

© 2000 Prentice Hall PTR
Prentice-Hall, Inc.
Upper Saddle River, NJ 07458

Prentice Hall books are widely used by corporations and government agencies for training,
marketing, and resale. The publisher offers discounts on this book when ordered in bulk quantities.
For more information, contact

     Corporate Sales Department,
     Prentice Hall PTR
     One Lake Street
     Upper Saddle River, NJ 07458
     Phone: 800-382-3419; FAX: 201-236-7141
     E-mail (Internet): corpsales@prenhall.com

Printed in the United States of America

10 9 8 7 6 5 4 3 2 1

ISBN 0-13-085859-5

Prentice-Hall International (UK) Limited, London
Prentice-Hall of Australia Pty. Limited, Sydney
Prentice-Hall Canada Inc., Toronto
Prentice-Hall Hispanoamericana, S.A., Mexico
Prentice-Hall of India Private Limited, New Delhi
Prentice-Hall of Japan, Inc., Tokyo
Pearson Education Asia Pte. Ltd., Singapore
Editora Prentice-Hall do Brasil, Ltda., Rio de Janeiro

To my older sister, Bess, my younger sister, Ardyth, and my brother Jed—I love you all, and hope that one of these days we will all be able to take enough time out of our crazy lives to get to know each other all over again. It was good to know you when we were kids, but even better to know you now that we are all (mostly) adults.

Contents

Preface   xxiv

    To the Reader   xxiv

    About this Book   xxv

    Conventions   xxvii

Acknowledgments   xxviii

CHAPTER 1   The New Features of Visual C++ and Visual Studio   1

    1.1   Understanding Microsoft's Goals with Visual Studio 6.0   1

    1.2   Overview of Key Technologies   3

        1.2.1   Multitier Enterprise Applications   3

        1.2.2   Briefly Introducing the Component Object Model (COM)   6

    1.3   Microsoft Visual Studio 6.0 Specifics   7

        1.3.1   Complete Suite of Tools for Component-Based
                Application Development   8

        1.3.2   Enhanced Lifecycle Productivity   9

        1.3.3   Enterprise Database Tools   11

        1.3.4   Enhanced Support for Team
                Development — All Kinds of Teams   13

1.3.5 Integration with Application Services   14

1.4   Visual C++-Specific Improvements in Version 6.0   15

1.4.1 Edit and Continue Debugging   15

1.4.2 IntelliSense Technology   15

1.4.3 Support for MTS Within AppWizard   16

1.4.4 Support for Internet Development   16

1.4.5 New Database Support   17

1.4.6 Miscellaneous Improvements to the Environment   17

1.5   Summary   18

CHAPTER 2   Debugging As a Development Consideration   20

2.1   Understanding the Different Types of Programming Errors   21

2.2   Understanding the Components of a Useful Debugger   22

2.3   The Visual Studio Integrated Debugger   24

2.3.1 Preparing an Application for Debugging   24

2.3.2 Using the Debugger When You Run an Application   27

2.4   Introducing the Various Debug Windows and Their Uses   28

2.4.1 The Variables Window   29

2.4.2 The Watch Window   30

2.4.3 The Registers Window   31

2.4.4 The Memory Window   31

2.4.5 The Call Stack Window   32

2.4.6 The Disassembly Window   33

2.5   Using Breakpoints and Single-Stepping When Debugging   34

2.5.1 Using the QuickWatch Window
and the DataTips Information   39

2.5.2 Using the Threads and the Exceptions Dialog Boxes
When Debugging   40

2.6   Simple Debugging Techniques   42

2.6.1 Using Message Boxes to Speed Debugging   42

2.6.2 Debugging Output   42

2.6.3 Using Assertions   43

2.6.4 Object Dumping   44

2.6.5 Detecting Memory Leaks and the CMemoryState Class   44

2.6.6 Using MFC Tracing   45

2.7 Additional Features of the Visual C++ Debugger   46

2.7.1 Just-in-Time Debugging   46

2.7.2 Edit and Continue Debugging   47

2.7.3 Remote Debugging   48

2.8 Advanced Debugging Considerations   50

2.8.1 Debugging Windows NT Services   50

2.8.2 Debugging Multithreaded Applications   51

2.9 Summary   53

CHAPTER 3 Using Callback Functions and
Dissecting the Message Loop   56

3.1 Understanding Callback Functions   57

3.2 Common Uses for Callback Functions   60

3.2.1 A Windows API Callback Function Example   60

3.2.2 Using Callback Functions Within Your Own Classes   61

3.2.3 Callback Functions Within MFC   63

3.3 The Fundamentals of the Windows Message Loop   65

3.4 Messages the Message Loop Receives   70

3.5 Using Multiple Message Loops with Multiple Windows   72

3.6 Optimizing Message Loops   76

3.7 Summary   76

CHAPTER 4 Creating and Using Advanced Dialog Boxes   78

4.1 Handling Dialogs in MFC   79

4.1.1 Creating Dialog Template Resources   80

4.1.2 Creating a CDialog-Derived Class   81

4.1.3 Displaying the Dialog Box   84

4.1.4 Dialog Box Coordinates   85

4.1.5 Changing the Input Focus and Default Buttons   86

4.2 Dialog Data Exchange and Validation   86

4.2.1 Mapping Member Variables to Controls 87

4.2.2 The Data Exchange and Validation Mechanism 90

4.2.3 Initializing the Dialog Controls 91

4.2.4 Retrieving Data from the Controls 93

4.2.5 Responding to Control Notifications 94

4.2.6 Dynamically Mapping Controls 95

4.2.7 Responding to OK and Cancel 96

4.3 Derived Control Classes in Dialogs 97

4.3.1 Creating a Derived Control 97

4.3.2 Customizing the Derived Control 98

4.3.3 Using the Derived Control in a Dialog Box 99

4.4 Modeless Dialog Boxes 101

4.4.1 Modeless Dialog Resource Templates 101

4.4.2 Creating and Destroying Modeless Dialog Boxes 102

4.4.3 Tracking Modeless Dialog Boxes 103

4.4.4 Dialog Bars 105

4.5 Using and Expanding the Common Dialogs and Common Controls 106

4.6 Working with Common Dialog Classes 106

4.7 Customizing the Common Dialogs 118

4.8 Customizing the Open Dialog Box for Greater Power 118

4.9 Understanding MFC Control Classes 123

4.10 Modifying Control Behavior 124

4.11 Summary 126

CHAPTER 5 Creating and Using Property Sheets
with Your Controls 128

5.1 Understanding Property Sheets 129

5.1.1 Creating a Property Sheet 131

5.1.2 Creating the Property Page Resources 131

5.2 Creating CPropertyPage-Derived Classes 134

5.2.1 Creating a CPropertySheet-Derived Class 135

5.2.2 Adding the Property Pages 136

5.2.3 Creating a Modeless Property Sheet 138

5.3   Responding to Property Sheet Messages   139

    5.3.1   Initializing the Property Pages   139

    5.3.2   Property Page Activation and Deactivation   140

    5.3.3   Handling Messages from OK, Apply, and Cancel Buttons   141

    5.3.4   Sending Messages Between Property Pages   142

5.4   Customizing the Standard Property Sheet   144

    5.4.1   Property Page Management   145

    5.4.2   Creating a Wizard-Mode Property Sheet   146

    5.4.3   Using the New CPropertySheetEx and
        CPropertyPageEx Classes   148

    5.4.4   Adding Help Buttons and Help Support   153

5.5   Summary   155

CHAPTER 6   Working with Device Contexts and GDI Objects 156

6.1   Device Contexts in MFC   157

    6.1.1   The CDC Class   158

    6.1.2   The CClientDC Class   160

    6.1.3   The CPaintDC Class   161

    6.1.4   The CMetaFileDC Class   161

6.2   Brushes and Pens   162

    6.2.1   Pens and the CPen Class   163

    6.2.2   Selecting Pens into the Device Context   165

    6.2.3   Using Stock Pens   165

    6.2.4   Drawing with Pens   166

    6.2.5   Brushes and the CBrush Class   169

    6.2.6   Selecting Brushes into the Device Context   170

    6.2.7   Using Stock Brushes   170

    6.2.8   Drawing with Brushes   171

6.3   MFC Classes for GDI Operations   171

    6.3.1   The CPoint Class   172

    6.3.2   The CSize Class   173

    6.3.3   The CRect Class   173

6.3.4 The CRgn Class and Clipping   174

6.4 Working with Fonts   176

6.4.1 Fonts and the CFont Class   176

6.4.2 Selecting Fonts into the Device Context   177

6.4.3 Stock Fonts   177

6.4.4 Device Context Font Interrogation Functions   178

6.4.5 Text Rendering Functions   178

6.5 Creating and Loading Bitmaps   179

6.5.1 Creating a Bitmap Resource with the Resource Editor   180

6.5.2 Loading a Bitmap   181

6.5.3 Creating Bitmaps   181

6.6 Drawing with Bitmaps   182

6.6.1 Bitmap Copying   182

6.7 Creating a Device-Independent Bitmap Class   183

6.7.1 Creating a DIB   184

6.7.2 Creating a DIB from a Device-Dependent Bitmap   187

6.7.3 Drawing with a DIB   189

6.8 Summary   191

CHAPTER 7 Working with Documents and Views   192

7.1 Understanding the Two Document-Interface Structures   193

7.2 Complex Combinations of Documents, Views, and
Frame Windows   197

7.3 Working with Multiple-Document Types   197

7.3.1 Understanding the CDocument Class   198

7.3.2 Declaring a Document Class in Your Application   199

7.3.3 Using CDocument's Member Functions   200

7.3.4 Better Understanding Documents and Message Processing   202

7.3.5 Overriding Virtual Document Functions   203

7.4 Working with Complex Document Data   204

7.4.1 Understanding the Benefits of CCmdTarget and CDocItem   208

7.5 Understanding How Your Applications Manage
Documents and Views   210

7.5.1   Working with the CSingleDocTemplate Class   211

7.6   Understanding the CMultiDocTemplate Class   212

7.7   Working with Frame Windows   212

    7.7.1   Understanding the CMDIFrameWnd and
CMDIChildWnd Classes   213

    7.7.2   Understanding the Role of AfxGetMainWnd()   215

7.8   Understanding the Document Template Resources   216

    7.8.1   Considering the Document Template Lifecycle   217

    7.8.2   Advanced Work with Templates   217

    7.8.3   Working with Multiple Templates   218

    7.8.4   Destroying Documents Added with the
AddDocTemplate() Member Function   220

7.9   Understanding and Using the CView Class   221

    7.9.1   Declaring a View Class   221

    7.9.2   Analyzing the CView Member Function   223

    7.9.3   Working with Views and Messages   225

    7.9.4   MFC-Derived Variants of the CView Class   225

7.10   Understanding Splitter Windows   227

    7.10.1   Differentiating Between Splitter Windows   228

    7.10.2   Understanding Specifics of the CSplitterWnd Class   228

    7.10.3   Creating Dynamic Splitters   230

    7.10.4   Using Different Views in Dynamic Panes   232

    7.10.5   Using a CRuntimeClass Object   233

    7.10.6   Using Splitters with Views Associated
with More Than One Document   233

7.11   Using Static Splitters   234

    7.11.1   Creating a Static Splitter   235

    7.11.2   Understanding Shared Scrollbars   236

    7.11.3   Determining Actual and Ideal Sizes   238

    7.11.4   Understanding Performance Issues with Splitters   238

7.12   Using MFC to Subclass Windows   238

7.13   Alternatives to the Document/View Architecture   240

7.14   Summary   241

CHAPTER 8   Printing Output After You Create It   244

8.1   Windows API Printer Support   245

8.1.1   Obtaining Printer Information   247

8.1.2   Understanding the Importance of Text Characteristics   248

8.2   Printing with MFC   249

8.2.1   Understanding Your Role and the
Framework's Role in Printing   249

8.2.2   Understanding the MFC Printing Sequence   250

8.2.3   Further Insight into MFC Default Printing   253

8.2.4   The Printing Protocol   254

8.2.5   Overriding View Class Functions and Pagination   254

8.2.6   Understanding the CPrintInfo Class   256

8.3   Understanding Printer Pages Versus Document Pages   257

8.3.1   Implementing Pagination   258

8.3.2   Adding the Helper Functions   261

8.3.3   Print-Time Pagination   263

8.3.4   Revisiting the Printing of Headers and Footers   264

8.3.5   Allocating GDI Resources for Printing   265

8.3.6   Enlarging the Printed Image   266

8.4   Understanding the Print Preview Architecture   266

8.4.1   The Print Preview Process   267

8.4.2   Modifying Print Preview   267

8.4.3   Enhancing an Application's Print Preview   269

8.5   Understanding the CPrintDialog Class   270

8.6   Summary   272

CHAPTER 9   Manipulating Threads and Managing Processes   274

9.1   Understanding What Threads Are   275

9.1.1   Understanding Thread Priorities   276

9.1.2   Switching Contexts   280

9.2   Understanding the Difference Between Processes and Threads   280

9.3   Determining Applications You Should Multitask   282

9.3.1   Specific Times When You Should Not Multitask   282

9.3.2 Threads and Message Loops 283

9.3.3 Times When You Should Use Multithreading 284

9.3.4 Applying Threads Within Your Application 285

9.4 Creating Threads 286

9.4.1 Using Your Own Threads 286

9.4.2 Handling Thread Messages 287

9.5 MFC Creation Benefits 288

9.5.1 Worker Threads 289

9.6 Understanding the Controlling Function 291

9.6.1 Creating Threads at Runtime 292

9.6.2 Terminating a Thread 294

9.6.3 Handling Premature Thread Termination 294

9.6.4 Threads Are Like Sharp Objects — Play Carefully 295

9.6.5 Checking Return Codes 296

9.7 Thread Synchronization 298

9.7.1 Critical Sections 298

9.7.2 Working with Mutexes 300

9.7.3 Semaphores 301

9.7.4 Events 303

9.7.5 Setting the Event's State 304

9.7.6 Other Waitable Objects 305

9.8 More on Processes 306

9.8.1 Process Creation Flags 307

9.8.2 Understanding What Comprises Process Information 309

9.9 Creating a Process 309

9.10 Closing on Threads and MFC 311

9.10.1 Wrapping Objects 313

9.11 Summary 314

CHAPTER 10 Using Advanced Memory
Management Techniques 316

10.1 Processes and Memory 317

10.1.1 Separate Address Spaces 318

10.1.2 Address Spaces   319

10.1.3 Virtual Memory   320

10.2 Understanding Differences Between 16- and 32-Bit Programs   322

10.2.1 Understanding the Differences in Integer Size   323

10.2.2 Changes in Type Modifiers and Macros   323

10.2.3 Differences in Performing Address Calculations   324

10.2.4 Managing Library Functions   324

10.3 Understanding the Win32 Memory Model   325

10.3.1 Using Selector Functions to Directly
         Manipulate Physical Memory   325

10.4 Overview of Simple Memory Management Techniques   325

10.4.1 Using malloc() and new() to Allocate Memory   326

10.4.2 The Problem of Stray Pointers   327

10.4.3 Sharing Memory Between Applications   328

10.5 Returning to Virtual Memory and Advanced Memory Management   328

10.5.1 Win32 Virtual Memory Management   329

10.5.2 Windows API Virtual Memory Functions   329

10.5.3 Functions   331

10.5.4 Windows API and C Runtime Memory Management   333

10.5.5 Miscellaneous and Obsolete Functions   333

10.5.6 Memory-Mapped Files and Shared Memory   334

10.5.7 Shared Memory and Based Pointers   336

10.6 Threads and Memory Management   337

10.6.1 Interlocked Variable Access   337

10.6.2 Thread-Local Storage   337

10.7 Accessing Physical Memory and I/O Ports   338

10.8 Summary   338

CHAPTER 11   Working with the File System   340

11.1 File System Overview   341

11.1.1 The FAT File System   342

11.1.2 Protected Mode FAT   343

11.1.3 The FAT-32 File System   343

11.1.4 The HPFS File System   344

11.1.5 The NTFS File System   344

11.1.6 The CDFS File System   344

11.2 Networked File Systems and Mapped Volumes   345

11.2.1 The DFS File System   346

11.2.2 File System Compression   346

11.2.3 Disk Quotas   347

11.2.4 Differences in Functions Among File Systems   347

11.2.5 Determining the File System and Drive Types   347

11.3 Win32 File Objects   347

11.3.1 Basic File I/O   348

11.3.2 Asynchronous I/O   352

11.4 Compatibility I/O   354

11.4.1 Low-Level I/O   355

11.4.2 Stream I/O   358

11.4.3 The I/O Stream Classes   358

11.5 Serial Communications   360

11.5.1 Opening and Configuring Serial Ports   361

11.5.2 Asynchronous Communications   362

11.5.3 Setting Communication Timeouts   365

11.5.4 Communication Events   365

11.6 Using Consoles   366

11.6.1 Allocating a Console   366

11.6.2 Console I/O   367

11.6.3 Customizing the Console Buffers and Display   368

11.7 Summary   368

CHAPTER 12   Opening Pipes and Mailslots for
              Communications   370

12.1 Communicating with Pipes   372

12.2 Creating Pipes   372

12.2.1 Connecting to Named Pipes   373

12.2.2 Transferring Data Through Pipes 375

12.3 Working More with Named Pipes 375

12.4 Understanding Microsoft Remote Procedure Call (RPC) 379

12.4.1 RPC Fundamentals 379

12.4.2 Implementing Communications over a Proxy-Stub Pair 380

12.4.3 Specifying the Interface 381

12.4.4 Implementing the Server 383

12.4.5 Implementing the Client 386

12.5 RPC Exception Handling 387

12.5.1 Advanced RPC Features 388

12.6 Working with Mailslots 389

12.7 Summary 390

CHAPTER 13 Managing the System Registry 392

13.1 Understanding the Registry's Structure 394

13.1.1 Considering the Role and Format of Registry Values 395

13.1.2 Registry Capacity 395

13.2 The Predefined Registry Branches 396

13.3 Editing the Registry Manually 399

13.4 Commonly Used Registry Keys 400

13.4.1 Considering the Subtrees in HKEY_LOCAL_MACHINE 400

13.4.2 Subtrees in HKEY_CLASSES_ROOT 401

13.4.3 Subtrees in HKEY_USERS 402

13.4.4 Subtrees in HKEY_CURRENT_USER 403

13.5 The Registry and INI Files 403

13.6 Writing Application Programs That Manipulate the Registry 404

13.6.1 Opening a Registry Key 404

13.6.2 Querying a Value 405

13.6.3 Setting a Value 407

13.6.4 Creating a New Key 407

13.6.5 Other Registry Functions 409

13.6.6 Working with Registry Hives 412

13.7 Summary 415

CHAPTER 14   Performing Advanced Exception Handling   416

14.1 Exception Handling   417

14.1.1 Hiding the Error Handling Mechanism   419

14.1.2 Multiple Catch Statements   419

14.2 Exceptions and MFC   420

14.2.1 Exception Handling with Macros   421

14.3 Understanding the MFC CException Class   423

14.3.1 Understanding the CMemoryException Class   424

14.3.2 The CFileException Class   425

14.3.3 Saving a CFileException   427

14.3.4 Purposefully Throwing a CFileException   428

14.3.5 The CArchiveException Class   428

14.3.6 The CNotSupportedException Class   430

14.3.7 The CResourceException Class   431

14.3.8 The CDaoException Class   431

14.3.9 The CDBException Class   432

14.3.10 The COleException Class   433

14.3.11 The COleDispatchException Class   434

14.3.12 The CUserException Class   434

14.4 Throwing an MFC Exception   434

14.4.1 Common Exception Features   435

14.5 MFC and Exceptions   436

14.6 The Visual C++ 6.0 Solution   437

14.6.1 Exceptions and Win32   438

14.7 Using the ASSERT Macros for Exception Handling   443

14.7.1 Using the ASSERT_VALID Macro   444

14.8 Summary   444

CHAPTER 15   Fundamental Principles of COM and DCOM   446

15.1 Understanding the Origins and Uses of ActiveX   448

15.2 Understanding the Various ActiveX Technologies   449

15.2.1 Understanding Automation Servers   450

15.2.2 Understanding Automation Controllers 450

15.2.3 Defining ActiveX Controls 451

15.2.4 Understanding Component Object Model (COM) Objects 451

15.2.5 Understanding ActiveX Documents 452

15.2.6 Understanding ActiveX Containers 453

15.3 Understanding What ActiveX Can Do for You 453

15.4 Determining What Type of ActiveX Component You Need 455

15.4.1 Using Automation Servers and Controllers 455

15.4.2 Using ActiveX Controls 456

15.4.3 Using COM Objects 457

15.5 Different Techniques for Creating ActiveX Components 458

15.5.1 Using Microsoft Foundation Classes to
Create ActiveX Components 458

15.5.2 Using the ActiveX Template Library to
Create ActiveX Components 459

15.5.3 Using the BaseControl Framework to
Create ActiveX Components 460

15.5.4 Create Your Own Framework 462

15.6 Basic ActiveX Component Architecture 462

15.6.1 ActiveX Automation Servers 463

15.6.2 ActiveX Controls 465

15.7 Better Understanding COM 465

15.7.1 COM Objects Implement Interfaces 467

15.7.2 Interface Definition Language 469

15.7.3 Understanding the IUnknown Interface 471

15.8 Moving on to DCOM 474

15.8.1 Using DCOM to Communicate
Out-Of-Process and Across Computers 475

15.8.2 Understanding How to Reduce Round Trips 477

15.8.3 Understanding Singletons 478

15.9 Understanding the COM Threading Model 479

15.10 Summary 480

CHAPTER 16   Creating In-Process ActiveX Servers
Using MFC   482

16.1 Creating the Basic Project   483

16.1.1 Adding an Automation Interface to the Application   486

16.1.2 Registering the Server   489

16.2 Writing the Support Code for the Sample Server   491

16.2.1 Adding Methods to Your Server   494

16.2.2 Adding Properties to the Server   500

16.3 Generating OLE Exceptions   502

16.3.1 Understanding Dual-Interface Servers   504

16.3.2 Generating Dual-Interface OLE Exceptions   513

16.4 Server Instantiation Using C++   517

16.4.1 Common Problems When Instantiating
OLE Servers Using C++   518

16.5 Creating Shareable Servers   519

16.6 Working with Single-Instance Servers   523

16.7 Summary   524

CHAPTER 17   Supporting OLE Drag-and-Drop
with Applications   526

17.1 Drag-and-Drop Basics   527

17.2 Creating a Container Application   528

17.2.1 Creating the Application   529

17.2.2 Adding Positioning Support   529

17.2.3 Adding Selection Support   532

17.3 Adding Drag-and-Drop Support   532

17.3.1 Implementing a Drag Source   533

17.3.2 Implementing a Drop Target   535

17.4 Summary   542

CHAPTER 18   Database Access with Visual C++   544

18.1 OLE DB as a Component Technology   546

18.1.1 Understanding Consumers   547

18.1.2 Understanding Providers   547

18.1.3 Base Consumer Functionality   548

18.1.4 More on Providers   548

18.1.5 Minimum Provider Functionality   552

18.2 Defining Base Providers   554

18.3 Additional Important OLE DB Concepts   555

18.3.1 Data Source Objects   555

18.3.2 Understanding Transactions   556

18.3.3 Understanding Sessions   556

18.3.4 Understanding Commands   558

18.3.5 Understanding Rowsets   560

18.3.6 Rowset Properties   563

18.3.7 Understanding Enumerators   563

18.4 Understanding OLE DB Error Objects   564

18.4.1 The ERRORINFO Structure's Contents   564

18.4.2 Error Parameters   565

18.4.3 Custom Error Objects   566

18.4.4 Dynamic Error ID   566

18.4.5 The Lookup ID   566

18.5 Extended Interfaces for OLE DB Providers   567

18.6 Using OLE DB from Within Applications   570

18.7 Using ActiveX Data Objects (ADO)   570

18.7.1 The ActiveX Data Objects Model   571

18.8 Introduction to ADO with Visual C++ 6.0   571

18.8.1 Implementing ADO with #import   573

18.8.2 Defining and Instantiating ADO Objects with #import   574

18.8.3 Creating an ADO Project with #import   576

18.9 ADO with MFC OLE   578

18.9.1 Creating an ADO Project with MFC OLE   578

18.9.2 ADO with COM Functions   579

18.9.3 Creating an ADO Project with the COM API   579

18.10 ADO and COM   581

18.10.1 Reading the Type Library   581

18.10.2 Viewing a Type Library with the OLE COM Object Viewer   581

18.10.3 Default Properties and Collections   582

18.10.4 The ADO Type Library and COM Implementations   584

18.10.5 COM Data Types Used By ADO   585

18.10.6 Converting Variants to Native Data Types   586

18.10.7 Using SAFEARRAYS   586

18.10.8 Error Handling with ADO   587

18.10.9 Specifics on ADO Exception Handling   588

18.10.10 Unrecoverable Exceptions with ADO   590

18.11 Taking a Closer Look at #import   591

18.11.1 #import and COM   591

18.11.2 Using the Type Library with the #import Directive   592

18.11.3 Analyzing the Contents of the .tlh and .tli Files
          Generated by #import   593

18.11.4 Single Versus Double Quote in SQL Statements   596

18.12 Summary   596

CHAPTER 19   Using Scripting and Other Tools to
             Automate the Visual C++ IDE   598

19.1 The Developer Studio Object Model   600

19.1.1 The Objects Exposed in Developer Studio   600

19.2 Using VBScript To Write Developer Studio Macros   602

19.2.1 Declaring Variables   602

19.2.2 VBScript Subroutines   602

19.2.3 Using Functions in VBScript   603

19.2.4 Creating a VBScript Macro   604

19.2.5 Removing a Developer Studio Macro File   605

19.2.6 Example Macros Included with Visual C++   606

19.2.7 Debugging a Visual Studio Macro   607

19.2.8 Adding a VBScript Macro to the Toolbar   607

19.3 Benefits of Custom AppWizards   607

19.3.1 The Custom Wizard Architecture   608

19.3.2 Types of Custom AppWizards   609

19.3.3 Using Custom Dialog Boxes   610

19.3.4 Understanding Classes and ClassWizard   612

19.3.5 Understanding the Class Information File's Contents   612

19.3.6 Using Macros in a Custom AppWizard   613

19.3.7 Text Templates   616

19.3.8 Binary Templates   617

19.3.9 Information Files   617

19.3.10 Directives   618

19.4 Creating a Wizard Project   619

19.4.1 Planning the Core Custom AppWizard   620

19.4.2 Beginning the Custom AppWizard Project   620

19.4.3 Editing the Dialog Box Resource   622

19.4.4 Providing an OnDismiss Function   623

19.4.5 Editing the Text Templates   624

19.5 Using the New Custom Wizard   626

19.6 Summary   626

INDEX   **628**

Preface

To the Reader

When Prentice Hall first approached me about writing a Core Visual C++ title, I must admit that I was a bit apprehensive — the language is so broad, and the amount of information necessary to do it justice so extensive, that I was concerned about my ability to put together an effective title that would yield real value to the reader. Add to that, Gary Cornell's programming works on writing with C++, and I wasn't quite sure where such a book would fit in. Obviously, they convinced me that it would.

But, in writing a book to meet their needs, it quickly became self-evident that we couldn't cover *all* of the topics important to Visual C++ programming. In fact, many peripheral topics about the compiler and programming over Windows, including the use of the Microsoft Foundation Classes (MFC) library, are substantial enough to demand their own books. Instead, it was necessary to tighten the scope of the book a bit. And so, I focused on a more low- to mid-level introduction to the language and the compiler, and on the issues virtually guaranteed to confront any developer using Visual C++.

To that end, I don't get into using ADO with databases, or using the DirectX family of COM objects for real-time graphical-interface design. Instead, I spent the time talking about crucial, real-world topics, such as memory management, thread management, and exception handling.

As a side note, when any book is being written, errors and inaccuracies are inevitable. I would very much like you, the readers, to tell me about any such problems you encounter with the code in this book. However, while I am happy for you to send me e-mail at lklander@lvcm.com, I would much prefer that you logon to my Web page, at http://www.larsklander.com/CoreVC, and place your information into the bug-and-problem information reporting tool on the page. To make your life easier, and mine, I will also place such information, after I have the chance to review it for accuracy, onto the same site, so you can review other people's thoughts. Finally, there are probably applications that tie closely in with the topics in these chapters which are not included herein. As such programs occur to me, or as I implement them in other areas of my business, I will happily place such code, as I am able, onto this site. I urge you to provide me with code you think will be helpful, as well.

About this Book

For starters, even though this book is written in an educational style, chapters in this book can almost certainly be read in any order you choose. The only exceptions that I would suggest are Chapter 1, which highlights some of the important technologies that we will be looking at over the course of the book's pages, and Chapter 2, which explains in-depth how to work with the Visual C++ Interactive Development Environment (IDE) and how to use the provided debugger to its best effect when designing your applications. Therefore, to help you navigate your way through the book, the following paragraphs provide short descriptions of each of the chapters.

I have started out the book with a brief introduction to Visual C++ 6.0 and Visual Studio, with an eye towards letting the reader know what's new in the product. Some of these new features are important because they will help the reader use the product more efficiently, others are important simply because of new functionality they expose. In Chapter 2, I move on to a discussion of debugging and the integrated debugger, because it is inevitable that the reader will have to use the debugger when writing programs in Visual C++.

After introducing the Interactive Development Environment and some of the tools that work with it, the book moves on to a discussion of the basic Windows programming environment in Chapter 3, with a focus on the nature of callback functions and the Windows message loop. Then the book discusses dialog boxes, common dialogs, and controls as the most fundamental interface design tools, in Chapter 4. In Chapter 5, I move on to a discussion of property sheets, how to build and use them, and focus on them primarily from the perspective of how you might use them in your applications to provide the user with choices, and how even the most complex property sheets are nothing more than a series of dialog boxes. In Chapter 6, I introduce you to graphic device interface (GDI) objects and discuss how you work with them, both from a Windows-native level and from the perspective of MFC classes and objects.

Once the fundamental interface tools are described — dialog boxes and controls — the book moves on, in Chapter 7, to the Windows document/view architecture, and how applications can use this architecture to more efficiently manage both the interface and the storage of data. Chapter 8 diverges briefly into a discussion of printing from the architecture, since output is an important and often neglected topic.

In Chapter 9, the book moves on to a more advanced topic, introducing you to the specifics of working with threads and thread management objects. The chapter includes discussions on multithreading, when and why to use it (or not use it), and the various constructs, such as mutexes and semaphores, necessary to implement and make effective use of multithreading support. Chapter 10 moves on to the consideration of a related topic, looking at the complexities of memory management in the Win32 model and how to make the most effective use of some of the constructs that Win32 provides for managing memory.

The file system, how to interact with it, and the classes and methods at the programmer's disposal for file work are discussed in Chapter 11. We take a look at the many different techniques available to you for file-system access, focusing on the implementations provided by MFC and the Windows API for simplifying file management, creation, and so on. In Chapter 12, a brief introduction to network issues, in the form of file-system derivative objects such as pipes and mailslots, begins to open up your programming universe to some of the innate complexity and power of the Win32 networking environment.

Chapter 13 explores one of the most important programming issues when designing over any of the variants of the Win32 platform — working with the Windows registry. How to manage the registry is a very important consideration for applications that maintain any ongoing data about their activities. Chapter 14 steps back a little from all the operating-system and network operating-system discussions in the previous chapters, instead detailing specifics about exception-handling issues with Visual C++, including the MFC exception classes and their uses.

In Chapter 15, the tone changes a little, letting you move into working with slightly more advanced implementations of Visual C++ and address more complex programming topics. Chapter 15 discusses the nature of Component Object Model (COM) and Distributed Component Object Model (DCOM) programming, and introduces you to some of the issues that you will need to consider when using either from Visual C++.

In Chapter 16, I take the general knowledge discussed in Chapter 15 and apply it to the specifics of the design on dynamic link libraries (DLLs) — in-process servers. The design of in-process servers is one of the most common activities that component-based development entails. In Chapter 17, I move away from the COM focus of the previous two chapters and discuss how to implement OLE drag-and-drop support. Such support has been commonplace enough to be an expected feature, not a "bell or whistle." So making sure you know how to implement such support is important.

Finally, the last two chapters wrap it all up by taking a brief look at some of the finishing techniques at the reader's disposal when programming with Visual C++ — creating an installation tool and performing scripting within the IDE to automate repetitive processes.

All in all, the book is designed in a manner that tries to manage a logical progression through Windows programming topics — from the most fundamental to some of the more advanced and powerful actions. Unlike many books, it is directed at the programmer who is somewhat knowledgeable in other programming languages (or even C/C++), but without significant experience in Visual C++.

Conventions

As is common throughout the *Core* series, I use `courier` type to represent computer code.

There are *Core Notes* in this book that examine some of the differences between Visual C++ and other language implementations, including Visual Basic and Java. You can skip over these if you have no experience or interest in either of these languages. Notes are tagged with this icon:

Acknowledgments

I have published several books, and have rapidly learned — much more so than I ever realized when I was only *reading* books — just how much work is involved in the creation and shipment of a given work before it reaches the shelves. Authors get most of the "glory" (such as it is), but without these other people, my words and thoughts would likely be a bunch of scribbles on a yellow pad.

I can't do any kind of acknowledgment without first acknowledging my wife, Brett, without whom I wouldn't really have much reason to go to work in the morning (or in the evening, or at night). While it seems rather odd, I also need to acknowledge all of my "faithful companions," for always being ready for a stroke or two when I reached a difficult point, and for putting up with a 5A.M. walk when I needed to clear my head, since they, like everyone else, thought it was a more appropriate hour for sleeping.

That being said, Jill Pisoni, the executive editor who brought me in on this project, really started the whole thing, and has been wonderful to work with. Moreover, she relocated in the middle of the project, so it was nice to work with an editor whose schedule got as messed up in the middle of a book as mine usually does.

Next on the list, the technical editor, my close friend Mark Linsenbardt, who fulfilled his usual role in my life in a bit more formal fashion this time — making sure that I didn't make too much of an idiot out of myself.

To Vanessa Moore, the project editor, and the whole rest of the team at Prentice Hall, thanks for making the book look good. Unfortunately, while content is king, inevitably appearance is still a big player in a person's decision to buy and read a book, and their work made this book look much better than I could have done in a year.

Last but not least, I always like to acknowledge my agent, David Fugate, because he does an excellent job for me, and is always looking out for my interests. Thanks everyone for all of your work, and I look forward to next time.

THE NEW FEATURES OF VISUAL C++ AND VISUAL STUDIO

Topics in this Chapter

- Understanding Microsoft's Goals with Visual Studio 6.0
- Overview of Key Technologies
- Microsoft Visual Studio 6.0 Specifics
- Visual C++-Specific Improvements in Version 6.0
- Summary

Chapter 1

With the release of Visual C++ 5.0 and its accompanying Visual Studio, Microsoft took a major leap forward in making Visual C++ a very powerful, very useful development environment. The addition of the Active Template Library (ATL), for example, was a significant new advance in the establishment of Visual C++ as a serious component development platform.

Visual C++ 6.0 also takes significant steps forward, both by adding new Microsft Foundation Classes (MFC) (such as CHtmlView) and by adding additional environmental tools (such as Edit and Continue debugging) to make the development environment even more powerful and easier to use.

1.1 Understanding Microsoft's Goals with Visual Studio 6.0

Today, information technology is helping organizations to dramatically reduce their cost structures, to reengineer their business processes, and to expand their product and service offerings to their business partners and customers directly over the Internet. Microsoft refers to companies that have harnessed technology to provide these competitive advantages as having a *Digital Nervous System.* The Microsoft Digital Nervous System relies on connected PCs and integrated software to make information flow rapidly and accurately throughout an organization and to its customers and partners. It helps employees act faster and make more informed decisions. It prepares a company to react to unplanned events. It helps close the gap between the corporation, its customers, and its business partners. And it lets organizations focus on business, not technology. Creating a true Digital Nervous System takes commitment, time, and imagination. Figure 1-1 shows the components of the Digital Nervous System.

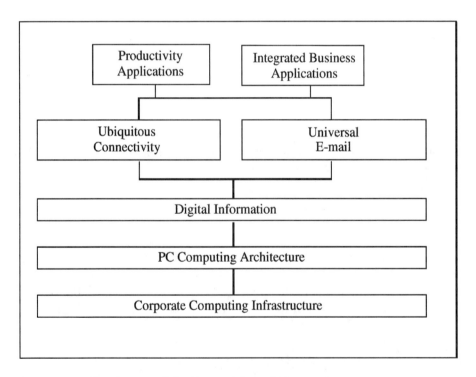

Figure 1-1   The elements of the Microsoft Digital Nervous System.

Development tools play a fundamental role in the effective use of information technology to build a Digital Nervous System. Development tools enable organizations to create, customize, and integrate the corporate applications that can turn information technology into a strategic edge in the marketplace. While all the development tools within the Visual Studio environment provide significant computing power to developers, Visual C++ is still the tool of choice for developers creating robust, full-featured applications.

In March 1997, Microsoft introduced the Visual Studio 97 development system, a complete suite of development tools. Visual Studio, Professional Edition, enables developers to take full advantage of Microsoft Windows operating systems (Windows 95, Windows 98, and Windows NT) and Web development. Visual Studio, Enterprise Edition, is the complete suite of tools for rapidly building data-centric, enterprise solutions. It offers higher-end enterprise features including enterprise database development and design tools, team development support, application design and performance analysis tools, and development versions of Microsoft BackOffice family application servers.

Visual Studio 6.0 is the next generation of the Microsoft enterprise development tools suite. It takes the implementation that Microsoft achieved with Visual Studio 97 one step further, improving greatly several of the component technologies. Most notably, Visual C++ is much easier to work with, Visual InterDev is virtually a brand-new product compared to the 1.0 release in 1997, and the support for database integration throughout the development cycle is vastly improved.

1.2   Overview of Key Technologies

Most developers and businesses today use some combination of tools when developing. For example, many businesses will use Visual Basic to rapidly design prototypes of programs they intend to develop later in Visual C++. In addition, many organizations today will use Visual Basic to design the front ends of their applications (because of its ease of use) and use Visual C++ to design components for the application front-end or back-end processes that require more speed, scalability, and robustness. Determining what applications you should use Visual C++ to write, and how to use Visual C++ within your organization's development process, is a key task. The first step in making that determination is understanding the specific technologies that Microsoft has targeted Visual C++ at as a development platform.

1.2.1   Multitier Enterprise Applications

Integrated enterprise applications are a primary element of a Digital Nervous System. Building such applications requires up-front attention to the design process and also requires modular, open application architecture. As the use of information technology changes to meet new business needs, the very definition of "enterprise applications" is also evolving. While enterprise infrastructures and applications vary widely across organizations, common attributes of modern enterprise applications are as follows:

- Enterprise applications should be component-based for flexibility and scalability.

- All applications require "lifecycle support," including design, development, management, and analysis.

- Enterprise applications require more sophisticated database architectures and are specifically designed to support such architectures.

- Most enterprise applications are developed by teams, with different groups or individuals within the teams handling the development of specific components within the entire application.

- Enterprise applications are, by nature, distributed applications, which must integrate with disparate back-end systems (for example, modern client/server database products such as Oracle and SQL Server and legacy data on mainframes).

To meet these requirements, an enterprise application architecture must include intelligent application partitioning, the use of modular and reusable components, scalability, cross-platform client support, and open interoperability with custom and packaged applications.

Recently, Microsoft introduced the Windows Distributed interNet Applications (DNA) architecture. Using the DNA architecture, enterprise developers can build scalable, multitier business applications that can be delivered over any network, provide open access to diverse data sources across different platforms, and be freely accessed by any client computing platform. Most importantly, Windows DNA helps organizations to leverage their existing technology infrastructure, while also adopting new technologies (such as the Internet and World Wide Web), to meet new business requirements and business models. Developers using Visual Studio can build applications based on the DNA architecture. Figure 1-2 shows how the different levels in the DNA model interact with each other and how the components in Visual Studio interact among and manage the levels in the model.

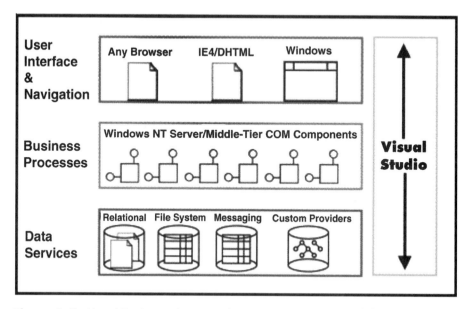

Figure 1-2 Visual Studio combines application programming, middle-tier, object creation, back-end processing, and Internet design capabilities to help you develop Windows DNA-compliant applications.

From both the developer's perspective and management's perspective, the Windows DNA architecture provides several fundamental benefits:

- Developers can cleanly partition their application into independent layers for the user interface, middle-tier business logic, and data access. Dividing the application into layers provides flexibility and modularity so that applications can be easily adapted to changing requirements—and changing environments.

- Developers can build thin-client applications that their applications can then deliver (over the Internet, a corporate Intranet, or any other network) to any browser on any platform. They can also build desktop-specific applications that take maximum advantage of the Windows desktop operating system.

- Applications can now use OLE DB and ADO (the successors to ODBC) to access all major database systems, running on any platform, using a simple, consistent programming model.

- Developers can encapsulate all business logic into reusable Component Object Model (COM) components. Your applications can work hand-in-hand with the operating system to transparently distribute COM components across middle-tier servers on a network (using DCOM or a server product such as MTS). Moreover, a COM component created in one language can be easily reused in any other.

- Middle-tier business components can be run within Microsoft Transaction Server (MTS), which provides seamless support for distributed database transactions based on the XA standard, and thread/resource pooling for servicing thousands of concurrent users. Developers are freed from the underlying programming for XA transactions and thread/resource pooling, as MTS provides these capabilities automatically.

- DNA applications can be process-isolated from each other, so that if a single application on a server fails, the others remain unaffected. Individual COM components within a single application can also run in dedicated processes for additional fault tolerance. The levels of fault tolerance that you can support within your applications will also provide you with significantly increased scalability for your components.

1.2.2 Briefly Introducing the Component Object Model (COM)

In recent years, as applications have become more complex and processing has been distributed more and more across multiple computers, the necessity for component-based development has grown. Microsoft has taken the basic concepts of component-based development and encapsulated them within a standard that Microsoft calls the Component Object Model (COM). COM is such an important concept that there are entire books, in fact entire *shelves* of books, dedicated to the principles and applications of COM development, particularly the ActiveX technologies that Microsoft has derived from the COM standard.

COM, at its most basic level, is about *interfaces*. Every COM object that you create will expose certain interfaces for other objects and applications to access. An interface lets other applications and objects access the COM object's properties, methods, and events without providing those applications with information about the COM object itself. You will learn more about

COM in later chapters of this book; however, it is worthwhile for you to be able to visualize how applications interact with COM objects, as shown in Figure 1-3.

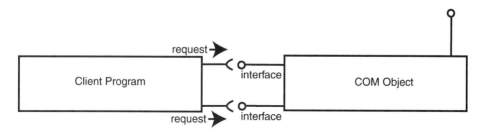

Figure 1-3 A very simple model of how applications interact with COM objects.

In this book, we will work only minimally with COM—the concepts that you must understand, and the techniques that you must use, are quite advanced and require extensive programming experience.

1.3 Microsoft Visual Studio 6.0 Specifics

Visual Studio 6.0 addresses all aspects of Windows DNA application development, including integrated tools for multitier application design, user interface development, middle-tier component development and assembly, database programming and design, performance analysis, and team-based development support. The features in Visual Studio 6.0 center around the following core design themes:

- Complete suite of tools for component-based development
- Enhanced lifecycle productivity
- Enterprise database tools
- Enhanced support for teams
- Integration with middle-tier application services

The following sections explain each of these themes in detail.

1.3.1 Complete Suite of Tools for Component-Based Application Development

Visual Studio 6.0 is a complete suite of tools for developing multitier applications based on components. Visual Studio 6.0 includes:

- The Visual Basic 6.0 development system, for rapid development of Windows client/server applications, as well as middle-tier business components.
- The Visual C++ 6.0 development system, the leading C++ tool for building the highest performance applications and components.
- The Visual J++ 6.0 development system for Java, Microsoft's new visual development tool for building applets, applications, and components using the Java language.
- The Visual InterDev 6.0 Web development system, an integrated, team-based Web development tool for building Web applications based on HTML, server-side and client-side script, and components created in any language.
- The Visual FoxPro 6.0 database development system, for building workgroup database applications and developing components using the XBASE language.

All the tools within Visual Studio can create and use COM components. For example, a COM component created in Visual C++ can in turn be reused by developers using Visual Basic or Visual FoxPro (or any other tool in the suite). The reusability of COM components lets organizations and developers choose a language based on the existing skills in their organization, as well as the technical requirements of a specific component. No matter what language is chosen, organizations can reuse any component in any other language or tool.

Visual Studio, Enterprise Edition, also includes a set of enterprise tools (in addition to the tools within the Professional Edition) that address a broad range of development lifecycle requirements. These tools are integrated throughout all of the languages in the suite and include:

- Enterprise database tools, most notably Universal Data Access for connectivity to all major RDBMS systems including Microsoft SQL Server, Oracle, Sybase, DB/2, and most other database platforms, as well as new graphical schema design tools for designing tables, relationships, and stored procedures and functions on SQL Server and Oracle databases.
- Application design and performance analysis tools, including the Visual Modeler 2.0, a Unified Modeling Language (UML)-based modeling tool for designing multitier applications, and Visual Studio Analyzer, a graphical performance analysis tool for analyzing distributed applications to quickly locate potential performance bottlenecks.
- Team-based development features, including the Visual SourceSafe 6.0 version control system, the Microsoft Repository, and the Visual Component Manager for managing all aspects of a team-based development project.
- Integrated application services, including development versions of BackOffice 4.5 application servers. Integrated application services include database, messaging, transaction, message queuing, distributed processing, Web application services, security, and SNA connectivity services.

Most of the chapters in this book require only that you have the Professional Edition of Visual Studio. However, some of the later chapters in the book (particularly those that focus on database management and interaction) may require that you use the Enterprise Edition of Visual C++ to achieve full benefit of the code. Throughout this book, if a specific feature requires the Enterprise Edition, the text will alert you to that requirement.

1.3.2 Enhanced Lifecycle Productivity

Visual Studio 6.0 supports a broad spectrum of the development lifecycle. In addition to application programming, Visual Studio includes several important tools to expedite both the design and analysis of applications, including:

- Visual Studio supports logical application design based on the Unified Modeling Language (UML) with the Visual Studio Modeler. In addition, Visual Studio 6.0 includes physical Web site diagramming and design for Microsoft Internet

Information Server and database design tools supporting both SQL Server and Oracle databases.

- Rapid application development support is included in all of the Visual Studio 6.0 development tools. The tools share a relatively common look, allowing developers to easily capitalize on their knowledge base from tool to tool. All tools support component development and assembly based on COM. It is important to recognize, however, that while all the tools in Visual Studio support rapid application development, some support it more fully than others. For example, while Visual C++ wizards will help you quickly design frameworks and achieve basic application functionality, implementing useful components and applications still requires significant programming.

- The Visual Studio Analyzer allows developers to visualize distributed solutions, understand their structure and component flows, locate problems, and isolate performance bottlenecks.

- The Microsoft Repository and the Visual Component Manager manage components written in any language in the suite. Developers can use the Visual Component Manager to publish, catalog, and search for components, designs, specifications and other elements of a project to or from the Repository.

- Visual Studio 6.0 includes enhanced build, package, and deploy functionality across the tools, enabling developers to easily deploy distributed components to staging servers for testing. For runtime deployment, Visual Studio enables components to be packaged for automatic replication via Microsoft Site Server, enabling staging servers to be easily replicated across many servers in the organization. Microsoft Systems Management Server can additionally be used to automate deployment of client-side applications and components.

Figure 1-4 shows a basic model of how the components within Visual Studio interact with each other to support all aspects of the development lifecycle.

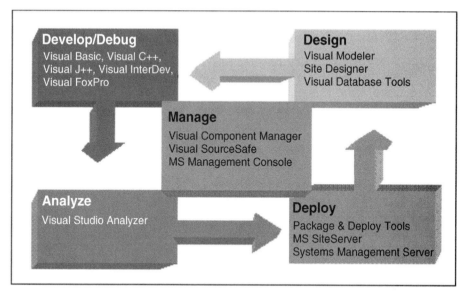

Figure 1-4   Different components within Visual Studio 6.0 support all aspects of the application development lifecycle.

1.3.3 Enterprise Database Tools

Visual Studio includes broad support for databases within the enterprise. Generally, the database tools within Visual Studio can be divided into two categories: universal data access tools and visual data access tools.

Universal Data Access is Microsoft's strategy for providing high-performance access to all types of information (including relational and nonrelational data) across organizations, from the desktop to the enterprise. Universal Data Access enables all Visual Studio tools to access virtually any data source on virtually any platform. Universal Data Access consists of three core technologies: OLE DB, ActiveX Data Objects (ADO), and Open Database Connectivity (ODBC).

OLE DB is Microsoft's system-level programming interface to diverse data sources. OLE DB specifies a set of COM interfaces that encapsulate, or hide, various database management system services. OLE DB is designed for non-relational as well as relational information sources on disparate platforms. These platforms can include electronic mail and file system stores, text, graphical data, geographical data, and custom business objects.

ODBC, Microsoft's low-level technology for database access, continues to provide standard access to most relational database systems on the market. In addition, the OLE DB Provider for ODBC uses existing ODBC drivers to access relational data. However, many developers are moving to the OLE DB model from the ODBC model because of its speed and usability.

ADO is Microsoft's strategic, high-level interface to data, completely isolating developers from the underlying OLE DB and ODBC technologies. ADO supplies an open, application-level data access object model that allows corporate programmers to write database applications over OLE DB data using any language. All of the Visual Studio tools can use ADO to access data. Through ADO, developers now have easy access to more types of data than in previous versions of Visual Studio and will, generally, need to spend far less time writing complex client/server code. Figure 1-5 shows a model of how the three data access technologies work to provide applications with access to data.

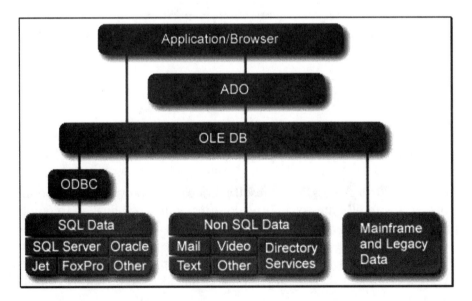

Figure 1-5 The Universal Data Access Architecture provides a unified layer of interoperability across multiple, traditional, and nontraditional data sources.

On the other hand, the Visual Database Tools, integrated into all members of the Visual Studio suite, provide extensive support for building data-centric applications rapidly. The Microsoft Visual Database Tools include the following features:

- The Data View control, which lets applications connect to and explore any ODBC or OLE DB database.
- The Query Designer, which lets developers easily design, execute, and save complex SQL queries.
- The Database Designer, which lets developers create and modify Microsoft SQL Server and Oracle database schemas from within Visual Studio, including individual tables, relationships, indexes, and keys, as well as entire database schemas.
- The Stored Procedure Editor, which lets developers create and edit Microsoft SQL Server stored procedures and Oracle subprograms and functions using a color-coded editor for Transact-SQL (SQL Server) and PL/SQL (Oracle).
- Support for Stored Procedure Debugging, which lets developers remotely debug stored procedures on Microsoft SQL Server 6.5/7.0 databases.

1.3.4 Enhanced Support for Team Development — All Kinds of Teams

Team development is a critical requirement for an enterprise development tools suite. Not only must the tool set support basic team features for networked environments, the tool set must also accommodate the diverse roles that make up such teams. For example, most Intranet and Internet applications are developed by teams that include programmers and nonprogrammers alike. With Visual Studio 6.0, a rich, team-based project model is supported that provides true team development inclusive of the Visual Studio tools targeted at developers and technical architects. If you add the Microsoft FrontPage Web site creation and management tool, which enables content authors and editors to work as integrated members of the project team, you can present team content even more easily.

Source code control is another team feature integrated throughout the Visual Studio suite. Visual SourceSafe 6.0 is provided in the box and enables developers to secure source code, manage revisions, and prevent editing conflicts (through file locking) during the development process. In addition to providing source code control for components developed in Visual J++, Visual Basic, Visual C++, and Visual FoxPro, Visual SourceSafe also fully integrates with Visual InterDev Web projects to secure and manage all elements of a dynamic Web application. The project-oriented features of Visual SourceSafe increase the efficiency of managing the day-to-day tasks associated with team-based application and Web site development.

The Microsoft Repository allows component information to be shared—not only by multiple team members, but also by multiple tools. By providing an open, extensible framework for storing software components and information about them (such as their methods, data types, and relationships to other components), Microsoft Repository enables tool interoperability across the application lifecycle. More benefits of component-based development can be realized, including more effective component management and higher levels of automation. Visual Studio 6.0 provides access to repository components through the Visual Component Manager (VCM), which is integrated throughout the tools in the suite. The VCM makes it easy for teams of developers to share a wide range of component types, enabling effective component and code reuse both within a development team and across an entire organization. The VCM allows developers to easily publish, find, and catalog components, including ActiveX controls, COM components, Java applets, HTML and ASP pages, UML models, specifications, and source code.

The Visual Component Manager's native store is the Microsoft Repository 2.0, allowing components to be stored on either SQL Server or Access databases. The VCM allows many repository databases to be open simultaneously, so the developer is able to maintain a set of component repositories, including for example, a personal component repository on Access, a project team component repository on SQL Server, and an organization-wide repository on SQL Server. Both the VCM and the Repository are extensible through SDKs, allowing third parties and end users to build repository applications and VCM handlers to manage their specific component types.

1.3.5 Integration with Application Services

It is critical that the enterprise development toolset let developers easily integrate middle-tier components with the rich set of application services required to support diverse application scenarios. Microsoft Visual Studio provides a set of integrated application services that make it much easier for developers to take advantage of critical application services such as data access, distributed processing, transactions, message queuing, messaging/workgroup services, security, Web application services, and SNA connectivity. These services are provided as programmable COM objects integrated into the development environment. In addition, Visual Studio (Enterprise Edition only) includes a development version of the Microsoft BackOffice suite of application servers, making it easy to take full advantage of these services from any development workstation.

1.4   Visual C++-Specific Improvements in Version 6.0

As earlier parts of this chapter indicated, Microsoft has mostly "stayed the course" with Visual C++ 6.0. The latest version of Visual C++ combines significant improvements in productivity and speed with a proven development environment. And this is good news for any development team that's building a version 1.0 product or application. You need to be able to rely on a software development tool that is mature and stable, with broad industry support, to reduce the complications your immature product is likely to present.

1.4.1 Edit and Continue Debugging

Edit and Continue debugging may be the most significant improvement in Visual C++ 6.0. Edit and Continue debugging will let you make several changes to source code during a debugging session, then resume the debugging execution without recompilation. If your source code files are large, and presumably they will be in an enterprise development environment, this is a major time-saving feature. You will learn more about Edit and Continue debugging in Chapter 2.

1.4.2 IntelliSense Technology

One of the most helpful technologies in recent editions of Visual Basic has been IntelliSense technology. In Visual Basic, IntelliSense monitors your typing and displays information about functions, procedures, or objects when it recognizes your entry — a significant benefit for avoiding missed parameters, invocation of unsupported object methods, and so on.

For Visual C++ 6.0, Microsoft has added IntelliSense to the Visual C++ IDE. IntelliSense completes code statements, with a full display of class members, function prototypes, identifier declarations, and comments both available and selectable as you type. IntelliSense also has a concept of scope, meaning that it is generally a good indicator of whether or not you are making a valid invocation within your program. Figure 1-6 shows the Visual C++ IDE with IntelliSense suggesting a function reference.

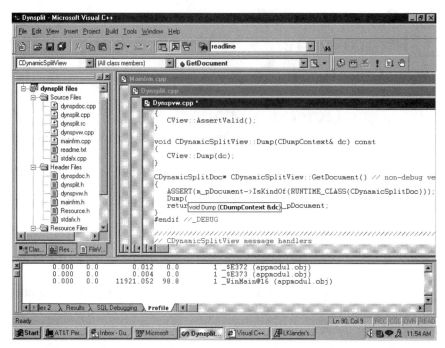

Figure 1-6   IntelliSense speeds code entry and helps avoid skipping back and forth between source and header files.

1.4.3 Support for MTS Within AppWizard

For enterprise developers, the next major improvement in Visual C++ 6.0 is the ATL COM AppWizard's support for MTS components. With the impending release of Windows NT 2000 and the likely full-scale use of the Microsoft Management Console (MMC), having the ability to generate project settings to support this critical multitier technology is going to be very important for enterprise developers.

1.4.4 Support for Internet Development

Microsoft has indicated clearly (as has much of this chapter) that they are moving their developer support emphasis to the middle-tier and back end, which is consistent with Internet development trends. Despite this shift, Visual C++ 6.0 still provides strong support for client-side development. In fact, the MFC AppWizard now includes support for Internet Explorer 4.0-style "Rebar" controls and Internet Explorer 4.0 HTML/DHTML functions. MFC support for the new `CHtmlView` class, together with extensive support for Dynamic HTML development and Web database development, helps make Visual C++ an even more useful tool for creating DNA-style applications.

1.4.5 New Database Support

Despite all the enhancements to the Visual Studio suite and the Visual C++ IDE, arguably the most important enhancement to Visual C++ 6.0 is support for OLE DB (which you have may used with the Visual C++ technology preview, released in the Fall of 1997). OLE DB support makes a significant difference in the ease of data access within Visual C++ to non–DAO-compliant databases. As managing data becomes the primary focus of many applications (often called the data-centric program model), Visual C++ support for OLE DB promises to be an important enhancement for many enterprise developers. As you will learn in later chapters, you can easily add OLE DB support to your application through the ATL Object Wizard.

Complete OLE DB support in the wizard generates code to build a full-featured OLE DB provider, including the underlying COM. Microsoft claims its wizard will reduce the amount of manually required code for database support from 6,000 lines to 100 lines.

1.4.6 Miscellaneous Improvements to the Environment

In addition to the features outlined previously, there are two other especially significant changes to the development environment. Firstly, Visual C++ 6.0 performs dynamic ClassView window updating. In real time, methods, properties, and even new classes will appear within the window as you enter them in the Code Editor.

Secondly, Visual C++ 6.0 posts significant gains in performance at compile time. In fact, Microsoft claims a 30% improvement on debug projects and 15% on nondebug projects. Microsoft also claims that compiled Visual C++ code will execute faster, based on new optimized keywords.

1.5 Summary

Organizations need the ability to harness information technology to provide a competitive advantage. Microsoft's vision for corporate computing encompasses a corporate Digital Nervous System to provide free flow of information that empowers corporations to react faster to changing business needs, make more informed decisions, get closer to customers and business partners, and focus on business, not technology. Development tools play a crucial role in enabling corporations to achieve a Digital Nervous System. Microsoft's enterprise development strategy centers on the Visual Studio development tools suite, in conjunction with the Windows Distributed interNet Application (DNA) framework. Together, Visual Studio and Windows DNA enable organizations to rapidly build well-architected solutions that can provide a competitive edge in the market.

As a Visual C++ programmer, your biggest concern (while the interoperability of the studio is important) is likely to be the performance and usability of the Visual C++ IDE. Microsoft has made significant improvements in many different parts of the Visual C++ compiler and editor, and careful use of the new improvements is likely not only to speed your ability to write clear and concise code, but also to result in applications that are more reusable, scalable, and robust.

Philosophically, many programmers creating enterprise applications feel that the application's *design* is where they must focus the majority of their time, as opposed to *writing* the applications themselves. While programmers will never be free from writing the code to implement the designs for applications that they create, Visual C++ 6.0 helps simplify the move from design to writing by providing you with additional tools to make your design a reality.

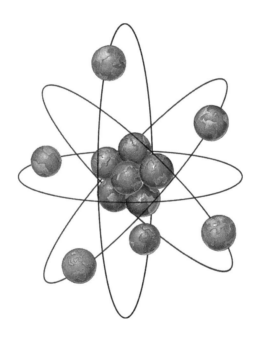

DEBUGGING AS A DEVELOPMENT CONSIDERATION

Topics in this Chapter

- Understanding the Different Types of Programming Errors
- Understanding the Components of a Useful Debugger
- The Visual Studio Integrated Debugger
- Introducing the Various Debug Windows and Their Uses
- Using Breakpoints and Single-Stepping When Debugging
- Simple Debugging Techniques
- Additional Features of the Visual C++ Debugger
- Advanced Debugging Considerations
- Summary

Chapter 2

Throughout this book, you will work closely with the Visual C++ development system to create Visual C++ applications. However, it is almost inevitable that during your learning process you will encounter mistakes in your program code. Resolving program code mistakes is known as *debugging*. Because debugging is such a crucial topic for good software design, it is worth discussing the tools and techniques that you will most commonly use with this product. Throughout this chapter, we will analyze both the tools at your disposal and effective techniques for using them. While talking about debugging may seem premature—after all, we haven't even discussed any programming, yet—good use of the debugging tools will simplify development so significantly that it is worth covering here, early in the book.

2.1 Understanding the Different Types of Programming Errors

When you write programs in any language, it is virtually certain that you will make mistakes during the initial programming. There are two basic types of errors that you will make when you write programs: syntax errors and logic errors. Syntax errors tend to be much simpler than logic errors and are generally easier to locate. In fact, when you compile programs that you write within

Visual C++, the compiler will advise you of syntax errors within your program code. For many syntax errors, the compiler will not compile executable code for your program because it cannot interpret the error.

Logic errors, on the other hand, are not so easy for you to track down and solve. A logic error may be relatively simple to locate, or it may be very difficult. For example, the following logic error is relatively straightforward:

```
cout << "This is the first line."
     << "This is the second line.";
```

The code will print both lines of text on the same line. Solving a logic error of this simplicity is relatively easy. However, solving a logic error similar to the following can be substantially more difficult:

```
if (a!=c)
  cout << "A is not equal to C";
  cout << "You must make A equal to C!";
```

When the program code executes, the program will always display the text Make A Equal to C! The logic error is in the lack of brackets around the two output statements. Even this second error, however, is very simple compared to the logic errors that you can make within a complex Windows program. Luckily, Visual C++ includes an excellent, integrated symbolic debugger. The Visual C++ debugger includes many powerful features, such as Just-in-Time debugging (the ability to debug programs that crash while launched outside the development environment) or remote debugging. The debugger is also fully integrated with other features of Visual Studio, such as the Source Browser and source editors.

When you are faced with the task of having to identify performance bottlenecks, a very specific type of logic error, you will use another tool, the Source Profiler, to identify the location of the performance bottlenecks.

2.2   Understanding the Components of a Useful Debugger

Clearly, debugging applications can be a complex and difficult process. As applications have become more complex and larger, the need for powerful debugging tools has only increased. As a rule, to be useful, a debugger should have at least four capabilities:

1. Tracing
2. Breakpoints
3. Watching variables
4. Changing values

Probably the most important facility a debugger can offer is a trace utility. A trace utility lets you run an application and at the same time watch exactly where the execution pointer is in your actual source code. In Visual C++, you have several different means of tracing program execution, from stepping through each line of code individually to executing entire programs until the program reaches a certain point.

As you can imagine, simply tracing through a program, line-by-line, can be very tedious, particularly when you know that some (or even most of the) code in the program works correctly. Even a small program (say, 1,000 lines) could take a very long time to step through, looking for one particular area of concern in the program. For larger programs, one can conceive of actually stepping through thousands of lines of code, taking hours just to reach a single routine that is not executing correctly. Because of the size of many program files, an efficient means of stopping the program's execution at some predetermined point in the source code or when some specific condition happens is a second important tool in any debugger. Most debuggers handle such stopping of program execution through the use of *breakpoints.*

Clearly, watching an application step through a series of instructions and understanding what execution path leads to a certain error is a very useful debugging technique. However, you will generally find that understanding *why* an error occurs is as valuable, if not more valuable, than understanding *what* happened before the error. A good debugging tool should let you view the current values or contents of all program variables having scope or context at the current point of execution within the program file. After you understand how the contents of a variable can negatively impact program performance (for example, oversize values, undefined values, and so on) or cause an exception, you will often find it helpful to be able to change that variable's contents on-the-fly to ensure that values within the correct range do not also cause an error. The fourth valuable feature of a debugging tool is that it lets you change the values or contents of variables during program execution, giving you the ability to check your program's reaction to a broad spectrum of variable values without your needing to rerun the program for each value set.

As you will learn through the rest of this chapter, the Visual Studio integrated debugger provides you with all of the capabilities already identified as necessary for a good debugging tool, as well as many others.

2.3   The Visual Studio Integrated Debugger

Visual C++ and the Visual Studio shell launch the integrated debugger whenever you run an application in debug mode. As you will learn later in this chapter, the shell will also launch the integrated debugger whenever you select the Debug button on an "Illegal Operation" dialog box. Within Visual C++, to launch an application in debug mode, you can select the Go, Step Into, or Run to Cursor commands from the Build menu's Start Debug submenu. However, before you can start the debugger, you must ensure that Visual C++ has included debugging informations when it compiles the application that you intend to debug.

2.3.1 Preparing an Application for Debugging

As the previous section indicates, in order for the symbolic debugger to function correctly and you to be able to use debugging information with your Visual C++ projects, you must instruct the compiler to compile the application with debugging information. If the application you want to debug is an MFC application that you originally created through AppWizard, chances are that you do not have to do anything: the AppWizard already created a debug configuration for your project and made it the default configuration.

However, if you created the project from scratch, or it is not an MFC application, and you must create a debug configuration yourself, you can do so in the Project Settings dialog box. You must set the appropriate compiler and linker options within this dialog box, After you do so, the Visual C++ IDE will let you debug the application.

To set the compiler options, select the Project menu Settings option. Visual C++ will display the Project Settings dialog box. Within the Project Setting dialog box, select the C/C++ tab. Visual C++ will change the display on the dialog box to reflect the C/C++ project settings. On the left-hand side of the dialog box, select the Win32 Debug option within the combo box. Within the Debug info combo box, select the Program Database for Edit and Continue option. Then, in the Optimizations combo box, select the Disable

(Debug) option. Figure 2-1 shows the Project Settings dialog box after you enable debugging.

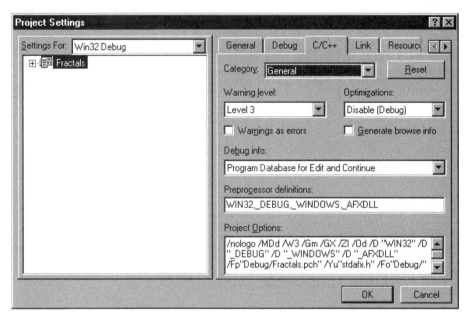

Figure 2-1 The Project Settings dialog box as it appears after you set the debug options.

If you wish to use Visual Studio's Source Browser features, you may also set the Generate browse info check box. Visual C++ automatically turns off the Generate browse information switch to save compiler time when it generates a new application through the AppWizard.

If you are using the compiler from the command line or from within a custom makefile, you may need to set the debugging options manually. To turn off optimization, use the /Od compiler option. To turn on the generation of debugging information, specify the /Zi option. You can learn more about command-line compiler directives in the Visual C++ help file.

Another setting that is important for you to keep in mind when setting debugging options is the option that lets you specify that your project should be linked with the debug version of the C runtime library during compilation. To instruct the compiler to use the debug library, change the selection within the Category combo box to the Code Generation option. Next, select the debug library option that is correct for your application within the Use runtime library combo box. Figure 2-2 shows the Project Setting dialog box and the possible selections for runtime library choices.

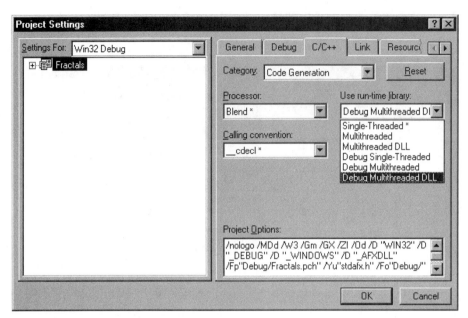

Figure 2-2   The Project Setting dialog box during the selection of the correct runtime library linking.

Again, to set the correct option from the command line, you would use the /M compiler switch. To select the debug DLL option, select the /MDd command-line option. To select the debug single-threaded library option, select the /MLd command-line option. Finally, to select the debug multithreaded library option, select the /MTd command-line option.

When you create a project for debugging, you must also modify the linker settings for the project to compile and link correctly. You can also set the linker settings from within the Project Settings dialog box. Select the Link tab and the General option with the Category combo box. To turn on the generation of debugging information, set the Generate debug info check box. Figure 2-3 shows the Project Settings dialog box after you set the Linker for debugging.

Just as you can set the debug options from the compiler command line, you can set the debug options in the linker from the linker command line. To do so, specify the /debug switch on the linker command line.

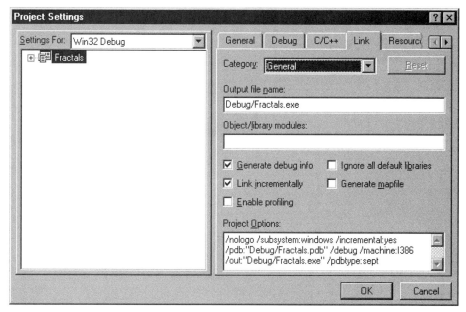

Figure 2-3   The Link panel after you set the linker for debugging.

2.3.2 Using the Debugger When You Run an Application

After you recompile your application with the debug settings, you can run the application in debug mode by using any of the commands (except the Attach to Process command) within the Build menu Start Debug submenu.

You can also control how the debugger runs the application through the Project Settings dialog box. Within the Debug tab of the Project Settings dialog box, you can control certain factors about how the program executes within the debugger. One of the fields of special interest on the Debug panel is the Executable for debug session field. You can use this field to debug dynamic-link library (DLL) projects. Instead of specifying the name of the DLL, however, you should specify the name of a program that loads and accesses the DLL. For example, to debug an ActiveX control (a special type of DLL), you can use the Visual C++ utility TSTCON32.EXE as the debug session executable. You can select the TSTCON32.EXE container from the right arrow next to the Executable for debug session field, as shown in Figure 2-4. (The textual reference is "ActiveX Control Text Container.")

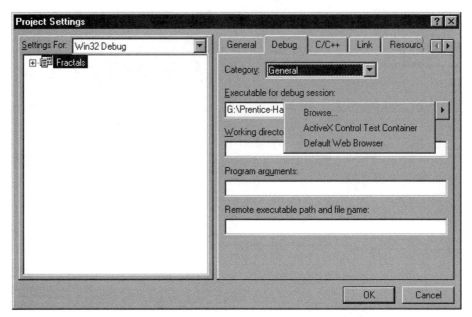

Figure 2-4   Setting the Debugger to debug an ActiveX control within the test control container.

When you begin a debug session, depending on your Visual Studio settings, any one of a variety of debug windows may appear within the Visual Studio window. Other windows (such as the Project Workspace window) that are normally present may also disappear. The Visual Studio menu bar also changes; the debug menu replaces the Build menu.

The application that you select for debugging starts executing and will continue to execute until either the debugger reaches a breakpoint or until you select the Break option from the Debug menu and interrupt the application's execution.

2.4   Introducing the Various Debug Windows and Their Uses

During a debugging session, Visual Studio presents debugging information in a series of debug windows. If Visual Studio is not currently displaying any or all of these windows, you can use the Visual Studio View menu to instruct the IDE to display each or all of the windows. You can display all of the debugging windows that you will learn about in this section as either normal windows or as docking windows. If you set the windows to display as docking windows, the windows will also appear in the toolbar pop-up menu, the menu that Visual Studio will display if you right-click an empty toolbar area.

Source windows are regular source editor windows. However, during a debugging session, special debugging functions are also available through the pop-up menu that you invoke by right-clicking inside a source window. You can set, clear, or enable and disable breakpoints from the source window pop-up menu. You can also execute single-stepping commands (that is, execute a single line of program at a time). You can also invoke the Disassembly windows and the QuickWatch dialog from the source window pop-up menu.

2.4.1 The Variables Window

The Variables window presents a look at variables that have definition within the current function. The window has three panels: the Auto panel, the Locals panel, and the `this` panel. The Auto panel displays variables that are declared locally (and thus, created on the stack) within the current procedure. The Locals panel shows all variables that have local definition within the current function, including both locally defined variables and function parameters. The `this` panel, as you might expect, shows the object to which the this pointer currently points. Figure 2-5 shows the Variables window with the Auto panel selected.

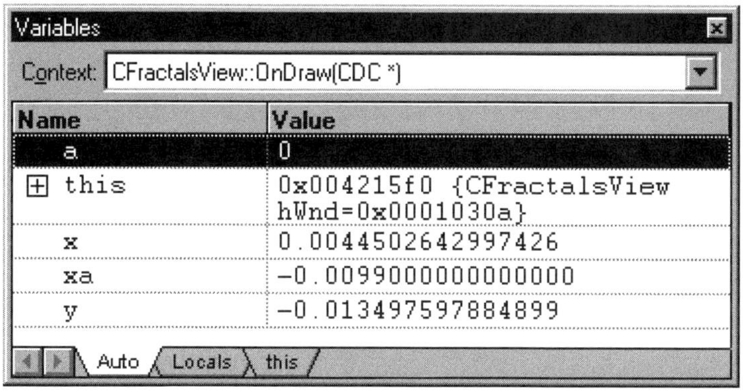

Figure 2-5   The Variables window shows the Name and Value of variables having definition in the current function.

You can also use the Variables window to view variables in the scope of functions that called the currently executing function. In addition, as you single-step through your code within the currently executing function, the Variables window will display all changed variables in a different color.

Finally, you can use the Variables window to modify the values of data items that are of a simple type (such as int, double, or pointer types). To modify a value, double-click the value in the Variables window. If the debugger will let you modify the value, the IDE will display a text cursor within the window.

2.4.2 The Watch Window

During a debugging session, you can use the Watch window to monitor the values of expressions. You can use the keyboard to enter an expression within the Watch window's Name field, or you can drag the expression or paste it from a source window. Figure 2-6 shows the Watch window.

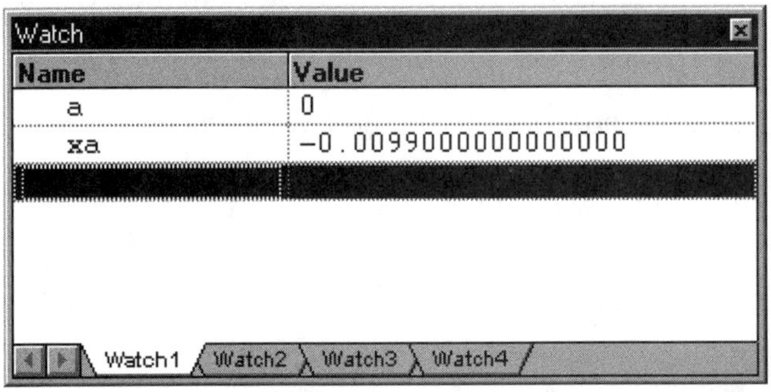

Figure 2-6 The Watch window displays information about expressions' current values.

As you can see, the Watch window has four panels. During a debugging session, you can use these panels to maintain four different sets of watch expressions. As your programs become more complex and you use custom classes and objects, being able to watch different expression sets will become more and more valuable to you.

Like the Variables window, the Watch window uses a different color to mark expressions whose values change as you single-step through your code. In addition, you can use the Watch window to modify the values of data items of a simple type just as you would the Variables window.

2.4.3 The Registers Window

The Registers window shows the current values of the registers in the computer's processor, including its floating-point registers (if you should decide to include them). Just as with the Variables window and the Watch window, the Registers window will change the color of values that change during single-stepping. Figure 2-7 shows the Registers window.

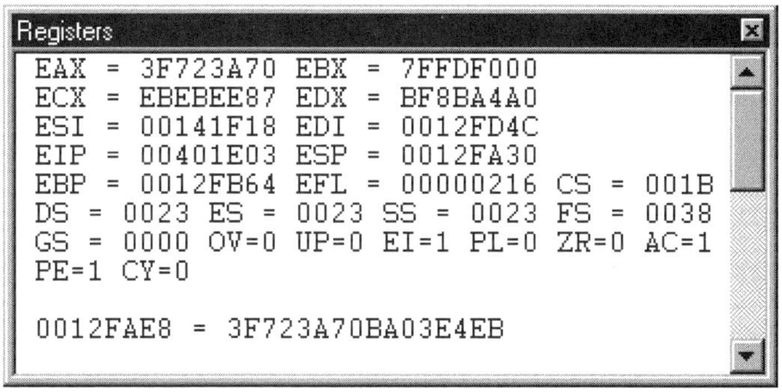

```
Registers                                              ☒
EAX = 3F723A70 EBX = 7FFDF000                          ▲
ECX = EBEBEE87 EDX = BF8BA4A0
ESI = 00141F18 EDI = 0012FD4C
EIP = 00401E03 ESP = 0012FA30
EBP = 0012FB64 EFL = 00000216 CS = 001B
DS = 0023 ES = 0023 SS = 0023 FS = 0038
GS = 0000 OV=0 UP=0 EI=1 PL=0 ZR=0 AC=1
PE=1 CY=0

0012FAE8 = 3F723A70BA03E4EB                            ▼
```

Figure 2-7 The Registers window shows the current values within the processor registers.

Registers are storage locations built into the computer's processor—storage locations that, typically, can store small integers (classic registers were actually only a single byte in size). Registers are used in conjunction with the computer's stack for the internal management of variable values.

2.4.4 The Memory Window

The Memory window lets you view memory contents in the address space of the process (application, DLL, or other program) that you are debugging. The Memory window can display memory contents in byte format, word (short hex) format, and double word (long hex) format. If you choose byte format, the Memory window will also display the ASCII characters that the bytes you are viewing represent along the window's right-hand side. You can use the Memory window pop-up menu to select the format that the Memory window will use to display values. To invoke the pop-up menu, right-click anywhere within the Memory window. Figure 2-8 shows the Memory window starting at this pointer's location in memory.

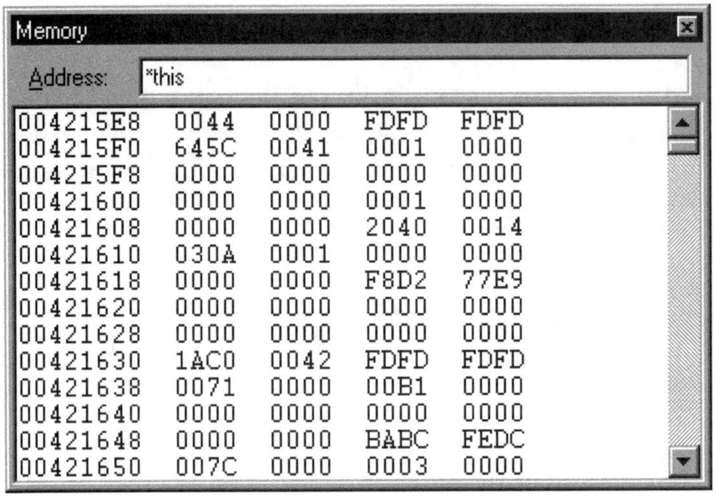

```
Memory                                              [x]
Address:  *this
004215E8   0044   0000   FDFD   FDFD        [▲]
004215F0   645C   0041   0001   0000        [▓]
004215F8   0000   0000   0000   0000
00421600   0000   0000   0001   0000
00421608   0000   0000   2040   0014
00421610   030A   0001   0000   0000
00421618   0000   0000   F8D2   77E9
00421620   0000   0000   0000   0000
00421628   0000   0000   0000   0000
00421630   1AC0   0042   FDFD   FDFD
00421638   0071   0000   00B1   0000
00421640   0000   0000   0000   0000
00421648   0000   0000   BABC   FEDC
00421650   007C   0000   0003   0000        [▼]
```

Figure 2-8 The Memory window displays values within process memory.

To display memory at a specific location, type an expression in the Address field of the Memory window's toolbar. Note that the Memory window may display memory locations that precede the specified address. Because the window might display as a symbolic expression (such as a variable name), it may be difficult for you to interpret the Memory window's contents. However, the window will automatically position the text cursor at the location that corresponds to the beginning of that expression's memory location, so you can use the cursor's position as a guide to where the block of memory you want to analyze begins. Like the other debug windows you have learned about, the Memory window will display changed memory contents in a different color as you single-step through a project.

2.4.5 The Call Stack Window

The Call Stack window lists the hierarchy of function calls that led to the current function the application is executing. If you double-click a function within the Call Stack window, the debugger will update source windows and other debug windows to reflect the context of the function you select. Selecting a function in the Call Stack window (by single-clicking) and pressing the F7 key executes code until the program reaches the specified function. Figure 2-9 shows the Call Stack window.

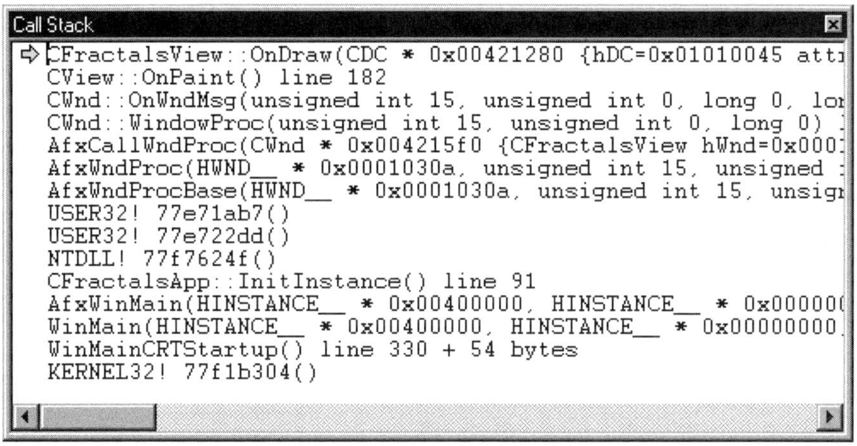

```
Call Stack                                                          ☒
⇨ CFractalsView::OnDraw(CDC * 0x00421280 {hDC=0x01010045 att⌐
  CView::OnPaint() line 182
  CWnd::OnWndMsg(unsigned int 15, unsigned int 0, long 0, lor
  CWnd::WindowProc(unsigned int 15, unsigned int 0, long 0)
  AfxCallWndProc(CWnd * 0x004215f0 {CFractalsView hWnd=0x000⌐
  AfxWndProc(HWND__ * 0x0001030a, unsigned int 15, unsigned
  AfxWndProcBase(HWND__ * 0x0001030a, unsigned int 15, unsigr
  USER32! 77e71ab7()
  USER32! 77e722dd()
  NTDLL! 77f7624f()
  CFractalsApp::InitInstance() line 91
  AfxWinMain(HINSTANCE__ * 0x00400000, HINSTANCE__ * 0x000000(
  WinMain(HINSTANCE__ * 0x00400000, HINSTANCE__ * 0x00000000
  WinMainCRTStartup() line 330 + 54 bytes
  KERNEL32! 77f1b304()
◄                                                                  ►
```

Figure 2-9 The Call Stack window displays the function call series that led to the currently executing function.

When you debug your programs, you can use the Call Stack window as a very effective tool in determining what call series caused a specific bug.

2.4.6 The Disassembly Window

The Disassembly window provides a view of the assembly language code that the compiler generates when it compiles your application. While the Disassembly window has the focus (that is, it is the currently selected window), you can use the single-stepping functions of the debugger to step through the assembly language code (rather than the actual program code) one instruction at a time. Stepping through assembly language code may help you determine what part of an expression is causing an error. Figure 2-10 shows the Disassembly window.

You can access a special feature of the Disassembly window through the pop-up menu that Visual Studio will display each time you right-click within the window. The Set Next Statement option lets you alter the processor's instruction pointer. With the Set Next Statement option, you can set the next instruction for the processor to perform to whatever instruction is under the text cursor. For example, you can use this feature to skip portions of your program code. However, you should use this feature with extreme care. If you set the statement to be one in the body of another function, or if you fail to maintain the stack correctly, the results will be unpredictable and the application you are debugging will probably crash.

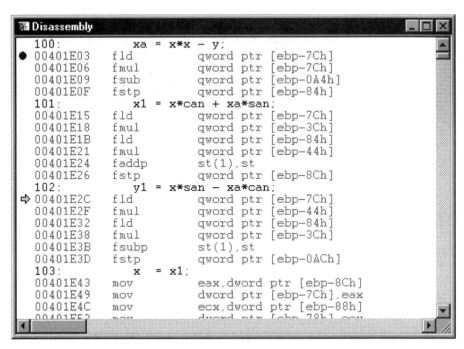

Figure 2-10   The Disassembly window shows the actual assembly language code for your program.

2.5 Using Breakpoints and Single-Stepping When Debugging

The two most fundamental features of any debugger, and two of the most powerful features of the integrated debugger that comes with Visual C++, are the capability to insert breakpoints into program code and the ability to execute program code step-by-step (a single instruction at a time).

The simplest way for you to place a breakpoint into your code is to move the text cursor in the source window to the specific location where you want to set a break. After placing the text cursor, press the F9 key to set the breakpoint. Visual Studio will place a large reddish-brown dot to the left of the line to indicate the breakpoint. Figure 2-11 shows a source window with two breakpoints set within it.

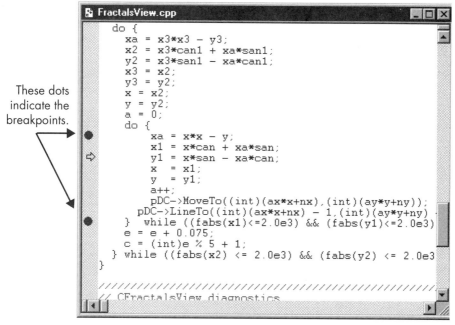

These dots indicate the breakpoints.

```
FractalsView.cpp
do {
    xa = x3*x3 - y3;
    x2 = x3*can1 + xa*san1;
    y2 = x3*san1 - xa*can1;
    x3 = x2;
    y3 = y2;
    x = x2;
    y = y2;
    a = 0;
    do {
        xa = x*x - y;
        x1 = x*can + xa*san;
        y1 = x*san - xa*can;
        x  = x1;
        y  = y1;
        a++;
        pDC->MoveTo((int)(ax*x+nx),(int)(ay*y+ny));
        pDC->LineTo((int)(ax*x+nx) - 1,(int)(ay*y+ny)
    }  while ((fabs(x1)<=2.0e3) && (fabs(y1)<=2.0e3)
    e = e + 0.075;
    c = (int)e % 5 + 1;
} while ((fabs(x2) <= 2.0e3) && (fabs(y2) <= 2.0e3
}
////////////////////////////////////////////////
// CFractalsView diagnostics
```

Figure 2-11 Two breakpoints are set in this source window.

There are two important things to note about simple breakpoints before you learn about more complex breakpoints. First, you can set a breakpoint at any location within a source file, on a comment line, on a bracket, and so on. Simple breakpoints have the result that, when you run the program in debug mode, execution will always halt whenever one is encountered. Second, Visual Studio lets you set breakpoints within the Disassembly window.

You can achieve much finer control over breakpoint settings through the Edit menu's Breakpoints option. If you select the Breakpoints option, Visual Studio displays the Breakpoints dialog, where you can set three different kinds of breakpoints.

Location breakpoints are breakpoints that interrupt program execution at a specific location. Location breakpoints are the breakpoints that you use the F9 key to set within your source code. You can also add a conditional check to a location breakpoint. If you add a conditional check, the breakpoint will only interrupt execution if the specific condition evaluates as true.

Data breakpoints interrupt program execution when a specific expression's value changes. For both data and location breakpoints, you can click the triangular button next to the breakpoint identifier to invoke the Advanced Breakpoint dialog box. Within the Advanced Breakpoint dialog box, you can specify the context of the breakpoint, including the function within which the breakpoint applies, the source file that contains the breakpoint, and the executable file in which the breakpoint is located. Figure 2-12 shows the Advanced Breakpoint dialog box.

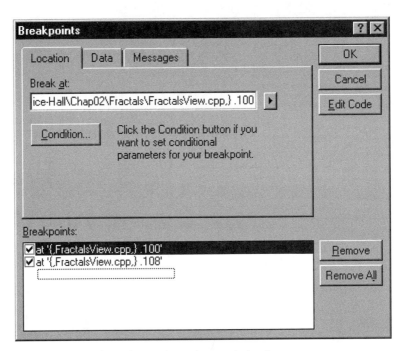

Figure 2-12   The Advanced Breakpoint dialog box.

The third type of breakpoint that you can set within your program is called a *message breakpoint*. A message breakpoint interrupts your program's execution whenever one of your program's window procedures receives a specific message (windows receive messages from the operating system all the time; each time the user presses a key while the window is active, for example). Setting message breakpoints lets you stop program execution only when a certain action (such as an OLE drag-and-drop action or the user's pressing of a key combination such as Alt+F10) occurs and ensures that the window in question processes the action correctly. Figure 2-13 shows the Breakpoints dialog box during the setting of a message breakpoint.

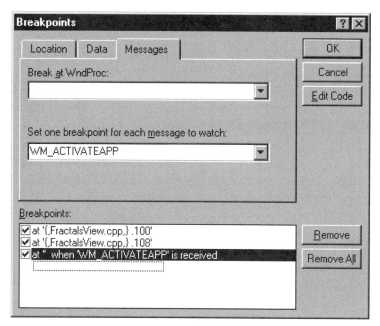

Figure 2-13   Setting a message breakpoint to halt execution when the window receives the WM_ACTIVATEAPP message.

A breakpoint can be either active or disabled. When a breakpoint of any type is active and your application is executing in Debug mode, the Breakpoints dialog box will display a checkmark next to the breakpoint. If you click the checkmark next to a breakpoint, the breakpoint will become inactive. Visual Studio will display inactive breakpoints as a hollow red circle in the source window.

In addition to using breakpoints, you can use the Debug menu Break option to interrupt program execution at any time. However, such an interruption is asynchronous by nature and will often interrupt the program deep inside a series of nested system function calls. In such cases, you can use the Debug menu's Step Out option to step out of such system functions until you reach a recognizable location in your code.

The Debug menu's Step Out option is one of several single-stepping commands that you can use to execute your program one step at a time. The most basic single-stepping command is the Step Into command, which executes the next line in the program's source file or the next instruction in the Disassembly window (depending on what window has the focus). If the next line in the program or instruction in the Disassembly window is a function call (or a

JMP statement), the program will step into the body of the function on the next Step Into command.

The Step Over command is similar to the Step Into command, except the Step Over command will not step into the body of a function. Rather, the debugger will execute all the code within the function (and any other functions it calls) and resume step-by-step execution at the first statement following the function call in the original (calling) function.

The Run to Cursor command effectively places a one-shot breakpoint at the cursor's current location in a source window or the Disassembly window. The debugger will continue executing the program code until it reaches the cursor position or until the debugger encounters another breakpoint.

You can use the Step Into Specific Function command to control which function the program's execution enters in the case of nested function calls in a single source line. If the debugger's execution pointer is not currently on a line that calls nested function calls, the Visual Studio IDE will disable the Debug menu's Step Into Specific Function option.

Many of the Debug menu's step commands have keyboard shortcuts. As you will learn, stepping through a program will generally be much simpler if you use the keyboard shortcuts. Table 2-1 shows the keyboard shortcuts for the Debug menu's Step commands.

Table 2-1 Keyboard Shortcuts for the Single-Stepping Commands

Command	*Function Key*
Step Over	F10
Run to Cursor	Ctrl+F10
Step Into	F11
Step Out	Shift+F11

While the program is halted within the debugger, you can specify the instruction at which the program's execution should continue. To do so, you should use the Set Next Statement command in either a source window or the Disassembly window. As you have learned, you must be careful when you use the Set Next Statement command. Placing it in another function or in a way that corrupts the stack will cause serious errors.

2.5.1 Using the QuickWatch Window and the DataTips Information

Despite the power that the debug windows you have learned about put at your fingertips to help you debug program code, there will nevertheless be times when you require information about a specific symbol within an executing program that does not appear in either the Variables or Watch windows. The Visual C++ integrated debugger provides you with two additional tools you can use for getting information in such situations: the QuickWatch window and the DataTips information.

DataTips are similar to the tooltips with which you are probably familiar, which show hints for a button or other user-interface object when the pointer rests over the object for a brief period of time. If during a debugging session you position the mouse cursor over the name of a symbol that can be evaluated, the IDE displays the symbol's value in a tooltip-like window. Figure 2-14 shows a DataTip display.

```
do {
    xa = x3*x3 - y3;
    x2 = x3*can1 + xa*san1;
    y2 = x3*san1 - xa*can1;
    x3 = x2;
    y3 = y2;
    x = x2;
    y = y2;
    a = 0;
    do {
        xa = x*x - y;
        x1 = x*can + xa*san;
        y1 = x*san - xa*can;
        x  = x1;                  can = -0.44118354009746
        y  = y1;
        a++;
        pDC->MoveTo((int)(ax*x+nx),(int)(ay*y+ny));
      pDC->LineTo((int)(ax*x+nx) - 1,(int)(ay*y+ny)
    } while ((fabs(x1)<=2.0e3) && (fabs(y1)<=2.0e3)
    e = e + 0.075;
    c = (int)e % 5 + 1;
 } while ((fabs(x2) <= 2.0e3) && (fabs(y2) <= 2.0e3
}
//////////////////////////////////////////////////
// CFractalsView diagnostics
```

Figure 2-14 A DataTip displays information about a local variable in the function.

The function and appearance of the QuickWatch window is similar to that of the Watch window. Just as with the Watch window, you can alter the values of simple types within the QuickWatch window. However, as the previous paragraph indicates, you can also choose specific symbols to add to the QuickWatch window. Figure 2-15 shows the QuickWatch window.

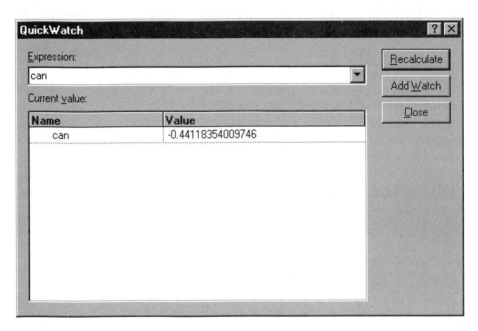

Figure 2-15   The QuickWatch window displaying a single expression.

2.5.2 Using the Threads and the Exceptions Dialog Boxes When Debugging

As you probably know, the Windows 32-bit programming environment is a multithreaded environment. Debugging multithreaded applications creates additional difficulties that can make effective debugging even harder. The Visual C++ debugger includes the Threads dialog box, which you can use to set the focus to a specific thread within a multithreaded application when you are debugging that application. You invoke the Threads dialog box through the Debug menu Threads option. Figure 2-16 shows the Threads dialog box.

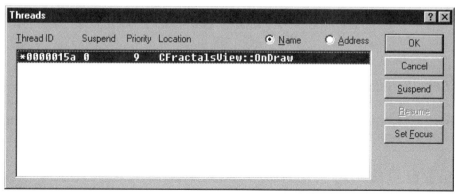

Figure 2-16 The Threads dialog box with the current thread highlighted.

In addition to the Threads dialog box, Visual C++ provides the Exceptions dialog box. You can use the Exceptions dialog box to specify how your program responds to exceptions during a debug session. You can select a standard exception or a user-defined exception. Within the dialog box, specify the action the debugger should take when the program notifies the debugger of a specific exception. By default, the debugger sets most exception types to Stop if not handled. Figure 2-17 shows the Exceptions dialog box.

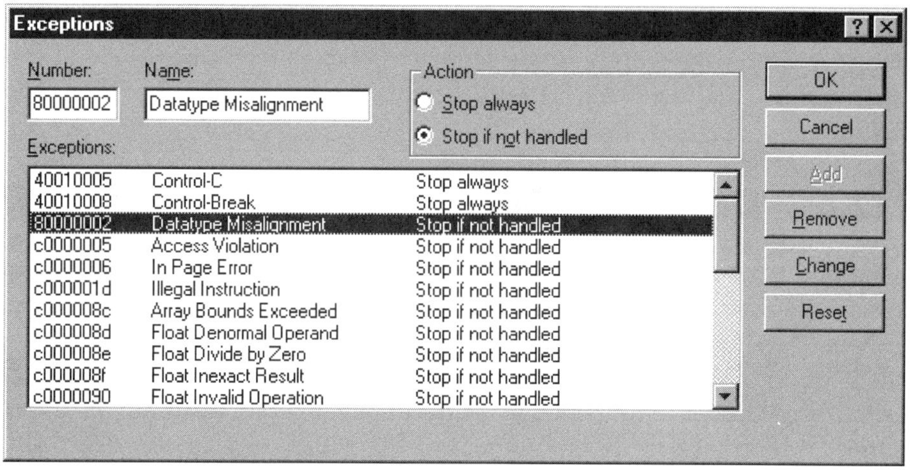

Figure 2-17 The Exceptions dialog box.

2.6   Simple Debugging Techniques

The Visual C++ integrated debugger and the various debugging features that Microsoft built into the Microsoft Foundation Classes provide for a variety of debugging techniques. The following sections detail some of the more common debugging techniques that you can use when debugging your programs.

2.6.1   Using Message Boxes to Speed Debugging

Although the integrated debugger provides great power and usability, sometimes it is not convenient for you to use the debugger when debugging your programs. For example, the debugger window's presence might interfere with your program's execution, or perhaps the bug you are trying to eliminate appears only in the release version of your program. In such cases, a message box may be all you need to effectively catch the bug. For example, if you determine that a two-parameter function called `ErrFunc()` misbehaves, you can easily verify that the function is receiving the correct parameters by adding a call to `AFXMessageBox()`, as shown in the following code:

```
char temparr[100];
wsprintf (temparr,
    "Calling ErrFunc (x = %d, y = %d)", x, y);
AfxMessageBox (temparr);
ErrFunc (x, y);
```

The message box will display the string before the function call, which might let you break the execution sequence, change the values of x and y, or simply verify that the error is internal to `ErrFunc()` and not in the calling values.

2.6.2   Debugging Output

One of the nice features that Microsoft built into the Microsoft Foundation Classes is that most MFC functions will automatically generate debugging output. You can also use either the `TRACE` or the `TRACE0`, `TRACE1`, `TRACE2`, and `TRACE3` macros to generate debugging output within your own program code. The debugger sends debugging output to the `afxDump` object, which is a predefined object of the MFC class `CDumpContext`. Visual Studio usually sends output from the `afxDump` object to the Output window. To see the output, select the Debug tab in the Output window. For example, to examine the values the calling program passes to the `ErrFunc()` function, you would write code similar to the following:

```
TRACE2("Calling ErrFunc(x = %d, y = %d)", x, y);
ErrFunc(x, y);
```

You will only be able to view the output from `TRACE2` if you have compiled your application for debugging. In addition, you must launch the application from the debugger, even if you do not want to use the other debugging features the debugger offers.

You should generally use the `TRACE0`, `TRACE1`, `TRACE2`, and `TRACE3` macros when doing so is appropriate, as each of these macros requires less memory than `TRACE` does. The `TRACE0` macro takes a format string (and only a format string) and can be used for simple text messages that the application dumps to `afxDump`. The `TRACE1` macro will process a format string plus one argument (one variable that the macro dumps to `afxDump`). The `TRACE2` macro takes a format string plus two arguments (two variables that the macro dumps to `afxDump`). The `TRACE3` macro, as you might expect, takes a format string plus three arguments (three variables that the macro dumps to `afxDump`). You can use the `TRACEn` macros when you know how many variables you intend to dump. Also, the `TRACEn` macros are useful in Unicode builds because you must use the `T` formatting character with `TRACE` in a Unicode build, but you do not need to with the `TRACEn` macros.

Furthermore, you cannot use any member of the `TRACE` family if you do not build the program for debugging; release compilations will ignore `TRACE` macros altogether.

2.6.3 Using Assertions

One of the most commonly used and most powerful tools in the debugger's arsenal is the `ASSERT` macro. You can use the `ASSERT` macro to interrupt the execution of your application when a specific condition evaluates as false. You can use the `ASSERT` macro within debug versions of your application to verify, for example, that a function receives the proper parameters. Again using the `ErrFunc()` example, you might place the `ASSERT` macro at the function's very beginning, as shown here:

```
void ErrFunc(int X, int y)
{
  ASSERT (x>=0 && y<100);
```

You can also use the ASSERT_VALID macro to verify that a pointer points to a valid CObject class-derived object. For example, when you have a function within your application called GetDocument() that returns a pointer to an object of type CSampleDoc, you may need to verify that the pointer is valid with the ASSERT_VALID macro. You might use code similar to the following to do so:

```
CSampleDoc *pDoc;
pDoc = GetDocument();
ASSERT_VALID(pDoc);
```

Both ASSERT and ASSERT_VALID will display a message box that indicates the line number within the program at which the assertion failed. The debugger will interrupt program execution and leave the execution pointer at the line containing the ASSERT macro. Like the TRACE macro, neither ASSERT macro has any effect if you do not build the application with debugging support.

2.6.4 Object Dumping

The CObject class has a member function, Dump, that dumps the contents of an object to the debugging output window (through the afxDump object). If you intend to dump the contents of objects you derive from the CObject class, you should implement the Dump member function for those objects. For example, if you derive a custom document class from the MFC CDocument class that you call CSampleDoc, and that class includes two member variables, m_xPos and m_yPos, your CSampleDoc::Dump implementation might look similar to the following code:

```
#ifdef DEBUG // check that it is a debug build
void CSampleDoc::Dump (CDumpContext& dc) const
{
  CDocument:Dump(dc);
  dc << "m_xPos = " << m_xPos << endl;
  dc << "m_yPos = " << m_y Pos << endl;
}
#endif // DEBUG
```

2.6.5 Detecting Memory Leaks and the CMemoryState Class

You can use the CMemoryState class to detect memory leaks that occur due to a program's inappropriate use of the C++ new or delete operators for memory allocation and retrieval. To take a snapshot of memory allocation at any point, you can create a CMemoryState object and call its Checkpoint member function. Later, you can call the DumpAllObjectsSince member function to dump the contents of all objects the program allocated space to since the last time the program called the Checkpoint member function. For example, to dump any objects that the SloppyFunc() function allocates and then fails to deallocate, you could use code similar to the following:

```
CMemoryState memState;
memState.Checkpoint();
SloppyFunc (x,y);
memState.DumpAllObjectsSince();
```

If you do not require a complete dump of all objects allocated between Checkpoint invocations, you can also use the DumpStatistics member function. You can call DumpStatistics after your program evaluates the difference between two memory states with the Difference member function. To use DumpStatistics, you must create, in total, three CMemoryState objects. You will use the first two to take snapshots of the state of memory and the third to evaluate the differences between the two. You might use code similar to the following to check the state of memory:

```
CMemoryState msBeforeCall, msAfterCall, msDifference;
// other code here
msBeforeCall.checkpoint();
SloppyFunc (x,y);
msAfterCall.Checkpoint();
if (msDifference.Difference (msBeforeCall, msAfterCall))
  msDifference.DumpStatistics();
```

Core Note

You cannot use CMemoryState *objects to detect memory leaks that result from incorrect program call sequences to the C++* malloc() *and* free() *statements or incorrect calling sequences to the Win32 API functions* GlobalAlloc() *and* GlobalFree()*, or* LocalAlloc() *and* LocalFree()*.*

2.6.6 Using MFC Tracing

As you learned earlier in this chapter, the debug version of the MFC Library sends a variety of trace messages to the Debug panel in the Output window. You can use the MFC Tracer application, TRACER.EXE, to enable or disable some or all of the MFC trace messages. You can use the Tools menu to invoke the Tracer application. The Tracer application displays a simple dialog-box interface that lets you specify the MFC TRACE messages you want to enable or disable. Figure 2-18 shows the MFC Trace Options dialog box that lets you specify when MFC should generate trace messages.

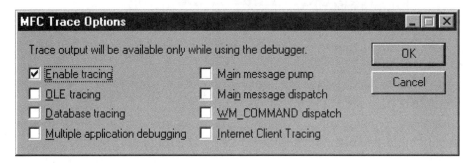

Figure 2-18 The MFC Trace Options dialog box for the Tracer application.

2.7   Additional Features of the Visual C++ Debugger

In addition to the features described so far, the Visual C++ debugging environment provides some important enhanced features—from features that let you debug a program while it is executing in debug mode to features that let you remotely debug an application on another system. The following sections detail some of these advanced features.

2.7.1 Just-in-Time Debugging

Just-in-Time debugging describes the Visual C++ compiler's ability to attach itself to a running program that just halted because of an unhandled exception. Just-in-Time debugging is a useful tool to help you debug applications that were not originally launched from within the integrated debugger or that were not built with debugging information.

You can turn on Just-in-Time debugging from the Tools menu Options command inside Visual Studio. In the Options dialog, select the Debug tab and set the Just-in-Time debugging check box.

Core Note

Visual Studio automatically enables Just-in-Time debugging when you install Visual Studio onto your computer.

2.7.2 Edit and Continue Debugging

As Rapid Application Development (RAD) tools such as Visual Basic have become more popular, many of their characteristics have carried over into the Visual Studio interface. In fact, Microsoft is currently trying to design a single, unified interface for Visual Basic, Visual C++, Visual FoxPro, Visual J++, and Visual InterDev. One of the Visual Basic compiler's most commonly used features is the Edit and Continue feature, which lets you make changes to an application as it executes and use those changes to resolve application errors.

Now, with Visual C++ 6.0, you can actually use Edit and Continue with debug builds of your Visual C++ applications. Unlike Visual Basic, however, the Visual C++ debugger has one major limitation on its use within programs. When you use the edit and continue feature of the debugger, you must ensure that you replace the exact same number of bytes with your change as the application had when you built it originally. For example, you could replace a number with another number, but you could not replace a string constant (such as 'A') with a string variable (such as A) because the replacement is one byte longer than the original (because of the trailing NULL character that C++ appends to strings).

VB TIP

It's true that Visual Studio's Edit and Continue debugging is similar in concept to the Visual Basic debugging environment. However, it is important to recognize that, in the vast majority of situations, while the VB debugger might let you make a change and continue without impact, many changes you make to an executing Visual C++ program will force you to recompile the program, rather than let you continue. Specifically, coding changes that result in a change to the byte values that make up the program will force recompilation every time.

If you make a change that Edit and Continue cannot support directly, Visual Studio will alert you and ask you to recompile the project or cancel the change.

Core Note

Visual Studio Edit and Continue debugging only works if the debugger successfully compiles the application, meaning you can only use it to capture logic errors, not syntax errors. The compiler catches syntax errors for you before you ever start to execute the application.

2.7.3 Remote Debugging

Often, you may work on or help debug programs that reside on another user's machine. *Remote debugging* lets you debug program code that is running on a machine to which your machine is connected. The local and the remote machines must be connected either through a serial connection, a local area network, or across any known TCP/IP connection. The local machine must run Visual C++ and the integrated debugger, while the remote machine runs the application that you wish to debug and the Visual C++ debug monitor. Figure 2-19 shows the communications process between the local machine and the remote machine during remote debugging.

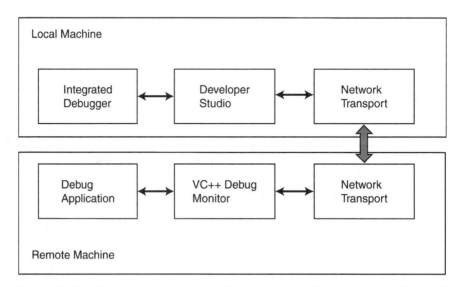

Figure 2-19 The communications path between the local, debugging machine and the remote application.

As the previous paragraph indicates, the remote machine must run the Visual C++ Debug Monitor application, Msvcmon.Exe, for the machine to support remote debugging of the application. In order for the Msvcmon.Exe application to run properly, you must also install the following DLLs on the remote computer: Msvcrt.Dll, Tln0t.Dll, Dm.Dll, Msvcp60.Dll, and Msdis100.Dll. You must copy all the files into a directory that is on the system path, preferably the Windows system directory.

Core Note

Visual Studio installs all the files automatically onto any computer on which you install Visual Studio. Default installation places the Msvcmon.Exe application into the Visual Studio directory's Common\MSDev98\Bin subdirectory.

To use remote debugging, you must run the Debug Monitor on the remote computer before you run the program that you wish to debug. When you execute the Debug Monitor, it will display a dialog box within which you must specify the settings for the debugging session—most notably, how the debugging computer will be connecting to the computer to be debugged. You will most often use remote debugging over a TCP/IP network connection. After you select the connection, you can click the Settings button to specify the details of the connection, including the machine running the program to be debugged's name or address, the debugging machine's name or address, and an access password, if any.

After you select the target machine, click the Connect button. The Debug Monitor will then wait for an incoming connection. To configure the local computer to request the connection, you must first run Visual Studio on the local machine.

After you have run Visual Studio, select the Tools menu Remote Connection command. Visual Studio will display the Remote Connection dialog box. Within the Remote Connection dialog box, you should specify the type of connection (in this case, a Network TCP/IP connection) and then set the parameters for the connection. Click the Settings button to set connection parameters. Figure 2-20 shows the Remote Connection dialog box.

Core Note

When you set a network connection, both the Debug Monitor and the Remote Connection will ask you to supply a password for the connection. Make sure that both passwords are the same or the two computers will be unable to communicate properly.

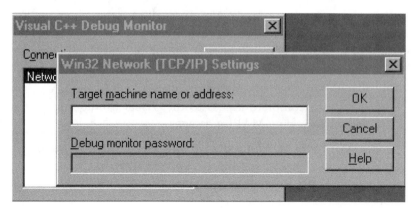

Figure 2-20 The Remote Connection dialog box.

The major advantage of remote debugging is that the application runs in a machine unaffected by the presence of the debugger. Remote debugging is ideal, then, for debugging applications that take over the Windows display, keyboard, sound drivers, and so on, such as full-screen game applications. Remote debugging is also ideal for debugging applications that work properly when you compile them as Win32 Debug applications but don't work correctly when you compile them as Win32 Release applications.

2.8   Advanced Debugging Considerations

Throughout this chapter, we have discussed the specifics of debugging with the Visual C++ debugger—particularly as it relates to the development of standard executables. However, particularly when you are developing for real-world deployments, you will often find that you are developing other types of applications. In the next couple of sections, you will look more closely at debugging two specific types of programs: Windows NT services and multithreaded applications. Debugging such programs brings its own set of concerns—concerns you should be aware of before you try to develop them.

2.8.1 Debugging Windows NT Services

As you have learned, the integrated debugger lets you debug any application that you can design in Visual Studio, not just standard executable applications. An excellent example of another application type that you can debug if it fails during execution is a Windows NT service.

The easiest way to begin debugging a service on Windows NT Server is to artificially run it as a console application — in other words, from a command prompt. Doing so lets you step through the service's code from the first instruction, provides more complete access to the Visual Studio debugger, and supplies a window for viewing MAPI messages.

To set up your service as a console application, you need to handle the return codes from the Windows NT service control manager and then take the appropriate code path in your startup code.

In other words, when an application runs as a service on Windows NT Server, the operating system usually calls the service control manager to find the application's main function. If the process is artificially running as a console application, calls to the service control manager fail. When calls to the service control manager fail, you should branch within the debugger and call your main function explicitly.

To run your service application as a console application, you must include the Winwrap.Lib library in your makefile (or your application's external dependency list). Doing so will handle the service control manager calls. If you do not include this library, look at the library's source code and make the necessary changes to your application's main function.

2.8.2 Debugging Multithreaded Applications

In later chapters, you will learn about how difficult writing multithreaded applications is. You will never write an application with more than one thread and then never have to debug it. Ever.

If you have worked with the debugger at all, you are probably used to using breakpoints to stop your code so you can inspect variables or step through the instructions your program has within it. In a multithreaded application, a breakpoint will be tripped whenever any thread crosses it. When the debugger gains control of the application to let you begin examining the code and its variables, it suspends all of the other running threads. If you let the application continue executing, any of the threads involved in the application might begin executing first — but only unblocked threads may start running.

Because of the concurrent nature of your multithreaded program, even single-stepping through what you will perceive to be a single thread can give other threads in the application a chance to run. If the goal of your debugging session is to track down a fault, you will quickly realize that single-stepping might not be the best way to approach the problem: Tracing from one seemingly benign statement to another innocuous piece of code lets other code run. If that other code is the source of the fault, you will be pretty surprised by the trap messages the debugger generates.

An easy way around this aspect of multithreaded development is to be very liberal in placing breakpoints. Set breakpoints just before and just after you spawn a new thread—right before you call `AfxBeginThread()`, for example, and then right after it so you can trap the spawning thread. You can also set a breakpoint in your thread's controlling function, in the constructor for its managing class, or in the `InitInstance()` member function where you let it get work done.

The debugger manages thread focus for you as you work with your application. Thread focus in the debugger has nothing to do with the threads in your application; it simply lets you know what thread you're watching execute. The thread that's executing the code identified by the yellow arrow in the source window of your debugging session has thread focus. If a thread hits a breakpoint, that thread will receive focus as the debugger wakes up to show you the code and the variables the thread is using. When you use the Break command in the Debug menu, whatever thread is currently running in your application at that exact instant will be displayed.

At any time the debugger has your program stopped, you can use the Threads... command in the Developer Studio's Debug menu to see what threads are extant (that is, created and not yet destroyed) within your application. The command results in the Threads dialog box shown earlier in Figure 2-16.

The thread that has focus is identified in this dialog by an asterisk. You can use the Set Focus button in the box to give focus to a different thread; just highlight that thread in the list box before clicking the Set Focus button. You will see the debugger, in the background, open the source file that contains the code that thread is currently executing. The debugger will place the yellow arrow indicating the next statement to execute at the appropriate place in that file to let you know what code is next to execute in that thread. At the instant you stop the program, the thread might be anywhere—someplace obvious in your application or deep in the code the runtime library contains. You will likely find that your code will stop in places where it does lots of looping, just because the odds are that it's in the middle of executing a lengthy loop. Finding that a thread's current execution point is somewhere in the message pump is quite common, particularly if the thread is responsible for the application's user interface.

The list box in the Threads dialog will show you which function each thread is executing; you can use the Address radio button at the top of the dialog to have the dialog show you the exact physical address of execution for the thread.

The list also includes a suspend count for the thread. Windows manages a suspend count for threads to help the scheduler manage their execution. The thread is runnable when the suspend count is exactly zero; any other number means that the thread is suspended. The number is always positive and can be increased by using the Suspend push button or decreased by using the Resume push button. Be careful when using these buttons—if you resume a thread that is suspended because it's waiting on an object, you will let your application execute code in a context for which you probably never planned. On the other hand, when you apply it carefully, this dialog box is a great way to work your application through a blocking condition that's misbehaving.

2.9 Summary

In this chapter, you have learned about the Visual C++ integrated debugger and the benefits that it provides you in debugging and testing your programs. The debug windows provide you with, in many cases, more information than you could ever need about a problem. The ASSERT macros, breakpoints, data tips, and more provide you with instant feedback about your application's performance.

However, all the debugging in the world is not a substitute for good, solid programming. The more solid your code is when you write it initially, the less time you will spend working with the debugger and the less time another programmer will spend with the debugger whenever they make additions or changes to your programs. The integrated debugger will help you solve many logic errors, but you should make every effort to learn from those errors so that you don't repeat them in other programs in the future.

Visual Studio and the Windows operating systems provide you with valuable tools to ensure that your applications are running as efficiently as possible and as correctly as possible. From additional information provided at every point during the debugging process to the ability to debug fully compiled executables from a remote location, both Visual Studio and the operating system will assist you in writing the most seamless, error-free applications.

In Chapter 3, we will move on to a discussion of callback functions and the Windows messaging loop, two concepts that are crucial for your understanding of program construction in Windows. Throughout the remainder of the book, you will find yourself regularly using the debug capabilities discussed in this chapter to maintain your code.

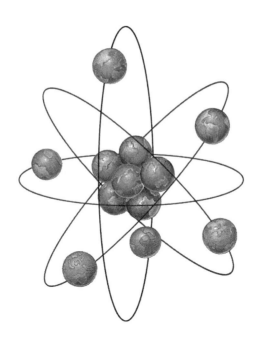

USING CALLBACK FUNCTIONS AND DISSECTING THE MESSAGE LOOP

Topics in this Chapter

- Understanding Callback Functions
- Common Uses for Callback Functions
- The Fundamentals of the Windows Message Loop
- Messages the Message Loop Receives
- Using Multiple Message Loops with Multiple Windows
- Optimizing Message Loops
- Summary

Chapter 3

Application programmers typically access the services provided by an operating system, or subroutine library, through calling functions from within their own programs. Callback functions are used for the exact opposite: they allow the operating system, or library, to request a service from the application. In Windows, callback functions have a dominant presence in the form of *window procedures*. In the MFC library, callback functions are used even more extensively. Understanding them is thus crucial if you wish to understand how the MFC library works and how its many features can be used efficiently.

3.1 Understanding Callback Functions

It's best to begin our consideration of callback functions with a simple example. Suppose you wish to develop a library function that can sort "things." These "things" are identified simply by pointers, while the actual sorting is accomplished using a comparison method supplied by the user. Your library function would look similar to the following:

```
void sort(void **pThings, int nThings,
    int (*CompareThings)(void *, void*));
```

The first parameter supplies an array of `void` pointers, which is the array that needs to be sorted. The second parameter specifies the number of items in the array (alternatively, you could just prescribe that the array be terminated with a `NULL`–pointer.) The interesting part is the third parameter: it is a function pointer that contains the address of an as-yet-undefined comparison function.

How would this library function be used? Suppose you have an array of strings (an array of character pointers). A trivial comparison function would then use `strcmp()` (assuming, for the sake of simplicity, that `Compare-Strings()` and `strcmp()` have the same semantics):

```
int CompareStrings(void *str1, void *str2) {
   return strcmp((char *)str1, (char *)str2);
}
```

With this function written, you are now ready to use your library to sort strings:

```
const int nStrings = 100;
char *ppszStrings[nStrings];
... // populate the string array here
sort((void **)ppszStrings, nStrings, CompareStrings);
```

It should be clear by now that in this example, `CompareStrings()` is nothing but a callback function. The library subroutine `sort()` will make use of this function as necessary, calling it for many pairs of strings as it sorts the string pointers in `ppszStrings`.

The flexibility of the callback function mechanism can be easily demonstrated. Suppose you want to sort things backwards using the `sort()` function. All you need to do is to create a new comparison function:

```
int CompareStringsBackwards(void *str1, void *str2) {
    return -strcmp((char *)str1, (char *)str2);
}
```

Now you're ready to call `sort()`:

```
sort((void **)ppszStrings(ppszStrings,
    nStrings, CompareStringsBackwards);
```

It is just as simple to use the sorting function for sorting things other than strings; all it takes is writing a new comparison function.

Core Note

As you might imagine, more elegant solutions exist for the problem presented here, for instance, solutions that utilize operator overloading or C++ templates. The basic concepts, however, remain the same.

It is important to realize that callback functions are not in any way special. They are ordinary functions that are used in a somewhat unusual manner.

What a callback function is also often depends on your perspective. This is best demonstrated by looking at the role operating system API functions play from the operating system's perspective: they are all callback functions. To understand this better, consider the following example: the operating system (perhaps in response to a user action) loads an application into memory and calls a subroutine in it that happens to be called `main()` (or `WinMain()`, for graphical Windows applications.) As the application executes, it in turn calls other functions that are part of the operating system.

Of course, viewing operating system functions as callback functions is going overboard a little. Normally, the concept is reserved for functions that are part of an application's code base, which may be called from the operating system or libraries. Often, an even more restrictive definition is used: only those functions whose address is passed to the operating system or library explicitly, as in the example presented in Figure 3-1, are called callback functions.

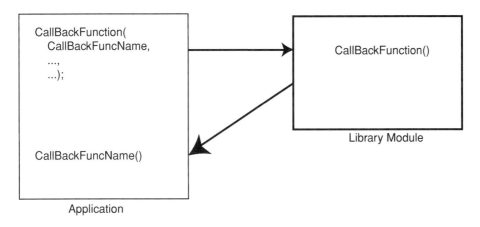

Figure 3-1   Visualizing how callback functions work.

3.2   Common Uses for Callback Functions

The example presented in the previous section demonstrates one of the most common uses of callback functions: their use enables library programmers to create subroutines whose behavior can be altered to suit the needs of their users. Indeed, in many cases in the Windows API callback functions are used precisely for this purpose. Let's take a look at how this works.

3.2.1   A Windows API Callback Function Example

Passing the address of a user-defined comparison function to a library sub-routine is a fairly common example of callback function use. Equally common is the passing of the address of a user-defined enumerator function. The basic concept is simple: an operating system or library function enumerates a specific set of objects, calling the user-defined function once for each object found.

Examples in Windows are very common. For instance, if you wish to list (perhaps in a combo box) the set of available fonts on your system, all you have to do is call the GDI function `EnumFonts()`. It is declared in the Windows API as follows:

```
int EnumFonts
    (HDC hdc,                    // handle to device context
     LPCTSTR lpFaceName,         // pointer to typeface name
     FONTENUMPROC lpFontFunc,    // pointer to callback function
     LPARAM lParam);             // address of app-supplied data
```

There it is, the third parameter, which contains a pointer to a user-defined callback function. That callback function must, in turn, be defined as follows:

```
int CALLBACK EnumFontsProc
    (const LOGFONT *lplf,        // logical-font data
     const TEXTMETRIC *lptm,     // physical-font data
     DWORD dwType,               // font type
     LPARAM lpData);             // application-defined data
```

In case it wasn't clear, it is important to emphasize that `Enum-FontsProc()` is a function *you* write; once it's completed, you can pass its address to the `EnumFonts()` function. In fact, for different situations, you may write several different versions of this procedure that perform different types of processing depending on how the EnumFonts() procedure was called.

Here is a simple example that shows how this function can be used from within your own program. Suppose you wish to list the fonts that are installed on the user's computer. Your EnumFontsProc() function might then look similar to the following:

```
int CALLBACK EnumFontsProc
    (const LOGFONT *lplf, const TEXTMETRIC *lptm,
    DWORD dwType, LPARAM lpData)
{
  printf("%s\n", lplf->lfFaceName);
  return 1;
}
```

A simple program that makes use of this newly created function might look similar to the following:

```
void main(void)
{
  EnumFonts(GetWindowDC(NULL), NULL, EnumFontsProc, 0);
}
```

That's all it takes to list the fonts installed on the system—though, honestly, this program isn't very useful as written, since it only displays, and even that only to a console window.

3.2.2 Using Callback Functions Within Your Own Classes

Now that you have a little better idea about how callback functions work, let's take a brief look at the role callback functions play in C++. C++, like all object-oriented languages, associates objects with methods: member functions in C++ parlance. What this means is that when you pass the address of (or a reference to) a C++ object to a function, you do much more than merely pass the address of a block of memory. Implicitly, you also pass the address to all the methods associated with the class to which the object belongs.

This is even more pronounced in the case of virtual member functions. The addresses of these functions are actually recorded along with data members in the memory block associated with the object. When you pass a pointer to an object that has virtual member functions, you also implicitly pass the address of this table of virtual function pointers, the so-called vtable.

Passing the addresses of functions—clearly this is very similar if not identical to the types of activities that we were performing in the last section. To be sure, these are not normally called callback functions, but they are often used for the same purpose and, in the same fashion, as "ordinary" callback functions in plain C programs.

The syntax of C++ can also be used to streamline the way these "callback" functions are defined or used. Consider the example, presented earlier, of a simple general-purpose sorting function. The use of a callback function in C, however efficient, is not very elegant: the arcane syntax when it comes to defining function pointers as arguments can be very difficult to read.

To understand how C++ makes this process a little more clear, let's consider how one would create a general-purpose sort function, usable with arguments of arbitrary type, in C++. The following template definition shows one way to do it:

```
template <class T>sort(T *pThings, int nThings);
```

Templatizing is good because it lets your programs use the sort() function in a handful of different ways. However, there doesn't seem to be much happening here in the way of callback functions. On the other hand, if you consider a possible implementation of the sort() function, as shown here, it becomes a bit more clear::

```
template<class T> void sort(T *pThings, int nThings)
  {
    // Straight insertion: a very inefficient
    // but simple algorithm.
    for (int j = 1; j < nThings; j++) {
       T p = pThings[j];
       int i = j - 1;
       while (i >= 0 && pThings[i] > p) {
          pThings[i + 1] = pThings[i];
          i--;
        }
       pThings[i + 1] = p;
     }
  }
```

Look closely at the line containing the while statement. Notice that it contains a reference to the comparison operator, >. Now remember that in C++, you can overload operators in any way you like, at least for your own types. This sorting function can now be used to sort an array of objects of an arbitrary type T, as long as a suitable comparison operator is defined for this new type. For instance, your new type may be a string type defined along the following lines:

```
class str
{
public:
   str(int nSize = 11) {m_str = new char[nSize];};
   ~str() {delete m_str;};
   operator char*() {return m_str;};
   operator const char*() const {return m_str;};
   bool operator>(const str &str2)
      {return strcmp(m_str, (const char *)str2) > 0;};
   friend ostream& operator<<(ostream&, const str&);
private:
   char *m_str;
};
```

If you have a library that contains a `sort()` function like the one defined above, then in order to sort an array of `str` objects, all you need to do is call the `sort()` function like this:

```
str pStrings[N];
...
sort(pStrings, N);
```

Through the power of C++, the `sort()` library function will implicitly reference the `str::operator>` function you defined as part of the `str` class. Although no function addresses were passed as parameters, the mechanism is practically identical to the mechanism seen in C programs.

3.2.3 Callback Functions Within MFC

Although the Microsoft Foundation Classes make little use of templates (much of the MFC was written before templates became part of the official ANSI C++ standard), the implicit callback mechanism shown in the previous section appears frequently within the library. Indeed, it often appears that an MFC-derived class is nothing but a collection of callback functions—generally callback functions to lower-level API functions.

Consider, for instance, dialogs implemented using a class derived from MFC's `CDialog`. Consider an application that uses a collection of such dialog classes to present a visual representation of a series of graphical values. One of the simpler classes in such an application project might manage a page in a tabbed dialog that provides controls for saving, recalling, or resetting a particular dialog box's state. This class, then, might be declared as follows:

```
class CSettingsView;
class CSettingsFileDlg : public CDialog
{
// Construction
public:
    CSettingsFileDlg(CWnd* pParent = NULL,
        CSettingsView *pView = NULL);

// Dialog Data
    //{{AFX_DATA(CHP8594EFileDlg)
    enum { IDD = IDD_DEFAULTIMAGEFILE };
        // NOTE: the ClassWizard will add data members here
    //}}AFX_DATA
    CSettingsView *m_pView;

// Overrides
    // ClassWizard generated virtual function overrides
    //{{AFX_VIRTUAL(CSettingsFileDlg)
    protected:
    virtual void DoDataExchange(CDataExchange* pDX);
    virtual void PostNcDestroy();
    //}}AFX_VIRTUAL

// Implementation
protected:

    // Generated message map functions
    //{{AFX_MSG(CSettingsFileDlg)
    afx_msg void OnPreset();
    virtual void OnOK();
    virtual void OnCancel();
    afx_msg void OnSave();
    afx_msg void OnRecall();
    //}}AFX_MSG
    DECLARE_MESSAGE_MAP()
};
```

Look at the member functions in this class. These were added through the ClassWizard. Each of these member functions would be documented as "This function is called when . . ." For instance, OnPreset() is called when the user clicks on the Preset button in the dialog. DoDataExchange() is called by the framework when the dialog is expected to initialize its controls or read control values or settings entered by the user. And so on.

Perhaps these functions aren't called callback functions in the MFC documentation, but they certainly work like callback functions. So, you say tomato, Microsoft says Tomatoe, but the long and short is that the functions work the same way. However, one issue does remain in the whole thing—while it is easy to say that a function like OnPreset() *is called* when the user clicks a button, it is most important for us to understand who, or what, is responsible for this call, for determining which class, and subsequently which member function is to handle such a highly specific event. To address this issue, it is necessary to examine how Windows informs applications of system events through the use of messages, and how applications are expected to handle, and dispatch, messages that they receive from the operating system.

3.3 The Fundamentals of the Windows Message Loop

In the previous section, you learned about callback functions and, in particular, how MFC utilizes a callback function-like mechanism to allow classes, such as a dialog class, to respond to system events. One question, however, remained unanswered—where the events originate from in the first place. This question leads to the second central topic of this chapter: the Windows message loop, and its role in your programs.

The problem that the developers at Microsoft needed to address when they began to build the Windows operating system (among a whole series of other problems) is that applications running under a graphical user interface must be able to respond to all kinds of events. These include, but are not limited to, keyboard events, mouse movement and clicks, changes in the layout of the application's windows or the desktop on which they reside, sizing and moving of windows, redrawing of window areas that are uncovered as a result of user action, timer events, and more.

Compare this with the typical text application that responds to keyboard events only and does not need to share the display with other programs. The solution to this problem—handling graphical events versus text events—also defines a fundamental characteristic of Windows: It is a message-passing operating system. Information about events is sent to corresponding applications in the form of messages, simple data structures of a fixed format.

At the core of every Windows program with a graphical interface (and many programs without a graphical UI) is a short program loop. This loop typically calls the Windows API function GetMessage(). As its name implies, GetMessage() retrieves the next message awaiting the application's attention. GetMessage() receives messages in the form of an MSG structure. Applications examine the contents of this structure and *dispatch* the event according to rules that best reflect the application's needs.

The MSG structure is very simple. Its six members are defined as follows:

```
typedef struct tagMSG {
    HWND    hwnd;
    UINT    message;
    WPARAM  wParam;
    LPARAM  lParam;
    DWORD   time;
    POINT   pt;
} MSG;
```

The first of these parameters is a unique identifier of the window to which the message applies: the window handle. The second parameter identifies the type of message: it typically contains a predefined value such as WM_MOUSEMOVE. The third and fourth parameters are message-specific: for instance, the WM_MOUSEMOVE message uses the wParam parameter to store the keyboard's state at the time the mouse was moved (so application programs can distinguish, for instance, between mouse movements with or without the Control key depressed, to determine whether the user wishes to execute a move or copy operation.) The lParam parameter contains the mouse cursor's position during the move in window client-area coordinates.

Core Note

The wParam *and* lParam *values are thus named because in 16-bit windows,* wParam *was a 16-bit parameter (a* WORD*) whereas* lParam *was a 32-bit* LONG. *In 32-bit versions of Windows, they are both 32-bit long words; furthermore, the use of the portable types* WPARAM *and* LPARAM *ensures compatibility with future Windows versions where — conceivably — the type of these parameters may again change (the impending release of 64-bit Windows within the next several years seems likely to result in such a change).*

The remaining two parameters of the MSG structure identify the system time at which the message was posted and the screen coordinates of the mouse cursor at that time.

Because applications can receive quite literally thousands of different messages, it would be difficult indeed if they had to respond explicitly to each. Fortunately, that is not the case: Windows provides several helper functions that render most message loops trivially simple. And this is where callback functions enter the picture.

Here is an example from one of the first Windows programs that most Windows C programmers write. Its main body, the `WinMain()` function, is only a few lines long—but if you are going to program in C in Windows, this framework is the basis from which all of your other Windows programs will descend:

```
int PASCAL WinMain
    (HANDLE hInstance,       // current instance
     HANDLE hPrevInstance,   // previous instance
     LPSTR lpCmdLine,        // command line
     int nCmdShow)           // show-window type (open/icon)
{
  MSG msg;                   // message
  if (!hPrevInstance)        // Other instances running?
     if (!InitApplication(hInstance))
                             // Initialize shared things
        return FALSE;        // Exits if fails

  /* Perform initializations that apply to a specific instance */
  if (!InitInstance(hInstance, nCmdShow))
     return FALSE;

  /* Acquire and dispatch messages until WM_QUIT is received. */
  while (GetMessage(&msg,        // message structure
                    NULL,        // handle of receiving window
                    NULL,        // lowest message to examine
                    NULL))       // highest message to examine
  {
    if (!TranslateAccelerator(hWnd, hAccTable, &msg)) {
       TranslateMessage(&msg); // Translates virtual key codes
       DispatchMessage(&msg);  // Dispatches message to window
    }
  }
  return msg.wParam;            // PostQuitMessage value
}
```

At the heart of this function is a `while` loop, containing a call to `Get-Message()`. That's hardly surprising: what is perhaps somewhat less expected is that at this stage the `MSG` structure is still treated as opaque. Rather than examining its members, the application calls a series of Windows API functions to process it.

TranslateAccelerator() and TranslateMessage() are merely helper functions that make it easier to process certain keyboard-related messages. (TranslateAccelerator() processes keystrokes corresponding to accelerator keys, such as CTRL+N or ALT+F4; TranslateMessage() turns virtual key event messages into character messages.) Far more important is the role played by DispatchMessage().

As its name implies, DispatchMessage() is the Windows API function that determines what needs to be done with individual messages. Let's take a quick look at just how that works. The key consideration is the window handle member of the MSG structure, hwnd.

Windows associates a function address with every window present on the system: the address of the window procedure. That is not to say that it is necessary to write a new function for every new window created: several windows can share the same window procedure. For this purpose, Windows defines the concept of *window classes*. When a new window is created, it is always associated with a window class, and unless a specific window procedure is defined for this window, the window procedure associated with the class will be used.

Many predefined window classes exist, and the associated window procedures often define the class's behavior. For instance, most buttons in dialogs are windows of the BUTTON class; the window procedure of this predefined class is responsible, for instance, for translating mouse events (such as a mouse click within the button's area) into command messages that the application can process.

Armed with this information, you can almost write your own version of DispatchMessage(). If you do, the result will undoubtedly look similar to the following:

```
LONG MyDispatchMessage(CONST MSG *lpmsg)
  {
    WNDPROC wndProc =
        (WNDPROC)GetWindowLong(lpmsg->hwnd, GWL_WNDPROC);
    if (wndProc != NULL)
        return wndProc(lpmsg->hwnd, lpmsg->message,
                       lpmsg->wParam, lpmsg->lParam);
    else
        return 0;
  }
```

Core Note

The Windows API documentation states that the window procedure address should not be called directly; instead, `CallWindowProc()` *must be used. This, like so many other anachronisms in the Windows API, is required for compatibility with 16-bit Windows (where* `GetWindowLong()` *retrieves not the actual function address but instead a handle to the function, which* `CallWindowProc()` *can resolve).*

So if you should write a function of this nature, determining the most important part of the function is pretty straightforward—the call to `GetWindowLong()` retrieves the address of the Window procedure for the window reference passed in. While you might not think of this as a callback function explicitly, in reality that is what it is doing. In other words, calling into the Windows API from your programs also often acts as the invocation of a callback function, even when it is not explicitly obvious.

The last key issue to address, then, with regard to the message loop and how it works is what window procedures look like. Let's take a look at the simplest construction of a window procedure to get the answer to this question:

```
long FAR PASCAL MainWndProc
    (HWND hWnd,          /* window handle */
    unsigned message,   /* type of message */
    WPARAM wParam,      /* additional information */
    LPARAM lParam)      /* additional information */
{
  switch (message) {
    case WM_DESTROY:
      PostQuitMessage(0);
      break;
    default:
      return DefWindowProc(hWnd, message, wParam, lParam);
  }
  return 0;
}
```

The archetypal window procedure is written in the form of a series of extended `switch` statements. *Extended* is the right word, because depending on your application's complexity, its window procedures may need to be able to process dozens, perhaps hundreds, of different types of messages.

Yet it could be worse. Fortunately, it is not necessary to process messages unless you really intend to do something with them; for the rest, you can simply call `DefWindowProc()`. As its name implies, `DefWindowProc()` calls the default window procedure for the specified window, which ensures that every message the window receives actually gets processed at some level—even if it is simply Windows' default handling that is in effect.

Armed with this knowledge, it is at last possible to understand how member functions in MFC classes are invoked. Deep inside the bowels of the MFC framework is a message loop and series of window procedures not unlike the ones presented in this chapter. Through clever use of macros and virtual functions, member functions corresponding to specific messages are invoked. These functions that the MFC calls message handlers can easily be added and managed through the ClassWizard. In the end, you don't *have to* understand the mechanism responsible for dispatching messages in order to add message handlers to your own classes; however, by being able to tell what happens "behind the scenes," you will be able to program far more efficiently.

3.4 Messages the Message Loop Receives

As mentioned previously, the number of different messages a Windows application can receive is in the range of thousands. Fortunately, this is not an arbitrary collection: messages fall into well-defined groups or categories.

Perhaps the easiest way to see messages at work is through using one of the most useful utilities that comes with Visual C++, the Spy++ application, as shown in Figure 3-2.

Spy++ is a utility that allows you to view the hierarchy of windows present on your system and to monitor the messages received by these windows. Its message selection dialog, shown in Figure 3-2, organizes messages into more than 30 distinct groups.

Many of these groups contain messages that are highly specific to certain areas of Windows programming. Other groups are specific to certain predefined window classes. Yet other groups are more generic in nature, containing messages that are processed by most window procedures.

For instance, selecting the Mouse message group in Spy++ (and deselecting all other groups) highlights the following fourteen messages:

```
WM_LBUTTONDBLCLK
WM_LBUTTONDOWN
WM_LBUTTONUP
WM_MBUTTONDBLCLK
WM_MBUTTONDOWN
WM_MBUTTONUP
```

```
WM_MOUSEACTIVATE
WM_MOUSEMOVE
WM_MOUSEWHEEL
WM_PARENTNOTIFY
WM_RBUTTONDBLCLK
WM_RBUTTONDOWN
WM_RBUTTONUP
WM_SETCURSOR
```

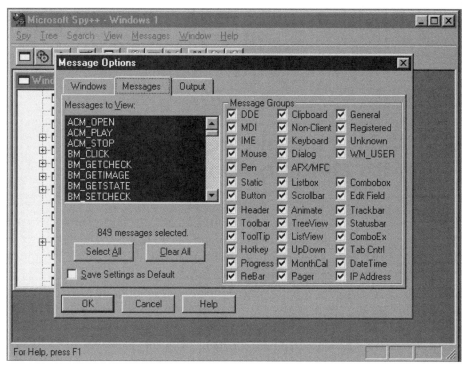

Figure 3-2 Using Spy++ to monitor Windows messages.

Needless to say, all these symbols are really numeric constants, defined in Windows header files such as `winuser.h`. The `WM_MOUSEMOVE` constant, for instance, is defined as the constant `0x0200`.

Clearly this is all very interesting and very detailed, but the operative issue at the center of this discussion is *when* exactly the application receives one or more messages. Most of the time it is the operating system that sends messages. However, it is also possible for applications to send messages to themselves (for instance, the window procedure of one window may cause a message to be sent to another window inside the same application) or to each other.

For use by an application internally, the range between WM_USER and 0x7FFF can be utilized. In this case, the meaning of a message is specific to a window procedure; for instance, WM_USER+1 may mean one thing to the window procedure associated with a button, and something different to the window procedure associated with an edit box.

It is also possible to define a named message that is guaranteed to be unique throughout a system, through a call to RegisterWindowMessage(). For instance, consider the following invocation:

```
RegisterWindowMessage(_T("WM_THISAPPLICATIONSUNIQUEMESSAGE"));
```

The return value of this function is a message code in the range of 0xC000 to 0xFFFF (or 0 if the call was unsuccessful). This mechanism of registering messages is typically used by cooperating applications that pass messages to each other.

3.5   Using Multiple Message Loops with Multiple Windows

The discussion in the previous section may create the impression that each Windows application is built around a single message loop. This is not so. In fact, this wasn't even so back in the days of 16-bit Windows; in the multi-threaded 32-bit environment, the picture is even more complex.

Perhaps the problem is with the terminology. The operative concern here is whether it's an application that receives a message, or a window, or a thread. To clarify what's going on, it's necessary to turn to the concept of the *message queue*. The name speaks for itself: it is the message queue where messages are temporarily stored before they are retrieved through a call to a function like GetMessage().

A message queue is associated with each thread of an application. Messages for a particular window are placed in the message queue of the thread that created that window. You can use EnumThreadWindows() to determine which windows a thread owns or GetWindowThreadProcessId() to identify the thread that owns a particular window.

Not all messages are placed in message queues. Some messages (often appropriately referred to as *nonqueued messages*) are passed to a window procedure directly.

This behavior is reflected by the two functions PostMessage() and SendMessage(). Calling PostMessage() allows you to place an arbitrary message in the message queue of the thread owning a specified window. Calling `SendMessage()` instead calls directly the window procedure associated with the window you specify. `PostMessage()` returns right away, while `SendMessage()` returns only after the message has been processed.

This difference in behavior can be utilized for different purposes. For instance, if you wish to have a window repainted, you can post a `WM_PAINT` message to that window. When this message actually gets processed is irrelevant; you know that the window will be repainted soon, perhaps when the system goes idle. On the other hand, if you wish to read the contents of an edit control, you send to it a `WM_GETTEXT` message using `SendMessage()`. When `SendMessage()` returns, the message will have been processed, and the buffer (a pointer to which was passed as the `lParam` parameter along with `WM_GETTEXT`) contains the requested text.

So if threads have message loops, it stands to reason that the call to `GetMessage()` must be made from the same thread with which the message queue is associated. But there is no reason at all to limit the number of `GetMessage()` calls to one. Your application (or, to be precise, its main thread) may have a primary message loop and auxiliary message loops that implement special operating modes.

For instance, your application may be performing a complex, time-consuming calculation:

```
for (int i = 0; i < 1000000; i++) {
   // Do something time-intensive 1,000,000 times
}
```

Implemented this way, your application will become entirely unresponsive while the calculation is running. Although you know that the application works as intended, all indications to the user will suggest otherwise. The application will not respond to mouse clicks in the menu bar, will not repaint its windows, will not resize or respond in any other way. There is a much better alternative, as shown in the following code:

```
for (int i = 0; i < 1000000; i++) {
   // Do something substantial 1,000,000 times

   // Now check if there are any messages that need to be processed
   while (PeekMessage((LPMSG)&msg, NULL, NULL, NULL, PM_REMOVE)) {
      if (!TranslateAccelerator(hWnd, hAccTable, &msg)) {
         TranslateMessage(&msg);
         DispatchMessage(&msg);
      }
   }
}
```

You may want to filter messages that should not be processed while the lengthy calculation is taking place. For instance, if the lengthy process changes the data managed by the application, you may wish to disable file load/save commands during its execution.

Core Note

The multithreaded environment offers several alternatives to the method presented here for keeping applications responsive during lengthy procedures. For instance, the lengthy calculation itself can be executed in a secondary thread, leaving the primary thread free to process the main message loop.

Secondary message loops need not be created explicitly. Some Windows API calls actually invoke a message loop implemented within Windows itself. Perhaps the simplest example comes in the form of the `MessageBox()` API function. With the help of this function, it is possible to create a simple but completely functional graphical Windows program in just a few lines:

```
#include <windows.h>

void main(void)
  {
    MessageBox(0, "Hello, World!", "This is Windows", MB_OK);
  }
```

If you compile and run this program, you'll find that it does not terminate until you close the window it creates. This activity is because `Message-Box()` internally implements a message loop processing all the messages that the message box receives. When the message box is destroyed, the message loop terminates and `MessageBox()` at last returns—and so the application exits thereafter.

Every time your application displays a message box using this API function (or the `AfxMessageBox()` function), it implicitly creates a new message loop. At this point, the logic of execution can become quite complex. Consider, for example, the following code fragment:

```
// Main message loop
while (GetMessage(&msg, NULL, NULL, NULL)) {
    if (!TranslateAccelerator(hWnd, hAccTable, &msg)) {
        TranslateMessage(&msg);
        DispatchMessage(&msg);
    }
}
```

```
...

// Inside main window procedure
switch (message) {
   case WM_COMMAND:
      switch (wParam) {
         case IDM_ABOUT:              /* Help/About selected */
            MessageBox(hWnd, "CoreVC++ App (c)1999",
                            "About", MB_OK);
            break;
          /* Other command messages are processed here */
          ...
       }
      break;
   case WM_PAINT:
     /* Repaint the application's window
     break;
 /* Other messages are processed here */
 ...
```

Let's take a brief look at what happens if the user selects the About menu command and then moves the message box around. First, selecting the About command causes a WM_COMMAND message with its wParam equal to IDM_ABOUT to be placed in the application's message queue. When this message is retrieved by the main message loop, the call to Dispatch-Message() invokes the window procedure associated with the application's main window. In that procedure, the command IDM_ABOUT triggers a call to MessageBox(), which temporarily takes over the function of dispatching messages from the main message loop.

If something, such as moving the message box around, uncovers parts of the application's main window, a WM_PAINT message is posted to the primary thread's message queue. When this message is retrieved by the message loop inside MessageBox(), it calls the main window's window procedure—again! Yes, this means that window procedures must be reentrant: during the processing of one message, the window procedure may be called again to process another. This is often seen in the call stack during a Visual C++ debugging session although even more often, due to stack switches or another message that has taken place inside system DLLs, only parts of the call stack remain visible.

The issue of reentrance must always be remembered when designing message loops or the behavior of functions called by message loops. Any function that invokes a secondary message loop implicitly is a potential candidate for reentrance. This is also true in the world of MFC. If an MFC message handler calls, for instance, `AfxMessageBox()`, it is possible that the message handler will be called again before `AfxMessageBox()` returns. Remember this and you can avoid the very annoying situation when a program under debugging seemingly goes mad, displaying, for instance, a runaway cascade of message boxes before it eventually dies, possibly bringing down the operating system with it by exhausting its resources.

3.6 Optimizing Message Loops

Optimization is usually not the first concern of application programmers when implementing a message loop. Although an application processes many messages, they are still relatively infrequent occurrences when compared with the processor's raw speed. However, it should never be forgotten that the processing of messages represents an occasionally significant overhead.

This overhead is due, in part, to the task and thread context switching that takes place in the background. Also called *marshalling* (at least in the context of ActiveX), this technique ensures that when a window procedure is activated due to a message, that activation takes place in the context of the thread that owns the window.

Another important thing to consider is how MFC applications process messages. Due to the way the MFC framework is implemented, the same message may be filtered through several message maps before it is finally processed by a message handler.

All this means that processing every single message can consume a considerable amount of valuable CPU time. Therefore, it is important not to use messages to implement processor-intensive functionality. Because of the simplicity, it may be tempting to utilize messages to implement communication between threads or processes. However, the implied overhead means that often it is better to utilize more complex but more efficient methods of interprocess communication (e.g., shared memory).

3.7 Summary

Callback functions provide a flexible mechanism for operating systems or library subroutines to request services for an application. Typical examples of callback function use include comparison functions and enumerator functions. Throughout the Windows API, callback functions are used for these and similar purposes.

Windows applications receive event notifications from the operating system (and each other) in the form of messages. Each of these messages is associated with a specific window and is processed by that window's window procedure. In that regard, the window procedure operates like a callback function: its address is stored when the window (or the window class to which the window belongs) is created, and the function is invoked when a message is dispatched to it by the operating system.

The MFC library further extends this mechanism in the form of message handlers. These functions are invoked by the MFC framework when the framework processes messages.

Messages are associated with individual windows and are deposited into the message queue of the thread that created the associated window. Several hundred predefined messages exist that fall into dozens of broad categories. Messages inform applications about cursor movement, keyboard events, and other occurrences.

Each Windows application that processes messages contains at least one message loop: a program loop that repeatedly retrieves and processes messages until the application terminates. An application can contain multiple message loops and may invoke message loops (implemented in the operating system or in libraries) implicitly. For example, calling the `MessageBox()` API function invokes a message loop that processes messages until the message box is closed by the user.

Window procedures must be reentrant. If the processing of a message results in the invocation of a second message loop, that loop in turn may dispatch a message to the first window procedure.

Processing of messages may involve considerable overhead. The MFC compounds this by filtering messages through multiple layers of message maps. Thus, although messages represent a flexible communication mechanism suitable even for interprocess communication, they should not be used in situations where efficient execution is of critical importance.

CREATING AND USING ADVANCED DIALOG BOXES

Topics in this Chapter

- Handling Dialogs in MFC
- Dialog Data Exchange and Validation
- Derived Control Classes in Dialogs
- Modeless Dialog Boxes
- Using and Expanding the Common Dialogs and Common Controls
- Working with Common Dialog Classes
- Customizing the Common Dialogs
- Customizing the Open Dialog Box for Greater Power
- Understanding MFC Control Classes
- Modifying Control Behavior
- Summary

Chapter 4

Dialog boxes remain the prime mechanism for detailed data exchange between the application and user. The MFC libraries provide extensive support for template-based dialog windows via the `CDialog` base class. Class Wizard is an excellent tool for creating dialog classes and automating the transfer between the dialog's controls and mapped member variables during dialog data exchange. However, there is only so much you can do with Class Wizard, and often you'll need to get down to the code to gain the full benefits of the dialog exchange and support mechanisms. This chapter focuses on some of these advanced techniques to help you exploit the dialog box to its full potential.

4.1 Handling Dialogs in MFC

Dialog boxes in MFC are usually based on dialog templates. These dialog templates are binary resources held in the structure defined by the Win32 `DLGTEMPLATE`, `DLGITEMTEMPLATE`, `DLGTEMPLATEEX`, and `DLGITEMTEMPLATEEX`. You can fill these structures with the positioning information, size, ID, and style flags required to describe every control on a dialog.

If these structures were created tediously by hand for every dialog box, user interface software would progress at a snail's pace. Fortunately, the Visual Studio dialog template editor is a powerful tool dedicated to this task.

Once you've created a dialog template resource, you can create a CDialog-derived class that uses the template to create the dialog box window and then manages the exchange between window controls and your dialog's member variables.

4.1.1 Creating Dialog Template Resources

You can create dialog boxes and add controls using the resource editor, as shown in Figure 4-1.

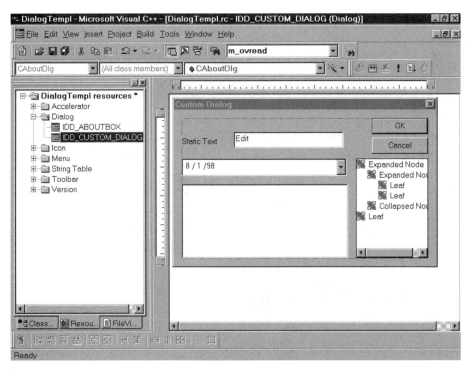

Figure 4-1   Editing a dialog with Visual Studio's dialog editor.

Once you've created the dialog, the visual studio saves the details in a text format in your project's `.rc` file. These details provide the source code required for the resource compiler to generate the required DLGTEMPLATE and DLGITEMTEMPLATE binary strucutures.

You'll rarely need to edit the .rc file directly, because the resource editor should solely maintain it. However, it is interesting to note the code produced after editing a dialog box, such as this entry produced for the dialog shown in Figure 4-1:

```
IDD_CUSTOM_DIALOG DIALOG DISCARDABLE  0, 0, 232, 135
STYLE DS_MODALFRAME | WS_POPUP | WS_CAPTION | WS_SYSMENU
CAPTION "Custom Dialog"
FONT 8, "MS Sans Serif"
BEGIN
    DEFPUSHBUTTON    "OK", IDOK, 175, 7, 50, 14
    PUSHBUTTON       "Cancel", IDCANCEL, 175, 24, 50, 14
    LTEXT            "Static Text", IDC_STATIC,7,23,44,8
    EDITTEXT         IDC_EDIT1,53,19,97,14,ES_AUTOHSCROLL
    LISTBOX          IDC_LIST1,7,64,147,64,LBS_SORT |
                     LBS_NOINTEGRALHEIGHT |
                     WS_VSCROLL | WS_TABSTOP
    CONTROL          "DateTime Picker1", IDC_DATETIMEPICKER1,
                     "SysDateTimePick32", DTS_RIGHTALIGN |
                     WS_TABSTOP, 7,42,146,15
    CONTROL          "Tree1",IDC_TREE1, "SysTreeView32",
                     WS_BORDER | WS_TABSTOP, 161,42,64,86
END
```

When you compile the resources, the compiler produces a file with a .res extension that holds the binary format of these dialog templates (and the other resources). This .res file is then linked with the program code (.obj files) to produce your target .exe, .dll, or .lib file.

4.1.2 Creating a CDialog-Derived Class

You can use Class Wizard to generate a CDialog-derived class by invoking the wizard while the new dialog is displayed in the resource editor. You could create the derived class by hand, but the wizard makes this process much easier.

Class Wizard automatically detects that there is no class currently held in the .clw file that uses the ID of the new dialog template resource and pops up a dialog to let you select an existing handler class, or to create a new one, as shown in Figure 4-2.

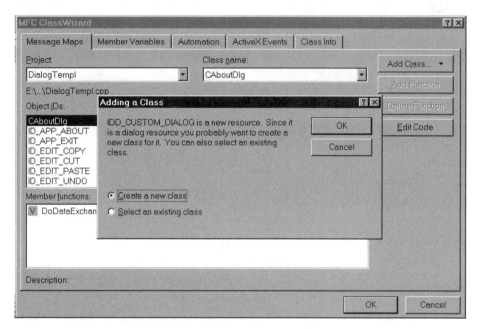

Figure 4-2 The Class Wizard prompting to create or select a dialog handler class.

Normally, you would create a new dialog handler class, but you may sometimes wish to select an existing implementation.

If you choose to create a new dialog handler class, the wizard then displays the New Class dialog box, as shown in Figure 4-3.

The New Class dialog box lets you change the name of the class and automatically generates filenames based on your name. You can change these auto-generated filenames if they aren't appropriate.

The `CDialog` base class and your dialog template ID are automatically selected. If your application is OLE enabled, you can also specify any OLE automation specific details for the new dialog.

After clicking OK to the New Class dialog, you'll see the new dialog handler class pop up in the ClassView pane. If you examine the new header, you'll see a minefield of `//{{AFX_...` comments created by the Class Wizard. When you subsequently add member variables and functions with Class Wizard, it will add the new code inside the appropriate comment sections.

You'll also notice that the dialog ID is enumerated as the `IDD` member with a value based on your dialog templates resource ID, such as:

```
enum { IDD = IDD_CUSTOM_DIALOG };
```

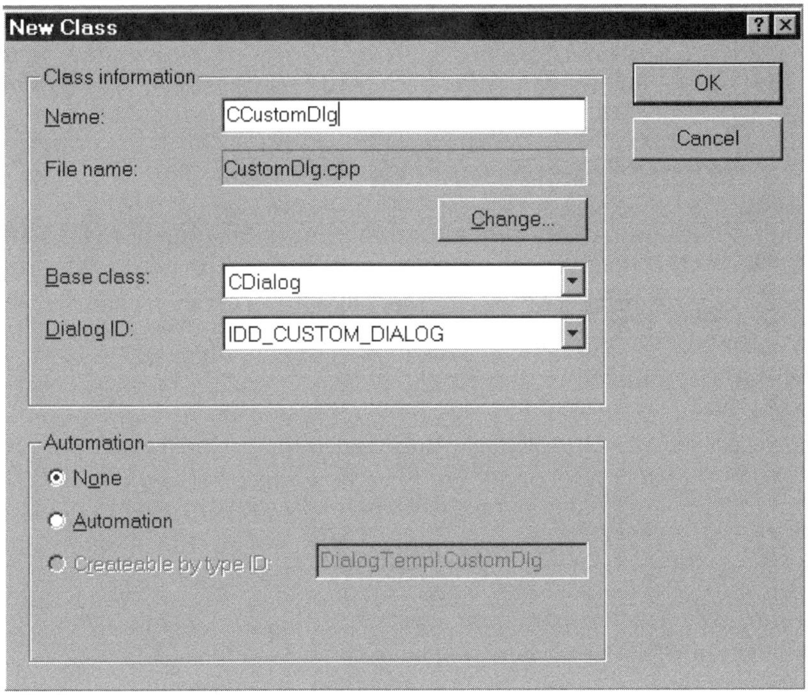

Figure 4-3 The New Class dialog box.

If you examine the dialog constructor function, you'll see that it passes this ID down into the `CDialog` base class along with an optional parent window pointer:

```
CCustomDlg::CCustomDlg(CWnd* pParent /*=NULL*/)
    : CDialog(CCustomDlg::IDD, pParent)
{
  //{{AFX_DATA_INIT(CCustomDlg)
    // NOTE: the Class Wizard will add member initialization here
  //}}AFX_DATA_INIT
}
```

The `//{{AFX_DATA_INIT` section in the constructor implementation is used by Class Wizard to initialize any member variables that you insert using the wizard.

The dialog class definition also includes a declaration for the virtual function `DoDataExchange()` (covered later in more detail) and a message map declaration:

```
DECLARE_MESSAGE_MAP()
```

This shows that the dialog box is ultimately derived from the `CCmdTarget` class (via `CWnd`). This is because the dialog box is a window, and your `CDialog`-derived class must process messages from its own window, and from the various dialog controls (which are child windows).

4.1.3 Displaying the Dialog Box

At this point you can create an instance of the dialog box handler class and display the dialog box. Dialog boxes are normally displayed in a modal sense (modeless dialogs are discussed later in this chapter). This means that when the dialog is displayed, the user is unable to interact with any other part of the application until they click OK or Cancel within the dialog box, thus dismissing the dialog box.

The `CDialog` class's `DoModal()` function initiates the modal process and ends when the `EndDialog()` member function is called. The default implementation of `CDialog` calls `EndDialog()` automatically in response to the user clicking the OK or Cancel buttons. You can use the integer value returned from `DoModal()` to find which button was pressed. This integer is actually returned from the parameter passed to `EndDialog()`, which by default is `IDOK` or `IDCANCEL` in response to the OK and Cancel buttons.

The following lines show how an object of the `CCustomDlg` class is constructed and displayed and the return code used to determine which button was clicked to close the dialog:

```
CCustomDlg dlgCustom;
if (dlgCustom.DoModal()==IDOK)
    AfxMessageBox("User Hit OK");
else
    AfxMessageBox("User Hit Cancel");
```

If you do want to use a dialog template constructed in memory, you should construct a `CDialog`-derived class calling the constructor with no parameters. Then you can call the `InitModalIndirect()` function passing a pointer to a `DLGTEMPLATE` structure in memory or a `HGLOBAL` handle to a global memory segment. If the initialization succeeds, `InitModal-Indirect()` returns a `TRUE` value. You can then call `DoModal()` as normal to display the modal dialog.

Core Warning

If you want to create more than 255 controls in a dialog, you must add the controls dynamically from within the `OnInitDialog()` function. Dialog templates in Visual Studio support a maximum of 255 controls.

4.1.4 Dialog Box Coordinates

When you edit a dialog box in the resource editor, you'll notice that the coordinates don't correspond to the current screen resolution. Dialog boxes use their own coordinate system based on the size of the font being used in the dialog. This helps with the problem of matching the sizes of controls and group boxes to the various font sizes.

When the dialog is displayed, the control positions and sizes will be converted from dialog units into real screen units depending of the size of font used. Most dialogs will use the default system font, but you can set different fonts when editing the dialog, or from within your code by calling the `CWnd` base class's `SetFont()` function, or by overriding the `CDialog` class's `OnSetFont()` function and supplying a pointer to your required dialog font.

These units are calculated from the average heights and widths of the current window font as one-eighth of the height and one quarter of the width. You can convert between these dialog box units and the real screen coordinates by passing a `RECT` structure holding the dialog box coordinates to the `MapDialogRect()` function. `MapDialogRect()` will then translate these dialog box coordinates into screen coordinates.

Core Tip

You may also find the `CWnd` base class's `ClientToScreen()` function useful when manipulating screen coordinates relative to the dialog box. `ClientToScreen()` converts client coordinates held in a `RECT` or `POINT` structure into screen coordinates. The corresponding `ScreenToClient()` function performs the opposite conversion.

4.1.5 Changing the Input Focus and Default Buttons

When you edit a dialog template in the resource editor, you can set the tab order by pressing Ctrl+D. This displays sequence numbers over the controls and lets you change the order by clicking on various controls in sequence. Whenever the user presses the Tab button while the dialog is displayed, the input focus is moved to the next control in this tab order. There is a set of member `CDialog` functions that let you change the current input focus from within your code based on this tab order.

You can set the focus to a specific control after the dialog is displayed by calling `GotoDlgClrl()` and passing a pointer to the control's window. You can find this pointer by ID by calling `GetDlgItem()`. For example, to set the input focus to the OK button, you could call the following from within your dialog class (after activation):

```
GotoDlgCtrl(GetDlgItem(IDOK));
```

The `NextDlgCtrl()` and `PrevDlgCtrl()` functions let you move forward and backwards through the tab order, setting the input focus to the next or previous control from the current control with input focus.

Normally, the OK button is the default button, so that when the user presses the Enter key, the OK button is pressed. You can change this behavior by passing a different button ID to `SetDefID()`, the alternative button will then become the default clicked when Enter is pressed. The corresponding `GetDefID()` returns the ID of the current default button.

If you are using context-sensitive help, you can set the context help ID for a dialog by calling `SetHelpID()` and passing the ID that corresponds to the documentation for that dialog.

4.2   Dialog Data Exchange and Validation

The controls in a dialog box are specialized windows that store their own copy of the data that the user enters or changes. In the lifetime of a dialog box, you'll normally want to initialize these controls with data from your program and then save that data back into those variables.

You'll probably also want to validate the values stored in the controls to ensure that they are within acceptable ranges when the user attempts to click OK to end the dialog box.

The first task in this process is to obviously add new member variables to the dialog handler class that will correspond to the controls.

4.2.1 Mapping Member Variables to Controls

You can use Class Wizard to add member variables and provide the mapping for most of the dialog controls via Class Wizard's Member Variables tab, as shown in Figure 4-4.

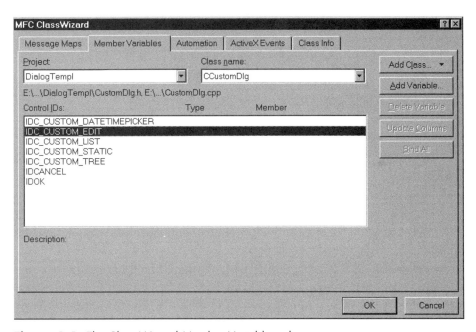

Figure 4-4   The Class Wizard Member Variables tab.

This tab lists the control IDs of the various controls by selecting one and clicking the Add Variable button. The Add Member Variable dialog is displayed, as shown in Figure 4-5.

You'll notice that the Add Member Variable lets you set a Category that can be either a value or a control and a variable type. The variable types available change depending on the setting of the Category drop list combo box.

If you set the category to indicate value mapping, the variable type combo will list member variable types that can be used with the type of control being mapped. These values are great for quick and easy value-oriented transfer, but often you'll need to map a control class to the control so that you can manipulate the control's more advanced features.

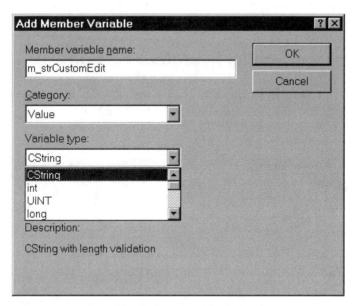

Figure 4-5 The Add Member Variable dialog box.

You can map a number of variables to the same control so that you can perform easy value transfer and allow control handler class mapping concurrently.

Once you've added the member variable map, you'll notice that the new member variable is inserted into your dialog handler class definition between the Class Wizard `AFX_DATA` generated comments. The new variable is also initialized within your dialog class's constructor function as shown here:

```
//{{AFX_DATA_INIT(CCustomDlg)
   m_strCustomEdit = _T("");
//}}AFX_DATA_INIT
```

You'll also see a new entry placed in the `DoDataExchange()` function that looks similar to the following:

```
void CCustomDlg::DoDataExchange(CDataExchange* pDX)
{
    CDialog::DoDataExchange(pDX);
    //{{AFX_DATA_MAP(CCustomDlg)
    DDX_Text(pDX, IDC_CUSTOM_EDIT, m_strCustomEdit);
    //}}AFX_DATA_MAP
}
```

The new `DDX_Text` macro entry automates data transfer between the control identified by `IDC_CUSTOM_EDIT` and your `m_strCustomEdit` member variable.

If you were to add a control map for the edit control, you would see a `CEdit` member variable entry added to the class definition and a corresponding `DDX_Control` macro to map it to the control ID. For example:

```
DDX_Control(pDX, IDC_CUSTOM_EDIT, m_editCustom);
```

If you insert other variable types, you will see different `DDX_` macros used to map the various types of control to various data types (some of which are shown in Table 4-1).

Table 4-1 Common Controls and Their Mapping Classes/Variables

Control	*Mapping Class*	*Allowable Mapped Data Types*
Static	CStatic	CString
Edit	CEdit	CString, DWORD, UINT, int, long double, float, BOOL, short, COleDateTime & COleCurrency
Button	CButton	–
CheckBox	CButton	BOOL
3-State CheckBox	CButton	int
Radio	CButton	int
ListBox	CListBox	CString, int
ComboBox	CComboBox	CString, int
Extended Combo	CComboBoxEx	
ScrollBar	CScrollBar	int
Spin	CSpinButtonCtrl	
Progress Bar	CProgressCtrl	
Slider Control	CSliderCtrl	int
List Control	CListCtrl	
Tree Control	CTreeCtrl	
Date Time Picker	CDateTimeCtrl	CTime, COleDateTime
Month Calendar	CMonthCalCtrl	CTime, COleDateTime

You can also add some simple validation maps to certain controls such as edit controls. Depending on the variable type mapped, the lower section of the Member Variables tab displays a section that lets you specify validation information.

For example, if you map a CString to an edit control, you can set the validation rules to limit the maximum number of characters allowed in the edit control. If you map an integer to the edit control, you can set upper and lower ranges for the entered value.

If you set any of these validation rules, Class Wizard will automatically add a DDV_ routine into the DoDataExchange() function to perform validation, as shown in the following example:

```
DDV_MaxChars(pDX, m_strCustomEdit, 10);
```

There are a number of different DDV_ routines for the various types of validation rule, member variable, and control type.

4.2.2 The Data Exchange and Validation Mechanism

The DoDataExchange() function is called several times during the lifetime of a dialog and performs a variety of tasks. First, when the dialog box is initialized it subclasses any mapped controls via the DDX_Control routine (discussed in more detail later). Then it transfers the data held in the member variables into the controls using the DDX_ routines. Finally, when the user clicks OK, the data from the controls is validated using DDV_ routines and transferred back into the member variables using the DDX_ routines again.

You'll notice that the DoDataExchange() function is passed a pointer to a CDataExchange object. This object holds the details that let the DDX routines know if they should be transferring data to or from the controls. The DDX_ routines then implement the Windows message required to set or retrieve data from the control associated with the given control ID.

When the m_bSaveAndValidate member is set to TRUE, the data exchange should transfer data from the controls to the member variables and perform validation. It is set to FALSE when data from the member variables should be loaded into the controls. You can add your own custom code to DoDataExchange() to transfer data to or from the controls and check the m_bSaveAndValidate member of the CDataExchange object to see if you should be transferring the data to or from the control.

Core Warning

When placing code in `DoDataExchange()`, *you should avoid changing the code inside the Class Wizard comment section, otherwise Class Wizard may become confused. You can safely add code after the Class Wizard section.*

The `DDV_` routines check `m_bSaveAndValidate` and perform the validation if it is set to `TRUE`. If validation should be performed, the `DDV_` macro calls the `CDataExchange` class's `PrepareCtrl()` function (or `PrepareEditCtrl()` for edit controls) passing the ID of the control to be validated. `PrepareCtrl()` and `PrepareEditCtrl()` find the HWND handle of the control associated with the passed ID and store it.

If the validation fails, this window handle is used to reset the focus to the control that caused the validation failure. When failing, the validation macro also calls the `Fail()` member variable, which throws a `CUserExeption` to escape the validation function and display a message box to inform the user as to why the validation failed.

The `DDX_` and `DDV_` routines can use the `m_pDlgWnd` member of the `CDataExchange` object to find the control associated with the specified ID by calling `GetDlgItem()`. `GetDlgItem()` is a `CWnd` function that will return a pointer to a child window of the parent window object (in this the dialog) when passed a control ID. The ID for each control is set in the `GWL_ID` window value of each control when it is initially created. You can use the `GetWindowLong()` and `SetWindowLong()` functions to get and change this control ID value for any of the dialog controls.

You can add your own custom `DDX_` and `DDV_` routines to handle custom data types. However, for most circumstances it is easier just to add validation code directly into the `DoDataExchange()` function to perform the same transfer and validation functions on your custom data type.

4.2.3 Initializing the Dialog Controls

Obviously the `DoDataExchange()` function must be initially called to load the default values from the mapped member variables into the controls. This initialization cannot be performed until the dialog window has opened because the controls don't exist yet. After the `DoModal()` function is entered and the dialog window is created, it enters a message loop to wait for interaction from the user. But the first message it will receive before the window is actually displayed is a `WM_INITDIALOG`. This message tells the dialog handler class that the dialog window and controls have all been created, but require initialization.

The base class implementation of CDialog handles this message and calls the UpdateData() function passing a FALSE value. UpdateData() is called to set up the starting conditions for a DoDataExchange() call. DoDataExchange() is never called directly (except from Update-Data()) because UpdateData() initializes the CDataExchange object and also handles the CUserException thrown by a validation rule violation. The FALSE parameter passed from the CDialog class's OnInitDialog() implementation ends up as the m_bSaveAndValidate member passed in the CDataExchange object to DoDataExchange().

In this way, the default OnInitDialog() implementation initializes the controls to their initial settings from the member variables. You can supply your own handler for OnInitDialog() in your derived class to extend to the default functionality.

When you add a handler for the WM_INITDIALOG message via the Add New Windows Message/Event Handler dialog, your CDialog-derived class gains an OnInitDialog() function that looks similar to the following:

```
BOOL CCustomDlg::OnInitDialog()
{
   CDialog::OnInitDialog();
   // TODO: Add extra initialization here
   return TRUE;   // return TRUE unless you set the focus
                  // EXCEPTION: OCX Property Pages return FALSE
}
```

You'll notice that the OnInitDialog() function first calls the base class implementation to initialize the controls. You can then add lines to perform your own specialized initialization. For example, you may wish to disable some of the dialog controls if you are using the same dialog in several difference circumstances. You can do this by passing FALSE to the EnableWindow() function of any of the control mapping classes (those mapped with DDX_Control) as shown here:

```
m_editCustom.EnableWindow(FALSE);
```

These mapping classes are all derived from CWnd, so you can perform any of the CWnd operations or any of the more specialized control specific operations. In the example above, m_editCustom is a CEdit object.

Alternatively, you may wish to initialize more sophisticated controls such as list or tree controls as shown here (where m_listCustom is a CListBox object):

```
m_listCustom.AddString("Dogs");
m_listCustom.AddString("Cats");
m_listCustom.AddString("Dolphins");
```

In both of the previous examples, Class Wizard will create `DDX_Control` maps to initialize the control mapping variables that look similar to the following:

```
DDX_Control(pDX, IDC_CUSTOM_LIST, m_listCustom);
DDX_Control(pDX, IDC_CUSTOM_EDIT, m_editCustom);
```

If you don't call the base class implementation of `OnInitDialog()`, you should at least call `UpdataData(FALSE)` before using any of the mapped control classes in `DoDataExchange()`. This is because the first pass of the `DDX_Control` routines is also responsible for initializing the HWND member variables of the control mapping classes. If you try to use these mapping classes without setting the HWND member, they won't work and will throw an assertion.

You'll also notice that `OnInitDialog()` must return a boolean value. If you return TRUE, Windows will set the input focus to the first control in the dialog (as defined by the tab order). If you return FALSE, you must set the input focus to a specific control yourself from within `OnInitDialog()`.

4.2.4 *Retrieving Data from the Controls*

You can call `UpdataData()` passing TRUE to retrieve and validate the current data from the controls. Once again `DoDataExchange()` is called from `UpdataData()`, this time passing a TRUE value for the `m_bSaveAndValidate` flag.

`UpdataData()` returns a TRUE value if the validation succeeded or FALSE if there was a problem validating the data. You can call `Update-Data()` at any time during the life of the dialog while the dialog window and controls are active.

This is often useful when you are responding to messages from one control (such as a combo box), but want to use the result from that control to update another. By the same token, you may find that `UpdateData()` is too sweeping and performs validation before the user has completed the whole dialog or overwrites values in controls or member variables.

For this reason, you will occasionally find that it is best to reserve the use of `UpdateData()` for initializing and finally closing the dialog. More precise data transfers can be performed by using the control mapping classes, including `CEdit`, `CComboBox`, `CListBox`, and so on. For example, the following lines use a `CEdit` control mapped object (`m_editCustom`) to retrieve the current contents of an edit control:

```
CString strText;
m_editCustom.GetWindowText(strText);
```

You could also set the text by using the `SetWindowText()` function. Each control mapping class has a large range of member functions to exchange and manipulate specific aspects of the control.

4.2.5 Responding to Control Notifications

You'll often wish to receive notifications from the controls on the dialog. These messages are sent from the control to the parent dialog window when the user performs a specific action such as changing the selection in a list box.

You can use Class Wizard again to help insert the message map entries for these notifications via the Message Maps tab. Selecting the ID associated with the required control will make Class Wizard display the possible notification messages available from that control. You can then add handler functions for these notifications by clicking Add Function, as shown in Figure 4-6.

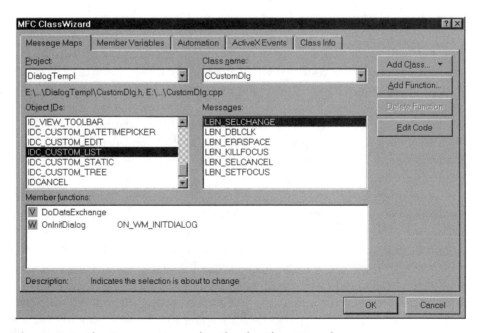

Figure 4-6 The Message Maps tab within the Class Wizard.

When you add the new message handler, a message handler function is generated in your dialog class along with a message map macro specific to the type of message selected. For example, a list box selection changed notification will result in the following message map entry:

```
BEGIN_MESSAGE_MAP(CCustomDlg, CDialog)
   //{{AFX_MSG_MAP(CCustomDlg)
   ON_LBN_SELCHANGE(IDC_CUSTOM_LIST, OnSelchangeCustomList)
   //}}AFX_MSG_MAP
END_MESSAGE_MAP()
```

When you click on a valid list box line, the control will post the `LBN_SELCHANGE` notification to the parent dialog window. This message map entry will then call your `OnSelchangeCustomList()` implementation.

Your implementation can then directly manipulate other controls via their control mapping objects. For example, you may wish to disable the edit control if the first item in a list box is selection, but enable it otherwise with a notification handler function as shown here:

```
void CCustomDlg::OnSelchangeCustomList()
{
   BOOL bEnable = (m_listCustom.GetCurSel()==0);
   m_editCustom.EnableWindow(bEnable);
}
```

Your dialog's message map entries can also include all of the messages sent directly to the dialog window itself, such as `WM_SIZE` messages if the dialog can be resized, or `WM_PAINT` if you want to implement some specialized rendering of your dialog box. If you don't add specific handlers for these messages, they will be passed down to the `CDialog` base class (and then the `CWnd` class) to be handled by the dialog's default implementations.

4.2.6 Dynamically Mapping Controls

Rather than using Class Wizard to generate member variable control mapping objects and their associated `DDX_` routine entries, you may wish to just create a local temporary map to a specific control. You can do this using the `GetDlgItem()` function and casting the `CWnd` pointer returned to the specific control mapping class.

For example, to change the text and disable the `OK` button via a dynamic map, you might add the following code in response to a control notification message:

```
CButton* pOK = (CButton*)GetDlgItem(IDOK);

if (pOK) {

  pOK->SetWindowText("Not OK");

  pOK->EnableWindow(FALSE);

}
```

If the control ID can't be found, `GetDlgItem()` returns a NULL value, which you should check or risk a crash caused by calling through a NULL pointer.

You can map any of the control mapping classes to their corresponding controls in this way and then call any of the control map member functions to send messages that manipulate the control. The corresponding `GetDlgCtrlID()` function will return the ID associated with any particular control.

4.2.7 Responding to OK and Cancel

When you click OK or Cancel, the framework normally calls `CDialog`'s `OnOK()` and `OnCancel()` virtual functions. The default implementation for `OnCancel()` is fairly simple and just calls `EndDialog()` passing `IDCANCEL`. This closes the dialog and returns `IDCANCEL` from the `DoModal()` function.

The default implementation for `OnOk()` calls `UpdateData(TRUE)` to save and validate the information from the dialog controls. If the validation fails, then the dialog remains open, otherwise `EndDialog()` is called and passed `IDOK` to close the dialog.

You can add your own `BN_CLICKED` handler function for the OK and Cancel buttons to perform specialized validation. If you do this, you will normally wish to call `UpdateData(TRUE)` yourself before your specialized validation to do the standard `DoDataExchange()` transfer and validation. Then you might perform your own special `OnOK()` code before calling `EndDialog()` to close the dialog. If you were to call the base class implementation from your overridden handler function, you may find that you've lost control over when the `UpdateData()` and `EndDialog()` functions are called.

You can call `EndDialog()` at any time during a modal dialog's lifetime to close the dialog.

4.3 Derived Control Classes in Dialogs

You can extend the functionality of any of the standard control classes by deriving your own classes and use these extended controls in your dialog. This technique can let you subtly (or drastically) modify the behavior of the standard Windows controls. Many third-party software vendors supply libraries full of these extended classes to greatly enhance the control capabilities.

4.3.1 Creating a Derived Control

You can use Class Wizard to create a new class derived from an existing MFC control class by clicking the Add Class button and selecting New... to display the New Class dialog box, as shown in Figure 4-7. After entering a name for your new control class, you can set the base class to one of the existing MFC control classes.

When you click OK, you'll see a new control class appear in your Class-View. This new class just consists of constructor/destructor functions and a message map derived from the existing MFC class.

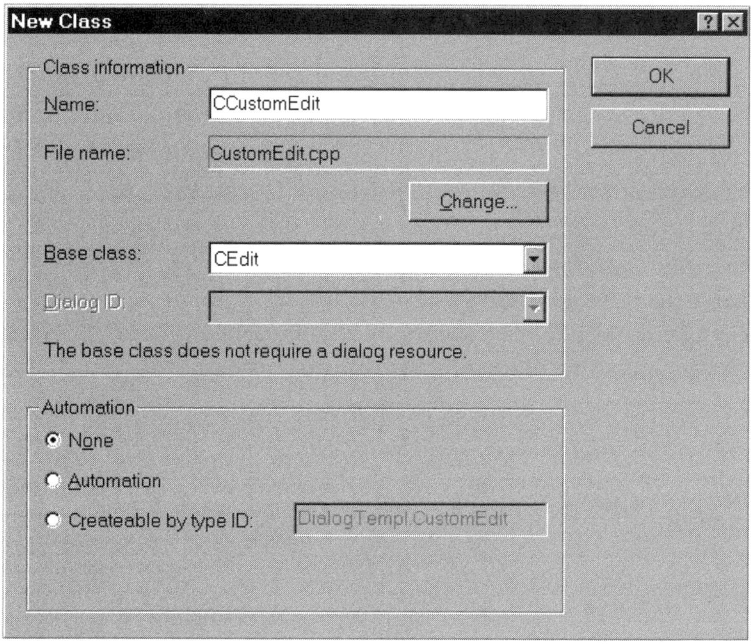

Figure 4-7 Deriving your own control class through the use of the New Class dialog box.

You don't have to use Class Wizard to generate this derived control class, but it certainly makes things easier especially when you come to incorporate the new control in a dialog box, as you'll see later.

Rather than deriving your custom control from another MFC control class, you can derive it from CWnd directly and write a new control from scratch. However, this is a fairly laborious job, and you would probably find it more beneficial to create the control as an ActiveX control.

4.3.2 Customizing the Derived Control

You change or extend the default functionality of your new derived class by adding message handler functions to intercept the Windows messages before they are passed to the base class. For example, you could create a custom edit control that automatically converts uppercase to lowercase letters. You could add a handler to catch the WM_CHAR messages and change any uppercase characters to lowercase, as shown here:

```
void CCustomEdit::OnChar(UINT nChar, UINT nRepCnt, UINT nFlags)
{
    if (nChar>='A' && nChar<='Z')
        nChar+=32;                        // Make it lowercase
    DefWindowProc(WM_CHAR,nChar,MAKELONG(nRepCnt,nFlags));
}
```

If you examine the source code for the MFC control base classes, you'll notice that most call a CWnd function called Default(). This function just calls the DefWindowProc() function passing the details of the last message sent to the window. The DefWindowProc() function then implements the default processing for the Windows message.

Rather than calling the base class CEdit::OnChar() function, the example above calls DefWindowProc() directly passing the modified nChar variable. You'll notice that a corresponding ON_WM_CHAR message handler macro was added to your derived control's message map, as shown here:

```
BEGIN_MESSAGE_MAP(CCustomEdit, CEdit)
    //{{AFX_MSG_MAP(CCustomEdit)
    ON_WM_CHAR()
    //}}AFX_MSG_MAP
END_MESSAGE_MAP()
```

This macro is responsible for separating the nRepCnt and nFlags word values from the original LPARAM parameter sent in the WM_CHAR message.

The MAKELONG macro used above merely recombines these values back into a single LPARAM parameter for the DefWindowProc() function.

You now have a simple customized CEdit-derived class that converts all uppercase characters to lowercase. Obviously this is quite a simple customization, but by catching other Windows messages in this way, you can customize the standard controls beyond recognition.

4.3.3 Using the Derived Control in a Dialog Box

Once you've derived a custom control, you can use it in a dialog as a mapped member variable as you would any standard MFC control. If you have used Class Wizard to create the derived control class, you'll find that your new class is available from the list of control variable types in the Add Member Variable dialog box as shown in Figure 4-8.

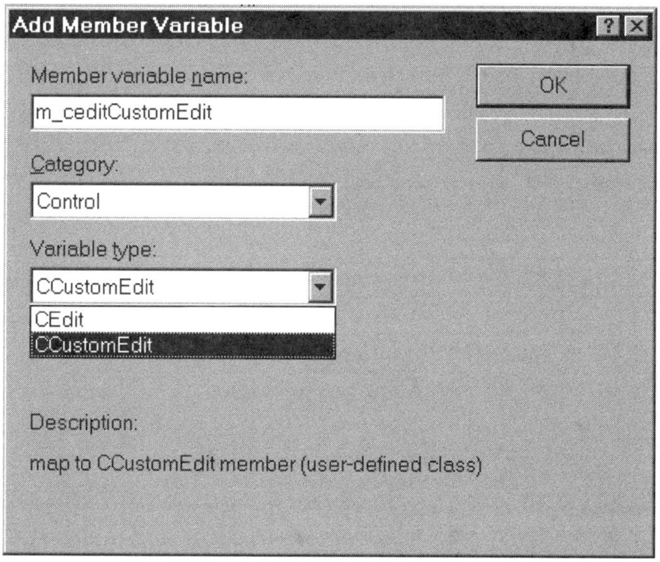

Figure 4-8 Mapping your derived class to a dialog control.

After clicking OK to map the new member variable to your derived class, you'll notice that Class Wizard adds the new member variable into the dialogs class definition as normal:

```
CCustomEdit    m_ceditCustomEdit;
```

Class Wizard also prompts you with a message box to remind you that you must manually add a #include for the custom controls class definition before the new member variable declaration. For example, if your new derived class is defined in the `CustomEdit.h` module, you should add the `#include` before your custom dialog definition:

```
#include "CustomEdit.h"
```

You should now find that when your new dialog is displayed, the behavior of your new customized control is changed accordingly.

You may not always wish to use Class Wizard (or be able to) to map your derived control class to a particular control. If not, you should manually add the member variable declaration for your derived class into the dialog class definition. You can then call `SubclassDlgItem()` from `OnInitDialog()` to hook your derived control class's message map into the specific Windows control.

The term subclassing in this circumstance is different from the object-oriented subclass term, and really means use this class to handle the Windows messages for this control. This subclassing is normally performed during the first pass of `DoDataExchange()` from inside a `DDX_Control()` routine. You must pass the control ID and a valid parent dialog window pointer to `SubclassDlgItem()`.

For example, to manually subclass the new custom edit box (`m_ceditCustomEdit`), your `OnInitDialog()` function may look as shown here:

```
BOOL CCustomDlg::OnInitDialog()
{
    CDialog::OnInitDialog();
    m_ceditCustomEdit.SubclassDlgItem(IDC_CUSTOM_EDIT,this);
    return TRUE;
}
```

Core Warning

You must only call `SubclassDlgItem()` *after your dialog and control windows have valid window handles. This means placing the subclass call after the call to the* `OnInitDialog()` *base class.*

If the subclassing succeeds, `SubclassDlgItem()` returns TRUE. If you already know the HWND handle of the control, you can call `Subclass-Window()` from the dialog instead, passing the controls window handle. `SubclassWindow()` also returns TRUE if the subclassing was successful.

You can also add an override for the `PreSubclassWindow()` virtual function in your derived control class. Your `PreSubclassWindow()` override will be called just before the control's messages are hooked into your derived class's message map. This lets you perform dynamic changes to the subclassing procedure or just some last minute initialization of your new control handler class.

You can call `UnsubclassWindow()` to make the control revert to using the original default (`CWnd`) handler object.

4.4   Modeless Dialog Boxes

So far you've seen how to create a modal dialog box using the `DoModal()` function. When a Modal dialog is displayed, the user is unable to interact with any other parts of the application's user interface until the dialog is closed.

However, you may wish to display a dialog like a control palette or to provide feedback such as coordinates from a drawing operation. To do this, you'll need a modeless dialog.

4.4.1 Modeless Dialog Resource Templates

There are a couple of differences you should consider when creating a dialog template for a modeless dialog.

First, you may not require OK and Cancel buttons for a modeless dialog because these are usually associated with modal operation. The user normally closes a modeless dialog via the system menu close (small x) in the upper right of the dialog. If you do decide to use OK and Cancel buttons, you must override the default `OnOK()` and `OnCancel()` message handlers and create your own that call `DestroyWindow()`. This is because the default functions call `EndDialog()`, which only closes a dialog in modal operation.

Second, if you want your dialog to be initially visible after creation, you should set the Visible flag on the dialog's properties (in the More Styles tab). By setting this flag, the dialog is created with the `WS_VISIBLE` style, otherwise the dialog window is created but remains invisible unless you call the dialog's `ShowWindow()` function passing `TRUE`.

Figure 4-9 shows the visible property for a modeless dialog with no OK and Cancel button.

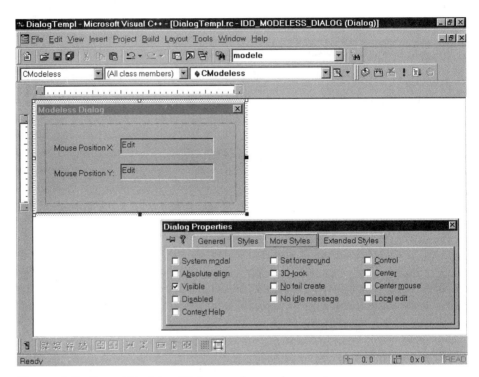

Figure 4-9 Typical Modeless Dialog template and properties.

4.4.2 Creating and Destroying Modeless Dialog Boxes

You can create a modeless dialog by using the Create() function to display the dialog rather than the DoModal() function. You should pass the dialog's template ID (or a resource name) to Create(), and optionally a pointer to a parent window. If the creation succeeds, Create() returns TRUE and the dialog window is created.

If you haven't specified the WS_VISIBLE flag on the dialog template, nothing will be displayed until you call ShowWindow(TRUE). If you have set this flag, the modeless dialog is displayed right away.

The Create() function returns immediately after the dialog is created (unlike the DoModal()). This has implications for the scope and lifetime of your modeless dialog class. You should never declare your modeless dialog as a local function variable like you might with a modal dialog. If you do, when the function returns, the dialog's handler object will be destroyed and the modeless dialog will be destroyed immediately by the `CDialog` base class destructor.

Instead, you can allocate the memory dynamically and, depending on your application requirements, track the memory or just let the dialog delete itself when it is closed. For example, if you don't track the dialog, you may create an instance from a menu handler function, as shown here:

```
void CDialogTemplDoc::OnShowdialogDisplaymodeless()
{
   CModeless* pDlgModeless = new CModeless;
   pDlgModeless->Create(CModeless::IDD);
}
```

If you allocate the memory in this way, you must delete it when the dialog is closed to avoid memory leaks. When the dialog is closed, the last message that is sent to your dialog handler class is WM_NCDESTROY. The default implementation of `OnNcDestroy()` then does some housekeeping and finally calls the `PostNcDestroy()` virtual function. You can override this virtual function to delete the C++ "`this`" pointer to the dialog box object itself. You can add an override to your `CDialog`-derived class using the Add Virtual Function dialog, then add the `delete` statement as shown in the following code:

```
void CModeless::PostNcDestroy()
{
   CDialog::PostNcDestroy();
   // Delete Ourselves
   delete this;
}
```

If you want to create the modeless dialog from a memory-based dialog template (rather than a resource), you can call the `CreateIndirect()` function passing a pointer to a `DLGTEMPLATE` structure or a global memory segment handle to memory containing the structures.

4.4.3 Tracking Modeless Dialog Boxes

The memory tracking technique in the last section is very simplistic and allows the user to create many instances of the modeless dialog, which is probably undesirable. Also, none of the instances can be destroyed from any objects in your code because the dialog object is the only thing that knows where its memory is located.

A more likely scenario is that your document would track the modeless dialog. To do this, you would add a member variable to your document to track the dialog so that you can destroy it from the document and send it messages to provide feedback from other elements of the user interface. You should also place a pointer back to the parent document so that you can inform the document of when the user closes the dialog.

For example, you could add a pointer to your CDocument-derived class to the modeless dialog handler class, and initialize it via the constructor as shown here:

```
CModeless::CModeless(CDialogTemplDoc* pParent)
   : m_pParent(pParent)
{
   Create(CModeless::IDD);
}


void CModeless::PostNcDestroy()
{
   CDialog::PostNcDestroy();
   m_pParent->m_pDlgModeless = NULL;
   delete this;
}
```

You'll notice that the constructor also calls Create() so that the modeless dialog is created and displayed when the object is constructed, thus simplifying the creation process from the calling object. The PostNcDestroy() function now uses the document pointer to NULL its pointer to the modeless dialog, indicating that the dialog is dead and gone.

The document can then track the modeless dialog with its own member pointer and close it from a menu handler as shown in these lines:

```
CDialogTemplDoc::CDialogTemplDoc() : m_pDlgModeless(NULL)
{
}


void CDialogTemplDoc::OnShowdialogDisplaymodeless()
{
   if (!m_pDlgModeless)
      m_pDlgModeless = new CModeless(this);
}


void CDialogTemplDoc::OnShowdialogClosemodeless()
{
   if (m_pDlgModeless)
      m_pDlgModeless->DestroyWindow();
}
```

This technique also lets you update the controls in the modeless dialog from other applications objects (such as a view to indicate the current mouse position) via dialog box member functions accessible through the document's pointer.

Only one instance of the modeless dialog box can be created at any one time because the document menu handler function checks the pointer to see if it already points to a modeless dialog box.

4.4.4 Dialog Bars

A dialog bar is a special form of modeless dialog that also encapsulates the functionality of a control bar (like a toolbar or status bar). This lets the modeless dialog dock naturally to the window frames or float with a small frame.

You can create a dialog template for a dialog bar like that for a normal modeless dialog. The only differences are that you should only set the `WS_CHILD` (the Child setting from the style drop combo) and not the `WS_VISIBLE` flag (visible from the More styles Tab).

You can then construct the dialog bar using the MFC `CDialogBar` class (inherited from `CControlbar`) or your own derived class. The default constructor doesn't require any parameters. You would normally embed the `CDialogBar` object inside a frame window class such as `CMainFrame` as you might a toolbar or status bar.

Once you've constructed the dialog bar, you can call its `Create()` function to create it. If you've embedded the dialog bar inside a frame window class, you would probably call the `Create()` function inside the frame's `OnCreate()` function just like a toolbar.

The dialog bar's `Create()` function differs from a modeless dialog's `Create()` function and is more like a control bar's `Create()`. The first parameter is a pointer to the parent window (normally a frame window). The second parameter is the ID of the dialog template resource that you want to use for the dialog bar (or a resource name string). The third parameter lets you specify a docking/alignment style; this is just like a control bar style and can be a flag value such as `CBRS_TOP`, `CBRS_LEFT`, or `CBRS_NOALIGN`. You should supply an ID for the control bar as the last parameter to uniquely identify the dialog bar.

You can handle the control and messages of a dialog bar as you would for a modeless dialog box. Dialog bars let you embed all the normal controls that you can use on a dialog template while letting you dock and reposition the bar like a toolbar.

4.5   Using and Expanding the Common Dialogs and Common Controls

A significant number of Windows API functions exist to support fundamental operations related to the creation and management of "raw" windows: rectangular areas on the screen with no associated predefined behavior. Although these operations by themselves are perfectly sufficient to create any application, it would be a very painful situation if you had to start from scratch when implementing the behavior of every button, text field, label, or other common window element.

Fortunately, this is not necessary. In addition to basic window operations, the Windows API provides a number of "ready-to-use" window types. These fall into two broad categories: common dialogs and common controls.

Common controls are simply things that typically appear in dialogs. The most commonly used common controls include buttons, edit boxes, list boxes, combo boxes, and static controls. With the introduction of Windows 95, Microsoft introduced a number of additional common controls, such as the tab control used to define the appearance of multipage "tabbed" dialogs. With Internet Explorer 4, yet another new set of common controls was made available to application programmers.

Common dialogs are dialogs that appear, either in an unchanged or a slightly customized form, in most applications. Perhaps the most visible of these is the file dialog, through which users can select a file for reading or writing. The Windows common dialog implementation allows extensive customization of both the appearance and behavior of common dialogs.

The Microsoft Foundation Classes (MFC) provide extensive support for common dialogs and common controls.

4.6   Working with Common Dialog Classes

Even without the Microsoft Foundation Classes, using common dialogs was fairly simple. For example, consider the following simple program:

```
#include <windows.h>
#include <stdio.h>
```

```
void main(void)
{
  OPENFILENAME ofn;
  char szFN[256];

  memset(&ofn, 0, sizeof(ofn));
  memset(szFN, 0, sizeof(szFN));
  ofn.lStructSize = sizeof(ofn);
  ofn.lpstrFile = szFN;
  ofn.nMaxFile = sizeof(szFN);

  if (GetOpenFileName(&ofn) != 0) {
    printf("%s\n", ofn.lpstrFile);
  }
}
```

This program, which can be easily compiled even from the command line (cl fileopen.c comdlg32.lib), returns a filename selected by the user through the common File Open dialog box, as shown in Figure 4-10.

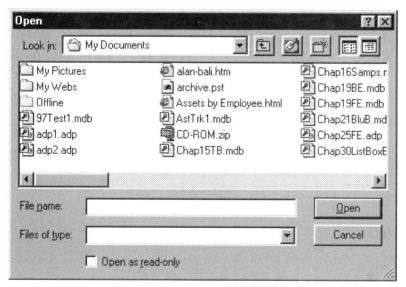

Figure 4-10 Invoking the File Open dialog box from a console application.

With MFC, using common dialogs has become a simple exercise — almost a trivial one, though nothing is ever truly trivial in Visual C++. The program shown in the previous example could thus be rewritten in the MFC as follows:

```
#include <afxwin.h>
#include <afxext.h>
#include <iostream>

using namespace std;

void main(void)
  {
    CFileDialog dlg(TRUE);
    if (dlg.DoModal() == IDOK) {
      cout << (LPCTSTR)dlg.GetPathName() << endl;
    }
  }
```

Because initialization is implicit in the `CFileDialog` constructor, you no longer need to worry about allocating an `OPENFILENAME` structure, initializing its values, and reserving memory for the filename.

Whether you are using the Windows API or MFC, the File Open dialog can be flexibly adapted to your application's requirements. For most simple applications, this flexibility is perfectly sufficient. In other cases, it may be necessary to subclass or otherwise customize the dialog; those techniques are discussed later in this chapter.

The most common customization in file dialogs is the use of filename filters. In its raw form, the File Open dialog allows the user to select any files. By adding filters, the selection can be restricted to specific file types, as shown in Figure 4-11. Consider the following example:

```
#include <afxwin.h>
#include <afxext.h>
#include <iostream>

using namespace std;

void main(void)
  {
    CFileDialog dlg(TRUE);
    dlg.m_ofn.lpstrFilter =
        _T("Text Files (*.txt)\0*.txt;*.lst\0All Files
           (*.*)\0*.*\0");
    dlg.m_ofn.lpstrTitle = _T("Open Text Files");
    if (dlg.DoModal() == IDOK) {
      cout << (LPCTSTR)dlg.GetPathName() << endl;
    }
  }
```

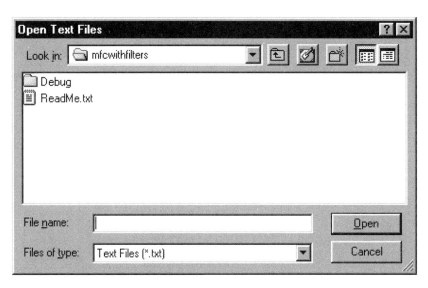

Figure 4-11 Using the File Open dialog with filters.

The File Open dialog has two modes: files can be opened for reading (as in the above examples) or writing. When using the Windows API, use `GetSaveFileName` in place of `GetOpenFileName` if you wish to display the Save As dialog. When using MFC, use `FALSE` as the first parameter of the `CFileDialog` constructor.

The specific behavior of the File Open dialog is controlled through a series of flags, supplied in the `Flags` member of the `OPENFILENAME` structure. For instance, specifying the `OFN_ALLOWMULTISELECT` allows the selection of multiple filenames in the dialog. Or using `OFN_CREATEPROMPT` causes the Save As dialog to display a prompt if the user selects a file that does not yet exist. (Note that some of these flags have meaning only for the Open or the Save As dialogs, whereas other flags are meaningful in both cases.) Flags can be combined using the binary OR (|) operator.

While the File Open dialog is probably the most commonly used of common dialogs, it is by no means the only one. Almost as frequently seen are the Print, and Page Setup dialogs. These two dialogs are typically used together to guide the user through the process of printing documents.

The Print dialog, as shown in Figure 4-12, is invoked through the Windows API function `PrintDlg`. As its single parameter, this function receives a pointer to the `PRINTDLG` structure, which governs the behavior of the dialog and is also used to return information about the user's choices.

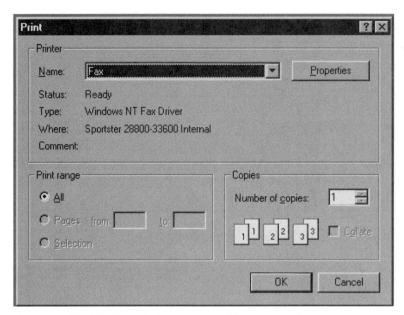

Figure 4-12   The Print dialog as invoked from a sample program.

MFC provides the wrapper class `CPrintDialog` for the Print dialog. Its use is demonstrated by the following program:

```
#include <afxwin.h>
#include <afxext.h>
#include <iostream>

using namespace std;

void main(void)
  {
    CPrintDialog dlg(TRUE);
    if (dlg.DoModal() == IDOK) {
        DEVMODE *pdm = (DEVMODE *)GlobalLock(dlg.m_pd.hDevMode);
        cout << pdm->dmDeviceName << endl;
        GlobalFree(dlg.m_pd.hDevMode);
      }
  }
```

This simple program, however, does not demonstrate one of the most useful features of the Print dialog—its ability to create, initialize, and return a device context (or an information context) for the printer requested by the user. For this, you must add the PD_RETURNDC (or PD_RETURNIC) flag to the flags in m_pd.Flags (the various flag values can be combined using the binary OR operator, as with the File dialog box).

This ability makes the Print dialog useful even when you do not wish to present a choice of printers and printer settings to the user. By specifying the PD_RETURNDEFAULT flag, you can ensure that the dialog is never displayed; however, parameters (including a device context, if requested) that correspond with the default printer are returned.

The Print dialog can also be presented in the form of a Print Setup dialog, as shown in Figure 4-13. Although the Win32 API documentation labels this use as obsolete, this is how the MFC framework implements the Print Setup command for AppWizard-generated applications. To invoke the Print dialog in Print Setup mode, specify the PD_PRINTSETUP flag or use TRUE as the first parameter of the CPrintDialog constructor.

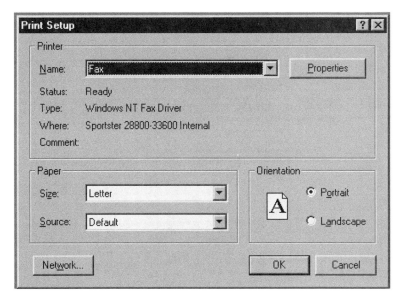

Figure 4-13   The Print dialog box when invoked with the PD_PRINTSETUP flag.

The reason why the Print Setup dialog is considered obsolete is because it has been superseded by the Page Setup dialog, as shown in Figure 4-14. Like the Print dialog, the Page Setup dialog is also supported by an MFC wrapper class: CPageSetupDlg. Use of this class is demonstrated by the following small program:

```cpp
#include <afxwin.h>
#include <afxext.h>
#include <iostream>

using namespace std;

void main(void)
 {
   CPageSetupDialog dlg;
   if (dlg.DoModal() == IDOK) {
      cout << (LPCTSTR)dlg.GetDeviceName() << endl;
    }
 }
```

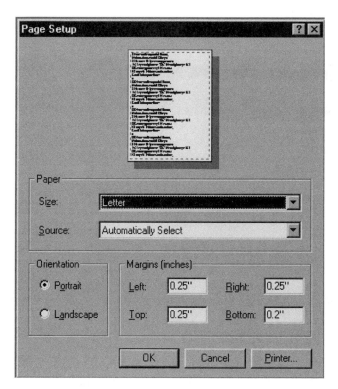

Figure 4-14   The Page Setup dialog box, which superseded the Print Setup dialog box.

An MFC wrapper class also exists for the Color Picker dialog box. Once again, the dialog is very simple to use; in most situations, it is sufficient to construct the MFC wrapper object, call its `DoModal()` member, and read the user's selection:

```
#include <afxwin.h>
#include <afxext.h>
#include <iostream>
#include <iomanip>

using namespace std;

void main(void)
  {
    CColorDialog dlg;
    if (dlg.DoModal() == IDOK) {
      cout << hex << setw(8) << setfill('0') << dlg.GetColor()
          << endl;
    }
  }
```

Finally, there is the Font Selection dialog box. Its use, again through the corresponding MFC wrapper class, can be demonstrated as follows:

```
#include <afxwin.h>
#include <afxext.h>
#include <iostream>

using namespace std;

void main(void)
  {
    CFontDialog dlg;
    if (dlg.DoModal() == IDOK) {
      cout << (LPCTSTR)dlg.GetFaceName() << endl;
    }
  }
```

As these examples demonstrate, the behavior of the common dialogs reviewed so far is very similar. If you are using the Windows API, you allocate a structure containing data specific to the common dialog you wish to use, initialize the structure's members, and call the appropriate API function. If you are using the MFC, you construct the dialog object, adjust settings by supplying parameters other than the defaults in the constructor, invoke the DoModal() method, and read the user's choices using other member functions.

Two other common dialogs, Find and Replace, work very differently. That is because these dialogs are nonmodal in nature. For instance, the Windows API function FindText() constructs a Find dialog but returns immediately afterwards; the dialog remains visible until it is dismissed by the user. When the user enters a search string, the dialog sends FINDMSGSTRING

messages (registered through the `RegisterWindowMessage()` function)
to its parent window. This allows you to create applications with behavior
similar to that of the Windows Notepad: users can keep the Find dialog on-
screen while working with the document.

Because of the difference in behavior, it is perhaps beneficial to first see
how these dialogs behave when used without the benefit of MFC wrappers.
This is demonstrated by the following simple program:

```
#include <windows.h>

int FR_FINDMSGSTRING;
FINDREPLACE g_fr;
HWND g_hwndFind;
char szFind[100];

LRESULT CALLBACK WndProc(HWND hwnd, UINT uMsg,
    WPARAM wParam, LPARAM lParam)
{
   if (uMsg == FR_FINDMSGSTRING) {
      if (g_fr.Flags & FR_FINDNEXT)
         MessageBox(hwnd, g_fr.lpstrFindWhat, "Find String", MB_OK);
   }
   else switch(uMsg) {
      case WM_COMMAND:
         switch (wParam) {
            case 1:
               if (!IsWindow(g_hwndFind)) {
                  g_fr.lStructSize = sizeof(g_fr);
                  g_fr.hwndOwner = hwnd;
                  g_fr.lpstrFindWhat = szFind;
                  g_fr.wFindWhatLen = sizeof(szFind);
                  g_hwndFind = FindText(&g_fr);
                }
               break;
            case 2:
               DestroyWindow(hwnd);
               break;
          }
         break;
      case WM_DESTROY:
         PostQuitMessage(0);
         break;
      default:
         return DefWindowProc(hwnd, uMsg, wParam, lParam);
   }
   return 0;
}
```

```
int WINAPI WinMain(HINSTANCE hInstance, HINSTANCE hPrevInstance,
                   LPSTR lpCmdLine, int nCmdShow)
{
   MSG msg;
   HWND hwnd;
   WNDCLASS wndClass;

   FR_FINDMSGSTRING = RegisterWindowMessage(FINDMSGSTRING);
   memset(&g_fr, 0, sizeof(g_fr));
   g_hwndFind = 0;

   if (hPrevInstance == NULL) {
      memset(&wndClass, 0, sizeof(wndClass));
      wndClass.style = CS_HREDRAW | CS_VREDRAW;
      wndClass.lpfnWndProc = WndProc;
      wndClass.hInstance = hInstance;
      wndClass.hCursor = LoadCursor(NULL, IDC_ARROW);
      wndClass.hbrBackground = (HBRUSH)(COLOR_WINDOW + 1);
      wndClass.lpszClassName = "HELLO";
      wndClass.lpszMenuName = MAKEINTRESOURCE(1);
      if (!RegisterClass(&wndClass)) return FALSE;
   }
   hwnd = CreateWindow("HELLO", "HELLO", WS_OVERLAPPEDWINDOW,
             CW_USEDEFAULT, 0, CW_USEDEFAULT, 0, NULL, NULL,
             hInstance, NULL);
   ShowWindow(hwnd, nCmdShow);
   UpdateWindow(hwnd);
   while (GetMessage(&msg, NULL, 0, 0)) {
      if (!TranslateAccelerator(hwnd, NULL, &msg)) {
         TranslateMessage(&msg);
         DispatchMessage(&msg);
      }
   }
   return msg.wParam;
}
```

This program requires the use of a simple resource script that defines the main window's menu, as shown in the following code:

```
1 MENU
BEGIN
   POPUP "&File"
   BEGIN
      MENUITEM "&Find", 1
      MENUITEM "E&xit", 2
   END
END
```

After it starts, this program first registers the window message FIND-MSGSTRING (a string value predefined in the window's header files). It also initializes the global structure FINDREPLACE. Why global? Because you must make certain that the structure does not go out of scope at the end of the function in which you create the Find dialog. (An alternative would be to allocate this structure on the heap using the new operator.) It is through members of this structure that the Find dialog communicates with your program.

When needed, the Find dialog is created through a call to FindText(). (If you wish to use the Replace dialog instead, just call ReplaceText().) Because the dialog is persistent, your code must ensure that no additional copies are created. In the present example, this is done by checking whether the handle of the Find dialog is that of a valid window. If it is, then it refers to a window that was created through a previous invocation of FindText(), so there's no need to call FindText() again.

When the user clicks the Find First button in the dialog, the dialog sends a FINDMSGSTRING message to the main window. The string entered by the user can be found in the buffer that was supplied to the dialog through the FINDREPLACE structure.

Using the Find or Replace dialogs from MFC applications is very similar. If you are using them from a standard, AppWizard-generated SDI or MDI application, you would normally invoke them when the user selects the Find or Replace command from the Edit menu. Make sure that you create the dialog object on the heap (that is, allocate it using the new operator); otherwise the object may go out of scope while the dialog is still being displayed, causing all sorts of trouble.

For instance, the Replace dialog may be invoked from a CView-derived class as follows:

```
void CMyView::OnEditReplace()
 {
    if (m_pdlgReplace && ::IsWindow(m_pdlgReplace.m_hWnd)) {
       m_pdlgReplace->SetFocus();
       return;
    }
    m_pdlgReplace = new CFindReplaceDlg;
    m_pdlgReplace->Create(FALSE, _T(""), NULL, FR_DOWN, this);
 }
```

The m_pdlgReplace variable would be declared as a member variable of type CFindReplaceDialog*.

Before the dialog is of any practical use, however, it is necessary to register the `FINDMSGSTRING` window message, and define a handler for it. The message is best registered as a global constant variable:

```
const int FR_FINDMSGSTRING = ::RegisterWindowMessage(FINDMSGSTRING);
```

Using this message requires that a handler be declared for it, adding to the class' message map, and defined. To declare the handler, add the following line to the view class's header file, just above the `DECLARE_MESSAGE_MAP` macro call:

```
afx_msg LRESULT OnFindMsgString(WPARAM wParam, LPARAM lParam);
```

To add this function to the view class's message map, insert a line in the implementation file, between the `BEGIN_MESSAGE_MAP` and `END_MESSAGE_MAP` macro calls, as follows:

```
ON_REGISTERED_MESSAGE(FR_FINDMSGSTRING, OnFindMsgString)
```

All you need to do now is to actually write the function. It should appear similar to the following:

```
LRESULT CMyView::OnFindMsgString(WPARAM wParam, LPARAM lParam)
{
   if (m_pdlgReplace->IsTerminating()) {
      m_pdlgReplace->DestroyWindow();
      m_pdlgReplace = NULL;
   }
   else {
      // Do something with the user's picks:
      MessageBox(m_pdlgReplace->m_fr.lpstrFindWhat);
   }
   return 0;
}
```

The call to `IsTerminating()` will help determine whether the dialog is still on-screen or has been dismissed by the user. The call to `Destroy-Window()` automatically destroys the dialog object as well (because of the implementation of `CFindReplaceDlg`), so it is not necessary to use the `delete` operator.

In addition to the dialogs demonstrated here, the MFC library also provides support for a series of OLE-specific common dialogs. These dialogs are defined as part of the OLE User Interface Library and facilitate OLE-specific operations such as the Paste Special command.

4.7   Customizing the Common Dialogs

Although the parameters and flags that govern the behavior of common dialogs allow for a great degree of flexibility, sometimes it is necessary to go beyond that level of customization. Fortunately, it is possible to customize common dialog behavior to a far greater extent with relative ease.

It is possible to alter the appearance of common dialogs by specifying new dialog templates; it is also possible to alter common dialog behavior by modifying the dialog's response to events and other messages.

The appearance of a common dialog can be modified by supplying a dialog template. In the old days, this template was a replacement for the built-in dialog template. This presented all kinds of problems, not only when a version upgrade altered the appearance of common dialogs in Windows, but also with localized versions of the operating system. In Windows 95 and Windows NT 4.0 (and, needless to say, in later versions) it is possible to supply a dialog template that is instantiated as a child dialog of the common dialog. So for instance, if you want to add a thumbnail control to the File Open dialog (the example presented in the next section), the dialog template need contain only this new control (and a dummy control used for positioning), not the complete set of controls that comprise the File Open dialog.

The behavior of a common dialog is modified through the addition of a hook procedure. A hook procedure is essentially a callback function, called by Windows in this case when the common dialog processes specific messages and events. The hook procedure needs to process only those messages and events for which the dialog's behavior is altered; all other messages and events can continue to be processed by the original dialog procedure that Windows supplies for the common dialog.

4.8   Customizing the Open Dialog Box for Greater Power

Many sophisticated applications modify the appearance of the File Open dialog, tailoring it to suit the application's needs. A commonly seen modification allows the user to preview files in a thumbnail form prior to opening them. The example presented in this section provides just such a thumbnail preview capability for enhanced metafiles (EMF), as shown in Figure 4-15.

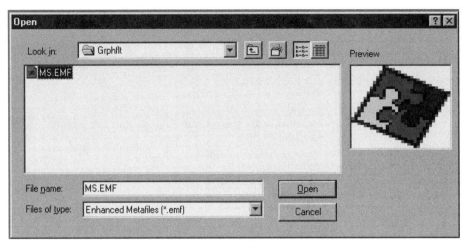

Figure 4-15 Displaying thumbnails for EMF files in the File Open dialog box.

The dialog template used for this customization contains only three controls. One of these is a placeholder. Its label, `stc32`, is recognized by Windows, which will treat the control as a placeholder for the standard controls in the dialog. The positions of the extra controls relative to the standard controls in the dialog will be the same as the extra controls' positions relative to the control labeled `stc32` in the template.

One of the other two controls in this custom template is just a text label. The other is a static control with the `SS_ENHMETAFILE` style; a control with this style is capable of displaying the contents of an enhanced metafile, scaled to the control's rectangle.

```
#include <windows.h>

16384 DIALOG DISCARDABLE  36, 24, 358, 134
STYLE DS_3DLOOK | DS_CONTROL | WS_CHILD | WS_CLIPSIBLINGS
FONT 8, "Helv"
BEGIN
   LTEXT    "",stc32,6,6,256,122
   LTEXT    "Preview",-1,265,15,88,12
   CONTROL ""‚16385,"Static",SS_ENHMETAFILE | WS_VISIBLE |
           WS_BORDER,265,27,88,66
END
```

To use this template and otherwise provide customization for the File Open dialog under MFC, it is easiest to just derive a class from the standard MFC

File Open dialog class, `CFileDialog`. The new class, `CEMFFileDlg`, will
have three member functions including the constructor:

```
#include <afxwin.h>
#include <afxext.h>

class CEMFFileDlg : public CFileDialog
 {
public:
   CEMFFileDlg(BOOL bOpenFileDialog, LPCTSTR lpszDefExt = NULL,
      LPCTSTR lpszFileName = NULL,
      DWORD dwFlags = OFN_HIDEREADONLY | OFN_OVERWRITEPROMPT,
      CWnd* pParentWnd = NULL);
   UINT HookProc(HWND hdlg, UINT uiMsg,
      WPARAM wParam, LPARAM lParam);
   static UINT CALLBACK OFNHookProc(HWND hdlg, UINT uiMsg,
      WPARAM wParam, LPARAM lParam);
 };

CEMFFileDlg::CEMFFileDlg(BOOL bOpenFileDialog, LPCTSTR lpszDefExt,
    LPCTSTR lpszFileName, DWORD dwFlags, CWnd* pParentWnd) :
   CFileDialog(bOpenFileDialog, lpszDefExt, lpszFileName,
      dwFlags | OFN_ENABLEHOOK | OFN_ENABLETEMPLATE |
      OFN_EXPLORER,
      _T("Enhanced Metafiles (*.emf)|*.emf|All Files (*.*)|*.*||"),
      pParentWnd)
 {
   m_ofn.lpTemplateName = MAKEINTRESOURCE(16384);
   m_ofn.lpfnHook = (LPOFNHOOKPROC)OFNHookProc;
   m_ofn.lCustData = (DWORD)this;
 }

UINT CALLBACK CEMFFileDlg::OFNHookProc(HWND hdlg, UINT uiMsg,
    WPARAM wParam, LPARAM lParam)
 {
   CEMFFileDlg *pDlg = NULL;
   switch (uiMsg) {
      case WM_INITDIALOG:
         pDlg = (CEMFFileDlg *)((LPOPENFILENAME)lParam)->lCustData;
         break;
      case WM_NOTIFY:
         pDlg = (CEMFFileDlg *)
            ((LPOFNOTIFY)lParam)->lpOFN->lCustData;
         break;
   }
   if (pDlg) {
      ASSERT_VALID(pDlg);
      if (pDlg->m_hWnd == 0)
         pDlg->Attach(hdlg);
      return pDlg->HookProc(hdlg, uiMsg, wParam, lParam);
```

```
      }
   else
      return 0;
 }

UINT CEMFFileDlg::HookProc(HWND hdlg, UINT uiMsg,
   WPARAM wParam, LPARAM lParam)
 {
   if (uiMsg == WM_NOTIFY) {
      LPOFNOTIFY lpofn = (LPOFNOTIFY)lParam;
      if (lpofn->hdr.code == CDN_SELCHANGE) {
         HENHMETAFILE hemf = NULL;
         CString strExt = GetFileExt();
         if (strExt.CompareNoCase(_T("EMF")) == 0) {
            hemf = ::GetEnhMetaFile(GetPathName());
          }
         HWND hEMF = ::GetDlgItem(hdlg, 16385);
         ::ShowWindow(hEMF, hemf ? SW_SHOW : SW_HIDE);
         if (hemf) {
            hemf = (HENHMETAFILE)::SendMessage(hEMF, STM_SETIMAGE,
               IMAGE_ENHMETAFILE, (LPARAM)hemf);
            if (hemf)
               DeleteEnhMetaFile(hemf);
          }
         return -1;
      }
   }
   return 0;
 }

int WINAPI WinMain(HINSTANCE hInstance, HINSTANCE hPrevInstance,
               LPSTR lpCmdLine, int nCmdShow)
 {
   AfxWinInit(hInstance, hPrevInstance, lpCmdLine, nCmdShow);
   CEMFFileDlg dlg(TRUE);
   if (dlg.DoModal() == IDOK) {
      ::MessageBox(NULL, dlg.GetPathName(), _T("File selected"),
         MB_OK);
   }
   return 0;
 }
```

As can be seen from the `WinMain()` function, altogether 4 lines long, the use of the new dialog class is just as simple as using the original MFC wrapper class. The magic of displaying a thumbnail picture for EMF files remains entirely hidden from the class' users.

This magic happens in part because of what takes place in the `CEMF-FileDlg` constructor. This constructor calls the constructor of the parent, `CFileDialog`, but some of the constructor's parameters are modified. In particular, the following three flags are added to the dwFlags parameter: OFN_ENABLEHOOK, OFN_ENABLETEMPLATE, and OFN_EXPLORER.

The first of these, OFN_ENABLEHOOK, specifies that a hook procedure will be used to process messages. The second, OFN_ENABLETEMPLATE, specifies that a custom dialog template will be used. Finally, OFN_EXPLORER prescribes that the dialog must behave like an "Explorer-style" File Open dialog, a behavior that the hook procedure relies on.

Along with these flags, it is also necessary to specify the identifier of the dialog template and the address of the hook procedure. This takes place in the CEMFFileDlg constructor. The 32-bit custom data field (lCustData) of the OPENFILENAME structure is used to store the address of the current dialog object, which will come in handy when the hook procedure is called.

The hook procedure, OFNHookProc(), is declared as a static member function because it is necessary to take its address and pass it to a nonmember function. The hook procedure retrieves a pointer to the OPENFILENAME structure (where this structure is stored depends on the type of message received) and uses it to obtain the dialog object's address, which was earlier placed in the lCustData member. A little bit of additional trickery is used to ensure that the dialog object is actually attached to the correct window handle. Finally, through the dialog object's address, the "real" hook procedure is called that does the actual processing of messages.

The intent, then, of the hook procedure (and thus the program) is to display a thumbnail representation of any EMF file that the user may select, so the message that needs to be processed, according to the Windows API documentation, is a WM_NOTIFY message with the notification code equal to CDN_SELCHANGE. This message is sent to the hook procedure every time the user clicks on a filename in the File Open dialog or otherwise causes a change in the currently selected file.

Because the dialog object is now properly attached to the corresponding handle, it is possible to use CFileDialog member functions such as GetPathName() or GetFileExt(). The filename extension returned by GetFileExt() can be checked to verify that the user indeed selected an EMF file with the proper extension. If so, a call to GetEnhMetaFile(), with the value returned by GetPathName() supplied as a filename parameter, can be used to obtain a metafile handle. If a valid handle was obtained, it is then passed to the static control that has the SS_ENHMETAFILE style; the control automatically displays the metafile data. Any previously opened metafile handles are closed using DeleteEnhMetaFile(). (Note that this function does not delete the disk file, only the memory representation of the metafile's bits.)

If the metafile handle is not valid, the static control is made invisible. This ensures that the control does not display the contents of a previously selected metafile when another file, itself not an enhanced metafile, has been picked by the user.

This simple customization exercise demonstrates the true power of common dialogs. With a few dozen lines of code, features can be added to your application that make it appear truly professional, easier to use, and a more pleasant experience for its users.

4.9   Understanding MFC Control Classes

Common controls are specialized windows that typically appear in dialogs. They include static controls, buttons, edit boxes, list boxes, combo boxes, Windows 95 controls such as the tree view, list view control, tab control, and the most recent set of controls that became available with Internet Explorer 4 and 5.

Most common controls are supported in the MFC through wrapper classes. These classes provide a C++ interface to most of the controls' functionality.

Take, for instance, the control that is perhaps the easiest to use and understand, the button control. Every button control in a dialog is actually a window that belongs to the built-in window class BUTTON. The window procedure of this class processes mouse events and sends notification (in the form of WM_COMMAND messages) to the control's parent when the user clicks or double-clicks the control.

Using a button control in an application is very easy, both with or without the benefit of the MFC. In a non-MFC application, you create the control either directly or indirectly (for instance, by creating a dialog from a dialog template that contains buttons). The dialog procedure must then process WM_COMMAND messages with the button control's identifier in the message's WPARAM parameter.

In an MFC application, you can use the Class Wizard to add handlers for WM_COMMAND messages. Normally, it is not necessary to make explicit use of the CButton class; all processing takes place using the control's identifier in the dialog. The CButton class is an MFC wrapper class for all windows of the BUTTON class. (Once again, make sure that you aren't confused by this unfortunate choice of terminology: a C++ class like CButton is not the same as a window class!) The CButton class enters the picture when you wish to perform some nonstandard processing with the control. For instance, you may wish to alter the text that the control displays in response to some user action. Or you may want to add handlers for messages not normally processed by the control.

The CButton class is derived from CWnd, MFC's main class representing windows in general. That means that most of the functionality available with other windows becomes automatically available for CButton objects as well. For instance, if you wish to alter the text displayed by a button, you can use CWnd::SetWindowText() for this purpose. You saw the various MFC wrapper classes and their functionality earlier in this chapter.

In addition to the classic MFC control classes, MFC supports classes for Windows 9x controls, including CAnimateCtrl (animation control), CHeaderCtrl (header controls like those used to label the columns in list view controls), CHotKeyCtrl (hot key windows), CImageList (image lists used, among others, with list view controls and tree view controls), CListCtrl (list view controls), CProgressCtrl (progress bars), CRichEditCtrl (edit boxes with paragraph formatting), CSliderCtrl (sliders), CSpinButtonCtrl (up/down controls), CStatusBarCtrl (status bars), CTabCtrl (tab controls like those used in multipage tabbed dialogs), CToolBarCtrl (toolbars), CToolTipCtrl (tooltip pop-ups), and CTreeCtrl (tree view controls.)

New to the MFC for Visual Studio 6.0 (and new to Windows, introduced only with Internet Explorer 4) are the classes CComboBoxEx (combo boxes with extended functionality), CDateTimeCtrl (date/time pickers), CDrag-ListBox (list boxes with repositioning functionality), CIPAddressCtrl (IP address controls), CMonthCalCtrl (calendar controls), and CRebar-Ctrl (Internet Explorer style "rebar" control bars.) These controls can only be used on systems that have a recent version of COMCTL32.DLL installed (such as the version distributed with Internet Explorer 4 or later).

4.10 Modifying Control Behavior

Before MFC, altering a control's behavior usually required that the control be subclassed. Subclassing a window class means substituting a new window procedure for the one originally associated with that window class.

Under MFC, such a replacement of the window procedure is rarely necessary. Because the processing of messages is already routed through the member functions of a window class, deriving your own C++ class from the appropriate window class, and overriding member functions or inserting additional message handlers is usually sufficient.

A somewhat crude but simple example is presented in the following few lines of code:

```
// Header
class CMyBtn : public CButton
  {
protected:
   afx_msg void OnKeyDown(UINT nChar, UINT nRepCnt, UINT nFlags);
   DECLARE_MESSAGE_MAP()
  };

// Implementation
BEGIN_MESSAGE_MAP(CMyBtn, CButton)
   ON_WM_KEYDOWN()
END_MESSAGE_MAP()

void CMyBtn::OnKeyDown(UINT nChar, UINT nRepCnt, UINT nFlags)
  {
   CString str;
   GetWindowText(str);
   switch (nChar) {
      case VK_PRIOR:
         str.Format(_T("%d"), atoi(str) - 1);
         SetWindowText(str);
         break;
      case VK_NEXT:
         str.Format(_T("%d"), atoi(str) + 1);
         SetWindowText(str);
         break;
      default:
         CButton::OnKeyDown(nChar, nRepCnt, nFlags);
   }
  }
```

What exactly does this code do? It modifies the behavior of the standard button control in such a way that the control now responds to the PgUp and PgDn keys (represented by the virtual key codes VK_PRIOR and VK_NEXT). It is assumed that the control's text label represents an integer; this integer is decremented or incremented when one of these two keys is pressed.

How would you use this class in your own programs (assuming that you have a need for a control with such a silly behavior)? You can insert a member variable for a button control through the Class Wizard, but this variable will be of type CButton. However, after insertion you can modify the variable's type to CMyBtn. (Don't forget to include the header file that contains the declaration of the CMyBtn class.) This is enough to alter the control's behavior; once an object of type CMyBtn is associated with the control, the object's message handlers are automatically called.

4.11 Summary

It is a rare Visual C++ application programmer who never needs to use dialog boxes. Understanding the intricacies and MFC behavior will help you customize and use the dialog mechanism to its fullest.

In this chapter, you've seen how to create dialog templates via the resource editor, and how (if necessary) you can alternatively create and use memory-based dialog templates.

You've seen how the font size affects the dialog control sizes and position, and how to convert between dialog coordinates and screen coordinates.

You've seen how the CDialog class can be used to display ordinary modal dialogs and how it exchanges data through the data exchange mechanism. It is important to understand the sequence of events when initializing the dialog, updating the individual controls during its lifetime, then performing validation and data transfer from the controls when the user clicks OK to close it.

You can map simple value holding variables to these controls for simple transfer, or map control mapping objects to enjoy all of the sophistication of the Windows control and its messages via an MFC C++ class specific to the type of control.

You can also extend these standard controls with your own derived controls to extend and specialize the functionality offered by the standard controls, then use Class Wizard to add your new derived control classes to the dialog.

You've seen how the subclassing mechanism attaches your derived class's message map to control so that it can catch and handle specific messages sent to and from the control.

Modeless dialog boxes let you leave the dialog open for use while the user uses other parts of your application. This is a handy technique for providing extra "floating" controls or feedback panels.

You can also use dialog bars that present an interface similar to a toolbar but with controls from a dialog template, allowing easier design and positioning of the controls than possible with an ordinary toolbar.

The ability of applications to provide a standardized "look and feel" at minimal cost in terms of programming effort is greatly enhanced by the presence of a variety of standard controls and dialogs provided by windows. These standard dialogs and controls are called common dialogs and common controls.

Common dialogs include the File Open dialog, the Print and Page Setup dialogs, the Font Selection dialog, the Color Selection dialog, the Find and Replace dialogs, and a variety of additional dialogs used for OLE.

Common dialogs can be used in their unaltered form with only a few lines of code. Their behavior can also be modified through a variety of flags and parameters. More extensive modifications can be accomplished by supplying custom dialog templates and hook procedures. The MFC provides wrapper classes for all common dialogs.

Common controls fall into three major categories. "Classic" common controls have been present in Windows since its 16-bit versions and include buttons, edit boxes, static controls, list boxes, combo boxes, and scroll bars. Windows 95 common controls include a variety of additional controls such as list views and tree views, tab controls, sliders, progress bars, the rich edit control, and more. Finally, with the introduction of Internet Explorer 4, yet another group of common controls was made available to application programmers.

The latest version of MFC provides support classes for all common controls. By deriving your own classes from MFC support classes, you can easily modify the behavior of a control. For instance, a button control can be made to respond keystrokes by altering its appearance through the addition of a simple message handler to a custom class derived from the MFC-supplied CButton class.

CREATING AND USING PROPERTY SHEETS WITH YOUR CONTROLS

Topics in this Chapter

- Understanding Property Sheets
- Creating CPropertyPage-Derived Classes
- Responding to Property Sheet Messages
- Customizing the Standard Property Sheet
- Summary

Chapter 5

Sooner or later, you'll find that a single dialog box doesn't offer enough screen space to display all the controls needed to maintain the properties of a particular object. Or you may find that a complex mass of controls is confusing and unstructured. In these situations a property sheet provides the ideal solution to this problem by letting you group common sets of controls into individual overlapping pages. The property sheet user can select between these pages by clicking on a titled tab representing each page. This representation is similar to what you might find in a filing system, a day planner, or some other similar tool.

5.1 Understanding Property Sheets

From a programmatic perspective, you should think of a property sheet as a collection of individual modeless dialog boxes (representing each page) held inside a larger modal dialog. The property sheet is implemented down at the Win32 level as a dialog window that contains a tab control (one of the common controls) and a set of controlling buttons such as OK, Cancel, Apply, and Help. The tab control handles the individual dialogs that make up the property sheet pages.

The rest of this section gives a brief overview of the structure and sequence of events down at the Win32 level. Unless you like a challenge and have loads of spare time, you won't actually need to implement a property sheet using the direct API calls and structures. You would more likely use the MFC (or ATL) wrapper classes (discussed in the following sections), which greatly simplify the process. However, it is worth a brief discussion of these events to understand the processes underlying the wrapper classes.

Before the property sheet is displayed, each page is added to a PROP-SHEETHEADER structure in memory as a pointer to a PROPSHEETPAGE structure and corresponding window handle.

When the property sheet is initially displayed, the first page is displayed and sent a WM_INITDIALOG message. If the user then selects another page, the first page is hidden and the new dialog displayed and also sent a WM_INITDIALOG message. If a previously displayed (but now hidden) page is subsequently reselected, the reselected page is redisplayed, but no WM_INITDIALOG message is sent.

This indicates that each of the dialogs comprising the pages of the property sheet is modeless with the overall modality controlled by the parent property sheet itself.

Except for the initial page, the dialog windows for each page are not created unless the user specifically selects the tab for that page. However, once created, the individual dialog windows exist until the property sheet is destroyed. The created dialog windows are merely hidden when their tab isn't currently active. You can see this in action using the Visual Studio Spy++ IDE tool to study the windows hierarchy while a property sheet (such as the Internet control panel applet) is displayed.

There are obviously occasions when you'll need to validate the details on a particular page before allowing the user to select another page. You can perform this validation from the currently active page when the tab control sends it a PSN_KILLACTIVE notification message. To keep the current page active, you can set a TRUE message result value in response to the notification. Alternatively, a FALSE message result allows the selection to continue resulting in a PSN_SETACTIVE notification being sent to the newly activated page. You can use the PSN_SETACTIVE notification to initialize or reinitialize any controls in the newly activated tab.

When the user clicks the OK or Apply property sheet buttons, a PSN_APPLY message is sent to each of the property pages to let you take whatever appropriate action is required for each page. When the OK, or Cancel buttons are pressed, the property sheet is closed and all of the property page and property sheet windows are destroyed. However, convention is that Apply should implement the changes specified by the modified control settings without closing the property sheet.

5.1.1 Creating a Property Sheet

The MFC wrapper classes `CPropertySheet` and `CPropertyPage` simplify the process of creating and displaying a property sheet and its pages. The `CPropertySheet` sheet class is directly derived from the `CWnd` class, although it has a lot in common with a normal `CDialog` class with a `DoModal()` function orchestrating the property sheets modal lifetime. However, the `CPropertyPage` class, used for creating each property page, is derived directly from `CDialog` and acts largely like a modeless dialog would.

By deriving your own classes from these two MFC base classes you can extend the specific functionality required for your application. Like dialog boxes, each property page needs a dialog template resource to define the user interface and layout of controls for that page. Creating this template is usually the first place to start the job of building a property sheet, because you can then use ClassWizard to automatically create your derived classes based on those templates, as shown in the following sections.

5.1.2 Creating the Property Page Resources

There is little difference between dialog template resources used in property pages and those used in normal dialog boxes. You can use the Resource Editor's Insert Resource dialog to add a property page specific template by selecting from the `IDD_PROPPAGE_LARGE`, `IDD_PROPPAGE_MEDIUM`, or `IDD_PROPPAGE_SMALL` standard options listed under the Dialog resource type as shown in Figure 5-1.

After inserting the property page dialog template, you can resize it as required, but you should bear in mind that the final size of the property sheet will be based on the largest property page it contains.

The initial difference from the usual dialog template that you'll notice is that there is no OK or Cancel buttons; these buttons will be automatically added to the property sheet and shouldn't exist on the individual pages. If you examine the Styles tab of the Dialog Properties for the new template, you'll also notice that the Style is set to Child and the Border is set to Thin, as shown in Figure 5-2.

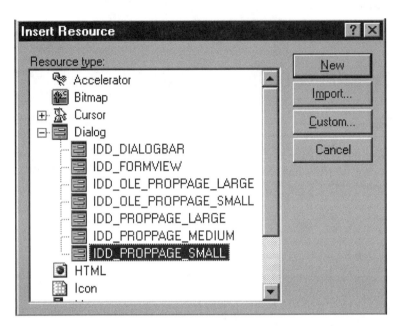

Figure 5-1 Inserting a standard property page dialog template.

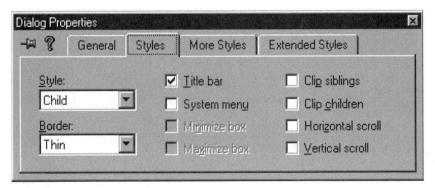

Figure 5-2 The property page template style and border settings.

The More Styles tab reveals that the Disabled style (see Figure 5-3) should also be set for a property page.

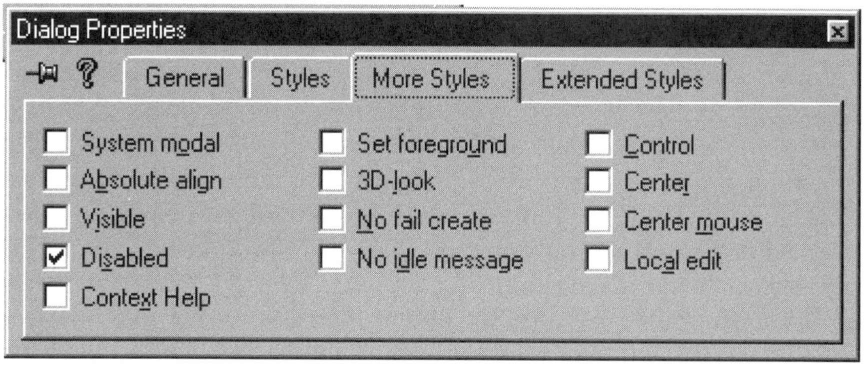

Figure 5-3 The property page template Disabled flag.

As with a normal dialog, you should set the resource ID and the Caption as appropriate to your application as shown in Figure 5-4. Your property page caption will appear in the tab for that specific page when the property sheet is displayed.

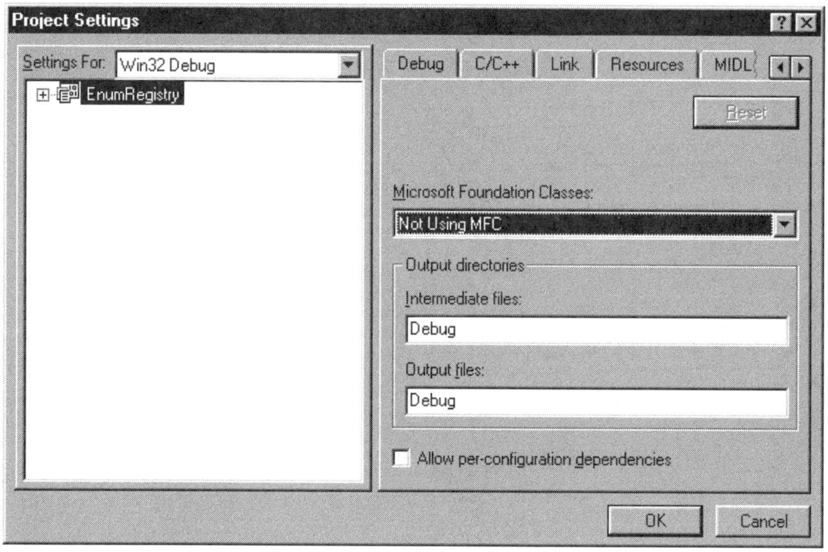

Figure 5-4 The property page template resource ID and caption.

You can add controls to the property page resource template in exactly the same way as you would an ordinary dialog. You can repeat the same process for each of the property pages that you wish to include in your property sheet. Each property page must be assigned a unique resource ID, as they are each individual dialogs in their own right.

5.2   Creating CPropertyPage-Derived Classes

For each property page you want to display, you'll need to create a class derived from the `CPropertyPage` base class to implement your application specific functionality. You can use ClassWizard to create this class quickly and easily, just as you would for a normal dialog box. If you invoke ClassWizard with the dialog template resource selected, ClassWizard will detect the new resource and offer the option of creating a new class or selecting from an existing implementation. If you decide to create a new class, the New Class dialog then lets you specify a specific name for your new class. You must remember to change the Base class combo to `CPropertyPage` rather than the default `CDialog` setting as shown in Figure 5-5.

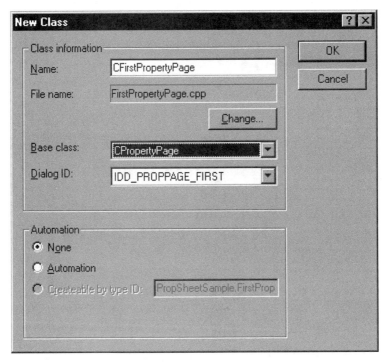

Figure 5-5   Creating a `CPropertyPage`–derived handler class for the property page.

You'll notice that the new `CPropertyPage`-derived class is very similar to a direct `CDialog` derivation. The ID of the dialog template resource is enumerated as the familiar `IDD` value in the class definition like this:

```
enum { IDD = IDD_PROPPAGE_FIRST };
```

The ID is then passed down into the `CPropertyPage` base class by the constructor function like this (excluding the ClassWizard lines):

```
CFirstPropertyPage::CFirstPropertyPage() :
    CPropertyPage(CFirstPropertyPage::IDD)
  {
  }
```

You'll also notice that, like a dialog, the property page has a `DoData-Exchange()` function so that you can exchange data between the controls and mapped member variables with the usual DDX macro entries. You can also validate that data using the normal DDV macros, which can both be easily generated using ClassWizard Member Variables tab.

A message map lets you handle messages from the the dialog controls and notifications from the parent tab control and property sheet. Again these message map entries have the usual ClassWizard comment placeholders to let you add handler functions from the Message Maps tab.

At this point, you can add mapping variables and event handlers for the various property page controls in just the same way as you would for a dialog box. You can repeat the same process of adding a property page handler class for each of the property pages in your property sheet as if they were individual dialogs.

5.2.1 Creating a CPropertySheet-Derived Class

Once you've created a `CPropertyPage`-derived class to handle each page in the property sheet, you can create a new class to extend the `CProperty-Sheet` functionality to cope with your application specific purpose and tie together the individual property pages.

It isn't strictly necessary to derive a new class from `CPropertySheet`, because the `CPropertySheet` base class has all of the functionality needed to display and tie together the various properties pages. However, for most applications, the various pages will probably be maintaining different attributes of the same object (like the resource editor's Dialog Properties property sheet describes dialog box attributes). Therefore, you'll probably find it desirable to embed the target object (or a pointer to it) inside the property sheet class. That way, each of the property pages can access the same target object via their parent property sheet.

Again, you can use ClassWizard to generate the `CPropertySheet` class just by setting the base class control to `CPropertySheet` and entering a specific name for your new class.

If you take a look at the new class definition, you'll see that it comprises a couple of very similar constructor functions and a message map. The two constructors are defined like this:

```
CSampleSheet(UINT nIDCaption, CWnd* pParentWnd = NULL,
    UINT iSelectPage = 0);
CSampleSheet(LPCTSTR pszCaption, CWnd* pParentWnd = NULL,
    UINT iSelectPage = 0);
```

The only difference between the two constructors is that the first needs an integer referencing a string table resource while the second takes a pointer to a string to specify the required caption. By overriding the default zero value in the `iSelectPage` parameter, you can make a property page other than the first display initially.

Now that you have a `CPropertySheet`-derived class and some `CPropertyPage`-derived classes, you have all the elements needed to construct and display a property page object.

5.2.2 Adding the Property Pages

After constructing a `CPropertySheet`-derived object, you can use its `AddPage()` function to add the `CPropertyPage`-derived objects. Once the pages have been added, the whole sheet can be displayed like a modal dialog by calling the `CPropertySheet`'s `DoModal()` function, as in this example:

```
#include "FirstPropertyPage.h"
#include "SecondPropertyPage.h"
// ...
void CPropSheetSampleDoc::OnPropertysheetDisplay()
  {
    CSampleSheet psSample("Sample Property Sheet");
    psSample.AddPage(new CFirstPropertyPage);
    psSample.AddPage(new CSecondPropertyPage);
    if (psSample.DoModal()==IDOK) {
      AfxMessageBox("Retrieve data from property sheet");
     }
    delete psSample.GetPage(0);
    delete psSample.GetPage(1);
  }
```

After the sample property sheet is constructed in line 6, two property page objects are instantiated and added to the property sheet in lines 7 and 8. The `DoModal()` call returns `IDOK` if the OK button was pressed just as it would for a normal dialog in line 9.

You'll also notice that the GetPage() function is used in lines 13 and 14 to return the pointer to the property page objects.

Adding the pages outside the property sheet gives you some flexibility as to which pages should be added. However, you could call AddPage() to add the property pages inside the property sheet's constructor function (as embedded objects). This solution may be more elegant for situations where the pages used in the property are always the same and the property sheet is instantiated in several places.

In this situation, you can embed the property sheet objects in your derived CPropertySheet class, like this class definition fragment:

```
protected:
   CFirstPropertyPage m_pageFirst;
   CSecondPropertyPage m_pageSecond;
```

Your property sheet constructor would be modified to add the two member property pages:

```
CSampleSheet::CSampleSheet(LPCTSTR pszCaption,
    CWnd* pParentWnd, UINT iSelectPage) :
        CPropertySheet(pszCaption, pParentWnd,
        iSelectPage)
 {
   AddPage(&m_pageFirst);
   AddPage(&m_pageSecond);
 }
```

The greatly simplified code required to display the property sheet is now like this:

```
CSampleSheet psSample("Sample Property Sheet");
if (psSample.DoModal()==IDOK)
   AfxMessageBox("Ok");
```

Core Warning

Windows 95 allows a maximum of 16,384 property pages in a property sheet.

If you need to create an array of property sheets, you can break the construction process down into two steps by using the Construct() function, which has parameters identical to the constructor. For example, the following lines create two property sheets and then set the caption in two stages; afterwards you can call DoModal() to display them as normal:

```
CSampleSheet arpsSample[2];
arpsSample.Construct("Sheet 1");
arpsSample.Construct("Sheet 2");
```

5.2.3 Creating a Modeless Property Sheet

You can create a modeless property sheet by simply calling the CProperty-
Sheet object's Create() function rather than its DoModal() function. A
modeless property sheet is created without the OK, Cancel, and Apply buttons,
but may be closed using the sheet's system menu or close button. If you need
these buttons on a modeless dialog, you'll need to override the CProperty-
Sheet's OnCreate() function and add them manually.

Another consideration is the scope of the property sheet object. Unlike a
modal property sheet, you can't declare your property sheet as a local variable
to a function. This is because the Create() function returns immediately,
leaving the modeless property sheet open for use. If it were defined as a local
variable, the property sheet object would be destroyed as soon as the invoking function returns. So as with modeless dialogs, a modeless property sheet
object should be created with the C++ new operator and tracked by a pointer
embedded in a holding class responsible for deleting the allocated property
sheet object after its window is closed.

You can force a modeless property sheet window to close programmatically by calling its DestroyWindow() function.

The following code fragment illustrates these concepts:

```
CPropSheetSampleDoc::CPropSheetSampleDoc() :
    m_pPSSample(NULL)
{
}


CPropSheetSampleDoc::~CPropSheetSampleDoc()
{
   if (m_pPSSample)
      delete m_pPSSample;
}


void CPropSheetSampleDoc::OnPropertysheetDisplay()
{
   if (m_pPSSample==NULL) {
      m_pPSSample =
          new CSampleSheet("Modeless Property Sheet");
      m_pPSSample->Create(AfxGetMainWnd());
   }
```

```
 }

void CPropSheetSampleDoc::OnPropertysheetClose()
 {
   if (m_pPSSample) {
      m_pPSSample->DestroyWindow();
      delete m_pPSSample;
      m_pPSSample = NULL;
    }
 }
```

This code assumes that the property pages are created inside the property sheet's constructor and that the m_pPSSample property sheet pointer is declared in the document class definition like this:

```
CSampleSheet* m_pPSSample;
```

The OnPropertysheetDisplay() function at line 10 is a menu handler function allowing the user to create the modeless property sheet, which is created as a child of the applications main window by the Create() call in line 15 if the object doesn't already exist.

The OnPropertysheetClose() function at line 19 is another menu handler function that demonstrates how the property sheet can be closed programmatically with a call to DestroyWindow().

5.3 Responding to Property Sheet Messages

There are a whole host of messages transmitted around a property sheet during its lifetime. These messages are essentially the glue that sticks together the various pages, header control, and the parent property sheet window. The pages themselves act like a series of independent dialog boxes, but there are also a set of activation messages sent from the header control to indicate when each is becoming active or inactive. Another set of messages is sent to the pages when the OK or Apply or Cancel buttons are pressed.

5.3.1 Initializing the Property Pages

Once the property sheet has been displayed, the first message that is sent to the initial property page is the WM_INITDIALOG message. You can trap this message in your `CPropertyPage`-derived class in a normal `OnInitDialog()` handler function.

Just like a normal dialog, your property page window and controls will be active after the call to the base class `CPropertyPage::OnInitDialog()` handler function. At this point you can call window-based functions on any of your sub-classed control-mapping objects (such as those added by ClassWizard), such as `EnableWindow()`. You can also subclass your own controls inside the `OnInitDialog()` handler.

As discussed earlier, the `WM_INITDIALOG` message is only sent once to a property page when it is first displayed. This means that any pages in the property sheet that haven't yet been displayed will not perform `OnInitDialog()`. Any attempt to access these uninitialized controls, for example, from the property sheet object or a different page object, will cause an assertion.

This only-on-demand initialization of property pages makes for fast and efficient property sheets that need to initialize only the pages that are actually selected by the user.

5.3.2 Property Page Activation and Deactivation

Whenever a particular property page is activated, either for the first time or on subsequent reselection, it is sent a `PSN_SETACTIVE` notification message from the header control. This notification is handled in the `CPropertyPage` base class, which then calls the `OnSetActive()` virtual function. You can provide an override for `OnSetActive()` in your derived class to perform any initialization required when that page is about to be redisplayed. Your override function should return a `TRUE` value if the page was successfully initialized or a `FALSE` if it was not.

The base class implementation of `OnSetActive()` calls `UpdateData(FALSE)` so that your overridden `DoDataExchange()` function is called to transfer data from your mapped member variables into the page's controls.

When the user then selects a different page, the currently active page will be sent the `PSN_KILLACTIVE` notification which the `CPropertyPage` base class translates into a call to the `OnKillActive()` virtual function. You can stop the new page selection at this point by returning a `FALSE` value from your own `OnKillActive()` override function.

The base class implementation of `OnKillActive()` calls `UpdateData(TRUE)`, this calls through the `DoDataExchange()` function in save and validate mode. By adding DDX_ and DDV_ macros to your derived class' `DoDataExchange()` function, you can transfer any data from the controls to your mapped member variables and perform validation specific to your property page. You can add any additional validation not performed in the `DoDataExchange()` function to `OnKillActive()`. You must remember to display a message box to inform the user why the validation may have failed and their new page not made active (or risk very irate users).

5.3.3 Handling Messages from OK, Apply, and Cancel Buttons

When the property sheet's OK button is pressed, an `OnOK()` virtual function is called for each of those property pages that have been displayed during the lifetime of the property sheet. Your property pages should override `OnOK()` to perform any OK handling specific to that page (and that page only). After all of the `OnOK()` functions have been called and returned in each of the property pages, the property sheet will be closed.

If you want to conditionally stop the property sheet from closing when OK is pressed, you should return a `FALSE` value from your `OnKillActive()` overridden function. The `OnKillActive()` is called for the currently active property page just before the `OnOK()` functions are called.

A corresponding virtual function, `OnCancel()`, is called in the same way when the Cancel button is pressed. However, the `OnKillActive()` function isn't called before `OnCancel()` so that the user can always close the property sheet (unless you explicitly disable the Cancel button). The `OnCancel()` function is actually called by another virtual function `OnReset()`; if you override `OnReset()` and don't call the base class function, `OnCancel()` isn't performed. `OnReset()` is called in response to the `PSN_RESET` notification.

You can prevent the user from closing the property sheet via the Cancel by adding an override for `OnQueryCancel()`, which is called just before the `OnCancel()` function. By returning `FALSE` from `OnQueryCancel()` you can stop the cancellation proceeding; a `TRUE` value lets the cancellation continue as normal.

The Apply button works differently than OK and Cancel. Apply means apply those changes without closing the property sheet. For example, the user may wish to change the color of a background window to see if it is pleasing without dismissing the property sheet and retaining the option of canceling the change. When the property sheet is opened, the Apply button is disabled. Whenever a setting in one of the property pages is changed, you should call that pages `SetModified()` function, passing a `TRUE` value.

This indicates that the page has been modified, and the Apply button will stay enabled as long as at least one page is set as modified. You can pass FALSE to SetModified() to reset the page's modified flag.

When the Apply button is pressed, a PSN_APPLY notification is sent to the property pages. This is routed by the base class to call the OnApply() virtual function for each of the initialized property pages (even if their modified flag isn't set). You can return a FALSE value from your OnApply() override to stop the changes from proceeding (and inform the user), otherwise you should apply the current changes to your application objects. However, remember that the user may wish to cancel those changes before closing the property sheet, so the original settings should also be preserved.

If you can't preserve the original settings, you can call the CancelTo-Close() member function of CPropertyPage after applying your changes. After calling this function, the OK button caption is changed to Close, and the Cancel button is disabled to indicate that the changes are irrevocable.

If you don't add an override for OnApply() to your derived property page class, the base class implementation automatically calls the OnOK() virtual function and resets the modified flag in each of the property pages.

You can programmatically simulate pressing one of these buttons by calling the CPropertySheet's PressButton() function from your derived property sheet object. The PressButton() function can be passed using either PSBTN_OK, PSBTN_CANCEL or PSBTN_APPLYNOW to simulate the OK, Cancel, and Apply buttons respectively. This function passes a PSM_PRESSBUTTON message to the property sheet.

You can also close the property sheet by calling the CPropertySheet's EndDialog() function, which actually posts a PSM_PRESSBUTTON message with a PSBTN_CANCEL value to the property sheet to close it.

Core Warning

A modeless property sheet doesn't normally have the same buttons as a modal property sheet and so won't respond to these messages in the same way.

5.3.4 Sending Messages Between Property Pages

You can send user-defined messages between the active property pages of a property sheet by calling the page's QuerySiblings() member function. This sends a PSM_QUERYSIBLINGS message to each of the other property pages in turn until one of the pages returns a nonzero value. Like other user-defined messages, PSM_QUERYSIBLINGS lets you pass two values, a WPARAM and a LPARAM, which can be passed in the two parameters of the QuerySiblings() function.

For example, consider that you have a property sheet with two property pages. You may want the second page to request the result of a multiplication from the first page.

The following code implemented in a button message handler in the second property page initiates the interpage communication:

```
void CSecondPropertyPage::OnMakeChange()
 {
    SetModified();
    int a = 123, b = 456;
    LRESULT lRes = QuerySiblings(a,b);
    CString strAnswer;
    strAnswer.Format("Result of %d * %d = %d",a,b,lRes);
    AfxMessageBox(strAnswer);
    // Save Changes...
 }
```

The call is made to QuerySiblings() on line 5, passing the two operands for the multiplication request. The result, lRes, returned from the query to the other pages, is then displayed in the message box in line 8.

The following code implemented in the first property page shows the corresponding message map entry and handler function for the query:

```
BEGIN_MESSAGE_MAP(CFirstPropertyPage, CPropertyPage)
    //{{AFX_MSG_MAP(CFirstPropertyPage)
    // NOTE: the ClassWizard will add message map macros here
    //}}AFX_MSG_MAP
    ON_MESSAGE(PSM_QUERYSIBLINGS,OnQuerySiblings)
    END_MESSAGE_MAP()

LRESULT CFirstPropertyPage::
    OnQuerySiblings(WPARAM wParam,LPARAM lParam)
 {
    AfxMessageBox("Got the message, Calculating!");
    return wParam * lParam;
 }
```

Notice the message map entry on line 5 for the PSM_QUERYSIBLINGS message and the corresponding handler function on line 8, which merely displays a message box and returns the result of the multiplication on line 11.

5.4 Customizing the Standard Property Sheet

There are a number of `CPropertySheet` member functions that let you change the standard property sheet appearance and a few that can radically change the standard functionality (such as setting the Wizard mode discussed in an upcoming section).

Normally you would set the property sheet title in the constructor, but you can use the `SetTitle()` member function to change this title. `SetTitle()` requires two parameters; the first is a pointer to the new caption and the second lets you optionally pass a `PSH_PROPTITLE` flag to prefix your title with the text "Properties for."

When the tabs of a property sheet cannot all be displayed along one line, the default action is to stack them to produce a number of rows of tabs as in Figure 5-6.

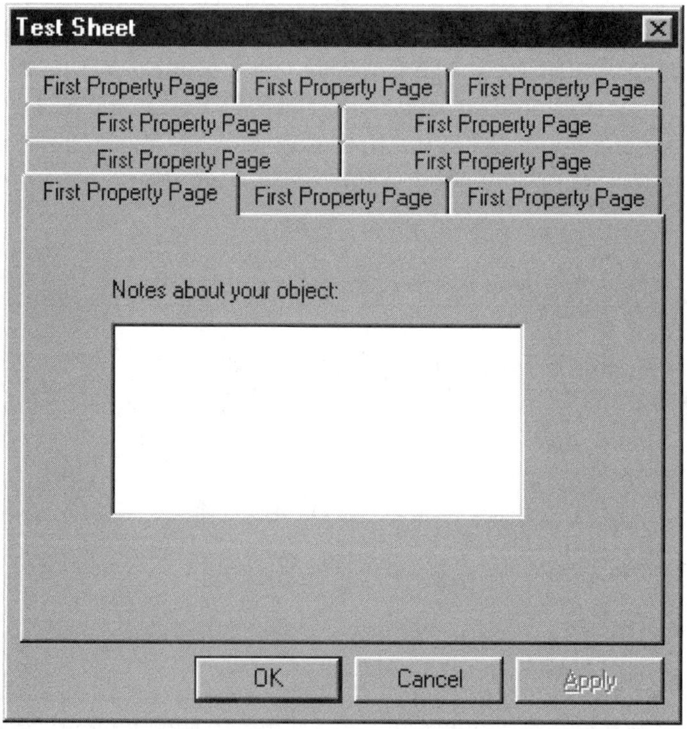

Figure 5-6   A property sheet with stacked tabs.

You can change this behavior by calling the property sheet's `EnableStackedTabs()` function passing a `FALSE` value. This will then display all of the tabs along the same line and add two scroll arrows to let the user scroll through the tabs as in Figure 5-7.

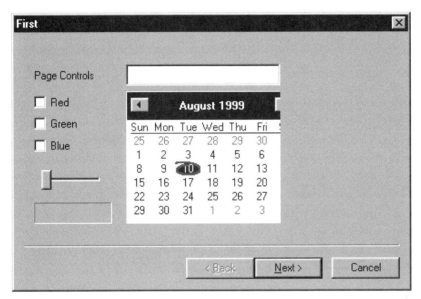

Figure 5-7   A property sheet with scrollable tabs.

5.4.1 *Property Page Management*

You can add a page at any time during the life of a property sheet, even after it has been displayed (although obviously this is easier with a modeless property sheet). The tab control is automatically updated after you call `AddPage()` so that the user can select it. Similarly, you can use `Remove-Page()` passing either a zero-based page index number or a pointer to a specific page to remove that page.

If you find the zero-based index for a specific page, you can use the `GetPageIndex()` function to return the index by passing the function a pointer to one of the sheet's `CPropertyPage` objects. The corresponding `GetPage()` function returns a pointer to the `CPropertyPage` object specified by an index value. You find the number of pages a property sheet holds, which is returned from the sheet's `GetPageCount()` function.

The current active page number is returned from `GetActiveIndex()`. If you would prefer a pointer to the active page, you can also find this directly by calling `GetActivePage()`. The corresponding `SetActivePage()` lets you set a new active page specified by either a zero-based index or a pointer to the desired page.

You can access and change the property sheet's tab control using the GetTabControl() function. This function returns a CTabCtrl pointer to the sheet's tab control object. Using this pointer, you can manipulate the full functionality of the tab control to add images to the tabs via SetImage-List(). You can only call GetTabControl() after the property sheet window is opened; this might cause difficulties when using DoModal() to display the property sheet. Fortunately, an OnInitDialog() override in the CPropertySheet class comes to the rescue, providing an excellent place to manipulate the tab control before the window is displayed.

For example, the following property sheet OnInitDialog() override adds an image to each tab from an image list (of 8 × 8 pixel images) held as a bitmap in IDB_IMAGE_LIST:

```
BOOL CImagePropertySheet::OnInitDialog()
 {
   BOOL bResult = CPropertySheet::OnInitDialog();

   m_ImageList.Create(IDB_IMAGE_LIST,8,8,RGB(255,255,255));
   CTabCtrl* pTabCtrl = GetTabControl();
   if (pTabCtrl) {
      pTabCtrl->SetImageList(&m_ImageList);
      for(int i=0;i<pTabCtrl->GetItemCount();i++) {
         TCITEM tcItem;
         tcItem.mask = TCIF_IMAGE;
         tcItem.iImage = i;
         pTabCtrl->SetItem(i,&tcItem);
      }
   }
   return bResult;
}
```

The m_ImageList member in this listing is defined as a CImageList object in the CImpagePropertySheet class definition. The example iterates through the tabs setting one of the images against each tab.

5.4.2 Creating a Wizard-Mode Property Sheet

Wizards are property sheets with **<Back** and **Next>** buttons rather than tabs to allow the user to sequentially traverse the property pages. You'll usually see them used in installation and configuration tasks where the user can only proceed to the next step when they have successfully completed the current page.

Turning a normal property sheet into a Wizard is simple; just one call to the property sheet's `SetWizardMode()` function is required before the sheet is displayed, and instantly the property sheet is transformed into a Wizard (as shown in Figure 5-8).

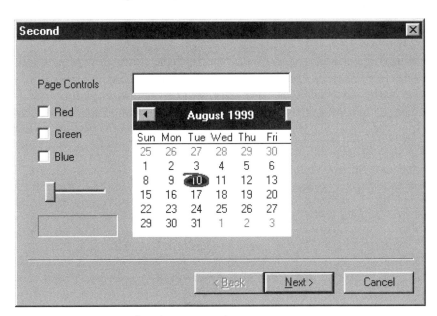

Figure 5-8 A Wizard-mode property sheet.

You'll probably want to disable some of the buttons at various stages and display a **Finish** button on the last property page. The property sheet's `SetWizardButtons()` function lets you do just that. You can pass and combine a set of flag values to specify the required customization as shown in Table 5-1.

Table 5-1 Flag Values for Customizing the Wizard Buttons

Flag Value	*Description*
PSWIZB_NEXT	Enable the Next> button
PSWIZB_BACK	Enable the <Back button
PSWIZB_DISABLEDFINISH	Show a disabled Finish button instead of the Next> button
PSWIZB_FINISH	Show the Finish button instead of the Next> button

You must only call `SetWizardButtons()` after the property sheet has been displayed because it manipulates the property sheet buttons directly. The `OnSetActive()` virtual function in the property sheet is a good candidate for calling `SetWizardButtons()`. You can use the windows `GetParent()` function to get to the property sheet object from a property page and access `SetWizardButtons()` through the pointer (after casting it) returned from `GetParent()`.

The following code fragment demonstrates these principles by overriding `OnSetActive()` in a derived `CPropertyPage` class. The example assumes that the same class (or base class) will be used to implement all the property pages in a property sheet. If this is true, the same function can test the current page to check if it is at the start or the end of a Wizard sequence. At the start it disables the **<Back** button, and at the end it displays the **Finish** button:

```
BOOL CWizProppage::OnSetActive()
 {
    CPropertySheet* pParentSheet
       = STATIC_DOWNCAST(CPropertySheet,GetParent());
    const int nPageNo = pParentSheet->GetActiveIndex();

    // Is this the first page, if so just enable next
    if (nPageNo == 0)
       pParentSheet->SetWizardButtons(PSWIZB_NEXT);

    // Is this the last page, if so just enable back and show finish
    if (nPageNo == pParentSheet->GetPageCount()-1)
       pParentSheet->SetWizardButtons(PSWIZB_BACK|PSWIZB_FINISH);
    return CPropertyPage::OnSetActive();
 }
```

You can further customize the **Finish** button by changing its caption with a call to `SetFinishText()` passing it a pointer to the required caption text. `SetFinishText()` also has the effect of removing the **<Back** button, so that only the button with your text and the **Cancel** button are displayed.

5.4.3 Using the New CPropertySheetEx and CPropertyPageEx Classes

The Visual C++ 6 MFC provides two new property sheet and page classes—`CPropertySheetEx` and `CPropertyPageEx`. These are introduced to support the new features introduced with Windows 2000 and Windows 98 (and will only work properly on these platforms). The new features let you set a background bitmap in a property sheet and let property pages display both titles and subtitles. However, at the time of this writing, these features are only available for Wizard-style property sheets.

Core Warning

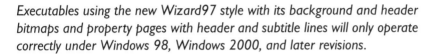

Executables using the new Wizard97 style with its background and header bitmaps and property pages with header and subtitle lines will only operate correctly under Windows 98, Windows 2000, and later revisions.

`CPropertySheetEx` extends `CPropertySheet`, and the only real difference is the additional constructor parameters. The first three parameters—the caption, parent window, and initial page—are identical. The next three (optional) parameters let you specify a `HBITMAP` handle for the background bitmap, a `HPALETTE` handle for the bitmap's palette, and a `HBITMAP` handle for the property sheet's header section. You can pass a `NULL` value to any of these parameters if they aren't required.

There is a corresponding `Construct()` function with parameters identical to the constructors for vectoring property sheets and an `AddPage()` function that takes a pointer to the new `CPropertyPageEx` pages.

You can access the `CPropertySheexEx` class' `m_psh` member to change the Win32 `PROPSHEETHEADER` structure directly. You must add the `PSH_WIZARD97` flag value to the `dwFlags` member of this structure before displaying the property sheet to use any of the new features.

There is a set of associated flag values that let you tailor the specific details of the new Wizard look as shown in Table 5-2. These flags can be combined with a logical OR to add or remove certain presentational aspects of the Wizard97 property sheet style.

The new `CPropertyPageEx` lets you specify both a title and subtitle for each property page as well as the normal caption. The `CPropertyPageEx` class extends `CPropertyPage` and supplies constructor functions to support the new features.

The `CPropertyPageEx` constructor lets you specify a resource dialog template ID, a string resource ID for a caption, another ID for the header title, and an ID for a subtitle. You can let all but the first parameter (the dialog template) default to zero if you don't need specific features.

As you'd expect by now, there is a corresponding `Construct()` function with identical parameters to allow for arrays of property pages.

Table 5-2 Flag Values for Customizing Wizard97 Property Sheet

Flag Value	Description
PSH_WIZARD97	Sets the Wizard97 mode. You must always set this flag if you want to use the new Wizard features.
PSH_WATERMARK	The watermark (background) bitmap style that should be used.
PSH_USEHBMWATERMARK	Used in conjunction with PSH_WATERMARK to specify that the hbmWatermark bitmap handle is used rather than using the pszbmWatermark string pointer to specify the watermark bitmap.
PSH_USEPLWATERMARK	Uses the supplied hplWatermark palette handle rather than the default palette.
PSH_STRETCHWATERMARK	By default the background image is tiled over the property sheet area. You can set this flag to stretch the bitmap to cover the property sheet.
PSH_HEADER	You should set this flag to use a bitmap in the property sheet header section.
PSH_USEHBMHEADER	Used in conjunction with PSH_HEADER to specify that the hbmHeader bitmap handle is used rather than using the pszbmHeader string pointer to specify the header bitmap.
PSH_USEPAGELANG	You should set this flag if you want the property sheet language settings to inherit from the first property page's resource template.

You can also access the m_psp PROPSHEETPAGE structure member to add some new flag values to the property page structure's dwFlags member. These flags are also used in conjunction with the Wizard97 property page style to customize appearance of each property page. The new flag values, which can be combined with a logical "or" are shown in Table 5-3:

Table 5-3 Flag Values for Customizing Wizard97 Property Page	
Flag Value	*Description*
PSP_HIDEHEADER	Hides the header section of the property page (when in Wizard97 mode). The property sheet background bitmap is then used to fill the entire property sheet.
PSP_USEHEADERTITLE	Displays the header text line.
PSP_USEHEADERSUBTITLE	Displays the subtitle line. The last two flags, PSP_USEHEADERTITLE and PSP_USEHEADERSUBTITLE, are automatically set as you pass the title and subtitle resource ID's to the property sheet constructor function. However, you may wish to set the PSP_HIDEHEADER flag to display a banner page in the property sheet's background watermark bitmap.

The following code lines show how two bitmap resources can be loaded and then displayed in the body and header section of the property sheet (note CBitmap pointers are cast into HBITMAP handles by their HBITMAP overloaded operator). Two property pages are constructed and added to the property sheet; the only difference is that one has the PSP_HIDEHEADER flag set. To simplify the code, only the base classes are used, however, in a real piece of code you would probably wish to derive your own classes from the CPropertySheetEx and CPropertyPageEx classes.

```
CBitmap bmHeader;
CBitmap bmBackground;
bmHeader.LoadBitmap(IDB_HEADER);
bmBackground.LoadBitmap(IDB_BACKGROUND);
CPropertySheetEx pex("New Property Sheet",
    NULL,0,bmBackground,NULL,bmHeader);
CPropertyPageEx* pNewPage =
    new CPropertyPageEx(IDD_PROPPAGE_FIRST,
    IDS_PAGE_CAPTION1,IDS_HEADER_TITLE1,
    IDS_SUBTITLE1);
pNewPage->m_psp.dwFlags |= PSP_HIDEHEADER;
pex.AddPage(pNewPage);
```

```
CPropertyPageEx* pNewPage1 =
    new CPropertyPageEx(IDD_PROPPAGE_FIRST,
    IDS_PAGE_CAPTION1,IDS_HEADER_TITLE1,
    IDS_SUBTITLE1);
pex.AddPage(pNewPage1);
pex.m_psh.dwFlags |= PSH_WIZARD97;
pex.DoModal();
```

When run, the code above displays the first property page without the header, with the property sheet background bitmap (IDB_BACKGROUND) filling the wizard dialog box, as shown in Figure 5-9.

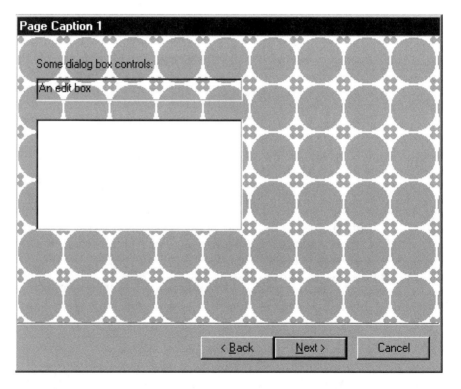

Figure 5-9   Wizard97 property page with the header hidden.

The second page is displayed with the new header style, showing the caption, header line, and subtitle line, as in Figure 5-10.

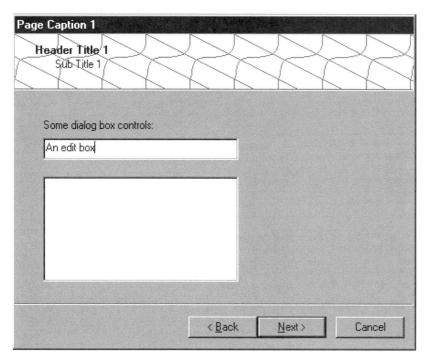

Figure 5-10 Wizard97 property page showing the header and subtitle lines.

5.4.4 *Adding Help Buttons and Help Support*

You can add the Help button to a property sheet by combining the
PSP_HASHELP flag value to each property page that will support help. You
should combine the PSP_HASHELP flag with the current dwFlags set in
the page's m_psp PROPSHEETPAGE structure before displaying the property sheet. For example, you could add a line like this into the property page
constructor:

```
m_psp.dwFlags |= PSP_HASHELP;
```

The Help button will then be added to the property sheet and enabled for
each page that sets the PSP_HASHELP flag, otherwise the button is disabled.

Alternatively, if you are dynamically adding pages after the property sheet
has been displayed, you can ensure that the help button is added by setting
the PSH_HASHELP flag into the property sheet's m_psh.dwFlags member. The Help button will then be displayed when the property sheet window
is created even though no current property pages implement help support.

Once you have added the help button, you can add a handler for the `ID_HELP` command message notification sent whenever the user presses the help button. ClassWizard doesn't automate this command message handler, so you must add the message map and handler function manually:

```
BEGIN_MESSAGE_MAP(CMyPropertyPage,CPropertyPage)
ON_COMMAND(ID_HELP,OnHelp)
END_MESSAGE_MAP


void CMyPropertyPage::OnHelp()
  {
    AfxMessageBox(IDS_HELP_RESPONSE);
  }
```

Rather than displaying the message box as shown above, you would normally invoke your application's helper application.

The user can access context-sensitive help from the property sheet by pressing the F1 key. This automatically generates a `WM_HELPINFO` message that can be handled by an `OnHelpInfo()` handler added to the property sheet or one of the property pages.

Core Tip

You can use ClassWizard to automatically generate an `OnHelpInfo()` handler function in response to the `WM_HELPINFO` message.

If you want to make the Help button use the same handler function as the context sensitive F1 help, you can add an `OnHelp()` handler function to the property sheet class and add code to send a `WM_COMMANDHELP` message to the active property page using `SendMessage()` like this:

```
#include "afxpriv.h"
void CSampleSheet::OnHelp()
  {
    SendMessage(WM_COMMANDHELP);
  }
```

Core Note

The `afxpriv.h` header file must be included to provide the definition of the `WM_COMMANDHELP` message.

When the active property sheet receives this message, its own `OnHelpInfo()` handler function will be called in response to a `WM_HELPINFO` message generated in response to `WM_COMMANDHELP`. By using this technique, you don't have to implement an `OnHelp()` handler in each of the property pages, and the standard framework `OnHelpInfo()` handler automatically invokes your application's helper application.

5.5 Summary

In this chapter you have learned how to build sophisticated, tabbed property sheets that let you group and present dialog templates as individual selectable pages. As you saw, property sheets are an invaluable tool for the developer when trying to build an easy to use but complex user interface. They let you hide and package many of the controls that might otherwise overwhelm the user if they were all presented on a single dialog.

You can dynamically add or remove property pages to further customize the property sheet presentation and share common pages while presenting other more specialized pages when applicable. Visual Studio's dialog editor makes good use of this technique; the control properties property sheet shows the same General and Extended Styles pages for all controls, but the Styles page is more specific to the type of control being edited.

You should use the various property sheet messages to control page selection and perform tasks such as validation before allowing the user to move off the current page. You can let the users apply their changes to your application to provide instant feedback as to the impact of those changes without losing the interface to revert to the old settings or make subsequent changes if needed.

Modeless property sheets let you keep the pages displayed while the user interacts with other parts of your application's user interface. This can give the users an extra control mechanism or a feedback mechanism to provide detailed information about the objects they click on and interrogate.

You can use the Wizard form of a property sheet to help guide the user through a series of forms and required fields when trying to configure parts of an application or install various software components.

The new Wizard97 background and header bitmaps let you present a better looking interface with clearer titles and subtitles on each of the pages.

WORKING WITH DEVICE CONTEXTS AND GDI OBJECTS

Topics in this Chapter

- Device Contexts in MFC
- Brushes and Pens
- MFC Classes for GDI Operations
- Working with Fonts
- Creating and Loading Bitmaps
- Drawing with Bitmaps
- Creating a Device-Independent Bitmap Class
- Summary

Chapter 6

The device context is the interface between an application that draws graphics and text on a two-dimensional surface and the device drivers and hardware that render those graphics. Applications can draw with the same Graphics Device Interface (GDI) functions, regardless of the actual hardware used, to achieve a consistent image to the best capabilities of the device. The device context can also be interrogated to inform an application of the capabilities and dimensions supported by the device. The device context can also use this dimensional information to allow an application to render images in real physical coordinate systems, such as inches and millimeters.

6.1 Device Contexts in MFC

Device contexts are Win32 objects; they are represented by HDC device context handles. The MFC provides wrapper classes for the device context object as the CDC base class and a number of more specialized derived classes.

The basic CDC class is huge and supports all of the GDI drawing, coordinate mapping, clipping, font manipulation and rendering, printer specific, path-tracking, and metafile playing functions.

The following sections briefly cover the various device context classes and when and how to use and obtain objects of these classes.

6.1.1 The CDC Class

The CDC base class encapsulates all of the device context functionality and drawing functions that use a Win32 HDC object. The actual Win32 device context handle is accessible via the public m_hDC member. You can retrieve this handle with the device context's GetSafeHdc() function.

You will often be handed a pointer to an initialized CDC object from MFC framework functions such as CView::OnDraw() and CView::OnBeginPrinting(). These objects are nicely clipped to the dimensions of the window client area so that the results of drawing functions do not appear outside the area of the window.

You can also obtain a pointer to a CDC object for the client area of a window using the CWnd::GetDC() function. If you want a CDC pointer for the entire window area (including the title bar and borders), you can use the CWnd::GetWindowDC() function instead. By calling the function GetDesktopWindow()->GetWindowDC(), you can even get a pointer to the entire Windows desktop.

A single Win32 device context object may be shared among windows of the same registered window class (windows registered with RegisterClass(), not to be confused with OO classes). It may be part of a parent window's device context, or it may be private to the specific window.

Once you have obtained a pointer to the device context, you can perform a number of drawing operations or other device context-specific functions.

However, if you have obtained the pointer to a window's device context via GetDC(), you must call CWnd::ReleaseDC() on the same CWnd object to release that window's device context for other applications to use.

Core Warning

Under some platforms (such as Windows 95), there are a limited number of common device contexts shared among applications. You may be returned a NULL pointer if the GetDC() operation cannot succeed. You should therefore always call ReleaseDC() to alleviate this situation by freeing the device context for other applications.

You can also use the `GetDCEx()` function, which retrieves the device context and lets you pass a flag value to control the clipping of the returned device context.

The `CDC` constructor function constructs an uninitialized device context, where the `m_hDC` member is invalid. You can then initialize it in a number of ways. The `CreateDC()` function lets you initialize the device context for a specific device with a driver and device name. For example, you can create a device context for the screen like this:

```
CDC dc;
dc.CreateDC("Display", NULL, NULL,NULL);
```

Or you could create a device context for a printer like this:

```
CDC dc;
dc.CreateDC(NULL,"Cannon Bubble-Jet BJ330",NULL,NULL);
```

The last parameter lets you pass a `DEVMODE` structure that can be used to set specific initialization defaults. Otherwise, the driver's own defaults are used.

If you just want to retrieve information regarding the capabilities of a device, you can use the `CreateIC()` and then `GetDeviceCaps()` to retrieve the capabilities of the specified device. The `GetDeviceCaps()` function can be used with any device context, but a device context created with `CreateIC()` is a special cut-down device context that only supplies information about a device and cannot be used for drawing operations.

You can use the `CreateCompatibleDC()` function to create a memory device context compatible with a reference device context supplied as a pointer to a real `CDC` object. The memory device context is a memory-based representation of the actual device. If you pass `NULL` as the reference device context, a memory device context is created that is compatible with the screen.

The most common use of a memory device context is to create an off-screen buffer to perform screen capture copy operations via bit-blitting (fast memory copying) or to copy images from the memory device context onto the screen device context.

Core Note

Memory device contexts created with `CreateCompatibleDC()` *are created with a minimum monochrome bitmap. If you want to copy color images between a memory device context and the screen, you must also create a compatible memory bitmap.*

If you have created a device context (rather than obtaining one via `GetDC()` or using a pointer to framework device context), you should delete the Win32 device context object after use by calling the `DeleteDC()` member function.

An uninitialized device context can also be initialized from a `HDC` device context handle using the `Attach()` function passing the `HDC` handle and detached calling the corresponding `Detach()` function, which returns the old `HDC` handle.

If you just want to quickly create and attach a temporary `CDC` object to a `HDC` handle, the `FromHandle()` function allocates and attaches a `CDC` object for you, returning the pointer. However, you should not keep any references to this object because it will be automatically destroyed the next time your program returns to the application's message loop by a call to `DeleteTempMap()`.

You can find the window associated with a device context by calling the device context's `GetWindow()` function, which returns a `CWnd` pointer to the associated window.

The device context maintains information relating to coordinate mapping modes, clipping rules, and the current GDI objects used for drawing (such as brushes, pens, bitmaps, and palettes). The details of these are discussed in subsequent sections. You can save and restore all these settings using `SaveDC()` and `RestoreDC()`. When you call `SaveDC()`, an integer is returned, identifying the saved instance (or zero if it fails). You can later pass this integer to `RestoreDC()` to restore those saved defaults.

6.1.2 The CClientDC Class

You can use the `CClientDC` class to quickly connect a `CDC` object to a window by passing a pointer to the desired window. This is equivalent to constructing a `CDC` object and attaching an `HDC` handle obtained from a window with the Win32 `::GetDC()` function.

If the constructor succeeds, the `m_hWnd` member variable is initialized with the handle of the window donating the `HDC` handle; otherwise an `CResourceException` is raised.

When the `CClientDC()` object falls out of scope or is deleted, the Win32 device context object (`HDC`) is automatically released.

For example, you might want to access the client device context of a view window from a view-based menu handler to draw a circle, like this:

```
void CCDCBaseView::OnDrawEllipse()
 {
   CClientDC dcClient(this);
   dcClient.Ellipse(0,0,100,100);
 }
```

You will notice that the C++ this pointer is simply passed to the CClientDC constructor to initialize the device context with the view's client device context. After initialization, the circle can be drawn in the view using the CDC::Ellipse() function. Finally, the destructor of the CClientDC object ensures that the view's HDC is released.

6.1.3 The CPaintDC Class

A CPaintDC object is constructed in response to a WM_PAINT message. If you add a handler for this message, you will see that ClassWizard automatically generates an OnPaint() handler starting with the following line:

```
CPaintDC dc(this); // device context for painting
```

The CPaintDC constructor automatically calls the BeginPaint() function for you. The BeginPaint() function is responsible for initializing a PAINTSTRUCT structure. PAINTSTRUCT holds information about the smallest rectangle that needs to be redrawn in response to an invalid portion of a window (usually when one window is moved to reveal a portion of the one behind).

This process is automated in the constructor so that you can immediately use the device context to redraw the invalidated area.

The PAINTSTRUCT information is available via the m_ps member, and the attached window handle can be found from the m_hWnd member.

When the object falls out of scope and is destructed, the EndPaint() function is called to complete the usual WM_PAINT procedure and mark the invalidated region as valid.

6.1.4 The CMetaFileDC Class

A Windows metafile is a file that contains a list of GDI drawing instructions required to render an image in a device context. The metafile can be stored on disk, reloaded on another computer with different display capabilities, and redrawn by repeating the drawing instructions to produce a similar image.

You can always play a metafile using the CDC base class's PlayMetaFile() and passing a handle to a metafile object. However, the CMetaFileDC class lets you also create and record metafiles.

To record a metafile, you should construct a `CMetaFileDC` object, then call `Create()`, or `CreateEnhanced()` to create a simple or enhanced metafile on disk passing a filename and a reference device context for the enhanced metafile.

Core Note

Enhanced metafiles store palette and size information so they can be reproduced more accurately on different computers with various display capabilities.

After creating the metafile, you can perform a number of drawing operations in the device context like any other device context. The details of these drawing operations will be stored in sequence in the metafile as you call each drawing function.

Finally, you should call the `CMetaFileDC::Close()` or `CMeta-FileDC::CloseEnhanced()` to close the metafile. The close functions return either a `HMETAFILE` or `HENHMETAFILE` handle, which can be used by the Win32 metafile manipulation functions, such as `CopyMetaFile()` or `DeleteMetaFile()`.

6.2 Brushes and Pens

So far you have seen the `CDC` base class and its derivatives and seen how to obtain and create device contexts in various situations. However, the main purpose of a device context is to provide a uniform drawing surface for the GDI rendering functions. These rendering functions use two main GDI objects to draw lines and filled areas. Lines are drawn with objects called pens and filled areas with objects called brushes.

These two objects are represented at the Win32 level by the `HPEN` and `HBRUSH` handles. All of the GDI objects, including pens and brushes, are wrapped by the `CGdiObject` MFC base class. Although the `CGdiObject` is not strictly an abstract base class, you would normally construct one of its derived classes, such as `CPen` or `CBrush`.

`CGdiObject` is responsible for manipulating these handles and provides member functions such as `Attach()` and `Detach()` to attach the object to a GDI handle and detach it after use.

The handle is stored in the `m_hObject` member, which you can retrieve by calling the `CGdiObject::GetSafeHandle()` function. A static function (similar to the device contexts) called `FromHandle()` lets you dynamically create a `CGdiObject` for the duration of a Windows message. This object is then deleted by `DeleteTempMap()` when the thread returns to Windows message loop.

You can find details about the underlying object by using the `GetObject()` function, which fills a structure with the object's attributes. The type of structure filled depends on the type of underlying object; the function just takes a `LPVOID` pointer to a buffer to receive the details and the size of the buffer.

The `DeleteObject()` function deletes the underlying GDI object from memory, so you are free to reuse the same `CGdiObject` by calling one of the derived classes `Create()` functions to create another GDI object.

The `CGdiObject` class is extended by the MFC `CPen` and `CBrush` classes, which greatly simplify creating and manipulating these two drawing objects. You can see how these classes are constructed and used in the following sections.

6.2.1 Pens and the CPen Class

Pens are used to draw lines, curves, and boundaries around filled shapes such as ellipses, polygons, and chords. You can create pens of various sizes, styles, and colors (even invisible pens for drawing shapes without outlines), then select a pen into the device context and draw with it. Only one pen can be selected into a device context at any time and the old pen is automatically swapped out when a new pen is selected.

There are two main pen types: cosmetic and geometric. The cosmetic pens are simple to create and quick to draw with. The geometric pens support more precise world units, and let you use complex patterns and hatching effects in a similar manner to brushes (described later).

You can create a variety of pens using the `CPen` constructor. There are two forms of the constructor. You can pass one form a set of style flags (as shown in Table 6-1), the pen width, and a `COLORREF` to indicate the color of the new pen.

Core Note

The *PS_DASH, PS_DASHDOT,* and *PS_DOT* styles work only with pens that have a width of one pixel; otherwise they are drawn as solid lines.

Table 6-1 Simple Pen Styles

Style	Pen Description
PS_SOLID	Solid color pen
PS_NULL	Invisible pen
PS_DASH	Pen with a dashed style
PS_DASHDOT	Pen with alternating dashes and dots
PS_DOT	Pen with a dotted style
PS_INSIDEFRAME	Line is drawn inside filled areas

The other constructor form lets you supply a pointer to a LOGBRUSH structure to initialize the attributes of a geometric pen. You can also pass an array of DWORD values to specify complex dot and dash patterns. You can also use some additional flags to change the mitering (how lines are joined) and end cap styles (how lines end). These flags are shown in Table 6-2.

Table 6-2 Advanced Pen Styles

Style	Pen Description
PS_COSMETIC	A cosmetic pen
PS_GEOMETRIC	A geometric pen
PS_ALTERNATE	Sets every other pixel (only cosmetic pens)
PS_USERSTYLE	The user-style DWORD array should be used to create the dash-dot pattern
PS_JOIN_ROUND	Round joined lines
PS_JOIN_BEVEL	Bevel joined lines
PS_JOIN_MITER	Miter joined lines
PS_ENDCAP_FLAT	The ends of lines should be flat
PS_ENDCAP_ROUND	The ends of lines should be round
PS_ENDCAP_SQUARE	The ends of lines should be square

You can also construct an uninitialized pen using the default constructor and then initialize it by using the `CreatePen()` and passing the same parameters as the two constructors, or by using `CreatePenIndirect()` and passing a pointer to a `LOGPEN` structure holding the pen initialization details.

6.2.2 Selecting Pens into the Device Context

Once you have created a pen, you must select it into a device context for the drawing functions to start using that pen. All of the GDI objects can be selected using the device context's overloaded `SelectObject()` function.

The `SelectObject()` function that accepts a `CPen` object returns a pointer to the currently selected `CPen` object. When you select your new object, the current object is automatically deselected, and you should save the pointer to this deselected object to reselect it when you have finished drawing with your pen.

Core Warning

You should never let a pen that is currently selected in a device context fall out of scope. The original pen should reselected into the device context so that your pen can be safely deleted after it is out of the context.

You can also use the device context's `SaveDC()` and `RestoreDC()` functions to reselect the original pens and release your created pen. (Remember that this will also restore all of the other GDI objects you have selected.)

6.2.3 Using Stock Pens

There are a number of common GDI objects that the operating system can lend out to applications called stock objects. These include a white pen, a black pen, and a null pen. You can select these straight into a device context by calling the `CDC::SelectStockObject()` function and passing the `WHITE_PEN`, `BLACK_PEN`, or `NULL_PEN` index values. As usual, the currently selected pen will be returned from `SelectStockObject()`.

You can also use the pen's base class `CGdiObject::CreateStock-Object()` function passing the same index values to create a stock `CPen` object.

Core Note

From Windows 2000 and Windows 98 on, you can use a new stock pen object called a `DC_PEN`. You can change the color of the `DC_PEN` using the global `::SetDCPenColor()` function passing the handle of the device context, and a `COLORREF` value. When selected, the `DC_PEN` will draw in the specified color. You can also retrieve this color by calling `GetDCPenColor()`. There is no equivalent `CDC` member function for this Win32 function in Visual Studio 6.0.

6.2.4 Drawing with Pens

There are a number of rendering functions that just use pens; others use brushes to fill an area, and pens to draw the outline of that area. You can also use the latter area-filling functions to draw only the outline of a shape by selecting a NULL brush.

The device context stores a current graphics cursor position, and many of the line-drawing functions use their starting point as the current graphics cursor position. You can change this position without drawing a line by using the device context's MoveTo() function. You can also find the current graphics position from GetCurrentPosition().

The LineTo() function draws a line from the current position to the specified position and updates the graphics cursor to the specified end point.

You can use the Polyline() function to draw a number of lines from coordinates stored in an array of POINT structures, and PolyPolyLine() to draw a number of independent line sections. The PolylineTo() function performs a similar task to Polyline() but also updates the current graphics cursor. You can plot a number of Bézier splines (a special type of curve) using the PolyBezier() and PolyBezierTo() functions. The PolyDraw() functions lets you draw a number of connected lines and Bézier splines.

You can draw elliptical arcs using the Arc(), ArcTo() and AngleArc(). You can also set the device context's default direction for these arcs to clockwise or counterclockwise by passing AD_CLOCKWISE or AD_COUNTERCLOCKWISE to the device context's SetArcDirection() function. This value also affects the rendering of chords drawn with the Chord() function. You can also find the current direction by the flag returned from GetArcDirection().

You can also call the area-filling functions to outline the areas with the current pen as discussed in the following sections about brushes.

The example `OnDraw()` function shown in the following program code draws a number of shapes using different drawing functions in a variety of pens.

```
void CPensDemoView::OnDraw(CDC* pDC)
 {
    CPen penRed(PS_SOLID,5,RGB(255,0,0));
    CPen penThick(PS_SOLID,10,RGB(0,0,255));
    CPen penDash(PS_DASH,1,RGB(0,128,0));
    CPen penDot(PS_DOT,1,RGB(255,0,255));
    CPen penDashDot(PS_DASHDOT,1,RGB(0,0,0));

    CRect rcClient;
    GetClientRect(&rcClient);
    int nSaved = pDC->SaveDC();
    pDC->SelectStockObject(NULL_BRUSH); // No Area Filling

    for(int i=0;i<rcClient.Height()/6;i++) {
        int x=i%3,y=((i%6)/3);
        int w=rcClient.Width()/3, h=rcClient.Height()/2;
        CRect rcDrw(x*w,y*h,x*w+w,y*h+h);
        rcDrw.DeflateRect(CSize(i,i));
        switch(i%6) {
            case 0:
                pDC->SelectObject(&penThick);
                pDC->MoveTo(rcDrw.TopLeft());
                pDC->LineTo(rcDrw.BottomRight());
                pDC->MoveTo(rcDrw.right,rcDrw.top);
                pDC->LineTo(rcDrw.left,rcDrw.bottom);
                break;
            case 1:
                pDC->SelectObject(&penRed);
                pDC->Ellipse(rcDrw);
                break;
            case 2: {
                POINT pts[] = {
                    {(short)rcDrw.left,(short)rcDrw.bottom},
                    {(short)rcDrw.right,(short)rcDrw.bottom},
                    {(short)rcDrw.left+rcDrw.Width()/2,
                    (short)rcDrw.top},
                    {(short)rcDrw.left,(short)rcDrw.bottom}};
                pDC->SelectObject(&penDash);
                pDC->Polyline(pts,sizeof(pts)/sizeof(POINT));
                break;
            }
```

```
        case 3:
            pDC->SelectObject(&penDot);
            pDC->Rectangle(rcDrw);
            break;
        case 4:
            pDC->SelectObject(&penDashDot);
            pDC->Pie(rcDrw,CPoint(rcDrw.right,rcDrw.top),
                rcDrw.BottomRight());
            break;
        case 5:
            pDC->SelectStockObject(BLACK_PEN);
            pDC->Chord(rcDrw,rcDrw.TopLeft(),
                rcDrw.BottomRight());
            break;
        }
    }
    pDC->RestoreDC(nSaved);
}
```

The preceding code produces similar output to that shown in Figure 6-1.

Figure 6-1   Drawing with various pen styles.

6.2.5 Brushes and the CBrush Class

Whereas pens are used to draw lines, brushes are used to fill areas and shapes. The CBrush class wraps the GDI brush object and, like other MFC GDI wrapper classes, is derived from the CGdiObject base class.

You can create brushes that fill an area with solid color, a pattern from a bitmap, or a hatching scheme. You can use one of three constructor functions to construct brushes initialized with one of these filling techniques. One form lets you pass a COLORREF value for a solid color brush. Another lets you pass a pointer to a CBitmap object to create a filling pattern. The third form lets you pass an index describing a hatching technique (as shown in Table 6-3) and a COLORREF value to specify the hatching pattern color.

Table 6-3 Brush Hatching Pattern Flags

Style	Brush Hatching
HS_DIAGCROSS	Diagonal crisscross
HS_CROSS	Horizontal crisscross
HS_HORIZONTAL	Horizontal lines
HS_VERTICAL	Vertical lines
HS_FDIAGONAL	Bottom left to top right lines
HS_BDIAGONAL	Top left to bottom right lines

You can also use the default constructor and then use the creation functions, such as CreateSolidBrush(), CreateHatchBrush(), or CreatePatternBrush(), to create the GDI brush object. The CreateBrushIndirect() function lets you initialize and pass a pointer to a LOGBRUSH structure to create the brush. You can set the desired style from a number of flag values to indicate what sort of brush you want with the lbStyle member of LOGBRUSH. The other members are lbColor for the desired color, and lbHatch to specify any hatching style flags. (Remember the same structure is also used with geometric pens.)

You can use the CreateDIBPatternBrush() function to create a patterned brush from a device-independent bitmap (DIB) (discussed in more detail later), and a CreateSysColorbrush() function to create a brush initialized with one of the current system colors specified by an index value.

Core Warning

While Windows NT lets you create patterned brushes using any size of bitmap (larger than or equal to 8 × 8 pixels), Windows 98 and Windows 95 can create only 8 × 8 pixel brushes; larger bitmaps will be truncated to the top size of 8 × 8 pixels.

6.2.6 Selecting Brushes into the Device Context

You can select a brush into a device context in the same way you would a pen. The device context's `SelectObject()` function has an overload that accepts a pointer to a `CBrush` object and returns the previously selected `CBrush` object.

Once the brush is selected, any of the drawing functions that draw filled shapes will draw with your new brush. As with the pen, you must ensure that a brush is also selected out of the device context before it falls out of scope or is deleted.

6.2.7 Using Stock Brushes

There are a number of stock brushes that you can select into a device context with the `SelectStockObject()` function as shown in Table 6-4.

Table 6-4 Stock Brush Objects

Stock Object Flag	Brush Description
WHITE_BRUSH	White
LT_GRAY_BRUSH	Light gray
GRAY_BRUSH	Gray
DKGRAY_BRUSH	Dark gray
BLACK_BRUSH	Black
HOLLOW_BRUSH, NULL_BRUSH	Transparent, like the NULL pen

You can also use the `CGdiObject` base class's `CreateStockObject()` function to create a `CBrush` object initialized from a stock object flag.

6.2.8 Drawing with Brushes

You can use a number of device context member functions with a brush to draw filled shapes. These shapes will also be outlined with the currently selected pen.

Some functions, such as `FillRect()`, let you pass a `CBrush` object by pointer to draw with that brush, and others draw a rectangle from a `COLORREF` value, such as `FillSolidRect()`. However, most use the currently selected brush, such as the `Rectangle()` function. `FillRect()`, `Rectangle()`, and `FillSolidRect()` all render a filled rectangle from a set of rectangle coordinates. The `RoundRect()` function lets you draw rectangles with rounded corners.

You can also draw filled polygons using the `Polygon()` and `Poly-Polygon()` functions that draw a single or number of filled polygons, respectively. These two functions are similar to the `Polyline()` functions in that they take an array of `POINT` variables to define the polygon's vertices. When drawing polygons, you can specify one of two filling techniques called winding and alternate. These affect which areas of a crisscrossing polygon are designated as filled. You can set these modes using the `SetPolyFillMode()` function passing either the `WINDING` or `ALTERNATE` flag values.

You can draw circles and ellipses using the `Ellipse()` function, pie segments using `Pie()`, and chord sections with the `Chord()` function.

The `FloodFill()` function lets you fill an area bounded by a specified color with the current brush. You can use the `ExtFloodFill()` to either fill an area bounded by a specific color or fill an area of a specific color with the current brush.

6.3   MFC Classes for GDI Operations

Many of the GDI functions use a set of sophisticated MFC helper classes that let you specify coordinates in a two-dimensional coordinate system. These classes also let you manipulate and perform arithmetic operations on sets of coordinates.

The `CPoint`, `CSize`, and `CRect` classes can hold point coordinates, size coordinates, or rectangles, respectively. They wrap `POINT`, `SIZE`, and `RECT` structures, and can be cast into each of these structures. Overloaded operator functions accept these structures as parameters, so arithmetic between the various classes can be performed interchangeably.

The following sections examine these MFC coordinate manipulation and storage classes in more detail.

6.3.1 The CPoint Class

The CPoint class wraps a POINT structure to hold a single two-dimensional coordinate specified by its x and y member variables. Many of the drawing functions can use CPoint objects as parameters.

You can construct a CPoint object from two integers specifying the x and y coordinates, or from another CPoint object, a SIZE structure, or from a DWORD value (using the low and high words). You can call the Offset() function to add an offset value to move the specified coordinates passing x and y coordinates, another CPoint object, or a SIZE structure.

Mostly, however, you would probably use the CPoint's operator overloads to add, subtract, or compare two CPoint objects. Many of these operators let you specify POINT, SIZE, or RECT structures as parameters, and return SIZE, POINT, or BOOL values as appropriate.

The CPoint operator functions available are shown in Table 6-5.

Table 6-5 CPoint Operator Overload Functions

Operator	Description
=	Copy the POINT
+=	Add a POINT or SIZE value to the point object
-=	Subtract a POINT or SIZE value from the point object
+	Add POINT, SIZE, or RECT values
-	Subtract POINT, SIZE, or RECT values
==	Compare for equality
!=	Compare for inequality

6.3.2 The CSize Class

The CSize class wraps a SIZE structure. This structure stores a two-dimensional size as cx and cy integer members, which are declared as public accessible members. You can construct a CSize object from two integers, a SIZE structure, a POINT structure, or a DWORD value.

You will find that many of the CPoint and CRect functions and operators can take SIZE structures objects as parameters for arithmetic manipulation. Some of the GDI and Windows functions require SIZE structures, usually to specify the size of an object (such as a window).

The CSize class implements the operators listed in Table 6-6.

Table 6-6 CSize Operator Overload Functions	
Operator	*Description*
=	Copy the SIZE
+=	Add a SIZE value
-=	Subtract SIZE value
+	Add POINT, SIZE, or RECT values
-	Subtract POINT, SIZE, or RECT values
==	Compare for equality
!=	Compare for inequality

6.3.3 The CRect Class

CRect is probably the most sophisticated of the coordinate-storing classes; it wraps a RECT structure that exposes its coordinates as two coordinate pairs. These pairs correspond to the top left and bottom right points in a rectangle and are accessible from the RECT structure as the top, left, bottom, and right member integers.

You can also obtain these coordinates as CPoint objects returned by the TopLeft() and BottomRight() functions. The CenterPoint() function is quite useful as it returns a CPoint object representing the center of the rectangle. You can find the width and height of the rectangle using the

`Width()` and `Height()` functions and the size represented as `CSize` object returned from the `Size()` function.

You can increase and decrease the size of the rectangle by using the `InflateRect()` and `DeflateRect()` functions, which are overloaded to take a variety of parameter types. The `OffsetRect()` function lets you move the position of the rectangle by an amount specified by a `SIZE`, `POINT`, or pair of integers.

There are also intersection, union, and subtraction functions provided by `IntersectRect()`, `UnionRect()`, and `SubtractRect()`. `IntersectRect()` makes the current `CRect` object the intersection rectangle of two source rectangles (where they overlap). `UnionRect()` makes the `CRect` object the union of two source rectangles (the smallest rectangle that encloses both). `SubtractRect()` sets its first `RECT` parameter's coordinates to the smallest rectangle that is not intersected by two overlapping rectangles (where the second rectangle encloses the first). Each of these functions requires that you have previously called `NormalizeRect()`. `NormalizeRect()` ensures that the top left point coordinates are lower than the bottom right coordinates, and if not, it sets them so. You may find some operations leave the coordinates in a condition where the width or height calculations may give negative results; if so, calling `NormalizeRect()` will fix them for you.

If you are implementing drag and drop or want to perform bounds checking, you will find the `PtInRect()` member function useful. This returns `TRUE` if the specified point lies within the rectangle.

There are also a number of operator overload functions, as shown in Table 6-7.

6.3.4 The CRgn Class and Clipping

The `CRgn` class is another `CGdiObject`-derived GDI object wrapper class, which wraps the `HRGN` GDI handle. You can retrieve the `HRGN` handle by casting a `CRgn` object.

Regions are used primarily for clipping; you can select a region into a device context using the device context's `SelectObject()` or `Select-ClipRegion()` functions. Thereafter, all GDI rendering functions performed in the device context will be clipped to the specified region.

You can specify complex regions that have overlapped borders, simple regions that do not have overlapping borders, or null regions where there is no specified region data. Many of the functions use and return the type of region specified by the `COMPLEXREGION`, `SIMPLEREGION`, and `NULLREGION` flag values. If an error occurs when combining or selecting regions, the `ERROR` flag is returned.

Table 6-7 CRect Operator Overload Functions	

Operator	Description
=	Copy the RECT
+=	Offset the rectangle by a POINT or SIZE value, or inflate each side by the coordinates of a RECT
-=	Offset or deflate
+	Offset or inflate returning a RECT result
-	As above
&=	Set to the intersection
|=	Set to the union
&	Return the intersection
|	Return the union
==	Compare for equality
!=	Compare for inequality

To create an initialized CRgn object, you must construct it using the default CRgn constructor and then use one of the various creation functions, such as CreateRectRgn() for rectangles, CreateEllipticRgn() for ellipses, CreatePolygonRgn() for polygons, or CreateRoundRgn() for rounded rectangles. There are other functions that initialize from structures or create multiple polygons.

You can also combine two regions using the CombineRgn() function. The two source regions specified by pointers to CRgn objects are combined using a logic operation specified by a flag as the last parameter. This flag value can be any one of the following: RGN_AND, RGN_OR, RGN_XOR, RGN_COPY, or RGN_DIFF (the nonoverlapping areas).

By using the PtInRegion() or RectInRegion() functions, you can perform complex bound checking.

The OffsetRgn() function can be used to move a region and the CopyRgn() to copy one region from another. You can test for equivalence between two regions with the EqualRegion() function.

Core Warning

You should bear in mind that regions (especially complex regions) can be fairly memory hungry and are limited to a maximum coordinate displacement of 32,767 pixels. Like other GDI objects, you can delete them after use with the `DeleteObject()` *function, which is called automatically when a* `CRgn` *object is deleted.*

6.4   Working with Fonts

Much of Windows graphical output consists of text in a variety of fonts. Like pens, brushes, and regions, a GDI handle (HFONT) also represents font object instances.

The fonts and their related rendering data for each character make a considerable memory footprint for each instance of a font object. To reduce the overhead of memory and processing time required to load, initialize, and store the details for each instance of a font, Windows uses a font mapper.

Whenever a new font object is created, the font mapper looks for the nearest match of the requested characteristics from the list of installed fonts. It then constructs a font that is as close as possible to the one you asked for.

6.4.1 Fonts and the CFont Class

The MFC CFont class is a wrapper for the HFONT GDI object. To create a font using CFont, you must first construct a CFont object with the default constructor and then call one of the font creation routines.

The quickest and easiest way to create a font is with CFont's Create-PointFont() function. You can pass a desired point size (in tenths of a point), a typeface name, and optionally, a reference device context pointer to create the font. You should pass a pointer to the device context to create an accurate point size match, otherwise the default screen device context will be used (which will be inaccurate when printing).

You can also use CreatePointFontIndirect() to create a font from the lfHeight member set in a LOGFONT structure.

A much more sophisticated font creation function is CreateFont(), which lets you specify a huge number of required attributes for the font. These specify the width, height, escapement, orientation, weight, effects, character set, clipping and rendering precisions, font family, pitch, and typeface in its 14 parameters.

Each of these parameters has several associated flag values to hone the type of font required. The font mapper will then use all of these attributes to try to find the best matching font for the requested specifications.

You can also initialize the LOGFONT structure with these specifications and pass a pointer to the LOGFONT structure to the CreateFontIndirect() function, which then performs the same actions. This creation form is especially useful when you have enumerated the currently installed fonts with one of the font enumeration functions, such as EnumFonts(). The callback functions for these enumerators are passed a pointer to a LOGFONT structure so that you can create a font object instance directly from it.

Once initialized, you can fill a LOGFONT structure with the details of a font using the GetLogFont() function.

The CFont class also has a HFONT operator to retrieve the underlying GDI handle when cast as a HFONT.

6.4.2 Selecting Fonts into the Device Context

As with the other GDI objects, you must select a font into the device context before use, and restore the previously selected font after use. You must also ensure that the font is not currently selected in a device context when it is deleted.

Once selected, the font will be used whenever any of the various text output functions are called.

6.4.3 Stock Fonts

A number of stock fonts can be selected with the SelectStockObject() function, as shown in Table 6-8.

Table 6-8 Stock Font Objects

Stock Object Flag	Font Description
ANSI_FIXED_FONT	ANSI fixed pitch
ANSI_VAR_FONT	ANSI variable pitch
SYSTEM_FONT	The current Windows system font
DEVICE_DEFAULT_FONT	The device's default font
OEM_FIXED_FONT	The OEM's fixed pitch font

6.4.4 Device Context Font Interrogation Functions

The device context has a number of member functions that let you retrieve information regarding the currently selected font.

With variable pitch fonts, you may need to know about the average and specific widths of characters when rendered in a specific device context. You can use the `GetCharWidth()` function to fill an array with the widths of individual characters for non-TrueType fonts or `GetABCCharWidths()` for TrueType fonts.

You can find the average widths, the height, and many other specific elements of a font from its `TEXTMETRICS` structure. The device context's `GetOutputTextMetrics()` function will fill such a structure for you with details of the currently selected font.

You can retrieve the typeface name of the currently selected font by calling the `GetTextFace()` function and passing a `CString` object by reference to receive the typeface name.

Kerning pairs specify the widths between two characters in a variable pitch font when placed together. These values may often be negative because characters such as "l" and "i" are thin and can be placed close together. The `GetKerningPairs()` function can fill an array of `KERNINGPAIR` structures to retrieve this information.

The `GetOutlineTextMetrics()` function returns an array of `OUTLINETEXTMETRICS` structures. These structures are full of information about TrueType fonts.

6.4.5 Text Rendering Functions

There are a number of text rendering functions that perform slightly different jobs in different circumstances. The simplest is `TextOut()`, which lets you specify an x and y coordinate, and a `CString` holding the text to display.

The device context's text alignment flags adjust the position of the text relative to the given coordinate. You can adjust these flags using the `SetTextAlign()` function and passing a combination of the alignment flags such as `TA_TOP`, `TA_CENTER`, `TA_RIGHT`, `TA_LEFT`, `TA_BASELINE`, and `TA_BOTTOM`. You can combine this flag value with the `TA_NOUPDATECP` and `TA_UPDATECP` to either not update or update the current graphic cursor position after the text rendering. The corresponding `GetTextAlign()` returns the current flag settings.

You can change the color of the rendered text with the device context's `SetTextColor()` and `SetBkColor()` function to set the foreground and background color to a specified `COLORREF` value. You can also make the background behind the text transparent or opaque by passing the `TRANSPARENT` or `OPAQUE` flag to the `SetBkMode()` function.

The `ExtTextOut()` function lets you clip text to a specified rectangle by using the `ETO_CLIPPED` flag. You can also supply an array of spacing value to separate the individual character cells to `ExtTextOut()`.

You can use `TabbedTextout()` to display a text string with embedded tab characters. These tabs are then expanded to positions specified by an array of tab consecutive positions relative to a specified origin.

The `DrawText()` function performs some quite advanced text formatting such as word wrapping and justification. You can pass a combination of formatting flag values such as `DT_WORDBREAK`, `DT_LEFT`, `DT_RIGHT`, `DT_TOP`, and `DT_CENTER` (and many others).

You can call the `GrayString()` function to draw grayed text using a specific graying brush and optionally pass a pointer to your own text rendering function.

You will often want to know the dimensions required by a text string without actually rendering it, and you can find these using the functions `GetOutputTextExtent()`, `GetTabbedTextExtent()`, or `GetOutputTabbedTextExtent()`. These use the device context to calculate and return a `CSize` object holding the size required to render the text using the currently selected font and device context settings.

6.5 Creating and Loading Bitmaps

Images are used extensively in Windows; a bitmap instance is another low-level GDI object represented by the `HBITMAP` handle.

Before you can use bitmaps in your application, you would normally create a number of bitmap resources that are bound with your .EXE or .DLL when linked. These bitmaps are then "loaded" from the current module ready for drawing.

Core Note

You should not confuse the "loading" terminology used here and expressed by the `LoadBitmap()` *function with loading and saving to specific disk files. However, device-independent bitmaps may be stored in individual disk files. The* `LoadBitmap()` *function will only load bitmap resources from the application's executable module and DLLs.*

6.5.1 Creating a Bitmap Resource with the Resource Editor

You can create a new bitmap resource from the Insert Resource dialog in the Visual Studio resource editor. You can change the size, the resource ID, and the source bitmap file name from the Bitmap Properties dialog.

You can then draw the bitmap using the resource editor drawing tools as shown in Figure 6-2. You can also open bmp, jpeg, gif, or many other common formats and copy and paste the image into a new bitmap.

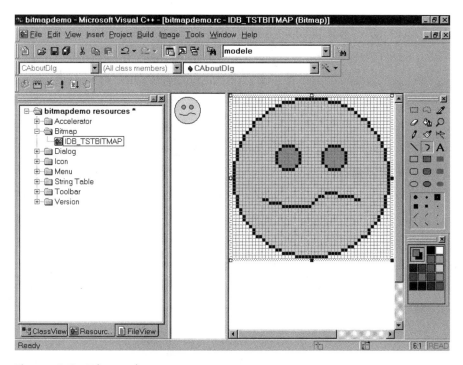

Figure 6-2   Editing a bitmap resource.

When you compile the program, the bitmap will be bundled into the resulting executable file.

6.5.2 Loading a Bitmap

Before you can use a bitmap, you must load the bitmap resource from the executable file. The CBitmap class is another CGdiObject-derived class and wraps the HBITMAP GDI object handle. You can construct a CBitmap object using its default constructor, then load a specific bitmap by calling its LoadBitmap() function, passing a resource ID (or resource name) that identifies the specific bitmap.

If the bitmap is found and loaded from the executable module, Load-Bitmap() will return a TRUE value and the HBITMAP handle will be valid. You can also use the LoadMappedBitmap() function to load color mapped bitmaps and specify a set of COLORMAP structures to define the remapped COLORREF values.

You can load a system stock bitmap with the LoadOEMBitmap() function passing a flag value that loads a few standard bitmaps.

6.5.3 Creating Bitmaps

You can create a bitmap image without an associated resource by using one of the bitmap creation functions. The CreateBitmap() function lets you create a bitmap in memory and specify its width, height, number of bit planes (color planes), the number of color bits per pixel, and optionally an array of short values to initialize the bitmap image.

Core Warning

When specifying the color planes or color bits, one or the other should be set to one; otherwise you will get a multiple of these values.

The CreateBitmapIndirect() function lets you specify these values in a BITMAP structure rather than via parameter settings.

You should use the CreateCompatibleBitmap() function to create bitmaps that are compatible with specific devices (such as the current display configuration). To do this, you must pass a pointer to a valid device context along with a width and a height. This will create a bitmap that has compatible color depth with the device attached to the device context.

6.6   Drawing with Bitmaps

Once you have created a GDI bitmap object, you can draw via a memory device context and then, using the bit blit (fast raster copy) functions, copy it from the memory device context into an onscreen device context.

As you read earlier in this chapter, you can create a compatible memory device context using the `CreateCompatibleDC()` function.

When a memory device context is initially created, it is automatically initialized with a monochrome bitmap. You should then select your custom bitmap into the device context (saving the pointer returned to the old bitmap) and then perform the copy into the screen device context. When you have finished, you must select the original monochrome bitmap back into the device context (thus deselecting your custom bitmap) before deleting the `CBitmap` object, or calling `DeleteObject()` to destroy the GDI bitmap object.

6.6.1   Bitmap Copying

Once you have selected a valid bitmap into a memory-based device context, you can use the `BitBlt()` device context function to transfer all or part of the image onto a display- or printer-based device context. `BitBlt()` lets you specify the source device context (your memory DC), the source coordinates to copy from (relative to the memory DC), the destination coordinates (relative to the destination DC), and the width and height describing the area to copy.

You can also specify a raster operation flag that can be used to invert the image during copying, merge the source with the destination image, just copy the source to the destination, or perform a number of other logical operations between the source and destination during the copy.

The `StetchBlt()` function lets you specify both a source width and height, and a destination width and height. The image will then be expanded or shrunk to fit the destination width and height, which provides a fast and easy way to perform zoom operations. You can change the technique used to copy the image area by passing a flag value to the `SetStretchBltMode()` function. This lets you perform color-averaging stretch copies that give a better image representation (at the expense of speed) or allow a number of other different stretching techniques.

You can use the `MaskBlt()` function to perform an image copy from a source device context through the holes in a mask provided by a monochrome bitmap into the destination device context.

The following code fragment shows how to create a memory device context, load a resource bitmap, and select it into the memory device context, and then use `StetchBlt()` to stretch it so that it fills the view.

```
void CBitmapdemoView::OnDraw(CDC* pDC)
  {
    // Create a compatible memory device context
    CDC dcMemory;
    dcMemory.CreateCompatibleDC(pDC);

    // Load and select the bitmap resource
    CBitmap bmImage;
    bmImage.LoadBitmap(IDB_TSTBITMAP);
    CBitmap *pbmOriginal = dcMemory.SelectObject(&bmImage);
    CRect rcClient;
    GetClientRect(rcClient);
    pDC->StretchBlt(0,0,rcClient.Width(),rcClient.Height(),
        &dcMemory,0,0,48,48,SRCCOPY);
    pDC->SelectObject(pbmOriginal);
  }
```

6.7 Creating a Device-Independent Bitmap Class

The bitmaps discussed so far are called device-dependant bitmaps because they rely on the current display device context for their palette colors and are dependent on the current display resolution to determine the displayed size.

A device-independent bitmap (DIB) not only stores the bitmap image, but also uses a `BITMAPINFO` structure to store the color depth, sizing information, and colors. The first part of the structure consists of one of the various header structures followed by an array of `RGBQUAD` structures that store the colors used in the bitmap. You can create a `BITMAPINFO` and associate it with a bitmap image to form a DIB.

Once you have created a DIB, you can transfer it onto different machines and display the same image, represented to the best capabilities of various devices, while preserving the original size and colors.

The following sections show some of the steps required in creating, displaying, and storing a DIB. The example code builds a DIB class derived from CBitmap to extend the bitmap functionality into a DIB.

6.7.1 Creating a DIB

To create a DIB, you must first initialize a BITMAPINFOHEADER structure or one of its more modern counterparts, such as the BITMAPV5HEADER (which requires Windows 2000 or Windows 98).

Core Warning

The BITMAPV5HEADER lets you specify advanced compression techniques such as JPEG. To support this, you will need Windows 2000 or Window 98. If your DIB will be used on older platforms, you should use either BITMAPV4HEADER for Windows NT4 or Window 95 or BITMAPINFOHEADER for older platforms.

There are a number of member variables you can initialize in the DIB header (BITMAPINFOHEADER structure) to specify the DIB width, height, number of bit planes, bits per pixel, compression technique, pixels per meter in the X and Y dimensions, and the actual number of colors used. There are even more members in the more modern versions to specify advanced compression techniques and gamma corrections.

Specifying the pixels per meter provides an important piece of information that lets you render the DIB to the correct size of various devices. Using the information about the resolution of the device or using one of the device context mapping modes (especially the MM_LOMETRIC or MM_HIMETRIC modes) will help you render the image to the correct size.

After specifying the header details, you should initialize the RGBQUAD structures that specify each color used in the bitmap. You may wish to use the colors from the palette selected in a specific device context by using the SetDIBColorTable() function. This function fills the RGBQUAD array for you from the specified device context handle.

The following code fragment shows a class definition for a DIB manipulation class:

```
class CDIB : public CObject
 {
public:
  CDIB();
```

```
   virtual ~CDIB();
   BOOL CreateDIB(DWORD dwWidth,DWORD dwHeight,int nBits);
   BOOL CreateDIBFromBitmap(CDC* pDC);
   void InitializeColors();
   int GetDIBCols() const;
   VOID* GetDIBBitArray() const;
   BOOL CopyDIB(CDC* pDestDC,int x,int y);

public:
   CBitmap m_bmBitmap;

private:
   LPBITMAPINFO m_pDIB;
 };
```

You will notice that the class uses a BITMAPINFO pointer (m_pDIB) to the buffer containing the DIB and has an embedded device-dependent bitmap (m_bmBitmap) for transferring the image from an existing bitmap resource (discussed in the next section).

You could then implement the CreateDIB() and associated functions to allocate the memory for a DIB and initialize the BITMAPINFO structure like this:

```
CDIB::CDIB() : m_pDIB(NULL)
 {
 }

CDIB::~CDIB()
 {
   if (m_pDIB)
      delete m_pDIB;
 }

BOOL CDIB::CreateDIB(DWORD dwWidth,DWORD dwHeight,int nBits)
 {
   if (m_pDIB)
      return FALSE;
   const DWORD dwcBihSize = sizeof(BITMAPINFOHEADER);
   // Calculate the memory required for the DIB
   DWORD dwSize = dwcBihSize +
        (2>>nBits) * sizeof(RGBQUAD) +
        ((nBits * dwWidth) * dwHeight);
   m_pDIB = (LPBITMAPINFO)new BYTE[dwSize];
   if (!m_pDIB)
      return FALSE;
   m_pDIB->bmiHeader.biSize = dwcBihSize;
```

```
m_pDIB->bmiHeader.biWidth = dwWidth;
m_pDIB->bmiHeader.biHeight = dwHeight;
m_pDIB->bmiHeader.biBitCount = nBits;
m_pDIB->bmiHeader.biPlanes = 1;
m_pDIB->bmiHeader.biCompression = BI_RGB;
m_pDIB->bmiHeader.biXPelsPerMeter = 1000;
m_pDIB->bmiHeader.biYPelsPerMeter = 1000;
m_pDIB->bmiHeader.biClrUsed = 0;
m_pDIB->bmiHeader.biClrImportant = 0;
InitializeColors();
return TRUE;
}
```

You will notice that dwSize is calculated from the size of the BITMAP-INFOHEADER structure, the size of the RGBQUAD array required for the specified color depth, and the size of the resulting bitmap buffer.

The BITMAPINFOHEADER structure is initialized with dimensions of 1000 × 1000 pixels per meter and uses the specified width, height, and color depth. The compression flag biCompression lets you specify the type of compression used in the DIB image buffer. The BI_RGB flag shown above indicates that no compression is used.

The colors could then be initialized (all to black) like this:

```
void CDIB::InitializeColors()
 {
   if (!m_pDIB)
      return;
   // This just initializes all colors to black
   LPRGBQUAD lpColors =
       (LPRGBQUAD)(m_pDIB+m_pDIB->bmiHeader.biSize);
   for(int i=0;i<GetDIBCols();i++) {
      lpColors[i].rgbRed=0;
      lpColors[i].rgbBlue=0;
      lpColors[i].rgbGreen=0;
      lpColors[i].rgbReserved=0;
   }
 }
```

You might want to initialize a specific set of RGBQUAD colors depending on the requirements of your DIB.

6.7.2 Creating a DIB from a Device-Dependent Bitmap

Once you have set the color values for the DIB, you can set the pixels for the image directly into a buffer (usually stored immediately after the BITMAPINFO structure) from within your code or from an existing device-dependent bitmap.

Although it is not necessary, it is usually desirable to keep the bitmap image information directly after the BITMAPINFO structure as shown in the CreateDIB() implementation above.

The following helper functions can help you retrieve the number of colors calculated from the color depth in the BITMAPINFOHEADER and a pointer to the bitmap image buffer calculated from the size of the header structure and the following color value array:

```
int CDIB::GetDIBCols() const
  {
    if (!m_pDIB)
       return 0;
    return (2>>m_pDIB->bmiHeader.biBitCount);
  }

VOID* CDIB::GetDIBBitArray() const
  {
    if (!m_pDIB)
       return FALSE;
    return (m_pDIB + m_pDIB->bmiHeader.biSize +
       GetDIBCols() * sizeof(RGBQUAD));
  }
```

You can find the size and color depth information from a device-dependent bitmap using the CBitmap class's GetBitmap() function. This function fills a BITMAP structure (passed by pointer) with the details about a specific GDI bitmap object.

You can then copy these details along with the extra DIB information into the DIB's BITMAPINFOHEADER to create a DIB with the same width, height, and color depth as the device-dependent bitmap.

The DIB color value information can then be initialized with the Set-DIBColorTable() from a reference device context.

After the DIB header and color values have been initialized from the bitmap, it only remains to copy the image bits The GetDIBits() function can perform this task for you. You need only pass the DIB information, a reference device context, and the GDI bitmap handle; GetDIBits() then copies the entire image bitmap into your supplied buffer.

If you want to perform the reverse operation of copying a DIB bitmap to a device-dependent bitmap, you can use the corresponding SetDIBits() function. You can even create a HBITMAP GDI object initialized from a DIB directly using the global CreateDIBitmap() function.

The following implementation for the CDIB class's CreateDIBFrom-Bitmap() function demonstrates these functions using the device-depen-dent m_bmBitmap member. The CreateDIBFromBitmap() function assumes that this CBitmap member has been previously initialized via a CreateBitmap() or LoadBitmap():

```
BOOL CDIB::CreateDIBFromBitmap(CDC* pDC)
{
  if (!pDC)
     return FALSE;
  HDC hDC = pDC->GetSafeHdc();

  BITMAP bimapInfo;
  m_bmBitmap.GetBitmap(&bimapInfo);
  if (!CreateDIB(bimapInfo.bmWidth,bimapInfo.bmHeight,
     bimapInfo.bmBitsPixel))
     return FALSE;
  LPRGBQUAD lpColors =
      (LPRGBQUAD)(m_pDIB+m_pDIB->bmiHeader.biSize);
  SetDIBColorTable(hDC,0,GetDIBCols(),lpColors);

  // This implicitly assumes that the source bitmap
  // is at the 1 pixel per mm resolution
  BOOL bSuccess = (GetDIBits(hDC,(HBITMAP)m_bmBitmap,
     0,bimapInfo.bmHeight,GetDIBBitArray(),
     m_pDIB,DIB_RGB_COLORS) > 0);
  return bSuccess;
}
```

You will notice the DIB_RGB_COLORS flag is also passed to the Get-DIBits() function. You can set this flag to either DIB_RGB_COLORS to indicate that the color values are literal RGB values or DIB_RGB_PAL to specify color index positions in the device context's current palette.

You might call the CreateDIBFromBitmap() function after loading a resource-based bitmap like this:

```
#include "dib.h"
CDIB g_DIB;

void CBitmapdemoView::OnInitialUpdate()
 {
   CView::OnInitialUpdate();
   CClientDC dc(this);
   g_DIB.m_bmBitmap.LoadBitmap(IDB_TSTBITMAP);
   g_DIB.CreateDIBFromBitmap(&dc);
 }
```

After calling the `CreateDIBFromBitmap()` function, the embedded DIB will be initialized in the memory pointed at by the m_pDIB pointer.

6.7.3 Drawing with a DIB

You can use several GDI functions to draw from a DIB directly into a normal device context. These are similar to the device-dependent blit functions you saw earlier.

The global `SetDIBitsToDevice()` function copies the image from a DIB buffer directly to a specified device context at a specified position. You can also specify the number of lines to copy, and the width, height, and position of the source DIB image. If it succeeds, `SetDIBitsToDevice()` returns the number of scan lines copied.

Core Warning

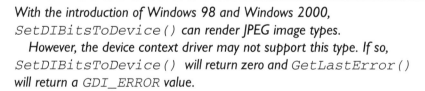

With the introduction of Windows 98 and Windows 2000, `SetDIBitsToDevice()` can render JPEG image types.

However, the device context driver may not support this type. If so, `SetDIBitsToDevice()` will return zero and `GetLastError()` will return a GDI_ERROR value.

You can also use `StretchDIBits()` in a similar way as `StretchBlt()` to stretch the DIB bitmap to the required size. This function is often useful when you are trying to preserve the original bitmap size. You can use the DIB's pixels per meter values to calculate the correct destination size and/or use a specific mapping mode to draw the image at a specific size.

The following example shows an implementation of the `CopyDIB()` function for the `CDIB` class defined previously. This function uses `StretchDIBits()` to render the DIB into a device context provided.

It maintains the standard size of the DIB by setting the mapping mode to MM_LOMETRIC. In this mapping mode, the logical unit size is 0.1 mm, so coordinates specified by the GDI functions will be converted by the device context to represent the correct specified size on the destination device. Therefore, the coordinates specified in the destination width and height should be multiplied by 10 so that each DIB pixel represents 1 mm to maintain the 1000 pixel per meter specification:

```
BOOL CDIB::CopyDIB(CDC* pDestDC,int x,int y)
{
   if (!m_pDIB || !pDestDC)
      return FALSE;

   int nOldMapMode = pDestDC->SetMapMode(MM_LOMETRIC);
   BOOL bOK = StretchDIBits(pDestDC->GetSafeHdc(),
      x,y,
      m_pDIB->bmiHeader.biWidth * 10,     // Dest Width
      m_pDIB->bmiHeader.biHeight * -10,   // Dest Height
      0,0,
      m_pDIB->bmiHeader.biWidth,          // Source Width
      m_pDIB->bmiHeader.biHeight,         // Source Height
      GetDIBBitArray(),m_pDIB,DIB_RGB_COLORS,SRCCOPY) > 0;

   pDestDC->SetMapMode(nOldMapMode);
   return bOK;
}
```

You could invoke this code from your applications view class in the OnDraw() and OnPrint() functions after previously creating the DIB from the loaded bitmap resource (as shown earlier) like this:

```
void CBitmapdemoView::OnPrint(CDC* pDC, CPrintInfo* pInfo)
{
   g_DIB.CopyDIB(pDC,50,-50);
}

void CBitmapdemoView::OnDraw(CDC* pDC)
{
   g_DIB.CopyDIB(pDC,50,-50);
}
```

Regardless of the device context passed to CopyDIB() and the ultimate destination device, the DIB should be rendered to the same size and with the same colors to the best capabilities of the device.

Core Warning

> *Mapping modes used with display monitors are usually very inaccurate, so the size of a displayed DIB may be physically wrong on a VDU. However, printer device contexts provide very accurate physical unit mapping so they should print the image to the correct size.*

6.8 Summary

In this chapter, you have seen how Windows maintains a common interface to applications to produce consistent output across a range of devices such as screens, printers, and plotters.

You saw how the CDC class wraps an HDC device context handle and provides member functions for the vast majority of API functions that use the device context.

You have seen how device context objects can be created directly for various devices, such as screens and printers, or obtained directly from windows to give you access to the client or entire rendering area of the window.

You have learned how to use the special CDC-derived classes that are used to get access to client areas, to handle window painting, or to play metafiles.

You saw how to create the basic GDI rendering objects, such as pens and brushes, to let you perform a wide range of graphical drawing operations using a variety of line-drawing and area-filling styles and techniques. You also saw how to use the various coordinate storing classes and regions in conjunction with the drawing functions to perform coordinate manipulation and clipping of the rendered output.

You saw how to draw text in a number of fonts using the various text-drawing functions of the device context, and how to create fonts, and the role of the font-mapper in their creation.

Finally, you have learned how to load device-dependent bitmaps from the application's resources or created and used in conjunction with memory device contexts. You have also seen the limitations of device-dependent bitmaps and how these limitations are solved with device-independent bitmaps with their additional information structures.

WORKING WITH DOCUMENTS AND VIEWS

Topics in this Chapter

- Understanding the Two Document-Interface Structures
- Complex Combinations of Documents, Views, and Frame Windows
- Working with Multiple Document Types
- Working with Complex Document Data
- Understanding How Your Applications Manage Documents and Views
- Understanding the CMultiDocTemplate Class
- Working with Frame Windows
- Understanding the Document Template Resources
- Understanding and Using the CView Class
- Understanding Splitter Windows
- Using Static Splitters
- Using MFC to Subclass Windows
- Alternatives to the Document/View Architecture
- Summary

Chapter 7

At the core of an MFC application is the concept of a *document object* and a corresponding *view window*. The document object usually represents a file the application has opened, while the view window provides a visual presentation of the document's data and accepts user interaction. The relationship between documents and views is a one-to-many relationship. In other words, a document can have many views, but you can associate a view with only one document.

Within your applications, you will represent document objects within classes that you derive from the MFC CDocument base class. You will derive your view window classes from the MFC CView class. In this chapter, you will learn about CDocument and CView and how to use them with simple, single-document interface (SDI) and multiple-document interface (MDI) applications.

7.1 Understanding the Two Document-Interface Structures

The built-in power of the document/view architecture, therefore, is that as users work with the application, they create and destroy instances of the file and user interface management code (and data) that define their very perception of the data with which they work.

A user-friendly application gives views to the application's data that make more sense to the user. For example, for most users it is probably difficult to imagine how cold it will be in South Dakota based on tabular temperature data from the entire United States. However, the common "blue is cold, orange is hot" weather graphs that appear in newspapers make it easy to guess what range of temperatures a traveler might expect with a quick glance at the right part of the map. The tabular data still has value, though. It's an easy way to enter the data in the first place, and it's the only way you might ever find out what the weather is like in South Dakota if you weren't completely sure where it was.

Core Note

Your applications may associate more than one instance of a particular view with a given document, and you may even associate instances of different views with the same document.

Single-document interface applications that you use AppWizard to produce only ever use one document and one view type, and only ever instantiate one of each of these classes. However, this is only true of the AppWizard-generated code — after the AppWizard creates your project, you can add as many views (and for that matter, documents) as you desire, if you decide that it's convenient to use multiple instances of each different view or document.

Multiple-document interface applications will make use of at least one document/view pair, but they may make use of additional documents and views in different combinations to enable the user to work with other files or to represent data in may different ways. As noted previously, you will learn more about multiple-document interface applications later in this chapter. Figure 7-1 shows which classes may support a simple SDI application that you implement using MFC objects.

In AppWizard-generated SDI applications, the CMainFrame class implements the frame window. In such cases, AppWizard will define the CMainFrame class for you in the Mainfrm.h header file and implement the class in the MainFrm.cpp source file. The CMainFrame class derives most of its functionality from the CFrameWnd class, which is the MFC wrapper class for a simple window. The CFrameWnd class does not do much in the single-document interface application. The notable exceptions are if you have added a status bar or dockable toolbars to the application, the CMainFrame class will handle the creation and initialization of those objects.

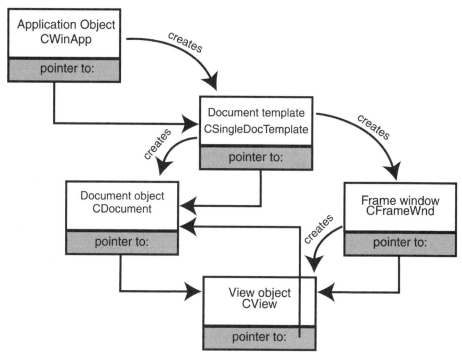

Figure 7-1 The model of the relationship between the five base classes for an SDI application.

While designing SDI applications is a useful exercise, SDI is generally only acceptable when you create small, simple applications. Within most applications that you design for actual use, whether for public use or within your own organization, you will require the ability to use multiple views, and generally multiple documents, to organize information. When you use multiple documents within a single application, you will use the multiple-document interface (MDI) model for the document/view structure. The layout of a multiple-document interface application is a little more complicated than the layout of a single-document interface application. Figure 7-2 shows the basic layout of the MDI application structure.

As you can see from Figure 7-2, multiple-document applications still use a main frame that holds the menu, toolbar, and status bars. However, in the MDI application, the CMainFrame class derives from MFC's CMDIFrameWnd class, instead of the CFrameWnd class. CMDIFrameWnd has the same visual characteristics as CFrameWnd, but it also implements the MDI frame protocol that Windows expects in an MDI application.

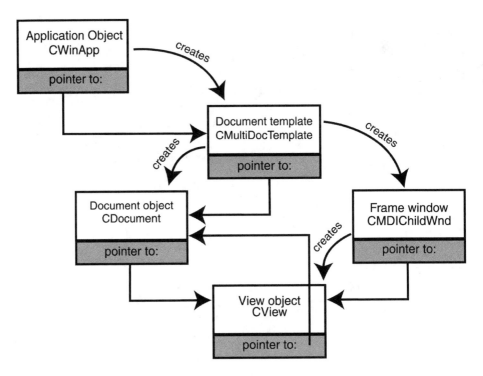

Figure 7-2   The basic layout of the MDI-application object structure.

The child windows that the figure depicts are also frame windows, but the child windows are instances of the MFC class CMDIChildWnd. This MFC class provides the child window that Windows MDI applications use in their client area to hold each instance of the MDI application's views. The frameworks will create one CMDIChildWnd to contain each view the application needs, just like the CMainFrame object wrapped the single view in the SDI application. The wrapped view may be of any type and can refer to any open document that the application is currently managing.

As a developer of MFC applications, it is your responsibility to decide exactly what kind of documents and views you will implement, and how they'll interact with the basic framework provided by MFC's implementation of the single-document or multiple-document interfaces. Your code alters and enhances the way the generic documents and views interact and behave. By tuning things to work the way you want them to, you will eventually develop the skeleton MFC provides into an application that does exactly what you need. Over the course of this chapter, you will learn more about the components of the MDI application and use a simple MDI application so that you can better decide what structure your applications require.

Conventional Windows applications written in C (and using the Windows API) would modify the way that Windows' own classes work. Within the application's body, your program code then would paint, draw, or store something as a direction to input messages (or combinations of input messages) to your application's windows. Fortunately, by using MFC, you are able to focus more closely on working with classes, rather than working with a series of system function calls. These MFC classes also support the ability to intercept those basic Windows messages and, when appropriate, do work at a much lower level.

7.2 Complex Combinations of Documents, Views, and Frame Windows

As you have learned, the standard relationship among a document, its view(s), and its frame window(s) is described in a relatively straightforward manner: a one-to-many relationship between documents and views, and a one-to-one relationship between each view and a frame window. Many applications need only to support a single document type (but possibly let the user open multiple documents of that type) with a single view on the document and only one frame window per document. But some applications may need to alter one or more of those defaults — creating multiple views on a single-document type, single views on multiple-document types, or multiple views on multiple-document types. It is worthwhile to consider the different situations that you may encounter when working with documents and views and how you should design your applications to respond appropriately.

7.3 Working with Multiple-Document Types

Whether you create an SDI or an MDI application, AppWizard will create only a single document class for you. In some cases, though, you may need to support more than one document type. For example, your application may need both worksheet and chart documents. Your application will probably represent each document type with its own document class and typically by its own view class or classes as well. When the user chooses the File menu's New option, the framework will display a dialog box that lists the application's supported document types. After the user chooses a document type, the application creates a document of that type. The application then manages each document type with its own document-template object.

To create extra document classes within your own applications, use the Add Class button in the ClassWizard dialog box. Choose CDocument (or COLEDocument) as the Class Type to derive form and supply the requested document information. Then implement the new class' data structures.

To let the framework know about your extra document class, you must then add a second call to AddDocTemplate() in your application class' InitInstance() member function. For example, an application with two documents would include code within its InitInstance() member function similar to the following:

```
CMultiDocTemplate* pDocTemplate;
PDocTemplate = new CMultiDocTemplate(
    IDR_OPAINTTYPE,
    RUNTIME_CLASS(CSample1Doc),
    RUNTIME_CLASS(CMDIChildWnd),
    RUNTIME_CLASS(CSample1View));
AddDocTemplate(pDocTemplate);
pDocTemplate = new CMultiDocTemplate(
    IDR_OPAINTTYPE,
    RUNTIME_CLASS(CSample2Doc),
    RUNTIME_CLASS(CMDIChildWnd),
    RUNTIME_CLASS(CSample2View));
AddDocTemplate(pDocTemplate);
```

7.3.1 Understanding the CDocument Class

The MFC-provided CDocument class provides the basic functionality for your application's document objects. The CDocument class' basic functionality includes the ability to create new documents, serialize document data, provide basic cooperation between a document object and view window, and more. MFC also provides a series of CDocument-derived classes that implement functionality specific to certain application types. For example, MFC provides the CRecordset and CDAORecordset types to simplify the creation of database views. You can visualize the relationship between documents and views as shown in Figure 7-3.

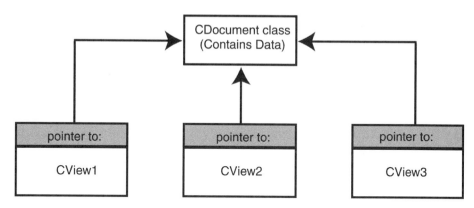

Figure 7-3 The one-to-many relationship between a document and its views.

7.3.2 Declaring a Document Class in Your Application

When you use the AppWizard to create your applications, you often do not need to worry about declaring your base document class — the AppWizard does it for you. However, it is still useful for you to understand the behavior of the CDocument class because more complex programs might very possibly require multiple instances of multiple derivations from CDocument. In addition, understanding the behavior of CDocument lets you easily enhance the AppWizard-generated application skeleton.

Core Note

Whether you create a single-document interface application or a multiple-document interface application, the AppWizard will only derive a single-document class for you from the MFC CDocument base class.

When you build a simple MFC application, it is often enough for you to make relatively minor modifications to your AppWizard-supplied document class. Often, you will not need to do much more to the class than add some member variables and some member functions that other portions of the program can use to access those member variables.

For example, the document object for a simple communications program (such as a terminal emulator) might contain member variables for settings. Those member variables would probably store information such as a telephone number, speed, parity, number of bits in each transmission segment, and so on. You could easily represent the communications settings with a set of simple member variables in the derived document class, as shown in the following code snippet:

```
class CSimpleTermDoc : public CDocument {
  protected:
    CSimpleTermDoc();
    DECLARE_DYNCREATE(CSimpleTermDoc)
  public:   CString_m_sPhoneNum;
    DWORD m_dwTransSpeed;
    WORD m_nTransParity;
    WORD m_nTransBits;
    DWORD m_dwConnectTime;
```

After you declare the member variables, you must ensure that the program initializes the variables to some default values in the `CSimpleTermDoc` class' `OnNewDocument()` member function. In addition, you must place code in the `Serialize()` function to ensure that the program serializes the variables properly.

For your simpler applications, you really need do nothing beyond the initialization and serialization of your member variables to have a complete, fully functioning document class.

7.3.3 Using CDocument's Member Functions

The `CDocument` class has several member functions, in addition to the serialization and initialization member functions that your applications will frequently use. The first set of member functions provides access to the associated view subjects. Every document object that you use within your applications will have a list of view objects that you associate with it. You can call the `GetFirstViewPosition()` member function for the document object to obtain an iterator to this list. The iterator will be of type `POSITION`.

You will use values of type `POSITION` throughout the MFC, primarily with collection classes. When your applications must traverse a list, you will typically request an iterator that the collection class associates with the first object on the list, and then use an iterator function to access the actual elements the list contains, one-by-one. `CDocument`, in this context, is a collection class; it maintains information about the collection of views associated with the class. Therefore, after you obtain the iterator to the first view of the `GetFirstViewPosition()` member function, you can repeatedly call the GetNextView() member function to work through the remaining views in the collection.

In other words, to process all the views that your program has associated with a given document object, your program code will generally look similar to the following:

```
POSITION posView = GetFirstViewPosition();
while (posView != NULL) {
  CView *pView = GetNextView(posView);
  // Do something with the pointer to the view
}
```

However, if all your program code is trying to accomplish is to notify all the views for the document that information within the document has changed, you can simply invoke the document object's UpdateAllViews() member function instead of iterating the views. Furthermore, you can also specify application-specific data that instructs the views to selectively update only portions of the view windows when you call the UpdateAllViews() function.

Some other view-related member functions for the document object that you will use much less frequently include the AddView() and Remove-View() functions. As their names indicate, the functions let you manually add and remove views from a document's list of views. In general, you will use the functions only rarely, as most developers simply use the default MFC implementation with little or no modification.

Whenever the document's data changes (either through a user's action or through internal program processing), your program should call the SetModifiedFlag() member function. Consistent use of SetModi-fiedFlag() will ensure that the MFC framework prompts the user before letting the user destroy an unsaved, changed document. Should you decide to override the framework, you can call the IsModified() member function to obtain the status of the flag.

You can use the SetTitle() member function to set the document object's title. The application, in turn, will display the title you set in the frame window (the main frame window in an SDI application, and the child frame window for the object in an MDI application).

You can also set the fully qualified path name for the document with the SetPathName() function and obtain the path name with the GetPath-Name() function. Finally, you can obtain the document template that the program associated with the document at the document's creation through a call to GetDocTemplate().

7.3.4 Better Understanding Documents and Message Processing

One of the most important features of a document is that a `CDocument` object is not directly associated with a window. Instead, a `CDocument` object is itself a command-target object — which means that the object can receive messages from the operating system. The view objects that you associated with a `CDocument` object are responsible for routing messages from the operating system to the document.

Because the view objects you associate with the document and the frame window that holds the document will receive messages before passing them through to the document, you have a great deal of control over which messages the frame window, views, and document process. However, there are some common-sense rules of thumb (as well as some simplicity issues) that provide you with a good starting point for how to process incoming messages.

When you consider messages, or for that matter any time that you are working with the document-view architecture, you should always keep in mind that a document is an abstract representation of your data — a representation, that is, which is independent of the visual representation of the data that the view window will provide. As importantly, a document may have one, many, or no views attached to it, so documents should respond only to messages that are global in nature. That is, a document should respond only to messages that have an immediate effect on the document's data, which messages' effect all the views attached to the document should reflect. On the other hand, views should respond to messages that are specific to that window's view only.

In practical terms, the division of responsibilities between documents and views generally makes it easier to determine how to process a given command. For example, if your application has a Save command, which the user would select to save the data in the object, the document should handle that command because the command is concerned with the data, not how the user sees the data.

On the other hand, if your application supports a Copy command, which the user would usually select to copy data the user has selected within the display, you would probably want to handle the command in the view. In fact, if a document supports multiple views, the data selected in each view might vary — making it even more clear that you should generally process the copy command separately for each view attached to a document.

Both cases we have considered already are relatively clean-cut — you are saving the data in the first example, and you are copying representation of the data from within one view to another view in the second example. However, there are some borderline cases. A common one is the Paste command. Determining whether the document class or the view class should handle it is slightly more complex. The Paste command impacts the entire document (you are inserting data into the document), not just a single view. On the other hand, the current view may have significant importance when pasting information into a document. For example, the paste action may actually replace existing, selected text within the view. In other words, the decision you must make about whether the document object or the view object should handle actions of this type is dependent on your application's design, and is usually something you should think through carefully.

Just to keep it interesting, there are also certain commands that you should not handle in either the document class or the view class, but rather in the frame window's code. Excellent examples of commands that you should handle within the frame window include commands to hide and display toolbars. The presence or absence of the toolbar is not particularly material to a document or its views. Rather, it is a configuration issue with effects global to the entire application.

7.3.5 *Overriding Virtual Document Functions*

As you learned earlier in this chapter (when working with OnNewDocument() and Serialize()), many of the member functions the CDocument class defines are virtual functions, meaning that you can override them in your own class declarations. The virtual functions in the CDocument class provide default processing that is sufficient for most needs. However, you will also find that your programs must perform specific processing for a certain document that the default processing does not provide.

For example, the CDocument class and its derivatives will call the OnNewDocument() member function whenever the program initializes a new document object (or when the program reuses an existing document object in an SDIU application). Your applications will typically call the OnNewDocument() function when handling a File New command. Similarly, your CDocument calls the OnCloseDocument() member function when the application is about to close a document. You should override this document within your own document classes if your application must perform any clean-up operations before destroying the document object.

Your document classes will call the OnOpenDocument() and OnSave-Document() functions to read a document from disk or to write a document to disk, respectively. You should override these functions only if the default implementation (which calls the `Serialize()` member function) is not sufficient. An excellent example of a situation in which you would override `OnOpenDocument()` and `OnSaveDocument()` is if you are encrypting data before you write it to the disk and decrypting it when you reload it from the disk.

The default implementations of both `OnOpenDocument()` and `OnCloseDocument()` call the `DeleteContents()` member function. The `DeleteContents()` member function deletes the document's contents without actually destroying the document object. Using `DeleteContents()` when opening a new document is more efficient (in terms of both memory usage and application speed) than actually closing and destroying the original document object and creating a new document object.

The `OnFileSendMail()` member function sends the document object as an attachment to a mail message. It first calls `OnSaveDocument()` to save a copy of the document to temporary disk file (in the directory set by your TEMP environment variable). Next, the program code within the member function attaches the temporary file to a MAPI message. The member function uses the `OnUpdateFileSendMail()` member function to enable the command that you identify with the constant `ID_FILE_SEND_MAIL` in the application's menu or remove it altogether if MAPI support is not available to the program. Both `OnFileSendMail()` and `OnUpdateFileSendMail()` are overridable functions, which lets you (relatively easily) implement customized messaging behavior within your applications.

7.4 Working with Complex Document Data

Earlier in this chapter you learned how to derive simple document classes from `CDocument`, within which you can store the document's data in a series of simple member variables. However, creating applications that you will use in the real world tends to be more demanding. Most applications you will develop will require significantly more advanced data than what you could ever possibly represent with a few variables of simple data types.

There are many different approaches that you will use to manage complex data types within a document object; however, arguably the best approach is to use a set of classes that you derive from the `CObject` class. Each derived class, then, will store the complex data objects. The document, in turn, will use a standard or custom-created collection class to embed the objects within the document class. For example, you might create data definitions similar to the following for an application:

```
class CAppObject : public CObject {
  // definitions
}

class CAppSubObject1 : public CObject {
  // definitions
}

class CAppSubObject2 : public Cobject {
  // definitions
}
```

Then, within the declaration of the document class, you would include a CObList member. The CObList class supports ordered lists of nonunique CObject pointers accessible sequentially or by pointer value. CObList lists behave like double-linked lists. Your document declaration, therefore, would look similar to the following:

```
class CSampleDoc : public CDocument {
  // code here
  public
    CObList_m_DataObList;

  // code here
}
```

In a complex situation such as the one just outlined, it is often not sufficient to simply declare member variables. Your document class is also likely to require member functions that provide methods to let views and other objects that must access the document's data do so. For example, you may not want to let other classes (such as a view class) directly manipulate the m_DataObList variable directly. Instead, you should usually provide a member function that the view class can access to iterate through the m_DataObList object as it needs to.

Such member functions should also ensure that each time the document's data changes, the application properly updates all the document's views. The member functions should also call the document's SetModifed member function to indicate to the document that an accessing function or class has changed the document's data. If your application will support an undo-type capability, you should also place your application's buffered undo data into its correct storage location while inside the member function. To understand this better, consider the following member function, AddNewObj(), which adds a new object to the document's object list:

```
BOOL CSampleDoc : AddNewObj(CAppObject *pObject)
{
  try {
    m_DataObList.AddTail((CObject *)pObject);
    SetModifiedFlag(TRUE);
    UpdateAllViews(NULL, UPDATE_OBJECT, pObject;
    return TRUE;
  }
  catch(CMemoryException *e) {
    TRACE("Doc—AddNewObj_memory allocation error.\n");
    e->Delete();
    return FALSE;
  }
}
```

Understanding the importance of the AddNewObj() member function is easier when you consider the relationship between the document and its views and how the program will pass control back and forth between the two.

First, the user will interact with the view, which might result in a new object being added, an existing object being modified or deleted, or some other action. For now, presume that the user's actions result in the need to add a new object to the document. To add a new object, the view object calls the AddNewObj() member function. After the member function adds the new object successfully, the document object will call the UpdateAll-Views() member function, which, in turn, will call the OnUpdate() member function of each view that you have previously associated with the document. The AddNewObj() member function passes a hint to the UpdateAllViews() member function through the use of the application-defined UPDATE_OBJECT constant and a pointer to a CObject. The hint assists all the views in most efficiently updating their component windows by instructing the views to repaint only those regions of the view directly and indirectly affected by the addition of the new object. Figure 7-4 shows the control-passing mechanism that the views and the document will use.

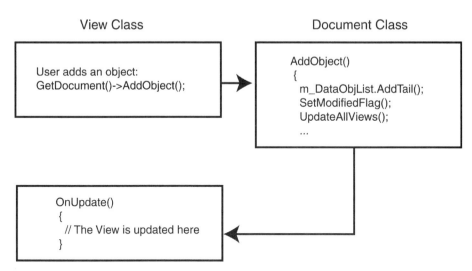

View Class   Document Class

Figure 7-4 Control passes from the view class to the document class and back.

Another advantage of using MFC collection classes within your application is that collection classes support serialization. For example, to load and save your document's data that is stored in CObject objects and referenced through a CObList object, all you need to do is to construct the document's Serialize() member function as shown here:

```
void CSampleDoc::Serialize(CArchive &ar)
{
  if (ar.IsStoring()) {
    // serialize any non-collection class data here
  }
  else {
    // serialize any non-collection class data here
  }
  m_DataObList.Serialize(ar);
}
```

You should be aware, however, that for this technique to work you must implement the Serialize() member function for all your object classes. A CObject-derived class will not serialize itself. If you decide to use one of the general-purpose collection templates, serialization is an issue that you must pay close attention to. The collection CArray, CList, and CMap rely on the SerializeElements() member function to serialize the objects within the collection. MFC declares this function as shown here:

```
template <class TYPE> void AFXAPI
    SerializeElements(Carchive &ar,
    TYPE *pElements, int_nCount);
```

Because the collection class templates do not require that you derive TYPE from CObject, they do not call the Serialize() member function for each element (because the Serialize() member function is not guaranteed to exist). Instead, the default implementation of SerializeElements() performs a *bitwise* read or write action. However, as you can imagine, in most cases, a bitwise read or write is not what you will want to perform. Rather, you should implement your own SerializeElements() function for your objects. You might implement such a function as shown here:

```
void SerializeElements(CArchive &ar,
    CAppObject **pObs, int_nCoutn);
{
  for (int i = 0; i< nCount; i++; pObjs++)
    (*pObs->Serialize(ar);
}
```

7.4.1 Understanding the Benefits of CCmdTarget and CDocItem

As you learned in the previous section of this chapter, you can use objects that you derive from the CObject class to store data within your documents. Unfortunately, if you wish your documents and applications to support OLE automation, the CObject class is insufficient. Instead, you must declare your objects as *command targets.* If you wish to support OLE automation, you may prefer to derive your data from the MFC CCmdTarget base class.

Alternately, and usually better, you may want to derive your data objects from the MFC CDocItem class. You can either create a collection of CDocItem objects yourself or rely on MFC's COleDocument class to create the collection. In other words, rather than deriving your document class from CDocument, derive it from COleDocument. You can use COleDocument in OLE applications where either the COleDocument class or a class previously derived from COleDocument is the base class for the OLE application's document class. Like CDocument, COleDocument is a collection class. COleDocument supports a collection of CDocItem objects, which are in turn either COleServerItem- or COleClientItem-derived. However, COleDocument supports CDocItem generically (that is, it doesn't care whether the item is a server or client item). COleDocument's generic implementation means that you can add your own CDocItem-derived objects to the collection without fear that doing so will interfere with normal OLE operations and behavior.

One nice thing about working with `COleDocument` is that it adds additional `CDOcItem` members for you automatically. If you use `AddItem()`, `RemoveItem()`, `GetStartPosition()`, and `GetNextItem()`, you can add, remove, and retrieve document items without further processing. The underlying MFC coding handles your other needs (such as serialization) without further programming on your part.

However, working with `COleDocument` is not without its pitfalls. Because of how you derive your document items and the OLE `COleClientItem` and `COleServerItem` objects, you may need to perform certain special programming actions to add certain functions to a given object. For example, suppose that you declare your object items as shown here:

```
class CSampleDocItem : public CdocItem {
   // more code here
   CRect m_Rect;
}
```

In addition, suppose that you also support the `m_Rect` member variable within your OLE client items, as shown here:

```
class CSampleClientItem : public ColeClientItem {
   // more code here
   CRect m_Rect;
};
```

Given these two declarations, you might suppose that you can create a function that takes an item from your document and manipulates its `m_Rect` member as shown here:

```
void sampFunc(CDocItem *pItem) {
   samp2Func(pItem->m_Rect);    //Error!
}
```

Because the `CDocItem` class by itself does not contain an `m_Rect` member variable, the compiler will halt the program's compilation with an error at the function declaration. Unfortunately, using a pointer to your own `CDocItem`-derived class doesn't really solve the problem either:

```
void sampFunc(CSampleDocItem *pItem) {
   samp2Func(pItem->m_Rect);
}
```

While declaring the function in this manner will support your derived class, it won't support OLE client items of type `CDocItem` — a significant issue. An obvious solution is to simply create two overridden versions of `sampFunc`, but maintaining two separate, identical versions of the same function is not only inelegant, it makes maintenance all that much more difficult. The best solution is to instead create a wrapper function that takes a pointer to a `CDocItem` object and uses MFC runtime type information to obtain the member variable, as shown here:

```
CRect_GetRect(CDocItem *pDocItem)
{
  if (pDocItem->IsKindOf(RUNTIME_CLASS(CSampleDocItem)))
    return_((CsampleDocItem *)pDocItem)->m_Rect;
  else if (pDocItem->
      IsKindOf(RUNTIME_CLASS(CSampleClientItem)))
    ASSERT(FALSE);
  return CRect(0, 0, 0, 0);
}


sampFunc(CDocItem *pItem)
{
  samp2Func(GetRect(pItem));
}
```

This solution, however, does require that you declare and implement both the `CSampleDocItem` and the `CSampleClientItem` classes with the `DECLARE_DYNAMIC` and `IMPLEMENT_DYNAMIC` macros. In general, however, that should not be an issue, because your document objects will typically support serialization. When you declare and implement a class with the `DECLARE_SERIAL` and `IMPLEMENT_SERIAL` macros, the `DECLARE_DYNAMIC` and `IMPLEMENT_DYNAMIC` macros are implied.

7.5   Understanding How Your Applications Manage Documents and Views

Now that you have learned about documents, and been introduced briefly to document templates, it is important to understand how MFC keeps track of the documents and views that comprise the application, and which documents and views are related to one another.

As the document/view architecture is the cornerstone of any document-based application (as you learned earlier, dialog-based applications perform differently than document/view applications), MFC must be able to create and destroy objects from the document/view implementation classes. As your application may handle more than one type of document/view relationship, MFC must have some way of knowing which document, view, and display classes you implement, what the relationships are between the classes, and how to create the implementations of the classes at runtime. After all, while one document might support many different types of views, associating other views with that same document might be nonsensical.

7.5.1 Working with the CSingleDocTemplate Class

To learn how MFC describes and maintains these associations, use the App-Wizard to create a simple single-document application. When you do, you will find source code that looks like the following:

```
CSingleDocTemplate* pdocTemplate;
pDocTemplate = new_CSingleDocTemplate(
    IDR_MAINFRAME,
    RUNTIME_CLASS(CSIMPLEDoc),
    RUNTIME_CLASS(CMainFrame),    // main SDI frame window
    RUNTIME_CLASS(CSIMPLEView));
AddDocTemplate(pDocTemplate);
```

The code dynamically allocates a new `CSingleDocTemplate` object. The constructor for `CSingleDocTemplate` takes four parameters. The first parameter is a resource ID. You will learn the significance of the resource ID later in this chapter. The second, third, and fourth parameters associated with the `CSingleDocTemplate()` constructor are pointers to runtime class information. The `RUNTIME_CLASS()` macro generates a pointer to the runtime class information for the application's document, main frame, and view classes. These pointers are all passed to the `CSingle-DocTemplate` constructor, which keeps the pointers so that it can create instances of the objects as needed to put together a complete document/view team.

The `CSingleDocTemplate` object lives as long as the application continues to execute. MFC uses the object internally and destroys any added document templates as the application's `CWinApp` object is destroyed. You can find the code that allocates `CSingleDocTemplates` to your application in its `CWinApp::InitInstance()` function, but you will never write code that deletes the document template objects if you use `AddDocTemplate()` to add the template, because the `CWinApp` destructor function will clean up that document template allocation for you automatically.

7.6   Understanding the CMultiDocTemplate Class

Much as the `CSingleDocTemplate` class defines a document template that implements the single-document interface, the `CMultiDocTemplate` class defines a document template that implements the multiple-document interface (MDI). An MDI application uses the main frame window as a workspace in which the user can open zero or more document frame windows, each of which displays a document.

An MDI application can support more than one type of document, and documents of different types can be open at the same time. Your application has one document template for each document type that it supports. For example, if your MDI application supports both spreadsheets and text documents, the application will have two `CMultiDocTemplate` objects.

The application uses the document templates when the user creates a new document. If the application supports more than one type of document, then the framework gets the names of the supported document types from the document templates and displays them in a list in the File New dialog box. Once the user has selected a document type, the application creates a document class object, a frame window object, and a view object and attaches them to each other.

Core Note

You do not need to call any member functions of `CMultiDocTemplate` *except the constructor. The MFC framework handles* `CMultiDocTemplate` *objects internally.*

7.7   Working with Frame Windows

Throughout this chapter you have learned about documents and frames. However, as you have probably gathered already, understanding the importance of frames in a document/view application is also important, even though you will not work with the frame class(es) anywhere near as frequently as you will work with the document and view classes.

In fact, the view your application implements is a window, but not a pop-up or frame window. Instead, it is a borderless child window that doesn't have a menu of its own, so it must be contained by some sort of frame window. MFC places the view window you create into the client area of the frame window identified in the document template constructor. In an SDI application, the frame window is always the main window for the application. Similarly, the frame window for views within a multiple-document interface application is an MDI child window.

When developing a Windows application, most programmers will not take the extra step of separating the client area of their application from the frame window. Instead, you would typically create a WS_OVERLAPPED-style window and paint right in its client area. To make MFC a little more modular, Microsoft implemented it so that it makes a distinction between the two types of frame windows that you might use. That is, MFC makes both an internal and an external distinction between a single-document interface frame window and a multiple-document interface frame window. You will learn more about frame windows later, but for now, it's enough to understand that the frame window is the one that receives all of the menu and window frame messages.

7.7.1 Understanding the CMDIFrameWnd and CMDIChildWnd Classes

The CMDIFrameWnd class provides the functionality of a Windows multiple-document interface (MDI) frame window, along with member functions that you will use within your applications to manage the window. To create a useful MDI frame window for your multiple-document interface application, you must derive a class for the main frame window from CMDIFrameWnd. After you derive the class, you will add member variables to the derived class to store data specific to your application (but not data specific to an individual document). In addition, you must implement message-handler member functions and a message map in the derived class to specify what happens when messages are directed to the windows, either by the operating system or by the document template.

You can construct an MDI frame window in two ways: by calling either the Create() member function or the LoadFrame() member function of CFrameWnd(). However, before you call Create() or LoadFrame(), you must use the C++ new operator to construct the frame window object on the heap. Before calling the Create() member function, you can also use the AfxRegisterWndClass() global function to register the window class and set the icon and class styles for the frame. You should use the

`Create()` member function to pass the frame's creation parameters as immediate arguments.

On the other hand, the `LoadFrame()` member function requires fewer arguments than the `Create()` member function, and instead retrieves most of its default values from resources that you create within the project, including the frame's caption, icon, accelerator table, and menu. To be accessed by `LoadFrame()` (and loaded into the definition for the new window), all these resources must have the same resource ID (for example, the MFC default resource ID `IDR_MAINFRAME` or any other resource ID such as `IDR_PARANTFRAME`).

Core Note

Although MFC derives the `CMDIFrameWnd` *class from the* `CFrameWnd` *class, you do not need to use the* `DECLARE_DYNCREATE` *macro when you declare a frame window class that you derive from* `CMDIFrameWnd`.

Similarly, the `CMDIChildWnd` class provides the functionality of a Windows multiple-document interface (MDI) child window, along with members for managing the window. An MDI child window looks much like a typical frame window, except that the MDI child window appears inside an MDI frame window rather than on the desktop. An MDI child window does not have a menu bar of its own, but instead shares the menu of the MDI frame window. The framework automatically changes the MDI frame window's menu bar to represent the currently active MDI child window's menu bar.

To create a useful MDI child window for your application, you must derive a class from `CMDIChildWnd` (or, if you do not intend to customize the window's actions, you can simply use the default `CMDIChildWnd` class). You will then add member variables to the derived class to store data specific to the document that the child window will be associated with within the application. Furthermore, you must implement message-handler member functions and a message map in the derived class to specify what happens when messages are directed to the window (otherwise, MFC will use the `CMDI-ChildWnd` class' default handlers to respond to messages the window receives). There are three ways to construct an MDI child window:

- Directly construct it using the `Create()` member function.
- Directly construct it using the `LoadFrame()` member function.
- Indirectly construct it through a document template.

Core Note

Unlike a frame window class that you derive from the `CMDIFrameWnd`
class, a frame window class that you derive from `CMDIChildWnd` must
be declared with the `DECLARE_DYNCREATE` macro for the
`RUNTIME_CLASS` creation mechanism to work correctly.

The only time your applications will not create a view within a real frame
window is when the view is active as an embedded OLE object. The view will
still have a frame in such situations, but the frame will be very different from
the standard frame windows you have learned about.

As you have learned, an SDI application usually creates a `CFrameWnd`
instance, while an MDI application typically creates a `CMDIFrameWnd`
instance as well as one or more `CMDIChildWnd` instances. On the other
hand, if you've written a dialog-based application, the dialog is the main window and your application doesn't have any frame window.

Due to the way command dispatching works, you will find that the frame
window often acts as a catch-all for choices in your command window. In
other words, any command from a menu that isn't handled by your view will
be offered to your frame window for it to handle.

You should implement handlers, ready for any frame message, no matter
which view the user is currently working with. If you have menu choices that
should react in different ways for different views, you can implement handlers in both the frame and the view classes. The view handler will be executed if the view object is active; otherwise, the frame's handler will be called.

7.7.2 Understanding the Role of AfxGetMainWnd()

Frames act as the main window for the thread that controls your process. If
you call `AfxGetMainWnd()` at any point in your program, you can retrieve
a pointer to the `CWnd` class that your application uses as its main window. You
will need to cast that pointer to the appropriate type if you need to access any
`CFrameWnd` or `CMDIFrameWnd` specific members.

A frame window is responsible for one or two more things than just making sure your application has a menu and a sizeable frame. It also serves as an
anchor for your window's toolbar and status bar. If your application has a status bar or a toolbar, you will find code in your main frame window that creates instances of `CStatusBar` or `CToolBar`. As you might guess,
`CStatusBar` creates a status bar and `CToolBar` handles a toolbar. In most

applications, the creation of these windows is handled in the OnCreate()
member of the application's frame window.

Core Warning

*Since the C++ objects are members of the frame windows, your application
will create them at the same time that it creates the frame window object.*

If you are working with an AppWizard-produced application, the status
bar in your application will be called m_wndStatusBar and your first toolbar will be called m_wndToolBar. Note that it is your *first* toolbar that
receives this name. Your frame is completely capable of handling more than
one toolbar — in fact, MFC will layout as many toolbars as you would like.

By the way, CStatusBar and CToolBar classes are dependent on a
frame window. Using them in other types of windows (such as dialogs) is
beyond the scope of this book. Doing so is not usually something that most
programmers would do because it results in a nonstandard interface. These
two classes are not really dependent on the document/view architecture, but
they do rely on the frame window associated with the document and view
classes. The classes use the frame window to lay themselves out in your application's user interface and they keep the view informed of the area it has
available to draw in.

7.8 Understanding the Document Template Resources

As you learned previously in Section 7.5.1, the first parameter to the
CSingleDocTemplate constructor is a resource ID. The first parameter
tells the frame that the template will use what kind of resources it must have
available to complete the link. This ID identifies the resources used to supply
the frame with an accelerator table, menu, and icon. The frame window that
your application uses should have the same resources ID for each resource
type it wishes to use.

If you examine HexView.rc, you will find that there's an accelerator
table, a menu, and an icon, each with the ID of IDR_MAINFRAME that corresponds to the ID the application passes to the CSingleDocTemplate
constructor. Having exactly the same frame window resource IDs is far more

convenient than requiring the constructor for `CSingleDocTemplate` to take six or seven parameters.

The resource ID is also the ID of an entry in your application's string table. The identified string has a very special format: it's really seven strings in one, each separated by a newline (`\n`) character.

7.8.1 Considering the Document Template Lifecycle

As you might imagine, `CSingleDocTemplate` is a lightweight class — that is, it takes very little memory. You shouldn't worry about keeping document template classes lying about, even if you have dozens of them.

`CSingleDocTemplate` and `CMultiDocTemplate` are used heavily by the application frameworks. After setting them up and getting them started, your application will depend on the templates to manage the document, view, and frame windows objects — but you will no longer need to manipulate the templates directly. As you saw earlier in this chapter, your application should register all of the document templates that it will use during its `CWinApp::InitInstance()` member function. By making them public members of your application object, you can access them later on when you need to juggle documents and views.

When you think about and manipulate document templates, probably the best single perspective for you to maintain is to let MFC do the work. In other words, you should ask MFC's code in the document template object to create the view and document you need, and hook up all of the associations. In a well-designed application, you should almost never have to directly create your own views, documents, and frames. The best applications let the document template do the work.

7.8.2 Advanced Work with Templates

Now that you understand the basics of templates, it is important to think about them from the perspective of application design. The way your application works really depends on your point of view. If your users have to do a lot of work to get to a view of the data they are interested in, they'll quickly get frustrated. Worse yet, if the views your application offers do not represent information in the way your users perceive as intuitive, your application will be seen as awkward, since the users will have to spend too much time thinking about how things should work instead of actually getting work done.

Out-of-the-box application frameworks that the AppWizard produces are too good not to use for most of your applications. Even after some modification, MFC will react to your changes in ways that are generally seen by the user as intuitive and consistent with the interfaces they are used to.

If you register several different document templates, you will get the extra dialog box to allow the user to choose their document type after selecting the File menu's New option. And once you have taken advantage of this simple opportunity, you will soon find that there are several other instances where you might want your application to differ slightly from the mainstream.

7.8.3 Working with Multiple Templates

You are always allowed to use more than one template when you are running an MFC document/view application. In general, your application will create any necessary templates as it handles `CWinApp::InitInstance()`. If your application initially came from the AppWizard, you will find that the function has been coded to create and register a template for the document/view pair that your application uses by default.

If you ever need to use documents or views in any other combination, you should add code to create a template for those particular document/view pairs. Doing so will make it much easier for you to create instances of the pairs at the user's request. The `CDocTemplate`-derived object you create is just that — an object — and as such, you will need to maintain a pointer to it after you use `new` to create it. In general, you should keep these pointers to document templates as instance data in your application's `CWinApp`-derived class. If you do, you can reference them at almost any time during the application's execution.

Each template you register with the frameworks using `CWinApp::AddDocTemplate()` is kept in a linked list. MFC uses this list to find templates when the user asks to create a new document or a new view, or performs any operation that requires that the application find an appropriate document template. For example, if more than one document template exists when `CWinApp::OnFileNew()` is called, the framework presents a list box that lets the user select the template for the type of document they wish to create.

The list is managed by an internal instance of an MFC collection class called `CDocManager`. This class is an undocumented implementation feature of MFC. Understanding how it works, though, can be quite useful. The `CWinApp`-derived object in your application creates an instance of the class. `CWinApp` holds a pointer to the `CDocManager` object. It destroys the object just before your application exits, in CWinApp's destructor function. CWinApp stores this pointer in the m_pDocManager member variable. In fact, you can use this pointer at any time to gain access to the document manager.

The document manager's main importance derives from its management of that linked list of template objects. The document manager stores the list in the public m_TemplateList member. You can walk the list using code similar to the following:

```
void CSampleWinApp::IterateEveryTemplate()
{
  CDocManager* pManager = AfxGetAp()->m_pDocManager;
  if (pManager == NULL)
    return;
  POSITION pos = pManager->GetFirstDocTemplatePosition();
  while (pos != NULL) {
    // get the next template
    CDocTemplate* pTemplate =
        pManager->GetNextDocTemplate(pos);
    // you can now do work with each pointer
    DoSomething(pTemplate);
  }
}
```

One of the most interesting things you can do with the list of templates is to drive a list of all active documents. This involves a nested loop, so that for each template you find, you can loop through the documents that the template has created. To do this, you might use some code similar to the following:

```
void CSampleWinApp::IterateEveryDocument()
{
  CDocManager* pManager = AfxGetApp()->m_pdocManager;
  if (pManager == NULL)
    return;
  POSITION posTemplate =
  pManager->GetFirstDocTemplatePosition();
  while (posTemplate != NULL) {
    // get the next template
    CDocTemplate* pTemplate =
    pManager->GetNextDocTemplate(posTemplate);
    POSITION posDoc = pTemplate->GetFirstDocPosition();
    while (posDoc != NULL) {
      CYourDocument* pThisOne = (CSampleDocument*)
          GetNextDoc(posDoc);
```

```
    // do some work with each document
    pThisOne->SomefunctionCall();
  }
 }
}
```

In both of these code fragments, you will retrieve a pointer to the manager by first getting a pointer to the application object with a call to `AfxGetApp()`. Next, you will examine the `m_pDocManager` member for the pointer to the template manager. This is, actually, more than a little duplicative, because the code fragments are member functions in `CSampleWinApp`, so they're presumably members of the very object that you are obtaining with the call to `AfxGetApp()`. Instead, you could have accessed the `m_pDocManager` member directly. However, the inefficiency lets you see the use of `AfxGetApp()` to retrieve information about the running application object. More importantly, however, you have learned how to implement the code in any function of any object in your application because the code does not presume that it is running within the `CWinApp`-derived object.

The code fragments above make use of the `CDocManager` member functions `GetFirstDocTemplatePosition()` and `GetNextDocTemplate()`, which should look familiar to you, as they perform similar processing to the `GetFirstViewPosition()` and `GetNextView()` member functions of the `CDocument` class that you learned about earlier in this chapter. `GetNextDocTemplate()` is the one that does the real work — it gets a pointer of type `POSITION` to the next document. As you can see, there is also some runtime casting in the code fragments because the second program fragment must promote the pointers to plain `CDocument` objects to pointers to the `CSampleDocument` class. It would be good programming to do `IsKindOf()` tests here, or use MFC's `DYNAMIC_DOWNCAST()` macro to make sure you get what you really wanted, but the code does not do so for simplicity's sake.

7.8.4 Destroying Documents Added with the AddDocTemplate() Member Function

If you use `AddDocTemplate()` to add your new template to the list that MFC manages for you, you need not worry about deleting the template when your application closes. However, in some circumstances, you may wish to have the template hidden from the user, and it is then that you will need to make sure your template is deleted. Deleting the template object during the program's execution of the destructor function of your application's CWinApp object is too good an opportunity to miss.

When designing your applications, don't worry about keeping templates around as long as you need them — as you have learned, templates are very lightweight. As with any other object, common-sense guidelines apply. A thousand templates are probably a little much (and a coding nightmare), but adding 10 or 20 templates to an application should not be overly burdensome, provided that you need the additional templates.

7.9 Understanding and Using the CView Class

As you have learned, for every CDocument-derived class that presents a visual interface to the user, there are one or more CView-derived classes that provide the interface. The CView-derived class provides the visual presentation of the document's data and handles user interaction through the view window.

The view window, in turn, is a child of a frame window. In an SDI application, the view window is a child of the main frame window. In MDI applications, the view window is a child of the MDI child window. In addition, the frame window can be the in-place frame window during OLE in-place editing, if your application supports OLE in-place editing. A frame window, in turn, may contain several view windows (for example, through the use of splitter windows).

7.9.1 Declaring a View Class

As earlier sections of this chapter have explained in detail, you should declare all data that is part of a document as part of the document's class. With that overriding precept in mind, however, it is important to recognize that there will likely be many data elements in your applications that pertain to a specific view. More importantly, most of those data elements will be nonpersistent, meaning you will not save them as part of the document.

Suppose, for example, that you create an application that is capable of presenting the data within the document at different zoom factors. The zoom factors will be specific to each individual view, meaning that different views may use different zoom factors even when the views are presenting information from the same document.

Given these considerations, you are probably best served to declare the zoom factor as a member variable of the view class, rather than as a variable in the document class, as shown here:

```
Class CZoomView : public CView {
  protected:
    CZoomView();
    DECLARE_DYNCREATE(CZoomView)
  public:
    CZoomableDoc* GetDocument();
    WORD m_wZoomPercent:
}
```

However, much more important than any member variables representing a setting is a member variable that represents the *current selection*. The current selection is the collection of objects within the document that the user has selected for manipulation. The nature and type of manipulation that the user might perform is entirely application-dependent, but it may include such operations as clipboard cutting and copying or OLE drag-and-drop placement support.

Arguably, the easiest way to implement a current selection is to use a collection class, just as you would in the document class. For example, you might declare the collection that represents the current selection, as shown here:

```
class CSelectableView : public CView {
  // more code here
  CList <CDocItem *, CDocItem *> m_SelectList;
  //
}
```

In addition to modifying the view class declaration, you must write one or more member functions so that your view class can respond to selection activities — filling and emptying the list, and so on. However, you must also always override the OnDraw() member function. The default implementation of OnDraw() performs no processing — you absolutely have to write code that will display your document's data items (even if the view class doesn't contain member variables of its own).

For example, if you derive your document class from COleDocument and use CDocItems to maintain the document's data, your OnDraw() member function for your class will probably look similar to the following:

```
void COleCapView::OnDraw(CDC *pDC)
{
  COLECapDoc *pDoc = GetDocument();
  ASSERT_VALID (pDoc);
  POSITION posDoc = pDoc->GetStartPosition();
  while (posDoc != NULL) {
    CDocItem *pObject = pDoc->GetNextItem(posDoc);
    if (pObject->IsKindOf(RUNTIME_CLASS(CNormDocItem))) {
      ((CNormDocItem *)pObject)->Draw(pDc);
    }
    else if (pObject->
        IsKindOf(RUNTIME_CLASS(COleDocItem))) {
      ((COleDocItem *)pObject)->Draw(pDc);
    }
  else
    ASSERT(FALSE);
  }
}
```

7.9.2 Analyzing the CView Member Function

Like the CDocument class, the CView class offers a wide variety of member functions that you can use in their default form and that you can override to provide specific functionality within your applications.

Among the most commonly used member functions in the CView class is the GetDocument() member function, which returns a pointer to the document object that you have previously associated with the view. Another commonly used member function is DoPreparePrinting(). The DoPreparePrinting() function displays the Print dialog and creates a printer device context based on the user's selections within the dialog. You will learn more about the DoPreparePrinting() function in Chapter 8.

GetDocument() and DoPreparePrinting() are the only CView member functions that are overridable. You can override any of the remaining CView member functions. These member functions supplement the large number of overridable functions that the CWnd class (which is the base class for the CView class) provides. In addition, the member functions handle the vast majority of user-interface events. Trying to list all the member functions here is a futile exercise, for there are far too many of them to make it worthwhile. However, among the member functions are functions to handle keyboard, mouse, timer, system, and other messages, clipboard and MDI events, and initialization and termination messages. Your application should override the view class member functions as needed. For example, if your application lets the user click and drag the mouse to place an object in a document, you should override the CWind::OnLButtonDown member function to support that functionality. In general, you can use the ClassWizard to create the override function, and simply add the appropriate code in the section the ClassWizard marks as TODO:

```
BOOL CSampView::IsSelected(const CObjedt* pDocItem) const
{
  return (m_SelectList.Find((CDocItem *)pDocItem) != NULL);
}
```

Another important member function that most applications will override is the OnUpdate() member function. During execution, the document class's UpdateAllViews() member function calls the OnUpdate() member function for each view associated with a document each time you invoke it. The default implementation of OnUpdate() simply invalidates the entire client area of the view window (which, in turn, results in rewarding the entire client area). To improve your application's performance, you may wish to override OnUpdate() and invalidate only the areas of the view window that the application must update. For example, you might implement OnUpdate() as shown here:

```
void CSampView::OnUpdate(CView *pView,
    LPARAM 1Hint, CObject *pObj)
{
  if (1Hint==UPDATE_OBJECT)    // app-defined constant
    InvalidateRect((CAppObject *)pObj)->m_Rect);
  else
    Invalidate();
}
```

Core Note

Normally, you should not do any drawing in the OnUpdate() member function. Instead, you should draw in the view's OnDraw() member function.

If your application supports nonstandard mapping modes such as zooming or rotating, the CView class OnPrepareDC() member function acquires special significance. In this function, you will set the view window's mapping mode before the application actually draws anything onto the window. You should always be sure, in the event that you create a device context for your view window, that your application calls `OnPrepareDC()` to ensure that the application applies the proper settings to the device context.

Similarly, your applications may often need to create a device context for the sole purpose of retrieving the current mapping of the view window. For example, you might need to convert the position of a mouse-click from physical to logical coordinates within the view's `OnLButtonDown()` member function, as shown here:

```
void CSampView::OnLButtonDown(UITN nFlags, Cpoint point)
{
  CClientDC dc(this);
  OnPrepareDc(&dc);
  dc.DPtoLP(&point);
  // further processing
}
```

7.9.3 Working with Views and Messages

In addition to those messages for which MFC provides default handlers in either `CView` or its parent class, `CWnd`, a typical view class will process many other system messages. Other messages typically include command messages that represent the user's selection of a menu item, toolbar button, or other user-interface object.

Whether it is the view or the document (or in some cases, the frame) that should handle a particular message is a decision left entirely up to you. Remember, however, that the most important criteria in making the decision is the scope and the effect of the message or command on the application's processing. If the command affects the entire document or the data stored within it, you should generally handle the command in the document class (except when the command's effect is *through* a specific view, as it might be in some implementations of a cut or paste command). If the command affects only a particular view (such as setting a zoom or rotation factor), the view object affected should handle the command.

7.9.4 MFC-Derived Variants of the CView Class

In addition to the basic `CView` class, MFC provides several derived classes that serve specific purposes, and that are intended to simplify handling of complex tasks. Table 7-1 summarizes the MFC-derived `CView` classes.

Table 7-1 MFC-Derived Variations of the CView Class

Class Name	Description
CCtrlView	Supports views that are directly based on a control (such as a tree control or edit control).
CDaoRecordView	Uses dialog controls to display database records.
CEditView	Uses an edit control to provide a multiline text editor.
CFormView	Displays dialog box controls. You must base CFormView objects on dialog templates.
CHtmlView	Provides a window in which the user can browse sites on the World Wide Web, as well as folders in the local file system and on a network.
CListView	Displays a list control.
COleDBRecordView	Displays database records using dialog controls.
CRecordView	Displays database records using dialog controls.
CRichEditView	Displays a rich-text edit control.
CScrollView	Enables the use of scrollbars for the user to move through the logical data in the document.
CTreeView	Displays a tree control.

Another rarely overriden variant of the CView class is the CPreviewView class. The MFC framework uses CPreviewView to provide print preview support to your applications.

All the CView-derived classes provide member functions that are specific to the class' goal. Member functions of view classes that derive from CCtrlView encapsulate Windows messages specific to the control class they represent.

CFormView and the classes that MFC derives from it (including CDataRecordView, COleDBRecordView, and CRecordView) support Dialog Data Exchange (DDE). You can use all four of these classes in a fashion similar to how you would use CDialog-derived classes, which you learned about in Chapter 4.

7.10 Understanding Splitter Windows

In a splitter window, the window is, or can be, split into two or more scrollable panes. A splitter control (or *split box*) in the window frame next to the scrollbars lets the user adjust the relative sizes of the window panes. Each pane is a view on the same document. In dynamic splitter windows, the views are generally of the same class. In static splitter windows, the views are more often of different classes. You will implement splitter windows of both kinds with the `CSplitterWnd` class.

Dynamic splitter windows let the user split a window into multiple panes at will and then scroll different panes to see different parts of the documents. The user can also unsplit the window to remove the additional views.

Static splitter windows start with the window split into multiple panes, each with a different purpose. For example, in the Visual C++ bitmap editor, the image window shows two panes side-by-side. The left-hand pane displays an actual-size image of the bitmap. The right-hand pane displays a zoomed or magnified image of the same bitmap. The panes are separated by a *splitter bar* that the user can drag to change the relative sizes of the panes.

Until now, you've learned only about applications that present one main window for their user interface. For some applications, it's interesting or valuable to have two related sections of the application's document visible in the application. Applications that can potentially render wide ranges of information to the user are common candidates for this sort of user interface. Microsoft Excel, for example, lets you split your view of a spreadsheet and independently scroll over each pane of the window (or over an entirely different portion of the sheet in each window).

Many of the applications that you will design, such as the `PaintObj` project just presented, could easily present more information than could possibly fit on one screen. Even though the application lets the user scroll within the window, the user might be interested in seeing two sections of the window simultaneously that are too far apart to ever show in a single window on a screen. By letting the user split their view of the window, you can pack more information onto the screen in the same amount of space.

Unfortunately, painting this kind of window without MFC support is tiresome, to say the least. You have to run the paint code twice, essentially fooling it into believing that the window is smaller than it really is — transposing the coordinates painted into each half of the split. Thankfully, MFC provides a simple solution: the `CSplitterWnd` class. `CSplitterWnd` is a special window class provided by MFC to live inside your application's frame window. Before you learn how to incorporate a splitter window into the design of your application, it is valuable to quickly review the different types of splitter windows that are available.

7.10.1   Differentiating Between Splitter Windows

First, programmers will generally call the `CSplitterWnd` class, and the windows it represents, splitters, so you should be aware of the different terms. Before you implement the `CSplitterWnd` class, it is worthwhile to take some time to think a little about the way a `CSplitterWnd` is used within your application, and the semantic rules that must be true for the class to make any sense and work properly.

When a user splits a window, he or she might decide to add another pane in the window either horizontally or vertically. In other words, the splitter will have to request that another view be created to fill the area to the right or below the divider. A user can also further divide a window, requiring three new views to be created immediately. This will fill the area to the right, beneath, and to the bottom right of the existing window, illustrating the quartering effect.

The `CSplitterWnd` class is capable of doing all of this work, because it records contextual information about the document template during its own creation. This lets the splitter know what document and which view class will be referenced by the new view windows. You can develop code to have the splitter generate different views for each pane in the window, or, alternatively, you can let it generate a new instance of the same view type used in the original window. You should first decide how you would like the user to approach the splitter window in your application. You will have two general choices for your splitter windows: a dynamic splitter or a static splitter.

7.10.2   Understanding Specifics of the CSplitterWnd Class

As you have learned, you will use the `CSplitterWnd` class within your MFC applications to provide users with the functionality of a splitter window, which is a window that contains multiple panes. A *pane* is usually an application-specific object that you derive from `CView`, but it can be any `CWnd` object that has the appropriate child window ID.

You will usually embed a `CSplitterWnd` object in a parent `CFrameWnd` or `CMDIChildWnd` object. Create a `CSplitterWnd` object using the following steps:

1. Embed a `CSplitterWnd` member variable in the parent frame.
2. Override the parent frame's `CFrameWnd::OnCreateClient()` member function.
3. From within the overridden `OnCreateClient()` member function, call the `Create()` or `CreateStatic()` member function of `CSplitterWnd` (depending on the splitter window type you intend to create).

Call the `Create()` member function to create a dynamic splitter window. A dynamic splitter window typically is used to create and scroll a number of individual panes, or views, of the same document. The framework automatically creates an initial pane for the splitter; then the framework creates, resizes, and disposes of additional panes as the user operates the splitter window's controls. When you call `Create()`, you specify a minimum row height and column width that determine when the panes are too small to be fully displayed. After you call `Create()`, you can adjust these minimums by calling the `SetColumnInfo()` and `SetRowInfo()` member functions.

Also, you can use the `SetColumnInfo()` and `SetRowInfo()` member functions to set an "ideal" width for a column and "ideal" height for a row. When the framework displays a splitter window, it first displays the parent frame, and then the splitter window. The framework then lays out the panes in columns and rows according to their ideal dimensions, working from the upper-left to the lower-right corner of the splitter window's client area.

To create a static splitter window, use the `CreateStatic()` member function. The user can change only the size of the panes in a static splitter window, not their number or order. You must specifically create all the static splitter's panes when you create the static splitter. Make sure you create all the panes before the parent frame's `OnCreateClient()` member function returns, or the framework will not display the window correctly.

The `CreateStatic()` member function automatically initializes a static splitter with a minimum row height and column width of 0. After you call `Create()`, adjust these minimums (just as you would with a dynamic splitter) by calling the `SetColumnInfo()` and `SetRowInfo()` member functions.

The individual panes of a static splitter often belong to different classes. A splitter window supports special scrollbars (apart from the scrollbars that

panes may have). These scrollbars are children of the `CSplitterWnd`
object and are shared between the two panes. You create these special scrollbars when you create the splitter window. For example, a `CSplitterWnd`
that has one row, two columns, and the `WS_VSCROLL` style will display a vertical scrollbar that is shared by the two panes. When the user moves the
scrollbar, `WM_VSCROLL` messages are sent to both panes. When the panes
set the scrollbar position, the shared scrollbar is set.

When creating either kind of splitter window, you just specify the maximum number of rows and columns that the splitter will manage. For a static
splitter, panes must be created to fill all the rows and columns. For a dynamic
splitter, the framework automatically creates the first pane when the application creates the `CSplitterWnd` object.

7.10.3   Creating Dynamic Splitters

As you learned earlier in this chapter, dynamic splitters let the user split the
window at his or her leisure. An application with dynamic splitters has small
boxes: one above the vertical scrollbar and one to the left of the horizontal
scrollbar. These can be dragged to split the window in one direction or the
other. Figure 7-5 shows an application with a dynamic splitter, after the user
has split the display into four window panes.

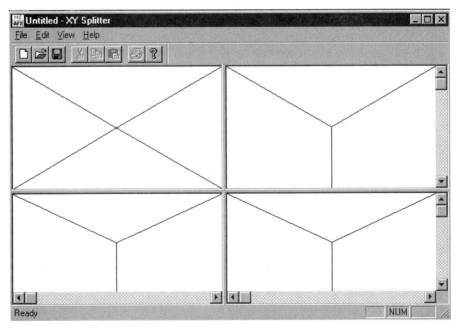

Figure 7-5   An application with dynamic splitter windows.

After dragging the box above the vertical bar down a little, the window splits and automatically creates another view: To set up this kind of splitter, you will need to declare an instance of `CSplitterWnd` in your application's frame window. For SDI applications, this would be the `CMainFrame` class, while for MDI applications, it would be within the `CMDIChildWnd` class for each view that implements dynamic splitter windows.

To initialize a dynamic splitter window, create the splitter window when the frame wants to create a client area of the frame window. Normally, the frame window will simply create the view and have it inserted into the client area of the frame, but you can have the splitter create and insert itself into the frame. The splitter will initialize a single view to populate itself, and will create more views when the user splits the window's content.

To get your frame to create the splitter, install an override of the `OnCreateClient()` function. For a dynamic splitter in an SDI application, the function just needs code similar to the following:

```
BOOL CMainFrame::OnCreateClient(LPCREATESTRUCT lpcs,
    CCreateContext* pContext)
{
    return m_wndSplitter.Create(this, 2,2,
        CSize(1,1), pContext);
}
```

The `CSplitterWnd::Create()` function accepts a few parameters. The first parameter is a pointer to the parent window of the splitter, which must be the frame. Your next two parameters are the maximum number of rows and columns that the splitter will support. You can force it to disallow horizontal splits by passing 1 for the maximum number of rows, or to avoid vertical splits by passing 1 for the maximum number of columns. Such a splitter window won't have a split box on the appropriate side of the window.

Core Note

Dynamic splitters in MFC are unable to support more than two rows and two columns. If you try to pass numbers larger than two to the `Create()` *function, MFC will* `ASSERT()` *your debug build and not compile the application.*

The value of `CSize()` that you pass to the function will cause the splitter to enforce lower size limits for the panes it creates. A size of 1 × 1, as the previous code fragment uses, effectively makes the splitter allow any window size. If, because of its content, your view has problems painting in terribly small windows, you may want to enforce a lower limit on your splitter by passing a larger `CSize()` to the creation function.

MFC won't let your user create a pane smaller than your passed `CSize()` values. It will snap the pane shut when the user lets go of the mouse while dragging a new size. Debug builds of MFC will display an appropriate warning within the debug window, such as the following:

```
Warning: split too small to create new pane.
```

Given the way all this works, with the splitter creating all of the views, there clearly must be a way for the splitter to know what view to create — and for the splitter to hook the view up to the right document. A `pContext` parameter gets passed about, from the `OnCreateClient()` parameter to the `Create()` function in `CSplitterWnd`. The `pContext` parameter points at the contextual information that tells the `CSplitterWnd` code who should handle the creation of the new view and its subsequent attachment to a document.

7.10.4 *Using Different Views in Dynamic Panes*

The code snippet from `CChildFrame::OnCreateClient()` shown in the previous section will result in a splitter that contains two instances of `CView`, registered in the document template that created the frame. You can use a different view in the extra panes of your splitter that lets you convey information in a different manner — side-by-side with information from the same document in a different view or even a different document in a different view.

When the user creates new panes in a dynamic splitter window, MFC calls the `CreateView()` member function of the `CSplitterWnd` class to perform the creation. Normally, `CreateView()` will simply create the required view, based on the context information you pass to it through the `pContext` parameter. If `pContext` is `NULL`, the function will determine what view is the currently active view and tries to create the same one.

You will need to derive your own class from `CSplitterWnd` if you want to have different views in the panes of your application's dynamic splitter window. You will have to override the `CreateView()` function, creating the view of your choice. Fortunately, the overriding code is simple — all you must do is pass the call along to `CSplitterWnd::CreateView()`, naming the `RUNTIME_CLASS` of the view class you wish to create for the splitter, as shown in the following code:

```
BOOL CMySplitterWnd::CreateView(int row, int col,
    CRuntimeClass* pViewClass, SIZE sizeInit,
    CCreateContext* pContext
{
  if (row == 0 && col == 0) {
    return CSplitterWnd::CreateView(row, col,
        pViewClass, sizeInit, pContext);
  }
  else {
    return CSplitterWnd::CreateView(row, col,
        RUNTIME_CLASS(CSecondView), sizeInit, pContext
  }
}
```

The code first checks to determine if the view is being created at row 0, column 0 in the splitter. If this is the case, the splitter is just now being initialized and you must create a view object of the class requested. If the code is indeed creating the first view for the splitter, it will create whatever view type the splitter originally wanted. But if the view is being created at a position other than the very first, the code will return the RUNTIME_CLASS() of the CSecondView class.

7.10.5 Using a CRuntimeClass Object

What the code in the previous section is doing is not necessarily very obvious because the calls to CreateView() supply a pointer to a CRuntime-Class object. A CRuntimeClass object describes the runtime type information for a class. Given this pointer, the code inside CreateView() can accomplish the construction of whatever object the runtime type information describes.

If you set a breakpoint on the CMySplitterWnd::CreateView() function and check the execution stream of an application that uses the code in the previous section, you will learn some important facts about the splitter window class. Most notably, you will find out that the splitter will destroy views that are no longer visible and recreate them later.

7.10.6 Using Splitters with Views Associated with More Than One Document

The whole process that the previous section details works fine for situations in which your new view will reference the same document as the existing views. However, if you want the second view to open another document, you have to handle the splitter's creation a bit differently. You will need to actually create the splitter and give it a different creation context. You must let it know that it must instantiate new documents and views, as well as move the view window to the correct coordinates, so that it fits with the rest of the window. Believe it or not, this last part is the most difficult portion of the process.

You can avoid doing all of this work by eliminating the call to `CSplitterWnd::CreateView()`. Instead, develop your own creation context to pass along to the `CreateView()` function, which lets it know exactly what it needs to do.

The `pContext` parameter is a pointer to a `CCreateContext` object. The `CCreateContext` object records which frame, object, and document should be used for the newly created document/view pair. The following code fragment builds its own `CCreateContext` object called `ctxSample1`. The object is initialized to have the view, document, and template information that the application should create in the new splitter panel:

```
BOOL CYourSplitterWnd::CreateView(int row, int col,
    CRun_timeClass* pViewClass, SIZE sizeInit,
    CCreateContext* pContext)
{
  CCreateContext ctxSample1;
  //if there is no active view, ASSERT
  CView* pOldView = (CView*)GetActivePane();
  ASSERT(pOldView == NULL);
  // you should test pOldView here and do something
  // reasonable with it. In this fragment, we
  // simply find out where the old view is
  ctxSample1.m_pLastView = pOldView;
  ctxSample1.m_pCurrentDoc = pOldView->GetDocument();
  ctxSample1.m_pNewDocTemplate =
  m_pCurrentDoc->GetDocTemplate()
  // pass call along
  return CSplitterWnd::CreateView(row, col,
  pOldView->GetRun_timeClass(),
  sizeInit, &ctxSample1);
}
```

7.11   Using Static Splitters

You should use static splitters in applications in which dynamic splitters are inadequate or inappropriate. Static splitters can be used when your application needs to show more than two split rows or two split columns. If you are interested in having your window split (no matter what column or row count), but refuse to allow the user to select how and where the splits should occur, you should use a static splitter instead of a dynamic splitter, because it's easier to code what you need using splitters than it is to write code to negate the actions of MFC.

Static splitters still use the CSplitterWnd class, but require a slightly different creation mechanism. You will still put a CCreateWnd instance in the CFrameWnd or CMDIChildWnd derivative of your application, but your override of the OnCreateClient() function will contain quite different code.

7.11.1 Creating a Static Splitter

To begin with, you should call CSpliterWnd::CreateStatic() instead of CSplitterWnd::Create(). The CreateStatic() function still creates and wires up the splitter, but you will need to create the content for the individual panes yourself. If you do not, MFC will ASSERT the application and stop its execution immediately. To create the pane, call CreateView() on the CSplitterWnd object you are using. You will need to make one CSplitterWnd call for each splitter pane you add. For example, code to create a static splitter with five rows and three columns, would look similar to the following:

```
BOOL CMAinFrame::OnCreateClient(LPCREATESTRUCT /*lpcs*/,
    CCreateContext* pContext)
{
  BOOL bRet;
  int nRow;
  int nCol;

  if(!m_wndSplitter.CreateStatic(this, 5,3))
    return FALSE;
  for (nRow = 0; nRow < 5; nRow++)
    for (nCol = 0; nCol < 3; nCol++) {
      bRet = m_wndSplitter.CreateView(nRow, nCol,
          RUN TIME_CLASS(CStaticSplitView),
          CSize(50,30), pContext;
      if (bRet == FALSE)
        return FALSE;
    }
  return_TRUE;
}
```

If you wanted to have different views in each pane, you would write the function's code to pass different RUNTIME_CLASS() information for each CreateView() call.

This chapter outlines ways to manually add a splitter window to your application mainly because a splitter window is most often an afterthought. If you are starting from scratch, you can check the Use Splitter Window in your application's MDI Child Frame or Frame Window page. You can reach this checkbox by pressing the Advanced... button in step four of the AppWizard request for information, as shown in Figure 7-6.

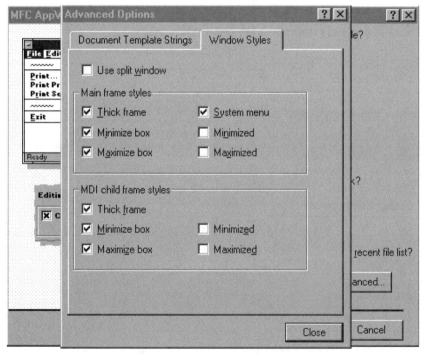

Figure 7-6   Creating splitter windows within the AppWizard.

7.11.2 *Understanding Shared Scrollbars*

The CSplitterWnd class also supports shared scrollbars. These scrollbar controls are children of the CSplitterWnd and are shared with the different panes in the splitter. For example, in a 1 row × 2 column window, you can specify WS_VSCROLL when creating the CSplitterWnd. A special scrollbar control will be created that is shared between the two panes, as shown in Figure 7-7.

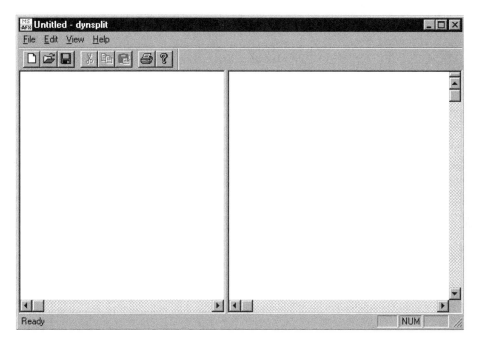

Figure 7-7   The splitter windows share a single scrollbar.

When the user moves the scrollbar, the framework will send WM_VSCROLL messages to both views. When the views set the scrollbar position, the shared scrollbar will be set.

Core Note

Shared scrollbars are most useful with dynamic or static splits that display two view objects of the same class within their different panes. If you mix views of different types in a splitter, then you may have to write special code to coordinate their scroll positions. Any CView-derived class that uses the CWnd scrollbar APIs will delegate to the shared scrollbar if it exists. The CScrollView implementation is one such example of a CView class that supports shared scrollbars. Non-CView-derived classes, classes that rely on noncontrol scrollbars, or classes that use standard Windows implementations (for example, CEditView) will not work with the shared scrollbar feature of CSplitterWnd.

7.11.3 Determining Actual and Ideal Sizes

The layout of the panes in the splitter window depends on the size of the containing frame window (which in turn resizes the `CSplitterWnd`). `CSplitterWnd` will reposition and resize the panes within the containing frame so that they fit as ideally as possible.

The row height and column width sizes set by the user, or that the application sets through the `CSplitterWnd` API calls, represent the ideal size. The actual size can be smaller than that ideal size (if there is not enough room to make that pane the ideal size) or larger than the ideal size (if that pane must be made larger to fill the leftover space on the right or bottom of the splitter window).

7.11.4 Understanding Performance Issues with Splitters

Splitters make it easy to divide the client area of your frame or MDI children to make the frame hold more than one view. However, this means that your view's painting code will be called many more times than before the split. Your view window will necessarily be smaller than it was before you adopted a splitter window, so you need to make sure your view does not do any drawing that is not absolutely necessary. Specifically, your view should not do any drawing beyond the bounds of the window. Limiting your drawing in such a manner will help ensure the greatest possible performance for your application.

Limiting the amount of redrawing that views must do is by far the most important consideration for applications that paint their views repeatedly in the different panes of a splitter window.

The likelihood that one view will change when another visible view must update its content for the same document is also much more likely when you are working with splitter windows. You should think about the different views in your application and try to ensure that your `UpdateAllViews()` or `UpdateView()` calls pass enough information to the updating view, thus ensuring that it can do the smallest amount of repainting required.

7.12 Using MFC to Subclass Windows

As you might expect, MFC provides an easy way for you to subclass any window that you derive from a `CWnd`-derived object. Rather than making the call to `SetWindowLong()`, you can simply invoke the `Subclasswindow()`

member function. Much as you would use SetWindowLong() with an API-created window, you call the Subclasswindow() member function to dynamically subclass a window and attach it to the CWnd object calling the member function. You must pass the window handle (HWND) of the window to subclass to the SubclassWindow() member function, which, in turn, will return a BOOL value that represents whether the subclassing was successful. When you dynamically subclass a window, windows messages will route through the CWnd's class first. Messages that are passed to the base class will be passed to the default message handler in the window.

On the side of the window being subclassed, the SubclassWindow() member function attaches the Windows control or window to a CWnd object and replaces the subclassed window's WndProc() and AfxWndProc() functions. The function stores the old WndProc() function in the location returned by the GetSuperWndProcAddr() member function. You must override the GetSuperWndProcAddr() member function for every unique window class to provide a place to store the old WndProc() function. You might subclass an existing edit control in a dialog box with a code similar to that shown in the following listing:

```
BOOL CSubbedDlg::OnInitDialog()
{
   ...Other initialization stuff

   // grab a pointer to the edit control
   CWnd* pEdit;
   pEdit = GetDlgItem(IDC_SSN);
   ASSERT(pEdit != NULL);

   // make the control use the system fixed-width font
   // because with numbers and dashed, it will look nicer

   HFONT hFont = (HFONT)
      ::GetStockObject(SYSTEM_FIXED_FONT);
   CFONT* pfont =:Cfont::FromHandle(hFont);
   pEdit->SetFont(pFont);

   // subclass the edit control so it is connected to the
   // custom CSubbedEdit class.
   m_Subbed.SubclassWindow(pEdit->m_hWnd);
   return_TRUE; // return TRUE unless you
             // set the focus to a control
}
```

From the point when this code is executed, the messages sent to the IDC_SSN control are offered first to the m_Subbed object, an instance of the CSubbedEdit class. CSubbedEdit is a class that subclasses (in the C++ way) from the MFC CEdit class. Since, after the SubclassWindow() call, the CSubbedEdit class is now an actual MFC window, it will start to receive messages via the CCmdTarget instance inside the CEdit class. You can perform the edits using ClassWizard to create message map entries for WM_CHAR and WM_KEYUP and to code whatever validation you need in response to those messages.

You can see that the CSubbedEdit class is a member of the application's dialog class. When the dialog initializes, the SubclassWindow() call is made against the social security number (IDC_SSN). The program code never does anything to undo the subclassing because the functionality is disconnected when the dialog window is closed.

One additional possibility would be to use a local instance of the CSubbedEdit class and call SubclassWindow() on that. This usually isn't acceptable, since the CSubbedEdit instance has to outlive the control that it subclasses. Locally declaring a subclassing MFC class to a function is almost worthless because there are very few functions that continue to run while messages are being dispatched. The subclassing code would never be installed while messages were being received.

When you want to return the subclassed window to its original state, you should call the CWnd::UnsubclassWindow() member function to unsubclass the window. The UnsubclassWindow() member function returns a window handle to the newly detached window.

7.13 Alternatives to the Document/View Architecture

While the document/view model is a good default and useful in many applications, some applications need to bypass it. The point of the document/view architecture is to separate data from viewing. In most cases, this simplifies your application and reduces redundant code. As an example of when this is not the case, consider porting an application written in C for Windows. If your original code already mixes data management with data viewing, moving the code to the document/view model is harder because you must separate the two. You might prefer to leave the code as it is. There are many approaches to bypassing the document/view architecture, of which the following are only a few:

- Treat the document as an unused appendage and implement your data management code in the view class. Overhead for the document is relatively low, as described below.

- Treat both document and view as unused appendages. Put your data management and drawing code in the frame window rather than the view. This is close to the C language programming model.

- Override the parts of the MFC framework that create the document and view to eliminate creating them at all. As you have learned, the document creation process begins with a call to `CWinApp::AddDocTemplate()`. Eliminate that call from your application class's `InitInstance()` member function and, instead, create a frame window in `InitInstance()` yourself. Put your data management code in your frame window class. This is more work and requires a deeper understanding of the framework, but it frees you entirely of the document/view overhead.

7.14 Summary

Most MFC applications are based on the *document/view model*. The document, an abstract object, represents the application's data and typically corresponds to the contents of a file. The view, in turn, provides presentation of the data and accepts user-interface events. The relationship between documents and views is one-to-many: a document may (and generally will) support several associated views, but a view is always associated with exactly one document.

Your applications will derive their document classes from the MFC-provided CDocument class. The CDocument class encapsulates much of the basic functionality of a document object. In the simplest case, applications need add only member variables that represent application-specific data and provide overrides for the `OnNewDocument()` (for initialization) and `Serialize()` (for saving and loading data) member functions to obtain a fully functional document class.

More sophisticated applications will generally rely on collection classes to implement the set of objects that comprise a document. In particular, applications can use the `COleDocument` class and rely on its capability to manage a list of `CDocItem` objects that MFC does not restrict to OLE client and server objects.

You will derive view classes from the MFC `CView` base class. View windows that `CView` objects represent are child windows. In an SDI project, the parent window is the main frame window; in an MDI project, the parent window is the controlling MDI child window.

A view object, in addition to containing member variables that represent view-specific settings (such as zoom and rotation settings), often implements a current selection. The current selection is the set of document objects that the user has designated or selected within the current view for further manipulation. As with documents, most complex applications will use collection classes to manage the current selection.

While a view class may, and generally will, override many member functions of the `CView` class from which it derives, every view class must override the `OnDraw()` member function. For OLE applications, you must also override the `IsSelected()` member function. In addition, you will generally override `OnUpdate()` and `OnPrepareDC()` within your applications.

Beyond `CView` implementations that you may derive, MFC provides several derivatives of the `CView` class that you may use within your applications to handle scrolling views, views based on dialogs, controls, and views representing database records. When you design your application, you should be sure to select the class most appropriate to your application as the base class for your view class.

You've also learned about splitter windows, a powerful tool for effectively using the limited "real estate" that users will grant your applications on their desktop. Effective splitter window use lets you increase and manage not only how much information you can present to your users within your application, but how you present the information.

Finally, you learned about subclassing windows, which lets you instruct the operating system and your application as to what windows should process messages, and how to respond when the user clicks certain windows. You learned that subclassing windows, while relatively simple from the Windows API, is very easy within MFC, and that the `CWnd` class from which you will derive most windows includes the `SubclassWindow()` and `UnsubclassWindow()` member functions.

In Chapter 8, you will go one step farther with your documents and views and learn how to add printing support to your applications, how to manage the MFC printing process, and how to generate attractive output from within your applications. In the next chapter, you will work with callback functions and messages to help you better understand how the operating system communicates with your application, independent of how you implement your application's interface.

PRINTING OUTPUT AFTER YOU CREATE IT

Topics in this Chapter

- Windows API Printer Support
- Printing with MFC
- Understanding Printer Pages Versus Document Pages
- Understanding the Print Preview Architecture
- Understanding the CPrintDialog Class
- Summary

Chapter 8

As you develop applications, you will find that most require some type of physical output — a permanent record of what the user has done. Generating and managing printing in your applications is a relatively simple process. Much of what you have already learned about Graphics Device Interface (GDI) management applies to printing; printers are merely a different type of device than a screen. In other words, sending output to a printer in a Windows program is almost the same as sending output to the screen. The same functions that work with screen output also work with printer output, except that the applications use a *printer device context* instead of a *screen device context*.

8.1 Windows API Printer Support

Before Win32, Windows used printer driver messages known as *escape sequences* and the Escape() API function to communicate with the printer. For the most part, in the Win32 API, the Escape() function is obsolete. Microsoft instead replaced the Escape() function with more specific functions, such as StartDoc(), EndDoc(), StartPage(), EndPage(), and so on.

As you might expect, an application must create a device context for a printer using the CreateDC() function before the application can print to the printer. After the application acquires a device context for a printer, the application can start the printing process by calling the StartDoc() function. The StartDoc() function requires as its parameter a DOCINFO structure that describes the document that the application is about to print. After you start to print, your application must call the StartPage() function to begin each page and the EndPage() function to end each page. You can think of a page as a drawing screen. The application must complete all the drawing for each page it prints before it begins to draw on the next page. When the application finishes printing the entire document, the application should call the EndDoc() function. The following code listing shows the Print2Page() function, a simple implementation of the steps necessary to print text information to a printer:

```
void Print2Page()
{
   HDC hDC;
   PRINTINFO di;

   // create a device context for the printer
   hDC = CreateDC("WINSPOOL", "HP Laser Printer",
       NULL, NULL);

   // set up PRINTINFO
   memset(&di, sizof(PRINTINFO));
   di.cbSize = sizof(PRINTINFO);
   di.lpszDocName = "Chapter 8 Sample Document";

   // start the printing
   if(StartDoc(hDC,&di) != SP_ERROR) {
      // Print Page 1
      StartPage(hDC);
      TextOut(hDC, 10, 10, "Core Visual C++", 18);
      TextOut(hDC, 10, 10, "This is on Page 1.", 18);
      EndPage(hDC);

      // Print Page 2
      StartPage(hDC);
      TextOut(hDC, 10, 10, "Chapter 8: Printing", 18);
      TextOut(hDC, 10, 10, "This is on Page 2.", 18);
      EndPage(hDC);

      // End Printing
      EndDoc(hDC);
   }
   DeleteDC(hDC);
}
```

Clearly, this type of simple implementation is suitable only for very small print jobs. For example, in applications with larger print jobs, an application should provide a way for the user to stop a print job currently in progress. You might display a dialog box with a Cancel button to alert users to the ongoing print job and give them the opportunity to interrupt the job. You could also use threads within your application to provide background printing on your print jobs so that users can continue working without waiting for the printing process to finish. You will learn more about creating and managing threads in Chapter 9.

If an application does not use threads, you can instead use an *abort procedure* — an application-defined function that processes messages while the application is printing. To set the abort procedure within your application, call the `SetAbortProc()` API function and pass the address of the abort procedure to the function prior to starting the print job. Windows, in turn, will periodically send messages to the abort procedure during the printing process. Using the abort procedure gives the application a chance to stop printing whenever it processes a specific message or set of messages. Typically, your application should watch for the activity in question, then call the `AbortDoc()` API function to stop printing. You might implement the code for a dialog box with a Cancel button.

8.1.1 Obtaining Printer Information

Although Windows generally shields the application from direct dealings with the printer hardware, a few situations may require that your applications interact directly with the device to retrieve hardware-specific information. For example, an application may need to determine the size of the paper, the number of paper bins, the graphic capabilities, and so on, of a printer.

Windows has two functions, `DeviceCapabilities()` and `GetDeviceCaps()`, that provide the information that your application might need about a printer. The `GetDeviceCaps()` function is a general function that provides information about displays, printers, plotters, and other output devices. The function retrieves information that is common among all types of devices, such as graphics capability, resolution, number of colors, and so on. The `DeviceCapabilities()` function, on the other hand, retrieves information that is specific to printers, such as information about paper bins, duplexing capabilities, paper size, and so forth. In versions of Windows previous to the Win32 implementations, `DeviceCapabilities()` was not directly supported by the operating system, but rather was part of the printer driver. Win32 moved the function into the operating system to simplify its use during application development. The APIPrint.cpp program includes a simple implementation within the `WndProc()` window procedure that checks an attached printer to see whether it supports font substitution.

8.1.2 Understanding the Importance of Text Characteristics

When an application outputs text, the application can control several characteristics of the text with the functions the Win32 API provides, including text placement, distance between characters, text color, the background color behind the text, and so on.

Each font has different sizing characteristics that you can determine with the `GetTextMetrics()` API function. TrueType fonts also contain more information about characteristics such as *kerning pairs*. Kerning pairs are pairs of characters that, when placed together in a string, have the spacing between them adjusted to get the best appearance. You can retrieve these character combinations with the `GetKerningPairs()` function. TrueType fonts also have other characteristics that are not applicable to other fonts. You can retrieve those characteristics with the `GetOutlineTextMetrics()` function.

When you scale and use fonts in an application, it is important that you understand the system of measurements that printers use to describe a character. Figure 8-1 shows two sample characters and the names of the measurements printers use to describe the characters.

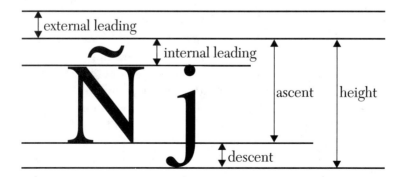

Figure 8-1   The measurements and metrics that you will use when you consider text characters.

8.2 Printing with MFC

After everything you have learned thus far in this text, it should not be surprising that Visual C++ 6.0 provides a set of MFC wrappers that you can use within your programs to support printing and device output. As you know, Microsoft Windows implements device-independent display. In MFC, this means that the same drawing calls, in the OnDraw() member function of your view class, are responsible for drawing on the display and on other devices, such as printers. For print preview, the target device is a simulated printer output to the display.

8.2.1 Understanding Your Role and the Framework's Role in Printing

Because you are using MFC wrapper classes, your responsibilities when programming MFC applications are not quite as broad as they are when you write printing code within a Windows program that does not use MFC. Specifically, it is your responsibility to ensure that your view class performs the following tasks:

- Inform the framework how many pages are in the document.
- When asked to print a specified page, draw that portion of the document.
- Allocate and deallocate any fonts or other graphics device interface (GDI) resources needed for printing.
- If necessary, send any escape codes needed to change the printer mode before printing a given page (for example, to change the printing orientation on a per-page basis).

The MFC framework, in turn, will handle the following tasks that are necessary for printing:

- Display the Print dialog box.
- Create a CDC object corresponding to the printer.
- Call the StartDoc() and EndDoc() member functions of the CDC object.
- Repeatedly call the StartPage() member function of the CDC object, inform the view class which page should be printed, and call the EndPage() member function of the CDC object.
- Call overridable functions in the view at the appropriate times.

The remainder of this chapter discusses how your programs should work with the MFC framework to support printing and print preview.

8.2.2 Understanding the MFC Printing Sequence

As you will learn later in this chapter, you will find that you often override member functions in the `CView`-derived class(es) of your applications to correctly support printing from those classes. You will generally overload, at a minimum, three member functions to support printing within your class — `OnDraw()`, `OnBeginPrinting()`, and `OnPrepareDC()`. These functions are critically important to the printing and print preview process. However, there are also other functions that enable you to add even more printing power to your applications. The functions important to the printing process are listed in Table 8-1, along with a brief description of each.

Table 8-1 Printing Functions of a View Class

Function	*Description*
`OnBeginPrinting()`	Override this function to create resources, such as fonts, that you need for printing the document. You can also set the maximum page count here.
`OnDraw()`	This function serves triple duty, displaying data in a frame window, a print preview window, or on the printer, depending on the device context sent as the function's parameter.
`OnEndPrinting()`	Override this function to release resources created in `OnBeginPrinting()`.
`OnPrepareDC()`	Override this function to modify the device context that is used to display or print the document. You can, for example, handle pagination here.
`OnPreparePrinting()`	Override this function to provide a maximum page count for the document. If you don't set the page count here, set it in `OnBeginPrinting()`.
`OnPrint()`	Override this function to provide additional printing services, such as printing headers and footers, not provided in `OnDraw()`.

To print a document, MFC calls the functions Table 8-1 lists in a specific order. First it calls `OnPreparePrinting()`, which simply calls `DoPreparePrinting()`. `DoPreparePrinting()`, in turn, is responsible for displaying the Print dialog box and creating the printer DC. The AppWizard implements the `OnPreparePrinting()` function as shown here:

```
BOOL CPrint1View::OnPreparePrinting(CPrintInfo* pInfo)
{
    // default preparation
    return DoPreparePrinting(pInfo);
}
```

As you can see, `OnPreparePrinting()` receives as a parameter a pointer to a `CPrintInfo` object. Using this object, you can obtain information about the print job as well as initialize attributes, such as the maximum page number. You can get all the information you will ever need about the members of the `CPrintInfo` class from the Visual C++ Help File.

When the `DoPreparePrinting()` function displays the Print dialog box, the user can set the value of many of the data members of the `CPrintInfo` class. Your program then can use or set any of these values. Usually, you will at least call `SetMaxPage()`, which sets the document's maximum page number, before `DoPreparePrinting()` so that the maximum page number displays in the Print dialog box. If you cannot determine the number of pages until you calculate a page length based on the selected printer, you have to wait until you have a printer DC for the printer.

After `OnPreparePrinting()`, MFC calls the `OnBeginPrinting()` member function, which is not only another place within which you can set the maximum page count, but also the function in which you should create resources, such as fonts, that you need to complete the print job. The `OnPreparePrinting()` member function receives as parameters a pointer to the printer DC and a pointer to the associated `CPrintInfo` object.

Next, MFC calls the `OnPrepareDC()` member function for the first page in the document. The call to `OnPrepareDC()` is the beginning of a print loop that the framework will execute once for each page in the document. `OnPrepareDC()` is the function in which you should control what part of the whole document prints on the current page. As you will learn, you handle this task by setting the document's viewport origin.

After `OnPrepareDC()`, MFC calls `OnPrint()` to print the actual page. Normally, `OnPrint()` calls `OnDraw()` with the printer DC, which automatically directs `OnDraw()`'s output to the printer rather than to the screen. You can override `OnPrint()` to control how the application and the framework print the document. You can print headers and footers in `OnPrint()` and then call the base class' version (which in turn calls `OnDraw()`) to print the body of the document, as shown here:

```
void CPrint1View::OnPrint(CDC* pDC, CPrintInfo* pInfo)
{
    // Call local functions to print a header and footer.
    PrintHeader();
    PrintFooter();
    CView::OnPrint(pDC, pInfo);
}
```

To prevent the base class version from overwriting your header and footer area, restrict the printable area by setting the `m_rectDraw` member of the `CPrintInfo` object to a rectangle that does not overlap the header or footer. You will learn more about printing headers and footers later in this chapter.

Alternately, you can remove `OnDraw()` from the print loop entirely by doing your own printing in `OnPrint()` and not calling `OnDraw()` at all, as shown here:

```
void CPrint1View::OnPrint(CDC* pDC, CPrintInfo* pInfo)
{
    // Call local functions to print a header and footer.
    PrintHeader();
    PrintFooter();
    // Call a local function to print the body
    // of the document.
    PrintDocument();
}
```

As long as there are more pages to print, MFC continues to call `OnPrepareDC()` and `OnPrint()` for each page in the document. After the last page is printed, MFC calls `OnEndPrinting()`, in which you can destroy any resources you created in `OnBeginPrinting()`. Figure 8-2 summarizes the entire printing process.

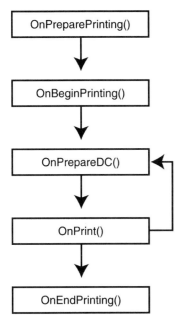

Figure 8-2   The MFC printing process uses a specific series of steps when printing any document type.

8.2.3 *Further Insight into MFC Default Printing*

As you learned in Chapter 7, in MFC applications the view class has a member function named OnDraw() that contains all the drawing code for that view. OnDraw() takes a pointer to a CDC object as a parameter. That CDC object represents the device context to receive the image produced by OnDraw(). When the window displaying the document receives a WM_PAINT message, the framework calls OnDraw() and passes it a device context for the screen (specifically, a CPaintDC object). Accordingly, OnDraw()'s output goes to the screen.

As you have learned, sending output to the printer is similar to sending output to the screen, because the Windows GDI is hardware-independent. You can use the same GDI functions for screen display or for printing simply by using the appropriate device context. If the CDC object that OnDraw() receives represents the printer, OnDraw()'s output goes to the printer.

The simplicity of passing a slightly different object into OnDraw() explains how MFC applications can perform simple printing without requiring extra effort on your part. The framework takes care of displaying the Print dialog box and creating a device context for the printer. When the user selects the Print command from the File menu, the view passes the default printer's device context to `OnDraw()`, which draws the document on the printer.

However, there are some significant differences between printing and screen display. When you print, you have to divide the document into distinct pages and display them one at a time, rather than display whatever portion is visible in a window. As a corollary, you have to be aware of the size of the paper (whether it's letter size, legal size, or an envelope). You may want to print in different orientations, such as landscape or portrait mode. The Microsoft Foundation Class Library cannot predict how your application will handle these issues, so it provides a protocol for you to add these capabilities.

8.2.4 The Printing Protocol

To print a multipage document, the framework and view interact in the following manner. First the framework displays the Print dialog box, creates a device context for the printer, and calls the `StartDoc()` member function of the `CDC` object. Then, for each page of the document, the framework calls the `StartPage()` member function of the `CDC` object, instructs the view object to print the page, and calls the `EndPage()` member function. If the printer mode must be changed before starting a particular page, the view object sends the appropriate escape code by calling the `Escape()` member function of the `CDC` object. When the entire document has been printed, the framework calls the `EndDoc()` member function.

8.2.5 Overriding View Class Functions and Pagination

The `CView` class defines several member functions that are called by the framework during printing. By overriding these functions in your view class, you provide the connections between the framework's printing logic and your view class' printing logic. You can do printing-related processing in other functions as well, but these functions are the ones that drive the printing process.

As you learned earlier in this chapter, the framework stores much of the information about a print job in a `CPrintInfo` structure. Several of the values in `CPrintInfo` pertain to pagination. Page numbers start at 1, that is, the first page is numbered 1, not 0. For more information about other members of the `CPrintInfo` class not explained in detail within this chapter, see the Class Library Reference.

At the beginning of the printing process, the framework calls the view's `OnPreparePrinting()` member function, passing a pointer to a `CPrintInfo` structure. As you learned, AppWizard provides an implementation of `OnPreparePrinting()` that calls `DoPreparePrinting()`, another member function of `CView`. `DoPreparePrinting()` is the function that displays the Print dialog box and creates a printer device context.

At the time of the call to `OnPreparePrinting()`, the application does not yet know how many pages are in the document. It uses the default values 1 and 0xFFFF (32767) for the numbers of the first and last page of the document. If you know how many pages your document has, override `OnPreparePrinting()` and call `SetMaxPage` for the `CPrintInfo` structure before you send it to `DoPreparePrinting()`. Setting the maximum page number lets you specify the length of your document.

`DoPreparePrinting()` then displays the Print dialog box. When the user exits the Print dialog box, the `CPrintInfo` structure contains the values the user specified within the dialog box. If the user wishes to print only a selected range of pages, he or she can specify the starting and ending page numbers in the Print dialog box. The framework retrieves these values using the `GetFromPage()` and `GetToPage()` functions of the `CPrintInfo` class. If the user doesn't specify a page range, the framework calls `GetMinPage()` and `GetMaxPage()` and uses the values returned to print the entire document.

For each page of a document to be printed, the framework calls two member functions in your view class, `OnPrepareDC()` and `OnPrint()`. The framework passes each function two parameters, a pointer to a `CDC` object and a pointer to a `CPrintInfo` structure. Each time the framework calls `OnPrepareDC()` and `OnPrint()`, it passes a different value in the `m_nCurPage` member of the `CPrintInfo` structure. In this way the framework tells the view which page should be printed.

The `OnPrepareDC()` member function is also used for screen display. It makes adjustments to the device context before drawing takes place. `OnPrepareDC()` serves a similar role in printing, but there are a couple of differences. First, the `CDC` object represents a printer device context instead of a screen device context; and second, the framework passes a `CPrintInfo` object as a second parameter. (This parameter is NULL when the framework calls `OnPrepareDC()` for screen display.) You must override the `OnPrepareDC()` member function to make adjustments to the device context based on which page is being printed. For example, you can move the viewport origin and the clipping region to ensure that the appropriate portion of the document gets printed.

The `OnPrint()` member function performs the actual printing of the page. As you have learned, the framework calls `OnDraw()` with a printer device context to perform printing. More precisely, the framework calls `OnPrint()` with a `CPrintInfo` structure and a device context, and `OnPrint()` passes the device context to `OnDraw()`. You must override `OnPrint()` to perform any rendering that should be done only during printing and not for screen display. For example, to print headers or footers (as you saw earlier, and will see more of later), you must place the header-printing code within the `OnPrint()` function rather than the `OnDraw()` function. After you place the header and footer into the printer device context, your program should then call `OnDraw()` from the program's overriden `OnDraw()` to do the rendering common to both screen display and printing.

The fact that `OnDraw()` does the rendering for both screen display and printing means that your application is a "what you see is what you get" application, commonly referred to by its acronym (WYSIWYG). However, there will be cases where you will not use a WYSIWYG application. For example, you might create a text editor that uses a bold font for printing but displays control codes to indicate bold text on the screen. In such a situation, you should use `OnDraw()` strictly for screen display. When you override the `OnPrint()` function, you should then substitute the call to `OnDraw()` with a call to a separate drawing function. That function will draw the document the way it appears on paper, using the attributes that you don't display on the screen.

8.2.6 Understanding the CPrintInfo Class

The `CPrintInfo` class stores information about a print or print preview job. The framework creates an object of `CPrintInfo` each time the Print or Print Preview command is chosen and destroys it when the command is completed. `CPrintInfo` contains information about both the print job as a whole, such as the range of pages to be printed, and the current status of the print job, such as the page currently being printed. Some information is stored in an associated `CPrintDialog` object; this object contains the values entered by the user in the Print dialog box.

A `CPrintInfo` object is passed between the framework and your view class during the printing process and is used to exchange information between the two. For example, the framework informs the view class which page of the document to print by assigning a value to the `m_nCurPage` member of `CPrintInfo`; the view class retrieves the value and performs the actual printing of the specified page.

Another example is the case in which the length of the document is not known until it is printed. In this situation, the view class tests for the end of the document each time a page is printed. When the end is reached, the view class sets the `m_bContinuePrinting` member of `CPrintInfo` to `FALSE`; this informs the framework to stop the print loop. `CPrintInfo` is used by the member functions of `CView`, as you have learned previously.

8.3 Understanding Printer Pages Versus Document Pages

When you refer to page numbers, it is sometimes necessary to distinguish between the printer's concept of a page and a document's concept of a page. From the point of view of the printer, a page is one sheet of paper. However, one sheet of paper doesn't necessarily equal one page of the document. For example, if you're printing a newsletter, where the sheets are to be folded, one sheet of paper might contain both the first and last pages of the document, side by side. Similarly, if you're printing a spreadsheet, the document doesn't consist of pages at all. Instead, one sheet of paper might contain rows 1 through 20, columns 6 through 10.

All the page numbers in the `CPrintInfo` structure refer to printer pages. The framework calls `OnPrepareDC()` and `OnPrint()` once for each sheet of paper that will pass through the printer. When you override the `OnPreparePrinting()` function to specify the length of the document, you must use printer pages. If there is a one-to-one correspondence (that is, one printer page equals one document page), then using printer pages is easy to do. If, on the other hand, document pages and printer pages do not correspond directly, you must translate between them. For example, consider printing a spreadsheet. When overriding `OnPreparePrinting()`, you must calculate how many sheets of paper will be required to print the entire spreadsheet and then use that value when calling the `SetMaxPage()` member function of `CPrintInfo`. Similarly, when overriding `OnPrepareDC()`, you must translate `m_nCurPage` into the range of rows and columns that will appear on that particular sheet and then adjust the document's viewport origin accordingly.

8.3.1 Implementing Pagination

Many of the basic applications you will design as you get used to working with printing are likely to be fairly simple applications, which support drawings or text entries, with each one fitting a single page. To illustrate pagination, you are probably best served to add a simple extension of your program that prints each screen object as a two-page document, a title page, and the drawing or text content itself.

To add pagination to a program, you will perform the following steps:

- Modify the OnPreparePrinting() member function.
- Override the default OnPrint() member function.
- Add two new helper functions: PrintTitlePage(), which prints the title page, and PrintPageHeader(), which prints a header on the actual page that contains content from the application.

You can try the code this section explains in any application you have created that supports the document/view architecture. For the code examples, the reference to the class name of CSampleView is simply to provide you with a context in which to review the code.

After you load your application, use the WizardBar to jump to the OnPreparePrinting() function definition of class CSampleView, and replace the existing comment and code with the following:

```
BOOL CSampleView::OnPreparePrinting(CPrintInfo* pInfo)
{
    BOOL bResult;
    CWinApp* pApp = AfxGetApp();

    // ask the app what the default printer is. if there
    //isn't any, punt to MFC so it will generate an error
    if (!pApp->GetPrinterDeviceDefaults(&pInfo->
        m_pPD->m_pd) ||
        pInfo->m_pPD->m_pd.hDevMode == NULL)
        return DoPreparePrinting(pInfo);

    HGLOBAL hDevMode = pInfo->m_pPD->m_pd.hDevMode;
    HGLOBAL hDevNames = pInfo->m_pPD->m_pd.hDevNames;
    DEVMODE* pDevMode = (DEVMODE*) ::GlobalLock(hDevMode);
    DEVNAMES* pDevNames =
        (DEVNAMES*)::GlobalLock(hDevNames);
```

```
LPCSTR pstrDriverName = ((LPCSTR) pDevNames)+
    pDevNames->wDriverOffset;
LPCSTR pstrDeviceName = ((LPCSTR) pDevNames)+
    pDevNames->wDeviceOffset;
LPCSTR pstrOutputPort = ((LPCSTR) pDevNames)+
    pDevNames->wOutputOffset;

CDC dcPrinter;
if (dcPrinter.CreateDC(pstrDriverName, pstrDeviceName,
    pstrOutputPort, NULL)) {
   pInfo->SetMaxPage(2);  //the document is 2 pages long
   dcPrinter.DeleteDC();
   bResult = DoPreparePrinting(pInfo);
  }
else {
   MessageBox("Could not create printer DC");
   bResult = FALSE;
  }
::GlobalUnlock(hDevMode);
::GlobalUnlock(hDevNames);
return bResult;
}
```

This function performs some pretty significant processing for your application. First, it makes sure that the user has specified a default printer. If the user has not done so, the code exits immediately by calling DoPreparePrinting() (so that MFC will, therefore, handle the error). After checking that a printer exists to design around, the program code obtains the driver name, the device name, and the output port of the printer, and tries to create a device context for the printer. If successful, the program code specifies the length of the document by calling the SetMaxPage() function for the pInfo parameter. Since, for this example, the program is specifying that all documents are two pages long, the function uses a numeric constant rather than a variable to represent the number of the last page of the document. The title page and the content page are numbered 1 and 2, respectively. In a real application, the SetMaxPage() assignment in this function is likely to be a call to another function that computes the real number of pages in the print job based on the amount of information within the document. After performing all those steps, the program code calls the DoPreparePrinting() function to display the Print dialog box and creates another device context for the printer that only DoPreparePrinting() uses.

After you override OnPreparePrinting(), you must next override the OnPrint() function. To override the OnPrint() function, use the WizardBar to open the SampleView.cpp file in the text editor. Next, click the arrow on the action button, located on the right end of WizardBar. On the menu, click Add Virtual Function. Visual Studio will display the New Virtual Override dialog box. Within the New Virtual Override dialog box, select OnPrint() from the New Virtual Functions list. Click the Add and Edit button. Visual Studio will display the OnPrint() function within the SampleView.cpp file. Replace the comments and existing code with the code the following listing contains:

```
void CHexViewView::OnPrint(CDC* pDC, CPrintInfo* pInfo)
{
    if (pInfo->m_nCurPage == 1) {
        PrintTitlePage(pDC, pInfo);
    }
    else {
        CString strHeader = GetDocument()->GetTitle();
        PrintPageHeader(pDC, pInfo, strHeader);
        /* PrintPageHeader() subtracts out from the
           pInfo->m_rectDraw the
           amount of the page used for the header. */

        pDC->SetWindowOrg(pInfo->m_rectDraw.left,
            -pInfo->m_rectDraw.top);

        // Now print the rest of the page
        OnDraw(pDC);
    }
    return;
}
```

The behavior of the OnPrint() member function depends on which of the two pages is being printed. If the title page is being printed, OnPrint() simply calls the PrintTitlePage() function and then returns. If it's the content page, OnPrint() calls PrintPageHeader() to print the header and then calls OnDraw() to do the actual drawing. Before calling OnDraw(), OnPrint() sets the window origin at the upper-left corner of the rectangle defined by m_rectDraw (which, as you will learn, was reduced in size by PrintPageHeader() to account for the size of the header). Reducing the size, as you have learned earlier in this chapter, keeps the drawing from overlapping the header.

Notice that the drawing isn't divided into multiple pages. Consequently, OnDraw() never has to display just a portion of the drawing (for example, it never has to display the section that fits on a particular page without displaying the surrounding sections). Either the title page is being printed and

`OnDraw()` isn't called at all, or else the content page is being printed and `OnDraw()` displays the entire drawing at once.

This also explains why `CSampleView` doesn't override the `OnPrepareDC()` member function — there's no need to adjust the viewport origin or clipping region depending on which page is being printed, because you are still effectively only using a single view page for the printing.

8.3.2 Adding the Helper Functions

The next step is to add the new helper functions. By using the Add Function pop-up menu command in ClassView, you can declare and define them in one step. As you learned earlier, the `PrintTitlePage()` function prints a title page, and the `PrintPageHeader()` function prints a header on the content page. To add the `PrintTitlePage()` helper function, perform the following steps:

1. In the ClassView, point to `CSampleView` and click the right mouse button.
2. From the pop-up menu, click the Add Member Function command.
3. In the Function Type box, type the return type of the function (in this case, `void`).
4. In the Function Declaration box, type the following:

   ```
   PrintTitlePage(CDC* pDC, CPrintInfo* pInfo)
   ```

5. In the Access area, select Public, and click the OK button. ClassWizard adds the declaration to the `public` section of the header file and creates a starter definition in the implementation file.
6. Expand `CSampleView` and double-click `PrintTitlePage()` to jump to the body of the definition so you can begin typing your application-specific code. Fill in the starter `PrintTitlePage()` function with the code shown in the following code fragment.

```
void CSampleView::PrintTitlePage(CDC *pDC,
    CPrintInfo *pInfo)
{
    // Prepare a font size for displaying the file name
    LOGFONT logFont;
    memset(&logFont, 0, sizeof(LOGFONT));
    logFont.lfHeight = 75;
```

```
CFont font;
CFont* pOldFont = NULL;
if (font.CreateFontIndirect(&logFont))
    pOldFont = pDC->SelectObject(&font);

// Get the file name, to be displayed on title page
CString strPageTitle = GetDocument()->GetTitle();

// Display the file name 1 inch below top of the page,
// centered horizontally
pDC->SetTextAlign(TA_CENTER);
pDC->TextOut(pInfo->m_rectDraw.right / 2, -100,
    strPageTitle);

if (pOldFont != NULL)
    pDC->SelectObject(pOldFont);
}
```

The `PrintTitlePage()` function uses m_rectDraw, which stores the usable drawing area of the page, as the rectangle in which the title should be centered. Notice that `PrintTitlePage()` declares a local `CFont` object to use when printing the title page. If you needed the font for the entire printing process, you could declare a `CFont` member variable in your view class, create the font in the `OnBeginPrinting()` member function, and destroy it in `EndPrinting()`. However, since this particular application will use the font for just the title page, the font doesn't have to exist beyond the `PrintTitlePage()` function. When the function ends, the compiler will automatically call the destructor for the local CFont object.

Now that you have added the `PrintTitlePage()` function, you must add the `PrintPageHeader()` function to the view class. To add the `PrintPageHeader()` function to the `CSampleView` class, from within ClassView, point the mouse to `CSampleView`, and click the right mouse button. From the pop-up menu, click the Add Member Function command. In the Function Type box, type the return type of the function as `void`. In the Function Declaration box, enter the following function declaration:

```
PrintPageHeader(CDC* pDC, CPrintInfo* pInfo,
    CString& strHeader)
```

In the Access area, select Public, and click the OK button. ClassWizard adds the declaration to the `public` section of the header file and creates a starter definition in the implementation file. Expand `CSampleView` and double-click `PrintPageHeader()` to jump to the body of the definition so you can begin typing your application-specific code. Fill in the starter `PrintPageHeader()` function with the code shown here:

```
void CSampleView:: PrintPageHeader(CDC* pDC,
    CPrintInfo* pInfo, CString& strHeader)
{
   // Specify left text alignment
   pDC->SetTextAlign(TA_LEFT);

   // Print a page header consisting of the name of
   // the document and a horizontal line
   pDC->TextOut(0, -25, strHeader);       // 1/4 inch down

   // Draw a line across the page, below the header
   TEXTMETRIC textMetric;
   pDC->GetTextMetrics(&textMetric);
   int y = -35 - textMetric.tmHeight;     // line 1/10th in.
                                          // below text
   pDC->MoveTo(0, y);                     // from left margin
   pDC->LineTo(pInfo->m_rectDraw.right, y);

   // Subtract from the drawing rectangle the space
   // the header uses from out of the rectangle.
   y -= 25;       // space 1/4 inch below (top of) line
   pInfo->m_rectDraw.top += y;
}
```

The `PrintPageHeader()` member function prints the name of the document at the top of the page, and then draws a horizontal line separating the header from the drawing. It adjusts the `m_rectDraw` member of the `pInfo` parameter to account for the height of the header. As you learned, the adjustments are important because the `OnPrint()` function uses this value to adjust the window origin before it calls `OnDraw()`.

8.3.3 Print-Time Pagination

In some situations, your view class may not know in advance how long the document is until it has actually been printed. For example, suppose your application isn't WYSIWYG, so a document's length on the screen doesn't correspond to its length when printed.

Such a situation can easily cause a problem when you override `OnPre-parePrinting()` for your view class. Because you don't know the length of a document, you can't pass a value to the `SetMaxPage()` function of the `CPrintInfo` structure. If the user doesn't specify a page number to stop at using the Print dialog box, the framework doesn't know when to stop the print loop. The only way to determine when to stop the print loop is to print out the document and see when it ends. Your view class must check for the end of the document while it is being printed, and then inform the framework when the end is reached.

The framework relies on your view class's OnPrepareDC() function to tell it when to stop. After each call to OnPrepareDC(), the framework checks a member of the CPrintInfo structure called m_bContinuePrinting. Its default value is TRUE. As long as it remains so, the framework continues the print loop. If it is set to FALSE, the framework stops. To perform print-time pagination, override OnPrepareDC() to check whether the end of the document has been reached, and set m_bContinuePrinting to FALSE when it has.

The default implementation of the OnPrepareDC() function sets m_bContinuePrinting to FALSE if the current page is greater than 1. This means that if the length of the document wasn't specified, the framework assumes the document is one page long. One consequence of this is that you must be careful if you call the base class version of OnPrepareDC(). Do not assume that m_bContinuePrinting will be TRUE after calling the base class version.

8.3.4 Revisiting the Printing of Headers and Footers

When you look at a document on the screen, the name of the document and your current location in the document are commonly displayed in a title bar and a status bar. When looking at a printed copy of a document, it's useful to have the name and page number shown in a header or footer. This is a common way in which even WYSIWYG programs differ in how they perform printing and screen display.

The OnPrint() member function is the appropriate place to print headers or footers because it is called for each page, and because it is called only for printing, not for screen display. You can define a separate function to print a header or footer, and pass it the printer device context from OnPrint(). You might need to adjust the window origin or extent before calling OnDraw() to avoid having the body of the page overlap the header or footer. You might also have to modify OnDraw() because the amount of the document that fits on the page could be reduced.

One way to compensate for the area taken by the header or footer is to use the m_rectDraw member of CPrintInfo. Each time a page is printed, this member is initialized with the usable area of the page. If you print a header or footer before printing the body of the page, you can reduce the size of the rectangle stored in m_rectDraw to account for the area taken by the header or footer. Then OnPrint() can refer to m_rectDraw to find out how much area remains for printing the body of the page.

You cannot print a header, or anything else, from OnPrepareDC(), because it is called before the program calls the StartPage() member function of CDC. At that point, the printer device context is considered to be at a page boundary. You can perform printing only from the OnPrint() member function.

8.3.5 Allocating GDI Resources for Printing

Suppose you need to use certain fonts, pens, or other GDI objects for printing, but not for screen display. Because of the memory such resources require, it's inefficient to allocate these objects when the application starts up. When the application isn't printing a document, that memory might be needed for other purposes. It's better to allocate them when printing begins and then delete them when printing ends.

To allocate these GDI objects, override the OnBeginPrinting() member function. This function is well suited to this purpose for two reasons: the framework calls this function once at the beginning of each print job and, unlike OnPreparePrinting(), this function has access to the CDC object representing the printer device driver. You can store these objects for use during the print job by defining member variables in your view class that point to GDI objects (for example, CFont* members, and so on).

To use the GDI objects you created, select them into the printer device context in the OnPrint() member function. If you need different GDI objects for different pages of the document, you can examine the m_nCurPage member of the CPrintInfo structure and select the GDI object accordingly. If you need a GDI object for several consecutive pages, Windows requires that you select it into the device context each time OnPrint() is called.

To deallocate these GDI objects, override the OnEndPrinting() member function. The framework calls this function at the end of each print job, giving you the opportunity to deallocate printing-specific GDI objects before the application returns to other tasks. As with every other object you create within your programs, you should be sure to add the deallocation code to the project — generally at the same time as you add the allocation code.

8.3.6 *Enlarging the Printed Image*

As you learned in previous chapters, when you specify a position for a GDI drawing function, you use logical coordinates. You have learned how CScrollView moves the origin of the logical coordinate system. You can also control the scale of this coordinate system, that is, the physical size of a logical unit. By default, GDI considers logical units to be equal to device units, meaning that 1 logical unit equals 1 pixel on the screen. This one-to-one interpretation of logical units is called the MM_TEXT mapping mode.

When AppWizard creates an application for you, the application will use the MM_TEXT mapping mode by default. That is, the application will consider a stroke that is 100 units long to be 100 pixels long. The physical size of the stroke depends on the device that displays it. For example, a device unit on a typical inkjet printer is 1/300 of an inch (while a laser printer is 1/600 of an inch), which is considerably smaller than a pixel on a typical screen. As a result, the images that AppWizard-created applications will produce on a printer are much smaller than those it displays on the screen.

To keep your applications from producing tiny images on the printer, you need a mapping mode that ensures that a drawing remains the same size no matter what device displays it. Windows provides several such mapping modes, known as metric mapping modes. In these modes, GDI considers logical units to be equal to real-world units (or metrics), such as millimeters or inches.

Core Note

When you refer to metrics and logical units when you manage printing from Windows, it is important that you recognize that you are not referring to the metric measuring system. Instead, metrics in this context refers to the measurements themselves.

8.4 Understanding the Print Preview Architecture

Print preview is somewhat different from screen display and printing because, instead of directly drawing an image on a device, the application must simulate the printer using the screen. To accommodate this, the Microsoft Foundation Class Library defines a special (generally undocumented) class derived from `CDC`, called `CPreviewDC`. All `CDC` objects contain two device contexts, but usually they are identical. In a `CPreviewDC` object, the two device contexts are different, with the first context representing the printer being simulated, and the second context representing the screen on which output is actually displayed.

8.4.1 The Print Preview Process

When the user selects the Print Preview command from the File menu, the framework creates a `CPreviewDC` object. Whenever your application performs an operation that sets a characteristic of the printer device context, the framework also performs a similar operation on the screen device context. For example, if your application selects a font for printing, the framework selects a font for screen display that simulates the printer font. Whenever your application would send output to the printer, the framework instead sends the output to the screen.

Print preview also differs from printing in the order that each draws the pages of a document. During printing, the framework continues a print loop until a certain range of pages has been rendered. During print preview, one or two pages are displayed at any time, and then the application waits; no further pages are displayed until the user responds. During print preview, the application must also respond to `WM_PAINT` messages, just as it does during ordinary screen display.

The `OnPreparePrinting()` function is called when preview mode is invoked, just as it is at the beginning of a print job. The `CPrintInfo` structure passed to the function contains several members whose values you can set to adjust certain characteristics of the print preview operation. For example, you can set the `m_nNumPreviewPages` member to specify whether you want to preview the document in one-page or two-page mode.

8.4.2 Modifying Print Preview

You can modify the behavior and appearance of print preview in a number of ways rather easily. For example, you can, among other things:

- Cause the Print Preview window to display a scrollbar for easy access to any page of the document.
- Cause print preview to maintain the user's position in the document by beginning its display at the current page.

- Cause different initialization to be performed for print preview and printing.
- Cause print preview to display page numbers in your own formats.

If you know how long the document is and call `SetMaxPage()` with the appropriate value, the framework can use this information in preview mode as well as during printing. Once the framework knows the length of the document, it can provide the Print Preview window with a scrollbar, allowing the user to page back and forth through the document in preview mode. If you haven't set the length of the document, the framework cannot position the scroll box to indicate the current position, so the framework doesn't add a scrollbar. In this case, the user must use the Next Page and Previous Page buttons on the preview window's control bar to page through the document.

For print preview, you may find it useful to assign a value to the `m_nCurPage` member of `CPrintInfo`, even though you would never do so for ordinary printing. During ordinary printing, this member carries information from the framework to your view class. This is how the framework tells the view which page should be printed.

By contrast, when print preview mode is started, the `m_nCurPage` member carries information in the opposite direction — from the view to the framework. The framework uses the value of this member to determine which page should be previewed first. The default value of this member is 1, so the first page of the document is displayed initially. You can override `OnPreparePrinting()` to set this member to the number of the page being viewed at the time the Print Preview command was invoked. This way, the application maintains the user's current position when moving from normal display mode to print preview mode.

Sometimes you may want `OnPreparePrinting()` to perform different initialization, depending on whether it is called for a print job or for print preview. You can determine this by examining the `m_bPreview` member variable in the `CPrintInfo` structure. This member is set to `TRUE` when print preview is invoked.

The `CPrintInfo` structure also contains a member named `m_strPageDesc`, which is used to format the strings displayed at the bottom of the screen in single-page and multiple-page modes. By default these strings are of the form "Page n" and "Pages n - m," but you can modify `m_strPageDesc` from within `OnPreparePrinting()` and set the strings to something more elaborate. See `CPrintInfo` in the Class Library Reference for more information.

8.4.3 *Enhancing an Application's Print Preview*

The default print preview capabilities are almost sufficient for most application's needs. To some extent, most of your application's print preview capabilities are enhanced when you enhance printing capabilities. Recall that in the override of `OnPreparePrinting()` earlier in this chapter, you called the `SetMaxPages()` function to specify the length of the application document. Specifying the application's pages, for example, lets the framework automatically add a scrollbar to the preview window.

Another enhancement you can make is to change the number of pages displayed when the user invokes the preview mode. To set the number of pages displayed in preview mode, edit the overloaded `OnPreparePrinting()` function so that it appears as shown in the following:

```
BOOL CSampleView::OnPreparePrinting(CPrintInfo* pInfo)
{
   BOOL bResult;
   CWinApp* pApp = AfxGetApp();

   // ask the app what the default printer is. if there
   //isn't any, punt to MFC so it will generate an error
   if (!pApp->GetPrinterDeviceDefaults(
       &pInfo->m_pPD->m_pd) ||
       pInfo->m_pPD->m_pd.hDevMode == NULL)
       return DoPreparePrinting(pInfo);

   HGLOBAL hDevMode = pInfo->m_pPD->m_pd.hDevMode;
   HGLOBAL hDevNames = pInfo->m_pPD->m_pd.hDevNames;
   DEVMODE* pDevMode = (DEVMODE*) ::GlobalLock(hDevMode);
   DEVNAMES* pDevNames =
       (DEVNAMES*) ::GlobalLock(hDevNames);

   LPCSTR pstrDriverName = ((LPCSTR) pDevNames)+
       pDevNames->wDriverOffset;
   LPCSTR pstrDeviceName = ((LPCSTR) pDevNames)+
       pDevNames->wDeviceOffset;
   LPCSTR pstrOutputPort = ((LPCSTR) pDevNames)+
       pDevNames->wOutputOffset;

   CDC dcPrinter;
   if (dcPrinter.CreateDC(pstrDriverName, pstrDeviceName,
       pstrOutputPort, NULL))      {
     pInfo->SetMaxPage(2);
     dcPrinter.DeleteDC();
     bResult = DoPreparePrinting(pInfo);
```

```
      /* Preview 2 pages at a time
         Set this value after calling DoPreparePrinting to
         Override value read from registry */
      pInfo->m_nNumPreviewPages = 2;
   }
  else {
    MessageBox("Could not create printer DC");
    bResult = FALSE;
  }
  ::GlobalUnlock(hDevMode);
  ::GlobalUnlock(hDevNames);
  return bResult;
}
```

The code assigns the value 2 to m_nNumPreviewPages. This causes the application to preview both pages of the document at once — the title page (page 1) and the drawing page (page 2). Note that the value for m_nNumPreviewPages must be assigned after calling DoPreparePrinting(), because DoPreparePrinting() sets m_nNumPreviewPages to the number of preview pages used the last time the program was executed; this value is stored in the application's registry entry.

8.5 Understanding the CPrintDialog Class

The CPrintDialog class encapsulates the services provided by the Windows common dialog box for printing. Common print dialog boxes provide an easy way to implement Print and Print Setup dialog boxes in a manner consistent with Windows standards.

If you wish, you can rely on the framework to handle many aspects of the printing process for your application. In this case, the framework automatically displays the Windows common dialog box for printing. You can also have the framework handle printing for your application but override the common Print dialog box with your own Print dialog box.

If you want your application to handle printing without the framework's involvement, you can use the CPrintDialog class "as is" with the constructor provided, or you can derive your own dialog class from CPrintDialog and write a constructor to suit your needs. In either case, these dialog boxes will behave like standard MFC dialog boxes because they are derived from class CCommonDialog.

To use a `CPrintDialog` object, first create the object using the `CPrintDialog` constructor. Once the dialog box has been constructed, you can set or modify any values in the `m_pd` structure to initialize the values of the dialog box's controls. The `m_pd` structure is of type `PRINTDLG`. For more information on this structure, see the Win32 SDK documentation.

If you do not supply your own handles in `m_pd` for the `hDevMode` and `hDevNames` members, be sure to call the Windows function `GlobalFree()` for these handles when you are done with the dialog box. When using the framework's Print Setup implementation provided by `CWinApp::OnFilePrint-Setup()`, you do not have to free these handles. The handles are maintained by `CWinApp` and are freed in `CWinApp`'s destructor. It is only necessary to free these handles when using `CPrintDialog` stand-alone.

After initializing the dialog box controls, call the `DoModal()` member function to display the dialog box and allow the user to select print options. `DoModal()` returns whether the user selected the OK (`IDOK`) or Cancel (`IDCANCEL`) button.

If `DoModal()` returns `IDOK`, you can use one of `CPrintDialog`'s member functions to retrieve the information input by the user. The `CPrintDialog::GetDefaults()` member function is useful for retrieving the current printer defaults without displaying a dialog box. This member function requires no user interaction.

You can use the Windows `CommDlgExtendedError` function to determine whether an error occurred during initialization of the dialog box and to learn more about the error. For more information on this function, see the Win32 SDK documentation.

`CPrintDialog` relies on the commdlg.dll file that ships with Windows versions 3.1 and later. To customize the dialog box, derive a class from `CPrintDialog`, provide a custom dialog template, and add a message map to process the notification messages from the extended controls. Any unprocessed messages should be passed on to the base class. Customizing the hook function is not required.

To process the same message differently depending on whether the dialog box is Print or Print Setup, you must derive a class for each dialog box. You must also override the Windows `AttachOnSetup()` function, which handles the creation of a new dialog box when the Print Setup button is selected within a Print dialog box. For more information on using `CPrintDialog`, see Common Dialog Classes in Visual C++ Programmer's Guide.

8.6   Summary

Most applications that you create, whether you use MFC or the Windows API, require some means that you can exploit to generate printed output. The Win32 API lets you manage printers using drawing and device contexts, just as you handle screen output — though there are some considerations in working with a physical page that are different from working with a virtual (screen) page.

As you learned in this chapter, you can create printer support within your applications in two ways: through the API support functions, or through the MFC wrapper classes. If you use the API to write printer support, you will typically use the Windows API functions such as `StartDoc()`, `EndDoc()`, `StartPage()`, `EndPage()`, and so on, together with functions such as `DeviceCapabilities()` and `GetDeviceCaps()`, to manage your printing output.

If you use MFC to manage your printing, the task is somewhat easier. The MFC framework handles much of the underlying processing on your behalf, letting you focus in more on generating the output and less on placing it onto the printer page. Overriding the `OnPrint()`, `OnPreparePrinting()`, `OnDraw()`, and other functions within your view class lets you easily add significant printing functionality to your classes. MFC also lets you easily add headers and footers to your documents when printing.

You can also manipulate print preview from the same member functions, with slightly different implementations against member variables.

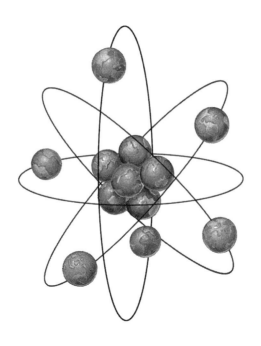

MANIPULATING THREADS AND MANAGING PROCESSES

Topics in this Chapter

- Understanding What Threads Are
- Understanding the Difference Between Processes and Threads
- Determining Applications You Should Multitask
- Creating Threads
- MFC Creation Benefits
- Understanding the Controlling Function
- Thread Synchronization
- More on Processes
- Creating a Process
- Closing on Threads and MFC
- Summary

Chapter 9

If you are not interested in writing multithreaded applications, you do not need to read this chapter. You can simply use the `CWinThread` class. However, even if you aren't of a multithreaded disposition, you might want to read the introductory sections to this chapter and skip the later details. Threads are an important part of the Win32 API and a crucial part of the system's operation as a whole.

Threads and synchronization objects are implemented on Win32 platforms like Windows 95 and Windows NT, but they are not available on Win32s. If you are planning a Win32s application, you won't be able to use threads or synchronization objects in your application.

9.1 Understanding What Threads Are

The term *thread* is shorthand for "a thread of execution." A thread represents the most fundamental information a running program needs while it is executing: a user-mode stack to hold temporary variables and return addresses for subroutines, a kernel-mode stack to hold addresses for interrupt service returns, and a set of processor registers. This information is collectively referred to as the *thread context*.

The information that the CPU needs to keep track of everything is largely stored in the CPU's registers; the registers themselves either contain information or flags, indicating the machine's current status, or they contain pointers out to that information in memory. The first important example of such a pointer is the *instruction pointer*, which lets the CPU know where in memory it will find its next instruction. The second important example is the *stack pointer*, which lets the CPU know where it can store or retrieve temporary values, such as local variables or the address of the routine that called the currently executing routine.

Since the operating system knows it needs to remember these things to switch between threads, it collects them into a thread context. The thread context, then, is everything that the CPU knows about.

A CPU doesn't know anything about switching threads, so once given a thread to execute, it will continue until the thread tells the CPU it is finished processing or until you tell it to stop processing that thread. It is the operating system that makes things seem as if there are multiple threads. It occasionally stops the CPU from working at one thread and has it start working on another. This process is buried deep in the operating system kernel in a routine known as the *scheduler*.

9.1.1 Understanding Thread Priorities

The scheduler knows which threads take precedence over others; it knows to give those threads all the time they need at the expense of the less important ones. This setup is usually referred to as the *thread priority*.

How much time the scheduler actually gives a thread is determined by a combination of the thread priority and the *process priority*. (You'll cover the differences between threads and processes a little later.) Process priorities always fall into the four categories that are listed in Table 9-1.

A thread always exists in the context of a process; Windows uses information about the process and the thread to make sure the thread gets time based both on its own needs and on the needs of the process it serves. Windows determines the thread priority, on a scale of 1 to 31, by the thread priority relative to the process priority. Tables 9-1 and 9-2 explain the rules and scores that Windows uses.

You can see that a process with `IDLE_PRIORITY_CLASS` and a thread with `THREAD_PRIORITY_IDLE` will score a 1. It will be scheduled when the operating system doesn't want to do anything else at all. It is important to understand that even the lowest thread priority does not mean that the thread will never run. If the system (or the specific processor if the program is running on a multiprocessor system) is not very busy, the thread will be scheduled to run quite often. However, the lower the thread priority, the more often every other thread with a higher priority will run.

Table 9-1 The Four Categories of Process Priorities

Process Priority Class	Base Priority Score	Description
REALTIME_PRIORITY_CLASS	24	
HIGH_PRIORITY_CLASS	13	
NORMAL_PRIORITY_CLASS	9 or 7	The value is 9 if the thread has a window in the foreground and 7 if it has a window in the background.
IDLE_PRIORITY_CLASS	4	Thread priorities, in turn, come in eight different types. The thread priority will increase or decrease the thread's priority score and is based on the base priority score. Table 9-2 lists the different types of thread priorities.

At the other extreme, your process might be running with REALTIME_PRIORITY_CLASS and your thread will have the priority THREAD_PRIORITY_TIME_CRITICAL. This nets you a priority score of 31. Windows will try to schedule your thread as often as possible — even, in some cases, to the point of starving other threads of time.

It is quite important to understand that thread priorities are designed to be used temporarily — you might create a thread that opens a few windows in response to the user. It is quite reasonable to use the CWinThread::SetThreadPriority() call to change the priority of the thread to something higher, so that the response to the user commands seems instantaneous, but after doing this, be absolutely positive that you drop down the thread priority — even in error conditions.

Table 9-2 The Eight Categories of Thread Priorities

Thread Priority	*Priority Score Adjustment*
THREAD_PRIORITY_TIME_CRITICAL	Indicates a score of 15 for IDLE_PRIORITY_CLASS, NORMAL_PRIORITY_CLASS, or HIGH_PRIORITY_CLASS processes, and a base priority level of 31 for REALTIME_PRIORITY_CLASS processes.
THREAD_PRIORITY_HIGHEST	Two above the base priority for the process.
THREAD_PRIORITY_ABOVE_NORMAL	One more than the base priority for the process.
THREAD_PRIORITY_NORMAL	Exactly the base priority score.
THREAD_PRIORITY_BELOW_NORMAL	One less than the base priority for the process.
THREAD_PRIORITY_LOWEST	Two points below the normal priority for the priority class.
THREAD_PRIORITY_IDLE	A score of 1 for IDLE_PRIORITY_CLASS, NORMAL_PRIORITY_CLASS, or HIGH_PRIORITY_CLASS processes, and a score of 16 for REALTIME_PRIORITY_CLASS processes.
THREAD_PRIORITY_ERROR_RETURN	Not used to adjust the priority score, but to indicate an error when querying a thread's priority.

If your application needs to create a couple of pop-up windows in response to a menu command, you might code a handler for that menu like this:

```
void CMyFrame::OnOpenWindows()
{
   CWinThread* pThisThread = AfxGetThread();
   pThisThread->SetThreadPriority(THREAD_PRIORITY_HIGHEST);
   m_pPopupOne = new CPopupTypeOne(this);
   m_pPopupTwo = new CPopupTypeTwo(this);
   if (m_pPopupOne->Create(/* params */) == NULL ||
```

```
    m_pPopupTwo->Create(/* params */) == NULL) {
      delete m_pPopupOne;
      delete m_pPopupTwo;
      m_pPopupOne = NULL;
      m_pPopupTwo = NULL;
    }
  else {
      m_pPopupOne->UpdateWindow();
      m_pPopupTwo->UpdateWindow();
    }
  pThisThread->SetThreadPriority(THREAD_PRIORITY_NORMAL);
  return;
}
```

As you can see, the program code uses the `AfxGetThread()` function to get a pointer to the currently running `CWinThread` object. By calling that object's `SetThreadPriority()` member, you can then raise the priority of the thread to `THREAD_PRIORITY_HIGHEST`. The program code does not use `THREAD_PRIORITY_TIME_CRITICAL` because the code's goal is simply to make the application respond quickly to the user. It is critical that all your thread manipulations recognize and respect the fact that there might be threads around which you really do need to respond to time-critical events, such as heart monitors or transmissions from a satellite.

You can assume that the two windows the program code creates are managed by the member variables `m_pPopupOne` and `m_pPopupTwo`. The code allocates the window objects and then creates them. If the creation for either window fails, the windows are deleted and the `m_pPopupOne` and `m_pPopupTwo` members are reset to `NULL` so that the program knows the windows aren't available.

After all this work, the program code calls `SetThreadPriority()` again to make the priority return to `THREAD_PRIORITY_NORMAL`. If there is a chance that the thread's priority wasn't `THREAD_PRIORITY_NORMAL` to start with, you might instead want to code a call to `GetThreadPriority()` to save the initial priority before changing it.

While it seems as if this function does almost no work, it does ensure that the initial update of the window happens at a higher priority than normal. The effects of this code will not be drastic on a system where there's not much happening, but on a system that is heavily loaded with threads that are not operating at a very high priority, the code will make the application's response to the user seem somewhat crisper.

If you are writing an application that responds to hardware or some other external event input, you might consider raising the thread priority permanently, but do this as sparingly as possible — you will be starving other threads of CPU processing.

9.1.2 Switching Contexts

When operating system developers talk about *context switching*, they are referring to the natural act of moving an operating system's execution focus from one thread to the next. The operating system must completely preserve the state of the current thread context when the operating system wants to stop executing that thread and start another.

Throughout its lifetime, each thread runs for a time and then pauses to let another one in. This starting and stopping could happen hundreds of times a second. Just as the many frames of still pictures per second in a motion picture make it seem as if you are really watching continuous action, these fast state transitions make it seem as if the threads are all running continuously and concurrently.

9.2   Understanding the Difference Between Processes and Threads

The operating system also enforces more arbitrary divisions: *processes*. At any given time, your Windows machine might be running several processes. You might be compiling a C++ program, playing Solitaire, and printing a report from your spreadsheet program while two users are connected to an SQL database on your machine, running queries or performing updates. Since these actions are all separate applications, your machine is running each one of these tasks as a separate process.

However, each one of those processes may consist of several threads (they all consist of at least one thread). The most likely candidate for a multi-threaded process in the previous example is the SQL database system. One thread in the database manager process may be servicing a user's request by reading or writing the database file while the other may be waiting for an I/O operation over the network. The process, what the user perceives as the SQL database server, owns both of those threads.

The process can dynamically create and destroy threads or the threads can decide for themselves that their work is done and terminate of their own accord. A thread must be owned by a process, even if the process in question is a part of the operating system. A thread cannot be owned by more than one process.

Processes are big. They are whole programs, or at least complete stand-alone executable images that are a part of a bigger program. They have their own private memory space, which they don't share.

Every process has at least one thread: the *primary thread*. It is created by the system when the process is loaded into memory and begins executing. This just makes sense: a process alone is just a memory image, but a thread is something that actually breathes life into that memory image and gets it to do some work. This structure is also the natural reason that `CWinApp` is a derivative of `CWinThread`.

A thread is smaller than a process because a process includes a range of logical address space that is completely dedicated to loading and running the program. One program, which might consist of several executable images including one .exe file and any number of .dll files, owns a range of memory. It is that memory range that defines the process that is running. A thread, on the other hand, doesn't own any memory besides some stack space.

As it is injected into the process, the primary thread brings with it all of the things that it needs: a stack, an instruction pointer, and an initial state for all of the registers in the CPU. Then it starts running. The first thread might start executing at `main()`, or `WinMain()`, or whatever symbol you have specified with the *Entry-point symbol:* option under the *Output Category:* on the *Link* tab of your *Project Settings* dialog when you built the application.

The primary thread might later decide to create more threads, which similarly need entry points. The Windows `::CreateThread()` API is the function used to create a new thread and get it running. It takes, among other parameters, an address for a function that will control the newly created thread. When that function returns, the thread ends.

While the threads are running, Windows is starting and stopping them to give the illusion that they are running at the same time. If a thread is stopped, it is said to be suspended.

Some people call the act of making a suspended thread run releasing the thread. If you have more than one CPU in your machine, the illusion fades and the threads really are running at the same time. One CPU might run Thread A, while the other might run Thread B. Windows might decide to suspend Thread A for a moment to let Thread C run on CPU number one, but can still let Thread B continue running on the second CPU.

From your perspective, your thread and all the others will get execution time almost arbitrarily from the operating system. They'll get time as often as their priority warrants when compared to other running threads, but there's very little way to predict exactly when your thread will execute.

To stop executing, a thread can call the `::Sleep()` API function if it realizes that it has no useful work to do and wishes to relinquish the rest of its time slice to other threads on the system. This API takes a single parameter: an integer that specifies the minimum number of milliseconds that the thread will rest. Remember that the number specifies a minimum number of milliseconds; the operating system might not necessarily schedule your thread to run again in exactly one second if you insert a `::Sleep(1000)` function call into your program.

9.3   Determining Applications You Should Multitask

If you consider it for awhile, you might wonder what the point is of using multiple threads. After all, it is not as if two things are really happening at once, and going through a lot of hoops to let the operating system pretend that two things can happen at once is more trouble than it is worth in many cases. In fact, there usually is no real reason to write a multithreaded application.

In fact, multithreaded applications have additional performance bottlenecks. The operating system has to take some amount of time to switch from thread to thread — you cannot get away from that. There are also a few things to worry about when you are trying to communicate between threads. So unless you really need the extra threads, there is really no point in creating multithreaded programs. You are, in most cases, slowing down your application and making additional work for yourself. That being said, there are certain situations when multithreaded applications are worthwhile or even necessary.

9.3.1 Specific Times When You Should Not Multitask

When you are adding threads to your application, there are lots of issues that you might not consider. For instance, you should be aware that threads often stall because of Windows APIs. If you were to think about the function of the API, you'd realize the problem immediately, but nobody, even experienced Windows programmers, is too caught up in thinking about problems from this angle.

There are samples and other writings that imply that it is a great idea to create one thread per window for your applications. This can be good in a few select cases, but is generally a pretty bad idea. MDI applications manage a frame window, a client area window, and a child window for each open document. These windows frequently send messages from one to the next. The `::SendMessage()` API function, which these windows use internally, causes the thread sending the message to stall until the receiving thread can get the message, process it, and return.

This adds a great deal of overhead. The sending window must stop executing and the scheduler must get around to starting up the receiving thread before the application can continue. In other words, using one thread per window introduces extra overhead just because it uses multiple threads. It would be a better idea to let the windows all run with one thread.

9.3.2 Threads and Message Loops

There are some very important relationships between a thread and a message loop that you should understand. A *message loop*, as you learned in Chapter 8, is a loop that retrieves messages from the thread's message queue and dispatches them to the appropriate function. MFC replaces much of that mechanism with code that efficiently dispatches the messages to the appropriate C++ object's member function for handling.

The message loop is just code in a loop that runs throughout the application's lifetime. The message loop needs a thread to be running. Each thread has its own message queue, so it must have its own message loop. If the thread stalls, no messages for that thread are retrieved or processed. They keep piling up until the message queue overflows (which can take a long time under Win32). If you have a worker thread that doesn't have any windows, it might not be sent any messages, so it is quite normal not to endow the thread with a message loop. However, if you have a user-interface thread, you must give it a message loop so that it can handle messages sent to windows that it owns.

This introduces a very important concept: any window that your application (or any other application) creates is owned by some particular thread. Only that thread can retrieve messages for the window. It might ask another thread to do work in response to the message, but no thread can retrieve messages sent to a window that it doesn't own.

A thread can, though, receive messages directly, even if that thread doesn't have any windows. You can do this using the `::PostThreadMessage()` API function. In addition to the regular message parameters (that is, the message number and its `WPARAM` and `LPARAM` parameters), the API takes the thread ID to which you are sending the message (instead of the handle of the destination window).

9.3.3 Times When You Should Use Multithreading

A great time to consider using a thread is when you have lots of work to do, but you also need to keep an eye on some external event, piece of hardware, or the user.

If you are writing a communications program, for example, you might have a few applications for threads. You might let the primary thread for your application handle the user interface for your application. It might also coordinate communications between other threads in your application. It would be a great idea to create another thread for handling the communications port. If there was something waiting at the port, the communications thread could retrieve it and store it in a private buffer. If there is not anything at the port, the thread could relinquish the rest of its time slice, giving the CPU back to other threads in the application or in the system.

The primary thread could query the subordinate thread for characters it has received. If the subordinate thread has any new characters, it could provide them to the user-interface thread to draw them on the screen.

This is a good architecture for two reasons. First, the extra code you will write to manage the two tasks is very logically separated. You are not using a thread for the sake of it, you are actually gaining benefit from it. If you didn't use two threads, you'd have to carefully architect your application to keep peeking at the communications port when it wasn't doing other work. The other work would stall while your application checked the communications port. On the other hand, with the threads in place, your application can naturally make simple checks for the other thread, or even set up a mechanism whereby the communications thread actively notifies the user-interface thread. That makes responding to information on the communications port almost as easy as handling a message.

Second, the use of threads is pretty natural. You are not constructing a dependency between the two threads to make one need information from another consistently before it can get work done. Some threaded applications stall because one thread actually spends all of its time waiting around for another. In this hypothetical application, that wouldn't be true — the main application thread has plenty of work to do in interacting with the user. When it has time, it can get information from the communications thread to digest later, but the threads can execute independently without much waiting.

This notion of independent execution is something you should strive for. You will find that good multithreaded applications have two very definite roles for threads. One role is where the thread is always running, independent of other threads, and makes some mechanism for providing results or data back to the original thread. The other is a thread that almost never runs — that is, it sleeps, or waits for an event to happen. When the event happens, the thread does some work quickly and then falls asleep again, or even terminates.

9.3.4 Applying Threads Within Your Application

Programming with threads seems simple at first: just decide what execution bottlenecks make your application slow and throw some threads at them. In reality, it is much more important to carefully approach the application design with threads in mind.

Almost all good multithreaded programs are attempts at maximizing the time for which a process is allowed to execute. If your application ever spends time waiting for input, output, or other events outside the direct context of the process itself, it can probably benefit from a multithreaded architecture. The time your application spends waiting for network I/O to complete could be used to update the user interface, perform more processing, or even begin another I/O operation.

If these blocking conditions exist in your application, then the workload should be split among many threads, getting more work done at the same time. If you have written a program that performs some unit of computation, writes the results of that computation to a disk file, and then loops to perform the same task again, you could benefit by allowing the I/O to take place in one thread and the computation to take place in another. The time spent waiting for the operating system to perform writes will block the I/O thread, but the computational thread will be free to continue processing.

On the other hand, if your program performs some computations, writes the results to disk, and then exits, it is a waste of time to implement threads. Your application will have to wait for the I/O operation to complete before returning to the user anyway, so using another thread will not help you. You gain nothing from the preemptive multitasking afforded while your I/O work completes.

In the Windows environment, I/O operations happen much more often than when you are just writing a file to disk. You may wish to use additional threads to maintain the user interface of your application while the primary thread processes data. This example is most applicable to situations in which output is extremely slow, such as printing.

Unfortunately, it is beyond the scope of this book to explain how to correctly apply threads in every circumstance, and perhaps even more unfortunately, no one can really completely describe when not to apply them.

Simply put, the best rule of thumb is that if you cannot prove that additional threads will benefit your application, do not use them.

9.4 Creating Threads

There are two ways to create threads in MFC applications. The first way is very MFC-centric and is particularly applicable to situations in which you need to have a thread running to service a particular window and the processing associated with it. The second approach involves creating a thread in an MFC application that follows the Win32 thread management APIs more closely, therefore offering you more control over the behavior of the thread, but making it somewhat more difficult to directly associate a thread with a window in your application.

The MFC technique for creating a thread is very much the same as the method for creating any other Windows object. MFC objects have a longer lifetime than their related Windows counterparts, being created before and destroyed after the existence of the Windows object. So, if you wish to create another thread for your process, you must first create an instance of the CWinThread class. The CWinThread's constructor simply initializes the CWinThread object — it doesn't create a thread.

9.4.1 Using Your Own Threads

The implementation of CWinThread is complete in that it wraps the Windows threading API for you; you needn't be concerned with the functions that Windows itself uses when it is creating, executing, or destroying threads. However, CWinThread's implementation is incomplete in that it does no work for you; you must derive a class in your application from CWinThread and override some functions to make sure you gain the functionality you need.

The only member function of CWinThread that you must override is InitInstance(). This function is similar to the InitInstance()

function of `CWinApp` in that it is called each time you create the thread that is wrapped by the instance of the thread class (in other words, it is called from `CreateThread()`, not the constructor). You should perform any initialization your thread needs in the `InitInstance()` member of your `CWinThread`-derived class. `CWinThread` has a corresponding `ExitInstance()` function, which is called when your thread terminates. This function is the appropriate place for any destruction code required by your thread.

Once your `CWinThread`-derived object is created, creating the actual Windows thread is only one step away; simply call the `CreateThread()` member function of `CWinThread`. The MFC approach to creating a thread may look something like the following:

```
CMyThread* pWinThread;              // derives from CWinThread
pWinThread = new CMyThread();       // _not_ CWinThread!
if (pWinThread == NULL) {
   MessageBox("Out of memory");
 }
else {
   if (pWinThread->CreateThread() == FALSE) {
      MessageBox("Couldn't Create Thread");
      delete pWinThread;
      pWinThread = NULL;
   }
 }
```

The MFC thread object, pointed to by the `pWinThread` pointer, is created by the new operator, but the actual Windows thread is not created until the call to `CreateThread()` returns.

9.4.2 Handling Thread Messages

You can override the `PreTranslateMessage()` function in your class to have a crack at messages the thread will process before they are grabbed by the normal Windows `TranslateMessage()` and `DispatchMessage()` APIs, but this is rarely necessary.

You do need to do this when you want to handle thread messages. Your application can use `::PostThreadMessage()` to send a message directly to a thread without targeting a specific window. This is great for sending messages to worker threads, even if they don't have a user interface.

Sending the message is easy enough, but how do you override `Pre-TranslateMessage()` in your `CWinThread`-derived class? `Pre-TranslateMessage()` takes a pointer to an `MSG` structure that contains information about the message sent. When a message is sent to a thread, the hwnd member of the MSG structure will be NULL. Since a thread can receive a message without having a window, and since thread messages are sent directly to threads and not to a window, the lack of a window handle lets you know without a doubt that the message is thread-specific. So, your Pre-TranslateMessage() routine can be very simple, as shown here:

```
BOOL CYourThread::PreTranslateMessage(MSG* pMsg)
{
   if (pMsg->hwnd == NULL) {
      // it is yours! do something interesting
      // pMsg->message is the message id
      // pMsg->wParam and ->lParam are params
      return TRUE;
    }
   else
      return CWinThread::PreTranslateMessage()
}
```

If the message has a NULL hwnd, you know that it is aimed squarely at your thread and that you can handle it. You can pick apart the MSG structure passed to you to get the juicy marrow inside. Otherwise, you should either call the base-class implementation of PreTranslateMessage() or use the CWinThread message map handlers to let the message dispatch proceed normally. You should handle the message in the PreTranslate-Message() override. Thread messages are always posted, so there's no need for you to return anything to the code that originally posted the message. On the other hand, you must return TRUE to the dispatch code that called PreTranslateMessage() so that code knows you processed the message and that it doesn't need to be dispatched to anyone else.

9.5 MFC Creation Benefits

The MFC thread-creation technique has some benefits. Most notably, if you create a thread with MFC, it is very easy to make the thread responsible for a particular window. Associating a thread with a window allows your application to process user input and output using one separate thread while others perform independent work in other portions of your program. The most appropriate way to realize this functionality is to have your InitInstance() function create the window it will be managing. Once the window is created, you should make the m_pMainWnd member variable of `CWinThread` equal to the pointer to the window you have created. This causes the message dispatch code built into `CWinThread` to manage the window exclusively.

Because the thread can only retrieve messages addressed to windows it owns, you cannot create a window before you create the thread you wish to use for it.

Aside from `m_pMainWnd`, `CWinThread` has some other useful and important member variables. You can get the Win32 handle to the thread represented by a given `CWinThread` object by examining the `m_hThread` member variable. This variable is `NULL` if the `CWinThread` instance has yet to actually create the thread. The standard MFC creation paradigm you have seen with most other MFC objects is at work here again; create the C++ object first, then create the Windows object, then destroy the Windows object, then destroy the C++ object.

The `m_bAutoDelete` member variable is `FALSE` by default. This means that the `CWinThread` object wrapping the thread object won't be destroyed by MFC when the Windows thread terminates. Setting this variable to `TRUE` can make managing threads a bit more convenient, since it will cause MFC to delete the `CWinThread` object as the thread terminates.

These member variables bring to light another advantage to the MFC method for creating threads: the member variables can be set directly before the thread is actually created. You can make these settings in the constructor for the thread or directly on the thread object after it is created but before calling the `CreateThread()` member.

When your Windows thread is finally created, the first thing it does is to execute the `InitInstance()` member of the thread class. Just like `CWinApp::InitInstance()`, `CWinThread::InitInstance()` can return FALSE if the initialization of the thread has failed. If, for example, the window creation for the thread failed, it would be a good idea to return `FALSE` so that work on it stops and the unused thread is destroyed.

In addition, you can also override the `CWinThread::Run()` function to have the thread do some work for you. If you do your own work here, don't call the base-class implementation of the function because it will just enter a message loop — and not return until your program has posted a `WM_QUIT` message.

9.5.1 Worker Threads

The MFC method for creating threads readily lends itself to the application of threads for handling a given window's events. However, this technique is not always appropriate, because sometimes you may wish to use a thread for some task that doesn't involve a window. For instance, you might want to create a thread to perform a task in the background, such as a long recalculation, a complex database activity, or a slow printing operation.

To provide for these circumstances, MFC also implements the `AfxBeginThread()` function, which lets you create threads without deriving your own version of `CWinThread`. You can also use the API to manage threads based around your own derivative of `CWinThread`. To this end, the function is implemented with two overrides.

The first overloaded version takes a pointer to a function that will control the thread. The prototype looks similar to the following:

```
CWinThread* AfxBeginThread(AFX_THREADPROC pfnThreadProc,
    LPVOID pParam, int nPriority = THREAD_PRIORITY_NORMAL,
    UINT nStackSize = 0, DWORD dwCreateFlags = 0,
    LPSECURITY_ATTRIBUTES lpSecurityAttrs = NULL);
```

This override also takes a `LPVOID` parameter. This parameter is handed to the controlling function as a parameter; you can use it to pass a pointer to a structure of information to the controlling function.

The other override takes a pointer to a `RUNTIME_CLASS` information structure, which is defined by the `CWinThread`-derived class you will be using to control the thread. The prototype for this overload of `AfxBeginThread()` looks similar to the following:

```
CWinThread* AfxBeginThread(CRuntimeClass* pThreadClass,
     int nPriority = THREAD_PRIORITY_NORMAL, UINT nStackSize = 0,
     DWORD dwCreateFlags = 0,
     LPSECURITY_ATTRIBUTES lpSecurityAttrs = NULL);
```

As you can see, the majority of the parameters are the same. Since they are common, it is worthwhile to discuss those first. These parameters are used to control exactly how MFC will perform its final internal Win32 `CreateThread()` call.

The `nPriority` parameter can be used to set the initial priority of the thread; certain values, such as `THREAD_PRIORITY_HIGHEST` and `THREAD_PRIORITY_ABOVE_NORMAL` can be used to allow Windows to more readily schedule time for the thread, while values such as `THREAD_PRIORITY_BELOW_NORMAL` and `THREAD_PRIORITY_LOYOUST` cause Windows to schedule time for the thread less often. The default value of `THREAD_PRIORITY_NORMAL` is adequate for almost all uses.

The `nStackSize` parameter dictates the initial size of the thread's stack (remember that each thread has its own stack). The default value of zero for this parameter causes Windows to allocate the same amount of stack space for the new thread as for the primary thread of the process. Although Windows will dynamically grow the stack, setting this value to gain more stack space can result in a slight performance improvement for the thread, since Windows won't have to allocate additional stack space for the process, little by little, as it executes and demands more space.

The `dwCreateFlags` parameter can either be zero or `CREATE_SUSPENDED`. If it is zero, which it is by default, the thread is created and immediately allowed to run. If the parameter is `CREATE_SUSPENDED`, the thread is suspended and doesn't run until the Win32 API `::ResumeThread()` function is called against the thread.

The `lpSecurityAttrs` parameter accepts a pointer to a security attributes structure. You will almost never need to use this parameter because threads almost never need anything more than the default security. If you do need to provide some security, you can allocate a `SECURITY_ATTRIBUTES` structure yourself and use the `::InitializeSecurityDescriptor()` call in the Win32 API to initialize the `lpSecurityDescriptor` field in that structure.

The security functions are not part of Windows 95 or Windows 98 APIs. All of the security functions return the failure code appropriate to the specific function and set the last error to `ERROR_CALL_NOT_IMPLEMENTED`.

`AfxBeginThread()` returns the address of the new object immediately after the new thread is created and the thread calling `AfxBeginThread()` runs concurrently with it. Since `AfxBeginThread()` always returns a pointer to a `CWinThread`, you may need to cast it to a pointer to the derived class of thread you actually wish to implement.

9.6 Understanding the Controlling Function

If you are using the `AFX_THREADPROC` version of `AfxBeginThread()`, you will need to provide a pointer to a function to control the thread. This is called the thread's *controlling function*.

The controlling function of a thread implements that thread. It is called to start the thread, and when it returns, the thread is terminated. The function doesn't need to do any work to start or terminate the thread, since this is handled by the operating system, but it does do all of the preparatory work for the thread's initialization. You may find this one of the most intuitive ways to implement a thread, since no extra work is required. The controlling function runs in the context of the thread.

The function that creates the thread can communicate with the controlling function using the second parameter to `AfxBeginThread()`. Neither MFC nor Windows make use of this parameter's value; they just send it along as a parameter to the controlling thread. As such, you can use it to send a number or a pointer to the thread pointer, or just set it to `NULL` if you don't need it. Of course, you may have to cast the parameter you wish to send to `LPVOID` if it is not a pointer. The prototype you should use for your controlling function is as follows:

```
UINT SomeControllingFunction(LPVOID pParam);
```

More often than not, the controlling function for a thread will be a global function not associated with a class. However, your controlling function can be a member function of a class, but only if it is a static member. Semantically, this means that you cannot make use of the this pointer, explicitly or implicitly, in the implementation of your controlling function. As a strategy to avoid this shortcoming, it is a very common practice to pass a pointer to any object the thread might use during execution. The other option is to make the function a friend of the class.

When you are designing your thread class, keep in mind the implications of the C++ language. Unless your controlling function is a member of the `CWinThread`-derived class you are using, you cannot access any variables or functions that are not declared as public.

9.6.1 Creating Threads at Runtime

In the previous section, you learned that there are two thread-creation mechanisms you can implement with the `AfxBeginThread()` function. To save you the trouble of looking back at the second implementation, here it is again:

```
CWinThread* AfxBeginThread(CRuntimeClass* pThreadClass,
    int nPriority = THREAD_PRIORITY_NORMAL, UINT nStackSize = 0,
    DWORD dwCreateFlags = 0,
    LPSECURITY_ATTRIBUTES lpSecurityAttrs = NULL);
```

You have already learned about all of the other parameters, so the only parameter you do not already know about is the `pThreadClass` parameter. This lets you offer the function runtime type information to identify the particular class you'd like to use to create your thread object. All you need to do is wrap the MFC-supplied `RUNTIME_CLASS()` macro around the name of your `CWinThread`-derived class.

If you want to use a class called `CPrinterThread` that you have based on `CWinThread` to control your thread, you could make your call like this:

```
pNewThread = (CPrinterThread*)
   AfxCreateThread(RUNTIME_CLASS(CPrinterThread));
```

The `AfxCreateThread()` function will create an object of the class you have specified by calling its default constructor, then it will start the thread and attach it to that object. Windows will use the newly constructed thread to enter your `CPrinterThread::InitInstance()` function. Your thread will run until it completes. For a thread created like this, completes can mean that the `InitInstance()` call returns `FALSE` because the initialization failed and the thread couldn't even get started the way it wanted to. Alternatively, it can mean that initialization succeeded and the `Run()` member of your class finally returned and the thread is done.

Like all other MFC objects, a `CWinThread`-derived object used in this manner usually outlives the inner Windows object. Your `CWinThread`-derived class creates an object before the real Windows thread is created and your object lives after the `CWinThread`-managed object terminates — if and only if you have set the `m_bAutoDelete` member of the object to `FALSE`. Otherwise, MFC will take care of deleting the thread object just after the thread stops running.

If you have a thread that you are sure will run to termination before your creating thread dies, you might consider using `m_bAutoDelete`. Be careful though — `m_bAutoDelete` removes all record of the thread. The pointer returned by `AfxCreateThread()` is no longer valid, so you can't use it to gain the handle to the thread from the `m_hThread` member — the key to getting the return code from the thread.

Normally, when you use the `CRuntimeClass*` overload of `AfxBeginThread()`, you will use the `dwCreateFlags` parameter to the function to make the thread create as suspended. This will let the `AfxBeginThread()` function return with a pointer to the new thread object before that object is actually set into motion. You can use that opportunity to initialize member variables of the thread, so the code in the thread class can later have information about your exact request. Once your initialization is done, you can call `ResumeThread()` against the suspended thread to get it running.

It offers you the ability to create a `CWinThread` object and get that object running with a different thread.

9.6.2 Terminating a Thread

Threads can terminate in one of two ways: naturally or prematurely. A thread ends naturally when its controlling function returns. For worker threads, this means that the controlling function has simply finished its work and returned. For user-interface threads, this means that the thread must call `PostQuitMessage()` to force the message loop in the MFC-supplied controlling function of the thread to exit. If the thread is managing an MFC window, MFC will automatically perform a `PostQuitMessage()` as the main window for the thread is destroyed.

In a worker thread, the controlling function can simply return or it can call `AfxEndThread()`. `AfxEndThread()` accepts one parameter: a `UINT`, which is the result code for the thread.

9.6.3 Handling Premature Thread Termination

Prematurely terminating a thread is a little more complicated. In both instances, if code within the thread knows it needs to terminate, it can call `AfxEndThread()`. The problem with this call is that it must be made from the thread that is to be terminated, but often the thread that created the secondary thread wants to terminate the thread asynchronously. The primary thread cannot call `AfxEndThread()` for the secondary thread, so it must set up some communication method with the secondary thread.

If, for example, you implement a secondary thread to take care of printing in your application, the primary thread will need to be able to shut down the secondary thread to give the user the opportunity to cancel printing.

For user-interface threads, the secondary thread may be able to trap a message to clean up any work currently in focus. The primary thread can then simply post that message to the window managed by the secondary thread to have it terminate.

Before a user-interface thread terminates, MFC calls the `ExitInstance()` function in the derived class, so some of the clean-up work can be placed there as well. Note that this is only true for user-interface threads, i.e., threads that don't have message loops or threads that don't receive `WM_QUIT` before they are terminated won't call their `ExitInstance()` member.

For worker threads, the problem is a little more complicated. The controlling thread has no direct method of communicating with the secondary thread, so you must provide the communication mechanism. You can solve this problem by avoiding it; have your printing thread also manage the dialog box. That way, the code that handles the Cancel button runs in the same thread that handles the printing and could cleanly use `AfxEndThread()`. On the other hand, if you are convinced you need two different threads, you might write some code that notifies one thread that the other needs some attention.

9.6.4 Threads Are Like Sharp Objects — Play Carefully

Some developers like to use APIs like `TerminateThread()`, which initially seems quite handy — it will let you end a thread from outside that thread. If you decide you don't like the work the thread is doing, you can just kill it with `TerminateThread()`.

However, you might notice that MFC's `CWinThread` class doesn't implement `TerminateThread()`. You could call it, if you had to, by using the `m_hThread` handle that is a member of the `CWinThread` object, but you should not.

MFC doesn't implement this function because it is too dangerous. `TerminateThread()` stops a thread, period. It doesn't let the thread clean itself up or let it release memory or other resources that it might have. It just stops executing. This is just miserable; not only will you leak the files and memory you have allocated, you run the risk of being in the middle of allocating one of those resources. If the resource is allocated and Windows hasn't yet assigned it to your thread, or if the C runtime libraries are in the middle of managing some pointers in the heap, or if the GDI is in the middle of passing some data back and forth between the system and a device driver, the game is probably almost over. Windows NT will protect the rest of the system, but Windows 95 cannot and there's nowhere to go but down. The next allocation, or the next paint, or the next file access can cause your application to just drop dead.

As mentioned, there are a couple of good ways to make sure that a thread quits safely. One way is to post a message to it. Exactly what you will do will depend on your threads. For user-interface threads with an identifiable main window, it is a good idea to just close the window. Your thread can clean up in `OnClose()` for that window. If you don't have an identifiable main window, or you are interested in terminating a worker thread, you can consider sending your thread a message directly. If your worker thread doesn't even process messages, you might consider setting up some synchronization object (see below) to let your thread know that it needs to quit.

9.6.5 Checking Return Codes

When your thread terminates, either by calling AfxEndThread() or by directly returning from the controlling function, the thread can offer a return value that can provide the primary thread with some information about the success or failure of the thread. By convention, most programmers use a return value of zero to indicate that the thread completed successfully and use some nonzero value to indicate an error code. This allows the nonzero error return to also provide more information, such as a code that indicates the exact cause of the failure. Of course, you are free to implement whatever return code semantics you wish.

To get the return code from a completed thread, you can call the Windows GetExitCodeThread() API. This API takes two parameters: a handle to the thread to be examined and a pointer to a DWORD, which will contain the return code from the thread. You might implement your controlling procedure like this:

```
DWORD SomeThreadProcedure(LPVOID pParam)
{
   CMyThreadObject* pObject = (CMyThreadObject*) pParam;
   if (pObject == NULL ||
      pObject->IsKindOf(RUNTIME_CLASS(CMyThreadObject))
         == FALSE) {
      return -1;
   }
   if (pObject->DoSomeWork()) {
      return 1;    // meaningful failure code
   }
   if (pObject->DoSomeMoreWork()) {
      return 2;    // meaningful failure code
   }
   return 0;
}
```

This thread-controlling function anticipates that it will be passed a pointer to a CMyThreadObject. If that pointer is NULL, or if the pointer is not pointing to an instance of CMyThreadObject, the function will immediately terminate the thread with a return code of -1.

The function continues by calling some member functions of your thread object class to get the work done. If any one of them fails, the function exits early and returns a nonzero code, but if things go well, the function returns zero. You can check for the status code returned by a secondary thread from its primary thread when the execution of the secondary thread ends.

Your main thread might create and execute this secondary thread by running code like this:

```
pNewMyThreadObject = new CMyThreadObject;
CWinThread* pRunningThread
   = AfxBeginThread(SomeThreadProcedure, pNewMyThreadObject);
```

The `AfxBeginThread()` call kicks off the controlling function for the second process, passing it a pointer to the thread object that would have been derived from `CWinThread`. Say, for instance, you wanted to see if the thread has terminated, you might use code like this:

```
DWORD dwRetCode;

if (GetExitCodeThread(pRunningThread->m_hThread, &dwRetCode)
    == FALSE) {
   // catastrophic failure!
 }
if (dwRetCode == STILL_ACTIVE) {
   // still running
 }
else {
   // done running ...
   // dwRetCode has return code from thread's controlling func
   // or AfxEndThread.
 }
```

Believe it or not, `STATUS_PENDING` turns out to be 0x103, so you will need to make sure you don't use that value as a status you want to return. Or you should carefully check to see if the thread is still running by using the `::WaitForSingleObject()` function against the handle to the thread. You could do that with a call like this:

```
if (::WaitForSingleObject(pRunningThread->m_hThread, 0)
    == WAIT_OBJECT_0)
   // the thread is done running
else
   // the object is still running
```

Remember that, more often than not, you will derive your own `CWinThread` to create your own thread classes. That's exactly what these code fragments have done, even though you haven't explicitly shown the overriding code. You'll see examples of this in subsequent sections of this chapter that make this very apparent.

9.7   Thread Synchronization

Synchronization objects are a very important aspect of thread programming; it is crucial that you understand them. Synchronization objects are a collection of system-supplied objects that allow threads to communicate with one another. There are four such objects in Windows: *critical sections*, *semaphores*, *mutexes*, and *events*.

All of these objects have different patterns of initialization, activation, and use but they all eventually represent one of two different states: signaled or unsignaled. (Sometimes it is convenient to say "cleared" instead of "unsignaled." Every object has slightly different rules for what the states represent.)

All of these objects, except for critical sections, are waitable. This means that a thread can stop executing and sit around until a particular instance of one of these objects becomes signaled. A sitting thread gets no work done at all; it doesn't even process messages. It relinquishes its time slice to the system so that other threads can run full-speed. Such a thread is said to be blocked.

9.7.1   Critical Sections

Critical sections are the simplest of synchronization objects. If two threads are going to share access to a particular resource, they will usually want to ensure that they don't touch the resource at the same time. If they did, they wouldn't be sharing, they'd be grabbing the resource from each other and overwriting the work that the other thread has just performed.

Maybe you have a multithreaded application in which one thread accepts input from the local user and the other accepts input from other users over the network. Both threads want to process this input and alter one of the open documents in the application. Maybe the document contains a linked list of stock prices, say. Both threads cannot access that CDocument instance at the same time. If one thread begins modifying the document by changing the head pointer in the list and the other steps in and makes a change based on that incorrectly set head pointer, the application will probably end up crashing because of the wrong pointer. Not only will it ruin the data structure, but the data structure will also be ruined for the first thread.

The problem with the access to the linked list is that operations against it aren't atomic. That is, they aren't simple enough to be executed without being interrupted by another thread. By using a critical section, though, you can ensure that the operation becomes atomic. Suppose a CDocument object contained a `CCriticalSection` object along with the linked list. This object can gain access to the linked list. The first thread, just before it decides to touch the list, can enter the critical section by calling the critical section object's `Lock()` function. Once it has marked the object as locked, the `Lock()` call will return immediately.

The thread can then begin modifying the list. If the system decides to activate the other thread, it will also try to lock the critical section before accessing the linked list. Since the critical section is already locked, the thread will block. It cannot execute, so the operating system will give its time slice to another thread.

Either immediately or after other threads have also executed, the first thread will begin executing again. It can finish modifying the linked list and can call `Unlock()` against the critical section. This will free it, allowing the `Lock()` call in the second thread to stop blocking. The second thread will similarly begin owning the critical section so that no other thread can interrupt it while it does its own work.

The critical section, then, synchronizes the access to the linked list. Properly using the critical section means that only one thread can access the object. But properly using the object is strictly up to you; you need to decide which accesses need to be protected and which don't.

Never, ever, underestimate the difficulty inherent in writing a multithreaded application. You must think of everything. You must protect yourself from any situation in which your thread could stop executing and another thread in your application can begin touching data structures important to the first one. You need to make sure you don't allow these situations to adversely affect your application. Depending on exactly what's happening, you need to choose one of the synchronization objects to protect your data or other resources that your threads share.

The `CCriticalSection` class has only a default constructor. The object is initially without a owner. A thread can gain ownership of it by calling `Lock()` against it and can release it by calling its `Unlock()` member. `Lock()` is the one that blocks — your call to `Lock()` won't return until the critical section is yours.

Critical sections are not waitable, so they are not said to be signaled or unsignaled. A thread may decide to enter a critical section — it is said to do so when it has acquired the critical section. When it exits the critical section, it releases it. The code executed while the critical section is owned is still not atomic — the operating system may still suspend the thread and let some other thread execute, but as long as all threads in the application are playing along and only accessing the thread through the critical section, everything is safe.

9.7.2 Working with Mutexes

Critical sections are almost all you need to write good multithreaded applications. They'll be the answer in about three-quarters of the situations in which you need to protect some data structure from multiple simultaneous access from separate threads.

Critical sections are, thankfully, very lightweight. They are really just a very small and special data structure that Windows implements and protects. This is a huge advantage when you need to toss around lots and lots of critical sections to protect lots and lots of different objects.

However, it turns into a disadvantage when you think about the other one-quarter of the situations in which you might need protection. The biggest disadvantage that critical sections have is that they are only visible within one process. That is, you can use critical sections to protect data accessed by two different threads in the same process, but you cannot use critical sections to protect data accessed by one thread in one process and one thread in another process.

You will also note that a critical section doesn't really fit the definition of a waitable object. You can call the Lock() member of a CCriticalSection object, but you might quite literally die waiting for the lock call to return. You cannot specify a timeout duration, nor can you wait for more than one critical section object at the same time.

To address these design issues, Windows implements a slightly larger flavor of critical sections called mutexes. Mutex is short for mutually exclusive.

Mutexes are quite similar to critical sections in their locking patterns: either you own it or you don't. At the expense of being bigger and more expensive, they address the cross-process shortcoming of critical sections that are outlined above. That is, a mutex is created and can then be shared across processes, as well as being shared across threads. By requesting the mutex by name, another process can also ask for access to the same mutex.

The aptly named CMutex class wraps access to mutexes for MFC applications. The class features this constructor:

```
CMutex(BOOL bInitiallyOwn = FALSE, LPCTSTR lpszName = NULL,
    LPSECURITY_ATTRIBUTES lpsaAttribute = NULL);
```

Since mutexes can be accessed by different processes, it makes sense to allow them to be initially owned from the instant they are created. As the previous section indicated, a common programming model is to use a synchronization object to protect data structures in your application. If you are protecting the data structure with a mutex, you might decide to hold the mutex in the same class that holds the data structure. In this design, you should consider keeping the gating mutex owned until the initialization of the underlying data structure is completed. For the linked list example, that might mean that you could sketch a CLinkedList class and give it a constructor similar to the following:

```
CLinkedList::CLinkedList(LPCTSTR pstrName)
    : m_mutex(TRUE, pstrName)
{
   // initialize the data strucutre
   // once it is ready, release the mutex
}
```

Initially, it might seem silly to be worried about protecting access to the list while it is being constructed, but the construction of the object is a very important time; it is making the transition from being some useless and uninitialized concept to something that you can actually touch. You should make sure it is not touched until you are completely ready! While I'm not planning on discussing how to initialize arbitrary data structures, in the next section I will explain what you should do to release the mutex — or any other MFC-wrapped shared object.

A mutex is identified within a handle returned by the operating system, though you need not concern yourself with that handle if you are using MFC's wrapper classes. The handle is created by the constructor and automatically closed by the destructor when the CMutex object is destroyed. If you create a mutex with the default constructor — that is, by supplying no name — you will always create a new mutex object. If you create a mutex and supply a name that doesn't exist anywhere on the system, you will also get a brand new handle. If that name does exist someplace on the system, though, and your process has privileges on that other mutex, you will actually get a handle that identifies the existing mutex without creating a new one.

That last situation is the mechanism that allows multiple processes to access the same mutex. Since the processes cannot directly share the handle for the mutex, they can just agree on a naming standard and refer to the mutex via the name. The third parameter is a pointer to a security information structure. As usual, this pointer describes a block of data that lets you carefully control access rights to the object.

9.7.3 Semaphores

You have learned that critical sections are pretty useful for indicating that a part of your code owns a resource. Your code can use critical sections to protect access to simple data structures. Critical sections are quite lightweight, but they have disadvantages for some designs. Most obviously, they are binary. That is, they are either owned or unowned. That's great for data structures that are owned or unowned, but not great for monitoring resources that are limited in quantity.

Many client/server-based applications, for example, will create more than one connection from the client to the server. This can greatly help the efficiency of the program, since the server usually manages some amount of context information and associates it with each connection and not with each client. With more than one connection, the server can reply to one client via the network, paw through memory in another thread, and do some disk I/O in a third thread. The bottom line is that all of the time that would normally be spent waiting for some hardware operation to finish can be better spent working on the numerous other in-memory tasks besieging the server.

A good approach to implementing this kind of application might involve writing some code that manages a pool of connections. The code could wrap a class around the connection information or simply hand out the same connection handles that the underlying transport layer might use. Whatever the specifics, the code knows it might have a limited number of connections: it might have six connections allocated, for instance.

Even if you are not embarking on the monumental journey of writing a server, you might use a semaphore to count other resources. If you need to complete six tasks, for instance, you might create a semaphore to share among the six threads completing those tasks. When the threads finish, they can notify the application's primary thread by incrementing the semaphore.

You might let threads throughout such applications request currently unused connections from a central function. That function can figure out what specific connection is not in use and return the first unused connection to the caller. If there are no connections available, maybe the function will just block until one is available or return an error condition to the requester. At any rate, the code needs to be thread-safe; if two threads make simultaneous calls to the connection manager function, the connection manager might end up handing out the same connection to two different requesting threads.

Critical sections and mutexes are obviously pretty useless in this situation. Critical sections are out because entering a critical section that is already owned would block your code; you might try coding the routine with a critical section just to protect it from other simultaneous access, but you would probably find that strategy is inefficient if your application code frequently requests connections — several threads would block while one thread is busy figuring out which thread to use. This would be particularly true if you were interested in dynamically creating new connections to the server as they were first needed; the act of getting a new connection is probably quite expensive, since it involves network access. That time-consuming work would be wrapped by the same critical section and therefore make the function a bottleneck for your whole application.

You could consider making an array of mutexes and protecting each individual connection that way, but your code would be quite awkward — it would have to try and lock each and every mutex and see which one let go first. Instead, a better approach would be to use a semaphore. A semaphore would let your application gate access to the function based first on the number of free items. Then, you might protect very small chunks of code with a critical section.

You can use the `CSemaphore` class to manage semaphores in your application. The constructor for the class takes four parameters, which looks like this:

```
CSemaphore(LONG lInitialCount = 1, LONG lMaxCount = 1,
    LPCTSTR pstrName = NULL,
    LPSECURITY_ATTRIBUTES lpsaAttributes = NULL);
```

The first parameter is the semaphore's initial count, which by default is 1. The maximum count for the semaphore is specified by the second parameter, also 1 by default. Obviously, the maximum count must be higher than or equal to the initial count. If you like, you can name the semaphore by specifying a string for the third parameter. If the third parameter is `NULL`, the semaphore is unnamed and cannot be seen by other processes. If the third parameter is not `NULL`, it is available to other processes by that same name.

The count of the semaphore is the mechanism by which it locks. If the count is zero, the semaphore is signaled; if it is not, the semaphore is unsignaled. The semaphore decreases its count whenever a thread that is waiting for the semaphore is released and allowed to run. The semaphore increases its count when you call `CSemaphore::Unlock()`. A semaphore's count never dips below zero.

9.7.4 Events

Event objects are useful for signaling the occurrence of an event. An event object lives in one of two states: signaled or unsignaled. Some people call the unsignaled state reset. You can create an event and leave it in its unsignaled state. Then, when the condition you wish to signal comes to pass, you can signal the event and any threads watching will know that the event is done.

Maybe you would use an event to indicate that printing is done, for example. If your application is asked to print, perhaps your user-interface thread will kick off a printing thread. That printing thread could then get to work. The primary thread could check an event object known to both the primary thread and the printing thread.

The thread that is using the event object to reflect its state will change the state of the object by calling functions against it. The threads that are watching the object can test its state without waiting or can block until the object becomes signaled.

MFC wraps Windows event objects with the CEvent class. The object has a constructor reminiscent of the other MFC synchronization objects:

```
CEvent(BOOL bInitiallyOwn = FALSE, BOOL bManualReset = FALSE,
    LPCTSTR lpszName = NULL,
    LPSECURITY_ATTRIBUTES lpsaAttribute = NULL);
```

We have seen the lpszName and lpsaAttribute parameters before; they are no different for the CEvent class. bInitiallyOwn can be TRUE if you want the event to be initially signaled.

It is the bManualReset flag that is most interesting, though. This parameter changes how the event object works pretty substantially. When bManualReset is TRUE, you are creating a manual-reset event. If it is FALSE or unspecified, you have created an auto-reset event.

9.7.5 Setting the Event's State

The CEvent class features a SetEvent() member that signals the event. Calling this function on an event object that was created with the bManual-Reset parameter set FALSE makes the event signaled, so any waiting thread is released and any threads that subsequently wait on the event will also immediately release. However, if bManualReset is TRUE, the event releases exactly one waiting thread before automatically resetting the event.

If you have created a manual-reset event object, you can reset it using the ResetEvent() member of the CEvent class. You should not need to use this function against auto-reset event objects.

CEvent also features a PulseEvent() member. This function will signal the event and then immediately unsignal the event in one atomic call. When PulseEvent() is called against an auto-reset event, the function resets the state and returns after releasing exactly one thread — just as SetEvent() would behave. On a manual-reset object, all waiting threads are immediately released. The function always makes the object unsignaled before the function returns.

`SetEvent()`, `ResetEvent()`, and `PulseEvent()` all accept no parameters and return zero if they were unsuccessful and nonzero if they were successful. Successful does not mean that the state changed; that is, calling `SetEvent()` twice in a row should return `TRUE` both times. These APIs will return only `FALSE` if they actually fail because the `CEvent` object is corrupt or hasn't been properly initialized — that is, they will fail only if the handle to the Win32 event object owned by the `CEvent` is invalid.

9.7.6 Other Waitable Objects

Windows implements many different system objects, but only a handful of them are waitable. Aside from mutexes, events, semaphores, and critical sections, there are four more waitable objects in Win32 systems:

- *Change notifications.* You can ask the system to provide you with an object that is attached to the file system. This object will signal when the identified file or directory is changed. Applications like File Manager or Windows Explorer use change notifications to spy on the current directory so they can update their representation of the file system as it changes.
- *Console input notifications.* If you have written a console application, you can avoid polling the console input by waiting on it instead.
- *Processes.* A process is signaled when it ends. You can query the exit state of the process even after it has terminated. Use the `GetExitCodeProcess()` API to retrieve this value.
- *Threads.* If you wait on a thread, your wait will be satisfied when the thread terminates. The thread's exit status can be queried using the `GetExitCodeThread()` API.

The mention of the exit codes for processes and threads in the list implies that the thread handle and process handle are valid after the process and thread exit. It turns out that Windows 95 and Windows NT will never reuse a handle value (or at least, almost never). You can write a program that does nothing but create threads and terminate them and not expect to see the same thread handle go by for months.

You should exercise good programming practice because a handle value might be reused, but you can expect that a handle given to you out of the blue is valid whether the object associated with the handle is brand-new or has been dead for weeks. If the one out of 2 billion odds are against you, your call to a function that does something to the handle will give you an ERROR_INVALID_HANDLE.

You can wait for changes or console input in your application to spy on what other parts of the system are doing, or what the user is about to do to you. They are not really designed to help with synchronization, though waiting on threads and processes can be a useful synchronization technique.

9.8 More on Processes

As you have learned, processes are whole living, breathing applications. It is quite common to need to run another program from your own, and when you do you will often need to be notified when the process ends and to know how the process ended. In Win32, you should use the CreateProcess() API function. This function is very powerful. Like all other powerful Windows functions, it takes a large number of parameters.

To solve the problem of creating an application and waiting until it is done, you can call CreateProcess() to get the process running and wait on the process handle you get back, which will signal when the process ends. The WaitForSingleObject() API function is the key to waiting for that handle. It is worthwhile to understand exactly how the creation and subsequent waiting is accomplished. The prototype for CreateProcess() looks like this:

```
BOOL CreateProcess(
    LPCTSTR lpApplicationName,
    LPTSTR lpCommandLine,
    LPSECURITY_ATTRIBUTES lpProcessAttributes,
    LPSECURITY_ATTRIBUTES lpThreadAttributes,
    BOOL bInheritHandles,
    DWORD dwCreationFlags,
    LPVOID lpEnvironment,
    LPCTSTR lpCurrentDirectory,
    LPSTARTUPINFO lpStartupInfo,
    LPPROCESS_INFORMATION lpProcessInformation
);
```

There are lots of parameters here. However, most of them can be NULL. The two most important parameters are lpApplicationName and lpCommandLine. The lpApplicationName parameter is a string that names the executable file. You must pass a full path name if the executable is not in the current directory; you cannot just pass an executable name and expect Windows to find the file for you on the path. The `lpCommandLine` parameter, meanwhile, contains a pointer to the command line you would like to send to the application. This command line is exactly what is passed to the running application, period.

The next two parameters, `lpProcessAttributes` and `lpThread-Attributes`, point to security attribute structures to control access to the newly created process and the thread object inside it. If you are writing a program for Windows 95, these are obviously ignored, since Windows 95 doesn't do any security work outside of the network. But if your application is running under Windows NT, these `SECURITY_ATTRIBUTE` blocks can describe who has what access to the process and thread, respectively.

The `bInheritHandles` parameter is a flag that lets you decide if handles owned by the creating process (your application) are assumed by the created process (the program you are running). Normally, this parameter will be `FALSE`. That will save a bit of memory and time by not forcing the operating system to duplicate all of the handles to objects your application has opened. But you may wish to make it `TRUE` if you are planning on letting the applications communicate via files, some shared memory, a named pipe, or another mechanism.

9.8.1 Process Creation Flags

The `dwCreationFlags` parameter is usually zero, but you can combine a few interesting flags to get some advanced work done. Some of the more important flags include `CREATE_SUSPENDED`, which lets you load and initialize the process and its primary thread, but not run the primary thread until you release it with `ResumeThread()` later. If there are timing issues or postinitialization things you need to take care of, this flag can be quite useful.

If you are using `CreateProcess()` to launch a Win16 or DOS application and you are running your application under Windows NT, you can specify the `CREATE_SEPARATE_WOW_VDM` flag to have Windows NT run the application in a separate virtual machine. That will get you some additional protection from crashing applications with a slight expense in resources. The flag has the exact same effect as the Run in Separate Memory Space checkbox in the Program Properties dialog box.

You might also specify `CREATE_NEW_CONSOLE` if you are running a console application. This will create a new console window instead of letting the new application share the current application's console window. You might want to forgo this flag and run your application with the

DETACHED_PROCESS flag so that the process runs without a console window. This is a great trick for processes that you need to run without a user interface. If the process needs a user interface, it can dynamically create a console window with the AllocConsole() API.

You will also need to use the dwCreationFlags to specify the process priority for the new process. As usual, you can use the following:

- HIGH_PRIORITY_CLASS
- IDLE_PRIORITY_CLASS
- NORMAL_PRIORITY_CLASS
- REALTIME_PRIORITY_CLASS

Each of the next three parameters specifies some aspect of the execution context of the process. lpEnvironment has a pointer to the environment (that is, the SET variables) for the process, and lpCurrentDirectory specifies the initial current directory for the new process. The parameters can be NULL if you wish the new process to inherit a copy of the same environment or the same current directory as the spawning process. The lpStartupInfo parameter points at a STARTUPINFO structure.

So all of these parameters work together to actually create the process. If the creation fails, the function returns FALSE and you can call the GetLastError() API to find out the exact cause of the failure. If the function returns TRUE, it will populate the PROCESS_INFORMATION structure that you passed as the last parameter of CreateProcess() with data that describes the created process.

The CreateProcess() and CreateProcessAsUser() APIs are very powerful and flexible. The explanation in this chapter only scratches the surface of that power. There are lots of details this chapter does not cover, particularly subtle variations between Windows 95/98 and Windows NT implementations of the function.

If you are writing a system with many different programs, you can use the handle to the thread returned to you from CreateProcess() in the PROCESS_INFORMATION structure. You will need to make sure you correctly create the process so that the primary thread is owned by the processes who need access to it. The easiest way to ensure that is to make sure you provide NULL for the LPSECURITY_ATTRIBUTES parameter. But if you really need security between the processes, you will need to make sure you hook up the correct attributes for the different accounts and groups running around in your system. You might have to call CreateProcessAsUser() to make the running process (or the system) think that the new process is running as a different user.

9.8.2 Understanding What Comprises Process Information

The PROCESS_INFORMATION structure is populated by the CreatePro-cess() function only if the function succeeds. The structure is pretty small. Its definition is as follows:

```
typedef struct PROCESS_INFORMATION {
    HANDLE hProcess;
    HANDLE hThread;
    DWORD dwProcessId;
    DWORD dwThreadId;
} PROCESS_INFORMATION;
```

The two HANDLEs can be used to identify the process and thread in later calls. You might call ResumeThread() on the hThread, for example, to get the primary thread running if you created the process with CREATE_SUSPENDED. The DWORDs are IDs. The DWORDs are particularly useful for keeping an eye on the process in a debugger or as parameters to the PostThreadMessage() API, but that's about it.

9.9 Creating a Process

The code to create a process is quite simple. It uses the CreateProcess() API function, as shown here:

```
UINT SpawnAndWait(LPVOID pParam)
{
    ...
    memset(&suInfo, 0, sizeof(suInfo));
    suInfo.cb = sizeof(suInfo);

    bWorked = ::CreateProcess(pInfo->m_strAppName,
        _T(""), NULL, NULL, FALSE, NORMAL_PRIORITY_CLASS,
        NULL, NULL, &suInfo, &procInfo);
    if (bWorked == FALSE)
        // something's wrong
    else
        // everything is just fine
}
```

As you can see, you can pretty easily get away with almost all of the parameters being `NULL`. The call will return `TRUE` if the process was created and started or `FALSE` if the process could not be initialized. The call can run any kind of process — regular Win32 program, a Win16 program, or a DOS program. If you are running Windows NT, you can also start any application for the Posix or OS/2 subsystems.

The addition of a thread to sit and wait is a big step in the right direction. But it has a problem: the waiting thread will block on the `WaitForSingleObject()` call forever. In the event the user shuts down the application, the creating program cannot abandon the thread; it will leak memory and resources. A great alternative is to use `WaitForMultipleObjects()`; with it, the primary thread can create a semaphore that is not signaled. The waiting thread can then wait on both the semaphore and the process. If either signals, it is done working. The waiting thread knows, then, that it is either time to quit and shut down, or time to quit and let the main thread know the subordinate application has finished.

Under this approach, you give the thread a pointer to a semaphore. The primary thread clears that semaphore on creation and will signal it as the user decides to leave the application. The waiting thread will wait both on that semaphore handle and the process handle for the spawned program. The code to do this is actually pretty simple. The code looks similar to the following:

```
HANDLE hArray[2];
hArray[0] = procInfo.hProcess;
hArray[1] = pInfo->m_psemClosing->m_hObject;

DWORD dwReturn = ::WaitForMultipleObjects(2, hArray,
    FALSE, INFINITE);
TRACE("Signaled with %d!\n", dwReturn);
```

The `::WaitForMultipleObjects()` call returns when either the process handle or the semaphore signals. The API returns an index into the array to indicate which object signaled. If the return from the function is 0, you know that the spawned process has finished running. If the return value is 1, the function knows that the application is shutting down.

The spawned process will take care of signaling itself when you are done running it. However, the program must manage the semaphore itself. In the SpawnProcess application, the program creates the semaphore as a member of the `CSpawnPrcDlg` class. It is initialized with an initial count of zero, meaning that it is signaled. The program can release it later, as the window is dying, with a call to its `Unlock()` function. Arguably, the best place to do that is in the `PostNcDestroy()` message handler in the application's dialog class, as shown here:

```
void CSpawnPrcDlg::PostNcDestroy()
{
    m_sfClosing.Unlock();
    CDialog::PostNcDestroy();
}
```

This code will work just fine; the wait in the thread will clear and the thread's controlling function will exit and get the thread shut down. To be completely safe, though, you should use `WaitForSingleObject()` to make sure the thread exits. If the code in the thread procedure after the `WaitForMultipleObjects()` call did any real work, it would be very likely to take a while to exit. But if you let the process terminate before that, it might not get to completely clean up after itself.

Solving the problem is pretty straightforward — you must simply wait for the thread after unlocking the semaphore. One additional call within the `PostNoDestroy()` function handles the problem, as shown here:

```
void CSpawnerDlg::PostNcDestroy()
{
    m_sfClosing.Unlock();
    ::WaitForSingleObject(m_pThread->m_hThread, INFINITE);
    CDialog::PostNcDestroy();
}
```

By making sure that the thread has enough time to properly finish executing, you can ensure that your application will run cleanly.

9.10 Closing on Threads and MFC

As mentioned earlier in this chapter, several rules surround the use of MFC objects in different threads. First, you should understand that Windows itself doesn't put any *real* restrictions on the use of different objects from different threads. That is, if Thread A creates a window or a GDI object or allocates some memory, Thread B can happily send a message to the window, select the GDI object, or write some data to the memory.

However, despite MFC's lack of real restrictions, there are some obvious ramifications to those actions mentioned. If Thread A creates a window, the only thing Thread B can really do is send or post messages to it. This is absolutely no problem; Windows takes care of suspending Thread B for sent messages and handles the queue management for posted messages. You have learned throughout this chapter about mechanisms you can use to protect access to shared resources like GDI objects or shared memory. You should not use the same GDI object in two threads at the same time, and you should not let one thread write to a data structure in memory while other threads might be reading it at the same time.

MFC, on the other hand, doesn't allow you to touch the C++ object that wraps a given Windows object from two different threads. So, if Thread A creates a new window and assigns it the pWindow pointer, and then gives that pWindow pointer to Thread B, Thread B cannot use it. If Thread B tries, it will trigger all sorts of ASSERTs in the MFC code. The reason lies in the way that MFC maps pointers to objects to the handles to the objects that Windows wants to use. MFC needs to manage such a map so that it can properly decide what function should handle any messages sent to the window. There are two such maps: the temporary map and the permanent map. So the reason this rule exists is because the entry in the map made during the pWindow->Create() call for Thread A doesn't affect the maps managed by any other thread.

However, you can pass the window handle from one thread to the other. So, Thread A might have code that does the creation; the code can then hand off to Thread B the m_hWnd handle from the object referenced by pWindow.

On the other hand, Thread B will need to create or allocate its own CWnd object and attach it to the handle provided. That attachment is done with the Attach() function. Thread B doesn't need to create the window because a real Windows object already exists; it was created by Thread A. Thread B does need to create, initialize, and manage an MFC C++ CWnd-derived object by itself, though. Thread B might use code similar to the following to accomplish this task:

```
CWnd* pMyWindow = new CWnd;
pMyWindow->Attach(hTheHandleFromThreadA);
```

Creating an MFC object and attaching it to an existing window in this way is just fine; it gets the job done. But you are responsible for managing that new CWnd object; when you are done with it, you can call CWnd::Detach() to divorce the MFC object from the real Windows object and then destroy the CWnd object. Or when you are done with the CWnd object, you can just destroy it and let MFC manage the detach itself — but this will have the side effect of destroying the actual window object.

You could, on the other hand, use the CWnd::FromHandlePermanent() function in Thread B. This call gets you a pointer to a permanently mapped

CWnd object for that thread. You won't have to manage the object; MFC will manage it for you. Since it is a permanent mapping, it doesn't disappear like a temporarily mapped object. That call would look like this:

```
CWnd* pThreadAWindow =
    CWnd::FromHandlePermanent(hTheHandleFromThreadA);
```

In this case, since you know the object referenced by pThreadAWindow, you can save it away anywhere you want and use it whenever you need to.

9.10.1 Wrapping Objects

The rule of not being able to access C++ objects from two different threads only applies to MFC objects that wrap Windows objects that are identified by handles. That is, it only applies to:

- CWnd-derived objects
- CMenu-derived objects
- CDC-derived objects
- CGdiObject-derived objects

Core Note

The exception to the rule is the CImageList class. Image lists are identified by a handle and wrapped by an MFC class, but MFC never lets that handle get mapped since it is never involved in the processing of messages.

So, you can access other objects from two different threads. You will certainly have no problem if they are not MFC objects, and you will certainly not have any problem if they are not in any of the above branches of the class hierarchy. You can even touch the objects we have identified as dangerous from different threads if you are doing something that doesn't involve the object's handle. If Thread A creates a CWnd-derived object that has some special member functions you have added, Thread B can call those special member functions if they don't ever touch the window handle. If they do, you will get the ASSERTs.

This should suggest something about the design of MFC programs to you: quite simply, you will have trouble accessing the same window from different threads unless you do some extra work to avoid those problems. (That extra work really amounts to nothing more than being careful with the MFC-created objects, as you have learned.) This implies that, if you want to go with the grain of MFC, you should not use more than one thread to manage the user interface of any single window. This is true: you will find that it is far more trouble than it is worth to paint into a window using two different threads.

Core Note

One last thing to consider when programming with threads (and processes, for that matter): Remember that sharing is important. If you have your primary thread create other threads, it will must be careful to shut them down correctly — don't resort to `::TerminateThread()`, *as you learned earlier.*

If different threads in your application share different resources, you will need to make sure that those resources are protected from being accessed in two different ways at the same time from two different threads. By using the synchronization objects you learned about in this chapter, you can ensure that you will stay out of trouble.

By focusing your design around your code's careful sharing and management of resources, you will always have less trouble when writing multithreaded applications.

9.11 Summary

This chapter has covered a great many details about the development of multi-threaded applications. By introducing extra threads to some applications, you can get a great performance benefit from your application, but you will also tremendously increase its complexity. That means more work for you, the developer, as you track down tricky synchronization problems and worry about resource leaks.

The most important thing to do when you are writing a multithreaded application is to concentrate very carefully on the design of the application. You must always consider the following issues:

- How threads will help solve the problem.
- How you will deal with killing threads in error situations.
- How the threads you create will get information back to their parent.

- What unseen things could cause the threads you have created to block.
- How your threads will react when the user suddenly closes the application.

By focusing your design around your code's careful sharing and management of resources, you will always have less trouble when writing multi-threaded applications.

In this chapter, you have learned how to create and manipulate threads and processes. You have also learned about the Windows waitable objects — not just critical sections, semaphores, mutexes, and events, but also processes and other special waitable objects.

You have focused on some of the issues involved in multithreaded development and have considered some of the most important questions to address when you consider using multiple threads in an application.

You have also learned that, in many cases, additional threads will not only degrade your processing, they may make it more difficult to solve problems with your program code.

Finally, you have learned about processes, and how you can manipulate processes from within your own program code. You have learned how to spawn processes, and the differences between processes and threads.

USING
ADVANCED
MEMORY
MANAGEMENT
TECHNIQUES

Topics in this Chapter

- Processes and Memory

- Understanding Differences Between 16- and 32-Bit Programs

- Understanding the Win32 Memory Model

- Overview of Simple Memory Management Techniques

- Returning to Virtual Memory and Advanced Memory Management

- Threads and Memory Management

- Accessing Physical Memory and I/O Ports

- Summary

Chapter 10

If you have done any Windows 3.x programming, you know that managing memory in the 16-bit mode on the Intel processor was a tricky game at best, with a single mistake in memory management enough to crash the entire operating system. While a single mistake, if catastrophic enough, can still crash 32-bit Windows operating systems, memory management has become much cleaner, more useful, and less dangerous than it used to be. In fact, memory management has become so greatly simplified that for most applications, `malloc()` or `new()` are all that you will need to allocate memory. Win32 memory management does have its own intricacies. However, programmers are no longer forced to learn about these intricacies to perform even the simplest tasks.

It is also worth noting that threads and processes, which you learned about in Chapter 9, are intimately tied to memory and memory management. In this chapter, you will learn about managing memory within your applications and more about the relationship between memory, processes, and threads.

10.1 Processes and Memory

Win32 provides a sophisticated memory management scheme. The two most distinguishing characteristics of this are the ability to run applications in separate address spaces, and the ability to expand the amount of memory available for allocation through the use of swap files. Both of these capabilities are part of Win32 *virtual memory management*. As you will learn, the entire Win32 memory model is fundamentally built around the virtual memory model and effective management of both virtual and physical memory.

10.1.1 Separate Address Spaces

For programmers familiar with 16-bit Windows, DOS, and other operating systems, one of the most difficult ideas to get used to when you start to do Win32 programming, is that an address in a Win32 program no longer represents a well-defined spot in physical memory. While one process may find a data item at address 0x10000000, another process may have a piece of its code running at the same address. Moreover, another process may regard that address as invalid, and even more importantly, the process address will generally refer to *three different addresses in virtual and physical memory*. Understanding how this is possible is crucial in developing a solid understanding of Win32 memory management.

Programmers generally refer to the addresses Win32 applications use as *logical addresses*. Every Win32 process has the entire range of 32-bit addresses available for its use (with some operating system specific restrictions, as you will learn later in this chapter). When a Win32 process references data at a logical address, the computer's memory management hardware intervenes and translates the address into a *physical address* (more on that later). The same logical address may (and under most circumstances, does) translate into different physical addresses for different processes. In general, each process has 4GB of available memory.

The Win32 memory management mechanism has several consequences. Most are beneficial, but some actually render certain programming tasks a bit harder to accomplish.

The most obvious benefit of having separate logical address spaces is that processes cannot accidentally overwrite code or data belonging to another process. Invalid pointers may still cause the offending process to halt, but those pointers cannot mangle data in the address space of other processes or the operating system.

On the other hand, the fact that processes no longer share the same logical address space renders the development of cooperating processes (that is, processes that work together and share data directly with each other) more difficult. In Win32 programming, you cannot simply send the address of an object in memory within one process to another process and expect that second process to be able to make use of the object. That address makes sense only in the context of the sending application; in the context of the application that receives it, it is meaningless, representing a random spot in memory.

Fortunately, the Win32 API offers a set of new mechanisms for cooperating applications to use. Among this set of mechanisms is the ability to use *shared memory*. Essentially, shared memory is a block of physical memory that is mapped into the logical address space of several processes. By writing data into, or reading data from, a block of shared memory, applications can cooperate with each other and easily share data.

Core Note

In addition to shared memory, you can share information between applications by using Object Linking and Embedding (OLE) technology.

10.1.2 Address Spaces

Earlier in this chapter, you learned that the use of 32-bit addresses within the logical address space of a process is not entirely unrestricted. Some address ranges are reserved for use by the operating system. Moreover, the restrictions are not the same in the different Win32 environments.

Using 32-bit addresses with byte-addressable memory means a total address space of 4GB (2^{32} = 4,294,967,296). Of this, Windows reserves the upper 2GB for its own use, while leaving the lower 2GB available for use by the application.

Windows 95 further reserves the lower 4MB of the address space. This area, often referred to as the *compatibility arena*, exists for compatibility with 16-bit DOS and Windows applications. As you have learned, Win32 applications run in separate address spaces. This is true, at least as far as the non-reserved areas of the logical address space are concerned. However, the situation of the reserved areas is somewhat different.

Under Windows 95, all reserved areas are shared. In other words, if one application finds a particular object at a memory location in one of the two reserved areas (lower 4MB or upper 2GB), all other applications are guaranteed to find the same object there. However, applications should not rely on this behavior; otherwise, the program will be incompatible with Windows NT (and thus not qualify for the Microsoft logo program). Besides, as you will see shortly, there are easy ways for applications to request a shared area in memory explicitly, and that mechanism works well under Windows NT, Windows 95, and Windows 98.

Windows 95/98 further divide the upper 2GB into two additional arenas. The arena between 2GB and 3GB is the *shared arena* that holds shared memory, memory-mapped files, and some 16-bit components (when necessary). The *reserved system arena* between 3GB and 4GB is where all of the operating system's privileged code resides. This arena is not addressable by non-privileged application programs.

10.1.3 Virtual Memory

In the previous sections, you learned quite a bit about memory — but the information carefully avoided a crucial issue — how Windows maps logical addresses to physical memory. After all, most computers do not have enough memory to hold several times the 4GB of memory that each application can address—in fact, most computers have only 128MB of memory or less in their physical memory storage. Moreover, many users do not even have 4GB (much less 12GB or 16GB) of available hard drive space on which to store all those addresses.

In fact, not all logical addresses of an application are actually mapped to physical storage, and those that are may not be mapped to physical *memory*.

Ever since the introduction of Windows 3.1, Windows has been able to use a *swap file*. The swap mechanism expands the amount of memory that the system can use by storing unused blocks of data on disk and loading them as needed. While swap files are several orders of magnitude slower than RAM, their use enables the system to run more applications or applications that are more resource-intensive than the application might be able to do otherwise.

The reason swap files can be used efficiently is that most applications allocate blocks of memory that are rarely used. For example, if you use a word processor to edit two documents simultaneously, it may happen that while you work on one document, you do not touch the other for extended periods of time. The operating system may free up physical memory in which the other document resides by *swapping* the document to disk. Doing so makes the physical memory available for other applications. When, after some time, you switch to the other document, you may notice some disk activity and a slight delay before the program displays the document. The delay is the result of the operating system loading the relevant portions of the swap file back into memory. At the same time, the operating system is likely swapping out other blocks of data not recently used to the swap file.

Figure 10-1 shows how the operating system and the computer's hardware accomplish the mapping of logical addresses. A table that is often called the *page table* contains information on all blocks or *pages* of memory. In effect, this table maps blocks in an application's logical address space to blocks in physical memory or portions of the swap file.

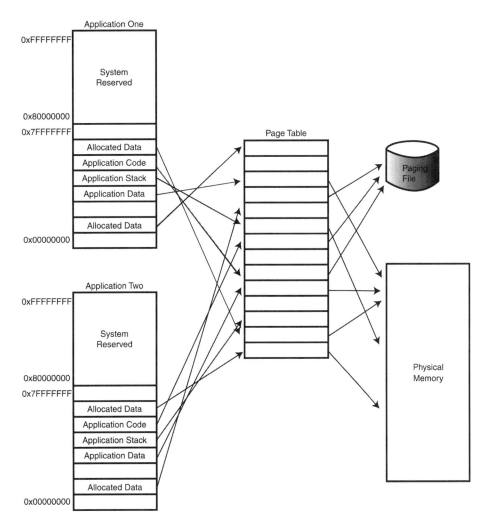

Figure 10-1 The operating system works with the computer's hardware to map logical addresses to physical memory, as shown here.

When the operating system maps a logical address to actual physical memory, the mapping is dereferenced and the data is read or written as requested. As the operation is supported by the processor's hardware, it does not require any extra time to resolve memory addresses this way.

When the logical address maps to a block in the system's swap file, a different series of events takes place. The attempt to reference such an invalid address triggers controls within the operating system. Windows then loads the requested block of data from the swap file into memory (while probably swapping out other blocks of data from memory to disk to make space). After the requested data is in physical memory and the operating system updates the page table to reflect the new address mappings, Windows returns control to the application. The application can then access the memory location successfully (because the map points to physical memory instead of the swap file). All the swapping and movement is completely transparent to the application, though not to the user, depending on the speed with which the operating system retrieves the data from the swap file. The only sign that would indicate that the requested block of memory was not readily available is the delay caused by the swapping operation.

The fact that logical addresses may map to physical memory locations, blocks of the swap file, or nothing at all implies some interesting possibilities. Furthermore, the existence of a mechanism that maps the contents of a file (namely, the swap file) to logical addresses also carries the potential for useful memory management—particularly if you can map the contents yourself, in addition to the operating system's default map. In fact, the Win32 API provides you with the means for your applications to explicitly manage virtual memory and to access disk data through *memory-mapped files*. The next section explores these and other memory management mechanisms.

10.2 Understanding Differences Between 16- and 32-Bit Programs

Because most Windows programmers have experience in programming 16-bit Windows (or some other 16-bit operating system), it is often helpful to begin an exploration of 32-bit memory management issues by considering the differences between 16- and 32-bit programs. A number of issues, such as integer size, the disappearance of the `far` and `near` specifiers (from the different DOS/Win16 memory models), and differences in address calculations will affect your coding practices when you write 32-bit programs.

10.2.1 Understanding the Differences in Integer Size

One of the most striking differences between the 16-bit and 32-bit environments can be demonstrated by the following simple example:

```
#include <iostream.h>

void main(void)
{
    cout << "sizeof(int) = " << sizeof(int);
}
```

When you run this program, it prints the following result:

```
sizeof(int) = 4
```

This is important, if you are a Win16/DOS programmer, because an integer was 2 bytes in length (16 bits) in those environments. In updating legacy code, you may face the difficulty of having to review older code for any signs of an explicit dependence on the 16-bit integer size.

One thing that has not changed is the size of types defined by Windows. Specifically, the types WORD and DWORD remain 16- and 32-bits wide, respectively. Use of these types when saving application data to disk ensures that the contents of a disk file remain readable by both the 16-and the 32-bit versions of the same application. In contrast, if an application used the int type when writing to disk, the contents of the disk file would be operating system dependent (because the operating systems would expect the values to be of different sizes).

10.2.2 Changes in Type Modifiers and Macros

One relatively obvious consequence of 32-bit addressing is that you no longer need to use type modifiers to distinguish between near and far pointers (a distinction of location within the 16-bit memory model), or to specify huge data. However, Microsoft has been kind enough to ensure that you do not need to modify existing programs to remove all references to the _near, _far, or _huge keywords. Instead, Visual C++ simply ignores these keywords to ensure backward compatibility.

Similarly, all the types that used to be defined in the windows.h header file, such as LPSTR for a far pointer to characters or LPVOID for a far pointer to a void type, still remain available. In the 32-bit environment, the header file simply defines these types as equivalent to their near counterparts. In other words, LPSTR is the same as PSTR, and LPVOID is the same as PVOID. To maintain backward compatibility (should you ever need to recompile your code with a 16-bit compiler), it is generally a good idea to continue using the correct types. This is further encouraged by the fact that the published interface to most Windows functions uses the correct (near or far) types.

10.2.3 Differences in Performing Address Calculations

Naturally, if your program performs address calculations specific to the segmented Intel architecture, you must modify it so that it does not do so any longer. If you do not, the applications will not work correctly. Moreover, such calculations would also be in violation of the platform-independent philosophy of the Win32 API, making it difficult to compile your program under Windows NT on the MIPS, Alpha, or other platforms.

A particular case that you must address regarding address calculations is the use of the LOWORD macro. In Windows 3.1, memory allocated with GlobalAlloc() was aligned on a segment boundary, with the offset set to 0. Some programmers used this fact to set addresses by simply modifying the low word of a pointer variable using the LOWORD macro. Under the Win32 API, the assumption that an allocated memory block starts on a segment boundary is no longer valid. The efficient yet questionable practice of using LOWORD in this manner will generally no longer work in Win32 programs.

10.2.4 Managing Library Functions

In the 16-bit environment, many functions had two versions. One version used near addresses, and one version used far addresses. It was often necessary to use both within a single program, or even within the same function (depending on the function's actions). For example, in medium-memory model programs, one frequently had to use _fstrcpy to copy characters from or to a far memory location. In the 32-bit environment, these functions are obsolete.

Core Note

If all this discussion of memory models, near and far pointers, and data types is meaningless to you, do not worry. Understanding the specifics of the Win16 and DOS memory models is not critical to working with the Win32 memory model. In fact, as you have learned, a solid understanding of the Win16 memory model may actually make it more difficult for you to manage memory under Win32.

The header file windowsx.h defines these obsolete function names to refer to their regular counterparts. By including this file in any program you compile that contains older source code, you can avoid having to manually line-check your source files and remove or change these obsolete function references.

10.3 Understanding the Win32 Memory Model

Ever since the introduction of the IBM PC, C/C++ programmers have had to learn a wide variety of compiler switches and options that control addressing behavior. Tiny, small, compact, medium, large, huge, and custom memory models, address conversions, 64KB code, and data segments size limitations all conspired to make writing programs in the 16-bit environment substantially more difficult than it probably needed to be. However, in 32-bit Windows, there is only one memory model (the virtual memory model), in which both addresses and code reside in a flat 32-bit memory space.

10.3.1 Using Selector Functions to Directly Manipulate Physical Memory

The Windows 3.1 API contains a set of functions (for example, `AllocSelector()` and `FreeSelector()`) that let programmers directly manipulate physical memory from within their applications. These functions are not available in the Win32 API. In fact, your 32-bit applications should generally not attempt to manipulate physical memory in any manner. In Win32 environments, the only applications that need to manipulate physical memory directly are device drivers.

10.4 Overview of Simple Memory Management Techniques

As you learned at the beginning of this chapter, memory allocation in the 32-bit environment is greatly simplified from memory management in the 16-bit environment. It is no longer necessary to separately allocate memory and lock it for use. The distinction between global and local heaps and allocations has disappeared. On the other hand, the 32-bit environment presents a set of new challenges for memory allocation and usage.

10.4.1 Using malloc() and new() to Allocate Memory

The memory management functions in earlier Windows versions, such as GlobalAlloc() and GlobalLock(), addressed a problem specific to *real mode* programming of the 80×86 processor family. Because applications used actual physical addresses to access objects in memory, there was no other way for the operating system to perform memory management functions. It was necessary for applications to abide by a convoluted mechanism by which they regularly relinquished control of these objects. This enabled the operating system to move these objects around as necessary. In other words, applications had to actively take part in memory management and cooperate with the operating system. Because malloc() not only allocated memory but also locked it in place, use of this function caused dangerous fragmentation of available memory.

Windows 3.1 uses Intel processes in *protected mode*. In protected mode, applications no longer have access to physical addresses. The operating system is able to move a memory block around even while applications hold valid addresses to it that they obtained through a call to GlobalLock() or LocalLock(). Using malloc() not only became safe, it became the recommended practice. Several implementations of this function also solved another problem. Because of a system-wide limit of 8,192 selectors, the number of times applications could call memory allocation functions without subsequently freeing up memory was limited. By providing a suballocation scheme, the newer malloc() implementations greatly helped applications that routinely allocated a large number of small memory blocks.

The 32-bit environment further simplifies memory allocation by eliminating the difference between global and local heaps. It is actually possible, although definitely not recommended by Microsoft or most programmers, to allocate memory with GlobalAlloc() and free it using LocalFree().

When you put it all together, it means that, in a Win32 application, you should generally allocate memory with malloc() or new(), release it with the corresponding free() or delete(), and let the operating system worry about all other aspects of memory management. For most applications, this approach is perfectly sufficient.

10.4.2 The Problem of Stray Pointers

Working with a 32-bit linear address space has one unexpected consequence. In the 16-bit environment, every call to GlobalAlloc() reserved a new *selector*. In protected mode in the Intel segmented architecture, selectors define blocks of memory; as part of the selector, the length of the block is also specified. Attempting to address memory outside the allocated limits of a selector resulted in a protection violation.

In the 32-bit environment, automatic and static objects, global and local dynamically allocated memory, the stack, and everything else belonging to the same application shares the application's heap and is accessed through flat 32-bit addresses. The operating system is less likely to catch stray pointers. The possibility of memory corruption through such pointers is greater, increasing the programmer's responsibility for ensuring that pointers stay within their intended bounds.

Consider, for example, the following code fragment:

```
HGLOBAL hBuffer1, hBuffer2;
LPSTR lpszBuffer1, lpszBuffer2;

hBuffer1 = GlobalAlloc(GPTR, 1024);
hBuffer2 = GlobalAlloc(GPTR, 1024);
lpszBuffer1 = GlobalLock(hBuffer1);
lpszBuffer2 = GlobalLock(hBuffer2);
lpszBuffer1[2000] = 'X';    /* Error! */
```

In this code fragment, the program code tries to write past the boundaries of the first buffer allocated that it allocated with GlobalAlloc(). In the 16-bit environment, this program code would result in a protection violation when the attempt is made to address a memory location outside the limits of the selector reserved by the first GlobalAlloc() call. In the 32-bit environment, however, the memory location referenced by lpszBuf1[2000] is probably valid, pointing to somewhere inside the second buffer. An attempt to write to this address will succeed and corrupt the contents of the second buffer.

On the other hand, it is practically impossible for an application to corrupt another application's memory space through stray pointers. This increases the overall stability of the operating system.

10.4.3 Sharing Memory Between Applications

Because each 32-bit application has a private virtual address space, it is no longer possible for such applications to share memory by simply passing pointers to each other in Windows messages. The GMEM_DDESHARE flag is no longer functional. As you learned, passing the handle of a 32-bit memory block to another application is meaningless and futile, because the handle only refers to a spot in the memory map for the private virtual address space of the recipient program.

If it is necessary for two applications to communicate using shared memory, they can do so using the DDEML library or by using memory-mapped files, which you will learn more about later in this chapter.

10.5 Returning to Virtual Memory and Advanced Memory Management

In the Win32 programming environment, applications have improved control over how they allocate and use memory. The Win32 API provides an extended set of memory management functions for programs to access. Figure 10-2 shows the different levels of memory management functions in the Win32 API.

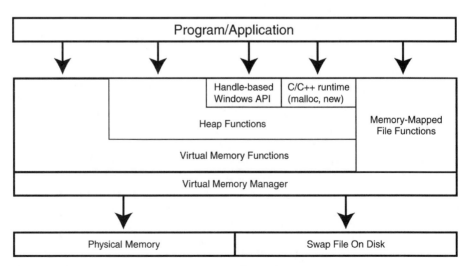

Figure 10-2 The relationship between application programs, memory management functions, and the virtual memory model in 32-bit Windows.

10.5.1 Win32 Virtual Memory Management

Figure 10-1, earlier in this chapter, might seem to indicate that pages of virtual memory must always be mapped to either physical memory or a paging (swap) file. However, despite the figure's simplicity, this is not always the case. Win32 memory management makes a distinction between reserved pages and committed pages. A *reserved page* of virtual memory is a page that is not backed by physical storage. In contrast, a *committed page* is a page that is backed by physical storage, either in physical memory or in the paging file.

However, understanding that there are two types of pages raises the question of why one would reserve pages without immediately committing them. One possibility is that you might not know in advance how much space the application will need to perform a certain operation. Using reserved pages lets you reserve a contiguous range of addresses in the virtual memory space of your process, without actually committing physical resources to that page until the application needs such resources. When the application makes a reference to an uncommitted page, the operating system generates an exception that your program can catch through structured exception handling. In turn, your program can instruct the operating system to commit the page, and then it can continue the processing that was interrupted by the exception.

Core Note

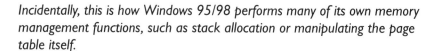

Incidentally, this is how Windows 95/98 performs many of its own memory management functions, such as stack allocation or manipulating the page table itself.

One commonly used example of reserved versus committed pages is when you are managing sparse matrices (two-dimensional arrays that have most of their array elements equal to zero). Sparse matrices appear frequently in technical applications. It is possible to reserve memory for the entire matrix but commit only those pages that contain nonzero elements, which has the net effect of significantly reducing the application's consumption of physical resources while still keeping the application code simple.

10.5.2 Windows API Virtual Memory Functions

An application can reserve memory through the `VirtualAlloc()` function. With this function, the application can explicitly specify the address and the size of the memory block about to be reserved. Additional parameters specify the type of the allocation (committed or reserved) and access protection flags. For example, the following code reserves 1MB of memory, starting at address 0x15000000, for reading and writing:

```
VirtualAlloc(0x15000000, 0x00100000, MEM_RESERVE, PAGE_READWRITE);
```

Later, the application can commit pages of memory by repeated calls to the `VirtualAlloc()` function. You can free memory that you allocate (whether it is reserved or committed memory) using the `VirtualFree()` function.

A special use of `VirtualAlloc()` concerns the establishment of *guard pages*. Guard pages act as one-shot alarms, raising an exception when the application attempts to access them. You can therefore use guard pages within your application to, for example, protect against accessing stray pointers that point past array boundaries.

You can use the `VirtualLock()` function to lock a memory block in physical memory (RAM), preventing the system from swapping out the block to the paging file on disk. Typically, you will use this function to ensure that the application can always access some block of critical data without disk I/O, no matter how much time has passed since you last accessed the data. You should not use this function because it can severely degrade system performance — if you restrict the operating system's capability to manage memory too greatly, the operating system will be unable to use the swap file effectively and will process data more slowly. You can unlock memory that you used the `VirtualLock()` function to lock with the `VirtualUnlock()` function.

An application can change the protection flags of committed pages of memory using the `VirtualProtect()` function. In addition, you can use the `VirtualProtectEx()` function to change the protection flags of a block of memory belonging to another process. Finally, you can use the `VirtualQuery()` function to obtain information about pages of memory, while you can use the `VirtualQueryEx()` function to obtain information about memory owned by another process.

You can create a simple application that uses virtual memory functions to manage a sparse matrix. This program could, for example, create a double-precision matrix of 10,000 × 10,000 elements. However, instead of allocating the total 800,000,000 bytes of memory that would be necessary to handle this matrix if every cell contained a value, it should only allocate memory on an as-needed basis. This mechanism is especially suitable for matrices that have very few nonzero elements; in this example, only 10 out of 100,000,000 elements would be set to random nonzero values.

This program first should reserve, but not commit, 800,000,000 bytes of memory for the matrix. Next, it should assign random values to 10 randomly selected elements. If the element falls on a page of virtual memory that is not yet committed (has no backing in physical memory or in the paging file), an exception would be raised. The exception would be caught using the C++ exception handling mechanism. The exception handler should check whether the value to be assigned is nonzero; if so, it should commit the page in question and repeat the assignment.

Core Note

In this simple example, the program would assume that the exception it will catch is always a Win32 structured exception indicating a memory access violation. In complex programs, this assumption may not always be valid and a more elaborate exception handling mechanism may be necessary to reliably identify exceptions. You will learn more about exception handling in Chapter 14.

In the last part of this program, the user may want to enter row and column index values. The program should then try to retrieve the value of the specified matrix element. If the element falls on a page that has not been committed, an exception would be raised; this time, it would be interpreted as an indication that the selected matrix element is zero.

This example program's output would look similar to that shown in Figure 10-3.

10.5.3 Functions

In addition to their default heap, processes can create additional heaps using the HeapCreate() function. Heap management functions can then be used to allocate and free memory blocks in the newly created private heap. A possible use of this mechanism involves the creation of a private heap at startup, specifying a size that is sufficient for the application's memory allocation needs. Failure to create the heap using HeapCreate() can cause the process to terminate; however, if HeapCreate() succeeds, the process is assured that the memory it requires is present and available.

```
MATRIX[91,4267] = 6334
MATRIX[6500,9169] = 15724
MATRIX[1478,9358] = 26962
MATRIX[4464,5705] = 28145
MATRIX[3281,6827] = 9961
MATRIX[491,2995] = 11942
MATRIX[4827,5436] = 32391
MATRIX[4604,3902] = 153
MATRIX[292,2382] = 17421
MATRIX[8716,9718] = 19895
Matrix populated, 10 pages used.
Total bytes committed: 40960

Enter row: 91
Enter column: 4267
MATRIX[41,8467] = 6334

Enter row: 41
Enter column: 8400
MATRIX[41,8400] = 0

Enter row: 1
Enter column: 1
Exception handler was invoked.
MATRIX[1,1] = 0

Enter row:
```

Figure 10-3   The output of the example sparse matrix program.

After a heap is created via HeapCreate(), processes can allocate memory from it using HeapAlloc(). HeapRealloc() can be used to change the size of a previously allocated memory block, and HeapFree() deallocates memory blocks and returns them to the heap. The size of a previously allocated block can be obtained using HeapSize().

It is important to note that the memory allocated by HeapAlloc() is no different from memory obtained using the standard memory allocation functions, such as GlobalAlloc(), GlobalLock(), or malloc().

Heap management functions can also be used on the default heap of the process. A handle to the default heap can be obtained using the GetProcessHeap() function. GetProcessHeap() returns a list of all heap handles owned by the process.

A heap can be destroyed using the function `HeapDestroy()`. This function should not be used on the default heap handle of the process that is returned by `GetProcessHeap()`. (Destroying the default heap would mean destroying the application's stack, global and automatic variables, and so on, with obviously disastrous consequences.)

The function `HeapCompact()` attempts to compact the specified heap by coalescing adjacent free blocks of memory and decommitting large free blocks. Note that objects allocated on the heap by `HeapAlloc()` are not movable, so the heap can easily become fragmented. `HeapCompact()` will not unfragment a badly fragmented heap.

10.5.4 Windows API and C Runtime Memory Management

At the top of the hierarchy of memory management functions are the standard Windows and C runtime memory management functions. As noted earlier, these functions are likely to prove adequate for the memory management requirements of most applications. Handle-based memory management functions provided in the Windows API include `GlobalAlloc()` and `LocalAlloc()`, `GlobalLock()` and `LocalLock()`, and `GlobalFree()` and `LocalFree()`. The C/C++ runtime library contains the `malloc()` family of functions (`malloc()`, `realloc()`, `calloc()`, `free()`, and other functions). These functions are safe to use and provide compatibility with the 16-bit environment, should it become necessary to build applications that can be compiled as both 16-bit and 32-bit programs.

10.5.5 Miscellaneous and Obsolete Functions

In addition to the API functions already described, a number of miscellaneous functions are also available to the Win32 programmer. Several other functions that were available under Windows 3.1 have been deleted or become obsolete.

Memory manipulation functions include `CopyMemory()`, `FillMemory()`, `MoveMemory()`, and `ZeroMemory()`. These are equivalent to their C runtime counterparts, such as `memcpy()`, `memmove()`, or `memset()`.

A set of Windows API functions is provided to verify whether a given pointer provides a specific type of access to an address or range of addresses. These functions are `IsBadCodePtr()`, `IsBadStringPtr()`, `IsBad-ReadPtr()`, and `IsBadWritePtr()`. For the latter pair, huge versions

(`IsBadHugeReadPtr()`, `IsBadHugeWritePtr()`) are also provided for backward compatibility with Windows 3.1.

Information about available memory can be obtained using `GlobalMemoryStatus()`. This function replaces the obsolete `GetFreeSpace()` function.

Other obsolete functions include all functions that manipulate selectors (for example, `AllocSelector()`, `ChangeSelector()`, `FreeSelector()`); manipulate the processor's stack (`SwitchStackBack()`, `SwitchStackTo()`); manipulate segments (`LockSegment()`, `UnlockSegment()`); or manipulate MS-DOS memory (`GlobalDOSAlloc()`, `GlobalDOSFree()`).

10.5.6 Memory-Mapped Files and Shared Memory

Earlier in this chapter, I mentioned that applications are no longer capable of communicating using global memory created with the `GMEM_DDESHARE` flag. Instead, they must use memory-mapped files to share memory. Let's take a look, then, at what memory-mapped files are.

Normally, the virtual memory mechanism enables an operating system to map nonexistent memory to a disk file, called the paging file. It is possible to look at this the other way around and see the virtual memory mechanism as a method of referring to the contents of a file, namely the paging file, through pointers, as if the paging file were a memory object. In other words, the mechanism maps the contents of the paging file to memory addresses. If this can be done with the paging file, it only stands to reason that you can also do it with other files. Memory-mapped files represent this natural extension to the virtual memory management mechanism.

You can create a file mapping by using the `CreateFileMapping()` function. You can also use the `OpenFileMapping()` function to enable an application to open an existing named mapping. The `MapViewOfFile()` function maps a portion of the file to a block of virtual memory.

The special thing about memory-mapped files is that they are shared between applications. That is, if two applications open the same named file mapping, they will, in effect, create a block of shared memory.

Isn't it a bit of overkill to be forced to use a disk file when the objective is merely to share a few bytes between two applications? Actually, it is not necessary to explicitly open and use a disk file in order to obtain a mapping in memory. Applications can submit the special handle value of 0xFFFFFFFF to `CreateFileMapping()` in order to obtain a mapping to the system paging file itself. This, in effect, creates a block of shared memory.

The following listings demonstrate the use of shared memory objects for intertask communication. They implement a simple mechanism in which one program, the client, deposits a simple message (a null-terminated string) in shared memory for the other program. This other program, the server, receives the message and displays it. These programs are written for the Windows 95 or Windows NT command line. To see how they work, start two MS-DOS windows, start the server program first in one of the windows, and then start the client program in the other. The client sends its message to the server; the server, in turn, displays the message it receives and then terminates.

```
// Intertask communication using shared memory: The server.
#include <iostream.h>
#include <windows.h>

void main(void)
{
  HANDLE hmmf;
  LPSTR lpMsg;

  hmmf = CreateFileMapping((HANDLE)0xFFFFFFFF, NULL,
        PAGE_READWRITE, 0, 0x1000, "MMFDEMO");

  if (hmmf == NULL) {
    cout << "Failed to allocated shared memory.\n";
    exit(1);
  }
  lpMsg = (LPSTR)MapViewOfFile(hmmf,
      FILE_MAP_WRITE, 0, 0, 0);
  if (lpMsg == NULL) {
    cout << "Failed to map shared memory.\n";
    exit(1);
  }
  lpMsg[0] = '\0';
  while (lpMsg[0] == '\0') Sleep(1000);
  cout << "Message received: " << lpMsg << '\n';
  UnmapViewOfFile(lpMsg);
}

// Intertask communication using shared memory: The client.
#include <iostream.h>
#include <windows.h>

void main(void)
```

```
{
    HANDLE hmmf;
    LPSTR lpMsg;
    hmmf = CreateFileMapping((HANDLE)0xFFFFFFFF, NULL,
                        PAGE_READWRITE, 0, 0x1000, "MMFDEMO");
    if (hmmf == NULL)
    {
        cout << "Failed to allocated shared memory.\n";
        exit(1);
    }
    lpMsg = (LPSTR)MapViewOfFile(hmmf, FILE_MAP_WRITE, 0, 0, 0);
    if (lpMsg == NULL)
    {
        cout << "Failed to map shared memory.\n";
        exit(1);
    }
    strcpy(lpMsg, "This is my message.");
    cout << "Message sent: " << lpMsg << '\n';
    UnmapViewOfFile(lpMsg);
}
```

These two programs are nearly identical. They both start by creating a file mapping of the system paging file with the name MMFDEMO. After the mapping is successfully created, the server sets the first byte of the mapping to zero and enters a wait loop, checking once a second to see whether the first byte is nonzero. The client, in turn, deposits a message string at the same location and exits. When the server notices that the data is present, it prints the result and also exits.

10.5.7 Shared Memory and Based Pointers

A shared memory-mapped file object may not necessarily appear at the same address for all processes. While shared memory objects are mapped to identical locations in the address spaces of Windows 95 processes, the same is not true in Windows NT. This can be a problem if applications want to include pointers in the shared data. One solution to this problem is to use based pointers and set them to be relative to the start of the mapping area.

Based pointers are a Microsoft-specific extension of the C/C++ language. A based pointer is declared using the __based keyword, in a fashion similar to the following:

```
void *vpBase;

void __based(vpBase) *vpData;
```

References through the based pointer always point to data relative to the specified base. Their utility extends beyond shared memory; based pointers can also be very useful when saving data that contains pointers to disk.

10.6 Threads and Memory Management

The multithreaded nature of 32-bit Windows presents some additional challenges when it comes to memory management. As threads may concurrently access the same objects in memory, it is possible that one thread's operation on a variable is interrupted by another's. Obviously, a synchronization mechanism is needed to avoid this. In other situations, threads may want private copies of a data object, instead of a shared copy.

10.6.1 Interlocked Variable Access

The first of the two problems I mentioned is solved in many cases by *interlocked variable access*. This mechanism enables a thread to change the value of an integer variable and check the result without the possibility of being interrupted by another thread.

Under normal circumstances, if you increment or decrement a variable within a thread, it is possible that another thread changes the value of this variable once again before the first thread has a chance to examine its value. The functions `InterlockedIncrement()` and `InterlockedDecrement()` can be used to atomically increment or decrement a 32-bit value and check the result. A third function, `InterlockedExchange()`, can be used to atomically set a variable's value and retrieve the old value, without the fear of being interrupted by another thread.

10.6.2 Thread-Local Storage

While automatic variables are always local to the instance of the function in which they are allocated, the same is not true for global or static objects. If your code relies heavily on such objects, it may prove to be very difficult to make your application thread-safe.

Fortunately, the Win32 API offers a mechanism to allocate *thread-local storage*. The `TlsAlloc()` function can be used to reserve a *TLS Index*, which is a `DWORD` sized space. Threads can use this space, for example, to store a pointer to a private block of memory through the `TlsSetValue()`

and `TlsGetValue()` functions. The `TlsFree()` function can be used to release the `TLS index`.

If this doesn't sound easy, don't despair. The Visual C++ compiler provides an alternative mechanism that is much easier to use. Data objects can be declared thread local using the thread type modifier. For example:

```
__declspec(thread) int i;
```

Using `__declspec(thread)` is problematic in DLLs because of a problem in extending the global memory allocation of a DLL at runtime to accommodate thread-local objects. It is recommended that you use the TLS APIs, such as TlsAlloc, in code that is intended to run in a DLL.

10.7 Accessing Physical Memory and I/O Ports

Programmers of 16-bit Windows are used to the idea of accessing physical memory or the input/output ports of Intel processors directly. For example, it is possible to write a 16-bit application that accesses a custom hardware device through memory-mapped I/O. It is natural to expect that those programming practices can be carried over to the 32-bit operating system.

However, this is not the case. Win32 is a *platform-independent* operating system specification. As such, anything that introduces platform (hardware) dependence is fundamentally incompatible with the operating system. This includes all kinds of access to actual physical hardware, such as ports or physical memory addresses.

So what can you do if your task is to write an application that communicates directly with hardware? The answer is that you require one of the various DDKs (Device Driver Kits). Through the DDK, it is possible to create a driver library that encapsulates all low-level access to the device and keep your high-level Win32 application free of platform dependencies.

10.8 Summary

Memory management in Win32 is markedly different from memory management in 16-bit Windows. Applications need no longer be concerned about issues related to the Intel segmented architecture. On the other hand, new capabilities mean new responsibilities for the programmer.

Win32 applications run in separate address spaces. A pointer in the context of one application is meaningless in the context of another. All applications have access to a 4GB address space through 32-bit addresses (although the different Win32 implementations reserve certain portions of this address space for special purposes).

Win32 operating systems use virtual memory management to map a logical address in an application's address space to a physical address in memory or a block of data in the system's swap or paging file. Applications can explicitly use virtual memory management capabilities to create memory-mapped files, or to reserve, but not commit, huge blocks of virtual memory.

Memory-mapped files offer a very efficient intertask communication mechanism. By gaining access to the same memory-mapped file object, two or more applications can utilize such a file as shared memory.

Special features address the unique problems of memory management in threads. Through interlocked variable access, threads can perform atomic operations on shared objects. Through thread-local storage, threads can allocate privately owned objects in memory.

Many of the old Windows and DOS memory management functions are no longer available. Because of the platform independence of Win32, applications can no longer access physical memory directly. If it is necessary to directly access hardware (as is the case when custom hardware is used), it may be necessary to utilize the appropriate Device Driver Kit.

WORKING WITH THE FILE SYSTEM

Topics in this Chapter

- File System Overview
- Networked File Systems and Mapped Volumes
- Win32 File Objects
- Compatibility I/O
- Serial Communications
- Using Consoles
- Summary

Chapter 11

Modern operating systems such as Windows provide a huge variety of services and features. However, if you were to ask what services comprise the core function of an operating system, providing a file system would surely be near the top of the list.

The dual requirements of file system evolution and backwards compatibility have littered the Windows operating system variants with a spectrum of old and new file systems.

To ensure that you can exploit the best file system features and still maintain compatibility across the various platforms, you should be aware of these differences and their implications on the behavior of file and device I/O functions.

11.1 File System Overview

Put simply, a file system turns a vast homogenous array of bits in a storage medium into a highly organized hierarchical structure more akin to the human mode of categorically orientated thinking.

It must also be fast and efficient, making good use of the underlying technology to provide rapid response to user requests to retrieve and store data.

Each file system occupies a storage device, such as a floppy or a CD drive, or an area on a hard disk called a volume. These volumes are labeled with drive names such as A:, B:, C:, D:, and so on.

File systems have evolved to offer many more advanced features, such as long filenames, file security via permissions and ownership, network volume mapping, virtual files, and file/directory compression.

This evolution has led to a number of file system types. Windows NT supports the largest set of file system types, providing support for both the latest innovative file systems and the older, simpler types. Windows 98 supports the next largest set with Windows 95 and Windows 3.11 bringing up the rear.

Things became more confused as support for some file system types were dropped in later versions of the operating system (for example, HPFS was dropped in NT 4.0).

The following sections attempt to clarify the various file system types and the operating system versions that support them.

11.1.1   The FAT File System

The FAT (File Allocation Table) file system is the simplest of all the file systems and is supported by all Windows operating systems.

The FAT file system (also known as FAT-16) is a holdover from the MS-DOS operating system. As its name suggests, it merely stores a table (and a backup table) of all the files and their positions on the disk. The table is stored at the beginning of a disk volume and must be updated whenever files are added or modified. New data is just allocated to slots large enough to contain it, leading to high fragmentation.

This simplicity leads to poor performance and limited robustness. The maximum size of a FAT file system is 4GB under Windows NT, but performance is seriously degraded for file systems larger than 200MB.

Core Note

The FAT file system was originally limited to 32MB partitions, until MS-DOS version 4 increased the size of the FAT entries. After version 4, FAT-16 was still limited to 4GB file systems. It was not until the release of FAT-32 and NTFS that larger file partitions were supported.

The basic FAT filenames are limited to eight characters followed by a dot and then a three-letter suffix. All lowercase letters in filenames are converted into uppercase when stored. Longer filenames are automatically truncated and made unique by conversion to a six-character name followed by a tilde and an auto-generated number to preserve uniqueness.

FAT file systems support only the very basic file attributes (such as read only, archive, hidden, and system). No security attributes or permissions can be assigned to files on a FAT file system.

It is unusual for modern Windows versions to create pure FAT file systems for their main hard disk partitions. But older systems (including early versions of Windows 95) may still use and preserve FAT file systems. Also, floppy disks still use FAT (Protected Mode) because it is the common denominator for file interchange and has a small footprint for small volume sizes (such as the common 1.44MB floppy disk standard).

11.1.2 Protected Mode FAT

Windows NT 3.5 and Windows 95 (and subsequent versions) use a clever trick to preserve long filenames by using several FAT entries to encode each file with a longer filename. This method of tricking the operating system is known as *protected-mode FAT* and allows filenames up to 256 characters in length.

These additional entries are marked with the hidden attribute so they appear invisible when browsing the directory entries. This system lets MS-DOS applications see the 8.3 component as normal, but more modern Windows versions can preserve longer names.

11.1.3 The FAT-32 File System

Originally, Windows 95 used the pure FAT file system (FAT-16). However, this was inefficient for the more common larger disk volumes because even a one-byte file would have to consume 32KB of disk space as the cluster size increased.

The FAT-32 file system was introduced with operating system release 2 (OSR2) of Windows 95. It liberates lots of disk space tied up in those large clusters by reducing the cluster size to 4KB (for up to 8GB disk volumes).

The other big advantage of FAT-32 is the ability to support much larger disk volumes up to a limit of 2TB (Terra Bytes) or 2,048GB.

Windows 98 supports both FAT-16 and FAT-32 file systems. FAT-16 is used by default, but FAT-32 can deliver more disk space and better performance.

11.1.4   The HPFS File System

The HPFS (High Performance File System) originated from the OS/2 operating system. It allowed access to larger disk volumes than FAT, and filenames up to 254 characters in length (and double-byte character sets such as Unicode in filenames).

HPFS also allowed flexible attribute information with a block of up to 64K available for user-defined attributes, but didn't have integrated file system level security.

HPFS gave a large performance increase over the FAT file systems, but performance degraded with larger volume sizes.

Support for HPFS was dropped from Windows NT 4.0 onwards, and previous versions of Windows NT didn't support security permissions for HPFS. Windows 95 and 98 have no support for HPFS.

11.1.5   The NTFS File System

The NTFS (New Technology File System) was designed with Windows NT to fully support the sophisticated NT security model at a low level. (However, lack of file encryption makes this fairly pointless as the volume can be interrogated freely from other operating systems.)

Filenames under NTFS can be up to 255 characters in length and preserve case (although they are not case sensitive). The theoretical volume size for NTFS exceeds any existing hardware allowing volumes of up to 16EB (about 16,777,216TB) and is thought to be very robust because it keeps multiple copies of the file information.

NTFS is fast and gives a good scaleable performance for file systems with volume sizes of 400MB or larger. There is no support for NTFS under Windows 95 or Windows 98, but Windows NT (obviously) supports it.

11.1.6   The CDFS File System

The CDFS (Compact Disk File System) is based on the ISO 9660 standard (but extends it to allow long and double-byte filenames). It appears to applications like a FAT file system.

Windows 95/98 and Windows NT 3.5 (and subsequent versions) support CDFS.

11.2 Networked File Systems and Mapped Volumes

The (modern) Windows family of operating systems (95/98 and NT) was designed with networked file system sharing from the ground up. Applications can specify filenames that conform to the Universal Naming Convention (UNC), which include the name of the host machine, the requested volume on that machine, and the path and filename of the target file.

The host name starts with the two backslash characters \\. The rest of the name is then separated by single backslashes as in an ordinary path name. For example, the UNC name `\\KlanNtServer\SampDriv\thefile.cpp` means find the file called `thefile.cpp` on the volume labeled `SampDriv` on the machine called `KlanNtServer`.

This name is submitted to the Multiple Universal Name Convention Provider (MUP), which attempts to resolve the name and hand the file access request over to a network redirector (RDR).

The RDR then contacts the host machine and passes the I/O request to the remote networked host machine to deal with. The host machine then passes the request to the file system for the specified volume, which then sends any return data back to the calling machine.

You can map one of these UNC names to a virtual volume on your local machine (as is done from Windows Explorer with the Tools/Map Network Drive... option).

This assigns a local volume letter to the UNC name and establishes a connection to the remote host machine specified. Once established, your applications can specify the volume name and destination filename without needing the full UNC name. This lets applications treat the remote volume as if it were just another local storage device, which is very useful for older UNC-unaware applications.

For example, if you were to map `\\KlanNtServer\SampDrive\` as `I:`, then you could access `thefile.cpp` from your application as simply `I:\thefile.cpp`. Because UNC naming allows subdirectory naming, you can also specify subdirectories to map, which then appear as complete volumes in their own right.

However, for operating systems such as Windows 95 and 98 that have little built-in security, allowing such freedom of access to a networked machine would have dreadful security implications. Therefore, your local machine can access only remote volumes that have been explicitly marked for sharing by a remote machine (which can be done from the Sharing... context menu option in Windows Explorer).

Because the host machine implements the actual file system access, networking allows interaction between normally incompatible file systems and platforms. For example, Windows 95 and 98 operating systems can easily access files on a Window NT NTFS via shared file systems because the actual file system access is performed by the Windows NT host machine.

11.2.1   The DFS File System

A DFS (Distributed File System) extends the concept of networked file systems and file mapping so that remote volumes can be mounted on a local file system transparently as subdirectories.

Other operating systems such as UNIX have had this design philosophy from their inception, however Windows has evolved from the MS-DOS drive name world and was forced by backwards compatibility issues to accept volume mapping by drive letter.

Windows NT server addresses the problems that drive letter mapping imposes (such as running out of letters in large networked file systems) by supporting DFS.

Windows NT Workstation and Windows 95/98 platforms can access files over a DFS but only via a Windows NT server.

DFS provides an excellent mechanism for large organizations to simplify the administration, backup, and virus scanning of a large number of individual PCs by mounting each PC as a subdirectory of an organization wide network.

11.2.2   File System Compression

Both Windows NT and Windows 95/98 support volume compression, although the technique used differs. Windows 95 and 98 use a special format called DriveSpace whereas Windows NT lets you set a compression attribute against each folder to compress that folder.

Unfortunately, Windows NT cannot access Windows 95/98 FAT file systems that have been compressed with the DriveSpace format (except via network access).

This can cause problems on dual boot machines and so compression should therefore be avoided.

Compression techniques also have a performance penalty depending on the type of compression and the file being accessed.

11.2.3 Disk Quotas

With NTFS version 5 (with Windows 2000) a technique called disk quotas will be supported. This means that administrators can assign specific limits to the amount of disk space available to individual users.

Write functions may fail when users reach their own quota limit even though sufficient disk space exists on the volume as a whole.

11.2.4 Differences in Functions Among File Systems

The various capabilities and drawbacks of all of these different file system types have implications that reach right down to individual operating system function calls. If you are designing an application that must work on a variety of platforms, you must be aware of these differences and respond to various return and error codes as appropriate.

Large parts of the API are ignored by lack of file system support, especially in the sophisticated areas of NT security.

11.2.5 Determining the File System and Drive Types

You can determine the file system type for a volume from within your code using the GetVolumeInformation() Win32 API function. You can pass the name of a file system's root directory to this function along with pointers to various buffers to retrieve lots of information regarding the file system's capabilities and type.

You can also find details about the type of device a particular root path belongs to by passing the root path name to GetDriveType(). The value returned will indicate whether the drive is a network drive, a CD-ROM drive, fixed disk, or other type of technology.

11.3 Win32 File Objects

The basic low-level file manipulation and device I/O functions provided by the Win32 API are CreateFile(), ReadFile(), WriteFile(),

`SetFilePointer()`, `LockFile()`, `UnlockFile()`, and `CloseHandle()`. There are many more, but these are probably the most commonly used.

These functions manipulate a Win32 file object referenced by a Win32 `HANDLE` type. The object can be of many various types such as:

- Simple disk (or RAM disk) file
- Directory (disk directories)
- Disk drive (physical floppy and hard disks accessed as raw data)
- Sequential communications device such as a serial or parallel port
- Console object that simulates a simple ANSI-style text terminal
- Named pipe (an interprocess communication (IPC) mechanism that allows one process to efficiently send data to another via shared memory)
- Mailslot (another IPC mechanism that lets one process send data to a number of others simultaneously)

11.3.1   Basic File I/O

`CreateFile()` is used to both create new files and open existing files, and returns a Win32 `HANDLE` to the open file.

The first parameter to `CreateFile()` is the filename, which can be a UNC file and path name or the name of a device such as COM1: or LPT1:.

The size of this filename is limited under Windows 95/98 to the maximum size defined by `MAX_PATH` (which is set to 260 characters). However, under Windows NT, you can prefix the path name with the characters `\\?\` to bypass this limitation.

The second parameter lets you specify the requested access mode, which can be `NULL` if you only wish to accept the default attributes of the file, or a combination of `GENERIC_READ` and `GENERIC_WRITE` for read and write access, respectively.

The third parameter lets you specify how you wish to share the file with other applications. If you want exclusive access, you can pass a `NULL` value, otherwise the `FILE_SHARE_READ` or `FILE_SHARE_WRITE` indicate that you will let other applications have read or write access to the file.

The fourth parameter to `CreateFile()` lets you specify security attributes by passing a pointer to a `SECURITY_ATTRIBUTES` structure. These attributes are only available under Windows NT and you would normally pass a `NULL` to this parameter to gain the same (default) attributes as the calling process. However, if your application spawns other processes and wants them to inherit this file handle, you should set the `bInheritHandle` member of this structure to `TRUE`, otherwise the child process will not be able to use the file. This also applies to Windows 95 and Windows 98.

The fifth parameter lets you specify how you want to open the file; you can pass any of the values from Table 11-1:

Table 11-1 File Open/Creation Flags	
Flag Value	*Description*
OPEN_EXISTING	Opens an existing file or device and returns an error if the specified name doesn't exist.
OPEN_ALWAYS	If the file doesn't exist, the function will create it as if you had passed the CREATE_NEW flag.
TRUNCATE_EXISTING	Opens an existing file and wipes out the contents so that the file becomes zero length.
CREATE_NEW	Creates a new file, but returns an error if the file already exists.
CREATE_ALWAYS	Creates a new file, regardless of any existing file with the same name.

The sixth parameter lets you set and combine specific file attributes such as hidden, archive, and read-only. Normally, you would use the `FILE_ATTRIBUTE_NORMAL` flag value.

You can also set a large number of flags in this parameter that change the way in which the subsequent file read and write functions work, such as:

- Data is written immediately without waiting for a write cache to be flushed.
- No buffering is performed.
- A special asynchronous mode called overlapping may be set in which read and write requests can return immediately even though the data hasn't been read or written to allow the calling program to perform some other processing after issuing the request (discussed later).
- The file is deleted when closed.

- Hints to increase performance when reading a file randomly or sequentially.

The seventh parameter lets you specify the handle of a template file that can be used to set the file attributes of a file being created. However, this functionality isn't supported on Windows 95 and will return an unsupported error code.

If `CreateFile()` successfully creates the file, a valid `HANDLE` to that Win32 file object is returned; otherwise `INVALID_HANDLE_VALUE` is returned. You can use the `GetLastError()` function to find out what went wrong and return an appropriate error code as with all of the file I/O functions.

You can then use the `HANDLE` value for subsequent `ReadFile()` and `WriteFile()` operations. The parameters for `ReadFile()` and `Write-File()` indicate a buffer to store or read the data from, the number of bytes to write or read, and a pointer to a `DWORD` value to store the number of bytes successfully read or written. There is also a pointer to an `OVERLAPPED` structure for overlapped I/O (discussed later). You can pass `NULL` for this parameter for normal blocking I/O (waiting for the function to complete). These functions return a simple boolean value to indicate success (`TRUE`) or failure (`FALSE`).

You can reposition the current file with the `SetFilePointer()` function. You can pass an amount to move by, and a flag value, or `FILE_BEGIN`, `FILE_CURRENT`, or `FILE_END` to indicate that the amount is relative to the start, current position, or end of the file.

This function lets you specify 64-bit amounts to move by. Normally (for files smaller than 4GB), you'd only use the second parameter to specify the low 32-bit value and pass zero to the third parameter. However, if you have truly huge files, you can pass the high order 32-bit word in the third parameter to access 2^{64} bytes of data!

If a call to `SetFilePointer()` fails, a value of `(DWORD)-1` is returned.

You can lock and unlock sections of a file using the `LockFile()` and `UnlockFile()` functions. These functions also let you specify two 64-bit numbers for the byte position to lock from, and the size of the locked region. A boolean return code indicates success or failure.

Finally, you can close the file with a call to the `CloseHandle()` function.

Files can be copied by passing the source and destination filenames to the `CopyFile()` function, or renamed with the `MoveFile()` function.

The following listing illustrates these various file handling functions with a program that uses a Win32 file object to calculate prime numbers (unusually getting faster with the higher primes!):

```
#include "stdafx.h"
#include "windows.h"
#include "iostream.h"

const DWORD dwPrimes = 50000;// Primes to 50,000

DWORD TestPrimes(HANDLE hFile);
DWORD DisplayError(LPSTR strError);

int main(int argc, char* argv[])
{
   HANDLE hPrimes = CreateFile(
       "Primes",                    // Filename
       GENERIC_READ|GENERIC_WRITE,  // Read & Write
       NULL,                        // No Sharing
       NULL,                        // Default Security
       CREATE_ALWAYS,               // Create it
       FILE_FLAG_DELETE_ON_CLOSE,   // Delete afterwards
       NULL);                       // No template
   if (hPrimes == INVALID_HANDLE_VALUE)
       return DisplayError("Creating");
   // Set the file size to the max number of primes
   char buf[100];
   memset(buf,0,sizeof(buf));
   DWORD dwBytesWritten;
   while(WriteFile(hPrimes,&buf,sizeof(buf), &dwBytesWritten,NULL))
       if (GetFileSize(hPrimes,NULL)>dwPrimes)
          break;
   TestPrimes(hPrimes);
   return CloseHandle(hPrimes); // Close the file
}

DWORD TestPrimes(HANDLE hFile)
{
   DWORD dwBytesRead,dwBytesWritten,dwTestPrime = 2;
   do {
       BOOL bFillMode = FALSE;
       DWORD dwPos = dwTestPrime;
       while(dwPos<dwPrimes) {
          if (SetFilePointer(hFile,dwPos,0, FILE_BEGIN)==(DWORD)-1)
             return DisplayError("Positioning");
          if (!bFillMode) {                // Is it a prime?
             BYTE byteTestByte;
            if (!ReadFile(hFile,&byteTestByte,1, &dwBytesRead,NULL))
                return DisplayError("Reading");
```

```
            if (byteTestByte == 0) {
                cout << dwPos << ";" << flush;
                bFillMode = TRUE;

                // Backup a byte
                if (SetFilePointer(hFile,-1,0,
                    FILE_CURRENT)==(DWORD)-1)
                    return DisplayError("Positioning");
            }
        }
        if (bFillMode) {              // Remove all the factors
            BYTE byteFill = 1;
            if (!WriteFile(hFile,&byteFill,1,&dwBytesWritten,NULL))
                return DisplayError("Writing");
        }
        dwPos+=dwTestPrime;
    }
    } while(dwTestPrime++ < dwPrimes);
    return 0;
}


DWORD DisplayError(LPSTR strError)
{
    DWORD dwError = GetLastError();
    cout << "An error occurred when " << strError
        << ", Errno = " << dwError;
    return dwError;
}
```

11.3.2 Asynchronous I/O

Asynchronous I/O under Windows is curiously termed overlapped I/O. Fundamentally, these terms refer to the ability to start a read or write request, then return from the read or write function immediately, without waiting for the request to finish. Given that I/O usually involves considerable waiting, asynchronous I/O can speed up a program by allowing it to perform some other processing while the I/O request is handled in the background. After your program has performed some other processing, it can check to see if the I/O request has completed, and either process the I/O or continue with other jobs.

Some single-threaded programs may need to perform asynchronous operations so that they don't block while waiting for input (such as characters from a serial port or keyboard).

Core Warning

Windows 95 doesn't support asynchronous I/O operation for disk files and consoles, although other objects such as serial ports, network sockets, and anonymous pipes are supported.

You can indicate that you wish to perform an asynchronous I/O operation on a Win32 file object by passing the FILE_FLAG_OVERLAPPED value to the sixth parameter of the CreateFile() function used to open the object. You must then provide a pointer to an OVERLAPPED structure for subsequent read and write operations.

The OVERLAPPED structure is then filled with internal information about the request when you call ReadFile() or WriteFile(). The Read-File() or WriteFile() function will return immediately, and your program can perform other tasks. The functions will return a FALSE value, indicating that an error has occurred with GetLastError() and returning an ERROR_IO_PENDING value. This is a normal return code for asynchronous operations and just indicates that the operation is in progress.

You can then periodically check if the operation has completed by using the HasOverlappedIoCompleted() macro, passing it a pointer to the OVERLAPPED structure.

You should ensure that the memory for this structure doesn't fall out of scope or become deleted before the function returns, otherwise a nasty crash or a blocked I/O situation can occur.

You can set the Offset and OffsetHigh DWORD members of the OVERLAPPED structure to specify a start position for a disk file transfer. You can also set the hEvent member to a manual-reset synchronization event handle that will be set to the signaled state when the operation has been completed. This lets you use the WaitForSingleObject() or WaitForMultipleObjects() functions to wait for the I/O to complete.

You can find more details about an asynchronous operation using the GetOverlappedResult() function. This function needs the handle of the file object, and a pointer to the OVERLAPPED structure as input. It can then return the number of bytes transferred so far into a pointer to a DWORD passed as the third parameter. The fourth parameter is a boolean value that you can use to make the function wait until the I/O operation is completed by passing TRUE. Otherwise, a FALSE value causes GetOverlapped-Result() to return immediately even though the I/O hasn't completed. If an error occurs during the I/O operation, GetOverlappedResult() will return a FALSE value and GetLastError() shows the reason for failure. However, this return code may also be ERROR_IO_PENDING if the operation is still in progress.

Core Note

In Windows 95/98, the hEvent member of the OVERLAPPED structure must be set if you want GetOverlappedResult() to wait for completion. This isn't strictly necessary on Windows NT, but is preferable to distinguish between multiple asynchronous requests, and to provide compatibility with the other platforms.

If you want to supply callback functions to be called when the I/O operation has been completed, you can use the ReadFileEx() and WriteFileEx() functions. These functions allow you to pass a pointer to an application CALLBACK function that will be passed any error codes, the number of bytes transferred, and a pointer to the OVERLAPPED structure, after the I/O request has completed.

You can find an example listing of asynchronous overlapped I/O in Section 11.5.2 later in this chapter.

Core Warning

ReadFileEx() and WriteFileEx() will only call the callback function when running on Windows 98 or Windows NT (not Windows 95).

You can cancel an asynchronous I/O operation in progress using the CancelIo() function and passing it the file object handle.

11.4 Compatibility I/O

The Windows range of operating systems support a range of I/O styles that provide compatibility with other operating systems, principally UNIX and DOS.

These functions can make it easier to port simple UNIX applications and old "C" style text-based applications onto Windows platforms. For simple batch file processing jobs, they can be easier to use than the sophisticated Win32 functions.

All of these functions ultimately make calls down to the Win32 functions discussed in the previous sections.

11.4.1 Low-Level I/O

The term low-level I/O is a misnomer because the real Windows Win32 API low-level I/O functions are the `CreateFile()`, `ReadFile()`, and `WriteFile()` functions. However, the low-level I/O functions refer to the "C" style low-level I/O functions inherited from the UNIX world.

The basic "handle" for these low-level functions is called a file descriptor and consists of an integer value. Three pre-defined "standard" handles are always available and always have the values 0, 1, and 2, respectively.

Core Warning

Although these file functions will inevitably use the Win32 subsystem I/O, there is no direct compatibility between low-level file handles and Win32 file object handles.

These handles are only available from console applications and run from an MS-DOS shell window. By default, the standard input descriptor (0) is the keyboard, the output descriptor (1) is the display, and the error descriptor (2) also sends output to the display.

However, these file descriptors can be redirected using the MS-DOS shells' pipe (|) and redirection symbols (< and >). This redirection provides a powerful tool to concatenate the input and output of programs together.

For example, consider the familiar MS-DOS command:

```
DIR | MORE
```

What this really means is the output handle (1) of the `DIR` command becomes the input handle (0) of the `MORE` command.

The following sort command redirects the input file descriptor (0) to read a file rather than the keyboard, and output file descriptor (1) is sent to a file rather than the display:

```
SORT < INPUT.TXT > SORTED.TXT
```

The shell is responsible for hooking these file handles to the appropriate input or output file or device and passing them to the command when it starts.

Your low-level I/O program can read and write to these handles using the `_read()` and `_write()` functions.

For example, the following console application garbles the input from descriptor (0) by incrementing all the characters with an ASCII code over 32 and then writes the result to the output descriptor (1):

```
#include "stdafx.h"
#include "io.h"
int main(int argc, char* argv[])
{
    char szChr;
    while(_read(0,&szChr,1)) {
        if (szChr>32)
            szChr++;
        _write(1,&szChr,1);
    }
    return 0;
}
```

You can run this code from the MS-DOS command line, piping the output of DIR into the standard input file descriptor like this:

```
DIR | GARBLE
```

You can create or open files with low-level I/O using the _create() and _open() functions. The _create() function requires a filename and a flag to indicate the file read and write permissions. You can combine the _S_IREAD and _S_IWRITE flag values to indicate these permissions. The _open() function requires a filename and a combination of the following flag values for its second parameter as shown in Table 11-2:

Table 11-2 File Open/Creation Flags

Flag Value	Description
_O_CREATE	Create and open for writing.
_O_APPEND	Open the file for appending.
_O_RDONLY	Open for read only.
_O_WRONLY	Open for write only.
_O_RDWR	Open for reading and writing.
_O_BINARY	Don't perform text conversions.
_O_TEXT	Perform text conversions.
_O_TRUNC	Open and truncate the file.

The optional third parameter lets you specify the _S_IREAD and _S_IWRITE flag values as in the _create() function. Both _create() and _open() return a file handle integer for use in subsequent functions, or a −1 value if the file couldn't be opened.

You can position the file using the _lseek() function passing the file handle, offset position, and origin flag in a similar manner to the Win32 SetFilePointer() function. The origin flags are SEEK_SET, SEEK_CUR, and SEEK_END to indicate that the file seek should be relative to the start, current, or end file positions. You can find the current file position using the _tell() function.

You should use _close() to finally close the file. The following example illustrates these functions by creating a file containing a text string, closing it, and then re-opening it to read the text string backwards and write the output to the console:

```
#include "stdafx.h"
#include "io.h"
#include "fcntl.h"
#include "sys\stat.h"
#include "string.h"
int main(int argc, char* argv[])
{
   // Create a file, setting read and write permissions
   int hFile = _creat("test.txt",_S_IWRITE|_S_IREAD);

   // Write some text to a file
   char* pszTxt = "This is my test text\n";
   _write(hFile,pszTxt,strlen(pszTxt));
   _close(hFile);

   // Re-open the file for reading
   hFile = _open("test.txt",_O_RDONLY);

   // Copy it backwards to the console
   _lseek(hFile,0L,SEEK_END);
   int nLen = _tell(hFile)-1;
   char szBuf;
   while(nLen>=0) {
      _lseek(hFile,nLen--,SEEK_SET);
      _read(hFile,&szBuf,1);
      _write(1,&szBuf,1);
   }
   return _close(hFile);
}
```

11.4.2 Stream I/O

The stream I/O functions provide compatibility for "C" style I/O. These functions access a "handle" in the form of pointers to FILE structures called streams. These structures themselves encapsulate the low-level file descriptor handle as the _file member of the FILE structure. The stream I/O functions use the low-level functions (which in turn use the Win32 functions), but provide extended capabilities and built-in buffering.

The standard input, standard output, and standard error file descriptors are mapped to the stdin, stdout, and stderr streams, respectively. These streams are just predefined pointers to FILE structures that map to the low-level standard 0, 1, and 2 handles. Therefore, you can use these standard streams for redirected and piped input and output.

You can use a whole host of stream functions to provide fairly sophisticated buffered file control. For example, the familiar printf() function is just a special case of fprintf() that always sends its output to stdout.

You can open files using _fopen() passing a file name and character string indicating the type of access, such as "r" for reading, "w" for writing and "r+" for reading and writing. If successful, a pointer to a FILE structure is returned, and can be used for subsequent operations. The low-level file descriptor can be found using the _fileno() function, and an existing descriptor used to open a stream via the _fdopen() function.

Other useful functions are _fread(), fgets(), fgetc(), and _fscanf() for reading in various ways, and the corresponding fwrite(), fputs(), fputc(), and fprintf() for writing.

You can position the file using _fseek(), and find the position using _ftell(). The _fflush() function flushes any unwritten output, and _fclose() closes the stream.

11.4.3 The I/O Stream Classes

Like MFC wraps many of the underlying Win32 functionality, the I/O stream classes are C++ classes that wrap the stream functionality.

The ios class is the base class for the other I/O stream classes and contains a number of common member functions for status testing and buffer manipulation. It also contains a number of enumerated flag values for manipulating the input and output stream data.

The istream class extends the ios class to provide a number of reading and repositioning functions such as get(), read(), peek(), putback(), seekg(), and tellg(). You can use the istream class directly, or derive your own classes from istream to add your application-specific functionality.

A corresponding `ostream` extends the `ios` class to provide writing orientated functions such as `put()`, `write()`, `flush()`, `seekp()`, and `tellp()`. Once again, you can inherit your own classes from this class to extend the write-only orientated functionality offered by `ostream`.

Using the sometimes frowned upon (but more widely accepted) practice of multiple inheritance, the `iostream` class combines the `istream` and `ostream` classes to give you a read- and write-capable class.

Before you use this jungle of classes, you'll notice that the constructors require a pointer to a `streambuf`-derived class. These classes provide the connection to the file, standard I/O channel, or character array in memory via the `filebuf`, `stdiobuf`, or `strstreambuf` subclasses. You must construct an object from one of these three classes (or a derivative) and then pass the pointer to the relevant `iostream()` derived classes' constructor function to initialize the manipulator object.

Rather than deriving from, or using the `istream`, `ostream`, or `iostream` classes directly, you would probably wish to use one of the more specific alternatives such as `fstream`, `stdiostream`, or `strstream`, which themselves derive from `iostream`. You could use `fstream` for file I/O, `stdiostream` for standard stream I/O, or `strstream` for character buffer manipulation. The big advantage of using these classes is that their constructor functions automatically create the `filebuf`, `stdiobuf`, or `strstreambuf` objects required, thus letting you create one-stop shop objects.

If all this sounds like a lot of hard work, you're right, it is. But you should remember that there are a lot of clever member functions in each of these classes that comprise a very sophisticated suite of file and character manipulation classes.

Like the low-level and stream I/O that they are based upon, there are three corresponding standard predefined objects that let you manipulate the standard input, output, and error channels as shown in Table 11-3:

Table 11-3 File Open/Creation Flags

Object	Class Type	Stream	File Descriptor
cin	istream	stdin	0
cout	ostream	stdout	1
cerr	ostream	stderr	2

These cin, cout, and cerr objects are actually created as objects of istream_withassign and ostream_withassign, which are classes that allow the objects to be assigned to other types of istream and ostream objects for piping and redirection to other program output or disk files.

There is also a clog object that is similar to cerr, but is fully buffered, whereas cerr is flushed immediately when data is assigned to it.

This example shows how to perform the equivalent text scrambling with a console application as in the low-level I/O section earlier, but using cin and cout:

```
#include "stdafx.h"
#include "iostream.h"
int main(int argc, char* argv[])
{
   char szChr;
   cin.flags(0);
   while(cin >> szChr) {
      if (szChr>32)
         szChr++;
      cout << szChr;
   }
return 0;
}
```

You'll notice that the cin.flags(0) is used to remove some rather unpleasant text-filtering flags from the input channel. The overloaded >> operator is used to read a character into the szChr single character buffer and the << operator writes it out after manipulation.

11.5 Serial Communications

Handling serial port I/O presents special problems because of the many different hardware-specific settings, the need for timeouts, and bi-directional asynchronous data transfer.

Parallel ports are a similar communications resource and, although they are generally used in more uni-directional applications (such as printers), they must still provide bi-directional asynchronous transfer.

The following sections discuss some of the aspects of serial data transfer.

11.5.1 *Opening and Configuring Serial Ports*

You can open a serial port device using the `CreateFile()` function by specifying a filename that refers to the specific port, such as "COM1" or "COM2."

When you open a serial port, it is automatically opened for exclusive access, so you should pass a zero for the `CreateFile()`'s third parameter and `OPEN_EXISTING` for the open mode (fifth parameter). You can add a combination of the special file mode flags to indicate overlapped I/O, or any special buffering requirements as normal.

If the serial port is opened successfully, a Win32 file object handle is returned, otherwise `INVALID_HANDLE_VALUE` is returned. The following example opens the port named by `m_strPort` for overlapped I/O and doesn't perform any buffering:

```
m_hCommPort = CreateFile(m_strPort,GENERIC_READ |
    GENERIC_WRITE, 0, NULL, OPEN_EXISTING,
    FILE_ATTRIBUTE_NORMAL | FILE_FLAG_OVERLAPPED |
    FILE_FLAG_NO_BUFFERING,NULL);
if (m_hCommPort == INVALID_HANDLE_VALUE)
   return FALSE;
```

Once you've opened a serial port, you must set the many flags required to configure the device. These flags are held in a device control block (DCB) structure. You can either fill in the entire DCB structure, or use one of the helper functions to fill in some of the details. The `GetCommState()` function fills in a DCB structure with the current settings from the hardware, and you can use a corresponding `SetCommState()` function to set the new settings from a DCB structure.

You can use the `BuildCommDCB()` to set some (but not all) of the settings from a command string, such as:

```
"baud = 9600 parity = N data = 8 stop =1"
```

The following example turns off all flow control (such as XON/XOFF, CTS/RTS, and DSR/DTR) and sets the baud rate, data bits, and parity settings from the `m_strBaud` command string:

```
DCB dcb;
memset(&dcb,0,sizeof(dcb));
dcb.DCBlength=sizeof(dcb);
GetCommState(m_hCommPort,&dcb);
if (!BuildCommDCB((LPCTSTR)m_strBaud,&dcb)) {
   TRACE("Unable to build Comm Port config = '%s', err = %d\n",
       (LPCTSTR)m_strBaud,GetLastError());
```

```
    return FALSE;
}

    // Common settings
    dcb.fOutxCtsFlow = FALSE;
    dcb.fOutxDsrFlow = FALSE;
    dcb.fDtrControl = DTR_CONTROL_DISABLE;
    dcb.fDtrControl = FALSE;
    dcb.fDsrSensitivity = FALSE;
    dcb.fOutX = FALSE;
    dcb.fInX = FALSE;
    dcb.fNull = FALSE;
    dcb.fRtsControl = RTS_CONTROL_DISABLE;
    dcb.fAbortOnError = FALSE;
    if (!SetCommState(m_hCommPort,&dcb)) {
        TRACE("Unable to set Comm Port config = '%s', err = %d\n",
            (LPCTSTR)m_strBaud,GetLastError());
    return FALSE;
}
```

You can also find the default communication settings by calling the `GetDefaultCommConfig()` function, which fills a `COMMCONFIG` structure. This structure holds a `DCB` structure, and a number of application-specific values. To change these settings, you can pass a `COMMCONFIG` structure with your customized settings to `SetDefaultCommConfig()`.

11.5.2 Asynchronous Communications

After configuring the serial port, you can start transferring data via `ReadFile()` and `WriteFile()` functions. However, you should remember that if you haven't specified the `FILE_FLAG_OVERLAPPED` flag in the `CreateFile()` flags parameter, then `ReadFile()` will block waiting for input. This is probably good if your program spawns another thread that specifically waits for incoming serial port characters, but not if you want to issue a `ReadFile()` and periodically check if any characters have arrived.

However, if you have specified the `FILE_FLAG_OVERLAPPED` flag, you must provide pointers to `OVERLAPPED` structures for the read and write functions and handle the asynchronous I/O.

The following example demonstrates asynchronous overlapped I/O. This console application issues a read request, then writes a string with the current time (in hours, minutes, seconds) out to the console. It then waits for either five seconds or for completion of the read request. If five seconds pass with no received characters, the loop repeats and writes the time again. If a character is received, a string is printed in response.

```
#include "windows.h"
#include "time.h"
#include "string.h"
#include "stdio.h"

BOOL SetCommDefaults(HANDLE hSerial);

int main(int argc, char* argv[])
{
    HANDLE hSerial = CreateFile("COM2",
        GENERIC_READ | GENERIC_WRITE,0,NULL,OPEN_EXISTING,
        FILE_ATTRIBUTE_NORMAL | FILE_FLAG_OVERLAPPED |
        FILE_FLAG_NO_BUFFERING,NULL);
    if (hSerial == INVALID_HANDLE_VALUE)
        return GetLastError();
    SetCommDefaults(hSerial);
    HANDLE hReadEvent = CreateEvent(NULL,TRUE,FALSE,"RxEvent");

    OVERLAPPED ovRead;
    OVERLAPPED ovWrite;
    memset(&ovRead,0,sizeof(ovRead));
    memset(&ovWrite,0,sizeof(ovWrite));

    ovRead.hEvent = hReadEvent;

    char szRxChar = 0;
    DWORD dwBytesRead = 0;
    DWORD dwBytesWritten = 0;

    while(szRxChar != 'q') {
        // Check if a read is outstanding
        if (HasOverlappedIoCompleted(&ovRead)) {
            // Issue a serial port read
            if (!ReadFile(hSerial,&szRxChar,1,&dwBytesRead,&ovRead)) {
                DWORD dwErr = GetLastError();
                if (dwErr!=ERROR_IO_PENDING)
                    return dwErr;
            }
        }

        // Write the time out to the serial port
        time_t t_time = time(0);
        char buf[50];
        sprintf(buf,"Time is %s\n\r",ctime(&t_time));
        if (HasOverlappedIoCompleted(&ovWrite)) {
            WriteFile(hSerial,buf,strlen(buf),
                &dwBytesWritten,&ovWrite);
        }

        // ... Do some other processing
```

```
        // Wait 5 seconds for serial input
        if (!(HasOverlappedIoCompleted(&ovRead)))
           WaitForSingleObject(hReadEvent,5000);
        // Check if serial input has arrived
        if (GetOverlappedResult(hSerial,&ovRead,&dwBytesRead,FALSE)) {
           // Wait for the write
           GetOverlappedResult(hSerial,&ovWrite,&dwBytesWritten,TRUE);

           // Display a response to input
           sprintf(buf,"You pressed the '%c' key\n\r",szRxChar);
           WriteFile(hSerial,buf,strlen(buf),
              &dwBytesWritten,&ovWrite);
        }

    }

   CloseHandle(hSerial);
   CloseHandle(hReadEvent);
   return 0;
}

BOOL SetCommDefaults(HANDLE hSerial)
{
   DCB dcb;
   memset(&dcb,0,sizeof(dcb));
   dcb.DCBlength=sizeof(dcb);
   if (!GetCommState(hSerial,&dcb))
      return FALSE;
   dcb.BaudRate=9600;
   dcb.ByteSize=8;
   dcb.Parity=0;
   dcb.StopBits=ONESTOPBIT;
   if (!SetCommState(hSerial,&dcb))
      return FALSE;
   return TRUE;
}
```

You'll notice in this example that the CreateFile() specifies the FILE_FLAG_OVERLAPPED flag for asynchronous I/O. A manual reset event (hReadEvent) is created to signal when incoming serial characters have been read by the overlapped ReadFile() function.

After ReadFile() is called, it returns immediately and other processing such as the WriteFile() can be performed before finally waiting in the WaitForSingleObject() function for a signal from the read event. This wait has a timeout of five seconds, so if no characters are read, the loop is repeated. The GetOverlappedResult() is used to check if characters are received, and a WriteFile() response is issued to any incoming characters.

11.5.3 Setting Communication Timeouts

You'll probably find that there are often times when you will need to set up various types of timeout, especially when implementing protocol-driven data transfer.

The `SetCommTimeouts()` function can help you simplify timeout implementation. The function requires a pointer to a COMMTIMEOUTS structure that contains a number of DWORD members that let you set timeouts in milliseconds, and multipliers for those timeouts.

The `ReadIntervalTimeout` member lets you set the maximum allowable time between reading two characters. If the timeout is exceeded, then the `ReadFile()` operation is completed. You can set this member to zero to indicate that you don't want to use interval timeouts. Alternatively, you can set it to MAXDWORD, and set the `ReadTotalTimeoutMultiplier` and `ReadTotalTimeoutConstant` members to zero to indicate that the `ReadFile()` should return immediately.

You can use the `ReadTotalTimeoutMultiplier` to specify a total timeout for the read operation. This millisecond value is multiplied by the total characters to be read to calculate an overall `ReadFile()` timeout. The `ReadTotalTimeoutConstant` value is added to the calculation to let you add a constant to the overall timeout duration. If you don't want to set an overall timeout, you can set these values to zero.

There are two corresponding members, `WriteTotalTimeoutMultiplier` and `WriteTotalTimeoutConstant`, which are used to calculate an overall timeout value for `WriteFile()` operations.

You can find the current timeout settings using the `GetCommTimeout()` function, which fills a passed COMMTIMEOUTS structure. The aptly named `BuildCommDCBAndTimeouts()` does just what it says, and lets you set both the DCB settings and timeouts in one go.

The `GetCommProperties()` function can fill a COMMPROP structure with details about specific driver settings, such as buffer sizes and maximum supported baud rates.

11.5.4 Communication Events

You can set an event mask to enable reporting of various types of communications events. The `SetCommMask()` function lets you specify a number of flag values such as EV_BREAK, EV_RXCHAR, or EV_CTS (break signal, received character, and clear-to-send signal).

Once you've set an event mask, you can use the `WaitCommEvent()` function to wait for one of those events to occur. This can be a useful way of waiting for received characters before issuing a `ReadFile()`. The `Wait-CommEvent()` function lets you pass a pointer to a `DWORD` variable to store the actual event received, and a pointer to an `OVERLAPPED` structure to let you issue asynchronous `WaitCommEvent()` operations that can be tested and completed using the `GetOverlappedResult()` function.

You can get the current mask settings by calling the corresponding `GetCommMask()` function.

If you want to issue special communication events, you can use a number of special functions, such as `SetCommBreak()`, `ClearCommBreak()`, and `EscapeCommFunction()`.

Any pending input or output characters can be purged by calling the `PurgeComm()` function. If any hardware errors are detected, the details can be retrieved with `ClearCommError()`, and the error condition is reset so that the device can continue.

11.6   Using Consoles

Consoles are a special type of window that emulate (and extend) the old 80×25 character DOS-style scrolling text display. An application can have only one attached console at any time as the applications' standard input and output channels are attached to the console.

You have probably seen the console in action when running the MS-DOS command prompt. These consoles let you change the font size and screen buffer size, and modify the display to a full-screen text mode. They also provide limited cut-and-paste editing support.

The consoles use selectable 8-bit code pages to display ANSI character set and national variants. You can also set attributes to show background and foreground colors.

11.6.1   Allocating a Console

Your application can start the console window simply by calling the `AllocConsole()` function, and detach itself from the console by calling `FreeConsole()`.

You can attach Win32 handles by calling `CreateFile()` and passing either `CONIN$` or `CONOUT$` as the filename, and using the

OPEN_EXISTING flag for the open mode parameter. Alternatively, the GetStdHandle() function will return the input, output, or error handles when GetStdHandle() is passed STD_INPUT_HANDLE, STD_OUTPUT_HANDLE, or STD_ERROR_HANDLE respectively. Alternatively, you can redirect the standard handles of a console window by using the corresponding SetStdHandle() function.

11.6.2 Console I/O

Once the console window is open and attached, you can use the low-level, streams-based, or Win32 I/O (covered in the previous sections) to communicate with it.

Alternatively, there are a set of console-specific functions such as ReadConsole() and WriteConsole(), which read characters from the keyboard and write character strings to the console window. You can use PeekConsoleInput() to read characters from the input buffer without removing them so that subsequent ReadConsole() functions retrieve the same "peeked at" characters.

You can call SetConsoleTextAttribute() to set the default color attributes of characters subsequently written to the console by passing combined attribute flags such as BACKGROUND_GREEN, FOREGROUND_RED, and FOREGROUND_INTENSITY. These let you set eight foreground and background colors, each with two levels of brightness, giving 16 overall colors.

You can reposition the consoles' cursors using the SetConsoleCursor-Postion() function, and passing the column (X) and row (Y) SHORT coordinates in a COORD structure. Your cursors' size and visibility can be changed with the SetConsoleCursorInfo() function after setting the dwSize and bVisible members of the CONSOLE_CURSOR_INFO structure. The SetConsoleCursorPostion() and SetConsoleCursorInfo() counterparts fill the appropriate structures to return the current settings.

With the SetConsoleCP() and SetConsoleOutputCP() functions, you can change the input and output code pages. These change the way keyboard characters are mapped for input and display characters are shown for output.

Special keyboard events, such as Ctrl-Break and Crl-C keys (specified by the CTRL_BREAK_EVENT and CTRL_C_EVENT flags), can be simulated by using the GenerateConsoleCtrlEvent() function. These events, whether generated by the user or from your code, can be handled by your supplied handler function. Your handler function must be registered with a call to SetConsoleCtrlHandler(), which can add a chain of event handler functions.

11.6.3 Customizing the Console Buffers and Display

There are a range of functions to set scrollable display buffers that are larger than the current display size. You can change the size of the window using the `SetConsoleWindowInfo()` function. The largest possible size can be found from `GetlargestConsoleWindowSize()` and the current settings found from `GetConsoleWindowInfo()`.

The scrollable buffer can be set larger than the visible console region. You can set this buffer size using `SetConsoleScreenBufferSize()` and passing a `COORD` structure holding the new number of rows and columns for the screen buffer. The `ScrollConsoleScreenBuffer()` function then lets you scroll the visible region from within your code to display various parts of the text buffer.

You can customize the title bar of your console window with a call to `SetConsoleTitle()`, passing a pointer to the new text string.

11.7 Summary

The evolution of the Windows operating system has spawned and supported many various file-system types to provide backwards (and sideward) compatibility and also to provide advanced security and performance (in Windows NT).

This evolution, although healthy, means that as a software developer, you must be aware of the potential differences in file I/O function across operating systems and file systems.

The fundamental Win32 file handling functions are both powerful and flexible tools for manipulating normal disk files and I/O devices with a common set of API tools. You can use overlapped (or asynchronous) I/O to improve the performance of your application and to let the operating system implement multithreaded I/O requests, rather than having to spawn new threads for handling blocking I/O.

The Win32 synchronization objects can be used in conjunction with the I/O API functions to provide flexible and efficient waiting and signaling support for your I/O problems. These are particularly useful when dealing with relatively slow communications devices such as serial ports.

Handling the complex hardware functionality of communication resources can be safely and easily delegated to the operating system. This leaves you with the more pleasant task of implementing your specific application requirements, rather than delving down to device level as was often required in previous platforms.

The low-level I/O, stream-based I/O, and C++ I/O stream classes provide compatibility with other operating systems such as UNIX and DOS. They can also simplify the implementation, file handling, and simple text-based applications.

You can use the Console window to help provide an emulation of old scrolling terminals and DOS consoles while gaining larger than screen size scrolling buffer support and an ANSI-compatible text mode display.

OPENING PIPES AND MAILSLOTS FOR COMMUNICATIONS

Topics in this Chapter

- Communicating with Pipes
- Creating Pipes
- Working More with Named Pipes
- Understanding the Microsoft Remote Procedure Call (RPC) Protocol
- RPC Exception Handling
- Working with Mailslots
- Summary

Chapter 12

P ipes offer an efficient, easy way for two cooperating Windows applications to communicate across a network. Pipes are easy to set up and use; they are one of the favored mechanisms for implementing client/server communications with server software running on Windows NT. Unfortunately, pipe support in Windows 9x is limited to client-side support.

In general, you will most frequently use *named pipes*. In addition to their other uses, named pipes also represent one of several mechanisms used by the Microsoft Remote Procedure Call protocol, or Microsoft RPC. RPC is a mechanism that provides applications with the ability to call procedures (functions) that are part of another application running on a different computer on the network. Apart from some initialization and housekeeping functions, using RPC is almost as simple as calling a local function.

A *mailslot* is a mechanism for one-way interprocess communications (IPC). A Win32-based application can store messages in a mailslot. The owner of the mailslot can retrieve messages that are stored there. These messages are typically sent over a network to either a specified computer or to all computers in a specified domain. A *domain* is a group of workstations and servers that share a group name.

You can (and often will) choose to use named pipes instead of mailslots for interprocess communications. Named pipes are a simple way for two processes to exchange messages. Mailslots, on the other hand, are a simple way for a single process to broadcast messages to multiple processes. One important consideration is that mailslots use *datagrams*, and named pipes do not. A datagram is a small packet of information that the network sends along the wire. Like a radio or television broadcast, a datagram offers no confirmation of receipt; there is no way to guarantee that a datagram has been received. Just as mountains, large buildings, or interfering signals might cause a radio or television signal to get lost, there are things that can prevent a datagram from reaching a particular destination. Named pipes, on the other hand, are two-way, verified transmissions.

12.1 Communicating with Pipes

Pipes offer a one- or two-way conduit of communication between cooperating applications. Programming with pipes is based on the client/server model; a typical server application creates a pipe and waits for client applications to request access to the pipe. You can envision a pipe as a means of crossing process boundaries to transmit data—something like a drainpipe going through a wall.

12.2 Creating Pipes

The Win32 API distinguishes between *named pipes* and *anonymous pipes*. The use of anonymous pipes is somewhat limited. When an application creates an anonymous pipe, it receives two handles; one of these handles must be passed on to another application in order for the two applications to be able to communicate. The most likely mechanism for passing a handle is inheritance. Therefore, anonymous pipes are often used for communication between a parent and a child process, or between child processes of the same parent process. Because anonymous pipes are identified by handles, they are, by their very nature, local, because a handle has no validity on another machine on the network. In contrast, named pipes are identified by a Universal Naming Convention (UNC) name that is valid across the entire network.

Anonymous pipes are created using the `CreatePipe()` function. This function returns two handles, one to the read end of the pipe, and another to its write end. You will implement the `CreatePipe()` function as shown in the following prototype:

```
BOOL CreatePipe(PHANDLE hReadPipe, PHANDLE hWritePipe,
    LPSECURITY_ATTRIBUTES lpPipeAttributes,
    DWORD nSize);
```

The `LPSECURITY_ATTRIBUTES` parameter accepts a pointer to a `SECURITY_ATTRIBUTES` structure on Windows NT machines; on Windows 9x machines, the function will ignore this parameter.

Named pipes are created by calling the `CreateNamedPipe()` function. Named pipes have names in the following form:

```
\\hostname\\pipe\\pipename
```

Servers cannot create a pipe on another computer. For this reason, the host name component in the pipe name, when the name is used in `Create-NamedPipe()`, must be set to a single period, indicating the local host:

```
\\.\pipe\pipename
```

A named pipe can be one-way or two-way. When the server creates the pipe, it indicates the directionality of that pipe by specifying either:

- `PIPE_ACCESS_DUPLEX`
- `PIPE_ACCESS_INBOUND`
- `PIPE_ACCESS_OUTBOUND`

Named pipes support asynchronous (overlapped) I/O operations. However, overlapped I/O is not supported by anonymous pipes.

When a named pipe is created, a server specifies the pipe's type. A pipe can be a byte-mode or a message-mode pipe. Byte-mode pipes treat data as a stream of bytes; message-mode pipes treat data as a stream of messages. The pipe's read mode can be byte-read mode or message-read mode; message-mode pipes support both read modes, but byte-mode pipes support only the byte-read mode.

The pipe's read mode and its wait mode (whether the pipe operates in a blocking or non-blocking mode) can be specified when the pipe is created and later modified using the `SetNamedPipeHandleState()` function. The current state of the pipe can be obtained by calling the function `GetNamedPipeHandleState()`. Further information about a named pipe can be obtained by calling `GetNamedPipeInfo()`.

12.2.1 Connecting to Named Pipes

After you create an anonymous pipe, the process creating it receives handles for both ends of the pipe. In contrast, when a server creates a named pipe, only one end of the pipe is opened; the server must wait for a client to make an attempt to connect to the pipe before either the server or the client can use the pipe. An overview of setting up, using, and shutting down named pipes is presented in Figure 12-1.

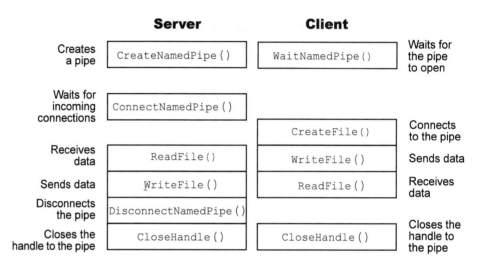

Figure 12-1   Setting up, using, and shutting down a named pipe.

To wait for a connection, servers issue a call to the `ConnectNamed-Pipe()` function. If you use this function synchronously, the server will wait until a client connects to the pipe, identifying the pipe by its name. However, you can also invoke `ConnectNamedPipe()` asynchronously, in which case the server is free to attend to other tasks while it is waiting for an incoming connection on the pipe.

Clients can determine whether a named pipe is available for the client to connect to using the `WaitNamedPipe()` function. Once the client application determines that a pipe is available, the application can use `Create-File()`, passing the name of the pipe as the filename, to open the connection, as shown here:

```
HANDLE CreateFile(LPCTSTR \\hostname\\pipe\\pipename,
    DWORD dwDesiredAccess, DWORD dwShareMode,
    LPSECURITY_ATTRIBUTES lpSecurityAttributes,
    DWORD dwCreationDisposition, DWORD dwFlagsAndAttributes,
    HANDLE hTemplateFile);
```

A server can subsequently break an established connection with the server by calling the `DisconnectNamedPipe()` function. When a server calls this function, the client-side handle of the pipe becomes invalid and all data that was not yet read by the client is discarded. To ensure that the client reads all data before `DisconnectNamedPipe()` is called, servers can call the `FlushFileBuffers()` function. After `DisconnectNamed-Pipe()` returns, servers can either close the pipe handle or reuse it in another call to `ConnectNamedPipe()`.

A client application can break the connection by simply calling the `CloseHandle()` function on the pipe handle they obtained through calling `CreateFile()`.

Servers can use several strategies for handling multiple connections, such as spawning separate threads or using overlapped I/O. Servers can create multiple instances of the same pipe by repeatedly calling `CreateNamedPipe()` with the same pipe name.

12.2.2 Transferring Data Through Pipes

After you create and connect the pipe, you can move on to the important step—actually passing data through the pipe. Your applications (both server and client) can write to or read from pipes using `WriteFile()` and `ReadFile()`. As indicated in the previous section, you can also use named pipes for overlapped I/O. In such situations, you may need to use the `WriteFileEx()` and `ReadFileEx()` functions (depending on your implementation).

For message-mode pipes, an alternative mechanism exists for quick and efficient message transfer. Clients can call the `TransactNamedPipe()` function to write a message to and read a message from the specified pipe in a single network operation. The `CallNamedPipe()` function combines into a single operation the calls to the `WaitNamedPipe()`, `Create-File()`, `TransactNamedPipe()`, and `CloseHandle()` functions. In other words, `CallNamedPipe()` will wait for the specified pipe to become available, then open the pipe, exchange messages, and close the pipe, all in a single function call.

12.3 Working More with Named Pipes

As you have learned, when you want to work with named pipes, you must create a pipe on the server, then connect to that pipe from the client—a fact that implies that there must be at least two applications for a named pipe to exist.

This section will detail two simple pipe examples that open a named pipe, then connect to it. The following program, if it was shown in it's entirety, would use a series of helper threads to implement multiple pipe instances. Each helper thread, as you might expect, would use its own `ThreadProc()` procedure. Within `ThreadProc()`, the code to create a named pipe is as follows:

```
hPipe = CreateNamedPipe ("\\\\.\\PIPE\\test", // Pipe name = 'test'
    PIPE_ACCESS_DUPLEX               // 2 way pipe.
    | FILE_FLAG_OVERLAPPED,          // Use overlapped structure.
    PIPE_WAIT                        // Wait on messages.
    | PIPE_READMODE_MESSAGE          // Specify message mode pipe.
    | PIPE_TYPE_MESSAGE,
    MAX_PIPE_INSTANCES,              // Maximum instance limit.
    OUT_BUF_SIZE,                    // Buffer sizes.
    IN_BUF_SIZE,
    TIME_OUT,                        // Specify time out.
    &sa);                            // Security attributes.
```

As you can see, the `CreateNamedPipe()` function creates a pipe named "test" on the server machine. The pipe is a two-way pipe, using overlapped I/O, which waits on messages. In the application, as written, no security attributes are passed into the function—though you could easily do so if you wanted to.

After the server component creates a pipe in a thread of its own, the client component must then connect to the newly created pipe. The program code that performs this processing is shown in the following code listing:

```
// Construct file/pipe name.
wsprintf (fileName, "%s%s%s", "\\\\", ShrName, "\\PIPE\\test");

// Do CreateFile() to connect to the named pipe.
hPipe = CreateFile (fileName, GENERIC_WRITE | GENERIC_READ,
    FILE_SHARE_READ | FILE_SHARE_WRITE,
    NULL, OPEN_EXISTING, FILE_FLAG_OVERLAPPED, NULL);
// Do error checking.
if ((DWORD)hPipe == 0xFFFFFFFF) {
    retCode = GetLastError();
    // This error means pipe wasn't found.
    if ((retCode == ERROR_SEEK_ON_DEVICE)
        || (retCode == ERROR_FILE_NOT_FOUND)) {
        LoadString(hInst, IDS_CANTFINDPIPE, lpBuffer,
            sizeof(lpBuffer));
```

```
         MessageBox (hDlg, lpBuffer, "", MB_OK);
      }
   else {                              // Flagging unknown errors.
      LoadString(hInst, IDS_GENERALERROR, lpBuffer,
         sizeof(lpBuffer));
      wsprintf (errorBuf, lpBuffer, retCode);
      LoadString(hInst, IDS_DEBUGTITLE, lpBuffer,
         sizeof(lpBuffer));
      MessageBox (hDlg, errorBuf, lpBuffer, MB_ICONINFORMATION
            | MB_OK | MB_APPLMODAL);
      }
   EndDialog (hDlg, 0);            // Kill app if pipe didn't connect.
 };

// Create and init overlapped structure for writes.
hEventWrt = CreateEvent (NULL, TRUE, FALSE, NULL);
OverLapWrt.hEvent = hEventWrt;

// Write the client name to server.
retCode = WriteFile (hPipe, ClntName, PLEASE_WRITE, bytesWritten,
    &OverLapWrt);
if (!retCode) {                    // Wait on overlapped if need be.
   lastError = GetLastError();
   if (lastError == ERROR_IO_PENDING)
      WaitForSingleObject (hEventWrt, (DWORD)-1);
 }
// Create a thread to read the pipe.
CreateThread (NULL, 0, (LPTHREAD_START_ROUTINE)ReadPipe,
    (LPVOID)&hPipe, 0, &threadID);
return (0);
```

However, connecting to the named pipe from the client side is not enough—the client program also needs to transmit and receive data down the pipe to and from the server. The code shown in the following example shows how to implement the function to read the pipe when data comes down from the server.

```
VOID ReadPipe (HANDLE *hPipe)
{
   CHAR inBuf[IN_BUF_SIZE] = "";    // Input buffer.
   DWORD bytesRead;                 // Used for ReadFile()
   DWORD retCode;                   // Used to trap return codes.
   CHAR  Buf[80];                   // Message box buffer.
   DWORD lastError;                 // Used to trap GetLastError.
   HANDLE hEventRd;                 // Event handle for overlapped
   OVERLAPPED OverLapRd;            // Overlapped structure.
   DWORD bytesTrans;                // Bytes transferred in read.
```

```
// Create and init overlap structure.
hEventRd = CreateEvent (NULL, TRUE, FALSE, NULL);
memset (&OverLapRd, 0, sizeof(OVERLAPPED));
OverLapRd.hEvent = hEventRd;

do {
   // Read the pipe handle.
   retCode = ReadFile (*hPipe, inBuf, IN_BUF_SIZE, &bytesRead,
      &OverLapRd);
   if (!retCode) {                     // Do error checking.
      lastError = GetLastError();
      // Check for 3 errors: IO_PENDING, BROKEN_PIPE, or other
      // If Error = IO_PENDING, wait for event handle success
      if (lastError == ERROR_IO_PENDING)
         WaitForSingleObject (hEventRd, (DWORD)-1);
      Else {
         // If pipe is broken, tell user and break.
         if (lastError == (DWORD)ERROR_BROKEN_PIPE) {
            LoadString(hInst, IDS_CONNECTBROKEN, lpBuffer,
               sizeof(lpBuffer));
            MessageBox (hWndClient, lpBuffer, "", MB_OK);
          }
         else {            // Or flag unknown errors, and break
            LoadString(hInst, IDS_READFAILED, lpBuffer,
               sizeof(lpBuffer));
            wsprintf (Buf, lpBuffer, GetLastError());
            LoadString(hInst, IDS_CLIENTDBG, lpBuffer,
               sizeof(lpBuffer));
            MessageBox (hWndClient, Buf, lpBuffer, MB_OK);
          }
         break;
       }
    }
   // NULL terminate string.
   GetOverlappedResult (*hPipe, &OverLapRd, &bytesTrans, FALSE);
   inBuf[bytesTrans] = '\0';

   // Write message to larger edit field.
   SendMessage (GetDlgItem (hWndClient, IDD_EDITREAD),
      EM_REPLACESEL, 0, (LONG)inBuf);
   // Add a new line.
   SendMessage (GetDlgItem (hWndClient, IDD_EDITREAD),
      EM_REPLACESEL, 0, (LONG)"\r\n");

 } while(1);

// When pipe is broken, send quit messages to Client dialog box.
PostMessage (hWndClient, WM_GO_AWAY, 0,0);
ExitThread(0);
}
```

You can test this application on a single machine running Windows NT (remember that Windows 95 does not support the server end of pipes) or on two machines across a network.

12.4 Understanding Microsoft Remote Procedure Call (RPC)

Microsoft's RPC extends the conceptual elegance and simplicity of a function or subroutine call by providing a similar mechanism for calls across the network. RPC servers offer a set of functions that can, in turn, be called by RPC clients.

The RPC mechanism is widely used in Windows. In particular, the RPC mechanism is the basis of Object Linking and Embedding (OLE) technology and is also the basis for the Distributed Component Object Model (DCOM).

12.4.1 RPC Fundamentals

The key to the RPC mechanism is the *stub function*. When an RPC client calls an RPC function, it issues a regular function call. However, the function that receives a call is an RPC stub (running locally on the client's computer). This stub function converts function arguments for transmission across the network (a procedure referred to as *marshaling*) and transmits the call request and the arguments to the server.

Stub functions on the server side *unmarshal* function arguments and call the server's implementation of the function. When the function returns, its return value is passed back to the client using a reverse mechanism. This entire procedure is illustrated in Figure 12-2, and is generally known as a *proxy-stub communication over RPC*.

When developing RPC applications, an element of central importance is the *interface*. Clearly, the stub functions on the client and the server sides must be based on identical function definitions; otherwise, the RPC process will fail. The tool that ensures that the stub functions on the two sides are compatible is the Microsoft Interface Development Language (MIDL) compiler.

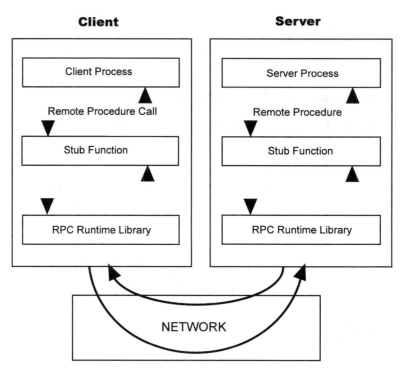

Figure 12-2   The proxy-stub communication over the RPC model.

12.4.2 *Implementing Communications over a Proxy-Stub Pair*

To help you better understand how Microsoft RPC works, this section will help you design a pair of applications (a client and a server) together with the appropriate proxy-stub configuration, to send data from a client to a server. When complete, the server will use RPC to receive string data from client applications, while the client will use RPC to send the data to the server.

As with any COM-based objects, the first step in developing this example is to specify the interface. This is done in the form of two files that represent the input files for the MIDL compiler. The MIDL compiler will produce three files: a header file that you must include in both the client and the server application, and two source files that implement the client and server stub functions. These files must be linked with the implementation of both the client and the server application to produce the final executables. This process is illustrated in Figure 12-3. (You will learn more about this process in Chapter 15.)

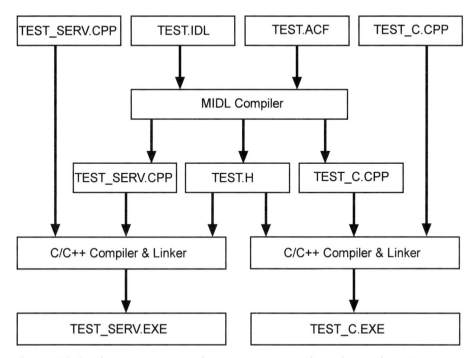

Figure 12-3 The necessary compilation steps to correctly implement the RPC connection.

12.4.3 Specifying the Interface

The interface for an RPC implementation is specified in the form of two files: the *Interface Definition Language File* and the *Application Configuration File*. These two files together serve as input for the MIDL compiler. The Interface Definition Language File for this example application is as shown here (although the UUID may differ on your computer):

```
[
  uuid (6fdd2ce0-0985-11cf-87c3-00403321bfac),
  version(1.0)
]

interface CallRemote
{
  void RemoteCallProc([in, string] const unsigned char *pszString);
  void Shutdown(void);
}
```

This file consists of two parts: the interface header and the interface body. The interface header has the following syntax:

```
[interface-attributes] interface interface-name
```

Perhaps the most important of the interface attributes is the interface's *GUID*, or *globally unique identifier*. The GUID is a 128-bit identifier that is supposed to be world-unique; in other words, no two applications in the world are supposed to have identical identifiers.

The Visual C++ distribution provides a tool, the executable program guidgen.exe, that is supposed to create such unique identifiers using, in part, information obtained from your computer's hardware, and in part a randomization algorithm.

The GUID is expressed in the form of a string of 32 hexadecimal digits. The specific form is 8, 4, 4, 4, and 12 digits separated by hyphens. The guidgen.exe program generates GUID strings in this form.

In addition to the GUID, another interface attribute specifies the interface's version number. The function of the version number is to identify potentially incompatible versions of the interface.

In the second part of the Interface Definition Language file, function prototypes are defined. The prototype syntax is similar to the syntax of the C language but it also contains extra elements. The `in` keyword indicates to the MIDL compiler that the following parameter is an input-only parameter; that is, it is sent to the server by the client. The `string` keyword indicates that the data sent is a character array.

The Application Configuration file is similar in syntax and appearance to the Interface Definition Language file. However, this file contains information on data and attributes not related to the actual transmission of RPC data. The Application Configuration file for the `CallRemote` project is as shown here:

```
[
    implicit_handle(handle_t CallRemote_IfHandle)
]
interface CallRemote
{

}
```

This file specifies a *binding handle* for the interface. This handle is a data object that represents the connection between the client and the server. Because the handle is not transmitted over the network, it is specified in the Application Configuration file.

The use of the keyword `implicit_handle` prescribes a handle that is maintained as a global variable. The client will use this handle in calls to RPC runtime functions.

You can compile the two files, `CallRemote.idl` and `CallRemote.acf`, with the MIDL compiler using a single command:

```
midl CallRemote.idl
```

The result of the compilation is three files produced by the MIDL compiler: `CallRemote_c.c`, `CallRemote_s.c`, and `CallRemote.h`. The files `CallRemote_c.c` and `CallRemote_s.c` provide the client and server-side implementation of stub functions, while the `CallRemote.h` header file provides necessary declarations.

By looking at these generated files, one can easily see just how much of the network programmer's work is automated by the use of the MIDL compiler. The generated stub functions perform all the required runtime library calls to marshal and unmarshal arguments and to communicate across the network. However, the real power and simplicity of the RPC mechanism are yet to become evident, as they will in the next sections when you implement the client and server.

12.4.4 Implementing the Server

The server must perform several steps to execute correctly. The most important of those steps is to initialize the RPC runtime library. Following initialization, the server should wait for incoming connections, using the three RPC runtime library calls to monitor the pipe. In the simple implementation, the runtime library calls are in the program's main function. The server application's implementation is shown here.

```
#include <stdlib.h>
#include <stdio.h>
#include "CallRemote.h"
void RemoteCallProc(const unsigned char *pszString)
{
   printf("%s\n", pszString);
}

void Shutdown(void)
{
   RpcMgmtStopServerListening(NULL);
   RpcServerUnregisterIf(NULL, NULL, FALSE);
}
```

```
void main(int argc, char * argv[])
{
    RpcServerUseProtseqEp("ncacn_ip_tcp", 20, "8000", NULL);
    RpcServerRegisterIf(CallRemote_v1_0_s_ifspec, NULL, NULL);
    RpcServerListen(1, 20, FALSE);
}

void __RPC_FAR * __RPC_USER midl_user_allocate(size_t len)
{
    return(malloc(len));
}

void __RPC_USER midl_user_free(void __RPC_FAR * ptr)
{
    free(ptr);
}
```

Core Note

You must implement the server program in its own file, rather than in the
`CallRemote_s.c` *file. When you compile the file, you must include the*
server implementation, the server-side RPC stub implementation (in the
`CallRemote_s.c` *file), and the RPC library (*`rpcrt4.lib`*).*

The first of the RPC runtime library calls is to the RpcServerUse-
ProtseqEp() function. This call defines the network protocol and endpoint that is to be used by the application. The example uses the TCP over IP
protocol (ncacn_ip_tcp) as a protocol because both Windows NT and
Windows 95 include default support for the protocol. However, the RPC
mechanism can utilize many other protocols. Table 12-1 lists the possible
RPC procotols you can implement and the associated string constants that
you will use in the call to RpcServerUseProtseqEp().

Protocols with a name that begins with ncacn are connection-oriented
protocols, while those with a name that starts with ncadg are datagram (or
connectionless) protocols.

Because Windows 95 supports named pipes for the client side only, the
ncacn_np protocol is only supported for RPC client applications. Windows
95 does not support ncacn_nb_ipx and ncacn_nb_tcp. The
ncacn_dnet_nsp protocol is supported only for 16-bit Windows and MS-
DOS clients.

The meaning of the endpoint parameter is dependent on the protocol. For
example, when you use the ncacn_ip_tcp protocol, the endpoint parameter represents a TPC port number.

Table 12-1 RPC-Supported Network Protocols

Protocol Name	Description
ncacn_ip_tcp	TCP over IP
ncacn_nb_tcp	TCP over NetBIOS
ncacn_nb_ipx	IPX over NetBEUI
ncacn_nb_nb	NetBIOS over NetBEUI
ncacn_np	Named pipes
ncacn_spx	SPX
ncacn_dnet_nsp	DECnet transport
ncadg_ip_udp	UDP over IP
ncadg_ipx	IPX
ncalrpc	Local procedure call

Starting up the server consists of two steps. First, the server interface is registered; second, it enters a state where it listens for incoming connections. Registering the server makes it available for incoming client connections.

The actual remote procedure, RemoteCallProc(), is implemented the same way a local function is implemented. In fact, it is possible to place the implementation of this function in a separate file; this way, applications that locally call the function could be linked with it, while applications that call this function through RPC link with the client-side stub instead.

The server implements another function, Shutdown(), that makes it easier for you to perform remote shutdown of the server. Server shutdown is accomplished by exiting the listening state and unregistering the server.

In addition to these two functions, the Microsoft RPC specifications require that the server implement two additional memory management functions. The midl_user_allocate and midl_user_free functions are used to allocate a block of memory and to free up allocated memory. In simple cases, these can be mapped to the C runtime functions malloc and free; however, in large, complex applications these functions enable finer control over memory use. Both of these functions are used when arguments are marshaled or unmarshaled.

Before you compile the server application, make sure that you include the
`rpcrt4.lib` file in the list of files to link.

12.4.5 Implementing the Client

Implementing the RPC client is only slightly more complicated than implementing an application containing a local function call. The client implementation for the example program is shown in the following code:

```
#include <stdlib.h>
#include <stdio.h>
#include <string.h>
#include "CallRemote.h"

void main(int argc, char *argv[])
  {
    unsigned char *pszStringBinding;
    if (argc != 3) {
       printf("Usage: %s hostname string-to-print\n", argv[0]);
       exit(1);
     }
    RpcStringBindingCompose(NULL, "ncacn_ip_tcp", argv[1], "8000",
        NULL, &pszStringBinding);
    RpcBindingFromStringBinding(pszStringBinding,
        &CallRemote_IfHandle);
    if (strcmp(argv[2], "SHUTDOWN"))
       RemoteCallProc(argv[2]);
    else
       Shutdown();
    RpcStringFree(&pszStringBinding);
    RpcBindingFree(&hello_IfHandle);
    exit(0);
  }

void __RPC_FAR * __RPC_USER midl_user_allocate(size_t len)
  {
    return(malloc(len));
  }

void __RPC_USER midl_user_free(void __RPC_FAR * ptr)
  {
    free(ptr);
  }
```

This client implementation (which avoids using the GUI purely for simplicity's sake) requires two command-line parameters: the name of the server
to connect to and the string to be sent to the server. Because of the protocol

being used (TCP over IP), the server name must be the host's Internet name or IP address. If you are testing the client and the server on the same host, you can use the default name for the local host, localhost, or its default IP address, 127.0.0.1.

The program combines the protocol name, host name, and endpoint into a *string binding* using the `RpcStringBindingCompose()` function. For example, the string binding representing the `ncacn_ip_tcp` protocol, the local host, and TCP port 8000 would appear as follows:

```
ncacn_ip_tcp:localhost[8000]
```

The `RpcStringBindingCompose()` function is merely a convenience function that saves you from the task of having to assemble the string binding from its components by hand. This string binding is used to obtain the binding handle for the interface in the call to `RpcBindingFromStringBinding()`. The receipt of the binding handle indicates that the connection is ready to be used.

Once the connection is established, using it is extremely straightforward. Calling a remote procedure becomes identical to calling a local function. In the client implementation shown previously, the program calls the function `RemoteCallProc()` with the second command-line argument; that is, unless that argument is the string SHUTDOWN, in which case the client program instead calls the `Shutdown()` function, which shuts down the remote server.

Like the server, the client must also provide its own implementations for `midl_user_allocate` and `midl_user_free`. Also, like the server, the implementations of both functions can be trivial for smaller applications, but should exercise a fine degree of control over allocation in larger appplications.

12.5 RPC Exception Handling

If you attempt to run the client application developed in the previous section alone, without starting up a server, a serious deficiency of the implementation becomes evident. Neither the client nor the server in this example performs any error handling; in particular, this means that the client does not respond well to situations in which no server is available.

Unlike other errors, which work under the presumption of the occasional unexpected occurrence, the unavailability of a server should be considered a likely occurrence that your client programs must handle effectively. The

Microsoft RPC implementation provides a special mechanism for this purpose that is very similar in its appearance to Win32 structured exceptions or C++ exception handling.

By protecting the remote procedure calls using the RPC exception handling macros, one can ensure graceful handling of network error conditions by a client application. For example, in the CallRemote application, the calls to `RemoteCallProc()` and `Shutdown()` on the client side should be protected using code similar to the following:

```
RpcTryExcept {
  if (strcmp(argv[2], "SHUTDOWN"))
     RemoteCallProc(argv[2]);
  else
      Shutdown();
 }


RpcExcept(1) {
   printf("RPC runtime exception %08.8X\n", RpcExceptionCode());
 }
RpcEndExcept
```

If you recompile the client application with this change, it will no longer crash when the server is not available. Instead, the application will gracefully terminate, printing the exception number.

12.5.1 Advanced RPC Features

Although the example application demonstrates the simplicity of using Microsoft RPC adequately, it only hints at the power and rich features of the RPC mechanism. This section mentions a few of the most notable features of Microsoft RPC.

The MIDL compiler can be used for specifying remote procedures that accept all kinds of arguments. This includes pointers and arrays; however, pointers and arrays require special consideration. Because the RPC stub functions must not only marshal the pointer arguments themselves but also the data they point to, it is necessary to define the size of the memory block a pointer points to in the interface specification. A series of attributes is available for specifying an array's size. For example, consider a remote procedure that takes the size of an array and a pointer to the first element as its parameters:

```
void simpleproc(short s, double *d);
```

You can identify the interface for such a procedure in your IDL file as follows:

```
void simpleproc([in] short s, [in, out, size_is ] double d[]);
```

Such an interface instructs the MIDL compiler to generate stub code that marshals a number of array elements. The `size_is` attribute is not the only attribute that assists in specifying array arguments. Others include `length_is`, `first_is`, `last_is`, and `max_is`.

The RPC mechanism can utilize the Microsoft RPC Name Service Provider on Windows NT. Through this mechanism, it is possible for clients to locate an RPC server by name. In particular, the use of the RPC Name Service enables you to develop clients that do not use an explicit binding handle (like the previous example did). Such clients would contain no RPC runtime library calls whatsoever and apart from being linked with the client-side stub, they look no different from programs that use local functions.

The MIDL syntax enables you to define interfaces that are derived from other interfaces. The syntax is similar to that used for deriving classes in C++:

```
[attributes] interface interface-name : base-interface
```

The derived interface inherits member functions, status codes, and interface attributes from the base interface.

12.6 Working with Mailslots

A *mailslot* is a mechanism for one-way interprocess communications (IPC). A Win32-based application can store messages in a mailslot. The owner of the mailslot can thereafter retrieve messages that are stored there. These messages are typically sent over a network to either a specified computer or to all computers in a specified domain. A *domain*, for purposes of this discussion, is a group of workstations and servers that share a group name.

You can choose to use named pipes instead of mailslots for interprocess communications. Named pipes are a simple way for two processes to exchange messages. Mailslots, on the other hand, are a simple way for a process to broadcast messages to multiple processes. One important consideration is that mailslots use datagrams, and named pipes do not. A datagram is a small packet of information that the network sends along the wire. Like a radio or television broadcast, a datagram offers no confirmation of receipt; there is no way to guarantee that a datagram has been received. Just as mountains, large buildings, or interfering signals might cause a radio or television signal to get lost, there are things that can prevent a datagram from reaching a particular destination.

There are three particular functions that you can use with mailslots. The `CreateMailslot()` function creates a mailslot with the specified name and returns a handle that a mailslot server can use to perform operations on the mailslot. The mailslot is local to the computer that creates it. An error occurs if a mailslot with the specified name already exists.

The `GetMailslotInfo()` function retrieves information about the specified mailslot. The `SetMailslotInfo()` function sets the timeout value used by the specified mailslot for a read operation.

The program code you would use to create mailslots would use a function call similar to that shown here:

```
hSlot = CreateMailslot (achMailSlotName, 0,
    MAILSLOT_WAIT_FOREVER, (LPSECURITY_ATTRIBUTES) NULL);
```

After the code creates a mailslot, it uses the `ReadFile()` function much as you did with pipes, except that the call passes in a handle to the mailslot, instead of a handle to a pipe, as shown here:

```
fResult = ReadFile(hSlot, achBuffer, cbToRead,
    &cbRead, (LPOVERLAPPED) NULL);
```

Needless to say, working with mailslots is nearly identical to working with pipes. The only significant difference is that you cannot wait on a mailslot, because it uses a connectionless protocol, as opposed to the connection-based pipe protocol.

12.7 Summary

Pipes represent a simple, efficient inter-application communication mechanism supported by Windows 95 (client side only) and Windows NT.

Pipes can be named and unnamed. Anonymous pipes are typically used between a parent and a child process or two sibling processes. The use of anonymous pipes requires communicating a pipe handle from one process to another (for example, by inheriting the handle). Because anonymous pipes are identified by handle alone, they cannot be used for communication across a network.

Unlike anonymous pipes, named pipes support overlapped I/O operations. A server can use a combination of techniques including overlapped I/O and using separate threads to serve several clients simultaneously.

Both servers and clients communicate on a named pipe using the pipe's handle and standard Win32 input and output functions.

Microsoft RPC is a mechanism for applications to call functions remotely. It provides a transparent interface where client applications can call remote functions in a fashion that is very similar to the calling of local functions.

The key to Microsoft RPC, in addition to the RPC runtime library, is the Microsoft Interface Definition Language (MIDL) compiler. The interface between a client and a server can be specified using a simple C-like syntax, from which the MIDL compiler generates server and client-side stub functions, freeing the programmer from the burden of complex network programming tasks and from having to maintain compatible versions of these functions on the server and client sides.

The actual implementation is through these stub functions. When a client calls a remote procedure, the call is handled by the corresponding client-side stub function. The stub function, in turn, calls the RPC runtime library that uses the underlying network transport to invoke stub functions on the server side. The client-side stub function also marshals function arguments for transmission over the network. The server-side stub function unmarshals these arguments and calls the actual function implementation. When the function returns, this process is played out in reverse, as return values are transported back to the client application.

Advanced RPC features include RPC Name Service, pointer and array function arguments, derived interfaces, and much more.

MANAGING THE SYSTEM REGISTRY

Topics in this Chapter

- Understanding the Registry's Structure
- The Predefined Registry Branches
- Manually Editing the Registry
- Commonly Used Registry Keys
- The Registry and INI Files
- Writing Application Programs That Manipulate the Registry
- Summary

Chapter 13

If you have done any programming in Windows 3.x or Windows 95, you are probably familiar with initialization (or INI) files. As their name suggests, initialization files provide initial information to programs—from word processors to the operating system itself.

In Windows 9x and Windows NT, Microsoft replaced initialization files (for the most part) with the Windows registry. In Win32, the registry contains initialization for all programs, the operating system, and hardware and other devices connected to the computer. The registry also contains information about OLE and ActiveX objects, and much more. You will work extensively with the registry in later chapters when you create your own ActiveX objects.

The registry also supports networking and lets individual users store preferences, so applications can customize the user interface for the current user. User registry data can be stored at a central location and imported into the workstation registry when a user logs on. Similarly, a system administrator can remotely access the registries of workstations to resolve conflicts.

In addition, applications and users can use the registry to associate shell actions (such as "compile," "edit," or "open") with document types. Using the Windows 9x/NT Explorer, when the user clicks the right mouse button on the icon of a document, a contextual menu appears that lists the programmed actions. Other important uses of the registry include internationalization (locale support), network protocols and binding, and plug-and-play support.

In this chapter, you will learn about the registry's responsibilities and com-position, and what you as a Win32 programmer must know to use the registry effectively.

13.1   Understanding the Registry's Structure

The registry is a hierarchically organized store of information—in short, it is a database that the operating system uses to maintain information. Because the registry is hierarchically organized, you can most easily visualize it as a tree-like information structure. Each entry in this structure is called a *key*. A key may contain any number of *subkeys*. A key can also contain data entries called *values*. In this form, the registry stores information about the system, its configuration, hardware devices, and software applications. It also assumes the role of the Windows 3.x INI files by providing a place where application-specific settings can be stored. Figure 13-1 shows the relationships between components of the registry.

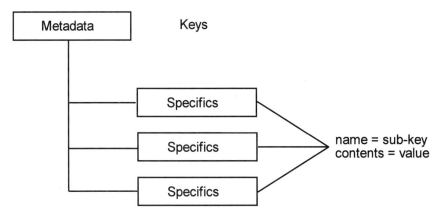

Figure 13-1   The relationships between keys, subkeys, and values.

Core Note

As you read books about Windows NT, you may encounter the term hive *in connection with the registry. The hive is simply another way of referring to the hierarchical tree-like structure that comprises the registry.*

A registry key is identified by its name. Keynames consist of printable ASCII characters, except the backslash (\), space, and wildcard (* or ?) characters. The use of keynames that begin with a period (.) is reserved by the operating system for its own use. Keynames are not case sensitive.

13.1.1 Considering the Role and Format of Registry Values

A value in the registry is identified by its name. Value names consist of the same characters as keynames. The value can be a string, binary data, or a 32-bit unsigned value.

There are some apparent differences between the behavior of the Windows 9x and the Windows NT registries. The Windows 9x registry appears to allow for the assignment of a value to a registry key (as opposed to a value name). This value then appears as the default value for that key. Upon closer examination, however, it turns out that this is really a superficial difference. The default value for a key is really a value with an empty name. Empty names are also permitted in the Windows NT registry. Perhaps the only difference is that the value with the empty name appears to be always defined for a key in the Windows 95 registry, while it must be explicitly created in the Windows NT registry.

Another apparent difference between the two registries is the existence of a variety of string types in the Windows NT registry, while Windows 95 appears to support only one string type. However, consider the following output (created by the registry reader program that you will examine later in this chapter):

```
Enter key: HKEY_CURRENT_USER\Environment\include
Expandable string: d:\msvc60\include;d:\msvc60\mfc\include
```

If you examine the same value using the Windows 9x Registry Editor, it will appear as a binary value. This, however, is a shortcoming of the Registry Editor, not the registry. Table 13-1 contains a list of all value types that can go into the Windows 9x and Windows NT registries.

13.1.2 Registry Capacity

In general, you should not store items larger than 1 or 2KB in the registry (and even that is generally not a great idea). For larger items, use a separate file, and use the registry for storing the filename.

Table 13-1 The Different Registry Value Types	
Symbolic Identifier	*Description*
REG_BINARY	Raw binary data
REG_DWORD	Double word in machine format (low- or little-endian on Intel)
REG_DWORD_LITTLE_ENDIAN	Double word in little-endian format
REG_DWORD_BIG_ENDIAN	Double word in big-endian format
REG_EXPAND_SZ	String with unexpanded environment variables
REG_LINK	Unicode symbolic link
REG_MULTI_SZ	Multiple strings ended by two null characters
REG_NONE	Undefined type
REG_RESOURCE_LIST	Device-driver resource list
REG_SZ	Null-terminated string

Under Windows 95, the registry is limited to 64KB in size. As you may have encountered when you installed Visual Studio 6.0, if you have been using a given machine for some time, it is possible to exceed the available registry space. Out of courtesy, when you design your own applications, keep their registry usage to a minimum.

Another consideration when using the registry is that storing a key generally requires substantially more storage space than storing a value. Whenever possible, organize values under a common key rather than using several keys for the same purpose.

13.2 The Predefined Registry Branches

The registry contains several predefined root-level keys. Any keys that you add to the registry should go in subkeys of these keys. In fact, most of your registry entries will end up in subkeys of subkeys of these keys.

The HKEY_LOCAL_MACHINE key contains entries that describe the computer and its configuration. This includes information about the processor, system board, memory, and installed hardware and software. You will generally write your key entries for your programs within a subkey of this branch. The HKEY_LOCAL_MACHINE key includes the SOFTWARE subkey. You will generally create additional subkeys under this key to store your own software-specific information. Figure 13-2 shows the Registry Editor displaying the HKEY_LOCAL_MACHINE key, SOFTWARE subkey, and Microsoft subkey.

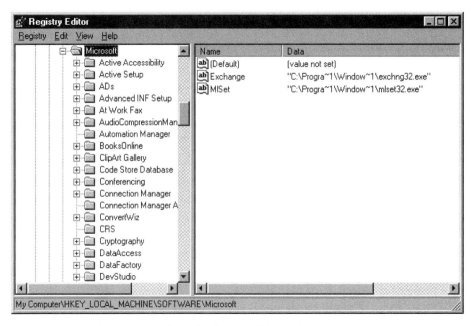

Figure 13-2   The Registry Editor displaying subkey information.

The HKEY_CLASSES_ROOT key is the root key for information relating to document types and OLE types. This key is a subordinate key to HKEY_LOCAL_MACHINE. (It is equivalent to HKEY_LOCAL_MACHINE\-SOFTWARE\Classes.) Information that is stored here is used by shell applications such as the Program Manager, File Manager, or the Explorer, and by OLE applications.

The HKEY_USERS key serves as the root key for the default user preference settings as well as individual user preferences. For example, color and sound configurations are stored within this key. The SOFTWARE subkey of HKEY_USERS corresponds to the SOFTWARE subkey of HKEY_LOCAL_MACHINE.

The HKEY_CURRENT_USER key is the root key for information relating to the preferences of the current (logged-in) user. Default users who do not have specific settings use the user settings for ".Default."

Under Windows 9x, there are two additional predefined keys. The HKEY_CURRENT_CONFIG key contains information about the current system configuration settings. This key is equivalent to a subkey (such as 0001) of the key HKEY_LOCAL_MACHINE\Config.

The HKEY_DYN_DATA key provides access to dynamic status information, such as information about plug-and-play devices. The Enum subkey records hardware data for each component of the system. The PerfStats subkey measures system performance. This data is generated when the HKEY_PERFORMANCE_DATA key is used in a call to RegQueryKeyEx().

Figure 13-3 illustrates the predefined keys and their relationships.

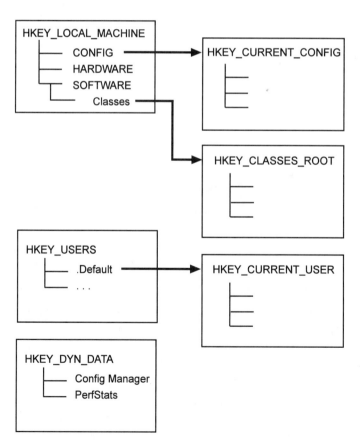

Figure 13-3   The predefined registry keys and their interlocking relationships.

13.3 Editing the Registry Manually

You can manually edit the registry using the Registry Editor. This program is named regedt32.exe under Windows NT and regedit.exe under Windows 9x. The Windows NT program regedit.exe is a version of the Registry Editor that offers behavior similar to the 16-bit Windows Registry Editor. This program is not very useful when editing the registry under Windows NT, as it only sees a subset of registry keys. When you double-click on a value within the registry, you can manually change that value, as shown in Figure 13-4.

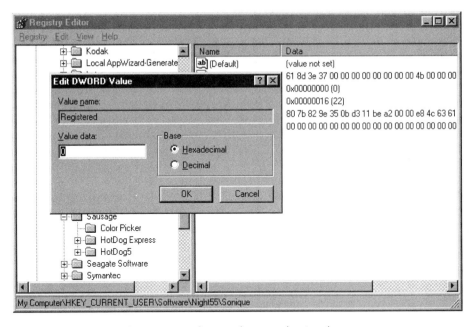

Figure 13-4 Using the Registry Editor to change a key's value.

Needless to say, using the Registry Editor is a last resort solution. Programmers may need to frequently access the registry this way (for example, to remove keys that have been placed there by applications that are under development). However, your applications should never require end users to change registry settings manually.

Core Warning

Editing and manipulating registry keys manually is a dangerous game, at best. In fact, almost every application that stores information in the registry will have one or more keys that, if changed to an invalid value, will result in the application not running correctly. Always use extreme caution when manipulating registry keys that you did not create.

Many registry settings are controlled implicitly through configuration applications such as the Control Panel. Other registry settings are created during application installation. OLE/ActiveX applications that have been created using AppWizard update their registry settings every time they run.

13.4 Commonly Used Registry Keys

Information about registry keys is often difficult to find. The registry is complex enough to write an entire book about (which several other authors have done). However, the following sections detail information on some of the most frequently used registry keys that are of interest to a programmer.

13.4.1 Considering the Subtrees in HKEY_LOCAL_MACHINE

As you learned earlier in this chapter, keys in HKEY_LOCAL_MACHINE contain information about the computer's software and hardware configuration. Of these, the Config and Enum subkeys are specific to Windows 9x and its plug-and-play capabilities. The Config subkey is where Windows 9x stores various hardware configurations, while the Enum subkey contains Windows 9x bus enumerators that the operating systems uses to build the tree of hardware devices.

Both Windows 9x and Windows NT maintain the System subkey under HKEY_LOCAL_MACHINE. The System\CurrentControlSet subkey contains configuration information for services and device drivers.

Other subkeys in HKEY_LOCAL_MACHINE include Software and Classes. The Software subkey is where information about installed software packages can be found (and where you will place the vast majority of information that you save in the registry). The Classes subkey is where HKEY_CLASSES_ROOT points to, and contains information about ActiveX and OLE objects. You will also use this key extensively, although much of the manipulation of values in this key will be handled for you by the AppWizard or by your MIDL files (which you will learn about in later chapters).

The `Software` subtree is of particular interest to application programmers. This is where you should store configuration and installation information specific to your application. Microsoft recommends that you build a series of subtrees under `HKEY_LOCAL_MACHINE\Software`. These subkeys should represent your company name, the name of your product, and the product's version number, as shown here:

```
HKEY_LOCAL_MACHINE\Software\PrenHall\CoreVC++\6.0
```

For example, configuration information pertaining to Microsoft Visual Studio can be found under the following key:

```
HKEY_LOCAL_MACHINE\Software\Microsoft\VisualStudio\6.0
```

What you store under such a key is entirely application-dependent. Note that you should not store anything here that is user-specific—instead, you should store user-specific information pertinent to your application under a subkey of `HKEY_CURRENT_USER`.

Of particular interest within the `Software` tree is the following key:

```
HKEY_LOCAL_MACHINE\Software\Microsoft\Windows\CurrentVersion
```

The `CurrentVersion` key describes the current Windows configuration. If you have an application that should run when Windows starts, for example, you would store the application under the following subkey of the `CurrentVersion` key:

```
HKEY_LOCAL_MACHINE\Software\Microsoft\Windows\CurrentVersion\Run
```

Another important key in the `Software` tree is the following key:

```
HKEY_LOCAL_MACHINE\Software\Microsoft\Windows NT\CurrentVersion
```

This key actually has a curious, unexpected role under Windows 9x. It allows debugger information stored under the following key within the Windows NT tree to affect debugger behavior under Windows 9x:

```
HKEY_LOCAL_MACHINE\Software\Microsoft\Windows NT\
   CurrentVersion\Aedebug
```

13.4.2 Subtrees in HKEY_CLASSES_ROOT

The `HKEY_CLASSES_ROOT` key contains two types of subkeys: subkeys that correspond to filename extensions and class definition subkeys. A filename extension subkey has a name that corresponds to the filename extension (such as .doc). The key typically contains one unnamed value, which holds the name of the class definition subkey. A class definition subkey describes the behavior of a document class. The information stored here includes data on shell-related and OLE-related properties.

A subkey under HKEY_CLASSES_ROOT is CLSID. This is the place where OLE class identifiers are stored.

When you create an MFC application using the Visual C++ AppWizard, a series of subkeys that are to be installed under HKEY_CLASSES_ROOT are also created. These identify the document type and filename extension of your new application and also its OLE properties such as the OLE class identifier. For example, creating an MFC application named Sample with a file extension .smp for its document files yielded the following Registry entries under HKEY_CLASSES_ROOT:

```
.SMP = Sample.Document
Sample.Document\shell\open\command = SAMPLE.EXE %1
Sample.Document\shell\open\ddeexec = [open("%1")]
Sample.Document\shell\open\ddeexec\application = SAMPLE
Sample.Document = Sample Document
Sample.Document\protocol\StdFileEditing\server = SAMPLE.EXE
Sample.Document\protocol\StdFileEditing\verb\0 = &Edit
Sample.Document\Insertable =
Sample.Document\CLSID = {FC168A60-F1EA-11CE-87C3-00403321BFAC}
```

Visual Studio will also create the following entries under the subkey HKEY_CLASSES_ROOT\CLSID:

```
{FC168A60-F1EA-11CE-87C3-00403321BFAC} = Sample Document
{FC168A60-F1EA-11CE-87C3-00403321BFAC}\DefaultIcon = SAMPLE.EXE,1
{FC168A60-F1EA-11CE-87C3-00403321BFAC}\LocalServer32 = SAMPLE.EXE
{FC168A60-F1EA-11CE-87C3-00403321BFAC}\ProgId = Sample.Document
{FC168A60-F1EA-11CE-87C3-00403321BFAC}\MiscStatus = 32
{FC168A60-F1EA-11CE-87C3-00403321BFAC}\AuxUserType\3 = Sample
{FC168A60-F1EA-11CE-87C3-00403321BFAC}\AuxUserType\2 = Sample
{FC168A60-F1EA-11CE-87C3-00403321BFAC}\Insertable =
{FC168A60-F1EA-11CE-87C3-00403321BFAC}\verb\1 = &Open,0,2
{FC168A60-F1EA-11CE-87C3-00403321BFAC}\verb\0 = &Edit,0,2
{FC168A60-F1EA-11CE-87C3-00403321BFAC}\InprocHandler32 = ole32.dll
```

13.4.3 Subtrees in HKEY_USERS

The key HKEY_USERS contains a subkey named .Default and zero or more subkeys corresponding to users on the system. The .Default subkey corresponds to the default user profile. Other entries correspond to profiles of existing users. User profiles store information about the user's system preferences, such as color and sound configurations, desktop settings, hardware profiles, and so on.

13.4.4 Subtrees in HKEY_CURRENT_USER

The `HKEY_CURRENT_USER` key corresponds to the profile of the currently logged-in user. This key has several subkeys, some common to both Windows 9x and Windows NT, some specific to one or the other.

Application configuration information specific to the current user should be stored under the subkey `Software`. Information should be organized by keys corresponding to company name, product name, and product version number. For example, user settings for Microsoft Excel 2000 can be found under the following key:

```
HKEY_CURRENT_USER\Software\Microsoft\Office\9.0\Excel
```

As you learned, the user's settings and preferences for Windows, its components, and applets can be found under the following key and its subkeys:

```
HKEY_CURRENT_USER\Software\Microsoft\Windows\CurrentVersion
```

13.5 The Registry and INI Files

In new applications that you design specifically for 32-bit distribution (which is clearly the vast majority of applications), the registry should be used instead of INI files. This is relatively obvious. However, it is important to understand how older applications (that is, applications that do not explicitly use the registry) behave under 32-bit Windows.

As it turns out, older applications behave differently under Windows NT than they do under Windows 9x. In order to maintain maximum backward compatibility, Windows 9x still maintains INI files, such as the win.ini file or the system.ini file. These files do not exist under Windows NT. Instead, Windows NT maps these files directly to the registry.

Which files Windows NT maps and which files Windows NT does not is determined by the settings under the following key:

```
HKEY_LOCAL_MACHINE\SOFTWARE\Microsoft\Windows NT\
    CurrentVersion\IniFileMapping
```

This key contains a subkey for every mapped INI file. Values under such a subkey correspond to sections in the INI file and typically point to other keys in the registry.

The mapping of INI files affects the operation of functions such as `Read-ProfileString()` or `WriteProfileString()`. If a mapping exists for the specified INI file, these functions will read from and write to the registry as opposed to an actual INI file.

13.6   Writing Application Programs That Manipulate the Registry

The Win32 API offers a variety of functions for manipulating the registry. Those functions let your applications read keys, write keys, create new keys, and perform just about any other action against the registry that your applications need to perform.

13.6.1   Opening a Registry Key

All access to the registry is performed through handles. In order to access a key in the registry, applications must use a handle to an existing, open key. There are several predefined key handles that are assumed to be always open. These handles include the following:

- HKEY_LOCAL_MACHINE
- HKEY_CLASSES_ROOT
- HKEY_USERS
- HKEY_CURRENT_USER

A registry key is accessed through the function `RegOpenKeyEx()`. For example, in order to obtain a handle to the registry key `HKEY_LOCAL_MACHINE\Software`, one would issue the following function call:

```
RegOpenKeyEx(HKEY_LOCAL_MACHINE, "Software", 0, KEY_READ,
    &hKey);
```

To access a subkey under the key `HKEY_LOCAL_MACHINE\Software`, it is necessary to call `RegOpenKeyEx()` again. For example, to obtain a handle to `HKEY_LOCAL_MACHINE\Software\Classes`, one would have to issue the following two calls:

```
RegOpenKeyEx(HKEY_LOCAL_MACHINE, "Software", 0, KEY_READ,
    &hKey);
```

```
RegOpenKeyEx(hKey, "Classes", 0, KEY_READ, &hSubkey);
```

Logical as it may appear, it is not possible to use concatenated key values delimited by a backslash as the keyname parameter to `RegOpenKeyEx()`. Thus, the following call is an error:

```
RegOpenKeyEx(hKey, "Key\\Sub-key", 0, KEY_READ,
    &hSubkey); // ERROR!
```

When an application is finished using a registry key, it should close the key by calling `RegCloseKey()`.

13.6.2 Querying a Value

Your applications can retrieve a registry value by calling the function `RegQueryValueEx()`. Before this function can be called, the appropriate subkey must be opened using `RegOpenKey()`.

`RegQueryValueEx()` offers a mechanism that enables applications to find out the memory requirements for storing a value before the value is actually retrieved. If you call this function with a `NULL` pointer passed as the data buffer pointer, the function will return the requested length of the data buffer without actually copying any data. Thus, it is possible to call `RegQueryValueEx()` twice for a single registry key value: first to obtain the length of the buffer, and next to actually copy the data, as in the following example:

```
RegQueryValueEx(hKey, "MyValue", NULL, &dwType, NULL, &dwSize);
pData = malloc(dwSize);
RegQueryValueEx(hKey, "MyValue", NULL, &dwType, pData, &dwSize);
```

The following code listing shows the program code from the Windows messaging procedure for the QueryValue program.

```
LRESULT FAR PASCAL WndProc( HWND hWnd, UINT uMsg, WPARAM wParam,
    LPARAM lParam )
{
   switch ( uMsg ) {
      case WM_COMMAND:
         switch ( wParam ) {
            case IDM_TEST:
               {                        // Test option.
                 LONG lRes1, lRes2;    // Holds results of key finds
                 char szBuffer[256];   // Buffer to store the values
                 HKEY hKeyIcons;       // RTF default icon key
                 HKEY hKeyFileType;    // RTF file key
```

```
                    // Open a key for rtffile.
                    lRes1 = RegOpenKeyEx( HKEY_CLASSES_ROOT,
                        "rtffile\\DefaultIcon", // icon name
                        0, KEY_ALL_ACCESS, &hKeyIcons );
                    lRes2 = RegOpenKeyEx( HKEY_CLASSES_ROOT,
                        "rtffile", 0, KEY_ALL_ACCESS,
                        &hKeyFileType );
                    if ((lRes1==ERROR_SUCCESS)
                        && (lRes2==ERROR_SUCCESS)) {
                      DWORD dwType;
                      LPTSTR lpszBuffer;
                      DWORD dwBytes = 128;
                      RegQueryValueEx( hKeyFileType, "", 0, &dwType,
                          szBuffer, &dwBytes );
                      // Make message.
                      lpszBuffer = &szBuffer[lstrlen(szBuffer)];
                      lstrcat(lpszBuffer, " icons are found in file ");
                      lpszBuffer = &szBuffer[lstrlen(szBuffer)];
                      dwBytes = 128;
                      RegQueryValueEx(hKeyIcons, "", 0, &dwType,
                          lpszBuffer, &dwBytes);
                     }
                    else
                       lstrcpy(szBuffer,
                           "Rich Text File Information Not Found" );
                    // Put message to screen.
                    MessageBox(hWnd, szBuffer, "Registry Query", MB_OK);
                   }
                break;
                case IDM_EXIT:
                   DestroyWindow( hWnd );
                   break;
            }
          break;
      case WM_DESTROY:
         PostQuitMessage( 0 );
         break;
      default:            // default windows message processing
         return DefWindowProc(hWnd, uMsg, wParam, lParam);
    }
   return(0L);
}
```

The code with the messaging procedure uses the `RegQueryValueEx()` function to query the registry for the name of the default icon that Rich Text Format (RTF) files use. If it locates the icon filename, it displays the filename within a message box. Otherwise, the program code displays an error message.

13.6.3 Setting a Value

A value in the registry can be set using the `RegSetValueEx()` function. Before this function can be used, the appropriate subkey must be opened with `KEY_SET_VALUE` access using `RegOpenKeyEx()`.

13.6.4 Creating a New Key

Applications can also create a new subkey in the registry. The function `RegCreateKeyEx()` creates the new key, opens it, and obtains a key handle. This function can also be used to open existing keys; thus it is ideal in situations when the application wishes to access a key, whether it already exists or not—during an installation procedure, for example.

Under Windows NT, when creating a new key, the application also assigns security attributes to it. The key's security attributes determine who can access the key for reading and writing. Security information can be obtained about an open key using `RegGetKeySecurity()` and set using `RegSetKeySecurity()` (that is, if the application has the necessary privileges).

The following code fragment shows the use of the `RegCreateKeyEx()` function.

```
LRESULT FAR PASCAL WndProc(HWND hWnd, UINT uMsg, WPARAM wParam,
    LPARAM lParam)
{
   switch(uMsg) {
      case WM_COMMAND:    // process menu items
         switch(wParam) {
            case IDM_TEST:
              {
                HKEY hKeyResult = 0;
                DWORD dwDisposition = 0;

                // Create "SampleDoc" shell interface.
                LONG  lResult = RegCreateKeyEx(HKEY_CLASSES_ROOT,
                    "SampleDoc\\shell\\&CheckKey\\command",
                    0, "", REG_OPTION_VOLATILE,
                    KEY_ALL_ACCESS, NULL,
                    &hKeyResult, &dwDisposition);
// Program the registry to use Notepad to open the document.
```

```
            if (lResult==ERROR_SUCCESS) {
               lResult = RegSetValueEx(hKeyResult, NULL, 0,
                  REG_SZ, "NotePad %1", lstrlen("NotePad %1"));
               RegCloseKey(hKeyResult);   // close SampleDoc key.
             }
            // Create .SDC file extension connection.
            lResult = RegCreateKeyEx(HKEY_CLASSES_ROOT, ".SDC",
               0, "", REG_OPTION_VOLATILE, KEY_ALL_ACCESS, NULL,
                  &hKeyResult, &dwDisposition);
            // Connect .SDC with SampleDoc type.
            if (lResult==ERROR_SUCCESS) {
               // Set the value of the .SDC key to "SampleDoc".
               lResult = RegSetValueEx(hKeyResult, NULL, 0,
                  REG_SZ, "SampleDoc", lstrlen("SampleDoc"));
               RegCloseKey(hKeyResult);
             }
          }
       break;
       case IDM_EXIT:
          DestroyWindow(hWnd);
          break;
     }
   break;
 case WM_DESTROY:
    PostQuitMessage(0);
    break;
 default:            // default windows message processing
    return DefWindowProc(hWnd, uMsg, wParam, lParam);
  }
  return(0L);
}
```

When the user selects the Set Key menu option, this sample program (of which the above is only a fragment) would create two entries in the Windows registry. The first entry would be for the document type SampleDoc and the second entry would be for the extension ".SDC." The program code would then link the file extension to the document type and the "&CheckKey" shell command. After the user creates the key entries, he would rename a text file with the .SDC extension. Next, the user would right-click the mouse on that file. Windows would display a context menu with the &CheckKey option. If the user selects the &CheckKey option, Windows would load the SampleDoc file into Notepad. The new shell registry key would show up under the HKEY_CLASSES_ROOT branch of the registry, as shown in Figure 13-5.

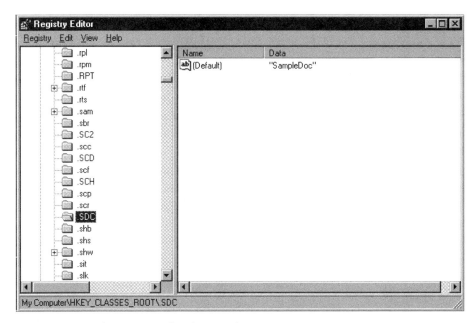

Figure 13-5   The Registry after the sample program executes.

13.6.5   *Other Registry Functions*

There are several other functions that assist in dealing with the registry efficiently. For example, the RegEnumKeyEx() and RegEnumValue() functions can be used to enumerate the subkeys and values under a specific registry key. Registry keys can be deleted using the RegDeleteKey() function. Several other functions exist to deal with saving and loading subkeys, connecting to remote registries, and performing other administrative functions. For example, the following code fragment shows the Enumerate-Registry() function.

```
EnumerateRegistry( HKEY hKey, HWND hWndListBox )
{
   DWORD dwcSubKeys, dwcValues, dwcMaxSubKeyName, dwcMaxValueName,
      dwcMaxValueData;
   char szLevel[33];           // demonstrates the subkey level
   static int iLevel = 0;      // Level counter
   char szBuffer[255];         // Format area for text output
   DWORD dwSubKeyIndex = 0;    // Counter for subkeys
   DWORD dwValueIndex = 0;     // Counter for values
   HKEY hNewKey = 0;           // New key to iterate
   LONG lStatus = ERROR_SUCCESS; // Status flag for enumeration
```

```
// make level string "========="
iLevel++;                              // Next level now.
FillMemory( szLevel, iLevel, '=' );
szLevel[iLevel] = 0;

// Find out how much space we need for key names and values
// in this subtree.
RegQueryInfoKey(hKey, szBuffer, NULL, 0, &dwcSubKeys,
    &dwcMaxSubKeyName, NULL,
    &dwcValues, &dwcMaxValueName, &dwcMaxValueData, NULL, NULL);
if (dwcValues!=0 || dwcSubKeys!=0) {
   LPTSTR lpszSubKeyName = HeapAlloc(GetProcessHeap(),
       HEAP_ZERO_MEMORY,
       dwcMaxSubKeyName+1);
   LPTSTR lpszValueName = HeapAlloc(GetProcessHeap(),
       HEAP_ZERO_MEMORY,
       dwcMaxValueName+1);
   LPTSTR lpszValueData = HeapAlloc(GetProcessHeap(),
        HEAP_ZERO_MEMORY,
        dwcMaxValueData+1);
   // Enumerate values before subkeys.
   do {
      DWORD dwType;
      DWORD dwcValueName = dwcMaxValueName + 1;
      DWORD dwcValueData = dwcMaxValueData + 1;

      lStatus = RegEnumValue( hKey, dwValueIndex,
          lpszValueName,&dwcValueName,
          NULL, &dwType, lpszValueData, &dwcValueData);
      if (lStatus==ERROR_SUCCESS) {
         wsprintf(szBuffer, "%s> VALUE [%s]=[%s], Type=%s",
             szLevel, lpszValueName,
             (dwType==REG_SZ) ? lpszValueData : "?",
             (dwType==REG_SZ) ? "REG_SZ" : "OTHER" );
         SendMessage(hWndListBox, LB_ADDSTRING, 0,
             (LPARAM) szBuffer);
      }
      dwValueIndex++;
   } while (lStatus==ERROR_SUCCESS);

   // Enumerate subkeys now.
   do {
      DWORD dwcSubKeyName = dwcMaxSubKeyName + 1;

      // Get data about the sub-key.
      lStatus = RegEnumKeyEx(hKey, dwSubKeyIndex, lpszSubKeyName,
          &dwcSubKeyName, NULL, NULL, NULL, NULL);
      if (lStatus == ERROR_SUCCESS) {
         wsprintf( szBuffer, "%s> %3d: Key=%s", szLevel,
             dwSubKeyIndex, lpszSubKeyName);
```

```
            SendMessage(hWndListBox, LB_ADDSTRING, 0,
                (LPARAM) szBuffer);
            if (RegOpenKeyEx(hKey, lpszSubKeyName, 0,
                KEY_ALL_ACCESS, &hNewKey) == ERROR_SUCCESS)
                EnumerateRegistry( hNewKey, hWndListBox );
            RegCloseKey( hNewKey );
        }
        dwSubKeyIndex++;
    } while (lStatus==ERROR_SUCCESS);

    // housekeeping - remove the data we allocated.
    HeapFree(GetProcessHeap(), 0, lpszSubKeyName);
    HeapFree(GetProcessHeap(), 0, lpszValueName);
    HeapFree(GetProcessHeap(), 0, lpszValueData);
    }
  iLevel--;          // Level is completed.
}
```

This sample EnumRegKeys program (of which the above is only a fragment) would create a window with a child list box. When the user selects the EnumKeys menu option, the Windows Messaging loop would invoke the EnumerateKeys() function, which in turn would display the contents of the HKEY_CLASSES_ROOT registry tree.

As you can see, the program uses a pair of Do-While loops to process the values of each key, and then moves forward to process the key's subkeys. The program would display keys and values with indentation within the list box, as shown in Figure 13-6.

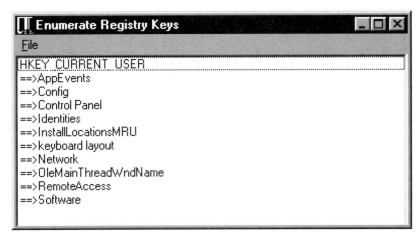

Figure 13-6   The list box within the sample EnumRegKeys program window after the user enumerates the registry keys.

13.6.6 Working with Registry Hives

As you learned previously in this chapter, many Windows NT programmers refer to the Windows NT registry as the *system hive*. In general, a hive is a collection of keys, subkeys, and values defined within a single file and a .log file. The Win32 API provides four functions for working with hives. You will use the `RegSaveKey()` function to create a hive, the `RegLoadKey()` function to load the hive into the registry, the `RegRestoreKey()` function to restore a key in the registry from the hive, and the `RegUnloadKey()` function to remove a hive key and its subkeys from the registry.

Creating hives is a useful way to store groups of registry key information offline—your applications can load the hive into the registry only when the application executes. In other words, your application might place only boot-strap information in the registry permanently, maintaining the remainder of the information it needs to execute offline in a hive, and then add the information to the registry only upon execution.

The following code sample shows the correct usage of the hive functions:

```
LRESULT FAR PASCAL WndProc(HWND hWnd, UINT uMsg, WPARAM wParam,
    LPARAM lParam)
{
  switch (uMsg) {
    case WM_COMMAND:
      {
        char szErrMsg[128]; // Buffer for message to
                            // print in message boxes
        HKEY hKey;          // Handle of key.
        LRESULT lResult;    // Tests function return values.
        switch (wParam) {
          case IDM_SAVE:
            {
              DWORD dwDisp;

              // Build the contents of the KeyRoot and its subkeys.
              RegCreateKeyEx( HKEY_CLASSES_ROOT,
                  "KeyRoot\\Test\\Test1", 0, NULL,
                  REG_OPTION_NON_VOLATILE, KEY_ALL_ACCESS, NULL,
                  &hKey, &dwDisp );
              RegSetValueEx(hKey, "Value1", 0, REG_SZ, "ABC", 14);
              RegSetValueEx(hKey, "Value2", 0, REG_SZ, "BCD", 14);
              RegCloseKey(hKey);
              RegCreateKeyEx(HKEY_CLASSES_ROOT,
                  "KeyRoot\\Test\\Test2", 0, NULL,
                  REG_OPTION_NON_VOLATILE, KEY_ALL_ACCESS, NULL,
                  &hKey, &dwDisp);
```

```
    RegSetValueEx(hKey, "Value1", 0, REG_SZ, "ZYX", 14);
    RegCloseKey(hKey);

    // Save key, "KeyRoot", in hive, "SampleHive".
    RegOpenKeyEx(HKEY_CLASSES_ROOT, "KeyRoot", 0,
        KEY_ALL_ACCESS, &hKey);
    RegSaveKey(hKey, "SampleHive", NULL);
    RegCloseKey(hKey);
  }
break;
case IDM_LOAD:
 {
    lResult = RegLoadKey(HKEY_LOCAL_MACHINE,
        "KeyRoot", "SampleHive");
    if (GetLastError()==ERROR_SUCCESS)
      MessageBox(hWnd,
          "Loaded SampleHive into HKEY_LOCAL_MACHINE",
        "MESSAGE", MB_OK);
    else {
      wsprintf(szErrMsg, "Error %d occurred",
          GetLastError());
      MessageBox(hWnd, szErrMsg, "ERROR", MB_OK);
    }
 }
break;
case IDM_UNLOAD:
 {
    lResult = RegUnLoadKey(HKEY_LOCAL_MACHINE,
        "KeyRoot");
    if (GetLastError()==ERROR_SUCCESS)
      MessageBox(hWnd, "SampleHive Was Unloaded",
          "MESSAGE", MB_OK);
    else {
      wsprintf(szErrMsg, "Error %d occurred",
          GetLastError());
      MessageBox(hWnd, szErrMsg, "ERROR", MB_OK);
    }
 }
break;
case IDM_RESTORE:
 {
    DWORD dwDisposition = 0;

    RegCreateKeyEx(HKEY_LOCAL_MACHINE, "KeyRoot", 0, "",
        REG_OPTION_NON_VOLATILE, KEY_ALL_ACCESS,
        NULL, &hKey, &dwDisposition);
    RegRestoreKey(hKey, "SampleHive", 0);
    if (GetLastError() != ERROR_SUCCESS) {
      wsprintf(szErrMsg, "Error %d occurred",
          GetLastError());
```

```
                    MessageBox(hWnd, szErrMsg, "ERROR", MB_OK);
                    RegDeleteKey(HKEY_LOCAL_MACHINE, hKey);
                  }
                else
                    MessageBox(hWnd, "The Hive was restored",
                        "MESSAGE", MB_OK);
                  RegCloseKey(hKey);
                }
            break;
            case IDM_EXIT:
                DestroyWindow(hWnd);
                break;
          }
        }
      break;
      case WM_DESTROY:
          PostQuitMessage(0);
      break;
      default:                  // default windows message processing
          return DefWindowProc(hWnd, uMsg, wParam, lParam);
    }
    return(0L);
}
```

The menu of this sample SampleHive application (of which this is only a fragment) would have four options: Save, Load, Unload, and Restore. Choosing the Save option would create some sample key entries and save them within a hive. The Load option, in turn, would load the hive into the registry. The Unload option would remove the hive, and (under Windows NT), the RegRestoreKey() function would return the key to its previous contents.

As you can see, the Save option would first create some registry keys, then save the keys into the hive file SampleHive. The other functions would simply manipulate the already created hive file.

Core Note

Windows 95 does not support the RegRestoreKey() *function. Invoking it under Windows 95 has no effect.*

13.7 Summary

The registry is a place where Windows and applications can store configuration data. The registry is a tree-like, hierarchically organized information store. Registry entries, or keys, are identified by a name and may contain any number of subkeys or values.

At the top level of the registry are the root keys `HKEY_USERS` and `HKEY_LOCAL_MACHINE`. `HKEY_CLASSES_ROOT`, `HKEY_CURRENT_USER`, `HKEY_CURRENT_CONFIG`, and `HKEY_DYN_DATA` are other predifined keys

A registry value can be a 4-byte integer, a string or a series of strings, or arbitrary binary data. Registry values are usually created by application programs, installation procedures, or configuration utilities such as the Control Panel. However, the registry can also be edited manually using the Registry Editor.

Applications typically store configuration information under `HKEY_LOCAL_MACHINE\Software` and user-specific data under `HKEY_CURRENT_USER\Software`. In both cases, subkeys should be created to correspond to a company name, product name, and product version number.

In addition, applications that manage specific document types create a file-name extension and a class definition entry under `HKEY_CLASSES_ROOT`. OLE applications also store OLE information here.

The Win32 API provides a series of functions for applications to access the registry. Using one of the predefined registry keys, applications can access any subkey for reading and writing, query values, and set values. Applications can also create new keys or delete existing keys.

PERFORMING ADVANCED EXCEPTION HANDLING

Topics in this Chapter

- Exception Handling

- Exceptions and MFC

- Understanding the MFC CException Class

- Throwing an MFC Exception

- MFC and Exceptions

- The Visual C++ 6.0 Solution

- Using the ASSERT Macros for Exception Handling

- Summary

Chapter 14

The Microsoft Foundation Classes Library provides two different forms of exception handling. It supports C++-style typed expressions, and it also supports exception handling through old-style MFC macros. Over the course of this chapter, you will briefly review C++-style exception handling as a crucial groundwork for and comparison with MFC-style exception handling. You will also learn about MFC's exception classes and how to use them within your MFC applications.

14.1 Exception Handling

Professionally written code always checks the result of any function called to make sure that it doesn't run into an error. Software should be robust. *Robustness*, when it comes to software, means that although a program cannot run in every possible situation, it should be able to detect those situations in which it cannot run correctly and do something useful about them (that is, respond to them). However, without exception processing, responding to all possible situations results in code that has to include `if` statements, which nest very deeply. Worse, the `if` statements will nest more and more deeply as you touch more and more things that might fail. For example, suppose you write the name of a book to a file, as shown here:

```
LPTSTR pstrName = NULL;
FILE *fOutput = NULL;
BOOL bSuccess = FALSE;

fOutput = fopen(_T("BOOK.DAT"), _T("w"));
if (fOutput != NULL) {
   pstrName = _tcsdup(_T("Core Visual C++ 6.0"));
   if (pstrName != NULL) {
      if (fputs(pstrName, fOutput) == _tcslen(pstrName))
         bSuccess = TRUE;
      free(pstrName);
    }
   fclose(fOutput);
 }
```

Even for this simple example, you can see that you must indent the code three levels to handle all of the possible errors. Adding to this simple example, implementing a more complicated (and more realistic) example would show the real weakness behind this method of programming.

To address the code quality, readability, and maintainability issues that if-based error checking raises, the C++ language introduced the concept of *exceptions*. The idea is that you can readily implement constructs that clean up the errors and release resources, avoiding the need to check return values from functions and the implied need for callers to know how their functions work internally. The code example to write a single book name to a file is slightly more readable if you use exception handling mechanisms, rather than if constructs, as shown here:

```
LPTSTR pstrName = NULL;
FILE *fOutput = NULL;
BOOL bSuccess = FALSE;

try {
   fOutput = fopen(_T("BOOK.DAT"), _T("w"));
   if  (fOutput == NULL)
      throw _T("Failed to open file!");
   pstrName = _tcsdup(_T("Core Visual C++ 6.0"));
   if (pstrName == NULL)
      throw _T("Failed to allocate memory!");
   if (fputs(pstrName, fOutput) == _tcslen(pstrName))
      throw _T("Failed to write data!");
   bSuccess = TRUE;
 }
catch(LPTSTR pstr) {
   PostErrorMessage(pstr); // fictitious function
```

```
   }
if (fOutput != NULL)
   fclose(fOutput);
free(pstrName);
return bSuccess;
```

The second code fragment is better program code than the first code fragment in several ways. First, the code does not indent all over the place and leave lots of questions about what will happen when an error is handled. Most programmers will quickly learn (or already have learned) to let their eyes hop down to the `catch()` block to see what is going to happen in the event of an error, which is much simpler than checking multiple `else` statements or blocks. The `catch()` block and all of its contents are known as the *exception handler*. The second fragment also lets the program naturally clean up from the work that it was doing. With a little careful coding, you can do all of the tidying for both error and nonerror conditions in one place.

14.1.1 Hiding the Error Handling Mechanism

The other interesting thing about the second code fragment is somewhat hidden, but is probably the most important. If you want to, you can code `throws` in any function, expecting that the caller of the function is making the call from within a `try` block to later catch the exception. This completely hides the error-handling mechanism (which, in this scenario, would likely be some sort of return-value setup). If you had used real C++ runtime library functions (like calling `new()` instead of `strdup()` or `_tcsdup()`), you would have been able to benefit from the exceptions that the standard implementation of the functions would throw, simplifying the code.

In the meantime, it is worthwhile to take a closer look at how the second example really works. The `throw` statements cause a jump to the appropriate exception handler. The `throw` keyword expects an expression, the type of which determines the exception handler that the program will subsequently invoke.

14.1.2 Multiple Catch Statements

A `try...catch` block might have more than one `catch` statement to handle different types of exceptions. You can just concatenate the extra `catch()` code to the end of the block. For example, you might want to handle the memory allocation error a little differently from other errors in the `try` block, as shown here:

```
try {
   // ... other code ...
   pstrName = _tcsdup(_T("Core Visual C++ 6.0"));
   if (pstrName == NULL)
      throw _tcslen(_T("Core Visual C++ 6.0"));
   // ... other code ...
 }
catch(LPTSTR pstr) {
   // ... throw string handler ...
 }
catch(size_t n) {
   _tprintf(_T("ERROR!  Couldn't get %d bytes\n"), n);
 }
// ... uninitialization code ...
```

The new throw statement takes a size_t expression, which will result
from the call to _tcslen(), to see how much memory wasn't available. The
additional catch statement accepts that size_t and formats a nice error
message with it. Note that, even though size_t is an integer underneath,
you don't catch an integer because it's always a good idea to catch a type that
is as unique as possible. In real life, you'll probably want to make your own
data type or class for your custom exception situations. You might consider
deriving your exception class from CException.

Note that CUserException (which you will learn more about later in
this chapter) is not designed to be a user-defined exception type. Here, user
refers to the USER module, one of the core components of Windows, and
not the user of the class library.

Since the catch statement is not limited to simple types, using
try...catch blocks gives you the ability to wrap almost any kind of functionality around the data surrounding the error. For example, you can use the
class to hold more information about the error or to provide more functions
to clean up or reset the state of the device that caused the error. MFC offers
several such error reporting classes.

14.2 Exceptions and MFC

MFC supported exception handling starting with MFC 2.0, which was bundled with Visual C++ 1.0. MFC provided this support using a set of macros,
even though the underlying compiler didn't support exceptions. The idea was
that MFC was a class library and wouldn't make much of an impact on the

world if it avoided the use of a C++ idiom which was, at the time, gaining lots of popularity. Without the compiler's support for exceptions under it, the Microsoft Foundation Class library had to implement its own exception handling macros and classes.

The macros that MFC defines to be used for exception handling are defined as macros with the same names as the C++ keywords. They are differentiated from the standard C++ keywords by being all uppercase. Since the macro implementation for exception handling keywords couldn't provide exactly the same functionality with the same set of keywords, there are a few extra macros for special situations. In modern versions of MFC, the macros map directly to real C++ exception keywords. The macros and keywords compare as shown in Table 14-1.

Table 14-1 Macro and Keyword Comparisons

MFC Macro	Standard C++ Keyword
TRY	try
CATCH	catch
AND_CATCH	catch
END_TRY	no equivalent
THROW	throw
CATCH_ALL	no equivalent

Note that the MFC `CATCH()` and `AND_CATCH()` macros take two parameters: the type of the catch and a data item in which to store that type of exception. Conversely, the normal C++ `catch` keyword accepts a data declaration there. You should also note that there is a special MFC macro, named `AND_CATCH`, that you can use when you need to catch another exception in the same exception handler.

14.2.1 Exception Handling with Macros

New applications should not use MFC exception-processing macros. That said, as there are probably many applications out there that rely on the old, macro-based exception handling mechanism, it is probably helpful to have a brief summary of how those macros can be converted into code following the C++ exception syntax.

The first and most obvious step is to replace the macro names with C++ keywords. The macros TRY, CATCH, AND_CATCH, THROW, and THROW_LAST should be replaced with the C++ keywords `try`, `catch`, and `throw`. The END_CATCH macro has no C++ equivalent; you should therefore simply delete it from your program code.

The syntax of the CATCH macro and the C++ `catch` keyword are different. When you use the CATCH macro, you will construct it as shown here:

```
CATCH(CException, e)
```

Using the C++ `catch` command, you would construct the exception trap as shown here:

```
catch(CException *e)
```

An important difference between the two forms of exception handling is that when you are using the C++ exception handling mechanism, you are supposed to delete the exception object yourself. You can delete objects of type CException by calling their Delete() member function. For example, if you have used MFC exception macros, you might use code similar to the following to catch an exception:

```
TRY {
    // Do something invalid here
  }
CATCH(CException, e) {
    // Process the exception here
  }
END_CATCH
```

Using the C++ `try...catch` combination, you will instead construct your exception blocks as shown here:

```
try {
    // Do something invalid here
  }
catch (CException *e) {
    // Process the exception here
    e->Delete();
  }
```

Core Note

Do not attempt to delete a `CException` *object in a* `catch` *block using the* `delete()` *operator. The* `delete()` *operator will fail if the exception object was not allocated on the heap.*

14.3 Understanding the MFC CException Class

The MFC exception macros revolve around the `CException` class. This class does not contain any very interesting member variables or functionality beyond the backbone of exception handling and cleanup. When a `CException`-derived class is thrown, `CException` prints a message to the trace device to show that the exception has been thrown. However, the real functionality comes as MFC uses various classes that are declared for each type of exception that may be thrown. These classes are used to indicate errors and abnormal conditions relating to memory, file management, serialization, resource management, data access objects (DAO), database functions, OLE, and other categories. MFC implements the following exception types:

- `CMemoryException`
- `CDBException`
- `CDaoException`
- `COleDispatchException`
- `COleException`
- `CUserException`
- `CNotSupportedException`
- `CFileException`
- `CArchiveException`
- `CResourceException`

The primary function of the `CException` class is to provide a distinct type for MFC Library exceptions. It could fulfill that function even as an empty class. It does, however, provide several member functions that can be utilized when processing an exception.

You can use the `GetErrorMessage()` member function within your applications to retrieve a textual description of the error. You can also use the `ReportError()` member function, which will retrieve the textual error message and display it in a standard message box.

Core Note

Not all exceptions caught by a CException *handler have a valid error message associated with them.*

The third member function that is important to know about is the Delete() function. You will use this function to delete an exception in a catch block if you process the exception. (You should not delete the exception if your program will subsequently use throw to pass it to another exception handler.)

Clearly, it is impossible to list all of the MFC functions that might throw an exception here, but you can get a good idea of what a given MFC function might do if you have a look at that function's documentation. If the declaration of the function shows a throw() statement, the call is capable of throwing that type of exception. That being said, it is worthwhile to take a quick peek at each CException type to see what it can do for you within your programs.

Core Note

The MFC Library does not directly support Win32 structured exceptions. If you wish to process structured exceptions, you may have to use the C-style structured exception handling mechanism or write your own translator function that translates structured exceptions into C++ exceptions.

14.3.1 Understanding the CMemoryException Class

Exceptions of type CMemoryException are thrown to indicate a memory allocation failure. In MFC applications, the new() operator throws CMemoryException exceptions automatically.

The CMemoryException class is thrown by any Microsoft Foundation Class or Library function that allocates memory. Most often, CMemoryException objects come out of MFC's OLE classes when your application receives a defective transfer buffer or interface from another application. Several other classes also generate CMemoryException objects. For example, a CEditView can throw one when the edit control in the view runs out of memory.

However, most memory exceptions are thrown when you call `new()` to get some memory. If the operating system cannot satisfy your request, the exception will be thrown. If you do not handle the exception, your application will likely become unstable or crash entirely.

Core Note

In Windows NT, you will have to completely exhaust physical, paged, and committed memory before `new()` finally fails. However, your code might be destined for some other 32-bit platform, like Windows 95 or Windows 98, which will not necessarily reserve as much memory for `new()` to allocate. In other words, it is always a good idea to include exceptions so your application can respond appropriately when the `new()` operator fails.

If you write your own memory-allocation functions, you are responsible for throwing such exceptions yourself. For example, the following code allocates some memory and then checks its validity:

```
char *p = malloc(1000);

if (p==NULL)
   AfxThrowMemoryException();
Else {
   // Populate p with data
 }
```

14.3.2 The CFileException Class

Exceptions of type `CFileException` indicate one of many file-related failures. To determine the cause of the exception, examine the `m_cause` member variable. For example, the following code opens myfile.txt for reading, and uses a single `catch` block and `m_cause` member to determine what caused the error:

```
try {
   CFile myFile("myfile.txt", CFile::modeRead);
   // Read the contents of the file
 }
catch(CFileException *e) {
   if (e->m_cause == CFileException::fileNotFound)
      cout << "File not found!\n";
   else
      cout << "A disk error has occurred.\n";
   e->Delete();
 }
```

Table 14-2 lists the possible values of m_cause for the CFileException class.

Table 14-2 Possible Values of m_cause for the CFileException Class	
Value	*Description*
None	No error.
Generic	Unspecified error.
fileNotFound	File could not be located.
badPath	Part of the path name is invalid.
tooManyOpenFiles	Maximum number of open files exceeded.
accessDenied	Attempt to open file with insufficient privileges.
invalidFile	Attempt to use an invalid file handle.
removeCurrentDir	Attempt to remove current directory.
directoryFull	Maximum number of directory entries reached.
badSeek	Could not set file pointer to specified location.
hardIO	Hardware error.
sharingViolation	Attempt to access a locked region.
lockViolation	Attempt to lock a previously locked region.
diskFull	The disk is full.
endOfFile	The end of the file was reached.

These m_cause values are operating-system independent. If you wish to retrieve an operating-system specific error code, you must instead examine the member variable m_iOsError.

Two member functions, OsErrorToException() and ErrnoToException(), can be used to translate operating-system specific error codes and C runtime library error numbers into exception codes. Furthermore, you can also use two helper member functions, ThrowOsError() and ThrowErrno(), to throw exceptions using operating-system specific error codes.

File I/O is one of the greatest sources of exceptions, next to memory allocation. Sometimes it seems as if almost anything can go wrong while you are working with a file. Such problems as lack of disk space, network volumes going offline, protection problems, file locking issues, and so on, all make file I/O a risky
place for your programs to work in. MFC will throw a CFileException from
any of its file I/O classes: CFile, CStdioFile, CMemFile, and
COleStreamFile are all suspects when a CFileException shows up.
Some other related classes, which depend on classes from the CFile tree, are
also probable causes of the error when a CFileException is thrown.

14.3.3 Saving a CFileException

As you have learned, when you catch a CFileException, you can examine
its member variable to see exactly what went wrong. The object contains two
data members: m_cause and m_iOsError. The latter code can be used to
retrieve an error from the system's _sys_errlist[] array. Code to get an
error message from the operating system might go something like the following:

```
catch(CFileException* e) {
   CString str;
   if (e->m_iOsError == -1)
      str.Format(_T("Can't: %d, %ld (%s)\n"),
         e->m_cause, e->m_iOsError,
         _sys_errlist[e->m_iOsError]);
   else
      str.Format(_T("Can't: %d, %ld (%s)\n"),
         e->m_cause, e->m_iOsError,
         _sys_errlist[e->m_iOsError]);
   MessageBox(str, _T("File Open Error"));
}
```

Core Note

*You must be careful to ensure that you spell the m_iOsError member
with a lower case i, rather than with a capital letter.*

The declaration for _sys_errlist[] comes from Stdlib.h, so you must
be sure to #include this file when you build your project. The Stdlib.h
header also provides many constant definitions, which in turn equate to the
different possible values for m_iOsError. You can test against these values

to react to specific errors in specific ways. On the other hand, m_cause is set to one of several MFC-defined constants, as you saw in Table 14-2.

14.3.4 Purposefully Throwing a CFileException

By the way, you can throw an error by creating a new CFileException object and setting its m_iOsError and/or m_cause members in the constructor. The CFileException constructor takes both of these values, but also provides defaults for both of them. The CFileException class constructor has this prototype:

```
CFileException(int cause=CFileException::none, LONG iOsError=-1);
```

You can also throw a CFileException by calling CFileException::ThrowOsError() and passing an operating system error number — any of the error number constants from Stdlib.h will do. MFC will automatically fill in the appropriate m_cause code as the library constructs the exception. You can translate an operating system error code to an m_cause code at any time by calling CFileException::OsErrorToException().

OsErrorToException() and ThrowOsError() are both static members of CFileException, so you don't even need a CFileException object to use the functions.

If you don't have an applicable m_iOsError value, you can call ThrowErrno() to throw the exception. Again, this member of CFileException is static, so you can use it at any time. CFileExceptions, which have an m_cause value but no m_iOsError, keep -1 in the m_iOsError member; you should make sure your code is able to deal with this eventuality.

AfxThrowFileException() is always available to create and throw CFileException objects as well, but it only provides a default parameter for m_iOsError — meaning that you must specify a value for the m_cause member.

14.3.5 The CArchiveException Class

The CArchiveException class is used in exceptions indicating serialization errors. These exceptions are thrown by member functions of the CArchive class. To determine the cause of the exception, examine the m_cause member variable. For example, you might place the following code within a CDocument-derived class' Serialize() member function:

```
CExceptDocument::Serialize(CArchive &ar)
{
   try {
      if (ar.IsLoading()) {
         // Load from the archive here
      }
      else {
         // Store in the archive here
      }
   }
   catch (CArchiveException *e) {
      if (e->m_cause == CArchiveException::badSchema) {
         AfxMessageBox("Invalid file version");
         e->Delete();
      }
      else
         throw;
   }
}
```

Table 14-3 lists the possible values of m_cause for the CArchiveException class.

Table 14-3 Possible Values of m_cause for the CArchiveException Class

Value	Description
None	No error.
Generic	Unspecified error.
readOnly	Attempt to store into an archive opened for loading.
endOfFile	The end of the file was reached.
writeOnly	Attempt to load from an archive opened for storing.
badIndex	Invalid file format.
badClass	Attempt to read an object of the wrong type.
badSchema	Incompatible schema number in class.

MFC's `CArchive` class is used to serialize data to or from persistent classes. The class may need to report an error if the object that is being recreated from serialization can't be created before its member data is read, or if your serialization code causes more than 32,767 objects to be written to the output file. This limitation is caused by the use of an integer-based `CMap` object to track the location of objects in the file.

14.3.6   The CNotSupportedException Class

Exceptions of type `CNotSupportedException` are thrown when a feature is requested that is not supported. No further information then is available on this error.

There are a few functions in MFC that are implemented without support. You can't call `Duplicate()` on a `CMemFile` object, for instance. There are also some actions or option flags that are not supported. For example, you cannot subclass a window more than once using MFC, and you cannot specify a versionable serialization when you are writing data to a serialization object. In these circumstances, MFC will throw a `CNotSupportedException`.

This exception is unlike others in MFC because it is designed never to be caught in release builds; it is for debugging purposes only. If, in testing, your debug code ever nets this exception, you should check to make sure that your code does not do anything silly.

This exception is frequently used in overridden versions of member functions in derived classes when the derived class does not support a base class feature. For example, the class `CStdioFile` does not support the base class feature `LockRange()`, and so you can catch it within your debug code as shown here:

```
try {
   CStdioFile myFile(stdin);
   myFile.LockRange(0, 1024);
   ...
 }
catch (CNotSupportedException *e) {
   cout << "Unsupported feature requested.\n";
   e->Delete();
 }
```

14.3.7 The CResourceException Class

MFC will throw a resource exception whenever it needs to find a resource but cannot. This most often occurs when it's looking for a string resource. You can throw a string resource exception by coding the following function:

```
AfxThrowResourceException();
```

Resource exceptions don't provide any information about the exception. Most CResourceExceptions are thrown from CDialog, CToolBar, and CControlBar and their derivatives. Note that MFC will also throw a resource exception in instances when a resource doesn't seem to be directly involved, particularly when trying to attach a C++ GDI object to a NULL or an unloadable Windows GDI object.

Exceptions of this type are used in conjunction with GDI resources. For example:

```
try {
   CPen myPen(PS_SOLID, 0, RGB(255, 0, 0));
 }
catch (CResourceException *e) {
   AfxMessageBox("Failed to create GDI pen resource\n");
   e->Delete();
 }
```

14.3.8 The CDaoException Class

CDaoException exceptions are used to indicate errors that occur when MFC database classes are used in conjunction with data access objects (DAO). All DAO errors are expressed in the form of DAO exceptions of the type CDaoException.

MFC provides classes that facilitate data access with DAO, in addition to other database access objects. Data access objects are OLE objects served by the system and allow your application to work with databases managed by the Jet database engine. The Jet engine is the database engine that is also shipped with Microsoft Access and Visual Basic.

When you use the DAO-related classes (which you will work with in-depth in later chapters), error conditions will throw CDaoException objects. The exact error code is returned as a SCODE in the m_scode member of the exception object. SCODE is a special data type used by OLE to convey error conditions.

The CDaoException object references some DAO-specific error information through its m_pErrorInfo member. This member points to information about the specific error that caused the exception to be thrown. Usually, the data access objects will report only one error at a time. However, in some circumstances, they will throw more than one at a time. You can find out how much error information is available by calling CDaoException::GetErrorCount().

You can find information about each specific error with a call to GetErrorInfo(). This function takes an integer parameter, which identifies the index of the error (which must be less than the total number of errors returned by GetErrorCount()). The function, however, does not return error information. Instead, it causes the m_pErrorInfo pointer to point to the error information.

To obtain detailed information about the error, examine members of the CDaoErrorInfo structure pointed to by m_pErrorInfo. Further OLE and extended MFC error codes can be obtained by examining the member variables m_scode and m_nAfxDaoError.

14.3.9 The CDBException Class

The database classes rely on some pretty complicated mechanisms to pass data around. In the simplest case, it is at least as complicated as getting data from or putting data into a file. In the most elaborate case, the database object is helping your program communicate with a far-off machine that is running powerful and complicated database server software.

The CDBException class encapsulates the error information that database errors generate. Since the MFC database classes lie upon ODBC (Microsoft's Open Database Connectivity API), the most important error code contained in CDBException mimics the RETCODE that all ODBC API functions return. This value is stored in m_nRetCode. The string associated with that error is stored in m_strError. Since all ODBC drivers don't share the same capabilities, some m_nRetCodes will have no corresponding error string, meaning that m_strError may be empty.

CDBException also contains information about the error that comes directly from the database software and isn't standardized to conform to ODBC's error code conventions. The m_strStateNativeOrigin member contains a string of the form "State: %s, Native: %ld, Origin: %s." The state value describes the state that caused the error. The value is a five character alphanumeric string, the meaning of which is defined by ODBC. This value corresponds to the szSqlState parameter of the ::SQLError() function.

(For more information, see Appendix A of the Programmers' Reference book in the ODBC SDK.)

The number following the word Native in the string is the native error number from the data source. This number isn't touched by ODBC; rather, it comes directly from the database software serving the query that failed. The second code corresponds to the `pfNativeError` parameter of `::SQLError()` and represents a native error code specific to the data source.

The final substring in `m_strStateNativeOrigin` is an indicator of the error's source. Each component in the multitiered ODBC architecture tacks on an extra string here, so the exact source for the error code can be readily identified. The code corresponds to error message text returned in the `szErrorMsg` parameter of `::SQLError()`. If something causes an error while accessing SQL Server, you might get "[Microsoft][ODBC SQL Server Driver][SQL Server]" as the error origin string. However, if the error was raised by the SQL Server driver and not by the database, the string would contain only "[Microsoft][ODBC SQL Server Driver]".

While `CDBExceptions` can be thrown with the `AfxThrowDBException()` function, they are not constructed like other MFC exceptions. The parameters to `AfxThrowDBException()` provide the exception with the `RETCODE` that caused the exception, a pointer to the `CDatabase` and the `HSTMT` context that caused the error. The function then constructs the `CDBException`. The constructing code will determine the string and source information from the database software and ODBC database driver before returning.

14.3.10 The COleException Class

The `COleException` class is used in exceptions indicating general OLE errors. To obtain information about the error, examine the `m_sc` member variable, which contains an OLE status code.

The static member function `Process` can be used to turn any caught exception into an OLE status code. For example, this function, when passed an object of type `CMemoryException`, returns the OLE status code `E_OUTOFMEMORY`.

14.3.11 The COleDispatchException Class

Exceptions of type COleDispatchException are used to indicate OLE errors related to the OLE IDispatch() interface. This interface is used in conjunction with OLE automation and OLE controls.

An error code specific to IDispatch() can be obtained by examining the m_wCode member variable. The member variable m_strDescription contains a textual description of the error.

Additional member variables identify a help context (m_dwHelpContext), the name of the applicable help file (m_strHelpFile), and the name of the application that threw the exception (m_strSource).

14.3.12 The CUserException Class

Exceptions of type CUserException are meant to be used by application programs to indicate an error caused by the user. Typically, these exceptions are thrown after the user has been notified of the error condition through a message box.

The CUserException class is a thin derivation of the CException class. A CUserException is thrown by MFC whenever a user-interface related problem arises. In the dialog data exchange routines, for example, a CUserException is thrown when validation fails against one of the fields involved in the data exchange operation. You can throw an exception by calling AfxThrowUserException(). CUserExceptions have no accessible member variables, so AfxThrowUserException() takes no parameters.

The MFC-supplied code in CWnd::DoDataExchange(), CDocument::ReportSaveLoadException(), and CWndProc::ProcessUserException() all have backstops that do nothing when handling a CUserException, but react and/or complain appropriately when handling other, more serious exceptions. As a result, you can throw a CUserException without causing your application to halt, but it still signals the exception and lets you out of the function or loop you're running.

14.4 Throwing an MFC Exception

If you wish to throw an MFC exception from your own code, you can do so by using one of the helper functions that are available in the MFC Library for this purpose. These helper functions are summarized in Table 14-4.

Table 14-4 Exception Handler Functions Used to Throw an Exception	
Function Name	**Action**
AfxThrowArchiveException()	Throws a CArchiveException
AfxThrowDaoException()	Throws a CDaoException
AfxThrowDBException()	Throws a CDBException
AfxThrowFileException()	Throws a CFileException
AfxThrowMemoryException()	Throws a CMemoryException
AfxThrowNotSupportedException()	Throws a CNotSupportedException
AfxThrowOleDispatchException()	Throws a COleDispatchException
AfxThrowOleException()	Throws a COleException
AfxThrowResourceException()	Throws a CResourceException
AfxThrowUserException()	Throws a CUserException

These functions take a varying number of parameters in accordance with the type of the exception being thrown. They construct an exception object of the specified type, initialize it using the supplied parameters, and then throw the exception.

Naturally, you can also elect to construct an exception object and throw the exception manually. This may be necessary if you derive a class from CException yourself.

14.4.1 Common Exception Features

All CException-derived exceptions feature a couple of interesting functions, which you learned about briefly earlier in this chapter: GetErrorMessage() and ReportError(). GetErrorMessage() has a prototype that looks like this:

```
BOOL GetErrorMessage(LPSTR lpszError, UINT nMaxError,
    PUINT pnHelpContext = NULL);
```

For the lpszError parameter, you'll need to provide a pointer to a buffer that you own. You can specify the size of that buffer with the nMaxError parameter. When you call GetErrorMessage() on a CException or

CException-derived object that you've caught, the function will populate your buffer with an error message that describes the exact error condition. If the function can successfully describe the error message, it returns TRUE. If it can't, it returns FALSE.

You have the option of providing the address of a UINT for the third parameter. If you do, your UINT will be populated with a help context ID that describes the error message. For most error messages that come from MFC, the UINT will be exactly equal to the identifier for the string resource where the error message was stored. Error messages from CFileExceptions, CDBExceptions, COleExceptions, and CDaoExceptions are formatted dynamically and will not have a help context ID with them. You can learn how MFC gets the text for these errors by reading up on the ::FormatMessage() function of the CStrings class.

GetErrorMessage() doesn't deal with CStrings, by the way, because there might not be enough memory to get a CString.

If you decide to make your own CException-derived classes to help you deal with problems in your application, you should make sure that you implement an override for GetErrorMessage() in that class so you can report errors easily, too.

14.5 MFC and Exceptions

The general recommendation is to use standard C++ exceptions (unless there is some specific benefit to using MFC exception macros, of which none are readily suggestible). You can use standard C++ exceptions even against the standard C++ types, plus any primitive or compound data type you can think of. All versions of the Microsoft Foundation Classes use macros to implement exception handling. Older versions of MFC used stock C++ code without the exception keywords but, starting with version 3.0, the macros equate to some compatibility code plus constructs that use the real C++ exception keywords. This means that real C++ exceptions are more compatible and they are used internally by MFC anyway.

There's a huge difference between MFC exceptions in previous versions of the compiler and standard C++ exceptions in new versions. In old versions, you would find that temporary objects were not destroyed when you used MFC exceptions to escape a function. Of course, the objects were removed from the stack, but data they might reference was not cleaned up because the runtime never invoked the objects' destructor functions. This could result in memory leaks, particularly if the objects contain dynamically allocated information, as CStrings do.

This is the reason behind the CString class' Empty() member function. You used to have to call this member for any CStrings that would go out of scope when you handled an exception. Otherwise, when the function died, all of the memory owned by the CStrings wouldn't be freed and you would be left with a large memory leak.

14.6 The Visual C++ 6.0 Solution

Thankfully, this awkwardness has been done away with. Visual C++ now (and for the last couple of versions) supports the normal semantics implied by standard C++ exceptions: the generated code will correctly call the destructors on local objects, allowing them to free their memory and resources. Visual C++ has featured such exception handling semantics since Version 2.0.

However, this functionality is only enabled when you use the /GX command line switch on the compiler. By default, this functionality is off, but the AppWizard-produced project files have the switch on. You can find the setting for your project by looking at the C++ tab in the Project Settings dialog. Check for the Enable Exception Handling check box when you have C++ Language selected in the Category drop-down. The dialog and page you must access are shown in Figure 14-1.

If you write programs that work with MFC, you should always use the /GX option. If you do not, your application can leak memory in some rare circumstances. Unfortunately, those circumstances are exactly when it's most dangerous to leak memory — that is, while handling error conditions. Never compile a program that uses MFC without the /GX option. You might find it tempting to not use /GX, especially if you find out that programs built without /GX don't have code to unwind exceptions and can be, in extreme cases, fifteen to twenty percent smaller than the same code with the /GX option. But don't do it — it's not worth it.

Now, back to the comparison. By far the biggest difference between MFC exceptions and standard C++ exceptions is that MFC exceptions can handle throws only from CException and its derivatives, while C++ exceptions can let you handle throws from any primitive or derived data type under the sun.

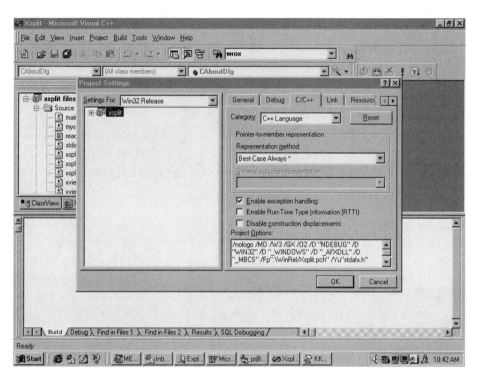

Figure 14-1   Enable exception handling within the Project Properties dialog box.

Note that after defining the `_AFX_OLD_EXCEPTIONS` flag, you can rebuild MFC to cause it to use the old, non-unwinding exception code. You should never need to do this; if you do, the code in question is broken and should be fixed. If you don't have time to do this, you can rebuild MFC while carefully making sure `_AFX_OLD_EXCEPTIONS` is defined; this will make MFC revert to the old exception code.

You should try to use standard C++ exception syntax when you can because it's slightly faster and results in a code image that's somewhat smaller than using the `CException` classes.

14.6.1   Exceptions and Win32

Both the `CException`-based MFC exceptions and the C++ standard exceptions are different than a third type of exception that is available to applications running under Windows NT or Windows 9x: you can also trap exceptions generated by the operating system. These exceptions are raised when your application does something that's trapped at the system level, such as divide by zero.

The syntax for catching the exceptions is very similar to the `try/catch` code that standard C++ code uses, but instead of `catch`, you'll need to use the `__except` keyword. To differentiate the two keywords, you will also need to use `__try` for operating system exceptions and `try` for C++ exceptions.

A typical exception trap might look something like the following:

```
double dCarefulDivide(double n, double d, double dNotANumber)
{
   double dResult;

   __try {
      dResult = n/d;
   }
   __except(GetExceptionCode() == EXCEPTION_FLT_DIVIDE_BY_ZERO)
{
      TRACE(_T("Bad divide attempt trapped!\n"));
      return dNotANumber;
   }
   return dResult;
}
```

As with standard C++ exception handling, the `__try` statement opens the block of code to watch for exceptions. When that block of code ends, the compiler expects to see one or more `__except` blocks that can handle the exception raised in the `__try` block. The statement in parenthesis governs the type of action that the exception handler will take.

Most exception handlers will be coded as the above example, with a comparison between a defined constant and a call to the `GetExceptionCode()` function. If the values are equal, the exception handler is executed and all other handlers are ignored. You can code any number of `GetExceptionCode()` handlers to trap any variety of handlers that you might need.

Unfortunately, the way `__except()` really works is slightly hidden by this technique. The expression inside `__except()` must evaluate to one of three values:

- `EXCEPTION_EXECUTE_HANDLER`,
- `EXCEPTION_CONTINUE_SEARCH`
- `EXCEPTION_CONTINUE_EXECUTION`

The first value, 1, is represented by `EXCEPTION_EXECUTE_HANDLER` (defined in Excpt.h) and causes the handler to be executed. Since the C++

equality operator evaluates to 1 when both sides of the operator are equal, the test that we used in the example evaluates to EXCEPTION_EXECUTE_HANDLER when the return from GetExceptionCode() equals the constant being tested.

If both sides of the operator are not equal, the == operator evaluates to a zero. This value is equal to EXCEPTION_CONTINUE_SEARCH; the code will continue to search through the handlers for an appropriate contender, and then up the stack for another block of handlers that might take care of the exception.

Finally, you can use __except(EXCEPTION_CONTINUE_EXECUTION) to force the code to continue executing where the exception occurred. Some exceptions can't be continued, in particular, invalid instruction traps. If you try to continue after such an exception, you'll throw a new exception with a code of EXCEPTION_NONCONTINUABLE_EXCEPTION.

The following table shows all of the exceptions that you can trap. These values are #defines from the Winbase.h header, which in turn uses information from the Winnt.h header, and match possible return values from GetExceptionCode(). The rest of the definitions you'll need for the GetExceptionCode() function (which is a macro in a function's clothing) and some other structures used when you throw your own operating system-level constructions are from Excpt.h, and are listed in Table 14-5.

Note that many of these exceptions have very different meanings; their exact meaning will depend on the architecture of the machine hosting Windows. What quantity exactly constitutes a division underflow, and which instructions are protected in which modes, varies between the Power PC, Alpha, MIPS, and Intel machines. Since Windows NT is available for all of these platforms, any operating system exception handling code you write is likely to be machine-specific.

Of course, you might only be trying to trap math errors. Since they're effectively the same on every machine, you can trap them with the same code, but using the EXCEPTION_SINGLE_STEP value to try to write a debugger for all platforms would be difficult at best.

Core Note

You cannot mix operating system exception handling code and C++ structured exception handling code in the same function — in other words, one function cannot have both __try and try blocks. Instead, you'll have to put your operating system trap-sensitive code in a function separate from any code that needs standard C++ exception handling.

Table 14-5 Operating System-Level Constructions for Structured Exception Handling	
Exceptions	*Description*
EXCEPTION_ACCESS_VIOLATION	The thread tried to read from or write to a virtual address for which it doesn't have the appropriate access.
EXCEPTION_BREAKPOINT	A breakpoint was encountered.
EXCEPTION_DATA_TYPE_MISALIGNMENT	The thread tried to read or write data that is misaligned on hardware that doesn't provide alignment. For example, 16-bit values must be aligned on 2-byte boundaries, 32-bit values on 4-byte boundaries, and so on.
EXCEPTION_SINGLE_STEP	A trace trap or other single-instruction mechanism signaled that one instruction has been executed.
EXCEPTION_ARRAY_BOUNDS_EXCEEDED	The thread tried to access an array element that is out-of-bounds and the underlying hardware supports bounds checking.
EXCEPTION_FLT_DENORMAL_OPERAND	One of the operands in a floating point operation is denormal. A denormal value is one that is too small to be represented as a standard floating point value.
EXCEPTION_FLT_DIVIDE_BY_ZERO	The thread tried to divide a floating point value by a floating point divisor of zero.

(continued)

Table 14-5 Operating System-Level Constructions for Structured Exception Handling

Exceptions	Description
EXCEPTION_FLT_INEXACT_RESULT	The result of a floating point operation can't be exactly represented as a decimal fraction.
EXCEPTION_FLT_INVALID_OPERATION	This exception represents any floating point exception not included in this list.
EXCEPTION_FLT_OVERFLOW	The exponent of a floating point operation is greater than the magnitude allowed by the corresponding type.
EXCEPTION_FLT_STACK_CHECK	The stack overflowed or underflowed as the result of a floating point operation.
EXCEPTION_FLT_UNDERFLOW	The exponent of a floating point operation is less than the magnitude allowed by the corresponding type.
EXCEPTION_INT_DIVIDE_BY_ZERO	The thread tried to divide an integer value by an integer divisor of zero.
EXCEPTION_INT_OVERFLOW	The result of an integer operation caused a carry or borrow out of the most significant bit of the result.
EXCEPTION_PRIV_INSTRUCTION	The thread tried to execute an instruction whose operation isn't allowed in the current machine mode.
EXCEPTION_NONCONTINUABLE_EXCEPTION	The thread tried to continue execution after a non-continuable exception occurred.

14.7 Using the ASSERT Macros for Exception Handling

Any discussion on exception handling would not be complete without a brief discussion of the ASSERT macro. While not pure exception handling, the ASSERT macro does provide you with an effective means of monitoring your program's activities during a debug session and can alert you safely to unexpected results within your code.

The most typical use of the ASSERT macro is to identify program errors during development. The argument given to ASSERT should be chosen so that it holds true only if the program is operating as intended. The macro evaluates the ASSERT argument and, if the argument expression is FALSE, alerts the user and halts program execution. No action is taken if the argument is TRUE.

When an ASSERT fails, a message box appears with the following text:

```
ASSERT failed in file <name> in line <num>
Abort Retry Ignore
```

In the message box, <name> corresponds to the name of the source file and <num> corresponds to the line number of the ASSERT that failed.

If you choose Abort, program execution terminates. If you choose Ignore, program execution continues. It is possible to break into the debugger after an ASSERT by clicking Retry. Neither Abort nor Ignore will activate a debugger, so they provide no way to examine the call stack.

If you are running under the debugger and choose Retry, a call to AfxDebugBreak() embedded in the code causes a break into the debugger. At this point, you can examine the call stack as you learned in Chapter 2.

The following example shows how the ASSERT macro could be used to check the validity of a function's return value:

```
int x = SomeFunc(y);
ASSERT (x >= 0);   // ASSERT fails if x is negative
```

You can also use ASSERT in combination with the IsKindOf() function to provide extra checking for function arguments, as in the following example:

```
ASSERT (pObject1->IsKindOf(RUNTIME_CLASS(CCore)));
```

The liberal use of ASSERT throughout your programs can catch errors during development. A good rule of thumb is that you should write ASSERT for any assumptions you make. For example, if you assume that an argument is not NULL, use an ASSERT statement to check for that condition.

The ASSERT macro will catch program errors only when you are using the debug version of the Microsoft Foundation Class Library during development. It will be turned off (and produce no code) when you build your program with the release version of the library.

The expression argument to ASSERT will not be evaluated in the release version of your program. If you want the expression to be evaluated in both debug and release versions, use the VERIFY macro instead of ASSERT. In debug versions, VERIFY is the same as ASSERT. In release versions, VERIFY evaluates the expression argument but does not check the result.

14.7.1   Using the ASSERT_VALID Macro

You will use the ASSERT_VALID macro within your applications to perform a run-time check of an object's internal consistency. The ASSERT_VALID macro is a more robust way of accomplishing the following action:

```
pObject->AssertValid();
```

Like the ASSERT macro, ASSERT_VALID is turned on in the debug version of your program, but turned off in the release version.

14.8   Summary

The MFC Library uses C++ style exceptions to communicate error conditions. Exceptions that are of a type derived from CException are thrown using a variety of helper functions and caught by your application.

Older MFC applications that predate C++ exception support in Visual C++ used a series of macros for this purpose. These macros can be easily translated into the C++ keywords try, throw, and catch.

The CException-derived classes that are used by MFC functions are summarized in Table 14-6.

For every one of these exception types, there is a corresponding helper function (for example, AfxThrowArchiveException() for CArchiveException). You can also construct a CException-derived object and throw an exception manually.

Table 14-6 Exception Helper Functions	
Function Name	*Action*
CArchiveException	Serialization errors
CDaoException	Errors occurring with data access objects
CDBException	Errors occurring during ODBC usage
CFileException	File system errors
CMemoryException	Memory allocation failure
CNotSupportedException	Notification of unsupported feature request
COleDispatchException	OLE IDispatch errors (automation, controls)
COleException	Generic OLE errors
CResourceException	Resource allocation failure (GDI)
CUserException	Errors caused by the user

In the exception handler, you are responsible for deleting the CException-derived object by calling its Delete() member function. You can also derive your own exception class from CException.

You also learned that you can use an operating-system based derivative of standard C++ exception handling (with the __try and __catch keywords) to perform structured exception handling.

Finally, you learned that you can use the ASSERT and ASSERT_VALID macros to evaluate expressions during debug builds and provide your applications with an efficient way to avoid errors in assumptions.

FUNDAMENTAL PRINCIPLES OF COM AND DCOM

Topics in this Chapter

- Understanding the Origins and Uses of ActiveX
- Understanding the Various ActiveX Technologies
- Understanding What ActiveX Can Do for You
- Determining What Type of ActiveX Component You Need
- Different Techniques for Creating ActiveX Components
- Basic ActiveX Component Architecture
- Better Understanding COM
- Moving on to DCOM
- Understanding the COM Threading Model
- Summary

Chapter 15

A s data has become the major focus of interface design, the data's content is what occupies the user's attention, not the application managing the data. In such a design, applications should not limit data to its native creation and editing environment. In other words, your applications should not limit the user to creating or editing data only within its associated application window. Instead, most applications should let users transfer data to other types of containers while maintaining the data's viewing and editing capability in the new container. Compound documents are a common example and illustration of the interaction between containers and their components, but they are not the only expression of this kind of object relationship that OLE can support. A *compound document* is any kind of document that contains components from multiple source locations. For example, you might create a document that includes text from a word processor, tabular data from a spreadsheet, a sound recording, and pictures created in other applications. Today, an ever-increasing number of documents that users create are compound documents. You can handle compound documents within your applications using items that you derive from the `CCmdTarget` MFC class. Compound documents are just one type of COM object — we will look at several different types in this chapter.

15.1 Understanding the Origins and Uses of ActiveX

From its name, you could easily guess that OLE technology supports two basic types of objects: embedded objects and linked objects. As you have learned, data objects that retain their native, full-featured editing and operating capabilities when moved or copied into a new location (such as a different application container), are called *OLE embedded objects*. Alternately, a user can link information rather than embedding it. An OLE linked object represents or provides access to another object that is in another location in the same container or in a different container.

In general, containers support any level of nested OLE embedded and linked objects. For example, a user can embed a chart in a worksheet, which in turn can be embedded in a word processing document. The model for interaction is consistent at each level of nesting.

Now that you understand a little more clearly what OLE really means, it is time to consider ActiveX. ActiveX and OLE have become synonymous. What people once referred to as OLE Controls (OCXs), they now refer to as ActiveX Controls. OLE DocObjects are now ActiveX Documents. In some cases, Microsoft has updated entire documents on how to implement OLE technologies to be ActiveX technologies, and the only material change that Microsoft made was to replace the term OLE with ActiveX.

ActiveX was not meant to replace OLE, but simply to broaden it to include the Internet, intranets, commercial and in-house applications development, and the tools used to develop these newer, broader-in-scope applications.

Although tremendous advances have been made and seemingly new technologies appear daily with regard to OLE and ActiveX, it is questionable whether the Internet was or is directly involved in many of these areas. The need for small, fast, reusable components (COM Objects) has been around for years. Microsoft first demonstrated distributed components (DCOM Objects) several years ago at the OLE 2.0 Professional Developer's Conference. The Visual Basic group played a major role in the enabling of ActiveX in its early days. In fact, the Visual Basic group developed the `BaseCtl` framework, which Microsoft included in the ActiveX Software Developer's Kit (SDK), to answer the group's need for small, lightweight controls to improve the load times of Visual Basic applications. The only contribution the Internet made came out of its need for a way to implement and publish Web pages. Practically every new feature with an ActiveX label can trace its roots back to a fundamental, global need for small, fast, reusable components, all of which started with OLE and COM.

Microsoft has published a number of documents regarding ActiveX development. The OC 96 specification defines how you should develop controls so that your controls provide faster startup times and better drawing capabilities. The specification also describes which interfaces a control must support to qualify as an ActiveX/OLE control and which interfaces are optional for you to implement. The *OLE Control and Control Container Guidelines* provide important information for control and container interaction. The Microsoft Web site, with its extensive knowledge base, white papers and articles, and MSDN online support, has become an extremely valuable source of information for developers who plan to create, use, or deploy ActiveX components.

In addition to the specific technologies for creating ActiveX components, Microsoft has set a standard for the use and integration of ActiveX components. Every product Microsoft releases, from Visual Basic to Microsoft Word to Microsoft's Visual J++ implementation of Java is inherently capable of using ActiveX components. Four years ago, it was almost impossible to find more than a handful of applications that were capable of integrating in such a relatively seamless fashion as is possible today.

15.2 Understanding the Various ActiveX Technologies

As you have learned, ActiveX technology is a continuation of and expansion on OLE technology. ActiveX technology can be, generally, divided into six basic component categories, as follows:

- Automation servers
- Automation controllers
- Controls
- COM objects
- ActiveX documents
- ActiveX containers

15.2.1 Understanding Automation Servers

Automation servers are components that other applications can drive programmatically. An automation server contains at least one, and possibly more, `IDispatch`-based interfaces that other applications can create or connect to. An automation server may or may not contain a User Interface (UI), depending on the nature and function of the server.

Automation servers can be *in-process* (executing in the process space of the controller), *local* (executing in its own process space), or *remote* (executing in a process space on another machine). The specific implementation of the server will, in some cases, define how and where the server will execute, but not always. A DLL can execute as either an in-process, local, or remote server, while an ActiveX EXE (more commonly known as COM EXE) can execute only locally or remotely.

Core Note

When designing automation servers, execution time is an important consideration. However, it is not the only consideration. For example, the fastest execution times are from servers that run in-process to the controllers using them. However, using an in-process automation server does not guarantee in-process performance. If an in-process automation server is created in one process space and then handed to a controller in another process space, the server becomes local and suffers from the same performance degradation as a local server. Determining how gracefully a server degrades when it is not in-process, or when it degrades from local to remote, is an important design consideration, especially in enterprise-based solutions.

15.2.2 Understanding Automation Controllers

Automation controllers are those applications that can use and manipulate automation servers. A good example of an automation controller is Visual Basic. With the Visual Basic programming language, you are able to create, use, and destroy automation servers as though they are an integral part of the language.

An automation controller can be any type of application, DLL or EXE, and can access the automation server either in-process, locally, or remotely. Typically, the registry entries for the server and controller and how you implement the automation server will determine which process space the server will execute within relation to the controller.

15.2.3 Defining ActiveX Controls

ActiveX controls are 32-bit controls that are equivalent to what is known as OLE controls or OCXs. A typical control consists of a user interface representation both at design time and runtime, a single `IDispatch` interface defining all of the methods and properties of the control, and a single `IConnectionPoint` interface for the events that the control can fire. In addition, the control may have support for persistence across its execution lifetimes and support for various user interface features, such as cut-and-paste and drag-and-drop features. In general, a control has a large number of COM interfaces that the using container must support in order to take advantage of the control's features. However, with the release of the OLE control and ActiveX guidelines for control development, a control is no longer limited to the feature set defined in the preceding text. Rather, the developer can now choose to implement only those features that are most useful and interesting to users of the applications. The control and container guidelines published by Microsoft list all the required interfaces and their specific requirements.

ActiveX controls always execute in-process to the container in which they reside. The extension of a control is typically OCX, but in terms of execution models, a control is nothing more than a standard Windows DLL.

15.2.4 Understanding Component Object Model (COM) Objects

COM objects are similar in architecture to automation servers and controllers. They contain one or more COM interfaces and probably little or no user interface. These objects, however, cannot be used by the typical controller application the way automation servers can. The controller must have specific knowledge of the COM interface that it "talks" to in order to use the interface, which is not the case for automation interfaces. The Windows 9x and NT operating systems contain hundreds of COM objects and custom interfaces as extensions to the operating systems. These COM objects control everything from the appearance of the desktop to the rendering of 3D images on the screen. COM objects are a good way to organize a related set of functions and data, while still maintaining the high-speed performance of a DLL.

Core Note

Automation servers can also benefit from COM interfaces. Servers that support COM interfaces are known as dual-interface servers. The IDispatch interface of the automation server also has a companion COM interface describing the methods and properties of the object. Automation controllers such as Visual Basic can take advantage of these dual interfaces to provide even greater performance when using the server. The one drawback to dual-interface servers is that they are limited to the set of data types supported by OLE automation when defining methods and properties.

15.2.5 Understanding ActiveX Documents

ActiveX documents, or *DocObjects* as they were originally called, represent objects that are more than a simple control or automation server. A document can be anything from a spreadsheet to a complete invoice in an accounting application. Documents, like controls, have a user interface and you must host documents within a container application. Microsoft Word and Excel are examples of ActiveX document aervers, and the Microsoft Office Binder and Microsoft Internet Explorer are examples of ActiveX document containers.

The ActiveX document architecture is an extension of the OLE linking and embedding model and allows the document more control over the container in which the user is hosting the document. The most obvious change is how the menus are presented. A standard OLE document's menu will merge with the container, providing a combined feature set; an ActiveX document will take over the entire menu system, thus presenting the feature set of only the document and not that of both the document and the container. The fact that the feature set of the document is exposed is the premise for all the differences between ActiveX documents and OLE documents. The container is just a hosting mechanism, and the document has all of the control.

Another difference between ActiveX documents and OLE documents is in printing and storage. An OLE document's designer intends for the document to be a part of the container's document that is hosting it. Therefore, Windows will print and store the OLE document as a piece of the host container's document. The operating system expects ActiveX documents to support their own native printing and storage functions and therefore does not integrate them with the container's document.

You should use ActiveX documents within a uniform presentation architecture, rather than within an embedded document architecture, which is the basis for OLE documents. Microsoft Internet Explorer is a perfect example of a uniform presentation architecture (that is, an architecture that supports ActiveX documents). Internet Explorer merely presents the Web pages to the users, but the users view, print, and store the pages themselves as a single entity, separately from the host container. On the other hand, Microsoft Word and Microsoft Excel are examples of the OLE document architecture. If an Excel spreadsheet is embedded in a Word document, the spreadsheet is actually stored with the Word document and is an integral part of it.

ActiveX documents also have the added capability of being published as Web pages on the Internet or on a corporate intranet. Imagine an in-house tracking system for purchase orders that users can run from the same Web browsers that they use to connect to the Internet and that fully integrates with the underlying data on purchase orders and which users can interact with as if it were a program on the desktop. Now you begin to see the bene-fits of ActiveX documents.

15.2.6 Understanding ActiveX Containers

ActiveX containers are applications that can host automation servers, con-trols, and documents. Visual Basic and the ActiveX Control Pad are examples of containers that can host automation servers and controls. The Microsoft Office Binder and Microsoft Internet Explorer can host automation servers, controls, and documents.

With the decreasing requirements that the ActiveX control and document specifications define, a container must be robust enough to handle the cases in which a control or document lacks certain interfaces. Container applica-tions may allow little or no interaction with the document or control they host, or they may provide significant interaction capabilities in both manipu-lation and presentation of the hosted component. This capability, however, is dependent upon the container hosting the component. The ActiveX control and document specifications do not indicate that such capability is required to qualify as a container.

15.3 Understanding What ActiveX Can Do for You

Understanding the power and capabilities of the different subtypes of ActiveX technologies is an important first step in determining what type of ActiveX object to create. Clearly, ActiveX components provide you with valuable tools in designing the best possible applications—and OLE support is critical for any application that you will use within the enterprise. In general, there are five considerations for you to take into account before you design an ActiveX component:

1. **Application requirements:** It is important to understand as many of the project's requirements as possible before starting your development project. Understanding the project's requirements will help you to better determine whether or not to use one or more ActiveX technologies during the project's design.

2. **Choosing the correct architecture and component type:** The various ways in which you can create and implement ActiveX components are crucial to a successful project. You don't want to do too much with a component (extending design times and expanding application space) or too little (resulting in bad program design or poor program implementation).

3. **Choosing the correct tool:** The tool you use to develop your component will also affect the project's success. Picking the right tool for the job is as important as understanding the job itself.

4. **Basic ActiveX component architecture:** Each ActiveX component type has its particular architecture and construction. Understanding this architecture is important, and can save you significant headache during the design of your application.

5. **Basic ActiveX support tools:** You will find a collection of development support tools that are invaluable to your ActiveX development — not only within Visual Studio, but also on the Microsoft Web site and other ActiveX-dedicated sites.

In short, you can no longer design a set of simple stand-alone applications that do not interoperate with each other — or that have a very uneasy set of interoperating rules. With OLE, ActiveX, and the Internet, users expect applications to be flexible, modifiable, and extendible, all in a manner that makes the applications very easy for the users to manipulate.

Spending a little extra time up front working out the design and architecture of your application, and any components that you design to use within your application, can and will make all the difference in the world. Very few applications that do not have a significant amount of forethought — regardless of whether that information is crammed into the head of one of your developers, scribbled on restaurant napkins, or written in formal documentation — ever make it to distribution or, even in the best-case scenario, distribute well. However, as a general rule, formal documentation or some other type of usable written record is probably the best policy — it makes it easier to explain to others the foundations of your great idea.

The basic principles of OLE and ActiveX are going to determine most of the specifics of the component architecture and design within your application. For example, you must develop ActiveX controls and documents within a specific set of parameters and rules so that they will interact with containers correctly. Similarly, automation servers and controllers have to conform to OLE automation rules and COM objects must support the basic fundamentals of COM. However, there are some issues that you will not be able to answer easily based on OLE and ActiveX fundamental principles. For example, determining the relationships between your components and the lifetimes of the components themselves will be a unique activity for each application. Determining which containers can access which interfaces, what security the component might support, wide-character support, and so on, are also all key issues to address.

15.4 Determining What Type of ActiveX Component You Need

When you begin to design one or more ActiveX components for use in your application, there are several decisions you must make, which the previous section outlined in broad strokes. The first thing you must decide is what kind of component best fits your requirements. Making such a decision requires a better understanding of the benefits and limitations of the different component types, which the following sections will help you achieve.

15.4.1 Using Automation Servers and Controllers

Automation servers and controllers probably have the greatest amount of flexibility of the different ActiveX technologies. Just about every major application available from Microsoft, and hundreds of other manufacturers, can use a server's `IDispatch` interface. Because the interface won't suffer from the same versioning requirements placed on strict COM interfaces, the interface also lends itself well to prototyping and modeling component interactions.

A dual-interface automation server created to be an in-process server that remains in-process throughout its lifetime is the fastest type of automation server. Dual-interface refers to the fact that a server contains two interfaces — one based on `IDispatch` and the other based on COM. The COM interface is actually the faster of the two. An in-process server means that the server resides in the same memory address space as the application that created it. The same-process residence of the server lets the application (through the operating system) invoke the server's methods significantly faster than it would if the server were out-of-process because there is no burden of having to cross process boundaries every time the application calls a method. For the same reason, in-process servers load faster than a similarly sized out-of-process server because of the minimal number of steps the operating system must perform to create the server and pass its `IDispatch` or COM interface pointer to the calling application.

Nothing inherent to automation architecture promotes the use of a user interface, and nothing prevents you from using a user interface either. You have complete freedom and control over how calling programs will implement and use your servers. Your automation servers could potentially contain a user interface in the form of a dialog, `CFormView` view class, or another similar dialog-based window.

Automation servers also lend themselves well to the increasingly popular multitiered application architectures that have become common in recent years. The separation of user interface from function is perfect for automation servers because you have complete freedom over how applications implement and use your servers. Creating servers with thin user interface layers that utilize other servers with no user interface to accomplish a task is at the heart of multitiered applications development — a technique that Microsoft makes specific adjustments to the COM standard for with the new COM+ standard. You should use automation servers just as you would any other DLL. The only difference between an automation server and a standard Windows DLL is the fact that the server uses only a restricted set of data types, while a DLL can use any type.

Designing automation servers that work without the need for a user interface also makes them prime candidates for Distributed COM (DCOM) and other distributing technologies (such as COM+).

15.4.2   Using ActiveX Controls

You should use ActiveX controls primarily as they were intended to be used. In other words, your ActiveX controls should generally be user-interface-based components to enhance or support a dialog, a form, or a document. Controls can be expensive to load because they can potentially require a large number of interfaces, depending on the functionality the control supports. The OC 96 specification added the `QuickActivate` interface to help with control load times, but the improvement was not significant. In addition, the OC 96 specification identifies a number of interfaces that are considered optional or conditional, depending on the type of control you are implementing. It is wise to review the specification to determine what you can and cannot remove from your implementation in order to improve its performance and overall size.

When creating controls, be sure to make them as lean as possible. If you do not intend to commercially distribute the control, for example, remove the "AboutBox" code. Also, see whether you can get away with relying on the property editor of the application's development tool that will be used, rather than supporting property pages. Avoid large amounts of persistence, and save the data only if you must. In other words (if you have not figured it out already), implement only those features that are truly useful and helpful for your control implementation.

15.4.3 Using COM Objects

COM objects (custom interfaces) are far more flexible than any other component type when it comes to interface design. They are also the fastest interfaces in terms of execution times, although the fastest COM objects are those in which the COM interface is in-process to the application using it — out-of-process COM objects suffer performance degradation just as other out-of-process ActiveX components do. COM objects can use any data type within their interface definitions and do not suffer from the same restrictions as automation servers. This situation does present a problem when crossing process boundaries because the object will then require its own proxy-stub marshaling code (because the Universal Marshaler, which handles proxy-stub relationships in automation servers, will only process simple data types).

Proxy-stub marshaling takes place when an application resides in a process space other than the application it is communicating with. It is necessary to translate function calls and data to a context that both applications can understand. This translation process is the responsibility of the proxy-stub code and is true for all types of OLE components. Moving any component out-of-process will have a profound effect on the application's performance because the operating system, the application, and the component are performing much more work to accomplish the same set of operations.

Automation servers rely on built-in proxy-stub marshaling code (within the Universal Marshaler), whereas COM interfaces must create their own. While you can create your own proxy-stub marshaling code, doing so does add to the development time and effort, maintenance of the code, distribution of the object, and overall performance of the application, so you must consider those issues when you decide what type of component to develop. If you plan to develop the COM object for out-of-process execution, you should probably consider using an automation server instead, because the performance will be comparable between the two — unless you are going to come up with your own marshaling code that significantly outperforms the built-in mechanisms.

COM objects are useful for the cases in which the limited set of data types available to automation servers has a significant impact on the type of interface that you can create. An example of a COM object might be a simple implementation that performs calculations of a large volume of user-defined data. Instead of copying the data and passing it to the COM object, it might be more useful to pass a pointer to the data and allow the COM object to manipulate the data directly. Automation server data-type restrictions would not allow for the creation of this kind of interface. COM does, however. Yet, keep in mind that, in this particular case, the COM object can execute only in-process because it needs direct access to the data and the pointer will have no meaning outside the process sphere. When creating your ActiveX components with Visual C++, you have four options, which are all described in the following sections.

15.5 Different Techniques for Creating ActiveX Components

As you might expect if you know the power of Visual C++ 6.0, the product provides you with several different tools at your disposal for the creation of ActiveX components. In the following sections, let's briefly consider those different tools and the benefits and limitations of each.

15.5.1 Using Microsoft Foundation Classes to Create ActiveX Components

The Microsoft Foundation Class Library (MFC) is the easiest choice of all the tools available for ActiveX development. The Visual C++ Integrated

Development Environment is designed specifically with MFC in mind and, as you have learned in previous chapters, provides the very useful AppWizard and ClassWizard to help you develop your application. MFC is robust and will probably cover 90 percent of your application's needs. Unfortunately, as with most software development or other creative projects, the last 10 percent of the project is where you spend 90 percent of your time.

Going outside the bounds of what MFC defines can be difficult and, in some cases, impossible. Take, for example, the requirement to have an object that is single-instance only. No matter how the object is created by the client application, you always want the same instance returned. Providing this kind of functionality is impossible with MFC without modifying the built-in Class Factory classes, which Visual Studio does not normally expose to the developer.

Supporting dual-interfaces in automation servers that you design with MFC is not impossible, but it does cause enough changes in your code so that you can no longer use the ClassWizard to completely maintain your methods and properties. MFC does provide a number of features and functions when developing ActiveX components, but be prepared to live by its rules. Occasionally, you can bend the rules, but you can almost never break them. The following chapters discuss how to successfully bend the rules in MFC and implement both single-instance and dual-interface servers.

A good rule of thumb when working with MFC to design ActiveX components is to avoid using the built-in classes as much as possible by utilizing the basic Windows API instead. Avoiding use of the MFC classes to solve your component application's problems has two benefits. The first is that your application will usually run faster; the second is that using the Windows API prior to moving the application code to an alternative development tool, such as ATL or `BaseCtl`, will let you avoid rewriting large amounts of MFC-dependent code. A large portion of the MFC classes have equivalent Windows API functions, especially in the area of GDI and drawing, and it is not that much of a departure from MFC to use the Windows API. Basic storage classes, such as lists and arrays, could be better provided by a general purpose class library, such as the Standard Template Library (STL), which can be used in combination with any and all of the ActiveX development frameworks (MFC, ATL, or `BaseCtl`).

15.5.2 Using the ActiveX Template Library to Create ActiveX Components

The ActiveX Template Library (ATL) is a relative newcomer to the ActiveX arena. It first appeared in the summer of 1996 and quickly became a favorite among developers. Based on the amount of development taking place by developers using ATL and the fact that, unlike the `BaseCtl` framework, ATL is actually a supported product, Microsoft and the industry have obviously seen ATL as a viable platform for creating ActiveX components. It should be around for a long time.

The initial implementation, versions 1.0 and 1.1, focused on the creation of small and fast automation servers and COM objects. With the introduction of 2.0, ATL expanded its coverage to include ActiveX controls and other ActiveX components. The level of integration with the Visual C++ IDE originally consisted only of an AppWizard that you would use to create the basic ATL project (which was, ironically, more complete than its MFC counterpart). In addition, you can use the ClassWizard to maintain the objects, methods, and properties as you do with MFC. Microsoft fully integrated ATL version 2.0 into Visual C++ 5.0 (including AppWizards, ObjectWizards, and ClassWizards) and maintains a consistent level of support for ATL within Visual C++ 6.0.

An added bonus to ATL is that you can integrate ATL components into existing MFC applications without dire consequences or enormous amounts of work. This capability gives you complete freedom to develop your component without the restrictions that MFC imposes, while still being able to use nice MFC classes and features (like structures, arrays, and lists, to name just a few).

15.5.3 Using the BaseControl Framework to Create ActiveX Components

BaseControl (`BaseCtl`) Framework and the ActiveX SDK is without a doubt the most difficult route to choose for ActiveX component development. The `BaseCtl` framework was first developed by the Visual Basic 4 development group in late 1995 and early 1996 in response to growing demands for better performance when using OCXs and Visual Basic. `BaseCtl` was intended as a bare-bones framework that knowledgeable developers could use to create lightweight OLE controls.

In an effort to meet the demand for tools to create OLE controls, the framework was put into the hands of various control developers and vendors who were in contact with Microsoft and the Visual Basic group. At the Internet Professional Developers' Conference, Microsoft packaged the `BaseCtl` Framework as part of the ActiveX Software Developer's Kit (SDK).

The `BaseCtl` has no integration with the Visual C++ environment. In fact, the version of the `BaseCtl` framework that ships with the ActiveX SDK is little more than a set of sample programs from which you can create new applications. The `BaseCtl` framework relies on a series of object and library files that you have to build before you can use them to develop components. All of the source files that come with the SDK, and those generated by the AppWizard, depend on command-line compilation. With a little bit of effort on your part, you can convert all the projects to Visual C++ projects, including the object and library files that come with the SDK — but before you start, you may want to ask yourself if such an effort is worthwhile. The documentation for the `BaseCtl` framework is rudimentary and somewhat cryptic.

Basic control development with the `BaseCtl` framework can be difficult, as well. A fair number of the functions and capabilities that you are probably used to working with in MFC development are not present in the `BaseCtl`. Worse yet, a number of the function names are different, and the architecture for persistence is completely different. `BaseCtl` is meant to get the job done with as little code as possible. As you probably have learned from your own development, getting the job done with as little code as possible typically means a bare-bones environment at best — and `BaseCtl` is no different. With the `BaseCtl` framework, you're expected to dig into the guts of the framework and build a lot of the functions yourself.

One thing the `BaseCtl` framework has going for it is a fair number of samples. When installing the `BaseCtl` framework, you should generally install the samples as well. Chances are that if you need to do something, it's in one of the samples. Another nice feature of the `BaseCtl` framework is the capability to access all the source code in the `BaseCtl` framework directly, so if you find a bug, you can fix it yourself and move on.

In addition, using the `BaseCtl` framework gives you much more freedom to model your control as you want. For example, suppose you have two controls that you want to develop. The first control is a Number control, which receives only basic numeric data input, while the second control is a Currency control, which receives only basic currency data input. Both can rely heavily on the C++ inheritance model at the code and interface levels if you create a BaseNumeric control and derive the code for the other two controls from it.

Clearly, MFC does not provide you with anywhere near that much freedom. However, do not let the freedom issue convince you to take the `BaseCtl` framework lightly — you can expect a lot of work when implementing a component with it. Even worse, the results may not justify the work. For example, converting an existing MFC Control to the `BaseCtl` framework might, in certain cases, result in a 40 percent improvement in the average load time from the MFC version to the `BaseCtl` version of the control. At first thought, a 40 percent improvement sounds pretty good. Unfortunately, with the speeds of modern computers and the amount of available memory, the reduction in load time might be negligible to the user. In other words, the load times might already be so low for the MFC version of the control that you literally have to place hundreds of controls on the application's form before the load-time difference between the two versions is noticeable.

15.5.4 Create Your Own Framework

The last method for control development is for you to just sit down and create the control. You can obtain code from the class libraries, samples, books, and so on, and come up with your own framework, tools, or whatever you want. But you can expect the work to be hard and time-consuming. To get an idea of how much work is actually involved, stop for a minute and take a look at some of the source files in MFC, ATL, and the `BaseCtl` framework. Literally thousands of lines of code have been implemented over the course of months and even years.

Due to the constantly changing nature of OLE and ActiveX requirements, it is usually wiser to choose an existing platform rather than trying to reinvent the wheel, unless you have an extremely compelling reason to create your own framework. Remember, the key to successful control development is not in the framework that you choose to develop in, but in how you apply it.

15.6 Basic ActiveX Component Architecture

Before moving on to the actual implementation of each type of ActiveX component, you should review some of the basic concepts and architecture surrounding each component. Even though you can develop a wide variety of ActiveX components — controls, servers, documents, and so on — one thing is true for every ActiveX component you design: Underlying every component is the Component Object Model (COM) architecture. COM defines the standard that all ActiveX components rely on when interacting with other ActiveX components.

In addition to COM, all ActiveX components are further defined or restricted by the operating system in how they are created and used. The type of ActiveX component you create will further define or restrict your options. A wide variety of choices are available to you as a developer, and it is important to understand the importance of your choices and how a choice can affect your development in a project.

15.6.1 ActiveX Automation Servers

Probably the easiest to implement and most flexible form of ActiveX component is the automation server. An *automation server* is an application that contains one or more `IDispatch`-based interfaces. An *interface* is a collection of related methods and properties and an `IDispatch` interface is the name of the COM interface that the component-using application uses to generically invoke the component's methods and properties. For more information on `IDispatch` interfaces, their use, and specifics of their implementation, you can review the Visual C++ books online that come with Visual Studio. The capability to define unique methods and properties for each server and have them be accessible through a generic mechanism is the real power of automation servers.

An automation server may or may not be directly createable by other applications using the `CreateObject()` function or a similar call. It is possible to have what are referred to as *nested objects*, or *object models*, that represent a hierarchy of objects. In such an environment, a single createable automation object is responsible for the creation and distribution of other automation objects. For example, an application may expose a document automation interface that can be created and manipulated by another application but that only exposes a `Page` interface as a method call to the document object. The lifetime of the `Page` object is less than or equal to the document object and cannot exist on its own.

Creating ActiveX automation servers using MFC is beyond the scope of this book. MFC is great for rapid development and ease of modification. Servers created with MFC will be the largest and slowest of the three types (MFC, ATL, and `BaseCtl`). Deviating from the standard MFC implementation of automation servers can also be a limiting factor when using this tool. MFC's greatest strength is its integration with the Visual C++ IDE and the speed with which an implementation can be up and running. In only minutes, developers can create a server and implement its methods and properties, assuming that they are familiar with the tools available.

Types of Automation Servers

When creating an automation server, you must decide how to implement the server relative to how it is going to be used. You can create two basic types of servers: DLL-based and EXE-based. If the server does not have to run as a stand-alone application and performance is a critical issue, you should implement your server as a DLL. A DLL-based server is typically referred to as an *in-process server* because of how it normally executes relative to its controller. If the server application does have a requirement to run as a stand-alone application, you must implement it as an EXE. An EXE-based automation server is typically referred to as a local server or *out-of-process server*, and it will execute in its own process space.

Automation servers also have an execution model that is independent of how the server is written. Automation servers can execute either in-process, locally, or remotely, relative to the application that has invoked or is using the server.

In-Process Execution

An in-process server is called *in-process* because it executes within the same process space as that of the application that created it. Only DLL-based automation servers can execute as in-process, but that is not a guarantee. This is very important to note when using nested objects or shared objects. If you create an object in a process space (for example, Process A), and you subsequently pass the object to another application in another process space (Process B), the server in Process A will execute as a local server relative to the application in Process B. Process B will treat the object as a local server — regardless of the fact that the server in Process A is a DLL-based server. This issue is critical since more times than not in-process servers are used to improve performance of the application using them.

Local Execution

Local execution occurs when an automation server is executing in a process space other than the process space of the controller application. As was stated earlier, a DLL-based server may execute locally to its controller, depending on how it was created, versus which application is using it. The main issue with local servers is performance, since all of the method calls have to cross process boundaries. This condition requires additional code overhead to move data back and forth between the server and its controller.

Remote Execution

Remote Execution occurs when the server is executing on a machine other than the application that is controlling it. As with local servers, performance is an issue with this type of execution.

15.6.2 ActiveX Controls

An ActiveX control, in general, is still the same OCX or OLE control as developers were creating several years ago. In fact, the only change from OLE controls to ActiveX controls is a decrease in the requirements to qualify as a control.

To qualify as an ActiveX control, a component must be a COM object, implement an `IUnknown` interface, and support registration and unregistration through the exported functions, `DLLRegisterServer()`, and `DLLUnregisterServer()`.

Even though your component may qualify as an ActiveX control, if all it supports is the preceding features, it will not do much more than take up space on your hard disk. If it needs user interface, persistence, events, or any other feature common to controls, the control must implement other categories of interfaces. The exact requirements are in the *OLE Control and Control Container Guidelines, Version 1.1* published by Microsoft. All of the guidelines for ActiveX development are available on the Internet at the Microsoft Web site or on the ActiveX SDK CD.

As you have learned, you have three tools at your disposal for creating ActiveX controls: MFC, ATL, and `BaseCtl`. As with ActiveX automation servers, each development tool has its strengths and weaknesses. With ActiveX controls you only have one option when creating and executing the control: as a DLL and in-process to the control's container application. Even though the extension of the control is .ocx, it is still in fact just a .dll.

15.7 Better Understanding COM

In later chapters, you will learn how to create ActiveX components, whether controls, ActiveX documents, ActiveX EXEs, or ActiveX DLLs. As you have learned, ActiveX is a technology built around the concepts of the Component Object Model (COM). However, before you begin designing components, it is worthwhile to focus on some concepts of COM, and also some basic concepts of DCOM. Before you write the projects in later chapters, you must first have a better understanding of how to create COM objects in Visual C++.

The most important concept that you must learn when you consider COM is the concept of an interface. You must know what an interface is before you do anything with COM. Conceptually, an *interface* is an agreement between a client and an object about how they will communicate. When you define a set of methods (that is, public functions that the object exposes) that reside on the interface, it becomes a communications channel between the client and the object. Within your program code, an interface is a collection of related procedures and functions. When you create objects that you build around COM and clients to communicate with such objects, both clients and objects must communicate exclusively through interfaces.

Before the use of interfaces was popular in large-system, object-oriented design, a client would work directly with an object's class definition. Programming directly with the object's class definition led to many shortcomings with code versioning and reuse. Because client code had too much "insider" information about the implementation details of the object, changes to an object's code often required changes to the client's code, making a system fragile and hard to extend. Today's component-based development often requires a client and an object to live in different binary executables, which makes reuse and versioning even more important.

COM uses the mechanism of a logical interface to eliminate any implementation dependencies between a client and an object. The logical interface results in systems that are less fragile and far easier to extend. An interface plays the role of a mediator between the client and the object. It is a contract that specifies what work the object must do, but it does not specify how the object should accomplish the work. An interface is also a communications protocol that defines a set of methods complete with names, arguments, and return types. Just as a network cable carries important data between computers on a network without knowledge of the specifics of the data, an interface lets important information, such as data and messages, pass between the client and the object. The object's implementation may change from version to version, but the object must continue to support every interface that it supports in earlier versions within its later versions. As long as an interface definition remains static, the established channels of communication remain unaffected between a client and an object from version to version. Figure 15-1 shows the logical model for communication between a client and a COM object.

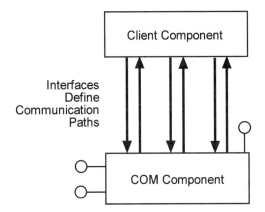

Figure 15-1   The logical model for communication between a client and a COM object.

15.7.1 COM Objects Implement Interfaces

As you learned in the previous sections, COM objects are built around interfaces the objects expose to clients. A COM object must implement at least one interface, although the object is free to implement as many interfaces as it may require. Objects can add support for new interfaces in later releases, which lets the objects evolve with demand. As long as the object continues to support every previously published interface in subsequent releases, client applications will not require modification. In a single stroke, then, interfaces solve the versioning problems of using classes directly and demonstrate one of the primary reasons Microsoft created COM. A client can test for a particular behavior and degrade gracefully if the object does not support the functionality. To test for a behavior, the client must query an object at runtime to see whether the object supports a particular interface. COM also supports *categories*, or collections of interfaces. If an object belongs to a category, you can assume that the object implements all the interfaces defined for the category. Interfaces and categories help you determine the capabilities of an object.

It is also possible for many different objects to implement the same interface. A single method that an interface defines can yield different behavior when invoked on implementations supplied by different objects. The one-to-many relationship between an interface and various COM objects makes it possible for COM to offer polymorphic behavior. As long as the client program uses interfaces to access objects, the program may switch between different object implementations with minimal impact on its code. Groups of objects that implement a specific interface or category are said to be *plug-compatible*. The polymorphic nature of COM makes COM objects highly reusable.

Another powerful feature of COM is language independence. COM clients and COM objects have the same layout and behavior at runtime, regardless of which language you use to produce the component. This lets you build systems with many different components that you or other programmers create in different languages, whether Visual Basic, C++, or Java. The language you use to create the component simply does not matter in COM. As a programmer, language independence offers you three major benefits. First, it lets you split up large systems into manageable subsystems early in the design phase. Second, it lets you implement each subsystem with a component that you create with any COM-capable tool. Third, it lets the individual teams working on each subsystem have complete autonomy.

COM defines the mechanism for client-object interaction in a language-independent way. The COM standard defines the standard memory layout for COM objects and also defines the way clients invoke method calls within the object. The definition of the standard COM object construction lets you write objects in any language, and write the client programs that access those objects in any language. Figure 15-2 shows the standard object construction for a COM object.

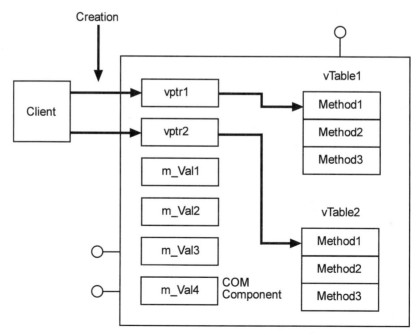

Figure 15-2 The standard construction of a COM object.

The object creates an array of function pointers called a vTable (the "v" stands for virtual), and passes a vTable pointer to the client. The client sees the vTable as the interface and uses the vTable pointer it received from the client to locate a particular function pointer. Once the client finds the function pointer, the client invokes the method directly. In other words, when programs access the COM object, they will always access the vTable and receive a vptr from the vTable. The actual method the vptr points to can change between program versions; so long as the client accesses the method through the interfaces that the vTable describes, the changes to the underlying methods are invisible to the client program.

When a client program accesses a COM object, it receives a pointer to an internal method within the object, and uses that pointer to execute the method itself.

15.7.2 Interface Definition Language

As the previous section details, COM is a definition standard that is language-independent, both when you define the COM object and when you define the client that will access the COM object. Even though COM is language-independent, there must be some official language for defining interfaces and COM classes (which COM programmers generally abbreviate as *coclasses*). COM uses interface definition language (IDL), which is similar to C, but offers object-oriented extensions that let you unambiguously define your interfaces and coclasses. C++ and Java programmers should always begin a COM-based project by defining the interfaces and coclasses with interface definition language. When you compile the COM-based project, the compiler feeds the interface definition language file to the Microsoft Interface Definition Language (MIDL) compiler, which produces a binary description file called a *type library*. For example, a typical interface definition language file might define two interfaces and a coclass, as shown here:

```
[ uuid("CVCCID1")]
  interface ICVCCInterface1
    {
      HRESULT CVCCMethod1();
      HRESULT CVCCMethod2();
    }
[ uuid("CVCCID2")]
  interface ICVCCInterface2
    {
      HRESULT CVCCMethod3();
    }
[ uuid("CVCCID3")]
  coclass CCVCCClass
```

```
{
  [default] interface ICVCCInterface1;
  interface ICVCCInterface2;
}
```

COM uses a unique identifier called a Globally Unique Identifier (GUID). Interface definition language uses the keyword *UUID* (for Universally Unique Identifier) instead of GUID, but do not let the different terminology confuse you — Globally Unique Identifiers and Universally Unique Identifiers are the same thing. Globally Unique Identifiers that identify coclasses are known as Class Identifiers (CLSIDs), while those that identify interfaces are known as Interface Identifiers (IIDs). Globally Unique Identifiers are long, 128-bit integers that you will use most frequently simply as a readable, 32-digit hexadecimal number, as shown here:

```
[ uuid(40C3E581-F26D-11D0-B840-0000E8A1E186)]
  interface IMyInterface1
  {
    HRESULT CVCCMethod1();
    HRESULT CVCCMethod2();
  }
```

Interface definition language, type libraries, and the Windows registry all use Globally Unique Identifiers to provide unique identification for COM entities such as type libraries, coclasses, and interfaces. Adding Globally Unique Identifiers to the registry is an important configuration issue on any COM-enabled machine. When you register a server component or type library on a client machine, you must store the Globally Unique Identifiers for the COM object, its interfaces, and its coclasses within the Windows registry.

Core Tip

One of COM's most important features is interface inheritance. Interface inheritance lets your programs inherit from many different interfaces within your COM class. Unfortunately, COM does not support implementation inheritance, which you would use to inherit the method implementations from another class. Under interface inheritance, you simply inherit the obligation to write the method implementations. This might seem strange at first because you are inheriting an obligation, rather than code already written. The key is that if you inherit from an interface, the client code that uses your object can use the interface pointer and be guaranteed that your object exhibits a certain behavior. Interface inheritance offers much higher levels of reuse than implementation inheritance. Preliminary indications from Microsoft are that the new COM+ standard (which is supposed to ship with Windows 2000) will support implementation inheritance.

15.7.3 Understanding the IUnknown Interface

As you have learned, all COM objects must implement at least one interface. All COM interfaces must inherit from a standard interface, IUnknown, which means that all COM interfaces must also contain the three methods in this interface in addition to their own methods. The IUnknown interface contains support for both reference counting and runtime type coercion (that is, forcing a value into a specific type). COM objects implement reference counting with two methods, AddRef() and Release(). These methods let objects maintain an internal count of connected clients and delete themselves from memory when no more clients are connected to the object. The third method, QueryInterface(), lets a client move between the different interfaces an object exposes. QueryInterface() is the cornerstone for polymorphism and versioning in COM. Clients can switch to a different interface to request different behavior from an object, and they can query an object to see if the object supports a certain interface. COM's support for runtime type inspection lets clients degrade gracefully if the object does not support the client-requested interface. Figure 15-3 shows the standard construction of an interface, including the three default methods all interfaces support.

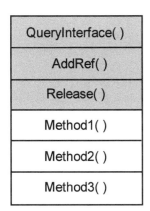

Figure 15-3 The standard interface construction that COM defines.

Most C++ programmers are used to calling the methods from IUnknown explicitly, but manual garbage collection is vulnerable to reference-counting bugs that are difficult, at best, to find. As you have learned, Microsoft has created direct COM support in the C++ compiler and frameworks such as the

Active Template Library (ATL), so programmers can create COM client applications without explicitly calling these methods.

Automation uses a standard COM interface called IDispatch. The vTable for an IDispatch interface always contains the same seven methods. The vTable is a single physical interface from which object implementers can create any number of logical interfaces. As long as the vTable bindings are consistent from one IDispatch interface to another, there's no need to generate new vTable bindings at compile time. Figure 15-4 shows the seven methods that comprise an IDispatch interface.

IDispatch vTable

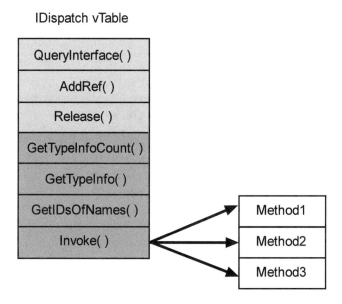

Figure 15-4   The seven methods that comprise an IDispatch interface.

The two key IDispatch methods are GetIDsOfNames() and Invoke(). GetIDsOfNames() lets a client get binding information at runtime. It takes a string argument containing the name of a function or property and returns a DispID, an integer value that uniquely identifies a specific method or property used in the call to Invoke(). When a client calls Invoke(), it must pass a painfully large and complex set of arguments. The arguments include the DispID, a single array of variants containing the values of the arguments; a variant for the return value; and a few other things that do not come into play here. When a client queries for these DispID values at runtime, the process is known as late binding. Going through IDispatch is inefficient, but essential for clients that cannot create vTable bindings at compile time.

Dual interfaces, or *duals*, simplify binding. Duals are interfaces that let sophisticated clients use vTable bindings, while still offering IDispatch to clients that do not support vTable bindings. Visual Basic and C++ clients can, therefore, communicate with your objects through vTable binding. VBScript clients can also communicate with your objects through IDispatch, which lets Web-centric environments such as Internet Explorer and Active Server Pages (ASP) control your dual-interface objects as well. Figure 15-5 shows how dual interfaces work. Note that the Method1, Method2, and Method3 methods are all part of the vTable, but are also accessible with calls to Invoke().

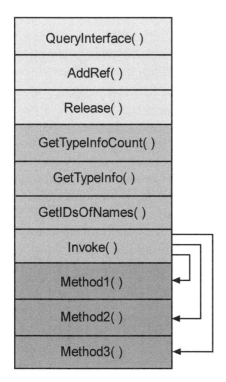

Figure 15-5 Dual interfaces let different client types access your objects.

A component that exposes coclasses to client applications is called a *COM server,* or an automation server. COM defines structures for two kinds of servers, in-process and out-of-process servers. In-process servers reside in the client application's address space. In-process servers create objects that reside in the same Win32 process as the client's program code. Out-of-process servers create their own Win32 processes. You can further divide out-of-process servers into local servers and remote servers. The distinction between local servers and remote servers tells you whether the client process and the server process run on the same computer or different computers. The Distributed Component Object Model (DCOM) lets the client and object communicate across computer boundaries, as with the case of remote servers.

You do not have to do anything special to differentiate between a local server and a remote server — the underlying architecture of DCOM takes care of most of the differences. But you must watch out for coding techniques that do not scale well across computer boundaries. An interface design that passes data inefficiently or incurs unnecessary round trips between the client and object can produce satisfactory performance in an in-process component or an out-of-process component on the same computer. The same interface design will usually result in unacceptable performance when used in an out-of-process component on a different computer.

In the next section, you will learn more about DCOM principles and the additional factors they add to the COM principles that you have already learned. However, before you continue with the next section, make sure that you clearly understand the three binding techniques COM uses to connect a client to an object. It is particularly necessary to understand the important performance differences between late binding and early binding. While there are many real-world scenarios in which late binding does not have a significant impact on performance, components in large-scale developments must be as efficient as possible. True `vTable` binding is always more efficient and more flexible than the two other COM communication methods that use `IDispatch`.

15.8   Moving On to DCOM

As you have learned, creating DCOM server components with Visual C++ is not particularly difficult. However, creating *scalable* DCOM server components with Visual C++ requires more complexity. Unfortunately, an object that does not scale well is not particularly useful for professional development.

Now that you have learned the basics of COM programming, it is worthwhile to learn more about DCOM programming, how it differs from COM programming, and additional issues you must consider when writing a scalable, multithreaded DCOM server component with Visual C++. You will also learn how to implement asynchronous method calls between a client and a remote object.

When a client application and a COM object exist in the same process, the client can invoke a method directly through an interface pointer. When a client creates an object from an ActiveX DLL, the client and object share the same call stack and memory addresses. When the client lives in one Win32 process and the object lives in another (as is the case whenever you work with out-of-process servers), the programming you must perform to manipulate the object becomes more complex. To correctly work with out-of-process servers, particularly remote out-of-process servers, a client must use DCOM's infrastructure to invoke a method on a remote object.

15.8.1 Using DCOM to Communicate Out-Of-Process and Across Computers

As you have learned, your programs can use DCOM to communicate with out-of-process components, whether on a local machine or on a remote machine. However, you will generally use DCOM to communicate with out-of-process servers on a remote machine. DCOM lets clients and objects communicate out-of-process with two helper objects, the proxy (at the client process) and the stub (at the server component process). These COM objects let the client and object pass the interface pointer across process boundaries. COM automatically inspects the type library for an object and uses the information within the library to create the proxy and stub at runtime. The client communicates with the proxy. The proxy, in turn, communicates with the stub, which communicates with the actual object. When information passes from the object back to the client, it follows the same process in reverse: object, stub, proxy, client. Figure 15-6 shows a logical model of proxy-stub communication between a client and an out-of-process COM component.

A proxy-stub pair exists for each interface pointer that the two programs (client and COM object) pass between processes. The proxy and stub, which assist your clients and objects by transporting method calls between processes, communicate by using an underlying protocol called Remote Procedure Call (RPC) across an RPC channel. RPC is an industry-standard communication protocol that has reached maturity on Windows, as well as many other non-Windows platforms. Microsoft has layered COM and DCOM on top of RPC. The proxy and stub communicate across the RPC channel for local servers and remote servers in a way that is transparent to your Visual Basic, Visual C++, or any other type of components.

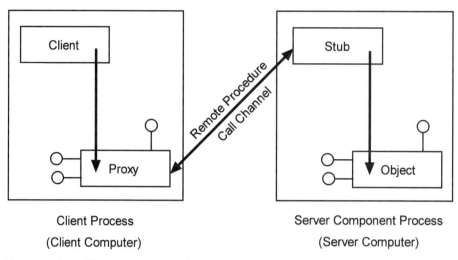

Figure 15-6   The communication between a client and an out-of-process COM component.

The best thing about the proxy and stub is that COM creates the proxy and stub transparently behind the scenes — the clients and objects will not even know that they are operating in different processes, on different machines, even in different cities. In-process and out-of-process objects have the same look and feel to both the client and the object — in other words, a client cannot tell the difference between an object's interface and the proxy for the interface, nor can an object tell the difference between a client and its stub. This means that when you create objects and clients, they automatically work for in-process as well as out-of-process communications.

A client interacts with an object the same way, regardless of whether the object is in-process, local, or remote. You can use classes written for a DLL in an out-of-process EXE without modification. You might assume, therefore, that you can create a remote server simply by changing your compilation target from a COM DLL to a COM EXE. Although such a translation will usually work, it is not necessarily the most efficient means of communication between the two out-of-process components. Many programming techniques work well in an in-process object, but do not scale when you extend the communications across process boundaries. You must consider two factors when creating remote servers: the overhead associated with a remote procedure call, and the requirements of moving large chunks of data across the network.

The proxy-stub architecture has a considerable amount of overhead associated with it. Much of this overhead is a function of the fact that the client's calling thread blocks (that is, stops executing) when the calling thread calls a method, and the calling thread does not get control back (resume execution) until after the call returns from the object. Programmers refer to the method call and the execution return from the remote object as a *round trip*. You can imagine that the time to make a round trip to an object and back increases by an order of magnitude as you move the object out-of-process and onto another machine. Distance impacts performance significantly. Even if you could communicate between two machines 5,000 miles apart at the speed of light, the time of a method call would increase by a factor of 10. The actual transmission speed, of course, is much slower than the speed of light.

15.8.2 Understanding How to Reduce Round Trips

As you learned in the previous section, the impact of round trips on your program performance is significant. When you design your interfaces, make sure that you design them to reduce round trips as much as possible. Never create multiple methods or properties when a single method can do the job just as well. For example, exposing three public properties, each of which requires a round trip, results in inefficient client code. Instead, you might provide a single method that lets the client accomplish the same task with fewer trips.

Moving data between the client process and the object process is known as *marshaling*. Marshaling is the responsibility of the proxy and stub. Your programs can use a COM-provided service called the *universal marshaler* to create the proxy and stub. Unfortunately, when you create the proxy and stub with the universal marshaler, there is nothing you can do to customize the behavior of the proxy or the stub. You can also write custom marshaling code to create proxies and stubs that are optimized for the data that the objects will transmit, and are therefore more flexible and more capable of transmitting user-defined types.

Marshaling a lot of data in a single round trip is far better than marshaling smaller amounts of data in multiple round trips. Although you should optimize round trips first, you should also be conscientious about the packets of data that you move back and forth. You must push some data from the client to the object, and you must pull other data from the object back to the client. Some data must move in both directions. Accordingly, COM defines parameters as being either *in* parameters, *out* parameters, or both *in* and *out* parameters.

15.8.3 Understanding Singletons

Sometimes you want many client applications to connect to a single object in a remote server. COM makes it easy for a client to create and connect to a new object, but connecting to an existing object takes a few additional steps. These single-instance objects are known as *singletons*. Each user creates a new connection object in the server, and each connection object provides a method to retrieve a reference to a global object stored in a global variable. A Visual C++ out-of-process server can readily implement this design, as shown in Figure 15-7.

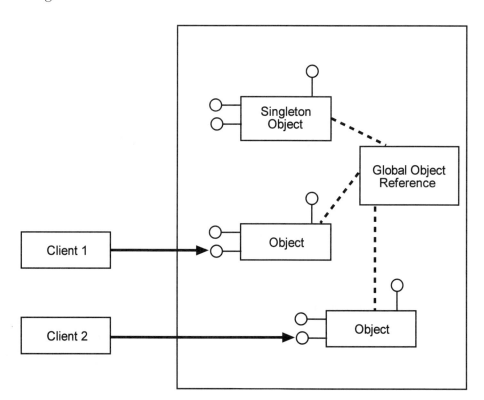

Figure 15-7   A client component communicates with a singleton object.

The code for this works well, as long as your server component is single-threaded. A multithreaded component won't give you the desired results if you use the same code, however, because every thread in your server process will own and maintain its own instance of global data.

15.9 Understanding the COM Threading Model

It's important to understand how the COM threading model works. Every COM object lives in an execution context called an *apartment*. Some COM processes have a single apartment, but others have more. A COM-enabled thread lives in only one apartment. COM allows apartments to be multithreaded or single-threaded. Multithreaded apartments can yield faster components, but they present synchronization issues that can be complex and problematic.

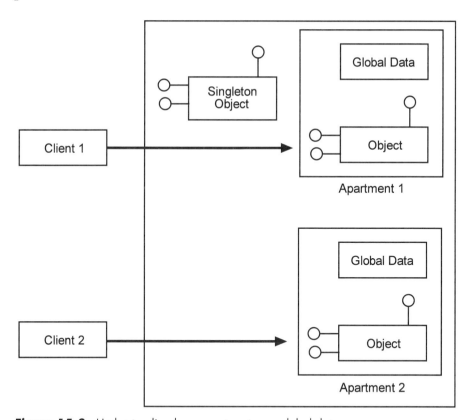

Figure 15-8   Understanding how apartments use global data.

Every single-threaded apartment has its own Windows message queue. COM invokes methods across apartment boundaries by posting messages in an apartment's message queue. The lone thread in each of these apartments retrieves these messages on a first-in, first-out basis. If three different clients invoke a method on an object, the methods are serviced first-come, first-served. Although the use of a message queue leads to an invocation architecture that is far from optimal, it does provide protection from synchronization problems: no object will ever be accessed by more than a single thread at a given time. There is also no chance that two threads will concurrently access an object and leave the data in an invalid state. In the context of a single-threaded apartment, every method call completes before another is started. This provides a multithreaded architecture that is slow, yet safe.

Each apartment maintains its own instance of global data. This implies that you cannot store a single reference to a global object and expect objects in distinct apartments to recognize it. The bottom line is that you cannot easily share data between objects in separate apartments.

15.10 Summary

In this chapter, you have learned about the different types of ActiveX components, including automation servers, automation controllers, ActiveX controls, COM objects, ActiveX documents, and ActiveX containers.

MFC allows for rapid component creation and implementation and the level of support built into the Visual C++ IDE for MFC is much stronger than that of ATL or `BaseCtl` (although Visual C++ 6.0 offers enhanced ATL support). MFC offers a very large and robust class library for solving most, if not all, of your development problems. MFC does, however, suffer from the problem that it is everything to everyone, which results in a slower application or one that cannot deviate from the "norm" fairly easily.

ATL provides a small and deliberate framework for creating ActiveX components. ATL, however, falls short in the area of common class and utility support, which is MFC's strength. In addition, ATL's integration with the Visual C++ IDE also leaves room for improvement (though it is greatly improved).

`BaseCtl` is similar to ATL in that it is focused specifically on small, fast component development. Like ATL, it lacks the same common class and utility support that makes MFC so attractive. `BaseCtl` has an added negative of being considered only as a sample and not as a supported product by Microsoft.

The level of experience of the development team and the intended life cycle of the code and applications will also affect the decision of which tool to choose to create ActiveX components. Take the time to investigate all of the options available to you before deciding on a platform and a direction.

After outlining the possible implementation options, the second half of this chapter focused on a discussion of the basic principles of COM and DCOM. As you learned, COM and DCOM both depend entirely on interfaces to provide access to calling clients.

CREATING IN-PROCESS ACTIVEX SERVERS USING MFC

Topics in this Chapter

- Creating the Basic Project
- Writing the Support Code for the Sample Server
- Generating OLE Exceptions
- Server Instantiation Using C++
- Creating Shareable Servers
- Working with Single-Instance Servers
- Summary

Chapter 16

As you learned in Chapter 15, MFC and Visual C++ provide a simple and easy to use framework for creating ActiveX objects. In fact, the Visual C++ development environment's AppWizard and ClassWizard were implemented with the creating of automation servers in mind. Creating and manipulating automation interfaces is one of the primary functions of Visual C++.

In this chapter, you will create a simple in-process automation server using MFC for logging string data to a file. Throughout this chapter, you can use an application such as Visual Basic to test your implementation. Visual Basic is perfect for accessing automation servers, since it takes so little time and code to do so. As you proceed through the chapter, you will expand on your implementation, highlighting some of the more advanced concepts of automation server creation.

16.1 Creating the Basic Project

When creating an automation server, the first step is to create a *basic project* upon which you will build your application's features and functionality. MFC provides an AppWizard that greatly simplifies this process. The AppWizard consists of a set of structured dialogs and choices that, in the end, will result in a set of files representing the basic application's project. To create the basic project, you need to open the Visual C++ Integrated Development Environment (IDE) and select the File menu's New option. Visual C++ will display the New dialog box. Within the New dialog box, select the Projects tab. Next, select MFC AppWizard (dll) as the project type. Enter the Project name as MFCAutoServer, and set the Location to the Chap16\MFCAutoServer directory. Click OK to continue. Figure 16-1 shows the New dialog box after you set it to create the MFCAutoServer program.

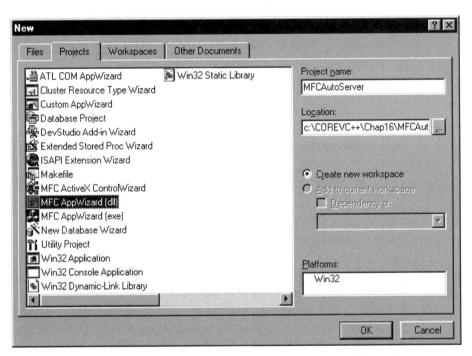

Figure 16-1   The New dialog box after you set it to create the MFCAutoServer program.

In the MFC AppWizard — Step 1 of 1 dialog box, you will define the specifics about how the AppWizard is going to create your application. For the type of DLL to create, select Regular DLL with MFC statically linked, which results in a slightly larger application, but one that should load faster because you won't have to load the MFC DLLs whenever the server is launched. Also, select the Automation check box, since that is the reason you are creating the application in the first place. Click the Finish button within the dialog box to continue. Visual C++ will display the New Project Information dialog box.

The New Project Information dialog lets you review your choices before creating the actual project. Click the OK button to complete the creation of your project. The MFC AppWizard will automatically create all the basic files that you will need to create a DLL-based automation server. Table 16-1 lists all the files that AppWizard creates for you and a brief explanation of what your applications will use the files for.

Table 16-1 Macro and Keyword Comparisons

Filename	Description
MFCAutoServer.clw	Visual C++ project file
MFCAutoServer.cpp	Main application source file and entry point for the DLL
MFCAutoServer.def	Standard application DEF file. This file contains the function export declarations needed for all in-process servers.
MFCAutoServer.dsp	Visual C++ project file
MFCAutoServer.dsw	Visual C++ project file
MFCAutoServer.h	Main application header file
MFCAutoServer.ncb	Visual C++ project file
MFCAutoServer.odl	Standard Object Definition Language (ODL) file
MFCAutoServer.rc	Standard resource file
ReadMe.txt	Text file that describes the project
Resource.h	Resource header file
StdAfx.cpp	Standard precompiled header source file
StdAfx.h	Standard precompiled header file. All the MFC-specific include files are added here.
Res\MFCAutoServer.rc2	Standard resource 2 file. This file contains all of the resource information that you cannot edit directly from within Visual C++.

After you create the default project, you can compile the project, but you can do very little with it because it does not contain interfaces, methods, or properties.

16.1.1   Adding an Automation Interface to the Application

To be an *automation server*, an application must contain at least one or more IDispatch-based interfaces. In MFC, you will use the CCmdTarget class to implement this interface (you learned about CCmdTarget in Chapter 8). You will use the MFC ClassWizard to add your automation interfaces to your application. To add the first automation interface, select the View menu ClassWizard option. Visual C++ will display the ClassWizard dialog box. Next, click the Add Class button, and select the New menu item. Visual C++ will open the New Class dialog box.

Within the New Class dialog box, enter the Name CTrackStr, and select CCmdTarget as its base class in the Base class combo box. Select the Automation radio button in the Automation radio button group. The Createable by type ID radio button and edit field are used to define the ProgID that you, and calling applications, will use to create and launch the automation server. The human-readable ProgID is used in place of the CLSID since it is much easier to write and remember. Be careful when defining a ProgID not to create duplicates. For your application, leave the ProgID set to its default value. Click the OK button to create your new class and add it to your application. Click the OK button in the MFC ClassWizard dialog box to close the ClassWizard. Figure 16-2 shows the New Class dialog box after you enter the class information.

When creating a new CCmdTarget class, MFC not only creates a header and source file with all of the appropriate information (in this case, TrackStr.h and TrackStr.cpp), but because you selected automation support for the class, it also updates the ODL file with the new dispinterface and CoClass entries of your automation server, as shown in the MFC-AutoServer.odl file:

```
// MFCAutoServer.odl : type library source for MFCAutoServer.dll

// This file will be processed by the MIDL compiler to
// produce the type library (MFCAutoServer.tlb).

[ uuid(2EE81064-F61D-11D1-8545-8FDA26F60349), version(1.0) ]
library MFCAutoServer
  {
```

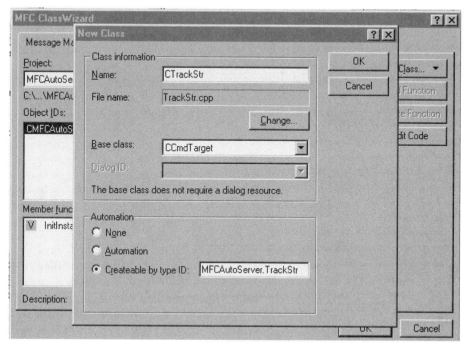

Figure 16-2 The New Class dialog box after you enter the class information.

```
importlib("stdole25-tlb");
  importlib("stdole2.tlb");

  // Primary dispatch interface for CTrackStr

  [ uuid(2EE81071-F61D-11D1-8545-8FDA26F60349) ]
  dispinterface ITrackStr
  {
    properties:
      // NOTE-ClassWizard maintains property information here.
      //    Use extreme caution when editing this section.
      //{{AFX_ODL_PROP(CTrackStr)
      //}}AFX_ODL_PROP

    methods:
      // NOTE-ClassWizard maintains method information here.
      //    Use extreme caution when editing this section.
      //{{AFX_ODL_METHOD(CTrackStr)
      //}}AFX_ODL_METHOD

  };
```

```
// Class information for CTrackStr

[ uuid(2EE81073-F61D-11D1-8545-8FDA26F60349) ]
coclass TrackStr
  {
    [default] dispinterface ITrackStr;
  };

//{{AFX_APPEND_ODL}}
//}}AFX_APPEND_ODL}}
};
```

The `dispinterface` is your primary `IDispatch`-based interface and is where the ClassWizard will add your new methods and properties. The `CoClass` interface identifies your class factory interface. The class factory is the part of the application that performs the actual creation of your automation server when it is necessary to do so. See the OLE and MFC documentation for more information on class factories and their role in OLE.

Notice from the code in the ODL file, however, that even though the MFC ClassWizard added the new interface to the server, it did not expose the interface to the outside world. Basically, what you have created thus far is an automation server that no application can create — which is, clearly, not very useful.

All ActiveX components are created through an object known as a *class factory*. MFC defines the class `COleObjectFactory` for its class factory support. However, you cannot add the `COleObjectFactory` class directly to your server implementation. Instead, MFC forces you to use two MFC-defined macros, `DECLARE_OLECREATE` and `IMPLEMENT_OLECREATE`.

To build your class factory, select the ClassView tab within the Project Workspace. Expand the class list, and double-click the `CTrackStr` class to open the TrackStr.h include file. Add the macro `DECLARE_OLECREATE` to your class definition. The macro takes a single parameter, which is your class name — in this case, `CTrackStr`. The following code implements the changed TrackStr.h header file:

```
// more code here

// NOTE-ClassWizard will add and remove member functions here.
//}}AFX_DISPATCH
  DECLARE_DISPATCH_MAP()
  DECLARE_INTERFACE_MAP()
  DECLARE_OLECREATE(CTrackStr)
};
```

Next, again within the Project Workspace window, select the FileView tab, expand the Source Files list, and double-click the TrackStr.cpp entry to open the file. Add the macro `IMPLEMENT_OLECREATE` to your source file. The `IMPLEMENT_OLECREATE` macro takes three parameters, the class name, the `ProgID` that applications will use to create the server, and the `CLSID` of the `CoClass` interface, as your ODL file defines. When AppWizard created the ODL file, it also generated a `CLSID` for the type library. When the Class-Wizard added the `CTrackStr` class, it created new `CLSID`s — one for the `DispInterface` and the other for the `CoClass`. You will implement the changes as shown in the following code. (Note that your `CLSID` should differ from the one used here.)

```
// more code here

// {11C82946-4EDD-11D0-BED8-00400538977D}
   static const IID IID_ITrackStr =
      { 0x11c82946, 0x4edd, 0x11d0, { 0xbe, 0xd8, 0x0, 0x40,
        0x5, 0x38, 0x97, 0x7d } };
   BEGIN_INTERFACE_MAP(CTrackStr, CCmdTarget)
     INTERFACE_PART(CTrackStr, IID_ITrackStr, Dispatch)
   END_INTERFACE_MAP()
   IMPLEMENT_OLECREATE(CTrackStr, _T("MFCAutoServer.TrackStr"),
       0x11C82947, 0x4edd, 0x11d0, 0xbe, 0xd8, 0x0, 0x40, 0x5,
       0x38, 0x97, 0x7d)

// more code here
```

You have now enabled your server implementation with a class factory, which lets other applications create the server. Before another application can create the server, however, OLE has to know where to find the server, which is done through the system registry. All ActiveX components that are publicly available to other applications must support registration and must create valid registry entries. You will learn more about server registration in the next section.

16.1.2 Registering the Server

ActiveX components have one or more registry entries that are used to describe various aspects of the application and how it can be used. The registry is critical to the successful launching and using of ActiveX components. Local servers rely on command-line options for registration support. It is the responsibility of the local server developer to check for the correct command-line option and take the appropriate action. Table 16-2 lists the command-line options for local server registration.

Table 16-2 Local Server Command-Line Options for Registration Support

Command-Line Option	Description
R	Register all components.
U	Unregister all components.
S	Perform registration in silent mode and do not display confirmation dialogs (which indicate successful registration). However, registration will still display error messages. You can combine this option with either R or U.

All in-process ActiveX components expose registration support through two functions the components export, the `DllRegisterServer()` function and the `DllUnregisterServer()` function.

The MFC AppWizard will automatically add the `DllRegisterServer()` function to the main application file of a project when AppWizard creates the project. You should register all of the components the application contains within this function. Further, each ActiveX component must be responsible for its own registration support.

The `COleObjectFactory` class automatically handles registration support. Even though you may not be aware of it, the `COleObjectFactory` class contains a singly linked list that it uses to keep track of all of the `COleObjectFactory` classes implemented in a single application. The linked list is a static member, which means that all instances of the class share the same class factory list. `COleObjectFactory` also contains a static function, `UpdateRegistryAll()`, that will cycle through the list of `COleObjectFactory` classes, instructing each to register themselves.

Unregistering the server is slightly more complex. The MFC AppWizard does not add the exported function, `DllUnregisterServer()`, to a project when AppWizard creates the project. This seeming oversight is actually probably due to an inherent limitation in MFC. The MFC group apparently did not feel it was necessary to add unregistration support to the basic MFC `COleObjectFactory` class. This is an odd decision, because all of the Microsoft logo requirements indicate that all applications that are installed and registered must also uninstall and unregister themselves in order to qualify for the logo.

To support server unregistration, you have to add the exported function, `DllUnregisterServer()` to the class and call the static function `COleObjectFactory::UpdateRegistryAll()`, passing `FALSE` as the parameter, to unregister the server. The actual unregistration code requires more work. This book does not include the unregistration code as a part of the sample code, but the implementation is straightforward. The first step is to create a new class that inherits from `COleObjectFactory`, and override the virtual function `UpdateRegistry()`. Within the overridden function, your code should check the parameter that the calling function passes to `UpdateRegistry()`, and based on its value, call the appropriate registration or unregistration code. MFC provides a basic registration helper function, `AfxOleRegisterServerClass()`, but does not define a companion helper function for unregistration. Searching the source files in MFC reveals a complete set of helper functions for the registry, but unfortunately they are not accessible from anything but an MFC-implemented ActiveX control. Since nothing is available from MFC, you are required to implement the registry updating code yourself (using Windows API calls). Remember, during the unregistration process, you must remove all of the registry entries that the server registration initially created, including the `ProgID`, the `CLSID`, and the type library.

16.2 Writing the Support Code for the Sample Server

Since your sample server is used to output data to a file, you first need to add some support code to your application before adding its methods and properties. The first step is to make some changes and additions to the TrackStr.h header file. You must add a set of member variables for storing the file handle and timer information that you will later use throughout the server implementation. You will implement the changes within the TrackStr.h header file as shown here:

```
// More Code Here
   DECLARE_OLECREATE(CTrackStr)
protected:
   FILE * m_fileLog;
   long m_lTimeBegin;
   long m_lHiResTime;
   long m_lLastHiResTime;
};
```

The next step is to update the source file for the class. You will add the include file mmsystem.h to the TrackStr.cpp file to support the functions that you are taking advantage of in the sample server implementation. You will also write a constructor and destructor for the server. You will implement the changes within the TrackStr.cpp file as shown, here:

```
// more code here

#include "TrackStr.h"

// needed for the high resolution timer services
#include <mmsystem.h>

#ifdef _DEBUG
  #define new DEBUG_NEW
  #undef THIS_FILE
  static char THIS_FILE[] = __FILE__;
#endif

/////////////////////////////////////////////////////////////
// CTrackStr
IMPLEMENT_DYNCREATE(CTrackStr, CCmdTarget)
CTrackStr::CTrackStr()
 {
   EnableAutomation();

   // make sure that the application won't unload until the
   // reference count is 0
   ::AfxOleLockApp();

   // setup the timer resolution
   m_lTimeBegin = timeBeginPeriod(1);
   m_lHiResTime = m_lLastHiResTime = timeGetTime();

   // get the current date and time
   CTime oTimeStamp = CTime::GetCurrentTime();
   CString cstrFileName;

   // create a file name based on the date
   cstrFileName.Format(_T("%s.tracklog"), (LPCTSTR)
   oTimeStamp.Format("%Y%m%d"));

   // open a file
   m_fileLog = fopen(cstrFileName, _T("a"));

   // if we have a file handle
   if(m_fileLog) {
```

```
      // output some starting information
      fprintf(m_fileLog, _T("************************\n"));
      fprintf(m_fileLog, _T("Start %s\n"),
          (LPCTSTR) oTimeStamp.Format("%B %#d, %Y, %I:%M %p"));
      fprintf(m_fileLog, _T("\n"));
    }
  }

CTrackStr::~CTrackStr()
  {
    // check to make sure a file handle exists
    if(m_fileLog) {
      // output some closing information
      CTime oTimeStamp = CTime::GetCurrentTime();
      fprintf(m_fileLog, _T("\n"));
      fprintf(m_fileLog, _T("End %s\n"), oTimeStamp.Format
          ("%B %#d, %Y, %I:%M %p"));
      fprintf(m_fileLog, _T("************************\n"));

      // close the file
      fclose(m_fileLog);
    }

    // if has created a valid timer services
    if(m_lTimeBegin == TIMERR_NOERROR)
      // reset the timer to its original state
      timeEndPeriod(1);

    // make sure that the application can unload the component
    ::AfxOleUnlockApp();
  }

// More code here
```

As you can see, you must also update the constructor and destructor of the server. The first function call to `EnableAutomation()` in the constructor is the result of your decisions in ClassWizard. Next, the program code must invoke the method `AfxOleLockApp()`, which ensures that the application will not be unloaded from memory until the reference count (that is, the number of currently open objects of the class) reaches zero. When you use OLE in MFC applications, you must always lock the application in memory by calling the locking method. This step is critical and you *must* include the function call in all MFC-based servers.

Next, the program code within the constructor creates a high-resolution timer and stores its current value in your member variables. The timer is useful for determining the number of milliseconds that have passed since the last method call was made. The timer output is great for tracking the performance of a particular action or set of actions.

You then get the current date and create a filename in the format of YYYYMMDD.tracklog. After successfully opening the file, you output some startup data to the file and exit the constructor.

The destructor does the exact opposite of the constructor. If there is a valid file handle, you write some closing information to the file and close it. Next, you terminate the timer. Remember to call the function AfxOleUnlockApp() to let the operating system remove the application from memory.

Finally, you must update the build settings for the project. Since the sample implementation is using some timer functions defined in mmsystem.h, you must also link your project with the appropriate library file that contains their implementation. To add the necessary linkage, select the Project menu Settings option. Visual C++ will display the Project Settings dialog box. In the Project Settings dialog box, from the Settings For drop-down list box, select the All Configurations entry. Select the Link tab, and add the file winmm.lib to the Object/library modules edit field. Click the OK button to close the dialog box.

The basic support code needed for the sample implementation is now added. The server will open a file in its constructor and leave the file open during its entire lifetime. When the server is destroyed, the destructor will be called and will close the file. The next step is to make the sample more meaningful by adding methods and properties, which you will use to output data to the open file.

16.2.1 Adding Methods to Your Server

An *automation method* consists of zero to *n* parameters and may or may not have a return value. The term *method* is synonymous with function or subroutine, depending on the particular language you are familiar with. Since your server is IDispatch-based, you are limited to a specific set of data types within your method calls. As you learned in the last chapter, you can only pass or return those data types that are valid VARIANT data types using a method.

As you learned at the beginning of this chapter, you will use the sample automation server to log strings of data to a file. The server will define the method OutputStrs(), which is used by the user of the server to supply the string data that the server writes to the file. The method will accept an array of strings and an optional indentation parameter and will output the strings to the file. The indentation parameter is used to offset the strings by *n* number of tab characters to provide simple, yet effective, formatting to the data as it is output to the file.

To add the method, select the View menu ClassWizard option. Select the Automation tab, and click the Add Method button. In the Add Method dialog box enter an External name of `OutputStrs` and a Return type of `BOOL`.

Core Note

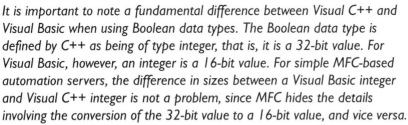

It is important to note a fundamental difference between Visual C++ and Visual Basic when using Boolean data types. The Boolean data type is defined by C++ as being of type integer, that is, it is a 32-bit value. For Visual Basic, however, an integer is a 16-bit value. For simple MFC-based automation servers, the difference in sizes between a Visual Basic integer and Visual C++ integer is not a problem, since MFC hides the details involving the conversion of the 32-bit value to a 16-bit value, and vice versa.

For dual-interface applications, though, the size difference poses a significant problem. When accessing the custom interface of a dual-interface server, the functions are called in the same fashion as any other function in an application. Basically, the operating system pushes the parameters of the function onto a stack, and then calls the function. When the function executes, the parameters are then popped off the stack. If Visual Basic calls a function in Visual C++, the stack will become corrupt because of the different sizes that each language uses for the Boolean data type. To be safe, Visual C++ applications should define all Boolean data types as type VARIANT_BOOL, which is defined by OLE as a 16-bit value and which is guaranteed to be the same size regardless of the language or tool being used.

The actual Boolean data value is different between Visual Basic and Visual C++ also. Visual Basic developers are used to Boolean values of 0 indicating FALSE and -1 indicating TRUE. For those of you who may be wondering why, the binary values are 0000000000000000 and 1111111111111111, respectively. For C++ programmers, Boolean data values are usually defined as 0 for FALSE and 1 or nonzero for TRUE.

The differences in Boolean data values can cause considerable problems when integrating Visual Basic and Visual C++ applications. In addition, Visual Basic 4 has some behavioral differences in its language, depending on the value being tested. Some Visual Basic functions do not test for 0 or nonzero and will test for the absolute value of 0 or -1, and vice versa, depending on the data type and function. When using Boolean data types, it is wise to also use the VARIANT_FALSE and VARIANT_TRUE constants to define the value of the variable.

You will define the `OutputStrs()` method to have two parameters, `varOutputArray` as a `VARIANT` passed by reference, which will contain a string array of data to output to the file, and `varIndent` as a `VARIANT` passed by value, which is also an optional parameter indicating the amount of indentation the server should use when writing the string data to the file. To add the method parameters, double-click the line in the Parameter list that is directly below the Name column, and type `varOutputArray`. Click directly under the Type column to activate the Type drop-down list box. Select `VARIANT *` from the list. Repeat the same process for `varIndent`, but set the data type to `VARIANT`. Figure 16-3 shows the Add Method dialog box after you perform your entries.

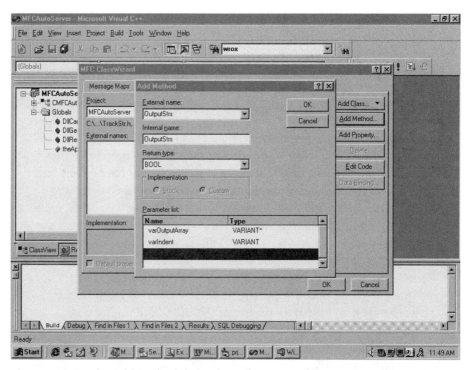

Figure 16-3   The Add Method dialog box after you perform your entries.

As you have learned, due to data type restrictions imposed by automation, you cannot pass arrays as parameters of methods, unless you write your own marshaling code. You can, however, pass `VARIANT` data types that can contain arrays. Therefore, in the sample server, you define `varOutputArray` as a VARIANT. In addition, you must define varOutputArray by reference because the array stored in the VARIANT does not get copied over when you pass the parameter by value.

As you also learned, optional parameters must fall at the end of the parameter list and must be of type VARIANT. The varIndent parameter is an optional parameter that indents the text output as an added formatting feature.

Remember that the ClassWizard added an entry to the ODL file as well as to the header and source files. It is a function of the ODL file to declare a parameter of a method as being optional. To be optional, a parameter must be declared with the optional parameter attribute. Remember, you must add the optional attribute by hand because ClassWizard will not add it for you. You will add the optional parameter attribute as shown in the following listing:

```
// NOTE - ClassWizard will maintain method information here.
// Use extreme caution when editing this section.
//{{AFX_ODL_METHOD(CTrackStr)
    [id(1)] boolean OutputStrs(VARIANT* varOutputArray,
        [optional] VARIANT varIndent);

//}}AFX_ODL_METHOD
```

Before you add the implementation of the OutputStrs() method, you first must add a member variable to the class definition. The server will use the new member, m_lIndent, to store the current indentation level between calls to the method OutputStrs(). You will add the new member to the TrackStr.h header file as shown here:

```
protected:
    FILE * m_fileLog;
    long m_lTimeBegin;
    long m_lHiResTime;
    long m_lLastHiResTime;
    long m_lIndent;

};
```

You also must update the constructor to initialize the member to a valid starting value (such as 0). After you perform the necessary steps to add and initialize the new member variable, you can write the OutputStrs() method. You will implement the OutputStrs() method as shown in the following code:

```
//////////////////////////////////////////////////////////////
// CTrackStr message handlers
BOOL CTrackStr::OutputStrs(VARIANT FAR* varOutputArray,
   const VARIANT FAR& varIndent)
{
  BOOL bResult = VARIANT_TRUE;
  // it is a file if the variant contains a string array
  if(m_fileLog && varOutputArray->vt ==
      (VT_ARRAY | VT_BSTR)) {
    // lock the array so we can use it
    if(::SafeArrayLock(varOutputArray->parray) == S_OK) {
      LONG lLBound;
      // get the lower bound of the array
      if(::SafeArrayGetLBound(varOutputArray->parray, 1,
          &lLBound) == S_OK) {
        LONG lUBound;
        // get the number of elements in the array
        if(::SafeArrayGetUBound(varOutputArray->parray, 1,
            &lUBound) == S_OK) {
          CString cstrIndent;
          CTime oTimeStamp;
          BSTR bstrTemp;
          // if we have an indent parameter
          if(varIndent.vt != VT_I4) {
            // get a variant for conversion purposes
            VARIANT varConvertedValue;

            // initialize the variant
            ::VariantInit(&varConvertedValue);

            /* try to  convert the data type to something
               useful-alternately you can use
               VariantChangeTypeEx() */
            if(S_OK ==
               ::VariantChangeType(&varConvertedValue,
               (VARIANT *) &varIndent, 0, VT_I4))
               // assign the value to our member variable
               m_lIndent = varConvertedValue.lVal;
          }
          else
            // assign the value to our member variable
            m_lIndent = varIndent.lVal;

          // if we have to indent the text
          for(long lIndentCount = 0;
            lIndentCount < m_lIndent;  lIndentCount++)
            // add a tab to the string
            cstrIndent += _T("\t");
```

```
            // for each of the elements in the array
            for(long lArrayCount = lLBound;
                lArrayCount < (lUBound + lLBound);
                lArrayCount++) {
                // update the time
                oTimeStamp = CTime::GetCurrentTime();
                m_lHiResTime = timeGetTime();

                // get the data from the array
                if(::SafeArrayGetElement(varOutputArray->parray,
                    &lArrayCount, &bstrTemp) == S_OK) {
                    // output the data
                    fprintf(m_fileLog, _T("%s(%10ld)-%s%ls\n"),
                        (LPCTSTR) oTimeStamp.Format("%H:%M:%S"),
                        m_lHiResTime - m_lLastHiResTime,
                        (LPCTSTR) cstrIndent, bstrTemp);

                    // store the last timer value
                    m_lLastHiResTime = m_lHiResTime;
                    // free the bstr
                    ::SysFreeString(bstrTemp);
                }
            }
        }
        else
          bResult = VARIANT_FALSE;
      }
    else
        bResult = VARIANT_FALSE;
      // unlock the array we don't need it anymore
      ::SafeArrayUnlock(varOutputArray->parray);
    }
  else
      bResult = VARIANT_FALSE;
  }
 else
    bResult = VARIANT_FALSE;
 // return the result
 return bResult;
}
```

First, the code within the method checks to see if it has a valid file handle and array of string data. The next step the code performs is to lock down the array so that you can perform operations on it. You must perform this step within all functions that you write that manipulate safe arrays. The next function call, `SafeArrayGetLBound()`, determines the starting point of the array, which can be either 0 or 1. This procedure is very important to implement since programming languages such as C++ define a base of 0 for arrays, and languages such as Visual Basic can define a base of 0 or 1. Next, you retrieve the number of dimensions in the array. Note that this value represents the number of dimensions and not the last dimension relative to the lower bound value.

After establishing the boundaries of the array, your code must check to see if the function also received an indentation value. You want to receive a long, VT_I4, but if you do not receive it, you try to convert the data that was given to you to a usable value. If you cannot convert the data, you simply use the value that the variable already contains. To indent the text, the function will concatenate from 1 to *n* tab characters into the beginning of the string.

For each of the elements in the array of strings, the function gets the current time and the data associated with each element, and then outputs the string along with the indentation string to the open file. Then, the function frees the string element when it finishes with it. Finally, the program code unlocks the array and exits the method with the proper return value.

It is worthwhile to review the documentation on ODL, automation, and VARIANT data types in the Visual C++ books online to see what kind of flexibility you have when defining methods and parameters. Now that you have added a method, you are ready to implement its counterpart — the property.

16.2.2 Adding Properties to the Server

A *property* can be thought of as an exposed variable that is defined in the automation server. Properties are useful for setting and retrieving information about the state of the server. You will implement properties within your server as a pair of methods — one to get the value, and the other to set the value. The m_lIndent member variable that you added to the class definition is a perfect candidate for the server to expose as a property.

As with methods, you can add properties to your server using the Class-Wizard in MFC. To add a property, select the View menu ClassWizard option. In the MFC ClassWizard dialog box, select the Automation tab, and click the Add Property button. In the Add Property dialog box, enter the external name of the property as Indent and select the type as long. Set the Implementation to Get/Set methods, and click OK to add the property to the server. Click the Edit Code button to close the MFC ClassWizard dialog and open the source file for editing. Figure 16-4 shows the Add Property dialog box after you make your entries.

Figure 16-4   Using the Add Property dialog box to add the Indent property.

The actual implementation of the Indent property is very easy. The GetIndent() function returns the value currently stored in the member variable, and the SetIndent() function stores the new value, after a little bit of error checking, in the member variable. You will implement the property-management functions as shown here:

```
long CTrackStr::GetIndent()
  {
    // return the member variable
    return m_lIndent;
  }

void CTrackStr::SetIndent(long nNewValue)
  {
    // if the new value is a least 0
    if(nNewValue >= 0)
      // assign the value to our member variable
      m_lIndent = nNewValue;
  }
```

Properties, like methods, have a wide variety of implementation options, including parameterized and enumerated values.

So far, you have added methods and properties to the server but have not really dealt with the issue of error handling in their implementation. In some cases, simply returning success or failure is not enough information for the developer to understand that an error occurred and what caused the error. You will communicate more error information through the use of OLE exceptions, which you will learn about in the next section.

16.3   Generating OLE Exceptions

While executing a method call or some other action, at times it is necessary to terminate the process due to some critical error that has occurred or is about to occur. For example, the controlling program calls a server method to write data to a file, but the server cannot open the file or write data to the file because there is not enough room on the hard disk to do so. It is necessary to halt further processing until the error can be resolved. An error of this kind is known as an *exception.* Any type of error can be treated as an exception. How you treat errors depends on the requirements of your application and how you choose to deal with the errors that may result.

You must become familiar with two forms of exceptions when creating ActiveX components. The first is a C++ exception. A *C++ exception* is a language mechanism used to create critical errors of the type described earlier and is confined to the application in which they are defined. The second is an OLE exception. *OLE exceptions* are used to communicate the same kinds of errors externally to applications that are using a component. The difference between the two is that C++ exceptions are entirely internal to an application's implementation, and you can use OLE exceptions both internally and externally, though you will generally use them to communicate errors to other applications.

The `IDispatch` interface contains specific parameters in its functions for dealing with exceptions and passing them to the controller application. The MFC implementation of the `CCmdTarget` class handles the details of generating OLE exceptions. The class' default definition traps any C++ exceptions that the class receives and translates the C++ exception to the proper `IDispatch` error information. You need only create a C++ exception of type `COleDispatchException` and `throw` the exception. MFC does all of the work for you. When you create dual-interface servers, you must handle exceptions somewhat differently. You will learn how to manage dual-interface server exceptions later in this chapter.

The first step you must take to prepare to handle OLE exceptions is to add an enumeration of the types of errors that the server can generate to the ODL file. Adding the enumeration to the ODL has the effect of publishing the error constants to the applications developer that is using the server. You add the constants in the form of an include file so you can use the same error constants file in the C++ source code implementation. You also add a UUID that is generated with the GUIDGEN.EXE program to the typedef so that it can be identified in the type library. You will implement the enumeration within the sample server program as shown here:

```
// more code here

[ uuid(11C82947-4EDD-11D0-BED8-00400538977D) ]
coclass TRACKSTR
  {
    [default] dispinterface ITrackStr;
  };

typedef [uuid(11C82948-4EDD-11D0-BED8-00400538977D),
    helpstring("TrackStr Error Constants")]
#include "trackstrerror.h"
//{{AFX_APPEND_ODL}}

};
```

The TrackStrError.h file, in turn, will contain a standard C/C++ enumeration of the errors that the application supports. The starting value of the errors falls into the range of valid user-defined errors. Be careful when you assign error numbers within your own applications because most tools will first look up the system-defined error message before using the message defined in the exception file. You will implement the TrackStrError.h file as shown here:

```
// Error enumeration
enum tagTrackStrError
  {
    MFCSERVER_E_NO_UBOUND = 46080,
    MFCSERVER_E_NO_LBOUND = 46081,
    MFCSERVER_E_NO_ARRAYLOCK = 46082,
    MFCSERVER_E_NO_FILE = 46083,
    MFCSERVER_E_BAD_ARRAY_PARAMETER = 46084,
    MFCSERVER_E_INVALID_VALUE = 46085
  }  TRACKSTRERROR;
```

After you define the exception values and set the ODL file to indicate the error values within the type library, the next step is to add the code that will generate the exceptions to all of the appropriate locations in the server code.

Instead of returning `VARIANT_FALSE` (or, worse yet, ignoring an error condition), the code will now generate meaningful errors and messages instructing the developer as to the source of the problem. The exception-generating code is fairly straightforward. First you create a pointer to a `COleDispatchException` object and set the appropriate members with the data that is necessary for the error that was generated (for information about other types of exceptions, see the Visual C++ documentation). For your implementation, you set the error code, the name of the file that generated the error, and the error message. You could also supply a help file-name and a help ID to further describe the error. Note the use of the `MAKE_SCODE` macro to generate a valid `SCODE` error number for the exception.

Exceptions are useful for communicating error conditions and problems back to the application and developer who are using an ActiveX component. Make use of them whenever you can to further enhance your implementation.

16.3.1 Understanding Dual-Interface Servers

A dual-interface server is exactly what it sounds like: The server implementation supports two interfaces with which to talk to the server. One interface, an `IDispatch` *interface*, is what you have been working with so far. The other, a *custom interface*, is a type of interface that you have not learned about yet. The dual portion refers to the fact that no matter which interface you choose, you are always talking to the same server, and you will always get the same response.

An `IDispatch`-based interface uses a generic mechanism for calling methods and properties in a server. When a method in a server is called, you pass the ID of the method to invoke and a structure describing its parameters and return type. This data is packaged and sent to the server, which unpackages the data and calls the appropriate method based on the ID supplied. A custom interface, on the other hand, is very different. When using a custom interface, you are talking directly to the server's functions and are not depending on a generic mechanism for invoking the methods or properties. The packaging of the parameters and return value are left to the compiler that created the applications.

Since the interfaces are written to access the same set of functions, the custom interface portion of a dual-interface server must conform to the same data type restrictions imposed by automation. This way, you are not required to create your own code to transfer data between the two applications, the controller, and the server. OLE does that for you with standard marshaling.

The major advantage to dual-interface is performance. The number of steps to call a method using the custom interface is far less than the number needed to call a method when using the `IDispatch` interface. The main disadvantage to dual-interface support in MFC servers is that they are not supported by the ClassWizard and will require manual changes for you to implement both interfaces. After you create the custom interface, the code involved with the interface is not too difficult to maintain.

Core Note

The advantage of using the custom interface of a dual-interface server loses its luster when executing across process boundaries. The custom interface is still faster, but not by much. The real performance benefit, a 25 to 50 percent improvement, is when the server is in-process to the calling application. The amount of improvement depends on the number and types of parameters that are being passed between the applications. If you are interested in seeing actual numbers regarding the amount of performance improvement, you can refer to the Microsoft Systems Journal archives (on Microsoft's Web site at http://www.microsoft.com/msj), which include several articles that specifically focus on performance differences between `IDispatch` *and custom interfaces.*

The first step when converting an MFC-based ActiveX server to dual-interface is to change the ODL file. It is not necessary to generate new UUIDs because the functionality of the server has not changed. You must add the `oleautomation` and `dual` attributes to the interface class, though. You must also add the `hidden` attribute, so this second interface will not be visible within Visual Basic. This is fine since Visual Basic will display the `CoClass` interface and will also show all of the methods and properties for the server. As a general rule, you should always hide your interfaces and leave visible the `CoClasses` the controller will use to create them. This is because applications like Visual Basic will display both interfaces, and the reality is that only the `CoClass` name is valid in Visual Basic. In other words, if you try to reference an object by its interface name, you will get an error. The necessary changes that you must make to the ODL file to support dual-interface are in the ODLList2.txt file.

You do not have to change the remainder of the ODL file entries to support dual-interface. However, because the server supports dual-interface, you must change your interface declaration to inherit from the `IDispatch` interface rather than declare the interface as type `dispinterface`, as in the original implementation. Dual-interface method and property declarations are different from `dispinterface` declarations, which are more like standard C++. Note that keywords such as `method` and `properties` are no longer within the interface declaration. Those terms are keywords related to the `dispinterface` keyword. As we stated earlier, properties are accessed using a pair of methods sharing the same `dispid`. The distinguishing factors are the method attributes `propget` and `propput`, which denote the direction of data flow. You must also change the `CoClass` to refer to `interface` and not `dispinterface`.

All dual-interface methods must return an `HRESULT` data type. If a method requires a return value, it must be specified as the last parameter of the method and must have the parameter attributes of `out` and `retval`. All parameters must have an attribute describing the direction of data flow. Table 16-3 contains a complete description of the possible attributes and combinations.

Table 16-3 Parameter Flow Attributes

Attribute	Description
in	Parameter is passed from caller to callee.
out	Parameter is returned from callee to caller.
in, out	Parameter is passed from caller to callee, and the callee returns a parameter.
out, retval	Parameter is the return value of the method and is returned from the callee to the caller.

Core Note

The changes that you have made to the ODL file will prevent the ClassWizard from updating the ODL file automatically when you add new methods and properties to the server. You are now responsible for maintaining the entries manually.

The ODL compiler has the capability of generating a C++ header file that describes all of the interfaces and enumerations that are contained in the type library that you have created for your server. The ODL-generated header file is useful for creating function prototypes that are required in the implementation of the server. You add the entry to the ODL file and compile it into a type library. Next, copy the new method from the header file into your class definition, make some minor changes, and everything is finished. In addition, you now have an interface file that can be used by other applications to access the custom interface of your server as well as the enumerations that are used when accessing specific methods and properties.

To generate the header file, you must update the build settings of your project. To update the build settings, select the Project menu Settings option. Visual Studio will display the Project Settings dialog box. In the Settings For drop-down list box, select All Configurations. Expand the MFCAutoServer project node and the Source Files node, and select the MFCAutoServer.odl file. Select the MIDL tab, and in the Output header file name edit field, enter the name TrackStrInterface.h. Whenever the type library is compiled, the compiler will regenerate the TrackStrInterface.h file to reflect the new implementation. Figure 16-5 shows the Project Settings dialog box after you make your changes.

After you make the changes to the build settings, you must include the new header file within the TrackStr.cpp source file. You must also remove the TrackStrError.h file because the error enumeration that you declared earlier in the chapter is also defined in the header file generated by the ODL compiler. The TrackStrInterface.h file must be included *before* or *in* the Track-Str.h file, as the `CTrackStr` class is dependent on the information in the TrackStrInterface.h file. In other words, your include statements should appear in the following order within the TrackStr.cpp file:

```
#include "MFCAutoServer.h"
// ODL generated interface file
#include "trackstrinterface.h"
#include "TrackStr.h"
// needed for the high resolution timer services
#include <mmsystem.h>
// more code here
```

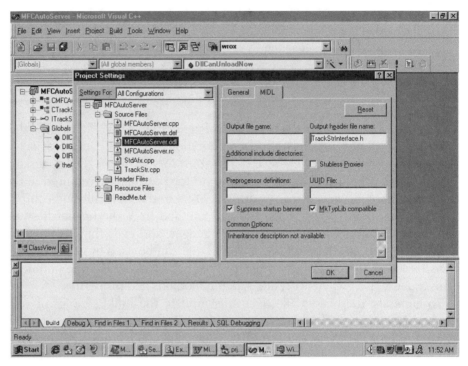

Figure 16-5 After you update the settings to create the C++ header file from the ODL file, the Project Settings dialog will display this information.

MFC defines a set of macros for describing interfaces within the context of an MFC component implementation. The interface macro defines the interface, its name, and the methods it contains. You must add the MFC interface declaration to your class definition to describe the custom interface portion of your server. You can add the interface declaration anywhere after the DECLARE_INTERFACE_MAP macro. You will implement the interface declaration within the TrackStr.h file as shown in the following code:

```
// more code here
// needed for dual interface support
BEGIN_INTERFACE_PART(SubDispatch, ITrackStr)
   STDMETHOD(GetTypeInfoCount)(THIS_ UINT FAR* pctinfo);
   STDMETHOD(GetTypeInfo)(THIS_ UINT itinfo, LCID lcid,
      ITypeInfo FAR* FAR* pptinfo);
   STDMETHOD(GetIDsOfNames)(THIS_ REFIID riid,
      OLECHAR FAR* FAR* rgszNames, UINT cNames, LCID lcid,
      DISPID FAR* rgdispid);
```

```
STDMETHOD(Invoke)(THIS_ DISPID dispidMember, REFIID riid,
    LCID lcid, WORD wFlags, DISPPARAMS FAR* pdispparams,
    VARIANT FAR* pvarResult, EXCEPINFO FAR* pexcepinfo,
    UINT FAR* puArgErr);
virtual /* [propget][id] */ HRESULT STDMETHODCALLTYPE
    get_Indent(/* [retval][out] */ long __RPC_FAR *Value);

virtual /* [propput][id] */ HRESULT STDMETHODCALLTYPE
    put_Indent(/* [in] */ long Value);
virtual /* [id] */ HRESULT STDMETHODCALLTYPE
    OutputStrs(
    /* [in] */ VARIANT __RPC_FAR *varOutputArray,
    /* [optional][in] */ VARIANT varIndent,
    /* [retval][out] */ VARIANT_BOOL __RPC_FAR *RetVal);

END_INTERFACE_PART(SubDispatch)
// more code here
```

The first parameter of the BEGIN_INTERFACE_PART macro, SubDispatch, is the name that is used to create a nested class within the class definition of the server. The second parameter is the name of the interface from which the nested class is inherited. The ITrackStr interface is declared in the TrackStrInterface.h header file that was created from the ODL file. The ITrackStr declaration in the header file contains a set of pure virtual functions that need to be copied into your interface declaration. When copying the functions, remember to remove the = 0 from the end of the function, since this is where you will implement them.

The header file contains the interface declaration, and the source file contains the interface implementation. The MFC AppWizard created a default interface implementation for the server when it was created. The original definition deferred to the default IDispatch interface defined in MFC. Since you have implemented an interface that inherits from IDispatch, it is necessary to route all IDispatch calls to the new interface. The interface map located in the server source file must be changed to reflect the new interface that you have declared. Change the interface from IDispatch to the name of the interface declared in the header file, in your case SubDispatch. Changing the name of the interface will have the effect of routing all calls to the IDispatch interface to your implementation of the interface first, which you can then implement yourself or pass on to the default implementation. You will implement the ITrackStr interface within the TrackStr.cpp file as shown here:

```
// more code here
BEGIN_INTERFACE_MAP(CTrackStr, CCmdTarget)
   INTERFACE_PART(CTrackStr, IID_IDispatch, SubDispatch)
   INTERFACE_PART(CTrackStr, IID_ITrackStr, SubDispatch)
END_INTERFACE_MAP()
```

Unfortunately, MFC does not allow for true C++ inheritance of the COM interfaces it contains, so it is necessary to route messages for a particular COM interface to the correct handler function in the server. Routing the messages is done through the `BEGIN_INTERFACE_MAP` macro. Since your implementation supports both an `IDispatch` interface and a custom interface, you are required to add two entries to the macro (one for each interface). In your case, you defer all `IDispatch` messages to the custom interface functions. The same is true of the custom interface messages.

The last step in adding dual-interface support to your server is to add the actual implementation of the functions declared in the interface. The first set of functions to implement is the base `IDispatch` functions that your server inherited from the `IDispatch` class. In all cases, you defer to the base class implementation of the method. You have the option of implementing these functions yourself or of relying on MFC to handle the methods for you. An important thing to note is the method you must use to call the basic `IDispatch` functions. Since the server captures all `IDispatch` messages and routes them to the custom interface implementation, you cannot call `GetIDispatch()` to retrieve the pointer to the `IDispatch` interface of the server (because doing so would result in a recursive call since the `IDispatch` functions are routed to your server implementation). Instead, the implementation must call the `IDispatch` functions `((IDispatch*)&pThis->m_xDispatch)->` directly, bypassing the message routing functions, which avoids the recursion problem. You will implement the functions as shown in the following:

```
///////////////////////////////////////////////////////////
// CTrackStr Standard IDispatch Dual Interface Handlers
ULONG FAR EXPORT CTrackStr::XSubDispatch::AddRef()
 {
   METHOD_PROLOGUE(CTrackStr, SubDispatch)
   return pThis->ExternalAddRef();
 }

ULONG FAR EXPORT CTrackStr::XSubDispatch::Release()
 {
   METHOD_PROLOGUE(CTrackStr, SubDispatch)
   return pThis->ExternalRelease();
 }
```

```
HRESULT FAR EXPORT CTrackStr::XSubDispatch::
    QueryInterface(REFIID riid, LPVOID FAR* ppvObj)
{
  METHOD_PROLOGUE(CTrackStr, SubDispatch)
  return (HRESULT) pThis->
      ExternalQueryInterface(&riid, ppvObj);
}

HRESULT FAR EXPORT CTrackStr::XSubDispatch::
    GetTypeInfoCount(UINT FAR* pctinfo)
{
  METHOD_PROLOGUE(CTrackStr, SubDispatch)
  return ((IDispatch*)&pThis->m_xDispatch)->
      GetTypeInfoCount(pctinfo);
}

HRESULT FAR EXPORT CTrackStr::XSubDispatch::
    GetTypeInfo(UINT itinfo, LCID lcid,
    ITypeInfo FAR* FAR* pptinfo)
{
  METHOD_PROLOGUE(CTrackStr, SubDispatch)
  return ((IDispatch*)&pThis->m_xDispatch)->
      GetTypeInfo(itinfo, lcid, pptinfo);
}

HRESULT FAR EXPORT CTrackStr::XSubDispatch::
    GetIDsOfNames(REFIID riid, OLECHAR FAR* FAR* rgszNames,
    UINT cNames, LCID lcid, DISPID FAR* rgdispid)
{
  METHOD_PROLOGUE(CTrackStr, SubDispatch)
  return ((IDispatch*)&pThis->m_xDispatch)->
      GetIDsOfNames(riid, rgszNames, cNames, lcid, rgdispid);
}

HRESULT FAR EXPORT CTrackStr::XSubDispatch::
    Invoke(DISPID dispidMember, REFIID riid, LCID lcid,
    WORD wFlags, DISPPARAMS FAR* pdispparams,
    VARIANT FAR* pvarResult,EXCEPINFO FAR* pexcepinfo,
    UINT FAR* puArgErr)
{
  METHOD_PROLOGUE(CTrackStr, SubDispatch)
  return ((IDispatch*)&pThis->m_xDispatch)->
      Invoke(dispidMember, riid, lcid, wFlags, pdispparams,
      pvarResult, pexcepinfo, puArgErr);
}
```

You should note that you must declare the nested class SubDispatch as XSubDispatch in the implementation. The X comes from the

BEGIN_INTERFACE_PART macros and has no particular significance. The same is true for the member variable m_xDispatch.

Note the use of the macro METHOD_PROLOGUE, which is required in MFC-based applications to ensure that MFC is in a valid state while the function is executing.

The last step in building your dual-interface server is to implement the functions that are specific to your server. You can simplify the implementation by calling the original MFC functions from the dual-interface implementations rather than reimplementing the functions using the new style. Doing so solves several problems. First, you can still rely on the MFC message mapping functions to invoke the methods when you call them through the IDispatch interface, and it does not require you to implement your own IDispatch code. Supporting the original MFC implementation also prevents you from having to change internal code that may rely on the already existing functions. As you will see a little later in this chapter, adding error handling to the dual-interface code is much simpler using this style. You will implement the ITrackStr functions within the TrackStr.cpp file as shown in the following code listing:

```
// CTrackStr interface handlers
HRESULT CTrackStr::XSubDispatch::get_Indent(LONG * Indent)
{
  METHOD_PROLOGUE(CTrackStr, SubDispatch)
  HRESULT hResult = S_OK;
  *Indent = pThis->GetIndent();
  return hResult;
}


HRESULT CTrackStr::XSubDispatch::put_Indent(LONG Indent)
{
  METHOD_PROLOGUE(CTrackStr, SubDispatch)
  HRESULT hResult = S_OK;
  pThis->SetIndent(Indent);
  return hResult;
}


HRESULT FAR EXPORT CTrackStr::XSubDispatch::
    OutputStrs(VARIANT FAR* varOutputArray,
    VARIANT varIndent, VARIANT_BOOL FAR* RetVal)
{
  METHOD_PROLOGUE(CTrackStr, SubDispatch)
  HRESULT hResult = S_OK;
  *RetVal = pThis->OutputStrs(varOutputArray, varIndent);
  return hResult;
}
```

After you compile the server and register it, you are ready to test its new dual-interface functionality. From C++, you will create the server as you did before, but now you may access its custom interface by using the `Query-Interface()` function and supplying the correct interface IID. From Visual Basic, you need only add the type library for the server to your list of references and change the name of the variable to the name that appears in the Object References dialog box. You can also create the server using the Visual Basic New operator instead of the `CreateObject()` method. In other words, the following Visual Basic program code will now execute properly:

```
Dim MyTrackStr as TRACKSTR
Set MyTrackStr = new TRACKSTR
```

In C++, you call the `QueryInterface()` function and pass the `IID ITrackStr` interface IID. The last step in your dual-interface conversion is to handle errors correctly. As a general rule, a server cannot throw C++ exceptions from the custom interface implementation of a dual-interface server. For that matter, it can't throw them from any interface. MFC just does the job of catching the C++ exceptions for you and converting them to OLE exceptions that are understood by OLE. Since you are supporting a custom interface in your server, you must do the same — that is, convert the C++ exceptions into OLE exceptions that your server can pass back through either interface to the controlling program.

16.3.2 Generating Dual-Interface OLE Exceptions

Dual-interface rules for handling errors and exceptions are slightly different for the custom interface portion of the interface. As you learned earlier in this chapter, you must change all of the methods in the custom interface to return an `HRESULT` in place of the function's normal return value. An `HRESULT` is used to indicate that an error or exception has occurred within the context of the method that was invoked. When an automation controller invokes a method in the custom interface of a server, it should check the return value of the function to see if it returned `S_OK`. If not, the controller has the option of checking to see whether the server supports extended error information via the `ISupportErrorInfo` interface. When a server that supports the `ISupportErrorInfo` interface creates an error, it does so by creating an `IErrorInfo` object containing the error information.

MFC does not support the `ISupportErrorInfo` interface by default, so you must add it yourself. You can create a set of macros to aid in adding the `ISupportErrorInfo` interface to your automation server. The macros are based on those defined in the `ACDUAL` sample included with MFC, and you can use them to simplify the `ISupportErrorInfo` implementation.

In addition, you must add a macro and a helper function to the class declaration of the server. The macro declares the `ISupportErrorInfo` interface, and the helper function is used to translate the exception into an `IErrorInfo` object. You will implement the changes within the TrackStr.h header file as shown here:

```
// more code here

    DECLARE_OLECREATE(CTrackStr)
    // add declaration of ISupportErrorInfo implementation
    // to indicate Server supports the OLE Automation
    // error object
    DECLARE_DUAL_ERRORINFO()
    HRESULT CreateErrorInfo(CException * pAnyException,
        REFIID riidSource);

    // needed for dual interface support
    BEGIN_INTERFACE_PART(SubDispatch, ITrackStr)

// more code here
```

Now that you have created your interface declaration within the header file, you must add the interface to the interface map. You must also add the implementation macro for the interface and add the implementation of the helper function. You will implement the changes within the TrackStr.cpp file as shown in the following:

```
BEGIN_INTERFACE_MAP(CTrackStr, CCmdTarget)
    INTERFACE_PART(CTrackStr, IID_ITrackStr, SubDispatch)
    DUAL_ERRORINFO_PART(CTrackStr)
END_INTERFACE_MAP()

IMPLEMENT_OLECREATE(CTrackStr, _T("MFCAutoServer.TrackStr"),
    0x11C82947, 0x4edd, 0x11d0, 0xbe, 0xd8, 0x0, 0x40, 0x5,
    0x38, 0x97, 0x7d)

// Implement ISupportErrorInfo to indicate server supports the
// OLE Automation error handler.
IMPLEMENT_DUAL_ERRORINFO(CTrackStr, IID_ITrackStr)

/* this code is based on the ACDUAL MFC\OLE sample application
    provided with Visual C++ */
HRESULT CTrackStr::CreateErrorInfo(CException * pAnyException,
```

```
   REFIID riidSource)
{
  ASSERT_VALID(pAnyException);
  // create an error info object
  ICreateErrorInfo * pcerrinfo;
  HRESULT hr = ::CreateErrorInfo(&pcerrinfo);

  // if succeessful
  if(SUCCEEDED(hr)) {
    // dispatch exception?
    if(pAnyException->
        IsKindOf(RUNTIME_CLASS(COleDispatchException))) {
        // specific IDispatch style exception
        COleDispatchException * e =
            (COleDispatchException *) pAnyException;
        // set the return value to the error
        hr = e->m_scError;

        // Set up ErrInfo object
        pcerrinfo->SetGUID(riidSource);
        pcerrinfo->SetDescription(e->
            m_strDescription.AllocSysString());
        pcerrinfo->SetHelpContext(e->m_dwHelpContext);
        pcerrinfo->
            SetHelpFile(e->m_strHelpFile.AllocSysString());
        pcerrinfo->
            SetSource(e->m_strSource.AllocSysString());
    }
    else if (pAnyException->
      IsKindOf(RUNTIME_CLASS(CMemoryException))) {
      // failed memory allocation
      hr = E_OUTOFMEMORY;

      // Set up ErrInfo object
      pcerrinfo->SetGUID(riidSource);
      CString cstrFileName(AfxGetAppName());
      pcerrinfo->SetSource(cstrFileName.AllocSysString());
    }
    else {
      // other unknown/unexpected error
      hr = E_UNEXPECTED;
      // Set up ErrInfo object
      pcerrinfo->SetGUID(riidSource);
      CString cstrFileName(AfxGetAppName());
      pcerrinfo->SetSource(cstrFileName.AllocSysString());
    }
```

```
   // QI for the IErrorInfo interface
   IErrorInfo * perrinfo;
   if(SUCCEEDED(pcerrinfo->
       QueryInterface(IID_IErrorInfo, (LPVOID *) &perrinfo))) {
       // set the error info object
       ::SetErrorInfo(0, perrinfo);
       // release the reference
       perrinfo->Release();
     }
   // release the reference
   pcerrinfo->Release();
   }
 // delete the exception
 pAnyException->Delete();

 // return the error value
 return hr;
}
```

The `CreateErrorInfo()` function translates any exception into an `IErrorInfo` object. The function is based on code that is part of the ACDUAL MFC sample application included with MFC. The primary responsibility of the function is to convert `COleDispatchExceptions` into `IErrorInfo` objects. It can, however, deal with any exception that it is passed, but the level of information about the error is far less. After the exception has been translated, it is set as the error information object for the currently executing thread.

The last step is to update the custom interface methods to defer all exceptions to the helper function that you just added. The additional code that you will need is straightforward and simple to implement. For each of the methods, you wrap the call to the basic implementation of the function with a `try...catch` block that will translate any exception into an `IErrorInfo` object and return the error code of the exception to the calling application. You will implement the additional code within the TrackStr.cpp file.

Thus far, we have covered all of the basics of ActiveX server creation and use by applications other than your own. However, there may be situations in which you must create and use the server from within the application in which it is defined. Or, there may be situations in which your application contains more than one server implementation, with only one server being exposed as a createable object and with the remaining servers being created only in response to a valid method call in the exposed server. These are referred to as *nested objects*. There are many techniques you can use to add additional power to your server objects. In the remainder of this chapter, you will consider three specific management cases for your automation servers: instantiating from C++, creating shared servers, and creating single-use servers.

16.4   Server Instantiation Using C++

While you have spent much of this chapter learning how to create and use automation servers with MFC and OLE, this is not the only method for creating and using automation servers that is available to you. You can also instantiate automation servers using C++ syntax.

At times, instantiating and using automation servers is necessary from within the application that defines the server. For example, there might be a situation in which an application contains three servers, only one of which is directly createable by outside applications using OLE. The remaining two servers can be created by the exposed server using C++ and returned via a method call to another application, which then uses the server as though it was created via OLE.

As you learned earlier in this chapter, for an application to be created by another application using OLE, the server must include the MFC macros DECLARE_OLECREATE and IMPLEMENT_OLECREATE. By removing or not including these macros, you can specify that other applications cannot instantiate the server using standard OLE server creation mechanisms. That fact, however, does not prevent the server from being created using C++ and MFC. Note, though, that you can create any OLE server in this fashion, as opposed to just those that are not createable through standard OLE mechanisms. MFC supports a facility for creating OLE servers using a helper class known as CRuntimeClass.

You can use the CRuntimeClass object to create servers that you will use internally to the application in which you define the servers and externally as a return or parameter value supplied to another application. To support CRuntimeClass creation of objects, a class must define either the IMPLEMENT_DYNAMIC macro, the IMPLEMENT_DYNCREATE macro, or the IMPLEMENT_SERIAL macro within their class implementation, which is true for any MFC class inherited for CObject, and not just those classes that utilize OLE.

The following listing is not included in the sample applications because of its simplicity. However, the listing does use the CTrackStr server as its example server. To create a server using the CRuntimeClass, you will use code similar to the following:

```
// create a CTrackStr runtime object
CRuntimeClass * pRuntimeClass = RUNTIME_CLASS(CTrackStr);

// create an CTrackStr OLE object
CTrackStr * opTrackStr =
    (CTrackStr *) pRuntimeClass->CreateObject();

// use the object as the application requires

// finished with the object - destroy it
delete opTrackStr;
```

After you create an object, you can also pass the object to another application. MFC supports two functions for retrieving OLE interfaces from a running server: the `GetIDispatch()` and `GetInterface()` functions. `GetIDispatch()` is defined and explained within the Visual C++ help file, but the `GetInterface()` function is not. `GetInterface()` accepts a single parameter — the IID of the interface that is being requested. `GetInterface()` will not increment the reference count of the pointer that is returned. The `GetIDispatch()` function gives you the option to increment the reference counter for the pointer.

16.4.1 *Common Problems When Instantiating OLE Servers Using C++*

Two problems arise when instantiating OLE components using C++: reference counting and in-process versus out-of-process execution. For reference counting, the problems can be that too many or too few reference counts exist on the server being used. Reference counting problems can arise regardless of how the server is instantiated, with either C++ or OLE. The problem is really relative to using servers in one-to-many relationships. All of the applications that use the same server must `AddRef()` and `Release()` the server properly to prevent problems. Reference counting problems manifest themselves as either the server terminating before it should or not terminating when it should. Be sure to check that all reference counts are being incremented and decremented correctly when creating and using objects in a one-to-many relationship or when a server is created and passed to another application.

The next problem that can arise is far more subtle and easier to miss, although the effects can be dramatic and obvious and involve the server's execution model. A server is not guaranteed to execute in-process to the application that is using it — only with the application that created it.

For example, Application A creates and uses an in-process server called Server 1. At some point, Application A creates an out-of-process server called Application B. Application A passes Server 1 to Application B. Server 1 will execute as an out-of-process server to Application B since the Server 1 object was created in the process space of Application A. This is important to keep in mind when creating and using nested objects or shared objects since the performance differences between the two is so great.

So far you have only looked at how to create individual instances of objects. Next you will look at how to share objects — that is, let multiple containers access a single running instance of an object.

16.5   Creating Shareable Servers

OLE defines a facility for sharing objects called the *Running Object Table.* Essentially, a shareable object will publish its CLSID and an IUnknown reference to itself in the Running Object Table. Any application that so desires can ask for the running instance of the object rather than create a new instance. Using shared objects is useful for applications that may need to work with a single running instance of an application rather than create multiple copies. The TrackStr object is a perfect candidate for this type of basic functionality. Multiple applications could use the same TrackStr object to log information, thus saving memory.

The first step in enabling shared-object support is to add a member variable to store the ID that will identify the object in the Running Object Table. This ID must be retained since it is used later in revoking the object from the Running Object Table when the object is destroyed. For the sample implementation, you add the variable as a public member of the class. You will add the variable within the TrackStr.h header file as shown here:

```
// more code here
END_INTERFACE_PART(SubDispatch)
public:
   DWORD m_dwRegister;

protected:
   FILE * m_fileLog;

// more code here
```

When registering a server in the Running Object Table, you use the CLSID of the CoClass object to identify the object in the table. Your implementation requires that you declare the CLSID of the CoClass object in the source file. The CLSID is copied from the TrackStrInterface.h header file and added to the source file. The line before the CLSID should be the include file initguid.h. The initguid.h file is needed to properly declare the CLSID and resolve it to the compiler. You will implement the CLSID declaration within the TrackStr.cpp file as shown here:

```
// more code here

static const IID IID_ITrackStr =
    { 0x11c82946, 0x4edd, 0x11d0, { 0xbe, 0xd8, 0x0, 0x40,
      0x5, 0x38, 0x97, 0x7d }
#include <initguid.h>

DEFINE_GUID(CLSID_TRACKSTR, 0x11C82947L, 0x4EDD, 0x11D0, 0xBE,
    0xD8, 0x00,  0x40, 0x05, 0x38, 0x97, 0x7D);
BEGIN_INTERFACE_MAP(CTrackStr, CCmdTarget)

// more code here
```

Next, you must add the code to the server that registers the object as running in the Running Object Table. The specifics of your server will determine the exact location where you register the server as running. For your implementation, the constructor is fine. Other implementations may be dependent on a particular state being reached in the server before registering the server. The decision is completely up to you and your specific implementation. You will implement the CTrackStr shared object support in the constructor of the CTrackStr class as shown here:

```
// more code here

EnableAutomation();
    // make sure that the application won't unload until the
    // reference count is 0
    ::AfxOleLockApp();

    // clear the member
    m_dwRegister = NULL;

    // QI for the IUnknown - remember no AddRef
    LPUNKNOWN pIUnknown = this->GetInterface(&IID_IUnknown);

    // if have an IUnknown
    if(pIUnknown) {
```

```
    // register the clsid as an active object so other
    // applications will get the same object
    if(::RegisterActiveObject(pIUnknown, CLSID_TRACKSTR,
        ACTIVEOBJECT_STRONG, &m_dwRegister) != S_OK)
      // make sure that the reference is clear
      m_dwRegister = NULL;
  }
  // setup the timer resolution
  m_lTimeBegin = timeBeginPeriod(1);
  m_lHiResTime = m_lLastHiResTime = timeGetTime();

  // more code here
```

In your implementation, the first step is to clear the member variable. The implementation is dependent on this member to identify whether the object was successfully registered as running or not. Next, you must retrieve the IUnknown reference for the object and, if successful, pass it along with an address of the member variable to the RegisterActiveObject() function. You specify a strong registration that will result in an extra reference count on the server to keep it in memory. If you didn't register the server, make sure to clear the member variable, just to be safe.

The last step is to call RevokeActiveObject() to remove the server from the Running Object Table. This step is the most critical aspect of shared object support. Do not add this code to the destructor of your server, as it will never be called. The destructor is called in response to the destruction of the server, which results from the server reference count reaching 0. Since the server has an extra reference count from the RegisterActiveObject() call, the server will never reach this state. To ensure that you properly remove the server from the table, your best course of action is to implement the revocation in the Release() function of the IUnknown implementation of your server so that the server's reference count can be monitored. You will implement the Release() function as shown in the following code to remove the object from the Running Object Table.

```
// more code here
ULONG FAR EXPORT CTrackStr::XSubDispatch::Release()
  {
    METHOD_PROLOGUE(CTrackStr, SubDispatch)

    // call the function and check the refcount
    long lRefCount = pThis->ExternalRelease();

    // if server running and this is the only refcount left
    if(pThis->m_dwRegister && lRefCount == 1) {
```

```
        // bump the refcount up so the routine doesn't destroy
        // the server until it is done
        pThis->ExternalAddRef();

        // get the registration ID
        DWORD tdwRegister = pThis->m_dwRegister;

        // clear the member variable to prevent hitting this
        // method again
        pThis->m_dwRegister = 0;

        // remove the interface from the running object table
        ::RevokeActiveObject(tdwRegister, NULL);

        // the revoke decremented the refcount by one
        // this call to Release destroys the server
        return pThis->ExternalRelease();
    }

    // exit
    return lRefCount;
}

// more code here
```

Each time the program calls Release(), the function begins its processing by making a call to decrement the reference count of the server, and the return value is saved. Next, the program code checks to see if the server has been registered as running, which is implied through a nonzero value in the member variable. Then, the program code checks to see if the reference count is 1. If the reference count is 1, the object is ready to be destroyed since the only application now referencing the object is the Running Object Table. Before calling RevokeActiveObject(), however, it is important to increment the reference count and clear the member variable. RevokeActiveObject() will result in a recursive call to Release(), and you do not want to actually destroy the object until you are finished with the first call to Release() (otherwise you will likely cause memory corruption and a program failure). After the RevokeActiveObject() call returns, you call the Release() function one last time to actually destroy the object and remove it from memory.

During the lifetime of the server, you can get the same instance of the server and use it from multiple applications. In Visual Basic, getting a running instance of a server is done with the GetObject() function, and in Visual C++, with the GetActiveObject() function. After the container retrieves the pointer to the server, the container can use the server as though the container created the server through normal OLE mechanisms.

This method of sharing objects is fine but requires that the application using the server take an active role in deciding to use the shared object versus an application creating its own instance of the object. Another approach can be taken: You can supply the instance of a running server to an application that calls `CreateObject()`, rather than relying on an application to call `GetObject()`. This approach is known as a single-instance server — because the container program can never create more than that single instance.

16.6   Working with Single-Instance Servers

To support single-instance servers, it is necessary to perform all of the steps you learned about earlier in this chapter in the Section 16.5, "Creating Shareable Servers," from within the class factory of the server and not from within the implementation of the server itself. By implementing the object sharing code within the class factory, you are able to control the number of instances of the server without having to rely on the user of the server to program specifically for those cases.

Unfortunately, MFC does not provide simple access to the `COleObjectFactory` class, which is responsible for creating OLE servers to allow for this kind of implementation. C++ inheritance, however, lets you create a new specialized version of the `COleObjectFactory` class that can support server instance sharing.

You must add two macros to the server class declaration and implementation to enable shared server support. `DECLARE_OLECREATE_SHARED` must replace the `DECLARE_OLECREATE` macro in the class header file, and `IMPLEMENT_OLECREATE_SHARED` must replace `IMPLEMENT_OLECREATE` in the server source file. The only difference between the new macros and the originals is that a class factory of type `COleObjectFactoryShared` will be added to the server implementation rather than a `COleObjectFactory` class. Creating the code to support single servers is relatively consistent with the code to create a shared server.

16.7   Summary

In this chapter, you learned how to create a basic implementation of an MFC automation server. You also learned how to expand upon the basic framework provided by MFC to create new and interesting features within your implementation.

Other areas in which your server development has room to expand are in adding a user interface to the server, possibly in the form of dialogs and event interfaces. The use of the basic MFC dialog classes can make implementation of UI a very easy and rewarding part of your implementations. However, currently, no container applications will recognize either of these features within an automation server. If your implementation has these requirements, you must decide how to implement them. The creation of services and remote servers also makes the prospect of implementing automation servers very enticing.

Every day more and more developers are enabling or integrating automation support as a basic feature of their applications. Any situation that calls for the transfer of data among applications can now be performed with OLE automation, whereas before data transfer would have required the exchange of data using DDE or, even worse, file import/export functions.

Automation servers provide an easy and flexible way to create lightweight ActiveX components for use by your applications. The support of both `IDispatch` interfaces and custom interfaces (a dual-interface server) also gives the user of the server a lot of flexibility in terms of implementation styles and methods.

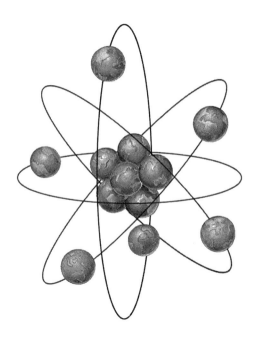

SUPPORTING OLE DRAG-AND-DROP WITH APPLICATIONS

Topics in this Chapter

- Drag-and-Drop Basics
- Creating a Container Application
- Adding Drag-and-Drop Support
- Summary

Chapter 17

O LE provides an elegant, simple, and standardized way to implement drag-and-drop capability in applications.

To explore drag-and-drop support in this chapter, we will build an OLE container application. This simple application is able to hold a series of container objects. Via the OLE drag-and-drop mechanism, this application supports dragging items between its view and another application, between its own view windows, and within a single view window.

17.1 Drag-and-Drop Basics

Drag-and-drop represents a technique of sharing data between applications that act as *drag sources* and applications that act as *drop targets*. Drag sources are applications that enable their items to be dragged from their windows to the windows of other applications. Drop targets are applications that accept items dragged from drag sources and released within their window, as shown in Figure 17-1.

Implementing a drag source using MFC is very simple. Implementing a drop target is somewhat more difficult, but it is still not an overwhelmingly complex task.

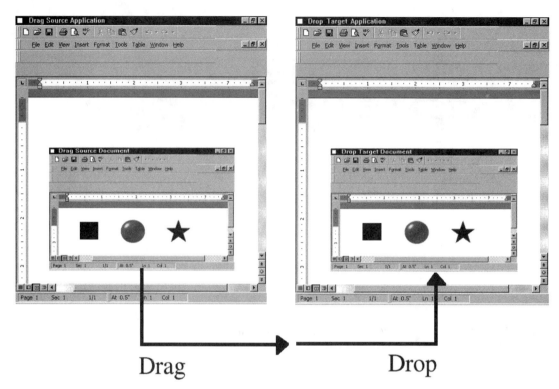

Figure 17-1 Drag-and-drop implementation.

The simple implementations presented in this chapter are based on the drag-and-drop support in the class `COleClientItem`. In applications that support drag-and-drop of native data or drag-and-drop of multiple items, you may decide to utilize the drag-and-drop support in `COleServerItem` instead.

Drag-and-drop functionality and clipboard functionality have many things in common. If you wish to implement clipboard cut, copy, and paste functions using OLE, you can share most of the clipboard support code and drag-and-drop code.

17.2 Creating a Container Application

The container application required for our purposes is based on the AppWizard-generated container application default, with a few modifications that make it possible to select items using the mouse, and that support persistent storage of item positions.

17.2.1   Creating the Application

To create the application, use AppWizard's defaults, except for specifying container application support in AppWizard Step 3. Let's briefly review the changes that need to be made to the AppWizard-generated skeleton to support persistent storage of embedded object positions and to support item selection using the mouse.

17.2.2   Adding Positioning Support

The default AppWizard-supplied implementation of a container application positions any inserted objects using a fixed rectangle. To make it possible for inserted items to be positioned anywhere in the drawing surface, a member variable of type CRect must be added to the class COCONCntrItem. This variable must also be serialized. The Draw member function of the view class must utilize this variable when drawing objects.

This variable should also be utilized in the COCONCntrItem member functions OnChangeItemPosition() and OnGetItemPosition(). Another change to COCONCntrItem is the addition of a new helper function, Invalidate(). This function, taking a CWnd pointer as its parameter, invalidates the item's rectangle in the specified window.

To add the new member variable to the COCONCntrItem class and to declare the new helper function, Invalidate(), use the following code:

```
class COCONCntrItem : public COleClientItem
{
    // different initializations
// Attributes
public:
    // member initializations
CRect m_rect;
...
// Operations
public:
    void Invalidate(CWnd *pWnd);
// Implementation
// more code here
```

This member variable must be initialized in the COCONCntrItem constructor, as shown:

```
COCONCntrItem::COCONCntrItem(COCONDoc* pContainer)
    : COleClientItem(pContainer)
{
```

```
// TODO: add one-time construction code here
m_rect = CRect(0, 0, 0, 0);
}
```

The modified versions of `COCONCntrItem::OnChangeItem-Position()` and `COCONCntrItem::OnGetItemPosition()`, shown in the following code, are used to reflect any changes in the item's size or position that were made during an in-place session. It also makes use of the `GetCachedExtent()` member function to update the item's size and position if it has not yet been initialized.

```
BOOL COCONCntrItem::OnChangeItemPosition(const CRect& rectPos)
{
   ASSERT_VALID(this);
   if (!COleClientItem::OnChangeItemPosition(rectPos))
      return FALSE;
   // TODO: update any cache you may have of the item's
   //   rectangle/extent
   m_rect = rectPos;
   GetDocument()->UpdateAllViews(NULL);
   return TRUE;
}


void COCONCntrItem::OnGetItemPosition(CRect& rPosition)
{
   ASSERT_VALID(this);
   // rPosition.SetRect(10, 10, 210, 210);
   if (m_rect.IsRectNull()) {
      CSize size;
      CClientDC dc(NULL);
      GetCachedExtent(&size, GetDrawAspect());
      dc.HIMETRICtoDP(&size);
      m_rect = CRect(CPoint(10, 10), size);
    }
   rPosition = m_rect;
}
```

The next code segment shows how you must modify `COCONCntr-Item::Serialize()` to support serialization of the new member variable.

```
void COCONCntrItem::Serialize(CArchive& ar)
{
   ASSERT_VALID(this);
   COleClientItem::Serialize(ar);
   if (ar.IsStoring()) {
      // TODO: add storing code here
      ar << m_rect;
```

```
  }
  else {
    // TODO: add loading code here
    ar >> m_rect;
  }
}
```

Finally, the addition of the new `Invalidate()` helper function concludes changes to the implementation of COCONCntrItem.

```
void COCONCntrItem::Invalidate(CWnd *pWnd)
{
  CRect rect = m_rect;
  rect.InflateRect(1, 1);
  pWnd->InvalidateRect(rect);
}
```

The following code, then, shows the changes to COCON-View::OnDraw(). The new version takes into account the items' stored positions and draws them accordingly. It also draws all items (as opposed to just the current selection). Furthermore, this version of the function uses a CRectTracker object to highlight the currently selected item.

```
void COCONView::OnDraw(CDC* pDC)
{
  COCONDoc* pDoc = GetDocument();
  ASSERT_VALID(pDoc);
  POSITION pos = pDoc->GetStartPosition();
  while (pos) {
    COCONCntrItem *pItem =
        (COCONCntrItem*)pDoc->GetNextClientItem(pos);
    pItem->Draw(pDC, pItem->m_rect);
    if (pItem == m_pSelection) {
      CRectTracker tracker;
      tracker.m_rect = pItem->m_rect;
      tracker.m_nStyle = CRectTracker::resizeInside |
        CRectTracker::solidLine;
      if (pItem->GetItemState() == COleClientItem::openState
        || pItem->GetItemState() ==
        COleClientItem::activeUIState)
        tracker.m_nStyle |= CRectTracker::hatchInside;
      tracker.Draw(pDC);
    }
  }
}
```

17.2.3 Adding Selection Support

In the previous section, we implemented highlighting the current selection. Adding support for selection of items using the mouse requires adding a handler for WM_LBUTTONDOWN events to the view class. This handler, shown in the following code, can be added using the ClassWizard.

```
void COCONView::OnLButtonDown(UINT nFlags, CPoint point)
{
  // TODO: Add your message handler code here and/or call default
  // CView::OnLButtonDown(nFlags, point);
  COCONDoc* pDoc = GetDocument();
  ASSERT_VALID(pDoc);
  COCONCntrItem *pSelection = NULL;
  COCONCntrItem *pItem =
      (COCONCntrItem *)pDoc->GetInPlaceActiveItem(this);
  if (pItem != NULL)
    pItem->Close();
  POSITION pos = pDoc->GetStartPosition();
  while (pos) {
     pItem = (COCONCntrItem*)pDoc->GetNextClientItem(pos);
     if (pItem->m_rect.PtInRect(point))
       pSelection = pItem;
  }
  if (pSelection != m_pSelection) {
     if (m_pSelection != NULL)
       m_pSelection->Invalidate(this);
     m_pSelection = pSelection;
     if (m_pSelection != NULL)
       m_pSelection->Invalidate(this);
  }
}
```

17.3 Adding Drag-and-Drop Support

Although the two areas of functionality are usually mentioned together, the requirements for a drag source application and for a drop target application are quite distinct. Of the two, implementation of a drag source is the easier task. However, both tasks are supported extensively, in part by the OLE architecture and in part by the MFC.

The support for implementing a drag source comes in the form of the DoDragDrop() member function of several classes, namely COleClient-Item, COleServerItem, and COleDataSource.

Drop target functionality is supported through a series of member functions of the `CView` class; namely, its member functions `OnDrop()`, `OnDragEnter()`, `OnDragOver()`, and `OnDragLeave()`. However, unlike the `DoDragDrop()` function, which can be called as is, these functions require customized implementations in your application.

17.3.1 Implementing a Drag Source

With the help of the `COleClientItem::DoDragDrop()` member function, adding drag source capability to an OLE container is almost embarrassingly simple. All we need to do is modify the handler function for `WM_LBUTTONDOWN` events, `COCONView::OnLButtonDown`. If and when a valid object is selected by the user using the mouse, we must call the object's `DoDragDrop()` member function to perform the drag-and-drop operation. We must also perform a minor housekeeping chore: If the object was moved from our application to another, we must delete it from the list of objects maintained by our document class. However, with `CDocItem`-derived objects, this is also a very simple task; it is sufficient to simply delete the object using the `delete` operator. The `CDocItem` destructor function ensures that the object is properly removed from the document's list of objects.

The modified version of `COCONView::OnLButtonDown()` is shown below:

```
void COCONView::OnLButtonDown(UINT nFlags, CPoint point)
{
  // TODO: Add your message handler code here and/or call default
  //  CView::OnLButtonDown(nFlags, point);
  COCONDoc* pDoc = GetDocument();
  ASSERT_VALID(pDoc);
  COCONCntrItem *pSelection = NULL;
  COCONCntrItem *pItem =
      (COCONCntrItem *)pDoc->GetInPlaceActiveItem(this);
  if (pItem != NULL)
    pItem->Close();
  POSITION pos = pDoc->GetStartPosition();
  while (pos) {
    pItem = (COCONCntrItem*)pDoc->GetNextClientItem(pos);
    if (pItem->m_rect.PtInRect(point))
      pSelection = pItem;
  }
  if (pSelection != m_pSelection) {
    if (m_pSelection != NULL)
      m_pSelection->Invalidate(this);
```

```
      m_pSelection = pSelection;
      if (m_pSelection != NULL)
         m_pSelection->Invalidate(this);
   }
   if (m_pSelection != NULL) {
      m_dragRect = m_pSelection->m_rect;
      if (m_pSelection->DoDragDrop(m_pSelection->m_rect,
         (CPoint)(point - m_pSelection->m_rect.TopLeft())) ==
          DROPEFFECT_MOVE) {
         m_pSelection->Invalidate(this);
         delete m_pSelection;
         m_pSelection = NULL;
      }
   }
}
```

Before we move onto the implementation of drop target functionality, I want to add a few notes concerning this drag source implementation.

Obviously, most applications have functionality above and beyond being an OLE container (if they implement container functionality at all). How would you implement drag source capabilities for those applications?

One possibility is to utilize the DoDragDrop() member function of COleServerItem. If your application is an OLE server, it already has a COleServerItem-derived class defined to represent your application's document in an embedded item. Modify this class to support representation of only the current selection (as opposed to the entire document). This modification is easy; you need only to change the Serialize() and OnDraw() member functions and create a constructor that takes a parameter representing the current selection. The utility of this class goes beyond drag source functionality; it can also be used to represent linked items and to facilitate the transfer of the current selection to the clipboard.

Once your COleServerItem-derived class is complete, you can create an item of this type in your WM_LBUTTONDOWN handler (or wherever you wish to implement drag source functionality). Subsequently, you can utilize the member function COleServerItem::DoDragDrop() to implement drag source capability just as simply as we did for OLE client items.

If you do not wish to use a COleServerItem-derived class for this purpose (for example, if your application is not an OLE server), you can also utilize the COleDataSource class. This class can be used to represent a selection for drag-and-drop and clipboard transfers. COleDataSource also has a DoDragDrop() member function, so implementing drag source functionality using this class is equally simple.

17.3.2   Implementing a Drop Target

Implementing an OLE drop target requires much more work than implementing a drag source. Several member functions of your view class require override versions. The view class must be registered as a drop target. Special considerations must be made to ensure that objects originating from within the application itself are handled properly and efficiently; for example, if the drag-and-drop operation effectively reduces to a move within the same window, it should be treated that way.

The set of CView member functions that require overrides is listed in Table 17-1.

Table 17-1 Drag-and-Drop Related Overridables in CView

Member Function	Description
OnDragEnter()	Called when an item is dragged into the window
OnDragLeave()	Called when a dragged item leaves the window
OnDragOver()	Called while an item is dragged within the window
OnDrop()	Called when an item is released in the window

Before we start madly writing code, here's a summary of exactly what we would like to see in our drop target application.

First, the obvious: If an object is released over our application's view window, we would like the object to appear at that location, preferably preserving its original size.

We would also like to see a tracking rectangle while the mouse is inside the view window. The rectangle will reflect the size of the object that is about to be dropped in the window.

Lastly, we would like to ensure that a drag-and-drop operation that reduces to merely moving an object within the same window is treated accordingly.

The implementation of the OnDragEnter(), OnDragLeave(), and OnDragOver() function overrides requires a few additional member variables. These variables will be used to remember the drag rectangle's size and position and other drag characteristics during a drag operation. In addition, a member variable of type `COleDropTarget` is also required in order to register the view window as a drop target. The declaration of these variables should be added to the declaration of the view class as follows:

```
class COCONView : public CView
{
// more implementation here
// Attributes
public:
    //more publics here
    COCONCntrItem* m_pSelection;
    COleDropTarget m_dropTarget;
    BOOL m_bInDrag;
    DROPEFFECT m_prevDropEffect;
    CRect m_dragRect;
    CPoint m_dragPoint;
    CSize m_dragSize;
    CSize m_dragOffset;
// more implementation here
```

The declarations for the overrides of `OnDragEnter()`, `OnDragLeave()`, `OnDragOver()`, and `OnDrop()` should be added using the ClassWizard.

Our first task in making the application work as a drop target is to register it as one. This is accomplished by adding a member variable of type `COle-DropTarget` and calling its `Register()` member function at the appropriate time. The most appropriate place for this is in the view class' `OnCreate()` member function. To implement this registration, create a handler for `WM_CREATE` messages using the ClassWizard, and add the code shown in the following code fragment:

```
int COCONView::OnCreate(LPCREATESTRUCT lpCreateStruct)
{
    if (CView::OnCreate(lpCreateStruct) == -1)
        return -1;
    // TODO: Add your specialized creation code here
    m_dropTarget.Register(this);
    return 0;
}
```

The `OnDragEnter()`, `OnDragLeave()`, and `OnDragOver()` member functions are used to manage visual feedback during a drag operation. `OnDragEnter()` attempts to retrieve the item's size by querying the item for the Object Descriptor clipboard type. This data type, when supplied, contains information about the transfer item, including its size and the offset of the mouse pointer relative to the item's upper-left corner.

```
DROPEFFECT COCONView::OnDragEnter(COleDataObject* pDataObject,
    DWORD dwKeyState, CPoint point)
{
    // Add your specialized code here and/or call the base class
    //  return CView::OnDragEnter(pDataObject, dwKeyState, point);
    ASSERT(m_prevDropEffect == DROPEFFECT_NONE);
    m_dragSize = CSize(0, 0);
    m_dragOffset = CSize(0, 0);
    HGLOBAL hObjDesc =
        pDataObject->GetGlobalData(cfObjectDescriptor);
    if (hObjDesc != NULL) {
        LPOBJECTDESCRIPTOR pObjDesc =
            (LPOBJECTDESCRIPTOR)GlobalLock(hObjDesc);
        ASSERT(pObjDesc != NULL);
        m_dragSize.cx = (int)pObjDesc->sizel.cx;
        m_dragSize.cy = (int)pObjDesc->sizel.cy;
        m_dragOffset.cx = (int)pObjDesc->pointl.x;
        m_dragOffset.cy = (int)pObjDesc->pointl.y;
        GlobalUnlock(hObjDesc);
        GlobalFree(hObjDesc);
    }
    CClientDC dc(NULL);
    dc.HIMETRICtoDP(&m_dragSize);
    dc.HIMETRICtoDP(&m_dragOffset);
    m_dragPoint = point - CSize(1, 1);
    return OnDragOver(pDataObject, dwKeyState, point);
}
```

This function makes use of the global variable `cfObjectDescriptor`. Declare this variable at the top of your view class' implementation file as follows:

```
static cfObjectDescriptor =
    (CLIPFORMAT)::RegisterClipboardFormat(_T("Object Descriptor"));
```

The next member function is `OnDragOver()`. This function is called every time the mouse moves while within the view window's client area. This function plays a dual role. First, it determines the currently applicable *drop effect*; based on the state of the Control, Shift, and Alt keys it determines whether the item, were it dropped in the window at this moment, should be copied, linked, or moved to this window:

```
DROPEFFECT COCONView::OnDragOver(COleDataObject* pDataObject,
    DWORD dwKeyState, CPoint point)
{
    // Add your specialized code here and/or call the base class
    // return CView::OnDragOver(pDataObject, dwKeyState, point);
    DROPEFFECT de = DROPEFFECT_NONE;
    point -= m_dragOffset;
```

```
  if ((dwKeyState & (MK_CONTROL|MK_SHIFT)) ==
      (MK_CONTROL|MK_SHIFT))
    de = DROPEFFECT_LINK;
  else if ((dwKeyState & MK_CONTROL) == MK_CONTROL)
    de = DROPEFFECT_COPY;
  else if ((dwKeyState & MK_ALT) == MK_ALT)
    de = DROPEFFECT_MOVE;
  else
    de = DROPEFFECT_MOVE;
  if (point == m_dragPoint)
    return de;
  CClientDC dc(this);
  if (m_prevDropEffect != DROPEFFECT_NONE)
    dc.DrawFocusRect(CRect(m_dragPoint, m_dragSize));
  m_prevDropEffect = de;
  if (m_prevDropEffect != DROPEFFECT_NONE) {
    m_dragPoint = point;
    dc.DrawFocusRect(CRect(point, m_dragSize));
   }
  return de;
}
```

The other role of this function is to actually draw visual feedback. This is accomplished by drawing a rectangle using the CDC::DrawFocusRect function.

The third function in this group is OnDragLeave(). This function, the simplest of the three, is called to mark the end of a dragging operation.

```
void COCONView::OnDragLeave()
 {
   // Add your specialized code here and/or call the base class
   // CView::OnDragLeave();
   CClientDC dc(this);
   if (m_prevDropEffect != DROPEFFECT_NONE) {
     dc.DrawFocusRect(CRect(m_dragPoint, m_dragSize));
     m_prevDropEffect = DROPEFFECT_NONE;
    }
 }
```

Now it's time to turn our attention to the OnDrop() member function. This function is by far the most important one in our implementation of drop target functionality. As its name implies, it is in this function that the actual insertion of a dropped item takes place.

```
BOOL COCONView::OnDrop(COleDataObject* pDataObject,
    DROPEFFECT dropEffect, CPoint point)
 {
   // Add your specialized code here and/or call the base class
```

```
   // return CView::OnDrop(pDataObject, dropEffect, point);
   ASSERT_VALID(this);
   COCONDoc* pDoc = GetDocument();
   ASSERT_VALID(pDoc);
   CSize size;
   OnDragLeave();
   CClientDC dc(NULL);
   point -= m_dragOffset;
   pDoc->SetModifiedFlag(TRUE);
   if ((dropEffect & DROPEFFECT_MOVE) && m_bInDrag) {
      ASSERT(m_pSelection != NULL);
      m_pSelection->Invalidate(this);
      m_pSelection->m_rect =
         m_dragRect + point - m_dragRect.TopLeft();
      m_bInDrag = FALSE;
      return TRUE;
    }
   COCONCntrItem* pItem = NULL;
   TRY {
      pItem = new COCONCntrItem(pDoc);
      ASSERT_VALID(pItem);
      if (dropEffect & DROPEFFECT_LINK) {
         if (!pItem->CreateLinkFromData(pDataObject))
            AfxThrowMemoryException();
       }
      else {
         if (!pItem->CreateFromData(pDataObject))
            AfxThrowMemoryException();
       }
      ASSERT_VALID(pItem);
      pItem->GetExtent(&size, pItem->GetDrawAspect());
      dc.HIMETRICtoDP(&size);
      pItem->m_rect = CRect(point, size);
      if (m_pSelection != NULL)
         m_pSelection->Invalidate(this);
      m_pSelection = pItem;
      if (m_pSelection != NULL)
         m_pSelection->Invalidate(this);
    }
   CATCH(CException, e) {
      if( pItem != NULL )
         delete pItem;
      AfxMessageBox(IDP_FAILED_TO_CREATE);
    }
   END_CATCH
   return pItem != NULL;
}
```

This function first terminates the drag operation by calling OnDragLeave() and notifies the document that the contents are changing by calling CDocument::SetModifiedFlag().

Next, it makes an attempt to determine if the drag-and-drop operation actually represents moving an object within the same window. For this, we make use of the m_bInDrag member variable; this variable is set in COCONView::OnLButtonDown() when a drag operation begins, as we will see momentarily. If the operation is a move, the function simply updates the affected item's rectangle and returns.

In the case of a genuine drop operation, an attempt is made to create a new item of type COCONCntrItem using the drop data. If the attempt is successful, the item's size is determined and the item's rectangle is updated.

As I mentioned, the key to determining whether a drag-and-drop operation reduces to a mere move is the m_bInDrag member variable. To set this variable, we have to implement yet another modification to COCON-View::OnLButtonDown(). This final version of this function is shown below:

```
void COCONView::OnLButtonDown(UINT nFlags, CPoint point)
{
    // TODO: Add your message handler code here and/or call default
//  CView::OnLButtonDown(nFlags, point);
    COCONDoc* pDoc = GetDocument();
    ASSERT_VALID(pDoc);
    COCONCntrItem *pSelection = NULL;
    COCONCntrItem *pItem =
        (COCONCntrItem *)pDoc->GetInPlaceActiveItem(this);
    if (pItem != NULL) pItem->Close();
    POSITION pos = pDoc->GetStartPosition();
    while (pos)
    {
        pItem = (COCONCntrItem*)pDoc->GetNextClientItem(pos);
        if (pItem->m_rect.PtInRect(point))
            pSelection = pItem;
    }
    if (pSelection != m_pSelection)
    {
        if (m_pSelection != NULL)
            m_pSelection->Invalidate(this);
        m_pSelection = pSelection;
        if (m_pSelection != NULL)
            m_pSelection->Invalidate(this);
    }
    if (m_pSelection != NULL)
    {
        m_bInDrag = TRUE;
```

```
    m_dragRect = m_pSelection->m_rect;
    DROPEFFECT dropEffect =
        m_pSelection->DoDragDrop(m_pSelection->m_rect,
            (CPoint)(point - m_pSelection->m_rect.TopLeft()));
    m_pSelection->Invalidate(this);
    if (m_bInDrag == TRUE && dropEffect == DROPEFFECT_MOVE)
    {
        delete m_pSelection;
        m_pSelection = NULL;
    }
    m_bInDrag = FALSE;
    }
}
```

As you can see, the m_bInDrag member variable is set to TRUE just before calling COCONCntrItem::DoDragDrop(). If, during the drag, a callback is made to the same view object, by looking at m_bInDrag we can determine that the source of the drag operation is the same view window.

The OnDrop() member function resets m_bInDrag to FALSE if a drag operation is successfully reduced to a move. In this case, OnLButton-Down() will not delete the selected item. That deletion is necessary other-wise, if the item was moved to a different window.

Finally, we need to initialize two of the member variables to ensure proper functioning of the view class. The following code shows the initialization of m_bInDrag and m_prevDropEffect in the view class' constructor.

```
COCONView::COCONView()
{
    // TODO: add construction code here
    m_pSelection = NULL;
    m_bInDrag = FALSE;
    m_prevDropEffect = DROPEFFECT_NONE;
}
```

This concludes our construction of an OLE container supporting drag-and-drop. The completed application, shown in Figure 17-2, can serve as a drop target (or drag source) for word processor objects, spreadsheet cells, drawings, and many other types of OLE objects.

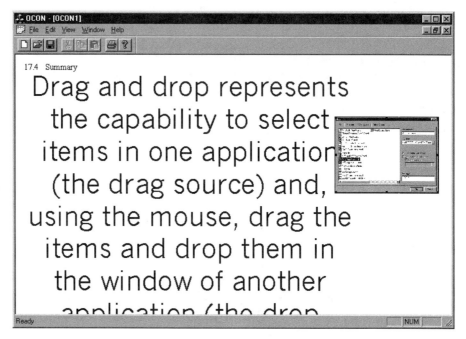

Figure 17-2   The OCON drag-and-drop application.

17.4 Summary

Drag-and-drop represents the capability to select items in one application (the drag source) and, using the mouse, drag the items and drop them in the window of another application (the drop target). Drag-and-drop, from the user's perspective, is a simpler mechanism for sharing data between applications than using the clipboard.

OLE provides extensive drag-and-drop support. This support is encapsulated in the MFC Library in the form of a series of drag-and-drop–related classes and functions.

The implementation of a drag source is relatively easy. For this purpose, you can utilize the member functions of `COleClientItem`, `COleServerItem`, and `COleDataSource`.

Use of `COleClientItem::DoDragDrop()` is recommended if the drag item is an embedded or linked OLE item represented by a `COleClientItem`-derived class. In this case, simply call the `DoDragDrop()` function for the object that the user selected for dragging, and the framework does the rest. Remember to delete the object if the return value of `DoDrag-Drop()` indicates that the selection has been moved (as opposed to copied or linked) to another application.

Use of `COleServerItem::DoDragDrop()` is recommended for applications that are OLE servers. This function is most useful if your `COleServerItem`-derived class is already capable of representing a selection (as opposed to the entire contents of a document). Just create a `COleServerItem`-derived object representing the drag selection and use its `DoDragDrop()` member function to perform the drag operation.

In applications that are not OLE servers, you can also consider using `COleDataSource` for implementing a drag source.

Implementing a drop target is a more involved operation. In addition to providing an override version of the `OnDrop()` member function of your view class, you must also override the `OnDragEnter()`, `OnDragLeave()`, and `OnDragOver()` member functions. The purpose of these functions, called by the framework while the mouse is over the view window during a drag-and-drop operation, is twofold: first, they are used to provide visual feedback during the drag; and second, they are used to inform the framework regarding the allowable drop operations.

In the simplest implementation of `OnDrop()`, you can create a `COle-ClientItem`-derived object representing the drop item. In more involved implementations, you may consider inspecting the item and identifying native data originating from within your own application, or data available in formats that your application can recognize.

In an application that acts both as a drag source and drop target, you should improve the application's efficiency by recognizing operations that reduce to a simple move. In this case, instead of removing the dragged item or items and creating new items, you can implement the operation as a simple position change.

DATABASE ACCESS WITH VISUAL C++

Topics in this Chapter

- OLE DB as a Component Technology

- Defining Base Providers

- Additional Important OLE DB Concepts

- Understanding OLE DB Error Objects

- Extended Interfaces for OLE DB Providers

- Using OLE DB from Within Applications

- Using ActiveX Data Objects (ADO)

- Introduction to ADO with Visual C++ 6.0

- ADO with MFC OLE

- ADO and COM

- Taking a Closer Look at #import

- Summary

Chapter 18

I n 1995, Microsoft released an interesting new technology for database developers. That technology was DAO, which stands for *data access objects*. Data access objects are really what their name implies: a set of OLE objects that allow your application to gain entry to different databases.

These objects do not allow direct access to a database, of course. Instead, they provide a way for your application to communicate with Microsoft's Jet Engine. Jet Engine is a database engine, which has for years shipped as part of Microsoft Access. By exposing a programming interface to Jet — other than through Access macros, forms, and Access Basic — Microsoft paved the way for more developers to get more work done with a better platform.

If you have read about DAO in the DAO SDK, you will note that it is very different from ODBC. ODBC is a call-oriented API, while DAO is an object-oriented database programming model. That is, the programming model is object-oriented — the databases involved are not. DAO was a significant step forward; however, it was still severely limited. To address issues with DAO's connectivity to non-Microsoft databases, Microsoft designed a new technology, called OLE DB, which includes an object model known as ActiveX Data Objects (ADO).

OLE DB, a set of interfaces for data access, is Microsoft's component database architecture that provides universal data integration over an enterprise's network — from mainframe to desktop — regardless of the data type. Microsoft's Open Database Connectivity (ODBC) industry-standard data access interface provides the underlying engine and a unified way to access relational data as part of the OLE DB specification.

OLE DB provides a flexible and efficient database architecture that offers applications, compilers, and other database components efficient access to Microsoft and third-party data stores.

OLE DB is the fundamental Component Object Model (COM)-based building block for storing and retrieving records and unifies Microsoft's strategy for database connectivity. It will be used throughout Microsoft's line of applications and data stores.

OLE DB defines interfaces for accessing and manipulating all types of data. These interfaces will be used not just by data-consuming applications but also by database providers. By splitting databases apart, the resulting components can be used in an efficient manner. For example, components called *service providers* can be invoked to expose more sophisticated data manipulation and navigation interfaces on behalf of simple *data providers*.

Core Note

OLE DB is a specification, not a library or program. The product that you receive on your Visual C++ 6.0 Enterprise Edition CD-ROM 2, within the MDAC2.0 folder, is the OLE DB software developer's kit. You must install it manually from the second CD-ROM, and the installation will automatically place the files in the c:\oledbsdk directory. You may need to update your environment as well as your Visual Studio directory settings to ensure that the OLE DB library and header files will be found by the compiler.

18.1 OLE DB as a Component Technology

To meet its goal of providing data access to all types of data in a COM environment, OLE DB is designed as a component technology. In OLE DB, data stores expose the interfaces that reflect their native functionality. Common components can be built on top of those interfaces to expose more robust data models. To define a component architecture, OLE DB identifies common characteristics between different data providers and services, and defines common interfaces to expose those characteristics. So, for example, while a rowset may be obtained through a number of very different mechanisms, the end result is still a rowset, with well-defined interfaces, methods, and characteristics. With OLE DB, navigating the result of a complex multitable join is no different than navigating a text file containing tabular data. Defining common interfaces in this manner allows components to more efficiently augment the individual data provider's native functionality.

Once the base functionality is defined, the next step is to view the additional functionality as incremental additions to this base functionality. Thus, the more sophisticated providers can expose these advanced features *in addition to* the base level interfaces. Furthermore, individual service components can be built to implement these features on top of the simpler providers.

18.1.1   Understanding Consumers

Developers writing OLE DB consumers can choose their level of interoperability with OLE DB providers. Consumers may be written to consume a specific provider, in which case they are designed to be aware of the functionality of the provider; or they may be written to consume generic providers. In order to consume generic providers, the consumer may be implemented in one of the following manners:

- Consume a minimum set of functionality and work with all OLE DB providers.
- Consume a higher level of functionality and query the provider for support of extended functionality.
- Consume a higher level of functionality and invoke service components to implement missing functionality, where such service components are available.

18.1.2   Understanding Providers

OLE DB providers can be classified broadly into two classes: data providers and service providers. A data provider is any OLE DB provider that owns data and exposes its data in a tabular form as a *rowset*, which is defined later in this chapter. Examples of data providers include relational DBMSs, storage managers, spreadsheets, ISAMs, and e-mail.

A service provider is any OLE DB component that does not own its own data, but encapsulates some service by producing and consuming data through OLE DB interfaces. A service provider is both a consumer and a provider. For example, a query processor is a service provider. Suppose a consumer asks to join data from tables located in two different data sources. In its role as a consumer, the query processor retrieves rows from rowsets created over each of the base tables. In its role as a provider, the query processor creates a rowset from these rows and returns it to the consumer.

18.1.3 Base Consumer Functionality

A consumer can expect a minimum level of functionality to be supported by a provider whenever it talks to any OLE DB provider. This functionality will vary by object. Every object, however, provides certain base interfaces. If the provider supports updating data, it will implement another set of interfaces for doing so. Providers not supporting update functionality are considered read-only providers. Table 18-1 lists the objects and interfaces that a consumer can expect.

The root enumerator interfaces, the data link interfaces, and the row position interface are always supported by common components in the SDK. They are never implemented directly by providers.

Consumers are guaranteed the functionality detailed in Table 18-1 in one of three ways:

- Data providers written in Visual Basic, Visual J++, C, or C++ by using the OLE DB Simple Provider (OSP) Toolkit automatically support all of the above functionality and more.
- Data providers natively written in C or C++ can expose the full set of interfaces listed in Table 18-1.
- Data providers natively written in C or C++ can implement the minimal provider functionality described in the section "Minimum Provider Functionality" on page 552. They rely upon service components to implement the additional functionality required for the base consumer functionality.

18.1.4 More on Providers

An OLE DB provider exposes OLE DB interfaces over some type of data. OLE DB providers include everything from a full SQL DBMS to a text file or data stream. Obviously, these data providers have different functionality, and it's important not to limit that functionality. But at the same time it's not reasonable to expect all providers that expose simple tabular data to implement a full-blown query engine as well.

Table 18-1 Minimal Functionality Expected from a Provider

Object	Base Interfaces Updatable
Root Enumerator	IDBInitialize
	IParseDisplayName
	ISourcesRowset
Data Links	IDataInitialize
	IPromptInitialize
Row Position	IRowPosition
Data Source	IDBCreateSession
	IDBInitialize
	IDBProperties
	IPersist
Session	IGetDataSource
	IOpenRowset
	ISessionProperties
Rowset	IAccessor
	IRowsetChange
	IColumnsInfo
	IConvertType
	IRowset
	IRowsetFind
	IRowsetIdentity
	IRowsetInfo
	IRowsetLocate
	IRowsetScroll
Rowset Behavior	DBPROP_CANHOLDROWS
	DBPROP_ REMOVEDELETED
	DBPROP_CANFETCHBACKWARD
	DBPROP_OWNUPDATEDELETE
	DBPROP_CANSCROLLBACKWARDS
	DBPROP_OWNINSERT

Providers support the native functionality of the data that they expose. This always includes, at the least, the functionality described later in this chapter. Additional interfaces should be implemented as appropriate. If the provider natively supports all of the functionality (listed in the section "Base Consumer Functionality" on page 548), then service components won't be needed to provide the minimal consumer functionality. In addition, providers may expose interfaces for extended functionality, which you will learn about later in this chapter.

All providers must support one of the three standard COM component models — either apartment, rental, or free-threaded. In addition, all providers must support aggregation of the Data Source, Session, and Rowset objects. If applicable, providers must support the aggregation of the Command and View objects.

Providers must support data conversions to the types returned in:

- `IColumnsInfo::GetColumnsInfo()` or `IColumnsRowset::GetColumnsRowset()` for rowset columns.
- `ICommandWithParameters::GetParameterInfo()` for parameters.
- `BTYPE_WSTR` for all column or parameter values other than those described as objects.

Providers that support binding to objects as `IStream` or `ILockBytes` must also support binding to those columns as `ISequentialStream`.

Core Tip

In general, the simplest way to view COM's threading architecture is to think of all the COM objects in the process as divided into groups called apartments. A COM object lives in exactly one apartment, in the sense that its methods can legally be called directly only by a thread that belongs to that apartment. Any other thread that wants to call the object must go through a proxy. There are two types of apartments: single-threaded apartments and multithreaded apartments.

The Apartment Model

In a single-threaded apartment, each thread that uses OLE is in a separate "apartment," and COM synchronizes all incoming calls with the Windows message queue. A process with a single thread of execution is simply a special case of this model.

In a multithreaded apartment, multiple threads in a single free-threaded apartment use COM, and calls to COM objects are synchronized by the objects themselves.

Single-threaded apartments consist of exactly one thread, so all COM objects that live in a single-threaded apartment can receive method calls only from the one thread that belongs to that apartment. All method calls to a COM object in a single-threaded apartment are synchronized with the windows message queue for the single-threaded apartment's thread.

Multithreaded apartments consist of one or more threads, so all COM objects that live in an multithreaded apartment can receive method calls directly from any of the threads that belong to the multithreaded apartment. Threads in a multithreaded apartment use a model called "free-threading." OLE does not provide any synchronization of method calls to COM objects in a multithreaded apartment. In particular, this means that the COM object must provide its own synchronization if needed.

A process can have zero or more single-threaded apartments, and zero or one multithreaded apartments. One way of looking at this is the following:

- A process that consists of just one single-threaded apartment is referred to as a *single-threaded process*.
- A process that has two or more single-threaded apartments and no multithreaded apartments is called an *apartment model process*.
- A process that has a multithreaded apartment and no single-threaded apartments is referred to as a *free-threaded process*.
- A process that has a multithreaded apartment and one or more single-threaded apartments is a *mixed model process*.

In reality, however, all processes are apartment-model. Some apartments have a single thread and some apartments have multiple threads. The threading model really applies to an apartment, not to a process. It can also apply to a class of objects, but it doesn't really apply to a component, such as a DLL, but to the object classes within the DLL. Different classes in a DLL can have different threading models.

In a process, the main apartment is the first to be initialized. In a single-threaded process, this remains the only apartment. Call parameters are marshaled between apartments, and COM handles the synchronization through messaging. If you designate multiple threads in a process to be free-threaded, all free threads reside in a single apartment, parameters are passed directly to any thread in the apartment, and you must handle all synchronization. In a process with both free-threading and apartment-threading, all free threads reside in a single apartment, and all other apartments are single-threaded apartments. A process that does COM work is a collection of apartments with, at most, one multithreaded apartment but any number of single-threaded apartments.

The threading models in COM provide the mechanism for clients and servers that use different threading architectures to work together. Calls among objects with different threading models in different processes are naturally supported. From the perspective of the calling object, all calls to objects outside a process behave identically, no matter how the object being called is threaded. Likewise, from the perspective of the object being called, arriving calls behave identically, regardless of the threading model of the caller.

Interaction between a client and an out-of-process object is straightforward, even when they use different threading models, because the client and object are in different processes and COM is involved in remoting calls from the client to the object. COM, interposed between the client and the server, can provide the code for the threading models to interoperate, with standard marshaling and RPC. For example, if a single-threaded object is called simultaneously by multiple free-threaded clients, the calls will be synchronized by COM by placing corresponding window messages in the server's message queue. The object's apartment will receive one call each time it retrieves and dispatches messages.

18.1.5 Minimum Provider Functionality

It is important for provider writers to implement the full set of interfaces that apply to their particular type of data. At a minimum, the provider must implement the interfaces and behaviors listed in Table 18-2 to be considered a generic OLE DB provider. Providers implementing the minimum provider functionality can rely on common service components available in the SDK to implement the base consumer functionality.

Core Note

Supporting `IConnectionPointContainer` *for* `IRowsetNotify` *is not strictly required for OLE DB 2.0 providers to satisfy the minimum requirements for an updatable provider. However, updatable providers are strongly encouraged to expose this connection point as some consumers will be forced to treat providers as read-only if they do not support rowset notifications by exposing the connection point for* `IRowsetNotify`.

Table 18-2 Minimum Interfaces a Provider Must Support To Be Considered a Generic OLE DB Provider

Object	Any OLE DB Provider	Updatable Providers
DataSource	IDBCreateSession	
	IDBInitialize	
	IDBProperties	
	IPersist	
Session	IGetDataSource	
	IOpenRowset	
	ISessionProperties	
Rowset	IAccessor	IConnectionPointContainer for IRowsetNotify
	IConvertType	IRowsetChange
	IColumnsInfo	
	IRowset	
	IRowsetIdentity	
	IRowsetInfo	
Rowset Behavior	DBPROP_CANHOLDROWS	DBPROP_OWNUPDATEDELETE
	DBPROP_OWNINSERT	
	DBPROP_REMOVEDELETED	

Supporting an interface means supporting all methods within that interface. No methods return E_NOTIMPL. Supporting a property means supporting the setting of and associated behavior of all possible values for a property.

Supporting the required rowset properties means that setting any combination of the required properties must yield a rowset that reflects at least those properties. It does not mean that those properties are always true for any rowset if the property has not been requested by the user.

18.2 Defining Base Providers

Providers that implement the full set of base interfaces can be consumed by general consumers without the support of additional service components, as shown in Figure 18-1.

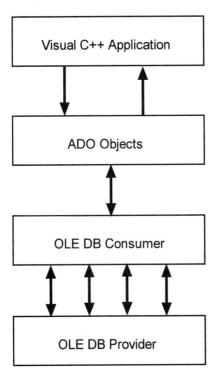

Figure 18-1   A general consumer consumes a provider that implements the full set of base interfaces.

Providers implementing the functionality described in Table 18-3, in addition to the minimum provider functionality described previously, are consumed as *base providers*. Note that providers that support the property:

`DBPROP_CANSCROLLBACKWARDS`

must also support the property:

`DBPROP_CANFETCHBACKWARDS`

Table 18-3 Interfaces That a Provider Must Include In Addition to the Minimum Interfaces To Be Considered a Base Provider		
Object	*Any OLE DB Provider*	*Updatable Providers*
Rowset	IRowsetFind	(same)
	IRowsetLocate	(same)
	IRowsetScroll	(same)
Rowset Behavior	DBPROP_CANSCROLLBACKWARDS	(same)
	DBPROP_CANFETCHBACKWARDS	(same)

18.3 Additional Important OLE DB Concepts

The OLE DB specification defines a series of component objects, all of which are important, whether you are designing providers or simply implementing consumers. The following sections detail some of the key objects.

18.3.1 Data Source Objects

The session of an OLE DB client begins by creating a data source object using the `CoCreateInstance()` function. This activates the corresponding OLE DB provider and prepares it for a session. Data source objects expose the `IDBProperties` interface, through which the object can communicate connection and authentication information (such as a data source name or a user password). They also expose the `IDBInitialize` interface, which the client can use to actually connect to the data source. Data source objects expose a number of other interfaces as well. The following prototype shows the COM interface definitions for the `DataSource` object:

```
CoType TDataSource
  {
    [mandatory] interface IDBCreateSession;
    [mandatory] interface IDBInitialize;
    [mandatory] interface IDBProperties;
    [mandatory] interface IPersist;
    [optional]  interface IDBDataSourceAdmin;
    [optional]  interface IDBInfo;
```

```
[optional]   interface IPersistFile;
[optional]   interface ISupportErrorInfo;
}
```

A data source object is the initial object that a provider instantiates when the consumer calls `CoCreateInstance` on the class ID for that provider. Consumers generally don't call `CoCreateInstance` directly, but instead they bind to the file moniker of a persisted data source object or to a moniker returned by the enumerator object. The code that performs the binding calls `CoCreateInstance` on behalf of the consumer. It is important to distinguish the data source object from the data source. The data source actually contains the data. For example, a data source might be a text file, an SQL database, or an in-memory array in an application.

18.3.2 Understanding Transactions

When working with databases, you will often use transactions as a tool for managing the way the database actually receives the information from the local user. When working with OLE DB providers, you will use the `Transaction` object to maintain information about transaction processing. The following prototype shows the interface declarations for the `Transaction` object:

```
CoType TTransaction
  {
    [mandatory] interface IConnectionPointContainer;
    [mandatory] interface ITransaction;
    [optional]  interface ISupportErrorInfo;
  };
```

Transactions are the mechanisms used to define persistent units of work within an application and to define how the different units relate to each other in a system with parallel activities.

18.3.3 Understanding Sessions

A session object acts as a factory for rowset, command, and transaction objects. However, its primary function is to define a transaction. The following prototype shows the interface declarations for the `Session` object:

```
CoType TSession
  {
    [mandatory] interface IGetDataSource;
    [mandatory] interface IOpenRowset;
```

```
    [mandatory]  interface  ISessionProperties;
    [optional]   interface  IDBCreateCommand;
    [optional]   interface  IDBSchemaRowset;
    [optional]   interface  IIndexDefinition;
    [optional]   interface  ISupportErrorInfo;
    [optional]   interface  ITableDefinition;
    [optional]   interface  ITransaction;
    [optional]   interface  ITransactionJoin;
    [optional]   interface  ITransactionLocal;
    [optional]   interface  ITransactionObject;
}
```

If the session supports `ITransactionLocal`, the consumer can call `ITransactionLocal::StartTransaction()` to start an explicit transaction. The session is then said to be in manual commit mode and any work done in the session must be explicitly committed or aborted. If `ITransactionLocal` is not supported or if the consumer does not call `StartTransaction()`, the session is said to be in auto-commit mode and any work done in the session is automatically committed; it cannot be aborted.

To create a session, a consumer calls `IDBCreateSession::Create-Session()` on the data source object. A single data source object can support multiple sessions and, therefore, multiple transactions. From a session, the consumer can do the following:

- Call `IDBCreateCommand::CreateCommand()` to create a command. A single session can support multiple commands. Note that some providers do not support commands.

- Call `IOpenRowset::OpenRowset()` to create a rowset. This is equivalent to creating a rowset over a single table and is supported by all providers.

- Create or modify tables and indexes with `ITableDefinition` and `IIndexDefinition`. Although providers are not required to support these interfaces, any provider built over a data source that supports creating and modifying tables and indexes should support them. For simple providers, such as a provider built over an array of data, `ITableDefinition` might be the only way to create or modify tables.

18.3.4 Understanding Commands

In OLE DB, data definition language (DDL) and data manipulation language (DML) statements are referred to as text commands. A command object contains a text command and encapsulates the query processing services available in today's DBMSs. Commands expose various interfaces representing different areas of functionality of a query processor including query formulation, preparation, and execution. Figure 18-2 illustrates a typical OLE DB query processor.

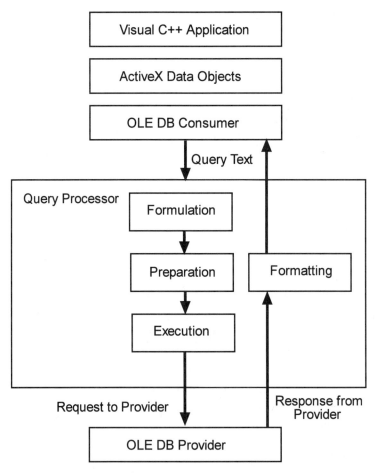

Figure 18-2 A typical OLE DB query processor.

The main purpose of a command object is to execute a text command. Executing a command such as an SQL SELECT statement creates a rowset, while executing a command such as an SQL UPDATE or CREATE TABLE statement does not create a rowset. Text commands are expressed in a provider-specific language, although this is typically ANSI SQL 92.

An OLE DB consumer that wants to use a command typically performs the following steps:

1. Obtains an interface on the command.
2. Builds a text string representing the command text.
3. Passes the text string to the command.
4. Requests properties to be supported by the resulting rowset, if any, including the interfaces it will expose.
5. Executes the command. If the command text specifies the creation of a rowset, the command returns the rowset to the consumer.

Notice that because providers can both consume and produce rowsets, it is possible to compose query processors that process distributed, heterogeneous, or parallel queries. It is also possible to compose specialized query processors, such as SQL query processors, text-search query processors, and geographical or image query processors.

The following prototype shows the interface declarations for the Command object:

```
CoType TCommand
  {
    [mandatory] interface IAccessor;
    [mandatory] interface IColumnsInfo;
    [mandatory] interface ICommand;
    [mandatory] interface ICommandProperties;
    [mandatory] interface ICommandText;
    [mandatory] interface IConvertType;
    [optional]  interface IColumnsRowset;
    [optional]  interface ICommandPrepare;
    [optional]  interface ICommandWithParameters;
    [optional]  interface ISupportErrorInfo;
  }
```

A command is used to execute a provider-specific text command, such as an SQL statement. It is important not to confuse a command, which is an OLE COM object, with its command text, which is a string. Commands are generally used for data definition, such as creating a table or granting privileges, and data manipulation, such as updating or deleting rows. A special case of data manipulation is creating a rowset, for example, an SQL SELECT statement.

Providers are not required to support commands. In general, providers built on top of a DBMS, such as an SQL DBMS, support commands and providers built on top of a simple data structure, such as a file or an array of data in an application, do not support commands.

18.3.5 Understanding Rowsets

Rowsets are the central objects that enable all OLE DB data providers to expose data in tabular form. Conceptually, a rowset is a set of rows in which each row has columns of data. Base table providers present their data in the form of rowsets. Query processors present the result of queries in the form of rowsets. This makes it possible to layer components that consume or produce data through the same object. The most basic rowset object exposes four interfaces, as follows:

- `IRowset`, which contains methods for fetching rows in the rowset sequentially.
- `IAccessor`, which permits the definition of groups of column bindings describing the way tabular data is bound to consumer program variables.
- `IColumnsInfo`, which provides information about the columns of the rowset.
- `IRowsetInfo`, which provides information about the rowset itself.

Using `IRowset`, a consumer can sequentially traverse the rows in the rowset, including traversing backward if the rowset supports it. Figure 18-3 illustrates the data structures a generic rowset object might support.

Other rowset interfaces expose additional rowset capabilities. For example, there is an interface to insert, delete, and update rows, and interfaces that expose richer row navigation models, such as direct access and scrollability. Rowsets are created in one of two ways. First, they can be created as the result of a query. Second, they can be created directly as the result of calling `IOpenRowset::OpenRowset()`. All providers support the latter method, while simple providers, such as those built over a base table, an index, a file, or an in-memory structure, generally do not support the former.

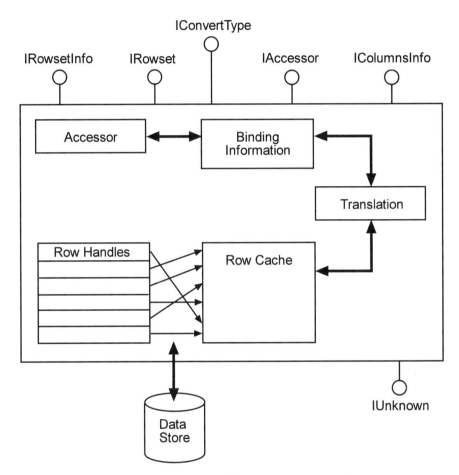

Figure 18-3 Data structures supported by a generic rowset object.

Index rowsets are rowsets whose rows are formed from index entries. Index rowsets have the additional property of allowing efficient access to contiguous rows within a range of keys. They are used primarily by query processor components. Indexes abstract the functionality of B-trees and indexed-sequential files. Indexes are traversed using the IRowset interface; information about the index entries is obtained through the IColumnsInfo interface; and insertions and deletions are performed through the IRowsetChange interface. Figure 18-4 shows the object model for the exposed rowset interfaces.

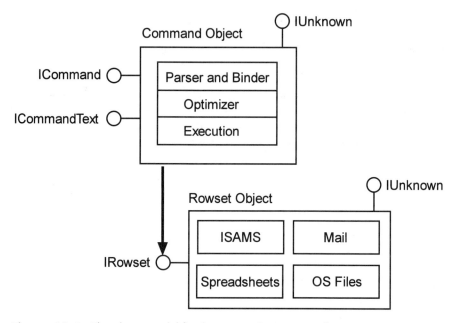

Figure 18-4 The object model for the exposed rowset interfaces.

The following prototype shows the interface declarations for the Rowset object:

```
CoType TRowset
  {
    [mandatory] interface IAccessor;
    [mandatory] interface IColumnsInfo;
    [mandatory] interface IConvertType;
    [mandatory] interface IRowset;
    [mandatory] interface IRowsetInfo;
    [optional]  interface IColumnsRowset;
    [optional]  interface IConnectionPointContainer;
    [optional]  interface IRowsetChange;
    [optional]  interface IRowsetIdentity;
    [optional]  interface IRowsetLocate;
    [optional]  interface IRowsetResynch;
    [optional]  interface IRowsetScroll;
    [optional]  interface IRowsetUpdate;
    [optional]  interface ISupportErrorInfo;
  }
```

18.3.6 Rowset Properties

During command formulation, OLE DB consumers can request certain properties to be satisfied by the rowsets resulting from a command. Common properties include the set of interfaces to be supported by the resulting rowset. Any rowset returned from a command exposes the mandatory interfaces `IRowset`, `IAccessor`, `IColumnsInfo`, and `IRowsetInfo` described earlier.

The basic `IRowset` interface supported by all rowsets enables consumers to, at minimum, navigate the rowset in a forward-only manner. Requesting the rowset property to scroll backwards enables a consumer to navigate the rowset in both directions. Supporting bidirectional rowsets puts additional requirements on the creation of the rowset object to support this functionality efficiently. A forward-only rowset can be fed directly from the query execution plan output. A bidirectional rowset might require materializing the result.

In addition to the default interfaces, a consumer may request interfaces to enable direct positioning within a rowset with bookmarks (`IRowset-Locate`), scrollability (`IRowsetScroll`), immediate updatability of rows (`IRowsetChange`), and deferred updatability of rows (`IRowsetUpdate`). It is also possible to request additional properties that specialize the behavior of certain interfaces — for example, to make some columns of the rowset updatable and the rest read-only.

18.3.7 Understanding Enumerators

An enumerator exposes the `ISourcesRowset` interface, which returns a rowset describing all data sources and enumerators visible to the enumerator. A root enumerator, shipped in the OLE DB Software Development Kit (SDK), traverses the registry looking for data sources and other enumerators. Other enumerators traverse the registry or search in a provider-specific manner. For example, an enumerator over the file system might search for subdirectories.

The following prototype shows the interface declarations for the Enumerator object:

```
CoType TEnumerator
  {
    [mandatory]  IParseDisplayName;
    [mandatory]  ISourcesRowset;
    [optional]   IDBInitialize;
    [optional]   IDBProperties;
    [optional]   ISupportErrorInfo;
  }
```

18.4   Understanding OLE DB Error Objects

OLE DB error objects extend the capabilities of automation error objects with the capabilities to return multiple error records and to return provider-specific errors. An error object is accessed by calling the `GetErrorInfo()` function exposed by the automation DLL and retrieving an `IErrorInfo` interface on the objects. Providers can also create error objects using `CoCreateInstance`.

Records in OLE DB error objects are numbered starting from zero. The methods in `IErrorRecords` allow consumers to specify the record from which to retrieve error information. As error records are added, they are added to the top of the list (that is, the number of the existing error records is increased by one and a new record zero is added), so consumers can start with the highest level of error information and then retrieve increasingly more detailed information.

Each error record is composed of five parts: an `ERRORINFO` structure, error parameters, a pointer to a custom error object, a dynamic error ID, and a lookup ID.

18.4.1   The ERRORINFO Structure's Contents

The `ERRORINFO` structure returns most of the basic information associated with an error:

```
typedef struct tagERRORINFO
  {
    HRESULT hrError;
    DWORD   dwMinor;
    CLSID   clsid;
    IID     iid;
    DISPID  dispid;
  } ERRORINFO;
```

The elements of this structure are used as shown in Table 18-4.

Table 18-4 The Elements of ERRORINFO Structure	
Element	*Description*
hrError	The code returned by the method. This might be different in different records in the error object. For example, suppose a query processor service provider opens rowsets provided by base table providers. If ICommand::Execute() in the query processor calls IOpenRowset::OpenRowset() in a base table provider and OpenRowset() fails with DB_E_NOTABLE, Execute() might return DB_E_ERRORSINCOMMAND.
dwMinor	A provider-specific error code.
clsid	The class ID of the object that returned the error.
iid	The interface ID of the interface that generated the error. iid can be different than the ID of the interface that defines the method the consumer called. For example, if a consumer calls Execute() in a query processor, and the query processor then calls OpenRowset() in a base table provider, Open-Rowset() may fail. If it does, iid is IID_IOpenRowset, not IID_ICommand. If the method that generates an error belongs to more than one interface due to inheritance, this is the ID of the first interface in which the method is defined. For example, suppose IRowsetLocate::GetRowsAt() is called through a pointer to IRowsetScroll, which inherits from IRowsetLocate. If GetRowsAt() fails, iid is IID_IRowsetLocate, not IID_IRowsetScroll.
dispid	If defined, this might indicate the method that returned the error.

18.4.2 Error Parameters

Error parameters are provider-specific values that are incorporated into error messages. For example, the provider might associate the following error message with a dwMinor value of 10:

```
Cannot open table <param1>.
```

In such a case, you would use the error parameters to supply the name of the table that could not be opened. Error parameters are substituted into error messages by a provider-specific error lookup service. Thus, the format of error parameters and how they are substituted into error messages is completely provider specific. The error lookup service is called by the code in `IErrorInfo`.

18.4.3 Custom Error Objects

A custom error object is associated with each error record. An interface pointer to the object is stored in the record. If no custom error object exists, this pointer is `NULL`. The custom error object is the mechanism by which OLE DB error objects are extensible.

When an error record is added, the error object calls `AddRef()` to add a reference to the custom error object. The provider that created the custom error object calls `Release` to release its hold on the custom error object. Thus, ownership of the custom error object is effectively transferred from the provider to the error object. The error object releases all custom error objects when it is released.

For example, ODBC-related providers can expose `ISQLErrorInfo` on a custom error object to return the SQLSTATE.

18.4.4 Dynamic Error ID

The dynamic error ID is the ID of an error message created at runtime by the error lookup service, as opposed to an error message hard-coded in the lookup service. The dynamic error ID is used by the error object to release the dynamic error message when the error object is released. In general, all error messages associated with a single error object have the same dynamic error ID.

18.4.5 The Lookup ID

The lookup ID is used by the error lookup service in conjunction with the return code to identify the error description, Help file, and context ID for a specific error. It can also be a special value, `IDENTIFIER_SDK_ERROR`, that tells the implementation of `IErrorInfo` that is shipped with the OLE DB SDK to ignore the provider's lookup service and use the description supplied in the error resource DLL shipped with the OLE DB SDK.

18.5 Extended Interfaces for OLE DB Providers

General-purpose providers may support additional functionality. It is advantageous that providers support as many extended interfaces as apply to their particular type of data.

In addition to common interface extensions, providers may expose specialized interfaces for the following sets of extended functionality:

- Rowset processing is exposed by providers that support native filter or sort capabilities.
- Command processing is exposed by providers that can execute more sophisticated queries or statements.
- Transaction processing is exposed by providers that can support transactional capabilities.
- Index navigation is exposed by providers built on indexed data to expose index functionality to service components, such as query processors. These interfaces are generally not directly consumed by OLE DB consumers other than service components.

Table 18-5 details the extended, specialized interfaces that providers may expose.

Generic consumers must be prepared for providers that don't support the extended interfaces. Consumers can handle such providers in several different ways:

- The consumer can invoke common services to implement extended functionality, where such service components are available.
- The consumer can implement extra code within the application to compensate for missing functionality.
- The consumer can reduce the functionality available to the user, based on missing functionality in the provider.
- The consumer can return an error indicating that the provider is not capable of supporting required functionality.

Table 18-5 Extended Interfaces That OLE DB Providers May Expose

Object	Any Provider/Updatable Providers	Transacted Providers
Data Source	IConnectionPointContainer for IDBAsynchNotify	
	IDBAsynchStatus	
	IDataSourceAdmin	
	IDBInfo	
	IPersistFile	
	ISupportErrorInfo	
Session	IAlterIndex	ITransactionLocal
	IAlterTable	ITransactionJoin
	IDBSchemaRowset	ITransactionObject
	IDBView	
	IDBCreateCommand	
	IIndexDefinition	
	ITableDefinition	
	ISupportErrorInfo	
View	IViewFilter	
	IViewSort	
	IColumnsInfo	
	IAccessor	
	ISupportErrorInfo	
	IViewRowset	
	IViewChapter	
Command	IAccessor	
	ICommand	
	ICommandPersist	
	ICommandText	
	IColumnsInfo	
	ICommandPrepare	
	IColumnsRowset	
	ICommandProperties	
	ICommandWithParameters	
	IConvertType	
	ISupportErrorInfo	

(continued)

Table 18-5 Extended Interfaces That OLE DB Providers May Expose		
Object	*Any Provider/Updatable Providers*	*Transacted Providers*
Command Behavior	MAXTABLESINSELECT > 1	
Custom Error	ISQLErrorInfo	
Multiple Results	IMultipleResults	
Rowset	IConnectionPointContainer for IRowsetNotify	
	IDBAsynchNotify	
	IColumnsRowset	
	IChapteredRowset	
	IDBAsynchStatus	
	IRowsetChapterMember	
	IRowsetIdentity	
	IRowsetLocate	
	IRowsetView	
	IRowsetIndex	
	IRowsetIndex	
	ISupportErrorInfo	
Rowset Behavior	DBPROP_LITERALBOOKMARKS	
	DBPROP_ORDEREDBOOKMARKS	
	DBPROP_LITERALIDENTITY	
	DBPROP_BOOKMARKSKIPPED	
	DBPROP_OTHERINSERT	
	DBPROP_OTHERUPDATEDELETE	
	DBPROP_STRONGIDENTITY	
BLOB Support	DBPROP_OLEOBJECTS	
	DBPROP_MULTIPLESTORAGEOBJECTS	
	DBPROP_STRUCTUREDSTORAGE	
	ISequentialStream	
	IStream	
	IStorage	
	ILockBytes	
	DBPROP_BLOCKINGSTORAGEOBJECTS =FALSE	

18.6 Using OLE DB from Within Applications

Clearly, OLE DB exposes a great number of interfaces that your applications can take advantage of to access data sources. Despite the power of OLE DB, Microsoft suggests that developers use the ActiveX Data Objects (ADO) wrappers to access the underlying COM interfaces. You will learn about ActiveX Data Objects in the next chapter.

18.7 Using ActiveX Data Objects (ADO)

Earlier in this chapter, you learned about OLE DB, Microsoft's new, preferred method of supporting access to data sources of all types. While OLE DB provides excellent support for accessing all types of database sources, Microsoft has gone an extra step and wrapped the OLE DB functionality within the ActiveX Data Objects (ADO) in an attempt to simplify database programming for Visual Basic, Visual C++, Visual J++, VBScript, and Java-Script developers.

ActiveX Data Objects (ADO) enables you to write a client application to access and manipulate data in a data source through a provider. ADO is ideally suited to consume data exposed by OLE DB providers, such as those written with the Microsoft OLE DB Simple Provider Toolkit. ADO's primary benefits are ease of use, high speed, low memory overhead, and a small disk footprint.

By using the Toolkit with ADO, you build a foundation for implementing flexible data-access strategies at a higher level. For example, you can combine ADO's ease of application programmability with the Simple Provider Toolkit's ease of developing providers to quickly build end-to-end, single, or multitiered applications that address your corporate, intranet, and other distributed processing needs.

18.7.1 The ActiveX Data Objects Model

The ActiveX Data Objects model uses a three-tiered architectural approach to separate the various components of a client/server system into three tiers of services. The user services, business and other middle-tier services, and data services are the logical tiers that collaborate in an application.

User services provide the visual interface for presenting information and gathering data in an application. The user services connect the user with the application and request the business and/or data services needed by the user to execute business tasks.

Business services respond to requests from the user (or other business services) in order to execute a business task. They accomplish this by requesting the data services needed and applying formal procedures and business rules to the relevant data. This protocol insulates the user from direct interaction with the database. Because business rules tend to change more frequently than the specific business tasks they support, they are ideal candidates for encapsulating in components that are physically separate from the application logic itself.

Data services maintain, access, and update data. They also manage and satisfy requests to manipulate data that are initiated by business services. Separating data services allows the data structure and access mechanisms to be maintained, modified, or, if necessary, even redesigned without affecting business or user services.

Figure 18-5 shows the integration of the ActiveX Data Objects with a three-tiered business model.

18.8 Introduction to ADO with Visual C++ 6.0

There are three ways to manipulate ADO within Visual C++: `#import`, the ClassWizard in MFC OLE, and COM in the Windows API. Of the three, `#import` is the most powerful and lets you generate simpler, cleaner code.

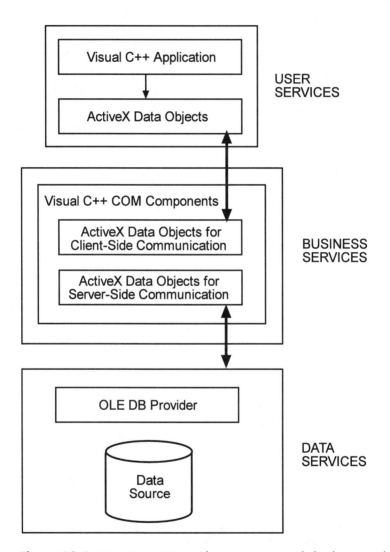

Figure 18-5 How ActiveX Data Objects integrate with the three-tiered expanded client-server model.

Before you can invoke an ADO object inside your application, you must initialize OLE. The following code fragment shows a global declaration you can add to one of the source files in your project to ensure that OLE is properly initialized and terminated (which should look pretty familiar, if you have read the earlier chapters on OLE and ActiveX).

```
struct InitOle {
   InitOle()   {::CoInitialize(NULL);}
  ~InitOle() {::CoUninitialize();}
 } _init_InitOle_;
```

18.8.1 Implementing ADO with #import

When you provide #import with the path or name of a file containing a type library, it generates definitions for globally unique identifiers (GUIDs), class wrappers for each ADO object, and enumerated types based on what it finds in the type library. For any type library you reference, Visual C++ generates the following two files at compile time:

- A header file (with .tlh extension) that contains enumerated types and definitions for objects contained in the type library.
- An implementation file (.tli extension) that has wrappers for each method in the type library's object model.

For example, if you generate #import on Msado21.dll, Visual C++ creates msado21.tlh and msado21.tli.

The #import directive also makes use of a new class, _com_ptr_t, also known as a *smart pointer*, which you learned about previously. Smart pointers automatically perform the COM QueryInterface(), AddRef(), and Release() functions. The _com_ptr_t class and the other helper classes available with #import are discussed in greater detail later in this chapter.

Failed HRESULT results returned by ADO cause #import to raise an exception. The _com_error class raised in the exception automates the task of querying the IErrorInfo interface to acquire details of the error. If you do not want exception handling in your code, you can override #import.

The #import directive generally does not support default values or optional arguments. This is actually a design limitation, because #import allows you to use default values if the argument is of type VARIANT. However, very few methods in which default values would most likely be used in ADO have arguments of type VARIANT.

The following code demonstrates how to use #import to add support for ADO in your application:

```
#import "c:\program files\common files\system\ado\msado21.dll" \
     rename ("EOF", "adoEOF")
```

Renaming the end-of-file constant (EOF) is required because in a typical Visual C++ application, the framework and the compiler have already defined EOF as a constant (-1) using #define. However, EOF is also defined within ADO as a property of type VARIANT_BOOL. Without the rename attribute redefining the string EOF for what #import generates on ADO's type library, you would get a compiler error, because it would replace the name of the property EOF with –1. The compiler does not accept this as a valid variable name and returns compiler error messages as a result.

Provided that you have already added the path "c:\program files\common files\system\ado" to one of your PATH, INCLUDE, or LIB environment variables (assuming the operating system has been installed on the C: drive), you could achieve the same results with the following line of code:

```
#import <msado21.dll> rename ("EOF", "adoEOF")
```

In the event that you will not actually use the "normal" EOF definition within your application, you can instead use the following alternate syntax, which eliminates the need for the rename attribute:

```
#undef EOF
#import <msado21.dll>
```

You could alternately assign EOF to a temporary variable, undefine EOF, import ADO, redefine EOF using the temporary variable you saved, and then undefine that temporary variable. However, this seems a terribly convoluted process, particularly when you can just rename the property as adoEOF.

18.8.2 Defining and Instantiating ADO Objects with #import

Manipulating an automation object takes two steps:

- Define and instantiate a variable to be used to manipulate a COM object.
- Instantiate an actual instance of a COM object and assign it to the variable.

With #import you can accomplish both steps in a single line of code, using the _com_ptr_t smart pointer's constructor to pass in a valid CLSID, or PROGID. You could also declare an instance of the object, and then use the _com_ptr_t::CreateInstance() method to instantiate the object. The following code fragment demonstrates both techniques for instantiating an ADO connection automation object:

```
#import <msado21.dll> rename("EOF", "adoEOF")
// other code here
struct InitOle {
   InitOle()   {::CoInitialize(NULL);}
   ~InitOle() {::CoUninitialize();}
 } _init_InitOle_;
// other code here
// Method #1: Declaring and instantiating a Connection object
_ConnectionPtr  Conn1(__uuidof(Connection));

// Method #2: Declaring and instantiating a Connection object
_ConnectionPtr  Conn1 = NULL;
HRESULT         hr    = S_OK;

hr = Conn1.CreateInstance(__uuidof(Connection));
```

The second technique is generally better, because the constructor of `_com_ptr_t` does not return a failed `HRESULT` if something goes wrong. The first method, as written, cannot test whether the creation of the ADO connection object succeeded or failed.

In both cases, use the Visual C++ extension `__uuidof(Connection)`, which in this case retrieves a GUID defined by `#import` in the .tlh file corresponding to the ADO connection object. By passing this value to `CreateInstance()`, you create a valid ADO connection object for the connection smart pointer. There are other forms you could pass into either the constructor or `CreateInstance()` to reference the ADO connection object and accomplish the same result.

The only flaw with the code shown previously is that it assumes you have imported only ADO. If you import multiple libraries and one or more of those libraries has an object with the same name, you must provide some differentiation between the two. For example, both ADO and DAO contain an object named `Recordset`.

Another attribute of `#import`, `no_namespace`, prevents the compiler from qualifying the classes in a namespace, which is to say the name of the library the type library defines. In the case of ADO, this is `ADODB`. Using `no_namespace` means you don't have to reference the namespace when initializing or defining variables whose types are defined by what `#import` generates. However, if you have many type libraries imported into your application, it is safer to omit the `no_namespace` attribute. To understand the difference between the two, consider the following code fragment, which uses the `no_namespace` clause.

```
#import <msado21.dll> no_namespace rename("EOF", "adoEOF")

void main()
 {
   HRESULT  hr = S_OK;
   _ConnectionPtr Conn1 = NULL;
   hr = Conn1.CreateInstance(__uuidof(Connection));
   Conn1 = NULL;
 }
```

On the other hand, the following code fragment shows how to perform the same operations when you omit the no_namespace clause:

```
#import <msado21.dll> rename("EOF", "adoEOF")

void main()
 {
   HRESULT hr = S_OK;
   ADODB::_ConnectionPtr Conn1 = NULL;
   hr = Conn1.CreateInstance(__uuidof(ADODB::Connection));
   Conn1 = NULL;
}
```

Note how the definition of the smart pointer and the establishing of the connection both require the object name be prefaced with the ADODB object library reference. While it may be more work to omit no_namespace, it does ensure your code will be more robust if it uses other automation servers whose objects might share the same name as an object found in ADO.

18.8.3 Creating an ADO Project with #import

Now that you understand a little better how to open and create a connection to an ADO object, it is worthwhile to create a simple project that lets you access some data. The project uses the VCUDemo database included on the companion CD-ROM. The following code sample shows the basic code that you need to create a console application that accesses a database through ADO.

```
#include <windows.h>
#import  <msado21.dll> rename("EOF", "adoEOF")
... Init Ole ...
void main()
 {
   HRESULT hr = S_OK;
   ADODB::_RecordsetPtr   Rs1 = NULL;
   _bstr_t Connect("DSN=VCUDemo;UID=admin;PWD=;");
```

```
   _bstr_t Source ("SELECT * FROM DemoTable");
   hr = Rs1.CreateInstance(__uuidof(ADODB::Recordset));
   Rs1->Open(Source, Connect, ADODB::adOpenForwardOnly,
       ADODB::adLockReadOnly, -1);
   Rs1->Close();
   Rs1 = NULL;
   ::MessageBox(NULL, "Success!", "", MB_OK);
 }
```

Disciplined COM developers may find the idea of setting a smart pointer to NULL to force an implicit release of the COM object somewhat disconcerting. Smart pointers make this unnecessary, but you may find it reassuring to explicitly release your objects rather than just setting them to NULL or letting them go out of scope.

The code declares an instance of the ADO recordset smart pointer named Rs1, but doesn't instantiate the actual ADO Recordset object until later with the CreateInstance() method. Note that #import generates the smart pointer definitions in the .tlh file with the _COM_SMARTPTR_TYPEDEF macro, as follows:

_COM_SMARTPTR_TYPEDEF(_Recordset, __uuidof(_Recordset));

To determine the name of any smart pointer that #import generates for use in your code, examine the list of _COM_SMARTPTR_TYPEDEF macros generated in the .tlh file and add a "Ptr" to have the name of the smart pointer class created by the macro. Thus, _Recordset in this definition equates to the smart pointer derived class _RecordsetPtr. The use of an underscore preceding an ADO object is not required; it depends on how the object was defined in the ADO type library.

The code defines two BSTR objects, one for the query statement and one for the connection string using the #import helper class _bstr_t. #import also offers a helper class for managing VARIANTs: _variant_t. After the code opens the Recordset object, it is closed and the recordset variable is released, deallocating the actual ADO object that was created by the CreateObject() method.

Finally, there is the fact that CreateInstance() is the one time you could receive a failed HRESULT from #import. Anytime you call a method of an object wrapped by a smart pointer, it raises a C++ exception with an instance of the _com_error class. The following macro combines the fact that well-written code should already be checking for exceptions raised by #import and eliminates the need to specifically test the HRESULT:

```
#define CREATEINSTANCE(sp,riid) \
 {
   HRESULT _hr =sp.CreateInstance(__uuidof(riid)); \
   if (FAILED(_hr))
   _com_issue_error(_hr);
 }
```

You will use this macro within your application as shown here:

```
CREATEINSTANCE(conn1, Connection)
```

18.9 ADO with MFC OLE

MFC OLE, like `#import`, generates class wrappers for a type library. Unlike `#import`, MFC OLE does not generate enumerated types from the type libaray, but it does implement ADO cleanly. The `CString` and `COle-Variant` MFC classes hide `BSTR`s and `VARIANT`s. However, your application carries along all of MFC as overhead (the Mfc42.dll), as opposed to the much leaner `#import`. Each class wrapper built by MFC OLE is derived from the `CPleDispatchDriver` class, and failed `HRESULTS` generated by ADO are wrapped inside the `COleDispatchException` class.

18.9.1 Creating an ADO Project with MFC OLE

The following ADO code fragment demonstrates how to get started with MFC OLE. The code assumes that you have already used the MFC Class-Wizard to generate classes against ADO 2.1:

```
AfxOleInit();
_Recordset rsADO1;
COleException e;
COleVariant Connect("DSN=VCUDemo;UID=admin;PWD=;");
COleVariant Source ("SELECT * FROM DemoTable");
rsADO1.CreateDispatch("ADODB.Recordset.2.0", &e);
rsADO1.Open((VARIANT) Source, (VARIANT) Connect, 0, 1, -1);
rsADO1.Close();
rsADO1.ReleaseDispatch();
AfxMessageBox("Success!");
```

The `AfxOleInit()` function is an MFC helper that initializes COM. The code declares an instance (rsADO1) of the ADO recordset class wrapper derived from `COleDispatchDriver()`, but doesn't instantiate the actual ADO `Recordset` object until later with the `CreateDispatch()` method. The name of a class wrapper generated by the ClassWizard is identical to the name of the object in the type library. Note the use of an underscore preceding an ADO object is not universally required; if the object is defined with an underscore in the ADO type library, the smart pointer class will require one.

The code defines two `COleVariants` for the Connect and Source variables. `COleVariant` has an operator that can cast to the `BSTR` type required by ADO for the `Recordset.Open()` method. After the `Recordset` object is opened, it is closed and the `Recordset` variable is released, deallocating the actual ADO object that was created by the `CreateDispatch()` method.

18.9.2 ADO with COM Functions

Both `#import` and MFC OLE provide wrapper classes around a given automation object, which is derived from a root class, `_com_ptr_t` or `COle-DispatchDriver`, respectively. You could, though, bypass these wrappers and directly manipulate the Windows application programming interface (API) to utilize ADO. Using `_com_ptr_t` or `COleDispatchDriver` is COM programming, but both classes encapsulate and hide much of the more common invocations of COM APIs, such as `CoCreateInstance()`, or use `QueryInterface()`, `AddRef()`, and `Release()` on a given COM interface. This section discusses what it would take to bypass these wrapper classes and use the Win32 API directly to manipulate a COM object.

To use ADO with COM directly, you need two header files (Adoid.h and Adoint.h) provided by the OLE DB 1.X SDK (for ADO 1.0 and 1.5) or the Microsoft Data Access SDK 2.0 (for ADO 2.0). These two files define the CLSIDs, interface definitions, and enumerated types that you need to manipulate the ADO type library. Though you do not link to a library, you must also use a `#include` statement on the `<INITGUID.H>` header.

18.9.3 Creating an ADO Project
with the COM API

The following ADO code fragment demonstrates how to get started with the COM API. The fragment presumes that you have already installed the OLE DB 1.X SDK or the Microsoft Data Access SDK on your computer.

```
#include <windows.h>
#include <initguid.h>   // Include only once in your application
#include "adoid.h"      // ADO GUID's
#include "adoint.h"     // ADO Classes, enums, etc.
... INIT OLE ...
void main()
 {
   HRESULT hr  = S_OK;
   ADORecordset* Rs1 = NULL;
   VARIANT Source;
   VARIANT Connect;

   VariantInit(&Source );
   VariantInit(&Connect);
   Source.vt = VT_BSTR;
   Source.bstrVal = ::SysAllocString(L"SELECT * FROM Authors");
   Connect.vt = VT_BSTR;
   Connect.bstrVal =
       ::SysAllocString(L"DSN=AdoDemo;UID=admin;PWD=;");
   hr = CoCreateInstance(CLSID_CADORecordset, NULL,
       CLSCTX_INPROC_SERVER,
       IID_IADORecordset, (LPVOID *) &Rs1);
   if(SUCCEEDED(hr))
      hr = Rs1->Open(Source, Connect, adOpenForwardOnly,
         adLockReadOnly, -1);
   if(SUCCEEDED(hr))
      hr = Rs1->Close();
   if(SUCCEEDED(hr)) {
      Rs1->Release();
      Rs1 = NULL;
    }
   if(SUCCEEDED(hr))
      ::MessageBox(NULL, "Success!", "", MB_OK);
 // More code here
 }
```

This code fragment demonstrates the inclusion of <INITGUID.H> in order for the application to run with Msado21.dll. Prior to ADO 1.5, a .lib file was provided to ensure that your application would use ADO; however, it is unnecessary when you use 1.5 or higher and include <INITGUID.H>. You can only include <INITGUID.H> once, or you will get multiple LNK2005 errors when building your application.

The code declares a Recordset interface variable and sets it to NULL, instantiating an ADO object with the call to CoCreateInstance().

ADORecordset is a definition provided by Adoint.h. The code defines two VARIANTs and assigns to them BSTR values for the query and connection information. After opening the Recordset object, the code closes it, releases the ADO Recordset object, and sets the interface variable to NULL.

Testing for a failed HRESULT is a significant difference between this code and #import or MFC OLE, which relies upon an exception being raised. See the section about error handling for more information.

18.10 ADO and COM

There are several important elements you need to know about COM when developing ADO applications, including reading the type library, implementing the ADO type library with COM, the importance and use of COM data types with ADO, and error handling steps that you must perform with ADO.

18.10.1 Reading the Type Library

Because ADO is a language-neutral automation server, the more you know about COM, the more you can accomplish with ADO. The ability to read and understand the ADO type library (contained within Msado21.dll for ADO 2.1 and later) greatly enhances your ability to fully utilize features of ADO.

Reading a type library is not hard, and there are excellent tools for doing so. VBA features an object browser in both Visual Basic and Microsoft Access. You can use #import, which returns the contents of the type library in a .tlh file. (This method is useful for non-#import Visual C++ developers so they can examine enumerated type definitions that MFC OLE might not otherwise provide.) Or you can use a language-neutral utility for viewing language-neutral object models, namely the OLE COM Object Viewer, which ships with Visual Studio.

18.10.2 Viewing a Type Library with the OLE COM Object Viewer

Within the OLE COM Object Viewer, select the File menu, and then the View TypeLib... option. Within the resulting dialog box, enter the path for the type library you wish to view, in this case Msado21.dll. Figure 18-6 shows the ADO type library within the OLE COM Object Viewer.

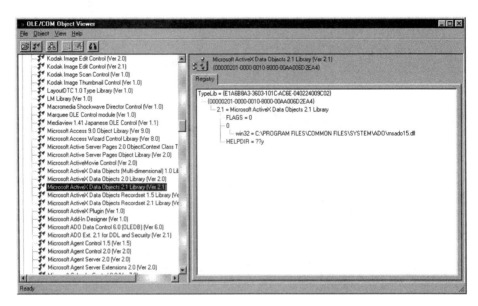

Figure 18-6   The ADO type library within the OLE COM Object Viewer.

In this case, use the OLE COM Object Viewer to examine the `Command.Execute()` method. You can observe from the type library that each of the arguments of `Command.Execute()` are optional, and that one has a default value. This is significant because not all COM implementation mechanisms take advantage of either optional arguments or default values; that is, you have to provide some value anyway. If you want to know what the default is, you may have to use the type library.

18.10.3 Default Properties and Collections

At times, an element in the type library may be the "default" property of a particular object or collection. In this case, you wouldn't need to see or use the element unless the implementation you are using doesn't recognize it as a default. An example is the `Item` property and its usage in `Collections`.

A Few Words About Hidden Type Library Elements, Default Values, and Optional Arguments

The type library viewer won't actually indicate which members of the ADO type library, whether values of enumerated type or actual interfaces, are hidden, and which ones are public. COM implementations for Visual C++ will typically expose all members, hidden or not, in any class wrappers that are generated. Most of the time, though, you will not need to use or know about hidden members of the type library.

Viewing the type library is useful for determining default values of a given property or argument of a method. It also lets you determine which arguments are optional. The COM implementation you use may not support either defaults or optional arguments; that is, you may have to specify every argument when calling a method call yourself. Viewing the type library is useful for understanding what ADO expects, or rather, what more robust COM implementations provide for free.

Many of the ADO enumerated types typically correspond either to arguments within the methods of ADO objects, or to properties of ADO objects. Not all arguments and properties have corresponding enumerated types, but most do. For any given enumerated type, the valid values are listed, and optionally, two special values, Unknown and Unspecified.

Unknown is usually for a property in a read-only state, and is indicative of an object that hasn't been initialized or which is in an unknown state. Unspecified tells ADO to either use the default value for the property or argument, or to use the value previously assigned to that property. Unspecified is actually a hidden member of a given enumerated type.

There is one special case for Unknown used with the Command-TypeEnum property, but this is an exception and not fully in-line with the rest of the ADO specification for the use of Unknown values within an enumerated type.

Occasionally, the argument of a method will have a corresponding property with the same object that the method belongs to. This scenario is the exception, not the rule, but it is important to understand how Unspecified may affect the behavior you receive from ADO. As a rule, ADO will use the value in the method and ignore the value you set in the property, unless you used one of the Unspecified enumerated values.

(continued)

The Command.Execute method, whose third argument also corresponds to the Command.CommandType property, demonstrates this. Specifying adCmdUnspecified in the third argument of Command.Execute tells ADO to use the value in the CommandType property. Otherwise, the value in the Execute method will be used and the CommandType property will be ignored. This particular example is further compounded by the fact that it is one of the rare cases in which ADO also allows you to specify an Unknown value for CommandType. In this case, giving ADO an adCmdUnknown in the CommandType property or in the Execute method's third argument tells ADO that the Command-Text to execute could be a query statement, could be a table name, or it could be a stored procedure name. ADO will try all three until one works.

Using Unknown slows performance because ADO takes time to test the actual type of the CommandText provided. You will have to specify values for each argument because COM does not take advantage of either optional arguments or default values for method arguments.

Typically, to reference an item within a collection (such as Fields, Properties, and Parameters) you provide an index to the Item property of the collection. The following code fragment, for example, retrieves the value of the first column in an open recordset.

```
// using #import
_variant_t v;

v = Rs1->Fields->GetItem(_variant_t(0L))->Value;
v = Rs1->Fields->GetItem(_variant_t("au_id"))->Value;
```

18.10.4 The ADO Type Library and COM Implementations

The need to view the type library is dependent upon the mechanism you choose to implement ADO. You must specify valid values for each argument of a given method. None of the three mechanisms in Visual C++ takes full advantage of default values or optional arguments:

- The Visual C++ #import precompiler directive generates class wrappers and enumerated data types based on what it finds in the type library.
- MFC OLE generates class wrappers that hide BSTR and VARIANT data types inside CString and COleVariant wrapper classes, respectively. MFC OLE, though, does not generate any definitions for a type library's enumerated types.
- For developers using COM, reading the Adoint.h file can be difficult. Using a type library viewer instead simplifies the definitions listed in Adoint.h.

18.10.5 COM Data Types Used By ADO

As you have learned, ADO uses three COM data types that you need to handle: BSTR, VARIANT, and SAFEARRAY. Of the three, SAFEARRAY is probably the most challenging to learn, and COM provides excellent support for it.

These considerations are important because, for example, you must create empty BSTR and VARIANTs for arguments with default values, as shown in the following code fragment:

```
// using #import
    _variant_t   vtEmpty (DISP_E_PARAMNOTFOUND, VT_ERROR);
    _bstr_t      bstrEmpty(L"");
    _bstr_t      Source(L"SELECT * FROM Authors");
    ADODB::_ConnectionPtr  Conn1 = NULL;
    ADODB::_RecordsetPtr   Rs1    = NULL;
    HRESULT hr =
        Conn1.CreateInstance(__uuidof(ADODB::Connection));
    Conn1->ConnectionString = "DSN=AdoDemo;UID=admin;PWD=;";
    Conn1->Open(bstrEmpty, bstrEmpty, bstrEmpty, -1);
    Rs1 = Conn1->Execute(Source, &vtEmpty, ADODB::adCmdText);
    Rs1->Close();
    Conn1->Close();
    ::MessageBox(NULL, "Success!", "", MB_OK);
 // More Code Here
```

In particular, note that you must define the empty VARIANTs using the parameters DISP_E_PARAMNOTFOUND and VT_ERROR; otherwise, you may get errors when you attempt to use them with ADO. The code fragment explicitly defines vtEmpty. However, #import automatically creates a variant of the exact same type called vtMissing. You could easily use vtMissing in place of the definition for vtEmpty. vtMissing was defined to be used for optional arguments of any method in a COM type library.

18.10.6 Converting Variants to Native Data Types

When you use Variants within Visual C++, however, you must eventually convert the Variant into native data types. The function ConvertVariant() was written to use MFC classes CString and COleVariant, but you can easily adapt it to non-MFC classes. In fact, COleVariant is just a class derived from the VARIANT data type.

18.10.7 Using SAFEARRAYS

SAFEARRAY is an automation data type used to pass data of varying types safely between client and server processes. Use them in ADO as optional ways to add records: with the AddNew() and OpenSchema() methods, and with the Parameters argument of the Command.Execute() method.

SAFEARRAYS are not complex, but can be more intimidating than other data types. Visual C++ handles them with the COM API and supports class wrappers such as COleSafeArray in the MFC OLE implementation. The following code fragment demonstrates how to use OpenSchema() to retrieve column information into a SAFEARRAY.

```
ADODB::_ConnectionPtr Conn1 = NULL;
ADODB::_RecordsetPtr  Rs1 = NULL;
HRESULT hr = S_OK;
_variant_t  vtEmpty (DISP_E_PARAMNOTFOUND, VT_ERROR);

hr = Conn1.CreateInstance(__uuidof(ADODB::Connection));
Conn1->Open(L"DSN=Pubs;UID=sa;PWD=;", L"", L"", -1);

// Create elements used in the array
_variant_t varCriteria[4];
varCriteria[0] = vtEmpty;
varCriteria[1] = vtEmpty;
varCriteria[2] = L"Authors";
varCriteria[3] = vtEmpty;
const int nCrit = sizEOF varCriteria /
    sizEOF varCriteria[0];

// Create SafeArray Bounds and initialize the array
SAFEARRAYBOUND rgsabound[1];
rgsabound[0].lLbound = 0;
```

```
rgsabound[0].cElements = nCrit;
SAFEARRAY *psa = SafeArrayCreate(VT_VARIANT,
   1, rgsabound);

// Set the values for each element of the array
for(long i = 0 ; i < nCrit && SUCCEEDED(hr);i++) {
   hr  = SafeArrayPutElement(psa, &i,&varCriteria[i]);
 }

// Initialize and fill the SafeArray
VARIANT vsa;
vsa.vt = VT_VARIANT | VT_ARRAY;
V_ARRAY(&vsa) = psa;

// call OpenSchema
Rs1 = Conn1->OpenSchema(ADODB::adSchemaTables,vsa);
Rs1->Close();
Conn1->Close();
```

Creating the SAFEARRAY in Visual C++ takes several steps. First, you must create an array of VARIANTs and set them to the values required by the particular schema you are opening. Next, you must create the boundary structure for the SAFEARRAY and use it to initialize the size and contents of the SAFEARRAY. Assign each element in the SAFEARRAY from your VARIANT array. Finally, assign the completed SAFEARRAY as a member of a VARIANT type to pass as the second argument to the OpenSchema() method. (While the above code listing uses the #import _variant_t class, you could just as easily use the VARIANT type.)

18.10.8 Error Handling with ADO

Error handling with ADO, just as with any other special feature of Visual C++, deserves careful attention. Any error condition you encounter will be raised through COM to the native error-handling mechanism you are utilizing. As a convenience, the errors collection lists additional warnings exposed by the underlying provider.

The ADO errors collection is available if you have instantiated an ADO connection object. This collection is reset and catches errors any time an unexpected condition is raised by an underlying provider (data or service) used by ADO. In addition, components underlying the provider may raise errors back to the provider, which it passes to ADO. For example, errors encountered by ODBC are raised to the OLE DB provider for ODBC, and from there to the ADO errors collection. A common misconception, though, is that errors ADO encounters are not placed in this collection but must instead be caught by whatever native error-handling mechanism the language or implementation you are using provides. Therefore, your error handling must check both the ADO errors collection as well as whatever native mechanism for raising and catching errors exists.

When an error condition is encountered, whether that error is raised to the ADO Errors collection or to your language's native error-handling mechanism, you may see an error message in one of three formats, as shown in Table 18-6. For example, the ADO error "No Current Record" is defined as having a numeric value of 3021, but it could also appear as an 8-digit hexadecimal value or as a negative long value. Table 18-6 presents all three valid results for 3021.

Table 18-6 Error Code Conversions with ADO	
Error Code	*Error Message*
3021	No Current Record
0x80040BCD	No Current Record
-2147218483	No Current Record

The value 0x0BCD is simply the hexadecimal conversion of the value 3021. The value shows up as 0x80040BCD because all ADO errors are prefixed with 8004. The long negative value, –2147218483, is simply a LONG conversion of 80040BCD.

18.10.9 Specifics on ADO Exception Handling

When calling an ADO method, regardless of language used, an error condition is typically returned as an HRESULT. This HRESULT is translated into an exception for #import (_com_error exception class) and MFC OLE (COleDispatchException class). With COM programming, you must review the returned HRESULT of each method to ensure that you have not encountered an error condition.

Exception handling within Visual C++ is recommended for all three implementations, although exceptions are far less likely to occur with native COM programming. Your application could raise two types of exceptions, Win32 and C++ exceptions. Whether you use #import, MFC OLE, or native COM programming, your application should have robust and comprehensive exception handling. The following code fragment gives an example of what it takes to ensure robust exception handling. This code provides working exception handling code you can add to your application.

```
#include <eh.h>             // Required for Win32 Exception Handling
#include <stdio.h>          // Optional
#include <afxwin.h>         // Required for MFC Exception Handling
#include <afxdisp.h>        // Required for MFC Exception Handling
#import  <msado15.dll> rename("EOF", "adoEOF")

// Class for Win32 Structured Exception Handling
class SEH_Exception {
private:
   unsigned int m_uSECode;
public:
   SEH_Exception(unsigned int uSECode) : m_uSECode(uSECode) {}
   SEH_Exception() {}
   ~SEH_Exception() {}
   unsigned int getSeHNumber() { return m_uSECode; }
};

// Raise Win32 Exception within a C++ Class SEH_Exception
static void MappingSEHtoCPPExceptions
 (
   unsigned int uExceptionCode,
   _EXCEPTION_POINTERS*
 )
 {
    throw SEH_Exception(uExceptionCode);
 }

// Sets up mapping between Win32 SEH & C++ Exception Handling
void LogEnable()
 {
   _set_se_translator(MappingSEHtoCPPExceptions);
 }

void main(void)
 {
   try {
      ADODB::_ConnectionPtr  Conn1 = NULL;
      Conn1.CreateInstance(__uuidof(ADODB::Connection));
      LogEnable();

      // To see each of the catch blocks work, comment out all
      // but one of the following 4 lines, each of which throws
      // an exception.
```

```
    // Bogus DataSource Name, raises _com_error
    Conn1->Open(L"", L"", L"", -1);

    // Explicitly raise MFC Exception
    AfxThrowMemoryException();

    // Explicitly raise SEH Exception
    RaiseException(EXCEPTION_ACCESS_VIOLATION, 0, 0, NULL);

    // Explicitly raise exception of a type not caught below
    // i.e. to the catch handlers, an "Unknown exception"
    throw 0L;    // Raises exception of type long
  }
// Catch Blocks -- All of which are a subset of the
//                 Exception Handling demonstrated in LOG.CPP
//                 in the C++ Rosetta Stone Samples
catch(CException *e) {
    CString         strName;
    CRuntimeClass   *pClass = e->GetRuntimeClass();

    printf("MFC Exception(%s) thrown\n",
        (LPCTSTR) pClass->m_lpszClassName);
  }
catch(_com_error &e) {
    printf("#import encountered failed HRESULT\n");
    printf("\tCode = %08lx\n",       e.Error());
  }
catch(SEH_Exception &e) {
    printf("Win32 Structured Exception Raised\n");
    printf("\t Error Code %08lx\n", e.getSeHNumber());
  }
catch(...) {
    printf("Caught an exception of unknown type\n");
  }
  ::MessageBox(NULL, "Success!", "", MB_OK);
}
```

18.10.10 Unrecoverable Exceptions with ADO

One weakness of the MFC OLE implementation for an automation server is that it is possible to generate an exception from which there is no recovery. That is, if you do not instantiate an actual ADO object, you can still invoke the methods of the helper class on that object. As long as the method is not returning another object, you will receive TRACE messages telling you, in a debug build, that you have not instantiated the object. Consider calling Connection.Execute, which returns a Recordset object. It is possible to create program code that generates an exception that triggers exceptions within exceptions, and there is no way to catch these — which can effectively crash your system, particularly in a debugging session.

18.11 Taking a Closer Look at #import

ADO is an excellent way to learn about COM, and #import is an excellent way to utilize COM. This section describes how to implement #import in COM.

18.11.1 #import and COM

The #import directive instructs the compiler to read a specified type library and generate two header files that are automatically included in your Visual C++ source file. Both header files are placed in the output directory and given the same timestamp as the type library. The type library header file has the name <typelibname>.tlh and contains a Visual C++ equivalent of the original type library. The type library implementation file has the name <typelibname>.tli and contains implementations of any wrapper functions.

The type library header (.tlh) file contains the definitions constructed from the type library items. It is divided into the following sections:

- The #include statement for Comdef.h, which defines the macros used in the header.
- Forward references and typedefs, structure declarations for interface IDs, and class names.
- Smart pointer typedef declarations, using the _COM_SMARTPTR_TYPEDEF macro to create typedefs of specialized _com_ptr_t template classes.
- Type library items, class definitions, and other items generated from the specified type library.
- Named GUID constants initializations, if the named_guids attribute was specified.

- An #include statement for the type library implementation (.tli) file.

- The type library implementation (.tli) file, which contains the inline implementations of the wrapper functions.

The functions that the compiler generates can be divided into two types: high-level error-handling functions, and low-level direct functions. The high-level wrapper functions invoke the low-level method, perform error checking of the returned HRESULT, and throw a _com_error C++ exception if an error occurs. The low-level functions call the method directly and return an HRESULT. High-level functions are generated by default, but you can change the default by specifying the raw_interfaces_only attribute in your #import statement.

18.11.2 Using the Type Library with the #import Directive

When you build the COM object server, the first utility that runs is the Microsoft Interface Definition Language (MIDL) compiler. The MIDL compiler creates a type library. To use the #import directive to import a type library into ADO 2.1, use code similar to the following:

```
#import <msado21.h> rename ("EOF", "adoEOF")
```

In MFC client applications, you can place the #import directive in the Stdafx.h file after the #include <afxwin.h> directive. The #import directive creates two header files that reconstruct the type library contents in C++ source code: a primary and a secondary header file.

The primary header file is similar to the one produced by the MIDL compiler, but it also contains additional compiler-generated code and data. This header file has the same base name as the type library, with a .tlh extension.

If the type library exposes custom interfaces and methods, their wrappers are placed in the secondary header file. This header file has the same base name as the type library, with a .tli extension. The secondary header file contains the implementations for compiler-generated member functions, and is included (#include) in the primary header file.

Both header files are placed in the output directory of the project. The files are read and compiled as if the primary header file was named by a #include directive.

You can import the type library (.tlb file), the DLL, or the executable file with the `#import` directive. It may be easier to import the .tlb file because it stays in the same place for both Debug and Release builds.

For more information about the contents of the primary and secondary header files, see the online help in Microsoft Visual Studio.

18.11.3 Analyzing the Contents of the .tlh and .tli Files Generated by #import

For any given type library, `#import` generates two files whose name matches the name of the file that contains the type library, and with the extensions .tlh and .tli, respectively. The .tlh (or type library header) contains forward references on GUIDs in the type library, smart pointer declarations, and other type library items. The .tli (or type library implementation) file contains wrappers for invoking methods and accessing properties for each object in the type library.

Forward references are created to type a GUID to a particular object within the type library. Consider the following forward references generated from ADO 1.5 for various connection objects defined in the ADO type library.

```
struct __declspec(uuid("00000515-0000-0010-8000-00aa006d2ea4"))
/* dual interface */ _Connection;

struct __declspec(uuid("00000516-0000-0010-8000-00aa006d2ea4"))
/* interface */ ADOConnectionConstruction;
// more code here
struct /* coclass */ Connection;
// more code here
```

Not all objects have multiple implementations, as this is specific to the connection object. For ADO, most interfaces are defined as dual interfaces and are what you typically use. In this case, `ADOConnectionConstruc-tion` is an internal interface used by ADO to bind to an OLE DB provider, and should not ever be used directly. It is unsupported, undocumented, and will remain so in the future. This raises one of the more interesting points about `#import` or reading the type library in general. Not all of the objects exposed are useful to ADO developers. Some are artifacts for backward compatibility, some are there out of necessity in order to actually implement ADO (such as `ADOConnectionConstruction`), and some are of limited use to ADO developers (such as `Unspecified` enumerated values). In general, though, the documented portions of the type library are what you should be using, and hidden or undocumented elements of the type library are usually undocumented for a reason. There is, simply put, no implicit advantage in using an undocumented element of the type library.

Following these forward references, you see the declarations of smart pointers for each object:

```
_COM_SMARTPTR_TYPEDEF(_Connection, __uuidof(_Connection));
// more code
```

Note that smart pointers are generated only on the dual interface and `coclass` connection objects. Typically, though, you use only the smart pointer created on the dual interface objects for ADO. To invoke the connection object you would use the following code to declare an instance of the smart pointer and create an actual ADO connection object:

```
// more code here
_ConnectionPtr conn1;
Conn1.CreateInstance(__uuidof(Connection));
```

The __uuidof clause refers back to the forward declaration for the connection object defined earlier in order to provide the correct GUID.

Other type library items are provided within the .tlh file, such as enumerated types defined within the type library. This is especially important for the Visual C++ developer. However, it can also expose items in the type library that you were not meant to see. Consider the following definition for `CommandTypeEnum`:

```
enum CommandTypeEnum {
    adCmdUnspecified = -1,
    adCmdUnknown = 8,
    adCmdText = 1,
    adCmdTable = 2,
    adCmdStoredProc = 4,
    adCmdFile = 256,
    adCmdTableDirect = 512
};
```

Following the declarations for enumerated types exposed by the type library, you see the declarations of the classes wrapped by the smart pointers defined previously. The following code is an excerpt of the _Connection object's smart pointer class.

```
struct __declspec(uuid("00000515-0000-0010-8000-00aa006d2ea4"))
    _Connection : _ADO
{
    // Property data
    __declspec(property(
```

```
    get=GetConnectionString,put=PutConnectionString))
  _bstr_t ConnectionString;
  // more implementation

  // Wrapper methods for error-handling

  _bstr_t GetConnectionString ();
  void PutConnectionString (
      _bstr_t pbstr);

  // Raw methods provided by interface

  virtual HRESULT __stdcall get_ConnectionString (
      BSTR * pbstr) = 0;
  virtual HRESULT __stdcall put_ConnectionString (
      BSTR pbstr) = 0;
  // more implementation
};
```

You can use various arguments with the #import statement to control whether you get the wrappers, raw interfaces, or by default, both. In this case the

```
declspec(property(get =GetConnectionString,
                  put =PutConnectionString))
```

invocation defines the methods for getting and putting the value of a property. In this particular example, it uses the GetConnectionString() and PutConnectionString() methods, which themselves are wrappers around the raw interface methods, as shown in the following excerpt from the .tlh file:

```
inline _bstr_t _Connection::GetConnectionString () {
   BSTR _result;
   HRESULT _hr = get_ConnectionString(&_result);
   if (FAILED(_hr))
      _com_issue_errorex(_hr, this, __uuidof(this));
   return _bstr_t(_result, false);
}

inline void _Connection::PutConnectionString (_bstr_t pbstr) {
   HRESULT _hr = put_ConnectionString(pbstr);
   if (FAILED(_hr))
      _com_issue_errorex(_hr, this, __uuidof(this));
}
```

You can disable these helpers, but they allow you to assign and retrieve the value of the ConnectionString property without actually invoking a method. These wrapper functions are typical of every implementation method found in the .tli file. That is, if a failed HRESULT is returned by the raw interface method, you will need to trap the _com_error exception that #import raises.

Within that exception is the value of the failed HRESULT as well as other information #import can collect about the description and origin of this error. You should still check the ADO errors collection for additional information. If the provider raises more than one error, only the first error is wrapped in an exception. If ADO generates the error, the _com_error exception smart pointer is your only way to trap the information ADO tries to give to you when it encounters.

18.11.4 Single Versus Double Quote in SQL Statements

If you have code that uses SQL syntax to make changes in a datastore, and you migrate that code from DAO to ADO, you might have to change some of the syntax, particularly double quote characters. With DAO, the Microsoft Jet database engine expects double quotes in SQL syntax. With ADO, the Microsoft Access ODBC Driver expects single quotes in SQL syntax. This example works within DAO (but not within ADO) to insert a new record into a table:

```
INSERT INTO DemoTable (DT_ID, Customer) VALUES (54,
   "Record # 54")
```

You must change the double quotes to single quotes for the example to execute successfully in ADO, as shown here:

```
INSERT INTO DemoTable (DT_ID, Customer) VALUES (54,
   'Record # 54')
```

Ironically, the OLE DB Provider for the Microsoft Jet Engine can handle either form of syntax.

18.12 Summary

In this chapter you learned about OLE DB, a set of interfaces for data access. OLE DB is Microsoft's component database architecture that provides universal data integration over an enterprise's network — from mainframe to desktop — regardless of the data type. Microsoft's Open Database Connectivity (ODBC) industry-standard data-access interface is the underlying technology that the OLE DB specification is built on top of.

OLE DB provides a flexible and efficient database architecture that offers applications, compilers, and other database components efficient access to Microsoft and third-party data stores.

OLE DB is the fundamental Component Object Model (COM) building block for storing and retrieving records and unifies Microsoft's strategy for database connectivity. It will be used throughout Microsoft's line of applications and data stores.

OLE DB defines interfaces for accessing and manipulating all types of data. These interfaces will be used not just by data-consuming applications but also by database providers. By splitting databases apart, the resulting components can be used in an efficient manner.

While you can write applications that access OLE DB directly, and may choose to do so in some cases (particularly if there is a need for the consumer to be extremely thin), Microsoft generally recommends that you use the ActiveX Data Objects (ADO) wrapper of the OLE DB interfaces for your applications.

While OLE DB provides excellent support for accessing all types of database sources, Microsoft has gone an extra step and wrapped the OLE DB functionality within the ActiveX Data Objects (ADO), in an attempt to simplify database programming for Visual Basic, Visual C++, Visual J++, VBScript, and JavaScript developers.

ActiveX Data Objects (ADO) enables you to write a client application to access and manipulate data in a data source through a provider. ADO is ideally suited to consume data exposed by OLE DB providers, such as those written with the Microsoft OLE DB Simple Provider Toolkit. ADO's primary benefits are ease of use, high speed, low memory overhead, and a small disk footprint.

Working with ActiveX Data Objects, more than any other consideration, simply requires an understanding of how to work with standard COM objects. Throughout this chapter, you learned specific examples of how you can use ADO within your applications, and you also learned about potential problems to watch for within your application when working with ADO.

USING SCRIPTING AND OTHER TOOLS TO AUTOMATE THE VISUAL C++ IDE

Topics in this Chapter

- The Developer Studio Object Model
- Using VBScript to Write Developer Studio Macros
- Benefits of Custom AppWizards
- Creating a Wizard Project
- Using the New Custom Wizard
- Summary

Chapter 19

Developer Studio is an open environment that you can customize to meet your own development needs. Using VBScript macros and Custom AppWizards, you can automate repetitive tasks, add additional features to the standard MFC AppWizard project, or even create new project types. This chapter discusses two different ways that you can extend Developer Studio:

- You can create VBScript macros that run inside Developer Studio. These macros can appear on toolbars and menus, and can be executed from the command line.
- You can create a Custom AppWizard DLL that integrates directly with Developer Studio. The new AppWizard can build on the standard MFC AppWizard project, or you can create new project types from scratch.

In this chapter, you will create a VBScript macro and look at the sample macros shipped with Visual C++. You will also create a sample project that demonstrates how you can create your own Custom AppWizard.

19.1 The Developer Studio Object Model

The macros used with Visual C++ projects make use of an object model that is exposed by Developer Studio. Developer Studio exposes two different types of objects:

- Singular objects that each represent a single object such as an application, a breakpoint, or a window
- Collections of objects, such as the breakpoints that exist in a project, or the set of windows that are currently open

Both types of objects can have properties, events, and methods associated with them. Methods and properties are used to set or collect data from the object. Events are sent from the object as a notification that something interesting has occurred inside the object.

19.1.1 The Objects Exposed in Developer Studio

The objects that make up the Developer Studio object model are shown in Figure 19-1.

The following objects are included in the Developer Studio object model:

- `Application` is the Developer Studio application.
- `Breakpoint` represents a debugging breakpoint.
- `Breakpoints` is a collection that contains all of the breakpoints.
- `BuildProject` is a project that contains build information.
- `Configuration` is an object that represents the settings used to build a project.
- `Configurations` is a collection of all `Configuration` objects in a project.
- `Debugger` is used to interact with a process being debugged in Developer Studio.
- `Document` is an open document.
- `Documents` is a collection of open `Document` objects; this collection also includes `TextDocument` objects.

- `Project` is a group of related files; the files share at least one `Configuration` object.
- `Projects` is a collection of `Project` objects in the current Developer Studio workspace.
- `TextDocument` is an open text file.
- `TextEditor` is the Developer Studio text editor.
- `TextSelection` represents the currently selected text in a `TextDocument`.
- `TextWindow` is a window that contains an open text file.
- `Window` is an MDI client window that contains a `Document` or `TextDocument`.
- `Windows` is the collection of all open windows.

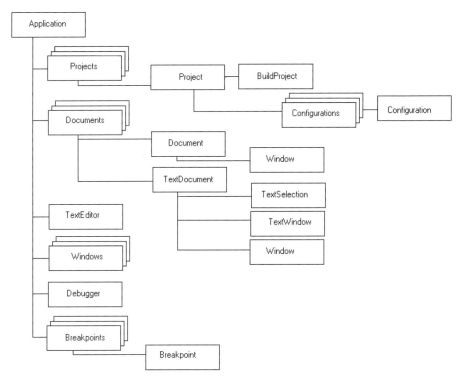

Figure 19-1 The Developer Studio object model.

19.2 Using VBScript To Write Developer Studio Macros

VBScript is an interpreted scripting language that is similar to Visual Basic. Like Visual Basic, it has loose rules about declaring subroutines and variable names. Unlike C++, it is not compiled, which means that each line is executed with the help of an interpreter.

VBScript macros are not stored as part of a Developer Studio workspace or project. When you write a VBScript macro, it is stored in a macro file with a DSM extension.

19.2.1 Declaring Variables

VBScript does not automatically require you to declare variables. This opens up a hole that makes it very easy to create new variables simply by misspelling an existing variable, thus introducing a bug that can be very difficult to fix.

You can change VBScript's default behavior so that it requires variables to be defined by changing the declaration mode to explicit, by inserting this line at the top of your VBScript source file:

```
option explicit
```

It's a very good idea to use explicit declarations, since it will prevent a common source of bugs in scripting languages.

To declare a variable, use the dim keyword:

```
dim strName
```

Unlike variable declarations in C++, you don't specify the type of the variable, just its name. All VBScript variables have the VARIANT type.

19.2.2 VBScript Subroutines

The VBScript equivalent of a C++ function is a subroutine. A subroutine always begins with the sub keyword, followed by the name of the subroutine and a pair of parentheses:

```
sub PrintName()
```

Any formal parameters used with the function are included within the parentheses, much as they are in a C++ function:

```
sub PrintNameAndAge(strName, ByVal nAge, ByRef strErr)
```

There are two differences in the way that formal parameters are declared for a VBScript subroutine when compared to a C++ function:

- The parameter name doesn't include a type.
- The parameter name is sometimes preceded by the `ByVal` or `ByRef` keywords.

Prefixing a parameter with `ByVal` indicates that the parameter is passed by value, just like in C++. If `ByRef` is used, the parameter is passed by reference, which is the same thing as using a C++ reference parameter. If no prefix is used, `ByVal` is assumed as the default.

Following the declaration of the subroutine is the body of the function, which consists of zero or more statements. For example, the following subroutine displays a message box:

```
sub dispMsg()
    MsgBox("Hello")
end sub
```

The end of the subroutine is marked by an `end sub` statement. When this line is encountered, the subroutine is completed, and flow of control returns to the caller.

You can exit a subroutine from inside the subroutine body with the `exit sub` statement:

```
exit sub
```

When `exit sub` is encountered, the subroutine is exited, and the flow of control is returned to the caller.

19.2.3 Using Functions in VBScript

VBScript also includes *functions*, which are exactly like subroutines, except that they return a value to the caller. A function looks very much like a subroutine, as shown in the following code:

```
function GetAge(strName)
  if strName = "Zaphod" then
    GetAge = 42
  elseif strName = "Ford" then
    GetAge = 84
  end if
end function
```

19.2.4 Creating a VBScript Macro

There are two steps to creating a VBScript macro. First, create a new macro file, then add a macro to it. To create a new macro file, use the following steps:

1. Select Macros... from the Tools menu. The Macros dialog box will be displayed.
2. Click the Options>> button to expand the Macros dialog box.
3. Click the New File... button. The New Macro File dialog box is displayed; enter a name and description for the new macro file. For this example, enter `Extended` as the macro file name, and click the OK button.

To add a macro to the Extended macro file, click the Edit button, and enter a description for the new macro. For this example, enter `numberLines` as the macro name and click OK. Developer Studio will open the macro file and create a skeleton of the new macro for you. Edit the macro file so that it looks like the source code shown in the following code.

```
option explicit
dim dsSelect

sub SelectNextLine()
  ' Selecting a line selects the entire line - including the
  ' carriage return. This can lead to skipping one line, so
  ' this function moves down one line, then up one line, to
  ' prevent this problem from occurring.
  ActiveDocument.Selection.SelectLine
  ActiveDocument.Selection.LineDown
  ActiveDocument.Selection.LineUp
  ActiveDocument.Selection.StartOfLine
end sub

sub numberLines()
  ' Line numbers that contain absolute line numbers. For example
  ' line 25 in the file is always line 25, even if a subset of
  ' the file is selected.
  dim lineFileCurrent 'The current file's line number
  dim lineFileEnd     'The last line in the file to be written
  ' Line numbers that are relative to the selected text. For
  ' example, line 25 might be referred to by a different number
  ' if a subset of the file is selected.
  dim lineFileWrite   'The current line number to be written
  dim CurrText
```

```
if ActiveDocument.type <> "Text" Then
  MsgBox("The active file is not a source file.")
else
  lineFileWrite = 1
  lineFileEnd = ActiveDocument.Selection.BottomLine
  lineFileCurrent = ActiveDocument.Selection.TopLine
  ActiveDocument.Selection.GoToLine lineFileCurrent, dsSelect
  do
    CurrText = ActiveDocument.Selection
    ActiveDocument.Selection = cstr(lineFileWrite) + _
        ": " + CurrText
    lineFileWrite = lineFileWrite + 1
    lineFileCurrent = lineFileCurrent + 1
    if lineFileCurrent > lineFileEnd then _
      exit do
    SelectNextLine()
  loop
  end if
end sub
```

To test the `numberLines` macro, open a source file and select a box of text such as a function. Next, open the Macros dialog box and double-click on the `numberLines` macro in the list box. Every line in the block of selected text will be prefixed with a line number, like this:

```
1:int getAnswer() {
2:  doSomethingForALongTime();
3:  return 42;
4: }
```

19.2.5 Removing a Developer Studio Macro File

There is no obvious way to remove a macro file once it has been loaded into Developer Studio. You can enable or disable the macro through the Macro dialog box, but if you really want to remove the macro, you must edit the registry.

You should only attempt the following steps if you are comfortable editing registry entries. You can easily render your machine inoperable if you make a mistake in the following steps. *You should always backup your registry before modifying it in any way.*

Macro filenames are stored at:

```
HKEY_USERS/Default/Software/Microsoft/Dev Studio/Macros
```

Developer Studio will query the value of this key to determine which macro files are to be loaded. By removing value entries from this key, you can trim the number of macro files loaded by Developer Studio.

19.2.6   Example Macros Included with Visual C++

Visual C++ includes example macros that illustrate how you can interact with the Developer Studio object model. The example macros include:

- `CloseExceptActive`, which closes all of the open editor windows except the currently active window.
- `CommentOut`, which can be used to comment out a block of text.
- `ToggleCommentStyle`, which is used to swap comment styles between the `/*` and `//` formats.

The example macro file is named SAMPLE.DSM, and can be found in the Common\MSDev98\Macros subdirectory, under the Visual Studio installation directory.

The sample macros are not loaded by default — you must load the macro file manually at least once. To load the sample macro file for the first time, follow these steps:

1. Select Customize... from the Developer Studio Tools menu. The Customize dialog box will be displayed.
2. Click on the tab labeled Add-ins and Macro Files. One of the items displayed on this property page is a list of the currently loaded macro files.
3. Click the Browse... button; a standard File Open common dialog box will be displayed. Navigate to the Common\MSDev98\Macros subdirectory and select the SAMPLES.DSM macro file.

After the macro file has been loaded, you can run individual macros by selecting Macros from the Tools menu. You can also add macros to the toolbar for easy access, as described later in the section, "Adding a VBScript Macro to the Toolbar" on page 607.

19.2.7 Debugging a Visual Studio Macro

There are two ways to debug Visual Studio macros:

- Add output statements to your macro so that your macro can print out information as it executes.
- Add message boxes to your macro so that execution stops while a message is displayed.

Neither of these two options is as sophisticated as the debugger included with Visual Studio. Since macros are generally fairly small, they usually require very little debugging.

19.2.8 Adding a VBScript Macro to the Toolbar

To add a VBScript macro to the toolbar, follow these steps:

1. Load the macro file, if it isn't currently loaded.
2. Select Customize from the Tools Menu.
3. Click the Commands tab, and select Macros from the Categories drop-down list; this will display a listbox containing all macros available for use.
4. Drag and drop the macro name to the toolbar that will contain the macro's button. The Button Appearance dialog box will be displayed to allow you to select the text or image that is displayed for the macro.
5. Select an image for the macro and click the OK button.

To remove a toolbar item, open the Customize dialog box and drag the item from the toolbar.

19.3 Benefits of Custom AppWizards

One of the ways that you can extend Visual C++ and Developer Studio is to create a Custom AppWizard. You can easily extend the options offered by the standard MFC AppWizard, or you can create completely new types of projects. Custom AppWizards are available only in Professional and Enterprise versions of Visual C++.

19.3.1 The Custom Wizard Architecture

Developer Studio offers a number of different options for new projects. When you select New from the File menu and click on the Projects tab, a list of the available project types is displayed, as shown in Figure 19-2.

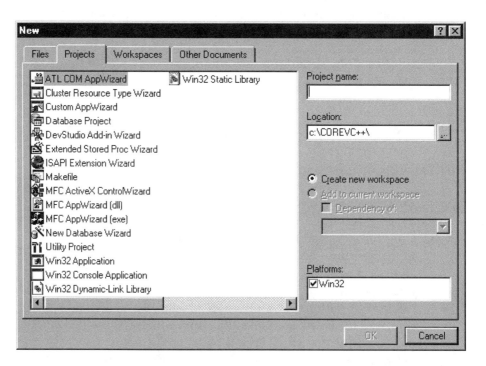

Figure 19-2 Developer Studio project types.

In addition to the default project types shown in Figure 19-2, Developer Studio will also display any available Custom AppWizards. The interface between Developer Studio and AppWizard is exposed through a set of classes and components that you can use to create Custom AppWizards. Custom AppWizards are implemented as DLLs that are placed in the Common\MSDev98\Template subdirectory, under the Visual Studio root installation directory.

The basic architecture for Custom AppWizards is shown in Figure 19-3. When you add a Custom AppWizard to Developer Studio, you don't modify or replace any of the existing Wizards used to create new projects.

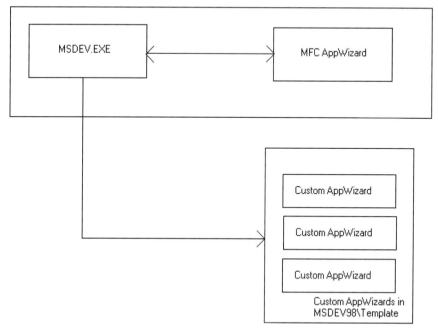

Figure 19-3   The Custom AppWizard architecture used with Developer Studio.

19.3.2   Types of Custom AppWizards

There are many different types of Custom AppWizards that can be created. Custom AppWizards generally fall into one of the following categories:

- Wizards that are generated from existing projects. In order to use this method, the project must have been built using MFC AppWizard.
- Wizards that add custom steps to the standard MFC AppWizard. A custom Wizard built using this approach will follow the default AppWizard logic, with additional custom steps added at the end of the sequence of Wizard pages.
- Wizards that offer completely new functionality or project types to the user. This is the most flexible approach to building a Custom AppWizard, and it's also the most difficult. You must create each dialog box used by the Custom AppWizard, and you must manage all data entered by the user.

Depending on the type of Custom AppWizard you create, you will need to modify or supply different Custom AppWizard components. Each component is used for a different purpose, so your Custom AppWizard may not need to interact with all parts of the Custom AppWizard architecture. If you're developing a Custom AppWizard that's based on the default MFC AppWizard, or a completely new AppWizard from scratch, you will need to understand the different components in the Custom AppWizard architecture, as shown in Figure 19-4. Each of these components is described in the following sections.

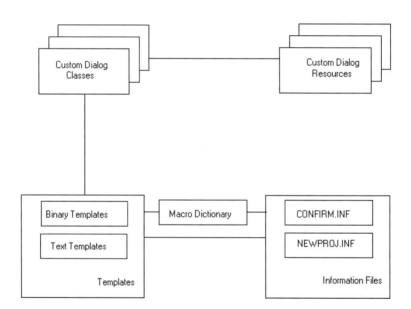

Figure 19-4   The components included in the Developer Studio Custom AppWizard architecture.

19.3.3 Using Custom Dialog Boxes

Custom dialog boxes are used to interact with your Custom AppWizard's user. As an AppWizard uses nested dialog boxes that are displayed as wizard pages to the user, you are responsible only for the interior dialog box. The exterior dialog box is maintained by the AppWizard framework. The relationship between your dialog box and the one provided by the AppWizard framework is shown in Figure 19-5.

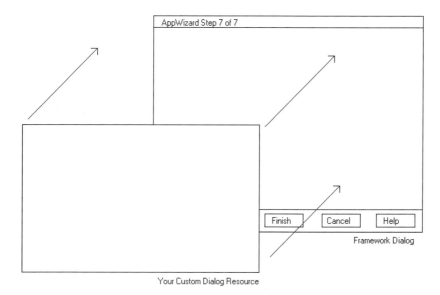

AppWizard Step 7 of 7

Finish   Cancel   Help

Framework Dialog

Your Custom Dialog Resource

Figure 19-5 A Custom AppWizard dialog box is nested inside the framework's wizard page.

The number of steps used by a Custom AppWizard is defined when a project is created. The AppWizard framework will create the necessary dialog boxes automatically. Each dialog box is managed by a class derived from `CAppWizStepDlg`.

As with any other MFC-based project, you can associate each control in the Custom AppWizard's dialog boxes with a member variable.

Each dialog box class includes an `OnDismiss()` member function. This function is called whenever the user attempts to leave the dialog box using the Next, Back, or Finish buttons. If this function returns `FALSE`, the dialog box won't be dismissed. If the function returns `TRUE`, the dialog box will be dismissed. To validate the data that has been entered by the user, you must edit the `OnDismiss()` function, like this:

```
BOOL CCustomDlg::OnDismiss()
 {
   if(!UpdateData(TRUE))
     return FALSE;
   if(m_strAuthor.IsEmpty() == FALSE)
     // Store a default value
   else
     // Store m_strAuthor
   return TRUE;
 }
```

In the preceding code fragment, the `OnDismiss()` function begins by calling `UpdateData(TRUE)`, which verifies the contents of controls and transfers the data into member variables. If the transfer is unsuccessful, `UpdateData()` returns `FALSE`, and `FALSE` is returned from `OnDismiss()` to prevent the user from switching to another page. If the transfer is successful, member variables such as `m_strAuthor` will contain valid data, and can be used in the Custom AppWizard. `TRUE` is returned so that the user can switch to another page in the wizard.

19.3.4 Understanding Classes and ClassWizard

All projects built with the default MFC AppWizard include a standard set of classes. If your Custom AppWizard extends the standard MFC AppWizard, it will need to interact with ClassWizard and the classes generated by the default MFC AppWizard.

In order to create classes for the project, you must manage two types of files:

- Text templates are used by a Custom AppWizard to define how text files containing classes (and other data) are generated. More information about text templates is provided later in the section "Text Templates" on page 616.
- The project's class information file is used by class wizard to manage classes and other resources. The class information file is created by Custom AppWizards using information in the NEWPROJ.INF file. Information files are discussed in the next section, and the NEWPROJ.INF file is discussed later in the section "Information Files" on page 617.

19.3.5 Understanding the Class Information File's Contents

As discussed in the previous section, ClassWizard uses the project's class information file to determine the classes that are used in a project. The class information file has the same name as the project, with a CLW extension. For example, the class information for a project named Foo is FOO.CLW.

The class information file is a text file containing the names of classes and other resources. The actual format of the class information file is not documented. However, the format is not difficult to decipher, and if you are making small changes, you can make the required changes easily.

The following code is an example of a class information file. Only the first part of the file is shown in this listing. You can get a good idea about how the different parts of the class information file relate to a Visual C++ project by opening the class information file for existing projects.

```
; CLW file contains information for the MFC ClassWizard

[General Info]
Version=1
LastClass=CADOMFC1View
LastTemplate=CDialog
NewFileInclude1=#include "stdafx.h"
NewFileInclude2=#include "ADOMFC1.h"
LastPage=0

ClassCount=6
Class1=CADOMFC1App
Class2=CADOMFC1Doc
Class3=CADOMFC1View
Class4=CMainFrame
Class5=CChildFrame
Class6=CAboutDlg

ResourceCount=3
Resource1=IDR_MAINFRAME
Resource2=IDR_ADOMFCTYPE
Resource3=IDD_ABOUTBOX
```

There is another option when dealing with the class information file. Developer Studio will efficiently recreate a class information file based on the files associated with a project. This option is useful if you are making extensive modifications to the standard class information file. It's also useful if you generate different classes than are specified in the NEWPROJ.INF file.

19.3.6 Using Macros in a Custom AppWizard

Macros are heavily used in a Custom AppWizard. These macros are not VBScript macros discussed in the first half of this chapter, rather they are more like C++ macros.

There are two types of macros:

1. Standard pre-defined macros that are used to track information entered by the user during standard AppWizard steps.

    2. Custom macros that are defined and used by your Custom AppWizard.

Macros are stored in an MFC `CMapStringToString` map collection named `m_Dictionary`, which is a member of the `CCustomAppWizard` class. The collection is used as a dictionary associating each macro name with a value. Information stored in the macro dictionary is available for use later in the Custom AppWizard.

Each macro name is used as a key into the `m_Dictionary` collection. For example, to create a new macro named `PROJ_DATE` that contains the project date, you can use a code fragment like this:

```
CTime theTime = CTime::GetCurrentTime();
CString strDate = theTime.Format("%A, %B, %d, %Y");
MyWizaw.m_Dictionary["PROJ_DATE"] = strDate;
```

The name of the Custom AppWizard instance is always the name of the project, plus aw. In the code fragment above, the name of the Custom Wizard is MyWiz, so the name of the Custom AppWizard instance derived from `CCustomAppWizard` is `MyWizaw`. The macro dictionary for a project named MyWiz is always accessed as:

```
MyWizaw.m_Dictionary
```

To retrieve a value from the dictionary, just use the macro name as the index:

```
strDate = MyWiz.m_dictionary["PROJ_DATE"];
```

After a macro has been defined, the macro value can also be used in text templates and project information files.

As discussed earlier, a Custom AppWizard is responsible for creating all of the classes and project information used for a new project. The Wizard will often need to know the name of the current project and other names that are specific to the project, as well as options that have been selected by the user. For example, the Custom AppWizard may be interested in knowing if the project is an MDI or SDI application.

There are literally hundreds of macros available to you. A complete list of the macros is documented in the Visual Studio help system. For this reason, a set of standard macros using a common naming convention are defined for every Custom AppWizard project. First, there is a set of prefixes that are used in macro names:

- `DOC` refers to the application's document class.
- `APP` refers to the application's `CWinApp`-derived class.
- `FRAME` refers to the application's main frame class.
- `CHILD_FRAME` refers to the application's MDI child frame class, if any.
- `VIEW` refers to the application's view class.
- `DLG` refers to the application's main dialog box class in dialog box-based applications.
- `DLGAUTOPROXY` refers to the automation proxy used by the application's main dialog box class in dialog box-based applications.
- `RECSET` refers to the application's main recordset class, if any.
- `SRVRITEM` refers to the application's main server-item class, if any.
- `CNTRITEM` refers to the application's main container-item class, if any.
- `IPFRAME` refers to the application's in-place frame class, if any.
- `TREEVIEW` refers to the treeview class used in an Explorer-style application.
- `WNDVIEW` refers to the view class in a `NODOCVIEW` MFC application.

Next, there is a set of component names that are combined with the prefixes from the previous list:

- `CLASS` refers to the class name.
- `BASE_CLASS` refers to the base class name.
- `IFILE` refers to the name of the implementation file. The file extension is not included in the name.
- `HFILE` refers to the name of the header file. The file extension is not included in the name.

Uppercase and lowercase versions of the `IFILE` and `HFILE` macros are provided. If the macro name is uppercase, its value is uppercase. If the macro name is lowercase, its value is lowercase, as shown in Table 19-1.

There is also a `ROOT` macro, which refers to the project name. Three versions of `ROOT` are provided. The macro `ROOT` is translated into the project name using all uppercase letters, `root` is translated using all lowercase letters, and `Root` is translated according to the capitalization used when the project was created.

Macro	Translation
APP_CLASS	CFooApp
VIEW_IFILE	FOOVIEW
DOC_HFILE	FOODOC
doc_ifile	foodoc
view_hfile	fooview

Table 19-1 Standard Macro Translations for a Project Named Foo

19.3.7 Text Templates

As discussed earlier, text templates are used to create files that will be used in text form in the user's new project. A text template is a mixture of macros, directives, and plain source code. Directives are discussed later in the section, "Directives" on page 618.

When a file is created, the text template for the file is read by a parser, which evaluates macros and directives, and writes the file into the project directory.

Macros found in text templates are always surrounded by dollar signs, like this:

```
$$MY_MACRO$$
$$VIEW_CLASS$$
```

When the parser reaches a pair of dollar signs, the macro is evaluated. If the symbol is a macro, a text substitution is made with the macro's value. For example, the following code fragment is a simplified version of the template used to create the OnNewDocument function for MFC AppWizard projects.

```
BOOL $$DOC_CLASS$$::OnNewDocument()
  {
    if (!$$DOC_BASE_CLASS$$::OnNewDocument())
      return FALSE;
    // TODO: add reinitialization code here
    // (SDI documents will reuse this document)
    return TRUE;
  }
```

As you can see, this code fragment is a mixture of macros and plain source code. As the parser scans the function, it makes the following substitutions:

- `$$DOC_CLASS$$` is replaced by the document class name. For example, if the project name is Foo, `$$DOC_CLASS$$` is replaced by `CFooDoc`.

- `$$DOC_BASE_CLASS$$` is replaced by the immediate base class of the document. For example, if this isn't an OLE document, the macro is replaced by `CDocument`.

All other text in this code fragment is written directly into the source file.

19.3.8 Binary Templates

Binary templates are used to create files that will be used in binary form in the user's new project. The Custom AppWizard uses binary templates to populate the new project with bitmaps, icons, cursors, and other binary data. By modifying the binary templates, you can change the appearance of projects created with your Custom AppWizard.

19.3.9 Information Files

Information files are used by a Custom AppWizard to create the project. An information file is very much like a "make" file; it's used to create projects and output based on user input stored in various macros.

There are two information files created as part of a Custom AppWizard project:

- NEWPROJ.INF contains directives and information used by your Custom AppWizard to create a project.
- CONFIRM.INF contains directives used to create the information displayed in the project confirmation dialog box.

Like the text template files, information files make heavy use of macros and directives. In most cases, you won't need to edit information files. The information file must be modified only when the rules for creating a particular file has been changed, or if a new source file has been added to the project.

19.3.10 Directives

Directives are used to control the flow of a text template or information file. A directive always begins with two dollar signs, just like macros:

```
$$IF(PROJTYPE_SDI)
```

A directive must always begin in the first column of a text template file. A directive can have one of the following values:

```
$$IF
$$ELIF
$$ELSE
$$ENDIF
$$BEGINLOOP
$$SET_DEFAULT_LANG
$$//
$$INCLUDE
```

The $$IF, $$ELIF, $$ELSE, and $$ENDIF directives are commonly used to control which lines of code are inserted into a source code module. For example, this code fragment is from the StdAfx.h text template:

```
$$IF(CRecordView)
#include <afxdb.h>            // MFC ODBC database classes
$$ELIF(CDaoRecordView)
#include <afxdao.h>           // MFC DAO database classes
$$ELIF(DB || PROJTYPE_DLL)

#ifndef _AFX_NO_DB_SUPPORT
#include <afxdb.h>            // MFC ODBC database classes
#endif // _AFX_NO_DB_SUPPORT

#ifndef _AFX_NO_DAO_SUPPORT
#include <afxdao.h>           // MFC DAO database classes
#endif // _AFX_NO_DAO_SUPPORT

$$ENDIF // database/DLL options
```

The $$IF and $$ELIF directives test a macro to determine if it is defined in the directory. If so, the directive evaluates as TRUE. The $$IF, $$ELSE, and $$ELIF directives are similar to the if, else if, and else statements used in C and C++, except that no braces are required. As shown in the previous code fragment, macros tested by the $$IF and $$ELIF directives can be combined using the logical or symbol, ||. For example, the line:

```
$$ELIF(DB || PROJTYPE_DLL)
```

evaluates as TRUE if DB or PROJTYPE_DLL is defined in the macro dictionary.

Macro names can also be preceded by the not symbol, !. Using ! changes a TRUE value to FALSE, and vice versa. For example:

```
$$(!PROJTYPE_DLL)
```

evaluates as TRUE if PROJTYPE_DLL is not defined in the macro dictionary.

Execution continues until the next directive. Each $$IF is terminated by an $$ENDIF. After an $$IF, there may be one or more $$ELIF directives, and a maximum of one $$ELSE directive that will be executed if none of the previous $$IF or $$ELIF directives are TRUE.

The $$BEGINLOOP and $$ENDLOOP directives are used to create loops in a text template or information file. Every $$BEGINLOOP must be matched with an $$ENDLOOP. These directives may not be nested. The macro that is tested must be a string that contains a numeric value. For example:

```
$$BEGINLOOP(NUM_LANGS)
    //Do some work...
$$ENDLOOP
```

executes NUM_LANG loops. If NUM_LANG contains the string "25," 25 loops are executed.

The $$INCLUDE directive is used to include other templates. This can be useful if you need to perform the same processing in multiple files. The macro used as a parameter must specify a filename:

```
$$INCLUDE(LOC_RC)
```

The $$// directive is used to indicate a comment in the template or information file. A comment marked with this directive is not written to the file. To write comments in a source file, just use comments without the $$:

```
$$// This is a template comment not written to the source file.
// This comment is written to the source file.
```

19.4 Creating a Wizard Project

In the next few sections, we will create a Custom AppWizard project named Core, which demonstrates how a Custom AppWizard is created.

The Core Custom AppWizard includes an expanded comment area at the beginning of every source file. The comment includes the author's name, the date the project was created, the purpose of the file, and a comment that is included in all source files.

```
/*

    This project was created using the "Core Visual C++"
    Custom AppWizard.

    This is the first Core AppWizard project.

    Author  : Zaphod
    File    : Foo.cpp
    Project : Foo
    Date    : Wednesday, October 18, 1999
    This file is the project's main cpp file.
*/
```

19.4.1   Planning the Core Custom AppWizard

Like any software project, it's a good idea to have a plan before you start coding. The Core AppWizard has two parts:

1. A Wizard page that collects information from the user.
2. Modifications to the text templates that control how the source code is generated.

The new wizard page collects the project author's name and a project-wide comment that will be added to every source file. This information, along with the current date, is stored in the macro dictionary. Every source code text template is modified to use the new macros when generating source code files.

19.4.2   Beginning the Custom AppWizard Project

Creating a Custom AppWizard is much like creating any other MFC project. Developer Studio includes a wizard that automates much of the process, so much of the hard work is done automatically.

The first step in creating the Core AppWizard is to create a Custom App-Wizard project. Begin by selecting New from the File menu. When the New dialog appears as shown in Figure 19-6, select the Projects tab. Select Custom AppWizard as the project type, and enter a project name and location. In Figure 19-6, the name of the project is CoreAppWiz, and the location is C:\COREVC++\CoreAppWiz.

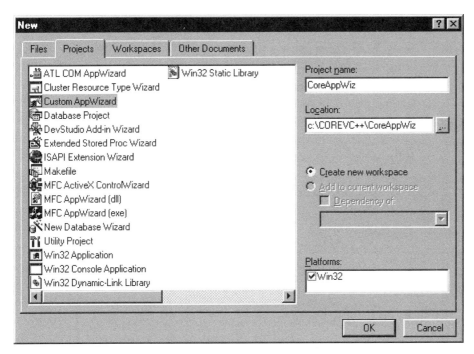

Figure 19-6 Starting a new Custom AppWizard project.

After you have filled in the information shown in Figure 19-6, click the Create button to generate the project. A wizard is displayed to help guide you through the process of creating a Custom AppWizard. The first wizard page is used to collect basic information about the new Custom AppWizard:

- The project starting point, which is either an existing project, the standard AppWizard steps, or completely custom steps. For the Core Custom AppWizard, select Standard MFC AppWizard steps.
- The name of the new Custom AppWizard as it will be displayed in the list of project types. The Core Wizard will keep the default name of `Core AppWizard`.
- The number of custom steps added in the new Custom AppWizard. The Core AppWizard adds one page; enter a 1 here.

When you're satisfied with the contents of the first wizard page, click the Next button. The contents of the second wizard page depend on the type of project selected on the first page:

- If the new AppWizard is based on an existing project, the second page will ask for a path to this project.
- If the new AppWizard is based on the standard AppWizard steps, the second wizard page collects two key pieces of information: the type of application built with the wizard, and the languages supported by the new wizard. For the Core AppWizard, select the MFC AppWizard Executable radio button, and English as the supported language.
- If the new AppWizard is based on completely new steps there is no second page; the only available buttons on the first wizard page are Cancel and Finish.

After you have completed the second wizard page, click the Finish button. The New Project Information dialog box will be displayed; click the OK button to dismiss this dialog and create the new Core AppWizard project.

At this point, the project will compile and run; however, it will have an extra, blank wizard page and the same functionality as the standard MFC AppWizard. To complete the Core AppWizard, the following steps are required:

- Edit the dialog box resource used for the seventh wizard page, and add class member variables for new controls that collect author and project information.
- Edit the new OnDismiss() member function to collect information from the new wizard page.
- Edit the text templates to make use of the information collected in the new wizard page.

These steps are covered in the next three sections.

19.4.3 Editing the Dialog Box Resource

The Core AppWizard has one dialog box resource, IDD_CUSTOM1, which was created as part of the original project. Open the IDD_CUSTOM1 dialog box resource by double-clicking on the IDD_CUSTOM1 icon in the Resource View tab in the project workspace. Add two edit controls as shown in Figure 19-7.

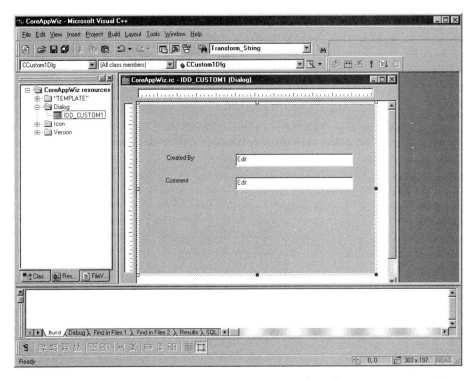

Figure 19-7 The IDD_CUSTOM1 dialog box resource from the Core AppWizard project.

Use the values from Table 19-2 to name the two new edit controls, and associate them with member variables in the CCustom1Dlg class.

Table 19-2 Member Variables Added to the CCustom1Dlg Class

Control ID	Name	Category	Variable Type
IDC_EDIT_AUTHOR	m_strAuthor	Value	CString
IDC_EDIT_COMMENT	m_strComment	Value	CString

19.4.4 Providing an OnDismiss Function

As discussed earlier, the OnDismiss() function is called when the user is moving from a new wizard page. This function should validate data contained in the dialog box controls, and store user input in the macro dictionary. The `CCustom1Dlg::OnDismiss` function used in the Core AppWizard is shown in the following code fragment:

```
BOOL CCustom1Dlg::OnDismiss()
 {
   if (!UpdateData(TRUE))
     return FALSE;
   if( m_strAuthor.IsEmpty() == FALSE )
     Coreaw.m_Dictionary["PROJ_AUTHOR"] = m_strAuthor;
   else
     Coreaw.m_Dictionary["PROJ_AUTHOR"] = "";
   if( m_strComment.IsEmpty() == FALSE )
     Coreaw.m_Dictionary["PROJ_COMMENT"] = m_strComment;
   else
     Coreaw.m_Dictionary["PROJ_COMMENT"] = "";

   CTime date = CTime::GetCurrentTime();
   CString strDate = date.Format( "%A, %B %d, %Y" );
   Coreaw.m_Dictionary["PROJ_DATE"] = strDate;
   strDate = Coreaw.m_Dictionary["PROJ_DATE"];
   return TRUE;
}
```

In addition to storing user input in the macro dictionary, `OnDismiss()` also calculates and stores the current time. The `PROJ_DATE` macro will be used to print the date that the project was created.

The next code listing adds three new macro names to the dictionary. However, `OnDismiss()` is called only if the user reaches your page. If the user clicks the Finish button prematurely, the function will never be called, and the macros won't be added to the dictionary. To avoid problems when generating the text templates, you must provide default values for the macros when the Core AppWizard is started. Add the source code from the following code fragment to the bottom of the `Core::InitCustomAppWiz` member function.

```
Coreaw.m_Dictionary["PROJ_AUTHOR"] = "";
Coreaw.m_Dictionary["PROJ_COMMENT"] = "";
Coreaw.m_Dictionary["PROJ_DATE"] = "";
```

19.4.5 Editing the Text Templates

Every Custom AppWizard project includes a Template subdirectory, which contains that information and template files used by the Custom AppWizard.

For the Core AppWizard project, text templates are modified to use the information entered in the new wizard page.

For the Core AppWizard, you will modify only the text templates that have .h or .cpp file extensions. These files will be used by the complete Core App-Wizard to generate source files for projects that it creates. The first few lines of each file are modified as shown below, which contains the changes to the ChildFrm.cpp text template. Most of the modifications shown below are used in all files, except for the parts that refer to a specific class or file.

```
/*

    This project was created using the "Core Visual

    C++" custom AppWizard.


    $$PROJ_COMMENT$$


    Author : $$PROJ_AUTHOR$$
    File   : $$child_frame_ifile$$.cpp
    Project: $$Root$$
    Date   : $$PROJ_DATE$$


    This file provides the implementation for the
    $$CHILD_FRAME_CLASS$$ class.

*/
```

The line:

```
File : $$child_frame_ifile$$.cpp
```

will be translated into:

```
File : ChildFrm.cpp
```

Every text template will have a different macro on this line, depending on the filename. In addition, the comment:

```
This file provides the implementation for the
    $$CHILD_FRAME_CLASS$$ class.
```

is slightly different for each text template file.

19.5 Using the New Custom Wizard

To use the Core AppWizard, first compile the Core AppWizard project. After the project is successfully built, the Core.awx DLL will automatically be moved into the Developer Studio Template subdirectory.

When a new project is started, a new selection named Core AppWizard is displayed as a new project type, as shown in Figure 19-8.

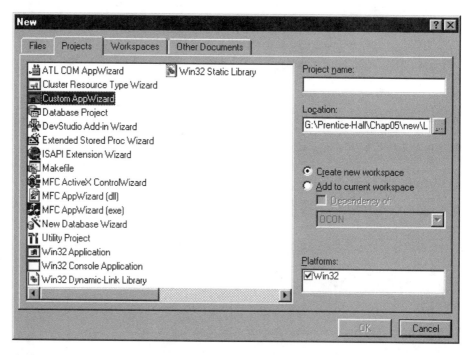

Figure 19-8   The New project property page, including the Core AppWizard project type.

19.6 Summary

This chapter discussed two ways that you can extend Developer Studio. Developer Studio macros use VBScript to automate repetitive tasks. The object model used by VBScript macros was discussed, as were the steps used to create and use VBScript macros.

Creating a Custom AppWizard is another way that you can interact and extend Developer Studio. You learned about the Custom AppWizard Architecture, and created an example AppWizard that added an extra step to the standard MFC AppWizard.

Index

A

Active Template Library, 1
   see also ATL
ActiveX, 6
   and VCM, 14
ActiveX components,
   ActiveX Template Library, 459
   designing with BaseCtl, 459
ActiveX containers, 453
ActiveX controls, IConnectionPoint interface,
    451
ActiveX Data Objects (ADO), 11, 570
   see also ADO
ActiveX documents, DocObjects, 452
address spaces,
   compatibility arena, 319

logical addresses, 318
physical address, 318
reserved system arena, 320
shared arena, 320
shared memory, 319
ADO, 5, 11
   business services, 571
   COM APIs, 579
   data services, 571
   error handling, 587
   exception handling, 588
   MFC OLE, 578
   objects model, 571
   type library, 581
   unrecoverable exceptions, 590
   user services, 571
   using #import, 573
AfxGetMainWnd(), role of, 215

allocating memory,
    free() or delete(), 326
    GlobalAlloc() and GlobalLock(), 326
    protected mode, 326
    real mode, 326
    selector, 327
    using malloc() and new(), 326
application services, integration with, 14
AppWizard,
    binary templates, 617
    Custom, 607
    custom types, 609
    information files, 617
    support for MTS components, 16
    text templates, 616
    using custom, 626
    using macros in custom, 613
ASSERT, IsKindOf(), 443
ASSERT macro, and debugging, 43
ASSERT_VALID macro, and debugging, 44
asynchronous I/O, 352
    asynchronous operations, 352
    OVERLAPPED structure, 353
    ReadFileEx() and WriteFileEx(), 354
ATL, 1, 459
automation controllers, 450
automation server, 463
    IDispatch interface, 450
    dual-interface, 456
    IDispatch interface, 455
    in-process, 450
    in-process servers, 464
    local, 450
    local execution, 464
    out-of-process servers, 464
    remote, 450

B

backwards compatibility, _near, _far,
        or _huge, 323
based pointers, __based keyword, 336
bitmaps,
    copying, 182
    creating, 181
    creating and loading, 179
    creating resources with the resource editor,
        180
    definition of, 179
    drawing with, 182
    loading, 181
bitmap class, creating a device-independent,
        183
breakpoint, message, 36
breakpoints,
    data, 35
    inserting into program code, 34
    location, 35
brushes,
    and CBrush class, 169
    and hatching pattern flags, 169
    drawing with, 171
    selecting into the device context, 170
    stock, 170

C

callback functions,
    common uses of, 60
    examples in Windows, 60
    role in C++, 61
    understanding, 57
    within MFC, 63
CClientDC class, 160
CCmdTarget class, 208
CDBException,
    AfxThrowDBException() function, 433
    SQLError() function, 432
CDC base class, GDI functions supported by,
        157
CDialog-derived class, creating, 81
CDocItem class, 208
CDocument class, 198
    member functions, 200
CEvent class, 304
CException, 420, 423
    Delete(), 424
    GetErrorMessage(), 423

purposefully throwing, 428
CHtmlView, 1
    MFC support for, 17
class information file, role in Visual Studio, 612
CMDIChildWnd class, 213
CMDIFrameWnd class, 213
CMemoryException, 424
CMemoryState class, 44
CMetaFileDC class, 161
CObject class, 44, 204
COM, 6
    and interfaces, 6
    apartment-threaded model, 550
    BaseCtl framework, 448
    OLE DB, 546
COM components,
    apartment-threading model, 479
    DLLRegisterServer(), 465
    DLLUnregisterServer(), 465
    dual interfaces, 473
    GetIDsOfNames(), 472
    IDispatch, 472
    interface definition language, 469
    interface inheritance, 470
    interfaces, 463
    IUnknown, 471
    nested objects, 463
    object models, 463
    plug-compatible, 468
    polymorphic, 468
    QueryInterface(), 471
    reference counting, 471
    type library, 469
    vTable, 469
command targets, 208
common controls, 106
common dialogs, 106
    Color Picker, 112
    customizing appearance of, 118
    customizing behavior of, 118
    File Open, 107
    Find, 113
    Font Selection, 113
    OLE-specific support of by MFC, 117
    Page Setup, 111

Print, 109
Print Setup, 111
Replace, 113
working with, 106
Compact Disk File System, 344
    see also CDFS
compatibility I/O, 354
    low-level I/O, 355
    stream I/O, 358
Component Object Model, and DNA
        architecture, 6
    see also COM
component-based application development, 8
compound document, CCMDTarget, 447
consoles, 366
    allocating, 366
    customizing buffers, 368
    I/O, 367
context switching, definition of, 280
control behavior, modifying, 124
CPaintDC class, 161
CPoint class, 172
    operator overload functions, 172
CPrintDialog class, 270
CPrintInfo class, and print or print preview
        jobs, 256
    and pagination, 254
CPropertyPage-derived classes, creating, 134
CPropertyPageEx class, using, 148
CPropertySheetEx class, using, 148
CRect class, 173
    operator overload functions, 175
CRgn class, and clipping, 174
critical sections, 298
CRuntimeClass object, 233
CSingleDocTemplate class, 211, 212
CSize class, 173
    operator overload functions, 173
CSplitterWnd class, 227
    specifics of, 228
    support of shared scrollbars, 236
CUserException, 420
CView class, 223, 225, 254
    MFC-derived variants of, 225
    using, 221

D

data access objects, 545
DCOM, 6, 379
DCOM components,
  marshaling, 477
  parameters, 477
  proxy-stub architecture, 475
  universal marshaler, 477
Debug Monitor, 48
debugger, using when you run an application, 27
debugging,
  advanced considerations of, 50
  and DataTips information, 39
  and Exceptions dialog box, 41
  and inserting breakpoints, 34
  and QuickWatch window, 39
  and single-stepping, 34
  and Threads dialog box, 40
  generating output using macros, 42
  multithreaded applications, 51
  preparing an application for, 24
  remote, 48
  settings, 25
  simple techniques, 42
  speeding, 42
debugging session,
  and Call Stack window, 32
  and Disassembly window, 33
  and Memory window, 31
  and Registers window, 31
  and Variables window, 29
  and Watch window, 30
  windows, 28
debugging tools, capabilities of, 22
derived control classes,
  creating, 97
  customizing, 98
  in dialogs, 97
  using in a dialog box, 99
device contexts, 157
  in MFC, 157
device-independent bitmap, 183
  see also DIB

dialog bar, 105
dialog box,
  and control notifications, 94
  and data exchange, 86
  and DoDataExchange() function, 90
  change the current input focus, 86
  common controls and their mapping
    classes/variables, 89
  coordinates, 85
  creating with the resource editor, 80
  derived control classes in, 97
  displaying, 84
  initializing the controls, 91
  in MFC, 79
  mapping controls, 95
  mapping the controls, 87
  modeless, 101
  responding to OK and Cancel, 96
DIB, 183
  creating, 184
  creating from a device-dependent bitmat,
    187
  drawing with, 189
Digital Nervous System, 2
  and integrated enterprise applications, 3
  components of, 2
DNA, 4
  and Visual Studio, 4
  benefits of, 5
document data, complex, 204
document object, 193
document template lifecycle, 217
document template resources, 216
document/view applications, vs. dialog-based,
    210
document/view architecture, 193
  alternatives to, 240
drag source, implementing with CDocItem,
    533
drag-and-drop,
  drag sources, 527
  drop targets, 527
  implementing with DoDragDrop(), 532
drive types, determining, 347

drop target, CView member functions, 535
dynamic splitters, creating, 230

E

Edit and Continue debugging, 15, 47
enterprise applications, attributes of, 4
enterprise database tools, 11
escape sequences, 245
event state, setting, 304
events, 298
    working with, 303
exception handler, defining, 419
exception handling keywords, macro imple-
        mentation, 421
exception handling, RPC, 387
exceptions,
    ASSERT macro, 443
    detailing, 418
    MFC supported, 420
    Win32, 438

F

File Allocation Table, 342
    see also FAT
File Open dialog, customizing, 118
file system, 342
    CDFS, 344
    determining, 347
    FAT, 342
    FAT-32, 343
    HPFS, 344
    NTFS, 344
    protected-mode FAT, 343
flag values,
    for customizing Wizard97 property
        page, 151
    for customizing Wizard97 property
        sheet, 150
fonts,
    and the CFont class, 176
    interrogation functions, 178
    selecting into the device context, 177
    stock, 177
    stock objects, 177
    text rendering functions, 178
    working with, 176
footers, printing of, 264
frame windows, working with, 212

G

GDI, 157
GDI operations, MFC classes for, 171
Graphics Device Interface, 157
    see also GDI

H

headers, printing of, 264
heap management functions,
    GetProcessHeap(), 332
    HeapAlloc(), 332
    HeapCompact(), 333
    HeapCreate(), 331
    HeapDestroy(), 333
    HeapRealloc(), 332
    HeapSize(), 332
helper functions, in printing, 261
High Performance File System, 344
    see also HPFS
HKEY_CLASSES_ROOT, 401
HKEY_LOCAL_MACHINE,
    Config subkey, 400
    Enum subkey, 400
hook procedure, 118

I

instruction pointer, 276
IntelliSense technology, 15
interface attributes, globally unique identifier,
    382
interface, binding handle, 382
interfaces, and COM, 6
IPC, 389

J

Just-in-Time debugging, 22, 46

L

lifecycle productivity, 9
lifecycle support, 4

M

macro, storage in the registry, 605
macros,
    adding to the toolbar, 607
    creating with Visual Studio, 602
    debugging, 607
    using VBScript, 606
mailslots, 371
    creating with CreateMailslot(), 390
    domain, 371, 389
    one-way communications, 389
managing memory, malloc(), 317
manipulating physical memory, selector
    functions, 325
mapped volumes,
    disk quotas, 347
    Distributed File System, 346
    Multiple Universal Name Convention
        Provider, 345
    network redirector, 345
    Universal Naming Convention, 345
    volume compression, 346
marshalling, 76
MDI, 193
memory leaks, detecting, 44
memory managing, new(), 317
memory-mapped file functions,
    CreateFileMapping(), 334
    MapViewOfFile(), 334
message loop, 283
    and threads, 283
    messages received by, 70
    multiple, 72
    optimizing, 76

messages,
    nonqueued, 72
    processing, 202
    queue, 72
    working with, 225
MFC, 1
    and document objects, 193
    and view window, 193
    CCmdTarget class, 208
    CDocItem class, 208
    CDocument class, 198
    CFont class, 176
    CPoint class, 172
    CRect class, 173
    CRgn class, 174
    CSingleDocTemplate class, 211, 212
    CSize class, 173
    printing sequence, 250
    support for common dialogs and common
        controls, 106
    support for Windows, 9x controls, 124
    using to subclass a window, 238
MFC classes, for GDI operations, 171
MFC control classes, understanding, 123
MFC thread-creation technique, benefits of,
    288
MFC Tracer, 45
Microsft Foundation Classes, 1
    see also MFC
Microsoft Repository, 10, 14
Microsoft Transaction Server, 6
    see also MTS
MIDL compiler,
    and Application Configuration File, 381
    and Interface Definition Language File,
        381
modeless dialog boxes, 101
    considerations when creating, 101
    creating and destroying, 102
    tracking, 103
MTS, 6
Multiple Universal Name Convention
    Provider, 345
    see also MUP

multiple-document applications, structure
    of, 195
multiple-document interface, 193
    see also MDI
multiple-document types, working with, 197
multithreaded applications, 282
    writing, 275
MUP, 345
mutexes, 298
    working with, 300

N

network redirector, 345
New Technology File System, 344
    see also NTFS

O

object, dumping, 44
ODBC, 5, 11
OLE, 379
    COleClientItem, 528
    COleServerItem, 528
    drag-and-drop, 527
    embedded object, 448
    linked objects, 448
    positioning support, 529
    selection support, 532
    shared memory, 319
OLE DB, 5, 11, 546
    consumers, 547
    data definition language, 558
    data manipulation language, 558
    data source objects, 555
    enumerators, 563
    error objects, 564
    extended provider services, 567
    providers, 547
    rowsets, 560
    sessions with, 556
    support by Visual C++, 17
    text commands, 558
    transactions with, 556

one-to-many relationship,
    between documents and views, 197
    between each view and frame window, 197
Open Database Connectivity, 11, 545
    see also ODBC
Oracle, 13
    databases, 10

P

pagination,
    implementing in a program, 258
    print-time, 263
parameters, in, 477
parameters, out, 477
Pen Demo program, 168
pens, 163
    advanced styles, 164
    and the CPen class, 163
    cosmetic, 163
    drawing with, 166
    geometric, 163
    selecting into the device context, 165
    simple styles, 164
    stock, 165
physical output, 245
pipes, 371
    anonymous pipes, 372
    connecting to, 373
    creating, 372
    datagrams, 372
    Microsoft RPC, 371
    named pipes, 371, 372
    SECURITY_ATTRIBUTES structure, 373
    transferring data through, 375
    two-way communications, 372
    Universal Naming Convention, 372
print preview,
    architecture, 266
    enhancing capabilities of, 269
    modifying, 267
    process, 267
print-time pagination, 263
printer device context, 245

printer information, obtaining, 247
printer pages, versus document pages, 257
printing,
    allocating GDI resources for, 265
    and enlarging image size, 266
    and Windows API support, 245
    functions of a view class, 250
    helper functions used in, 261
    of headers and footers, 264
    protocol, 254
    the programmer's role vs. the framework's role, 249
    vs. screen display, 254
    with MFC, 249
process,
    creating, 309
    creation flags, 307
    information structure, 309
process priorities,
    and HIGH_PRIORITY_CLASS, 277
    and IDLE_PRIORITY_CLASS, 277
    and NORMAL_PRIORITY_CLASS, 277
    and REALTIME_PRIORITY_CLASS, 277
    the four categories of, 277
processes, 306
    differences from threads, 280
programming errors,
    logic, 21
    syntax, 21
    types of, 21
property page,
    activation and deactivation, 140
    adding, 136
    adding controls to the resource template, 133
    initializing, 139
    management, 145
    sending messages between, 142
    sizing and Windows, 95, 137
    template, 131
    template Disabled flag, 133
    template resource ID and caption, 133
    template style and border settings, 132
property sheet,
    adding Help button and support, 153
    and Apply button, 130
    and Cancel button, 130
    and OK button, 130
    controlling buttons, 129
    creating, 131
    creating a modeless, 138
    customizing the standard appearance, 144
    customizing the standard functionality, 144
    flag values for customizing the Wizard buttons, 147
    handling messages from OK, Apply, and Cancel buttons, 141
    modeless, 142, 145
    responding to messages, 139
    understanding, 129
    creating Wizard-mode, 146

R

RDR, 345
registers, 31
registry,
    capacity, 395
    hive, 394
    HKEY_CURRENT_CONFIG branch, 398
    HKEY_CURRENT_USER branch, 398
    HKEY_DYN_DATA branch, 398
    HKEY_PERFORMANCE_DATA branch, 398
    initialization files, 393
    predefined branches, 396
    Registry Editor, 399
registry keys,
    creating, 407
    opening, 404
    querying, 405
    setting values, 407
registry structure,
    subkeys, 394
    values, 394
registry values, 395
remote debugging, 48

Remote Procedure Call,
    basis for DCOM, 379
    basis for OLE, 379
    interface, 379
    marshaling, 379
    proxy-stub communication over, 379
    stub function, 379
    unmarshaling function, 379
robustness, 417
RPC,
    exception handling, 387
    RPC Name Service Provider, 389
    RPC runtime library, 383

S

screen device context, 245
scrollbars, shared, 236, 237
SDI, 193
semaphores, 298
    working with, 301
serial communications, 360
serial ports,
    asynchronous communications, 362
    opening and configuring, 361
    setting communication timeouts, 365
sharing memory,
    DDEML library, 328
    GMEM_DDESHARE flag, 328
    memory-mapped files, 328
shared memory management, based pointers,
        336
single-document interface, 193
    applications, 194
    see also SDI
single-stepping, keyboard shortcuts for com-
        mands, 38
singleton objects, 478
Source Browser, 25
Source Profiler, and performance bottlenecks,
        22
SpawnProcess sample program, 309
splitter control, 227
splitter windows, 227

determining size of, 238
differentiating between, 228
dynamic, 227
performance issues, 238
static, 227
Spy++, 70, 130
SQL Server, 10
SQL statements, single versus double quotes,
        596
stack pointer, 276
static splitters,
    creating, 235
    using, 234
stream I/O, I/O stream classes, 358
synchronization objects,
    critical sections, 298
    definition of, 298
    events, 298
    mutexes, 298
    semaphores, 298
system hive, registry, 412

T

team development, 13
templates,
    using for advanced work, 217
    working with multiple, 218
text characteristics, and printing, 248
text rendering functions, 178
thread context, definition of, 275
thread priorities, 276
    and THREAD_PRIORITY_
        ABOVE_NORMAL, 278
    and THREAD_PRIORITY_
        BELOW_NORMAL, 278
    and THREAD_PRIORITY_
        ERROR_RETURN, 278
    and THREAD_PRIORITY_HIGHEST,
        278
    and THREAD_PRIORITY_IDLE, 278
    and THREAD_PRIORITY_LOWEST, 278
    and THREAD_PRIORITY_NORMAL,
        278

and THREAD_PRIORITY_TIME_
    CRITICAL, 278
the eight categories of, 278
threads,
    applying within applications, 285
    checking return codes, 296
    closing on, 311
    controlling function, 291
    creating, 286
    creating at runtime, 292
    definition of, 275
    differences from processes, 280
    messages, 287
    premature termination, 294
    synchronization, 298
    terminating, 294
    using multiple, 282
    using your own, 286
    when not to use multiple, 282
    when to use multiple, 284
    worker, 289
threads and memory,
    interlocked variable access, 337
    thread-local storage, 337
throw statements, 419
TRACE macro, and generating debugging
        output, 42
trace utility, 23
try...catch block, 419

U

UML, 9
UNC, 345, 372
Unified Modeling Language, 9
    see also UML
Universal Data Access architecture, 11
Universal Naming Convention, 372
    see also UNC

V

VCM, 14
view class, declaring, 221

view class functions, overriding in printing
        processes, 254
view window, 193
views,
    using different in dynamic panes, 232
    working with, 225
virtual functions, 203
    overriding, 203
virtual memory,
    memory-mapped files, 322
    page table, 320
    swap file, 320
virtual memory management, 318
    committed page, 329
    reserved page, 329
    sparse matrices, 329
    VirtualAlloc(), 329
virtual memory management functions,
    VirtualLock(), 330
    VirtualProtect(), 330
    VirtualQuery(), 330
    VirtualUnlock(), 330
Visual Basic, and source code control, 13
Visual Component Manager, 10, 14
    see also VCM
Visual Database Tools, features of, 12
Visual FoxPro 6.0, 8
    and source code control, 13
Visual InterDev, 3, 8, 13
Visual J++, and source code control, 13
Visual SourceSafe, 6.0, 13
Visual Studio Analyzer, 10
Visual Studio Modeler, 9
Visual Studio,
    class information files and, 612
    customizing the interface, 599
    design themes, 7
    Enterprise Edition, set of enterprise tools,
        8
    integrated debugger, 24
    object model exposed by, 600

W

waitable objects, 305
Win32, GlobalAlloc(), 324
Win32 file objects, 347
   manipulation functions, 348
   SECURITY_ATTRIBUTES, 348
window classes, 68
window procedures, 57
Windows Distributed interNet Applications
      architecture, 4
   see also DNA
Windows message loop, fundamentals of, 65
Windows metafile, 161
wrapping objects, 313

X

XBASE language, 8